ABM, MRV, SALT, and the Nuclear Arms Race

ABM, MRV, SALT,

and the

Nuclear Arms Race

Hearings
before the
Subcommittee on Arms Control,
International Law and Organization
of the
Committee on Foreign Relations

United States Senate
Ninety-First Congress
Second Session

March 16, April 8, 9, 13 and 14, May 18 and 28,
June 4 and 29, 1970

GOVERNMENT REPRINTS PRESS.
Washington, D.C.

© Ross & Perry, Inc. 2001 All rights reserved.

No claim to U.S. government work contained throughout this book.

Protected under the Berne Convention. Published 2001

Printed in The United States of America
Ross & Perry, Inc. Publishers
717 Second St., N.E., Suite 200
Washington, D.C. 20002
Telephone (202) 675-8300
Facsimile (202) 675-8400
info@RossPerry.com

SAN 253-8555

Government Reprints Press Edition 2001

Government Reprints Press is an Imprint of Ross & Perry, Inc.

Previously published as title "Department of Defense Dictionary of Military and Associated Terms".

Library of Congress Control Number: 2001094512
http://www.GPOreprints.com

ISBN 1-931641-92-7

∞ The paper used in this publication meets the requirements for permanence established by the American National Standard for Information Sciences "Permanence of Paper for Printed Library Materials" (ANSI Z39.48-1984).

All rights reserved. No copyrighted part of this publication may be reproduced, stored in a retrieval system, or transmitted, in any form or by any means, electronic, photocopying, recording, or otherwise, without the prior written permission of the publisher.

CONTENTS

	Page
Statements by—	
Barnett, A. Doak, senior fellow, The Brookings Institution	145
Brooke, Hon. Edward W., U.S. Senator from Massachusetts	2
Bundy, McGeorge, president, the Ford Foundation	66
Clark, Hon. Joseph S., president, World Federalists, U.S.A	354
Drell, Dr. Sidney D., deputy director, Stanford Linear Accelerator Center	534
Fisher, Adrian S., dean, Georgetown University Law School	234
Foster, Dr. John S., Jr., director of Defense Research and Engineering	424
Goldberger, Dr. M. L., professor of physics, Princeton University	525
Hornig, Dr. Donald F., vice president, Eastman Kodak Co., Rochester, N.Y.	380
Hsieh, Mrs. Alice Langley, Institute for Defense Analyses	120
Kistiakowsky, Dr. George B., professor of chemistry, Harvard University	389
Laird, Hon. Melvin R., Secretary of Defense	274
Panofsky, Dr. Wolfgang K. H., director, Stanford Linear Accelerator Center, Stanford University	176
Shulman, Marshall D., director, Russian Institute, Columbia University	19
Scoville, Dr. Herbert, Jr., Carnegie Endowment for International Peace	220
Wiesner, Dr. Jerome B., provost, Massachusetts Institute of Technology	394
York, Dr. Herbert, dean of the graduate school, University of California at San Diego	58
Insertions for the record—	
"The Limitation of Strategic Arms," article by G. W. Rathjens and G. B. Kistiakowsky, Scientific American, January 1970	42
Letter from Dr. John S. Foster, Jr., to Senator Edward W. Brooke, August 30, 1969	53
Opening statement by Senator Gore, April 8, 1970	55
"To Cap the Volcano," article by McGeorge Bundy, reprinted from Foreign Affairs, October 1969	67
"Safeguard and the 'accidental' attack," statement by Dr. Herbert York	109
"China Nuclear Strategy and a U.S. Anti-China ABM," prepared statement of Mrs. Alice Langley Hsieh	133
"United States versus Soviet Intercontinental Strategic Offensive Forces," table prepared by the Department of Defense	192
Letter from The American Assembly on Arms Limitations, enclosing final report—1970, and list of participants	249
Prepared statement of Adrian S. Fisher, with respect to the current Strategic Arms Limitation Talks	260
Prepared statement of Secretary of Defense Melvin R. Laird	285
Text of Senate Resolution 211	304
U.S.-U.S.S.R. force comparison, submitted by Department of Defense	307
"Military Update of Cambodian Operations, May 18, 1970" submitted by Department of Defense	327

Insertions for the record—Continued

	Page
"Rogers Rules Out Troops To Defend Cambodia Regime . . .," article by Peter Grose, the New York Times, May 13, 1970	334
"Report of Joseph S. Clark, president, World Federalists, U.S.A., chairman, Coalition on National Priorities and Military Policy," April 23, 1970	354
"Will '72 Elections Be Cancelled?" article by Don Demaio, the Distant Drummer, Philadelphia, Pa., May 21, 1970	361
"Citizens' Hearing on an Alternate Defense Budget for the United States; Report of the Panel of Inquiry"	364
Description of Coalition on National Priorities and Military Policy and Affiliated Organizations as of April 1, 1970	368
Prepared statement of Joseph S. Clark, president of World Federalists, U.S.A., chairman, Coalition on National Priorities and Military Policy, and attached correspondence with U.S. Government officials	371
"Soviet ICBM Force Trends," Chart prepared by Dr. George B. Kistiakowsky	399
Letter to Senator Claiborne Pell from John M. Fisher, president, American Security Council and attached "National Security Issues Poll—1970"	413
Sketch showing U.S. PAR Radar and U.S.S.R. Dog House Radar, submitted by Department of Defense	427
Chart showing present and future Soviet threat against Minuteman and estimated protection afforded by Safeguard Phase II-a, prepared by Dr. Wolfgang K. H. Panofsky	430, 544
"Ad Hoc Panel on Fiscal 1971 Safeguard Plan," submitted by Department of Defense	443
"Laird Seeks Industry Aid To Defeat Mansfield Amendment," article from Science Magazine, March 20, 1970	446
"Behavioral Science Work Units Fiscal Year 1970 and 1971," submitted by Department of Defense	450
Details of Defense Department sponsored research project, "Factors in Regional Change at the American University of Beirut in Lebanon," submitted by Department of Defense	500
Letter to Senator Gore from M. L. Goldberger, June 11, 1970, commenting on Dr. Foster's testimony	522
Letter to Senator Gore from Sidney D. Drell, June 5, 1970, commenting on Dr. Foster's testimony	522
"Contributions to Maximum Surveillance Range," chart prepared by Dr. Sidney D. Drell	543
"A Citizen Looks at the ABM," article by Henry Cabot Lodge, The Reader's Digest, June 1970	567
Letter to Senator Gore from Sidney D. Drell, July 6, 1970, commenting on "A Citizen Looks at the ABM"	572

Appendix I—
  Biographies of:

Mr. Marshall D. Shulman	581
Mr. McGeorge Bundy	581
Dr. Herbert York	582
Mrs. Alice Langley Hsieh	582
Mr. A. Doak Barnett	584
Dr. W. K. H. Panofsky	584
Dr. Herbert Scoville, Jr	585
Dr. Adrian S. Fisher	586
Hon. Joseph S. Clark	586
Dr. Donald F. Hornig	586
Dr. George B. Kistiakowsky	588
Dr. Jerome B. Wiesner	588
Dr. Sidney D. Drell	589
Dr. M. L. Goldberger	590
Letter and statements from Mr. Roman Kolkowicz, Institute for Defense Analyses	591

Appendix II—
    Department of Defense responses to questions submitted by Senators Case and Cooper_____ 603

ABM, MIRV, SALT, AND THE NUCLEAR ARMS RACE

Senate Resolution 211—Seeking Agreement With the Union of Soviet Socialist Republics on Limiting Offensive and Defensive Strategic Weapons and the Suspension of Test Flights of Reentry Vehicles

MONDAY, MARCH 16, 1970

UNITED STATES SENATE,
SUBCOMMITTEE ON ARMS CONTROL,
INTERNATIONAL LAW AND ORGANIZATION
OF THE COMMITTEE ON FOREIGN RELATIONS,
Washington, D.C.

The subcommittee met, pursuant to notice, at 2:30 p.m., in room 4221, New Senate Office Building, Senator Albert Gore (chairman of the subcommittee) presiding.

Present: Senators Gore, Fulbright (chairman of the full committee), Church, Symington, Case, Cooper, and Javits.

Senator GORE. The subcommittee will come to order.

OPENING STATEMENT

In early February this subcommittee began its study of the vitally important questions of ABM (anti-ballistic missile), MIRV (multiple independent reentry vehicle), the strategic arms limitations talks and the nuclear arms race. In the weeks ahead the subcommittee plans to hold a number of hearings in which notable authorities on these subjects will be invited to present their views.

The present series of hearings began with an executive session briefing on the SALT talks by the Director of the Arms Control and Disarmament Agency, Ambassador Smith. Two weeks ago CIA Director Richard Helms appeared in executive session to present the current U.S. intelligence assessment of Soviet and Chinese strategic capabilities and intentions. Our first open session was to have been an overall review of the nuclear arms race.

Last week, however, we learned to our surprise that the Administration, proceeding more rapidly than had been expected, plans to deploy the first MIRV equipped Minuteman missiles in June of this year. This announcement, made by Air Force Secretary Robert Seamans, was subsequently described by the Pentagon as a slipup. This is a rather important subject on which to have a slipup.

The MIRV deployment decision raises very serious questions regarding the Administration's attitude toward the SALT talks and regarding its concept of our future security in the nuclear age. We hope for reassurance on this critical matter.

We will be considering both ABM and MIRV in this series of hearings because together they threaten to undercut the SALT talks without providing any real additional security.

Our discussion today will focus on Senate Resolution 211, originally introduced by Senator Brooke and now cosponsored by 43 other Members of the Senate.

The subcommittee is pleased to have Senator Brooke appear before it today. In addition, the subcommittee is pleased and fortunate to have Prof. Marshall Shulman, director of the Russian Institute at Columbia University, who will follow Senator Brooke.

Before inviting Senator Brooke to begin, I wish to announce that the subcommittee will continue its hearings on April 8, at which time it will receive testimony on "The Arms Race, Past, Present, and Future" from two more distinguished authorities, Mr. McGeorge Bundy, president of the Ford Foundation and former Presidential Assistant for National Security Affairs, and Dr. Herbert York, chancellor of the University of California at San Diego and former Director of Defense Research and Engineering.

The committee is very pleased indeed to have Senator Brooke testify. Will you please proceed, Senator Brooke.

STATEMENT OF THE HONORABLE EDWARD W. BROOKE, U.S. SENATOR FROM MASSACHUSETTS

Senator BROOKE. Mr. Chairman, I am grateful for the opportunity to appear before this distinguished subcommittee and to discuss the most urgent issue of our times—the quest for a secure peace. The United States and the Soviet Union are now poised on the edge of decisions which will determine whether it is possible to build such a peace through restraining the nuclear arms race.

There is no more vital business before mankind than the strategic arms limitation talks (SALT) between our two countries. SALT comes at a unique juncture in the strategic arms race. Unless we can exploit the favorable conjunction of political interest, strategic balance, and technological opportunity, the arms race may well continue to feed on itself for many years to come.

SENATE ACTION ON NUCLEAR ARMS CONTROL URGED

I am here to urge this committee and the Senate to assert their leadership in the search for nuclear arms control. Twice in the past decade the Senate has paved the way to Soviet-American agreement by resolutions endorsing efforts to devise the nuclear test ban treaty and the Nonproliferation Treaty. Since the Senate must ultimately face the question of consenting to any treaty which may emerge from SALT, it is even more important that the Senate tender its advice on the character of the agreement which the United States should seek in these negotiations. Senate Resolution 211 is an essential vehicle for this purpose.

Senate Resolution 211 is cosponsored by 43 Senators and represents, I am confident, the majority opinion of the Senate. It recognizes that the technology of multiple independently targetable reentry vehicles (MIRV) is the most immediate and most serious threat to the strategic stability on which peace depends. It seeks to forestall deployment of such destabilizing weapons by proposing a mutual suspension, by both the Soviet Union and the United States, of the flight tests necessary to perfect such systems.

PRESENT CREDIBLE DETERRENT OF UNITED STATES AND RUSSIA

Before discussing the proposed MIRV moratorium in detail, let me make clear the context in which any arms control plan must be judged. As President Nixon has so forthrightly said, the security of the United States and the Soviet Union rest today on mutual deterrence. Neither side could rationally attack the other because neither side has the capacity to prevent devastating retaliation by the victim. This capacity to retaliate—to visit assured destruction on any nation which might launch a nuclear war—is the foundation of credible deterrence.

Today both sides possess a credible deterrent. Both sides will do what is necessary to maintain such a deterrent. Developments which seem to jeopardize either side's deterrent erode strategic stability and induce changes in the force postures of both sides.

EFFECT OF MIRV DEVELOPMENT

MIRV is precisely such a development. The principal incentive for the U.S. decision to proceed with MIRV development was the fear that the Soviet Union was deploying a heavy system of antiballistic missiles. By multiplying the number of warheads each missile could deliver, and the number of targets each missile could strike, MIRV was intended to guarantee U.S. capacity to penetrate the expected Soviet ABM.

That ABM system has not materialized. It could not be deployed for years, even if the Soviet Union chose to do so. It is public knowledge that the number of ABM launchers has remained at well under 100 for several years now. The United States has already countered the light Soviet defenses by targeting enough warheads on Moscow to exhaust the number of ABM missiles.

If the Soviet Union had moved to a massive ABM development, I would not be here today. Under those circumstances, MIRV might well be required and I would not oppose its testing or deployment. However, that is not the situation at present or in the foreseeable future. The anticipated threat has not emerged. MIRV is utterly unnecessary. Given the existing balance of forces, no responsible official would argue that MIRV is required. The system is now advocated merely as a convenient and cost effective modernization of U.S. forces which will serve as a hedge against possible future improvements in Soviet ABM capabilities. The leadtime for such ABM deployment is greater than the leadtime for U.S. deployment of MIRV.

But if MIRV is not now required for deterrence, it is positively hostile to the prospects for strategic stability, either through tacit arrangements or explicit arms limitations. Why is this so? The reasons are straightforward.

MIRV enables one missile to attack several targets. Given sufficient accuracy and reliability, these weapons could eventually pose a direct threat to the land-based missiles on which both notions have banked so heavily. Should the United States and the Soviet Union confront each other with highly accurate and dependable MIRV systems, the barriers to nuclear war would be weakened significantly. In moments of acute crisis, leaders on both sides might be under increased pressure to attempt a disarming first strike against the opponent's weapons, fearing that otherwise the opponent himself might launch such a counterforce attack. MIRV would scarcely make nuclear war rational, but it could increase the danger that preemptive war might erupt from some tense encounter.

Invulnerable and effective weapons are necessary for stable deterrence. By rendering land-based missiles more vulnerable, MIRV would certainly compel compensating changes in the offensive forces of both countries. Indeed, even the prospect of a Soviet MIRV, as the prospect of a Soviet ABM, has already generated major countermeasures by the United States. We have felt it necessary to make a start on an active ABM defense of our Minuteman force, on the apprehension that the large SS-9 missile might well present an accurate MIRV threat by mid decade. We have also begun to study possible changes in our offensive forces, including mobile land-based weapons and deceptive basing concepts. If such innovations are eventually required, they will create additional and extremely serious obstacles to adequate verification of an arms agreement. And in the absence of such agreement, such innovations on either side could so complicate the intelligence problem of counting the number of missiles in the inventory that force levels might expand drastically as a hedge against uncertainty.

Thus, the inexorable chain reaction might well continue, with consequences foreseen by no man. Such a process, if allowed to continue, might forever deny us the reasonable limitation of nuclear arms which both Moscow and Washington have termed desirable.

MUTUAL SUSPENSION OF MIRV TESTING AND DEPLOYMENT

Thorough study has convinced me that the best chance for breaking this chain reaction and for enhancing the security of both nations lies in the initiative proposed by Senate Resolution 211. A mutual suspension of MIRV testing and deployment is still timely. It could be invaluable in buying time for more extensive arms limitations to be negotiated. If a MIRV moratorium is not adopted, a freeze on the numbers of missiles may still be possible; but an expensive, dangerous and unnecessary deployment of multiple warheads may well undermine confidence in such a freeze.

The consensus of informed opinion on this proposal is much wider than on the related issue of ABM deployment. This committee has received uniform endorsements of Senate Resolution 211 from eminent and competent authorities: Dr. Jack Ruina, formerly Director of the Advanced Research Projects Agency and a senior consultant to the current Administration; Dr. Herbert York, formerly Director of Defense Research; Dr. Gordon MacDonald, recently a member of the President's Scientific Advisers Committee and newly appointed member of the Council on Environmental Quality and Dr. Freeman Dyson, distinguished scientist and weapons analyst. Dr. Dyson and Dr. MacDonald, one may note, supported last year's ABM decision, while Dr. Ruina and Dr. York indicated opposition to deployment of the Safeguard system. But on the question now before this committee, they were unanimous: The mutual MIRV moratorium contemplated by Senate Resolution 211 is feasible, verifiable, and vital.

The proposal has grown more imperative in recent weeks. As you know, the Department of Defense has revealed that it is continuing with its plan to begin deployment in June of the first generation MIRV weapon, the Minuteman III. This is a singularly unwise decision. No such action is required, nor should it be taken until we and the Soviets undertake a full exploration of potential controls over MIRV technology. With the resumption of the SALT negotiations next month, the issue should be addressed immediately, but agreement may take some time. We must not begin what might prove an irreversible deployment without affording SALT even the opportunity to address the issue.

There has been some suggestion that it is now too late for a test suspension to be effective. Nothing could be further from the truth. Our intelligence evaluation now indicates that the multiple warhead tests of the SS-9 have not yet demonstrated the accuracies required to threaten the Minuteman force. Years of additional testing are considered necessary, and probably major design changes as well.

Similarly, the U.S. development program has not approached a counterforce capability. The relatively small warheads and accuracies of the U.S. MIRV systems would be sufficient only for retaliatory purposes against soft urban targets. The test program to date has vindicated Dr. Ruina's testimony to this committee last year: it will take a number of years and many more tests than so far conducted for the U.S. MIRV systems to present a threat to hard targets.

It is, however, customary for missile accuracy to improve substantially after deployment through countinued proof testing and modifications of guidance systems, reentry vehicles, and other components. In the last decade accuracies improved by a factor of 10; in the coming years far less improvement in precision would be needed to make even small warheads a threat to land-based missiles. Both Soviet and American planners are already anticipating such accuracy growth and are no doubt adjusting their deployments accordingly.

For these reasons a suspension of MIRV testing and deployment remains workable and critical. Without many additional tests, neither the United States nor the Soviet multiple warhead technology can achieve the accuracies and reliabilities required for counterforce applications. Without additional tests, it would not be possible to train operational crews to the normal levels of proficiency. Without further tests, it is extremely unlikely that either nation could maintain such multiple-target killers in their inventories for any great period of time. In short, without further tests the destabilizing impact of MIRV can be avoided. No nation would risk its survival by attempting a counterforce war with weapons of uncertain accuracy and reliability, and fired by untrained crews.

VERIFICATION OF MUTUAL TEST SUSPENSION

There is considerable confidence among knowledgeable technical people in and out of Government that such a test suspension can be verified adequately. Substantial information is already gathered concerning Soviet test activities. If, as I believe, each side has a greater interest in dissuading the other from deploying MIRV than in deploying MIRV itself, it may be possible to agree on means for improving such verification. For example, I have suggested agreements on prior announcement of all missile tests, on limiting tests to specific ranges which facilitate observation by the other country, on exchanging observers at the small number of launch facilities on both sides, and possibly on the installation of suitable radars and other instruments near such facilities. Even without agreement on these details, experts believe we would have adequate verification, but we should certainly seek to reinforce mutual confidence in any moratorium that might be accepted. Some combination of proposals like these could be very valuable in this regard.

FREEZE ON NUMBER OF OFFENSIVE MISSILES

A central safeguard in such a moratorium would be a freeze on the number of offensive missiles themselves. That must obviously be an early objective in SALT. If the number of SS-9's does not grow much beyond present levels, calculations reveal that a Soviet violation of a MIRV moratorium would not jeopardize the U.S. deterrent. This is especially true if some hard-point defense is added to the Minuteman fields as a hedge against such a possibility. In other words, a MIRV moratorium could help preserve the credible deterrence we now have without a continued drain on precious resources and a continued exacerbation of international tensions.

EFFECT OF MIRV DEVELOPMENT ON SALT TALKS

Some commentators have implied that the U.S. plan to begin MIRV deployment this June might afford added leverage for our position in the SALT discussions. I could not disagree more completely. If the United States deploys MIRV—even a first generation system capable only of retaliation against cities—it is virtually certain that the Soviet Union will persist in its program to deploy a multiple-target weapon. To begin deployment prematurely would tend to remove from the bargaining arena the crucial question of MIRV. For the negotiations then would have to center on reduction or removal from the force of weapons already fielded. This would surely make more complex the problem of verification and increase the need for onsite inspection, one of the most formidable stumbling blocks to progress in arms control.

To begin the deployment of MIRV is not a strategy for effective diplomacy; it is a strategy guaranteed to stimulate parallel deployment by the Soviet Union. And it is such parallel deployments, I remind you, that we consider the gravest peril to our own deterrent. Since MIRV is not need militarily, a precipitate deployment now would be a reckless act of folly.

This question is one of ultimate importance to all our people. The Congress and the country have only begun to perceive its implications. It should not be resolved within the closed system of politics which have shaped too many decisions on our national security. I believe that, whether or not it is possible to arrange a mutual MIRV moratorium, no final decision on deployment should be made until the

Congress, as well as the Executive, has conducted an ample and careful review of the entire issue. I hope that this committee will lend its valued support to such a review.

PURPOSE OF SENATE RESOLUTION 211

Mr. Chairman, before concluding, let me call the attention of the committee to two aspects of the legislative history of Senate Resolution 211 which need to be emphasized. My statement introducing the resolution last June made clear that its purpose was to forestall deployment of MIRV systems through an effective test limitation. This point could well be underscored by modifying the relevant clause of the resolution to make it explicit.

The clause would then read:

> *Resolved further,* That the President of the United States should propose to the Government of the Union of Soviet Socialist Republics an immediate suspension by the United States and by the Union of Soviet Socialist Republics of flight tests and deployment of multiple independently targetable reentry vehicles, subject to national verification or such other measures of observation and inspection as may be appropriate.

Only the words "and deployment" need be inserted.

Secondly, the legislative history makes clear that Senate Resolution 211 intends to cover tests of any devices by which a single missile may deliver warheads against more than one target. That is the intended definition of the phrase, "multiple independently targetable reentry vehicles," as used in the resolution. While there is some confusion as to whether the Soviet Union has tested a MIRV similar to our own, I am satisfied that they have at least tested an intermediate technology which is more advanced than a simple cluster warhead. The wide dispersal of SS-9 warheads suggests that it probably could be used against several targets separated by some miles, although accuracies would not be great. The kind of controllable pattern of warhead dispersal which seems to be associated with the SS-9 is quite distinct from the single target capability of the Polaris A-3 missle which may employ more than one warhead but which could not disperse them for use against more than one target.

Thus the intent of the resolution is to cover missiles able to strike multiple targets, not missiles carrying multiple warheads but able only to strike a single target. I am advised that tests of these types of systems can be distinguished. This question would, however, have to be resolved to the satisfaction of both parties to the proposed moratorium. It should not prove insuperable.

NECESSITY OF MIRV MORATORIUM TO SALT PROGRESS

In my considered judgment a MIRV moratorium is a necessary, though not a sufficient, condition of major progress in the SALT talks. It cannot stand alone, but it can buy time for diplomacy to find the way to erect other walls in the structure of peace. If adequate verification were to prove impossible, if the Soviet Union were not interested in the plan, if a freeze on the total number of missiles were not accepted, if the Soviets were to deploy a thick ABM system—if any of these contingencies were to develop, then the United States might well be compelled to deploy MIRV. But these questions can only be answered fully in the SALT negotiations we have all labored so hard and so long to obtain. And a MIRV initiative could prove the decisive spur to constructive answers on each of them. How tragic and foolhardy it would be to crush the fragile prospects for far-reaching arms control by a senseless commitment to an unnecessary weapon on the eve of the meeting in Vienna. The prospect on MIRV deployment may well encourage diplomacy; the fact of MIRV deployment might well defeat it.

As a member of the Committee on Armed Services and the Subcommittee on the Strategic Arms Limitation Talks, I have devoted many months to analyzing the implications of MIRV and the implications of MIRV and the possibilities of success in SALT.

I have evaluated the classified details regarding both the U.S. programs and developments in the Soviet Union. I will be pleased, Mr. Chairman, to discuss these details further, if you wish, in executive session. I have reviewed the exchange at Helsinki and, as members of this committee may know, there has so far been no significant discussion of MIRV between ourselves and the Soviets. There is no substantial evidence, as some have implied, that the Soviet Union is not interested in a MIRV limitation. In fact my own surmise is that they would welcome a proposal on this score and might well respond favorably. But it is certain that we will never know their response, unless we make a proposal. The moratorium proposal is one which the United States can make safely and should make promptly.

SENATE RESOLUTION 211 CONVEYS SENATE'S COUNSEL

This Committee and the Senate of the United States have a weighty responsibility and a rare opportunity to catalyze such an initiative. Each of us respects the fact that the President is our country's principal agent in international affairs. Our respect for the diplomatic prerogatives of the Presidency is great indeed. Yet the President needs not only the Senate's respect; he needs its counsel. Senate Resolution 211 is a crucial means of conveying that counsel.

By stressing that any moratorium must be mutual, by leaving the President wide latitude to determine what kinds of verification are appropriate, by relating the MIRV proposal to progress in the larger SALT discussions, the resolution imposes no burdens on the President. Indeed, by sharing the political burdens and risks of choosing a course for the arms control effort, the Senate can relieve the President of certain damaging inhibitions. Senate Resolution 211 can expand the President's options by permitting him to advance the MIRV proposal with clear evidence of support in the body which must ultimately approve any arms agreement. It can create wider, rather than narrower, vistas for energetic negotiation. Thus, through the device of this resolution, we can effectively couple congressional and executive efforts in the search for a secure and durable peace.

ADMINISTRATION VIEWS ON MUTUAL MIRV MORATORIUM

Mr. Chairman, I have been on consultation with the President and other members of the Administration for many months. President Nixon has indicated, both in private and in his press conference of

June 19, that the United States is prepared to consider the possibility of a mutual moratorium on MIRV. Secretary Rogers reaffirmed this position in his press conference of August 20, and termed the proposal a helpful one. In a letter on August 30, Dr. John Foster emphasized that "there is no intrinsic objection on the part of the Department of Defense to a joint MIRV test moratorium, provided that appropriate collateral provisions are also implemented." As recently as last week, in commenting on the revelation that Minuteman III is to be deployed this June, the Department of Defense reaffirmed the Administration position that MIRV is still negotiable. I would respectfully submit that action on this resolution is compatible with the Administration's position and would be a valuable service to the President's effort to achieve meaningful arms control.

NO PRESENT NEED FOR MIRV DEPLOYMENT

In summary, Mr. Chairman, there is no present need for MIRV deployment by either the Soviet Union or the United States. U.S. deployment of such weapons will surely invite a similar deployment by the Soviet Union, resulting in immense hazards to our own national security. Mutual suspension of MIRV tests is a feasible and verifiable means of impeding deployment of weapons which, once they grow more accurate and reliable, will threaten mutual deterrence. Senate Resolution 211 is a sensible and suitable instrument for expressing the collective judgment of the Senate on these vital concerns. Mr. Chairman, I implore the committee to act favorably on the resolution and to report it to the Senate for prompt action.

COMMENDATION OF THE WITNESS

Senator GORE. Senator Brooke, the Chair wishes to express appreciation to you for your testimony and for the leadership you have shown, as well as the study you have devoted to this subject. The Chair with the approval of the committee will set a time on an appropriate date to exchange with you our views on the classified matters involved in this decision.

REASONS FOR LACK OF ACTION ON PREVIOUS RESOLUTION

The Chair would like to state to you publicly, as he did last year by letter and in person, his reasons for recommending that the committee not take action on the resolution which you introduced at that time. I felt that we had a chance to defeat funds for the deployment of the anti-ballistic-missile system and that that chance, close as it appeared, might be adversely affected by the injection of the MIRV issue.

Secondly, I thought that surely the Administration, interested as it was in initiating the SALT talks, would await some reasonable determination of the possibilities of agreement before actual deployment of MIRV, and I felt that you agreed and I certainly agreed that research and development should continue.

Thirdly, I thought that we had a chance to do something effective with respect to ABM while your consent of the Senate resolution with respect to MIRV was only advisory. This brings me to my question.

EFFECT OF SENATE PASSAGE OF SENATE RESOLUTION 211

Now that the Administration has announced deployment earlier than members of this committee I think anticipated, certainly earlier than I anticipated, action on your resolution certainly becomes a pertinent issue. What effect do you think passage of your resolution by the Senate would have?

Senator BROOKE. Well, Mr. Chairman, let me say that I certainly did understand your reasons last year and I certainly respected them. I do believe, however, that, perhaps even more than at that time, action on this resolution is vital. I think it will be of great assistance to the President. I think it will help the President as he proceeds to the SALT talks in Vienna. It will give the President support of the Senate that ultimately would have to act on any agreement that might be reached in the SALT talks, and I think it would help the President in finally arriving at a decision as to whether the United States can assume what risks there are in the moratorium on further flight testing and on the deployment of MIRV.

Now, we all know that even after deployment of MIRV, there will be a need for additional tests, tests for the perfection of accuracy and reliability. I think that the scientific community perhaps would be in agreement that this first generation of MIRV's would not be a first strike capability, that it very well may not be destabilizing initially, but it is potentially destabilizing. And I think that this is the great fear, that if we continue the testing of MIRV, even after deployment, say, that eventually we would be able to perfect it so that its reliability and its accuracy would be such that it would have first strike capability; namely, it would be able to be fired successfully against the ICBM's of the Soviet Union, and thus it would play havoc with our mutual deterrence.

Thus I think at this time more than ever we know that we are close to deployment and if we are to understand that this deployment can take place as soon as June of this year, then we should do all that we can to let the President of the United States and our negotiators at SALT, know that it is the sense of this body, the Senate of the United States, giving its advice in this instance, giving its counsel, that we believe we should enter into a mutual cessation of further flight testing and at the same time hopefully postpone the deployment of MIRV.

I think that this would have great importance, great impact, with the executive, and therefore I feel that it ought to be done at this time.

Senator GORE. All you seek to do, if I correctly understand your statement, is to render to the President the advice of the Senate with respect to a decision which it is in his power under law, and with appropriations already made, to make.

Senator BROOKE. Yes. Mr. Chairman, the President has advisers in the executive branch of the Government, those who are giving him advice for deployment and for continued flight testing of MIRV, and I think that this would strengthen the President's position and strengthen those who are advising him against deployment at this time and those who are advising him against further flight testing of this technology. I think that this is important. I think that we should do this. I think that this is our responsibility and I think that is an important step for us to take.

ADMINISTRATION POLICY ON MIRV DEPLOYMENT

Senator GORE. This question of arms control, limitation of nuclear arms, the control of nuclear pollution of the world's atmosphere, is certainly in no sense a partisan issue and no one is approaching it from that standpoint. My own personal experience has not varied over a period of years, serving in conferences as a representative of the Government during the Administrations of President Eisenhower, President Johnson, President Kennedy, and I am now a delegate to the 18-nation Disarmament Conference in Geneva during President Nixon's administration.

I have tried to help all, and I hope to assist this Administration in the SALT talks. It seems to me that one way to assist the Administration is to urge it to be very cautious of precipitate deployment in the face of the further initiation of the conference in Vienna on the 15th of next month.

In that connection I wonder if you have any information which you could impart to the committee with respect to the announcement that was made. Was this in fact Administration policy or a slipup? I don't quite understand. I am puzzled whether this really represented the President or whether it didn't. I am hoping that it didn't and seeking some assurance from you or from someone that this was in fact a slipup.

Senator BROOKE. I cannot be helpful in that regard, Mr. Chairman. I only know that we were certainly advised as to when the flight tests commenced. We also knew that they would take approximately 2 years for completion prior to deployment. We also knew that 2 years is about up or should be up around June or July of this year.

So it could very well have been expected that if things went along according to schedule, that MIRV could be deployed in June or July of 1970.

I have heard no evidence that these tests were not successful. To the contrary, I heard that the tests were successful and were going along generally according to schedule. So it did not come as any shock to me that in June we might be able to deploy the first generation of MIRV.

Now, whether the decision to deploy would be made or not was another matter and I frankly didn't know that the President would make that decision or that the President frankly has made that decision.

When I first read of it and heard of it as you did, Mr. Chairman, I immediately called upon the President to postpone deployment because the MIRV weapon is unnecessary at this time. So I can't, I am afraid, Mr. Chairman, help you as to the slipup.

EFFECT OF SENATE RESOLUTION 211 ON AGENDA FOR SALT

If I may, however, Mr. Chairman, revert to your previous question, I would think that the President at this time is preparing his agenda for the Vienna talks. We know that both sides when they went to Helsinki did not have specific agendas. The discussions were pretty general, as I understand, and it was agreed that the talks that we have now scheduled in Vienna to commence on April 16 would get into the substantive matters for discussion. So I presume the President is in the midst of preparation for the agenda and I for one am very hopeful that the President will make specific proposals for this agenda. So I think that the committee's favorable report on this resolution would be very helpful to the President in preparing that agenda.

It might help the President and insure us that the President would include a moratorium on operational testing of MIRV and even postponement of deployment of the first generation of MIRV as a high priority on that agenda.

Now, I know as a practical matter for the Senate it will take time for a committee to have its deliberations and report it out on the floor. I know what is presently on the floor. I know that it might be some time before the Senate could actually vote upon this resolution. And time is of the essence. The SALT talks begin on April 16.

I don't know, though I hope we would be able to get to it prior to the commencement of those talks, that some word or some act on the part of the responsible body would be made prior to the beginning of those talks. Therefore even a favorable decision of this committee, Mr. Chairman, in my opinion would be most helpful in seeing that these items were given top priority on the agenda for the Vienna talks.

Senator GORE. As you can tell from the committee meeting today, the committee is giving very serious consideration to your resolution.

The last thing I wish to do is take any action that would prejudice the SALT talks because the re-ordering of priorities by the United States cannot be taken in isolation. If there is to be a geniune re-ordering of priorities, it must stem from a modification of the equation between the United States and the Soviet Union, the two great nuclear powers that have the power to destroy each other. Unless we can reach some basic understanding to limit nuclear armaments, then a genuine re-ordering of our priorities is going to be very difficult. Here is an opportunity, I believe, and I wish to congratulate President Nixon upon the initiation of the SALT talks. I hope and pray for their success. I trust that this committee can add to the prospects for the success of that conference and your resolution may be an important part.

Senator Fulbright?

COMMENDATION OF THE WITNESS

Senator FULBRIGHT. Mr. Chairman, I would like to commend the Senator from Massachusetts for his initiative and energy in introducing this resolution. I think it has been the vehicle for a great deal of talk and soul-searching about this whole matter. Personally, I have been very favorably impressed by his past statements and his statement here today. I think it is very useful.

SOVIET ATTITUDE TOWARD U.S. MIRV DEPLOYMENT

This question of the arms race is an extremely difficult one. I am not sure I can attribute this to the President, but some of his supporters and spokesmen have stated that the MIRV along I think with the ABM is a chip to play in the game. We must go forward with ABM in order to have something to play in the game, as if we were playing poker with the Russians. I confess it doesn't appeal to me that mature people would be using analogies to a poker game or any other game. If it is true I don't understand it. There are so many other weapons in the armament factory, so much enormous capacity for destruction in other ways. I don't understand why this is taken very seriously. Yet fundamentally it seems to me these are not really technical questions so much as they are psychological and political problems as to how you approach it.

In the August 30 letter you mentioned from Dr. Foster, Director of Defense Research and Engineering, Department of Defense. Dr. Foster stated that our MIRV is a reaction to the Soviet ABM activity. It is designed to preserve our deterrent, while the Soviet MIRV falls in the category of a potential first strike weapon.

Do you think the Soviets could make the same kind of comparison between the purposes of their system and the purposes of ours?

Senator BROOKE. I certainly believe if we were sitting on the Soviet side of this issue, Mr. Chairman, that seeing that we are testing some MIRV technology and about to deploy it, that we would consider that even though the first generation may not have first strike capabilities, that we are well on our way to a first strike capability; namely, that MIRV ultimately will be able to attack their Soviet ICBM's, perhaps even on a 1-to-1 ratio, and I would think that they would certainly view our moves so far as MIRV is concerned as very definitely destabilizing as we are viewing their SS-9's.

Now, Dr. Foster went further, I think, in that letter or certainly in his testimony to state that because the Soviet Union was moving ahead I think at about 50 SS-9's a year and they possibly might be testing MIRV's—although I don't think Dr. Foster at any time has said, or anybody else for that matter, that there is clear evidence that the Soviets are testing MIRV's—that their SS-9's, since we do not have a city defense, are being developed ultimately for purposes of a first strike capability; namely, to knock out our Minuteman force.

I think Dr. Foster goes further and rationalized that since we don't have an ABM and that the only ABM that we are headed toward is namely a defense of our missile sites that this is stabilizing rather than destabilizing.

Well, I think the Soviets can turn that quite around and I am sure that they do. I think both sides are looking at the other side as being engaged in destabilizing technology and I think the Soviets certainly could very legitimately and logically conclude that if we perfect our MIRV's that we no longer have a balanced deterrent, that we don't have mutual deterrence. I think that is what they are doing and that is why I think it is so important particularly at this time that we do not deploy MIRV and that we stop flight testing the MIRV.

I think the leadtime is certainly there. The sole purpose for MIRV, as Dr. Foster has stated, and I think our Government still maintains, is to penetrate their ABM which we admit has really not developed and is at the least 5 years away. So certainly if we stop flight testing of MIRV and didn't deploy MIRV in June, we certainly would have ample time to get on with flight testing and deployment of MIRV in the event the Soviet Union did change and go into heavy deployment of a sophisticated ABM system which to date there is no evidence of.

DEFENSE DEPARTMENT VIEWS ON MIRV MORATORIUM

Senator FULBRIGHT. Dr. Foster's letter actually is a rejection. While he says, "I should mention at the outset that there is no intrinsic objection on the part of the Department of Defense to a joint MIRV test moratorium, provided that appropriate collateral provisions are also implemented", it seems to me he goes on from there and in the rest of the letter denies that there should be any moratorium. What testimony I have heard from Dr. Foster is quite consistent with this attitude. I don't believe he is really very enthusiastic for any kind of cessation or moratorium on any kind of weapons system.

What you say about the ABM is quite correct. I have seen no testimony that would indicate Russia has an effective ABM. This is simply an excuse for our going forward.

U.S. PSYCHOLOGICAL AND POLITICAL ASSUMPTIONS

Senator BROOKE. Mr Chairman, may I add that if we deploy a MIRV and combine it with an expansion of our ABM system to protect U.S. citizens, then it seems to me that it would make it rather clear at least to the Soviet Union that we want a first strike capability.

Senator FULBRIGHT. The only reasoning, I think, that could possibly counter what you have just said is the assumption that we are good people and would never harm anybody, and they are bad people.

Senator BROOKE. And I don't know that the Soviets are making that assumption.

Senator FULBRIGHT. We are. Mr. Foster apparently is because that is the only assumption that would justify his attitude. This is the crux of it. I said in the beginning that this involves a psychological, a political, question. It does involve the attitude of our people toward the Soviets. If the assumptions are that the Soviets are determined to have a first strike capability and that there is no possibility of ever doing business with a Communist country, of course there is no support for arms limitation.

You just go all out for every weapon you can think of. I don't know how we can put this game about how many missiles they have and how many we have and how many you can take out if you have such and such a system in a different context. It finally becomes utterly confusing and frustrating. It is the worst kind of numbers game, it seems to me. Then they talk about how many people they can kill. If they have a first strike, can they kill 50 million Americans or 100 million Americans, and how many can we kill? It comes down to the fundamental attitudes we are going to have toward the Russians and toward other people. I don't understand in any way the psychology that wishes to prolong the arms race. When we are just about to enter into negotiations after a year and a half of preparation and endless discussion by you and many people in the Congress, I don't understand the psychology that thinks we should announce MIRV and ABM. It has inspired a number of newspaper articles in the last few days in which the Russians are saying, at least, that we don't take the SALT talks seriously. Isn't that what they are saying? This is in a number of articles. It seems to me that is a logical conclusion, rather than the idea that this is a chip that we are going to play and they are going to put in their ABM and we are going to put in our ABM system. Of course, it is a matter that would be discussed inevitably, but our making this announcement does tend to raise a question about our good faith. I wish you could give thought to how you turn the arms race around and to reevaluate what is security.

ARMS BUILDUP LESSENS SECURITY

It is quite clear to me that the building up of this arms race in both big countries is lessening their security rather than increasing it. The only thing that would really give each of them security is a real moratorium on the arms race.

Senator BROOKE. We have much less security now, Mr. Chairman, than we had a long time ago.

Senator FULBRIGHT. We are going to have less when they build the ABM and MIRV. We are going in exactly the wrong direction.

REACTION TO ARMS CONTROL

Just to speculate a moment, what do you think would be the reaction from our people and from the Russians and from everyone if there were really a complete cessation on the part of both countries, of the nuclear escalation and hopefully a de-escalation? I don't know the proper word.

Senator BROOKE. Arms reduction.

Senator FULBRIGHT. I don't mean that we would get rid of all arms, but a reasonable control. I believe that there would be a tremendous reaction from every side. What is your idea?

Senator BROOKE. I agree with you. I certainly do not profess to be a Soviet expert. We have Dr. Shulman who will testify later, I understand, before the committee and he certainly qualifies in that regard, but from what I read and what I understand, the Soviets even now may be willing and somewhat eager to enter into an agreement on a moratorium on MIRV technology. I can't believe that the Soviet people don't want—I don't know so much about their government, frankly, but I can't believe the Soviet people, and that is your question, don't want to see an agreement on arms limitation and arms control, and as you say, not disarmament. We will never have that, but we certainly can have reductions in arms. We can have control on those that we do have.

It appears to me that we are somewhat near parity, somewhat close to it. I don't know that you ever really get to parity but we have some mutual deterrence and it seems further that we are going to have to maintain that mutual deterrence.

Once you don't have that deterrence, then, of course, you open yourself up to a nuclear holocaust. Some crises might come about and I can see a crisis that might take place which could result in one side or the other firing some of the nuclear missiles. Of course, if that is done, you have got the question of retaliation. We are talking—we don't want to get into numbers but we are talking about the destruction of millions and millions of people, with not only the immediate kill but the fallout, contamination, and all that results from it.

I think that the people in the Soviet Union and in the United States, in fact all over the world, are very hopeful that their governments will immediately think about limitations, arms limitation, anything that controls nuclear weapons.

Senator GORE. Senator Brooke, since we have reached this point of the exchange, I wonder if you would be willing, and if the subcommittee would be willing, for you to remain here and hear Dr. Shulman who is an expert in this particular field? Then the committee could question the two of you as a panel.

Senator BROOKE. Mr. Chairman, I would be more than pleased. I would like to hear Dr. Shulman's testimony. I have it, but I haven't read it. I have great respect and esteem for him.

Senator GORE. Unless there is objection——

COMMENDATION OF MASSACHUSETTS LEGISLATURE

Senator FULBRIGHT. I want to pay one compliment to the Senator from Massachusetts for the very wise action taken by your legislature in the last few days raising this question about the Vietnam war. Since you represent Massachusetts, and you were Attorney General of the State, you evidently have had a beneficial effect upon your colleagues in the State government there. I want to congratulate you.

Senator BROOKE. Thank you. I will pass that on to our legislature.

Senator FULBRIGHT. I think Massachusetts is giving leadership in that area as you are in this particular area.

COMMENDATION OF THE WITNESS

Lastly, you said you are not an expert on Russia. That may be, but you are an expert on human nature and people or you wouldn't be here. You wouldn't have been elected. Therefore, it seems to me, your judgment about reaction to your resolution or reaction to going forward with the MIRV and the ABM could be as good as anyone's because it is a matter of human qualities and human judgment as to how people react. They are people, whatever else you may call them. I think you are quite correct.

Senator BROOKE. Thank you, Mr. Chairman.

Senator CASE. There is one point, Mr. Chairman, I think I would like to address a question to our distinguished colleague from Massachusetts on. I don't think it is within the particular competence of Dr. Shulman, who is an expert in the political side and social side, I understand, rather than the scientific side of this problem. Is that correct?

Dr. SHULMAN. Yes, it certainly is.

Senator CASE. So we rely for our scientific information and instruction upon our distinguished colleague from Massachusetts.

Senator BROOKE. You are more than generous, Senator.

Senator CASE. Who has taken leadership in this field in a way that is not only commendable but enormously helpful to so many of us.

Senator BROOKE. Mr. Chairman, I should say together with Senator Case in this.

Senator CASE. Thank you very much. The Senator got something like 52 or 92 cosponsors and I got myself last year; so I joined him.

Senator BROOKE. Perhaps I proceeded on more political lines. There are many, certainly, who agreed with the distinguished Senator from

New Jersey on his resolution and I just counted heads as the Senator did on that, but I am very honored to have the Senator as cosponsor.

IS IT TOO LATE FOR MUTUAL SUSPENSION?

Senator CASE. You are most generous. Seriously, the question I had in mind, Senator, was the question to which you advert but don't deal with it at great length in your statement, and that is whether it is too late for this because either we are or we think we are, or they are or they think they are, or we think they are, or they think we are, too far advanced in testing to make it possible for us to monitor them or them to monitor us by external means and we never will get onsite inspection.

Would you develop that point a little bit?

Senator BROOKE. The Senator certainly poses a very important issue. I don't know where they think they are so far as their own development is concerned, but I think that we—and when I say we, I include certainly our Defense Department—we do not think that the Soviets are at the present time testing MIRV. At least we found no evidence of that. We do believe that they are testing MRV's and we have evidence to support that. I am sure that not only do they think, but I am sure that they know because we have admitted publicly that we are testing MIRV. We have admitted publicly what that flight schedule would be in general terms and most recently we have admitted publicly that we are now ready and intend to deploy MIRV in June of 1970.

So this is what is known by both sides.

I think that they can—they certainly can accept our word for it. I don't think they need disbelieve that fact, that we are testing MIRV and that we are ready perhaps to deploy MIRV.

I don't think that there is any real problem here insofar as an agreement between the Soviet Union and the United States on further testing of MIRV. I think they, by their intelligence, know the capability of our first generation MIRV.

They know that that MIRV will not be reliable and accurate enough to be aimed and successfully strike their ICBM's in silos in the Soviet Union. They perhaps also know that if we continue the testing of our MIRV technology that it will not be too long—I don't want to put a time on it because very frankly I do not know, Senator—but I am sure they know it will not be too long before we can improve that technology to the point where we can zero in and strike their missiles in silo, and that once we begin the perfecting of it, that we can add these refinements to the missiles, to our missiles, without it being known, that they won't be able to detect that. That is the same thing that would happen to them. That is one of the grave dangers of MIRV technology. Once you begin deployment of MIRV, No. 1, you cannot tell whether the other side has MIRV'ed its missiles unless you have onsite inspection and you dismantle the missile itself and look into it, remove, the shroud and look into it.

Whether it has been perfected and whether its capabilities have greatly increased will not be something that will be known by us. We will just have to speculate and guess on this.

STILL TIME FOR MUTUAL SUSPENSION

Senator CASE. Of course, the question I express again is, have we reached that point yet?

Senator BROOKE. No. I think——

Senator CASE. That is the question. A year ago we were talking about this and we were urging it then, that if it wasn't done within months, we would be over the hill.

Senator BROOKE. What we were urging then was if it would not be done in months, we would be able to deploy MIRV and that has come about. That is exactly what has happened. I wish we could back up and pass this resolution of June of 1969 when it was first introduced but we didn't do it then. Now we have gone down the road and we have achieved a degree of scientific development where we are now ready to deploy MIRV.

All I am saying to you is that we have not by any means achieved the ultimate in MIRV technology. We have only come to the first generation which will not be able to be a first strike capability, but if we continue with the testing, then we will have it.

So I say let's don't make the same mistake we made in June of 1969 in March of 1970. Let's stop it now before we get much farther down the road. The genie may be out of the bottle but the genie is not perfected.

Senator CASE. Well, I think you are very frank about this and this is a question we are going to have to face. We will get the argument from people who profess to be very competent in this area that we already are at the point where neither side dares trust the other because we can deploy, and perhaps they can deploy their kind of MIRV, and we won't know in a particular case whether they have or not without on-sight inspection, and therefore the time has gone by for the use of the formula which the Senator and I so strongly urged together last year.

U.S. ANNOUNCEMENT OF MIRV DEPLOYMENT

Senator BROOKE. And the strong point, Senator, that I think that knowing now, and I certainly will agree with the chairman that this was most untimely—if ever there was a moment to consider untimely, this was certainly it, 1 month or so before we enter into the substantive talks in Vienna, to announce deployment of MIRV. It certainly is not going to sit well with anyone who would be coming into an arms limitation talk to find out that the other side has stepped up and is ready to deploy MIRV. I think that is most unfortunate.

But the great danger now is that once we deploy MIRV and continue testing for perfecting of reliability and accuracy what else can we then expect the Soviet Union to do? The Soviet Union then, of course, has to begin testing MIRV for its SS-9's, and with MIRV'ed SS-9's with its superior megatonnage, then we end off through another gigantic spiral in the arms race and where is it going to stop?

Senator CASE. Mr. Chairman, thank you.

Senator GORE. Dr. Shulman, will you take your position.

Dr. Shulman is director of Russian Institute at Columbia University. We would be very happy to hear you and we appreciate the consideration of Senator Brooke in remaining and joining in the colloquy.

COMMENDATION OF THE WITNESS

Senator JAVITS. Mr. Chairman, before Dr. Shulman starts I would like to express our pride in Dr. Shulman, a most distinguished professor at Columbia University. I would like to mention also to the committee the degree of trouble which he took to come here on very short notice. He was only notified last Friday afternoon that his testimony was wanted today. I am delighted that he was able to come. It indicates a very measurable demonstration of cooperation with this committee, that Dr. Shulman was able to accept the chairman's invitation to be here and have such a distinguished prepared statement.

Senator GORE. I want to thank the distinguished senior Senator from New York because I sought him out and asked him to communicate our invitation to Dr. Shulman. I apprepreciate your efforts and appreciate the presence of Dr. Shulman.

STATEMENT OF MARSHALL D. SHULMAN, DIRECTOR, RUSSIAN INSTITUTE, COLUMBIA UNIVERSITY

Dr. SHULMAN. Mr. Chairman, thank you very much for the opportunity to be here. I appreciate the opportunity and I appreciate also Senator Javits' kind words. I respect deeply the work of this subcommittee and would be glad to come any time you want to hear me.

I do have a statement, Mr. Chairman, which I would like to put forward.

PRESENT OPPORTUNITY TO CHECK STRATEGIC ARMS RACE

The Soviet Union and the United States have a common enemy—the strategic arms race. Can anyone doubt the proposition that both countries would be better off, and more secure, if the strategic balance could be maintained at lower levels? And yet, the upward spiral continues, independent of will or reason. The problem is: where and how to initiate the process of checking and then reversing this upward spiral?

The answer is full of technical complexities, but it is fundamentally a political problem. If the will exists to reverse the present senseless trend, ways can be found to solve the technical obstacles. If the will does not exist, or is not strong enough, any technical rationalization will suffice as an epitaph.

It is not a question of trust: the level of mistrust is too high in both directions for that. The real question is whether enough reasonable men on each side can be brought to recognize and act upon their own rational self-interest.

The present moment offers a singular opportunity. Usually in the past, when one country has been ready to be serious about arms limitations, the other has been building up its arsenal; the moment passes, and the roles are reversed. Now, however, there is an unusual combination of circumstances: previous disparities have been greatly reduced; each side has more than enough weapons to deter the other; each side is under pressure to use its resources in more constructive ways; and we stand poised fleetingly before the entranceway to a new era in military technology—an era whose costs, tensions, and instabilities would reduce the security of both sides. In the course of the next 30 days, decisions will be made in Washington and Moscow that will determine whether the present opportunity will be explored to its utmost by men of common sense.

COMPLEXITY OF SOVIET DECISIONMAKING PROCESS

It is necessary to bring as much insight as we can into the circumstances in which these issues are being decided in the Soviet Union. Although there is much that we do not know about the process of decisionmaking in the Soviet system, we have been learning to appreciate the complex interplay of interests and pressures at work in the Soviet Union today. Like many industrialized countries, including our own, the Soviet Union is experiencing an increase in social tension resulting from the paradoxical rise in pressures for change and, at the same time, in strong conservative resistance to change.

As a result, there are contradictory tendencies to be observed in Soviet political life today. There are those who are concerned about the declining growth rate and the lag in advanced industrial technology, who are seeking to clear away archaic and cumbersome impedances to progress and to adapt the system to modern requirements. Among these men are to be found those who most keenly appreciate the incubus of the arms race upon Soviet economic progress. But there is also to be observed a backlash tendency of ultraconservatism, from those who fear that reform and adaptation will threaten the role of the Communist Party bureaucracy. They are responsible for an upsurge of dogmatic ideology reminiscent of the past; they are engaged in a campaign for orthodox conformity, for an extirpation of alien influence. Their answer to economic and social problems is the old tried and true method of exhortation and coercion, and this leads them to form political alliances with the military and with the police.

The top political leadership seeks to preserve its collegial unity at all costs, and to conciliate the contradictory pressures that bear upon it. The cost of this effort to maintain a consensus government has been an incapacity to act decisively to resolve major problems. Decisions are waiting to be made for the XXIV Congress of the Communist Party of the Soviet Union and the new 5-year plan for the economy, both involving fundamental, economic, and political issues. Serious concern about turbulence in Eastern Europe and even more so about relations with Communist China are major complications intertwined with the domestic problems facing Soviet leadership.

It would be vain to try to prophesy the outcome of these decisions, or to guess whether the system will find the vitality and the flexibility necessary to cope with its complex problems. But it is important to appreciate how deeply this interplay of conflicting forces and pressures affects Soviet-American relations, and also how much it is affected by what we do and say. Clearly the conflicting pressures of modernization and regression toward dogmatic orthodoxy create uncertainties and set limits on what the leadership can do. It is also evident that many of our old stereotypes about "the Russians" have little applicability, whether the wishful stereotype of Western-style liberalization or the simple stereotype of Stalinist total control.

FACTORS AFFECTING SOVIET ATTITUDES TOWARD SALT

Obvious, the complex currents of Soviet politics affect decisions about SALT above all, since these concern vital questions of security, relations with the Soviet Union's foremost adversary, and the allocation of resources as between military and industrial interests. The decision to enter into SALT was hard fought over a long period of time, and those who argue for entering into talks with the United States have always at their backs powerful ideologs who voice their suspicions of American intentions, and who fear the operational problems of preserving the muscularity of the Communist movement during periods of reduced tension with the United States. With the Chinese charging "collusion with the imperialists," the military reacting neurologically to every word and act of our military, and the party dogmatists hammering away at the iniquities of "American imperialism," it would be surprising if the Soviet leadership did not show reserve and hesitation in their negotiations with the United States.

There are in addition a number of other circumstances which also peculiarly affect Soviet decisionmaking in regard to SALT. Unlike the United States, the Soviet Union does not have people circulating in and out of government who can serve, while they are out of government, as an independent and knowledgeable lobby on arms control questions, nor does it have scientists who circulate in and out of defense responsibilities who can contribute critical technical experience to the public discussion of these issues. Unlike the United States, the Soviet Union has not had a great contribution to strategic military theory in the nuclear age from civilians; its discussions of these matters are conducted in professional military journals, many of which have limited circulation. In the compartmentalization of Soviet life, there is not much lateral transfer of information about military technology, particularly because of the extreme secrecy in which all military affairs are held. The consequence is that there has not been in the Soviet Union the kind of broad educational experience involving the interplay of scientific, military, and political factors involved in arms control questions, which this country has had, for example, as the result of the ABM debates. If we consider how long it takes for the ramifications of new weapons systems to sink into our consciousness, we must also allow for the learning time required for these ramifications to be absorbed by the Soviet political leadership and its staff. This process has something to do with the lags in reaction time which have characterized the action-reaction cycle between the two governments. It takes time for such concepts as the stability and instability of various new weapons systems to be diffused back and forth across the ocean, and to enter into personal and bureaucratic habits of thinking. We therefore have to allow for the incubation period of new ideas, if the negotiations are to have some chance of success.

One other factor affecting Soviet attitudes toward SALT and which sometimes gives rise to misinterpretation is the distinctive Soviet approach to negotiations and bargaining. It has often been the case that the Soviet Union will take elaborate pains to conceal its anxieties, for fear that it may confer a bargaining advantage upon its adversary. When, after a long delay, the Soviet Union reached a decision to enter into the SALT negotiations, its representatives pressed the United States on every occasion for an immediate response. This led to an interpretation abroad that the Soviet Union needed an easement of the burden of armaments more than the United States did, and that the United States could exact a political price for entering into the negotiations. The Soviet representatives thereupon received instructions to "play it cool," which they did with such elaborate casualness that many observers concluded the Soviet Union had lost all interest in the negotiations. It will be recalled, going back earlier, that when Stalin was first publicly informed by President Truman of the successful atomic explosion at Alamagordo, he reacted with such elaborate indifference as to lead many Western observers to conclude that he failed to appreciate the significance of the event. In retrospect, it became clear that he was anxious not to give an impression of Soviet concern lest the United States be encouraged to take diplomatic advantage of its lead. Many years later, it appeared to many observers that the Soviet Union had become reconciled to its status of strategic inferiority, because so little value was given to it in public. But it is now clear that the Soviet leaders felt a deep concern, and particularly after the rapid American buildup of the 1961–65 period, did everything possible to overcome the American lead, with consequences that we are now witnessing. Because of the timelag, however, the Soviet buildup was not seen as part of a process of interaction.

SOVIET ATTITUDES TOWARD MIRV

These general principles can be illustrated specifically in considering some prevailing assumptions about Soviet attitudes toward the MIRV issue. It has been widely argued here in Washington that the Soviet Union is indifferent to MIRV because its representatives did not show concern when the matter was raised at Helsinki. But there has been no indication that the question was clearly put by the United States, and it should not be surprising that the Soviet Union was not prepared to raise the issue, perhaps out of fear that its show of concern would confer a bargaining advantage upon the United States.

In unofficial discussions in the Soviet Union last October with Soviet defense scientists and officials, it was clear to the American participants that the complex ramifications of MIRV were beginning to be studied with lively interest in the Soviet Union, and that a learning process was at work. It may be that the incubation period has now passed, for there have been many indications that at least some in the Soviet Union fully appreciate what the consequences of MIRV deployments will be for both sides, and are as concerned about MIRV as they are about the deployment of antiballistic missiles.

It would be a mistake for us to conclude that a proposal for a ban on the testing and deployment of MIRV would be automatically rejected by the Soviet Union. It might be, if those in the Soviet Union who want to push ahead until they have reached our level of experience with MIRV testing prevail. But if the learning process has reached the point at which the Soviet leadership recognizes how costly this delay would be for them as well as for us, it is possible that the mutual advantages of heading off MIRV deployments will be seriously considered.

CLARIFICATION OF U.S. INTENTIONS REGARDING SALT NEEDED

One conclusion affecting our own policy which follows from these observations of the Soviet situation is that a clear signal of U.S. intentions regarding SALT is needed. A question often asked of Americans in Moscow is whether the U.S. administration is serious about the negotiations. There have been a number of articles in the Soviet press in recent days—in Pravda on March 7, Izvestia on the 13th and Red Star on the 14th—which are at least in part intended to influence the American discussion of these matters, but which also reflect the extent to which the uncertainty regarding American intentions toward SALT are involved in the intramural debates in Moscow. More specifically, the articles pose two questions: Whether the United States is now prepared to accept as a basis for negotiations a condition of approximate parity in strategic capabilities? Or whether those spokesmen who urge an intensified effort to gain a relative strategic advantage over the Soviet Union before and during the talks represent the Administration position?

Meanwhile, of course, the Soviet Union has continued to enlarge its strategic arsenal at an impressive pace. Perhaps it should not be surprising that as the two nations approach negotiations, they should each try to improve their bargaining position by improving their strategic capabilities. But wise men should recognize that unless this is stopped, there will be nothing significant left to negotiate.

U.S. SECURITY INTERESTS

This brings us directly to Senate Resolution 211. The essential question we must ask ourselves is this: Would our security be better served if both countries had MIRV capabilities, or if neither country did? It is not likely that we could preserve a unilateral advantage with this weapon for very long. The answer seems clear that if we both move into the MIRV era, we shall both be obliged, certainly by the time second generation of MIRV's makes its appearance, to enter upon a huge restructuring of our strategic forces to protect ourselves from the vulnerabilities to which MIRV will subject us. In time, several years and many billions of dollars later, we would doubtless reach a new equilibrium, but neither country will be more secure than it is now, and the costs, tensions, and instability may be very great.

Senator GORE. I hesitate to interrupt, but that is so precisely like an argument I listened to as to whether we should stop atmospheric testing that I just had to call it to your attention.

Dr. SHULMAN. Thank you for recalling that point.

PRESIDENT'S PROPOSED MORATORIUM

It would, therefore seem urgently desirable, in our own security interests, to try as strongly and as sincerely as we can to stop the present movement toward MIRV deployments. This points toward the wisdom of a proposal from the President of the United States to the Soviet Union at the earliest possible moment for a 24-month agreed moratorium including the following elements:
1. A ban on flight testing and deployment of MIRV's;
2. A hold at presently projected levels of ABM deployments; and
3. A hold at present levels of land-based fixed-site ICBM's which includes no new digging of silo emplacements for SS-9's.

Senator SYMINGTON. Excuse me, Professor. Did you purposely leave out "including and most importantly supporting radar installations"?

Dr. SHULMAN. No, sir. I intended that to be part of No. 2.

Senator SYMINGTON. So it still stands; does it?

Dr. SHULMAN. Yes, sir. As a matter of fact, I fear that a line was left out which referred specifically to that point. I am glad you caught it.

Senator SYMINGTON. I have the line here.

Dr. SHULMAN. It is left out of my text. How does it go, Senator? I haven't got it before me. How does that sentence go?

Senator SYMINGTON (reading). "Including and most importantly supporting radar installations."

Dr. SHULMAN. Thank you very much. I am so glad you referred to that because I think that is a critical point. The radar installation is the point that is most likely to be subject to observation.

Senator SYMINGTON. So do I.

Dr. SHULMAN. I put it down to the haste of getting this duplicated.
3. A hold at present levels of land-based fixed-site ICBM's— which includes no new digging of silo emplacements for SS-9's;
4. An agreed limitation on flight tests of all delivery vehicles to some moderate number, with the understanding that all tests would be conducted only in preannounced areas where they can be observed by national means of monitoring.

If this proposal were to have any chance of acceptance, it would be essential that the United States exercise restraint in the immediate future in regard to the early deployment of Minuteman III or a MIRV'ed Poseidon. The recently announced plan to deploy the first Minuteman III by June, with a rather slow rate of deployment for the balance of the year would not improve our capabilities significantly, and would only serve to forestall any possible negotiations about MIRV. The plan also suffers from the logical defect that if we fail to hold the line on MIRV, Minuteman seems destined for obsolescence in the foreseeable future.

OBJECTIONS TO PROPOSED MORATORIUM

A number of objections have been raised to a moratorium proposal along these lines: It is too late to stop MIRV. It is too difficult to agree what should be included in the prohibition. We need MIRV capabilities for our strategic arsenal. We would be losing a bargaining advantage if we did not proceed with MIRV and Safeguard Phase II. It would be difficult to resume our programs at the end of the moratorium period even if the conditions were not fulfilled. These are serious objections, and they deserve to be examined carefully.

Perhaps the most difficult objection is the feeling that it is too late. It is more difficult to reverse our course of thinking than it is to give in to the inertial force of on-going events. But unless it is more important to fulfill our presently programed weapons plans than it is to get an agreement to forestall MIRV deployments, this fatalistic argument is no more persuasive now than it was when it was first advanced in Washington at least a year and a half ago.

The difficulty of defining what is to be included and excluded in the agreement is a real one; should the prohibition include MIRV components tested singly, and if so would we be able to verify compliance with the prohibition? Should the prohibition extend to MRV's as well as MIRV's? The best judgments seem to be that these are real but disproportionate objections. Whichever way these problems of definition are worked out in the negotiations, it is not reasonable to fear that our security would be seriously compromised within the 24-month period of the moratorium even under the worst assumptions that can be made.

ARGUMENTS FOR PROCEEDING WITH MIRV

The argument that we need MIRV has at various times rested upon three rationales. The first is that we need more warheads to cover our present target obligations. This would be a persuasive argument only if we decided to depart from a deterrent posture; it is clear that retaliatory damage to the adversary does not greatly increase if numbers of delivered warheads are increased much beyond 1,000—or, indeed, above 500. There is no limit to what we could include in our target requirements if this is allowed to run free. A second rationale is that we need MIRV as a penetration aid, particularly if Soviet ABM's should be increased, and if the Soviet Union should upgrade its present surface-to-air missile air defense to ABM-level capabilities.

This argument neglects the disparity in time required between ABM's and MIRV's. We know from our own Safeguard plans that at least 7 to 8 years are required to install an ABM system, whereas a MIRV capability can be created in perhaps 3 or 4 years. The critical point about the upgrading of SAM's, surface-to-air missiles, would be the supporting radars rather than the interceptors, which might indeed be done under concealment. But if phased array radars made their appearance, these could not be as easily concealed, and the disparity in lead times would still leave us a reasonable margin of safety. The third rationale has been the need for MIRV's as hard target killers, and here it is most evident that the development of MIRV's capable of destroying adversary missiles would be destabilizing and therefore undesirable, since it would create understandable apprehensions on the Soviet side about our intentions, particularly if it were accompanied by an expansion of our ABM capabilities.

The argument that we should proceed with MIRV, and also with Safeguard Phase II, in order to have a bargaining counter in our hand is short-sighted. To enter upon these programs in order to have something to bargain with, or in order to apply pressure upon the Russians, is likely to have an effect opposite to what is intended. The logical

Soviet reaction to such actions would be to question our real intentions, and to redouble their own military efforts. If SALT proceeds over a long period, as it may do, and if both sides argue the need for continuing their build-up to improve their bargaining advantage, the effect of the SALT negotiations will be to leave us both worse off than if they had never been begun.

(I have an image here that Senator Fulbright anticipated in his questions before.)

Negotiating about strategic weapons is not entirely like a poker game—both sides *can* lose.

Finally, it is true that it may be politically difficult to resume our strategic programs at the end of a 24-month moratorium period, even if we have not been able to negotiate in the meantime a larger and more lasting arms control agreement, but the risk is by no means equal to the risk we run in letting present events take their course, and it must be left to our best judgment at the end of the moratorium period whether our security interests do or do not require a resumption of efforts to build MIRV and additional ABM systems under the conditions that then prevail.

Hopefully, it might be possible during the 24-months to work out the complex requirements for a freeze on strategic capabilities, and perhaps even to move toward some reductions. Without the moratorium, however, time would work against the possibility of any such agreements.

U.S. LONG-TERM RELATIONS WITH SOVIET UNION

The moratorium proposal, and the SALT negotiations generally, have an important place in the framework of a larger conception of our long-term relations with the Soviet Union. Given the present internal political conditions in the Soviet Union described earlier, it does not seem likely that an easement of political rivalry between the two countries can be expected in the near future. But progress in SALT or toward a moratorium on MIRV testing, does not require a détente, since the mutual interest in damping down the strategic arms race exists whether tensions in other fields are high or low. There is a tendency current now in the Soviet Union to link progress in SALT with our policy toward China; and a tendency in this country to tie SALT to Soviet restraint in the Middle East or some other problem.

This would represent a serious error or judgment in either direction, for our security interest in the success of SALT is not and should not be made dependent upon other problems, and this is equally true for the Soviet Union. However, if the SALT negotiations prove to be successful over a period of time, it is possible that the level of tension may be reduced sufficiently to open the way to an improvement in our relations with the Soviet Union. This is best viewed as a series of stages over a fairly long time-span. SALT is the major business of the present stage. If it is successful, it may open the way to an intermediate stage whose main business would be to introduce some restraints into our deep-seated political rivalry. This would in turn open up possibilities for more substantial cooperation, involving trade and technology, and hopefully common action through the United Nations in peace-keeping arrangements, economic development and environmental problems.

This longer-term perspective would, however, be extremely remote if we have not succeeded in the months immediately before us in levelling off the strategic arms race, beginning with MIRV. And this will not be possible without vigorous action on the part of those who perceive that at this moment and on this subject the rational self-interest of the United States and the Soviet Union meet. Thank you, Mr. Chairman.

SIMILARITY OF ARGUMENTS FOR MIRV TO THOSE AGAINST NUCLEAR TEST BAN

Senator GORE. Thank you, Dr. Shulman. The Chair feels that Senator Case did not conclude and therefore is entitled to recognition. I hope he will pardon the Chair to make one statement. First, I want to thank you very much for a very able statement. Secondly, I want to observe that those who argue now that deployment of ABM and MIRV would add to the security of the United States could in my opinion make identically the same arguments that it would add to our security to somehow renounce the atmospheric test ban and resume testing in the atmosphere so we could have bigger and better bombs. Would you agree with that?

Dr. SHULMAN. Yes, I do, Senator.

Senator GORE. I heard these same arguments over and over and over. The same fears were expressed about the conclusion of an agreement to stop testing in the atmosphere. Fortunately, we overcame the fears and now I think we have more security rather than less as a result of this treaty. We also have less pollution of the atmosphere.

Senator Case?

Senator CASE. Thank you, Mr. Chairman. I want to thank you, too, for this very good statement. It is impressive and gives strong support to the idea of an immediately agreed upon moratorium.

SPECIFIC ELEMENTS OF PROPOSED MORATORIUM

I am interested in your suggestion in your statement on specific elements of such a moratorium. You would—and I think it makes great sense—suggest a 24-month agreed moratorium to include a ban upon flight testing and deployment of MIRV's, and then a hold on present level for ABM, a hold at present levels on fixed-site ICBM's, which includes no new digging for Soviet SS-9's and an agreed limitation on flight tests of all delivery vehicles to some moderate number.

It seems to me the more I thought about this that, although anything that we can get in the way of restrictions or limitations accepted by each side would be good, the chance of getting limitation, for example, of ABM might well be improved by an agreement on the other side to limit MIRV's or stop MIRV testing and deployment, because the real counterpart of MIRV on one side is the ABM on the other and vice versa, and not the MIRV's on each side.

Dr. SHULMAN. That is right.

Senator CASE. So I think that is a very valuable contribution to our thinking here and I am sure that our colleague from Massachusetts would regard it as such.

Thank you, Mr. Chairman. That is all.

Senator GORE. Senator Church?

RUSSIAN ATTITUDE TOWARD MIRV DEPLOYMENT

Senator CHURCH. Thank you, Mr. Chairman.

Doctor, your testimony touched upon the question of what might be an indifference feigned by Russia toward the MIRV question.

I was interested in that because of what I read in Anthony Astrachan's article in the Washington Post of March 7. He reported on a commentary in Pravda regarding the SALT talks. According to Astrachan, the Pravda article emphasized Soviet concern over further deployment of the Safeguard system. This commentary mentioned Secretary of Defense Laird's backing for a new manned bomber plus a new underwater missile system, but did not mention MIRV.

Astrachan commented, "The article thus tended to confirm reports from both sides after the first round of SALT talks, that the Soviets were concerned about ABM's and bombers, but not about MIRV's."

I have seen in this particular account and in others as well the suggestion that the Russians really don't care much and, because they don't care much, we ought to proceed with our planned deployment of the weapon. Please amplify your argument on this score.

Dr. SHULMAN. Thank you, Senator. I would be glad to amplify this point and to suggest to you three reasons why I don't agree with the conclusion of that article.

First of all, there has been subsequent Soviet press comment referring to MIRV, particularly the most recent story that I referred to which was in response to Secretary Seaman's announcement about the date for the planned deployment of the first Minuteman III, and it was—there was no hesitancy at all on direct reference to MIRV in that story.

Second, there were two factors that seemed to me important that would lead me to be hesitant to conclude that because the Russians hadn't talked much about MIRV that they are not interested. One is that MIRV is a field in which they feel we have an advantage and, if my impressions of the Soviet conduct at these negotiations is right, I think their fear is that if they talk a great deal about MIRV that their feeling would be that we would act upon our presumed advantage and try to use it as a bargaining counter, and it seems to me that the characteristic pattern of Soviet behavior in such matters has been not to raise—at least not to express—their concern about matters where they feel they have a disadvantage or vulnerability.

Then there is another point and that is, and I stress that this is an impression. This is really a guess. I think that there has been a learning time involved. I suggested a number of reasons why it takes time for some of the basic conceptions involved in arms control to get a hearing in Moscow and get a substantial hearing.

Now, this was true, for example, on the ABM issue when, as I suggested, I belonged to a number of study groups that go back and forth to Moscow and talk to Soviet scientists and officials from time to time. When we first started talking to them about the ABM issue, we couldn't really get a hearing. We argued that, if they went ahead with what they were then talking about, the effect would be to trigger an arms race and it wouldn't do them much good, that there wouldn't be any increase in security because they would trigger a response from us. "How can we not do something that might save some lives?"

And that is a good simple answer, but the problem is a lot more complex than that. And it took, well, 3 years, 4 years before we began to see a real appreciation on the part of Soviet scientists and others about what the process of interaction would be.

Now I think the same kind of learning process has been going on about MIRV. MIRV is a complex issue. Not many of our own people really understand the issue very well. It hasn't really sunk in on us. It involves enormously complex technical aspects and I think it has taken time for those who are involved, not only directly immediately in preparing the negotiating position but the supporting people around them, the scientific community and others, to absorb what MIRV would mean.

RUSSIAN CONCERN OVER MIRV DEPLOYMENT

So my feeling is that, allowing for the learning-time period, and my impressions of our own conversations in Moscow last fall where there obviously was a learning process going on, people turning this around, looking at it, trying to study the ramifications of it, it was apparent to me that there really is a serious concern but it takes time before it gets registered, and before it gets sufficient support to be expressed in the official position.

So that is why I am hesitant to draw the conclusion that they don't see their self-interest in getting MIRV banned if possible.

Senator BROOKE. Senator Church, might I add that, if we can presume that the Soviet scientists understand MIRV technology, and the ramifications of it, then it is inconceivable that the Soviets would not be concerned about MIRV, because the whole problem is whether one side or the other has a first-strike capability. And if the scientists understood that MIRV technology is potentially a first-strike capability and potentially a destabilizing factor, then it seems to me again, as I said, inconceivable that they would not be concerned about it.

I think that what Dr. Shulman says is unquestionably correct. I do, of course, call the Senator's attention to the Washington Post article of March 15, where the Soviets attacked the United States on the MIRV decision once that decision had been made, that it was very clear that the Soviet Union said that American missile policy could jeopardize disarmament talks between the countries and then the article goes on further.

I read the article to which the Senator referred. I was rather concerned myself as to why—what importance had not been placed by the Soviets upon this whole question of MIRV and I have just had to conclude that they just wanted to soft-pedal it because we were so far ahead of them at the time and they just didn't want to raise it at that time. But indications are now, I think, very clear that the Soviets are not only concerned about it but apparently are of a disposition to entertain discussions leading to an agreement on it.

Dr. SHULMAN. Senator, could I mention one other point that I think might be interesting to you? My impression is that, when the Soviet delegation went to Helsinki, it went with a position which was very much of a compromise position, that there was a coalition that supported the decision to enter into the SALT talks, but it was a coalition of people who are not altogether agreed on the reasons why they wanted to go or on the substantive position to take.

So there was a rather limited mandate and my impression is that among the pressures bearing upon the leadership at the time were some from people in the Soviet Union who very much want to go ahead as fast as possible in their own MIRV test program and try to overcome the disadvantage in this, and I think that is part of the reason why they may not have been able to get written into their instructions an instruction to include MIRV in their discussions. At least—of course, this is just a guess, Senator, but I think it sounds plausible and it has some parallels with our own situation.

COMMENDATION OF THE WITNESS

Senator FULBRIGHT. Will the Senator yield for one comment? I want to express my appreciation to Professor Shulman for coming here and giving us the benefit of his observations. He has been one of the finest scholars of the Russian scene for a long time. I am sorry, but I have to go because I have another appointment. Thank you.

Dr. SHULMAN. Thank you, Senator.

SOVIET INTEREST IN MIRV MORATORIUM

Senator BROOKE. Senator Church, may I just add one matter? Mr. Nitze was before our committee and, though I am certainly not at liberty to discuss his testimony before the committee, nevertheless I think it is safe to say that in the manner in which the question of MIRV was raised at Helsinki, I don't believe that it is a fair conclusion that the Soviets did not indicate any interest in an agreement on MIRV at that time. In fact, I am saying that we did not propose a moratorium. I think that is public information at the present time.

Our delegation did not propose a moratorium on MIRV to the Soviet Union and in the context in which the whole question was raised together with many other facets, some of the members of our delegation did conclude that the Soviets were not interested. I don't believe that if the Senator were privy to the manner in which the question was raised, the context, that he would have drawn such a conclusion.

Senator CHURCH. I appreciate the comments. From a purely logical standpoint, the Russians should be as concerned about MIRV as we should be. However, I have seen these puzzling and seemingly contradictory arguments put forward by those who propose MIRV. One line states the deployment of MIRV will not jeopardize the commencing of the SALT talks because the Russians simply don't care that much and the other line says we should proceed deploying our weapons so that we will have a lever of great influence to use at the talks themselves.

EFFECT OF U.S. TECHNOLOGICAL LEAD ON MIRV MORATORIUM

I am concerned about one other aspect of this whole question. Has the time already passed when agreement between the two countries on MIRV might be obtained?

If we are to proceed with the deployment of MIRV's, at least in its first stage, how will the Russians rely upon any moratorium in which we simply undertake to promise not to deploy the weapon and not to proceed with further tests? The testing is presumably subject to verification on either side. However, if what I have understood of your testimony, there is no way to check upon the deployment of the weapon without onsite inspection and very intimate surveillance. Aren't we already in a position where it might appear to the Soviets the purpose of suggesting a moratorium is to enable us to proceed with the deployment, which they could not possibly check out while they have not tested sufficiently to proceed to a deployment on their part? And if that is so, then how can we reasonably expect the Russians to acquiesce in such a proposal?

Dr. SHULMAN. Senator, I agree that is a problem and it may affect the Soviet attitudes but there are two reasons why I think they might be expected to accept a proposal despite the advanced state of our own testing.

The first is that even if we had completed all the development testing we required for the penetration aid function of MIRV, that is, for the first uses of them, I believe it would be contrary to all our previous practice if we were to move ahead to deployment without the opportunity of confidence testing on a weapon as enormously complex, much more complex than anything else we have worked with. This is, of course, a matter subject to military testimony, I suppose, but my impression would be that the most responsible military men would not be willing to commit themselves to reliance upon a weapon which they were not able to test, to have confidence tests of even if they had completed their development.

The second reason stems partly from the asymmetry of our two situations. It is inconceivable to me, and I hope it would be inconceivable to the Russians, that the United States could cheat and get away with it in this kind of a society. I do not believe that we could actually, if once we committed ourselves to a test ban, then go ahead and deploy anyway in defiance of our commitment. I do not believe it could be kept secret in this society and I would hope the Russians would know that.

Senator BROOKE. I certainly would agree on both points, Senator Church. Certainly on the first point, the technology as we know it today is no more than a penetration aid. That is what our Defense Department has said. That is the purpose of MIRV in the first instance, that this would be a penetration aid in helping us with a sophisticated ABM system which does not now exist. But the Russians know that if this technology is to be really devastating to them in the sense that it goes beyond a penetration aid and becomes a hardpoint kill weapon, that we would have to continue further testing and that this testing could not really be concealed. I think Dr. Shulman would agree that even our crews would have to be given an opportunity to gain experience and expertise in addition to the weapon itself.

All of this would be ascertainable and verifiable by the Soviet Union. I think in addition to that we have only what the Soviets themselves have said most recently, Mr. Dobrynin in his statement, and others, that if the question of a moratorium on MIRV testing and deployment were to be presented, that they would be interested in such discussion of a possible agreement.

So obviously they don't feel that it has gone so far that it is at the point of no return.

PROBLEM OF ON-SITE INSPECTION

Senator CHURCH. I have one last question. Senator Gore mentioned earlier that during the long and tortuous discussions that finally led to the test ban treaty we focused on the question of onsite inspection, and the Russians were adamant against what they conceived to be an effort on our part to penetrate their society for purposes other than verifying suspicious explosions. It wasn't until we finally agreed to limit our objective to those tests which could be independently monitored without the need to penetrate the other country that the Russians proved willing to sign the treaty.

We face the same problem here. If we proceed to propose a moratorium which must be negotiated and which will involve inevitably some discussion of supplementary inspection over and above what may be available to either side, involving as Senator Brooke suggested certain penetration of the other country's territory, aren't we really asking for a repetition of that long argument? If so, wouldn't it be desirable, indeed ever preferable, for the President to say, before the talks commence in that he is undertaking unilaterally not to proceed with further testing or deployment of the MIRV weapon so long as the Russians refrain from commencing MIRV tests? He would thus be setting the ground for the negotiations which may be very long and very difficult on the question of inspection procedures. In view of the experience that we had with the test ban treaty, what would be wrong approaching it that way?

Senator BROOKE. Well, Senator, No. 1, let me say this, that at the present state of the art, technology of MIRV, we are really getting very little more than the penetration aid that the Defense Department has talked about and we really don't need it. We have I think—this is not classified information, but we have sufficient missiles at the present time to wreak havoc and unacceptable damage on the Soviet Union, so that you can understand that. In fact, both sides have that. We really don't get into a very serious problem so far as the Soviets are concerned until this technology is refined and perfected.

I just don't think that the first generation of MIRV's create that much problem for the Soviet Union.

Dr. Shulman, you may correct me if I am wrong, but from the best information I have, it does not really present to them this first strike capability.

Dr. SHULMAN. Providing they could know that this——

Senator BROOKE. Yes. Providing they know that we have stopped there, of course; yes.

Now, I say that, Senator Church, to say that if we stopped there, we are all right so far as the Soviets are concerned, I would presume, and they might want to build more SS-9's or more SS-11's, to be sure. They might want to increase their arsenal. But I don't know that they would be in too grave a danger as a result of our progress in

MIRV technology. But once we proceed further, then we get into a very serious situation, and this would necessitate further testing.

So at the present time there would be no need for onsite inspection. That is the point I am trying to make. We wouldn't need onsite inspection at this time but if we let them proceed and we get to the point where MIRV becomes a first strike capability, then, of course, nothing short of onsite surveillance by the Soviets would ever convince them of what we have in those silos.

MONITORING BY SATELLITE AND RADAR

Dr. SHULMAN. Could I add, Senator, there is one important difference I think between the situation now and the situation in 1963 when we talked about the partial test ban treaty, and that is the availability to both sides of satellite reconnaissance effective for this purpose plus our general radar competence on both sides, which means that on this issue the monitoring of flight testing can be done adequately without any intrusion of each other's territories.

There are only two elements involved here in the list of items that now are immediately before us that require monitoring. One is the question of whether there is a flight testing of MIRV's, multiple warheads. The one shortcoming there is, as I suggested, the possibility that the single component of the MIRV system could be tested individually and that might not be——

Senator SYMINGTON. I didn't hear that. Possibility of what?

Dr. SHULMAN. Of the single components of a MIRV system being tested individually; that is, not in multiples, but the warheads being tested separately which might not be subject to the kind of monitoring you are talking about. And we have to weigh how big a risk is that? Is that an acceptable risk? I think it is, but that obviously is subject to expert testimony.

The other element involved which requires testing has to do with a limitation on flight testing of other vehicles. I suggested that it should be at some moderate number and that each side should commit itself to conduct its tests in preannounced areas where it can be monitored.

Now, this is important for several reasons. For one thing it is a backup protection against the possibility of cheating on the MIRV flight testing. I mean, if either side were to use its limited number of tests for that purpose, it would be seriously limited on the other kinds of testing it could do. But that can be perfectly monitored so long as it is done in areas that are preannounced and where we are set up for it.

Apart from that, there would be no necessity in any of the matters that Senator Brooke or I have discussed today that would require onsite inspection that would raise the thorny issue of intrusive inspection of Soviet territory.

Senator BROOKE. And then the question of verification of monitoring would be the subject of negotiation. These are matters that could be negotiated in the agreement.

Senator CHURCH. That is all I have, Mr. Chairman.

Senator GORE. Senator Cooper?

COULD MIRV RESPOND TO RUSSIAN SS-9 DEPLOYMENT?

Senator COOPER. Thank you. I must leave in a few minutes. I want to say, though, I am very grateful to listen to testimony from both of you. I think the Senator from Massachusetts deserves great credit for bringing this matter before us again. And we are always glad to hear you, Dr. Shulman.

On the basis of hearing both of you now and also hearing a great deal of testimony about MIRV last year, your statement seemed to demolish any rational arguments that could be made for deploying MIRV's, but there is one question I would like to ask.

The Secretary of Defense at the beginning of last year and again this year has expressed great concern about Soviet deployment of an increasing number of SS-9's. I must say I share that concern. It is a threat. If they deploy enough of them and arm them with MRV's or MIRV's I think it would be a threat against our retaliatory capability—a threat which we thought last year would not be relieved by inferior ABM system in effect.

Now, is there any possible rationale that can be made for the continuing test flights and deployment of MIRV's as a response to the continued deployment of SS-9's?

Senator BROOKE. Senator, I think the answer——

Senator COOPER. Let me just say one more thing. It seemed to me that if we were not able to come to an agreement in the SALT talks and if the Soviets continue to deploy SS-9's, then we have to think about an effective way to meet that threat.

Senator BROOKE. Senator, I think the answer is "No" to that. Very frankly you say that the Soviets are continuing their deployment of SS-9's, and that is true. I think the rate that has been estimated, just guesses, is about at the rate of 50 per year of the SS-9's, and it is estimated now that they have a few more ICBM's, the Soviet Union at the present time, SS-9's, SS-11's, than does the United States. But if you look at the overall strategic forces and consider the B-52 bombers, our bombing force as compared to their strategic bomber force, if you look at our Polaris submarines now being converted to Poseidons as compared to their submarines, if you look at the tactical nuclear weapons in Europe at the present time which I think will be reliable, obviously we are still ahead of the Soviet Union.

I did respond earlier that we are probably as close to parity as one can be. It is just not strictly a numbers game. It is quality and megatonnage as well as numbers of missiles that either side has.

Senator GORE. It is also a question of when is enough enough.

Senator BROOKE. That is right. So if you say that we must continue our flight testing of MIRV, we must get into the deployment of MIRV in order to keep up with the Soviets who are continuing their testing and their deployment of SS-9's, this is a—this is the very spiral that we are trying to avoid.

I think someone is going to have to stop and I am suggesting that the MIRV gets us into a whole new field.

Now, if we were merely increasing our numbers of Minutemen, that would be one thing. We say as the Soviets increase the SS-9's we should increase our Minuteman force of if they increase their bombers, we increase ours, but here we get into a new technology which really revolutionizes it.

Senator COOPER. I didn't say it.
Senator BROOKE. I am sorry.
Senator COOPER. I didn't say anything like that.
Senator BROOKE. I'm sorry. I misunderstood.

POSSIBLE RESPONSE TO RUSSIAN SS-9'S

Senator COOPER. I agree wholly and I have been one of those who opposed——
Senator BROOKE. I know you did.
Senator COOPER (continuing). Opposed taking unnecessary steps that would continue the arms race. I hope with all my heart that we are successful in SALT, and I think that is the most important work before our country today because everything hinges, as you said, on it. But the Administration has made a statement that it is going to deploy this weapon in June. I hope they won't, before the SALT talks have had a chance. In the event that the SALT talks fail, it will be necessary to meet the threat of SS-9's, because our Minuteman will become obsolete, as the doctor says, and we either have to go into some feasible defensive weapon if that is technologically possible or equip our submarines with a better weapon.
Senator BROOKE. Senator, the Department of Defense has at no time said that MIRV is a response to the Soviet SS-9. The Defense Department has consistently said that MIRV is in response to what they believed the Soviet Union would have—an ABM system that the Soviet Union was developing. I don't think they have ever said it was in response to a SS-9 to my knowledge.
Senator COOPER. I didn't mean it that way. When Minuteman becomes obsolete, would you not then need some other retaliatory capacity to preserve the deterrent which would be underwater?
Dr. SHULMAN. Senator Cooper, could I add just one sentence to that?
Senator COOPER. Yes.
Dr. SHULMAN. If we are worried about the SS-9 and what the Soviet Union might do with it when MIRV'd, it seems to me the logic of that worry would be to have a greater rather than a lesser interest in getting the MIRV moratorium.
Senator COOPER. Thank you very much.

UNILATERAL CESSATION OF FLIGHT TESTING NOT PROPOSED

Senator BROOKE. Mr. Chairman, may I merely state to Senator Church, because he raised the—Senator Church raised the question of unilateral cessation and I don't think either Dr. Shulman or I addressed it. I just want to make it clear that this moratorium suggested in Senate Resolution 211 does not go to a unilateral cessation of flight-testing. This question was raised when it appeared before the committee the first time. Senator Symington is very much concerned about a unilateral moratorium. I have personally never favored the unilateral moratorium. In fact, I even changed the language of this resolution so that it would be very clear that this calls for a mutual cessation rather than a unilateral cessation of flight-testing.
Senator CHURCH. Yes, I understand that. I wanted to inquire about the hangup we have regarding inspection, but your answers

have clarified that point. At this present juncture, the problem of inspection would not be a very complicated nor difficult one, as I understood your replies.

Senator GORE. Senator Symington?

Senator SYMINGTON. Thank you, Mr. Chairman.

Senator Brooke, I am very interested in your resolution, although I wasn't present when Mr. Nitze testified before the committee we are both on, Armed Services. I was much impressed with your questioning, and thought it extremely penetrating.

Senator BROOKE. Thank you, Senator.

Senator SYMINGTON. I would like to support your resolution but am not exactly sure about the unilateral aspect, and would present to you why, and would like also to ask Dr. Shulman incident thereto.

U.S. DEPLOYMENT OF ABM AND MIRV

When the first ABM came out I was against it because it seemed silly; the idea we were going to defend our cities with a thin defense against China, and not worry too much about the Soviet Union.

When it was shifted—the name but not the design—it was a more logical application, but it was certainly not designed for point defense. That has now been proved by the fact they are changing the design of the radar and adding a number of missiles.

It would seem to me that any country which announced its intention to deploy an ABM and a MIRV both, whether the relatively small number on the head of a Minuteman or the much larger number on the head of a Poseidon, would be shooting for a first-strike capability. At least a possible enemy would so believe. I can't get that out of my mind. We all agree we must have, without any reservation of any kind, a second-strike capability, against anybody; but this double deployment would look like first-strike desire.

To me the MIRV is a second-strike weapon all the way through, especially considering the Poseidon. I worry about what is said about the SS-9. If it is what they say it is, which I personally doubt from the standpoint of accuracy—after all, it is really nothing more or less than the Titan, which we abandoned; it has a bigger warhead and is more accurate, no doubt, but so could have the Titan. They went for punch, we for numbers.

Now, a lot of the people who wanted to add to the arms race emphasized the importance of that punch. Do I make sense as you see it?

Dr. SHULMAN. Yes.

Senator SYMINGTON. To me the MIRV Minuteman is fundamentally a second strike weapon, especially as applied to the Poseidon. I was opposed to the ABM because I did not think it would work. But we have gone ahead with it and now are applying it to the area defense aspect as well as the point aspect. Although I am personally willing to listen to all the assurances of our Government that combined with the Poseidon, it does not represent a desire to have a first-strike capability, I doubt, if I was in the Kremlin, I would agree with those assurances. Certainly there is no way we can prove to them it is not the first step to a thick area defense.

Does that make sense to you?

Dr. SHULMAN. Yes.

PROPOSED U.S. POLICY FOR ARMS CONTROL NEGOTIATIONS

Senator SYMINGTON. Then why shouldn't we go ahead and express to the Soviets our willingness to talk about all this; but at the same time notify them, until there is a successful outcome to these talks, we intend to deploy our second-strike capability, through the MIRV's, just as they assure us, which some doubt, that they are deploying their SS-9's for a second-strike capability.

We say we are going ahead, now, with our Poseidons and our Minuteman III's. We know you know there is no first-strike aspect to that program; and we agree with you there is no first strike re your SS-9 increase; but just as you have to protect yourself, so we have to protect ourselves. What I am trying to say is, if we package our ABM concept with our MIRV concept, it is clear to me that they could think we were going for a first-strike capability. So also we have the right to think that if they proceed with an ABM as well as the SS-9's—perhaps even if they don't proceed with the ABM based on the way the SS-9 is cocked up—they are going for a first-strike capability.

So what I would like my able friend from Massachusetts to do is to say we are going ahead with our MIRV both ways, sea and ground, but would like to stop it—in our open society they know they could investigate whether or not we did—and if we reach agreement you would stop your deployment efforts in the ABM field. We in turn will stop ours, our deployment in the ABM field. Then you would have a real arms control program underway.

What would be the matter with that, as policy?

Dr. SHULMAN. Senator, I would think that the logic of your argument would lead you to package it a little bit differently; that is to say, it would involve I should think an agreement to hold on ABM, not to deploy the Minuteman III, but to go ahead with the Poseidon. That is, if the Minuteman III as you have suggested could be part of a counterforce strike whereas the Poseidon might not be, moreover, Minuteman III suffers from the vulnerability that it could become obsolescent, which the Poseidon would not be unless there were great advances in antisubmarine warfare.

Therefore, the negotiating package you are putting together I would think would involve holding on those two items, not going ahead now in June with the Minuteman III deployment but perhaps letting Poseidon come off the line in November or December, whenever it is scheduled to come off the line, unless there was a response from the Soviet Union.

I first want to make sure I have your proposition right.

Senator SYMINGTON. You are doing fine.

Dr. SHULMAN. All right. Now, the reason why I would hesitate to move along those lines is that although for our purposes we would have a clear distinction between a penetration aid function on the part—as part of our retaliatory capability, say, for the Poseidon, that the question on the other side always is not knowing how far we have gone with our R. & D. in our MIRV capability. I don't know whether they would be content with the impression that we were going to hold our MIRV development at a penetration aid level, whether there was not testing going on, where there wasn't R. & D. going on, which would make it possible for us, in a rather short time, to give it counterforce capability.

Senator SYMINGTON. Well, they have the same detection possibilities and more—being a closed society. They would have more capacity to cheat than we would.

Dr. SHULMAN. Sure. Well, the difficulty is that borderline there, and the reason why I would favor Senator Brooke's approach to this is that it is a lot easier technically to get the firebreak short of deployment than it is to get it midpoint in deployment between the penetration aid force function and the counterforce aid function, I think.

WEAPONS TO BE INCLUDED IN ARMS CONTROL AGREEMENT

Senator SYMINGTON. I can't figure how you can eliminate the Poseidon. That would be sort of like saying let's stop them holding up the corner drugstore, but let's not worry about the fact they are robbing a big bank.

In other words, the Poseidon is so much more a dangerous weapon to them than the Minuteman III would be, if we really want to make a deal which, of course, we do because we are talking about the most important subject in the world. Shortly we start hearings on this in the other committee, so I am trying to get a little ammunition. I don't see how you can have—and I say this with great respect to the Senator from Massachusetts—any true arms control agreement unless you pool the ABM development, the SS-9, the Minuteman III, and the Poseidon all together in a package of overall agreement.

Dr. SHULMAN. Well, I certainly do agree with you that these are closely related and that is why it seemed to me that there had to be those four elements that I suggested as part of the moratorium. It would include a hold on ABM, as I say, particularly on the radar. It would also mean that the Soviet program would not go forward on the SS-9's beyond present silo emplacements.

Now, the Secretary of Defense has indicated in his posture statement that at the present level of development, the SS-9 did not—he did not regard it as having counterforce capabilities and he argued in that posture statement that it would require great improvements in accuracy and much greater flexibility in order for it to have effective counterforce capability.

Now, that is why I think if these were made part of the moratorium package, to refer more specifically to the Poseidon point, Senator, what occurs to me as you speak is that it might be wise for us to return to a concept that we had in this Government a couple of years ago but which we didn't develop, and that was for considering the development of Poseidon as a single warhead missile, with its greater capability of range.

Senator SYMINGTON. That is the Polaris.

Dr. SHULMAN. Well, but the retrofitting that is now going on could be adapted to the new Poseidon with its greater range and could be——

Senator SYMINGTON. You mean a MRV and not MIRV or a——

Dr. SHULMAN. No, sir.

Senator SYMINGTON (continuing). Just a better Polaris?

Dr. SHULMAN. That is right.

Senator SYMINGTON. I see.

PRESENT RUSSIAN IDEOLOGICAL TENDENCY

I read a story about Mr. Suslov, our old friend—you are a Kremlinologist—coming back into authority. Does this mean the Stalinist line is becoming relatively stronger today in the Politburo than it was before?

Dr. SHULMAN. Since this field in which I work, which is mostly guesswork really, the first part of the answer is I don't know but the second part is yes. There was a story that went around on the wires that there was a letter signed by three men, of whom Suslov was one, critical of the two leaders, Kosygin and Brezhnev. The story has not been authenticated. It has been formally denied and I suppose all one can say is a questionmark. It would be highly unusual if there were such a letter. There may certainly be acute differences among the leadership. It seems to me unlikely that they would air it that way unless they were really ready to come apart at the seams.

My feeling would be not to give credence to it at this stage. However, it certainly is true that if you look at the Soviet press these days—I had occasion to go back and catch up after being away from it for a little while and I was startled at the rise in the vitriol, the rise of material of heavy ideological content. I think it would be too much to say it was a return to Stalinism but there was a lot of old-fashioned tub-thumping kind of primitive stuff and I was startled to discover that I myself was the target of an article of abuse just last month which was an old-fashoned piece just like the old days.

So while I don't think that is *"the* Russia" by any means, that is certainly one of the tendencies that is present in the Soviet Union today.

Senator SYMINGTON. Thank you, and congratulations to my colleague, Senator Brooke, for the fine work he has done in this field.

EFFECTIVENESS OF U.S. SECOND-STRIKE FORCE

Senator BROOKE. I thank you for your congratulations. I would much rather thank you for your support of this resolution. I have great respect for your knowledge particularly in this field. I am somewhat concerned about your conclusion, what seemed to me to be your conclusion that we need MIRV as a second strike-force. It just seems to me that we have ample retaliatory forces already and we certainly don't need MIRV for that purpose.

Senator SYMINGTON. When you say MIRV, do you include the Poseidon?

Senator BROOKE. Yes. I mean I am talking now about deployment.

Senator SYMINGTON. Then I say with respect I am not sure I could go along with your position. That is where we perhaps have a difference.

Senator BROOKE. Actually if you are talking about Minuteman III, obviously we would not need MIRV for this purpose because——

Senator SYMINGTON. I hope we can have the opportunity of discussing this further, either the two of us, or in executive session. Thank you. My time is up.

Senator GORE. Senator Javits?

Senator JAVITS. Mr. Chairman, I won't detain the committee at this hour. The witnesses have been very generous with their time. I think we are all very grateful to Dr. Shulman and Senator Brooke, our colleague, for their very fine analyses of this whole problem for us.

EFFECT OF U.S. DECISION ON MIRV ON SALT

I have one question, Dr. Shulman. In your statement you say something about the top political leadership in the Soviet Union conciliating the contradictory pressures that bear upon it, and so on. That is generally a characterization of it. Now, of course, I am thinking of a SALT agreement. It is a fact that, to make a SALT agreement, you have to make it with the leadership probably as it is now.

Could you tell us anything about their state of mind, their likely inducement to make an agreement, and how that will be affected by our deployment or failure to deploy MIRV? We are told—in that very chair where you are setting—we were told by the Director of the Disarmament Agency that the Russians couldn't care less about whether we deploy MIRV or not. They say go do as you like, it isn't going to affect our negotiations in the SALT talks.

Now, in your judgment is that right? Is it wrong? What do you think about it?

I have maintained that even though they might have said it isn't going to make any difference, it will, make a difference. If we took the position that we will not deploy, it could have a very great impact upon them even in terms of their own public opinion, even if the public opinion was their own party. But this is just my idea and I am interested in yours.

Dr. SHULMAN. Senator, I agree with you completely. I think that anyone who would argue that the Soviets are unconcerned with what we do on MIRV or would not be affected by it or would not take actions in response to such deployment is dead wrong. And if you ask what would be the effect on the Soviet leadership of our decision to go ahead as, for example, the announcement the other day from Secretary Seamans, I would say that it will make it very much harder for anyone in the Soviet system to argue in behalf of serious negotiations in SALT, to argue that the United States is serious, that if they have a forthcoming position, that we would be willing to meet it.

As I have suggested, I think there are good reasons in the Soviet self-interest for them to want to damp down the strategic arms race. I think the economic pressures are considerable. But as I suggested, there are also people present in the system who constantly voice suspicions about what we are up to and who will use this action to show that we are not serious. And there is also a curious kind of relationship between our military and their military. Every step that we take is used by their military people to prove their needs for appropriations as we move ahead.

I think the consequence of such an action on our part would be that, instead of winding down the arms race, we would find an acceleration to which we would then respond.

Senator JAVITS. Thank you, Dr. Shulman. Thank you, Mr. Chairman.

REQUEST FOR PROMPT ACTION ON S. RES. 211

Senator BROOKE. Mr. Chairman, I would like to take this opportunity, to thank Dr. Shulman for his very able and very helpful testimony before this committee, and I certainly thank you, Mr. Chairman, for holding these hearings.

I would like to refer, Mr. Chairman, to your distinction between the role of the Senate in the ABM issue and the role of the Senate so far as the MIRV is concerned as you referred to it last year. It is a very valid distinction, Mr. Chairman, and I raise it at this time for this reason.

In your opening statement today you mentioned that the committee would be considering both ABM and MIRV during the course of these hearings and you further stated that you wished to announce that the subcommittee would continue its hearings on April 8.

I would just like to say, Mr. Chairman, that we consider this matter as of very vital concern, that time is of the essence, that we can take care of the ABM issue in your committee and the Armed Services Committee and in the Appropriations Committee, but this resolution, of course, is merely a sense of the Senate resolution which hopefully will be directed to the Executive, the President of the United States, and I hope that the able chairman might see his way to have an executive meeting on this particular resolution without waiting until hearings have been concluded on ABM as well.

Of course, I feel very strongly that the effect of this particular resolution will be greatest if it is acted upon almost immediately and our delegation before going to the talks in Vienna might have the benefit of this committee's thinking on it, and hopefully of the Senate committee's action prior to the commencement of the Vienna talks.

Senator GORE. Senator, you have made a reasonable request and it will be the purpose of the chairman to have an executive session of the committee and consider whether we report your resolution. Before doing so I shall personally undertake to explore with the Administration the possibility that this was an inadvertent statement on deployment and not a high level one. The first thing I think you and I would agree should be our goal is to avoid taking any action which in any way would prejudice the opportunity of reaching agreement at the SALT talks. It is perhaps our last chance. I will explore that and then I will talk with you further.

I want to explore with you in executive session the classified matters, but I think you are entitled to a vote on your resolution. I shall call the committee together for that purpose in the very near future.

Senator BROOKE. I am very grateful to you.

Senator GORE. Thank you, Dr. Shulman and Senator Brooke, very much.

LIMITATION OF STRATEGIC ARMS

I will put in the record an article entitled "The Limitation of Strategic Arms," found in the Scientific American.

(The article follows.)

The Limitation of Strategic Arms

The long-term prospects for the strategic-arms-limitation talks would be greatly enhanced by an early agreement to ban further tests of multiple independently targeted reentry vehicles (MIRV's)

by G. W. Rathjens and G. B. Kistiakowsky

The preliminary phase of the strategic-arms-limitation talks ("SALT") between the U.S. and the U.S.S.R. was conducted in a convivial atmosphere and with a refreshing lack of familiar rhetoric. The road ahead for the negotiations nonetheless remains a steep and slippery one. The fact that the talks were delayed for as long as they were by both sides is not an encouraging sign. The initial unwillingness of the Russian leadership to negotiate because of the American involvement in Vietnam and the subsequent unwillingness of the American leadership to negotiate because of the Russian intervention in Czechoslovakia both reflect a failure to perceive the extraordinary and possibly fleeting nature of the opportunity presented at this particular juncture in the arms race and a failure to recognize that the strategic-arms confrontation can and should be largely decoupled from other sources of conflict between the two superpowers. More recent delays, first by the U.S. and then by the U.S.S.R., reinforce the view that on both sides there has been a fundamental failure in the ordering of priorities—a failure to recognize that the dangers to national security associated with arms-control agreements can be far less than those inherent in the ongoing arms race.

As the substantive phase of the arms talks is about to begin, it is still not obvious that policy-making circles of the two superpowers have consonant views about such basic questions as what objectives strategic forces serve, what relative roles offensive and defensive strategic forces play and what the desired effects of limitations on such forces are. If it should develop that there is no agreement on these points, it may not be possible to negotiate any meaningful limitation on strategic forces.

This article is written in the hope that by stimulating discussion of these questions the differences between the two powers may become more clearly understood and in time narrowed. Even if the talks fail to produce significant agreement, a better grasp of the issues involved will be in the ultimate interest of everyone.

A number of recent developments make the prospects for successful negotiations seem to be more favorable now than they might have been some years ago. Advances in the strategic reconnaissance capabilities of the superpowers (chiefly in the area of surveillance by artificial satellites) are steadily reducing the need for intrusive inspection to establish the degree of compliance with possible future agreements. Thus the thorny issue of verification may be less of a barrier to agreed arms limitation than it has been in the past. In addition the rapid growth of Russian offensive-missile forces has effectively erased a disparity with the U.S. that existed in the past, thereby making an arms-limitation agreement a more realistic possibility. Finally, there is the growing popular realization—at least in the U.S. and presumably also in the U.S.S.R.—that each side already has an enormous "overkill" capacity with respect to the other, and that further escalation in strategic-force levels would entail tremendous costs and new dangers at a time when both countries are confronted with a host of other pressing demands on their resources.

Although these developments would seem to favor successful negotiations, they are possibly outweighed by developments on the other side of the ledger. The most troublesome items are two emerging technical capabilities: multiple independently targeted reentry vehicles (MIRV's) and anti-ballistic-missile (ABM) defenses. It is frequently argued that the development and deployment of either (or particularly both) of these systems by one superpower could lead to a situation in which a decision to attempt a preemptive attack against the other's strategic forces might be considered rational. Indeed, some strategic planners contend that the threat is so great that offsetting actions must be started even before it is clear whether or not the adversary intends to acquire either a MIRV or an ABM capability. It is our belief that such arguments are largely fallacious and are made without real appreciation of the fact that a thermonuclear war between the superpowers, considering the vulnerability of the two societies, is a totally irrational policy choice. No combination of tactics and

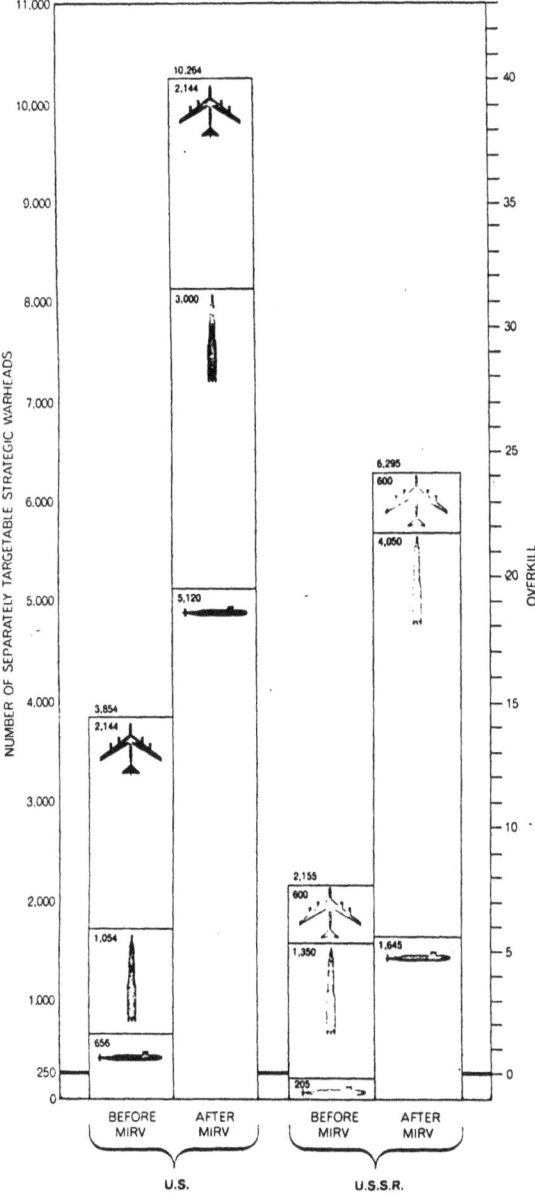

weapons, offensive and defensive, could provide either power with sufficient assurance that at least a small fraction of its adversary's weapons would not be successfully delivered, thus inflicting in retaliation damage that would be clearly unacceptable.

We are confronted here, however, with a paradox that will haunt the rest of this discussion. Unilateral decisions regarding the development and procurement of strategic-weapons systems, and hence planning for arms-control negotiations, have been and will continue to be greatly influenced by a fundamentally simpleminded, although often exceedingly refined, form of military analysis. This approach, sometimes characterized as "worst-case analysis," invariably ascribes to one's adversary not only capabilities that one would not count on for one's own forces but also imputes to him a willingness to take risks that would seem insane if imputed to one's own political leadership. Thus the U.S. will react to Russian MIRV and ABM programs, and vice versa, whether or not national security demands it. Even if the reaction is totally irrational, it nonetheless becomes as much a part of reality as if the decision were genuinely required to preserve a stable strategic balance. We reluctantly accept the fact that in both the U.S. and the U.S.S.R. policy will be influenced excessively by those military planners and their civilian allies who persist in behaving as if a thermonuclear war could be "won," and in asserting that responsible political leaders on the other side may initiate it on that assumption.

The development of a strategic nuclear capability by lesser powers, particularly China, seems also destined to complicate efforts to curtail the strategic-

STRATEGIC BALANCE between the U.S. and the U.S.S.R. is shown at left in terms of the numbers of separately targetable strategic nuclear warheads already deployed and the numbers projected for 1975 if present plans to deploy multiple independently targeted reentry vehicles (MIRV's) go into effect. The symbols indicate the means of delivery; the numbers give the actual total of deliverable warheads in each category. The scale at right suggests the enormous "overkill" capacity possessed by each side in either circumstance; it is calibrated in units of 250—a highly conservative estimate of the number of nuclear warheads required to devastate the 50 largest cities on each side. The chart includes only strategic (that is, intercontinental) nuclear warheads, not tactical or intermediate-range nuclear weapons.

arms race between the superpowers. Here there are essentially two problems. First, what was said earlier about the unacceptability of nuclear war between the superpowers may be less applicable to conflicts between emerging nuclear powers, because their political leadership will be less knowledgeable about the effects of nuclear warfare and because the nuclear stockpiles involved will, at least initially, not be large enough to ensure the destruction of entire societies. Thus, with proliferation, the probability of thermonuclear war is likely to increase, and the superpowers will have a real basis for concern about their becoming involved. Second, a phenomenon not unlike the much discussed action-reaction effects of ABM defenses and MIRV's is likely to come into play. Nuclear proliferation may complicate Russian-American efforts to curtail the strategic-arms race even more than the objective facts warrant, as each superpower overreacts not only to the development of new centers of nuclear power but also to the other's reaction to them.

In fact, the rising threat of nuclear proliferation is already increasing the pressure in the U.S. (and probably in the U.S.S.R.) to develop defenses that might be effective at least for a few years against emergent nuclear powers. The enthusiasts talk about neutralizing completely the effects of such developments; the realists propose measures aimed at reducing the damage that might be inflicted in the unlikely event of a nuclear attack by a smaller power. Unfortunately the capabilities that might prove effective, for instance an ABM system adequate to cope with first-generation Chinese missiles, would probably lead the other superpower to expand or qualitatively improve its strategic forces.

The other major considerations that will have a bearing on the prospects for SALT are domestic. As the failure of American policy in Southeast Asia and its implications become apparent, it seems likely that there will be a sharp reaction in an important segment of American society, with the polarization of attitudes proceeding even further than it has in the past year or two. It will be a difficult time for arms-control negotiations. Indeed, the strategic-arms-limitation talks are likely to be a divisive factor in the same way that the recent debate on the Safeguard ABM system was.

The situation in the U.S.S.R., although less clear, seems no more promising. The controversy between China and the U.S.S.R. might lead one to expect that accommodation and cooperation with the West would be increasingly attractive to the Russian leadership. But that controversy, like the recent Russian difficulties in eastern Europe, is also likely to be a factor in reinforcing the trend toward orthodoxy and conservatism within the U.S.S.R., which is hardly a favorable augury for an arms-control agreement.

Thus for SALT to be successful will require not only that the two governments be sincere in approaching the talks but also that they be prepared to display leadership and steadfastness of purpose in dealing with domestic opposition. On both sides there will have to be a rejection of many of the premises on which military policy has been at least partially based for two decades, for example the importance of "superiority" in strategic strength, the concept of "winning" a thermonuclear war, and the view that one can build meaningful defenses against a thermonuclear attack. The leadership in each nation will be confronted with arguments about the great risks inherent in various kinds of agreement—barely feasible (or at least not provably unfeasible) developments that might be taken advantage of by an adversary. Such arguments will undoubtedly resemble those to which the Kennedy Administration had to respond, when in connection with the nuclear-test-ban treaty it was asserted that the U.S.S.R. might conduct nuclear tests behind the moon or behind the sun to our great disadvantage. If agreement is to be reached, such arguments will have to be judged for what they are: nightmares of people who have focused so narrowly on such problems that they simply lack the perspective for weighing the risks of agreement against the risks implicit in continuing the arms race without any agreed constraints.

In the case of the U.S. the President will have a special problem and a formidable challenge, perhaps the greatest faced by any American leader since President Wilson's effort at the end of World War I to gain acceptance for his views regarding the Treaty of Versailles and the League of Nations. Although most Americans, including probably a majority of those who supported President Nixon in his campaign for the Presidency, would support him in his efforts to reach an arms-control agreement, almost certainly the conservative wing of the President's political supporters will counsel him to exercise extreme caution in approaching SALT. In so doing this latter group will give unwarranted weight to the technical and military risks that might be involved in any agreement under consideration. It is equally certain that the military will attempt to influence him with similar arguments, both through its direct channels and through its Congressional allies.

It is inconceivable that any meaningful agreement can be reached if the views of these groups should prevail. They need not, of course. Exercising broader judgment, the President can reject such advice and, as suggested above, draw on very substantial ...ationwide support for an agreement. Should he choose to do so, he will be in a better position to make his decision politically acceptable than would have been the case for any of his recent predecessors, or for that matter for his opponent in the last election. There is almost certainly a sizable segment of the American body politic that could accept a decision by President Nixon to conclude a very far-reaching agreement as a result of SALT that would not accept a similar position were it offered by, say, a liberal Democratic president.

President Nixon's prospects for such an achievement will be enhanced if the SALT negotiators make substantial progress in the next few months. With momentum established as a result of some limited agreement, and with the prospects of broader agreements before them, both the American and the Russian leadership might well make the judgment that it would be worthwhile to expend the political capital that might be required to effect broader agreements. If, on the other hand, the talks bog down in procedural discussions or in defense of obviously non-negotiable positions, the political leadership in both the U.S. and the U.S.S.R. will be in a weakened position in dealing with those who are most skeptical and fearful of an agreement. Thus the importance of early limited agreement in connection with SALT cannot be overestimated.

In what areas might such limited agreement be immediately feasible? In order to answer this question we must first examine some of the technical realities of the present strategic balance. We believe that for the foreseeable future technological considerations will continue to make nuclear offensive forces dominant over nuclear defensive forces. In other words, we assert that, as has been the case since the initial deployment of thermonuclear weapons, it will be easier to destroy a technologically advanced society than to defend one. What can and should be done both in structuring strategic forces in the absence of agreement and in agreeing to limitations is critically

21

dependent on whether or not this judgment is correct. There is some dispute about its correctness in the U.S. For example, some assert that with recent developments in ABM technology it may be possible to offset the effects of an incremental expenditure on offensive capabilities by a similar or even lesser expenditure on defenses. Nonetheless, we share the prevailing view that defense of population, at least against a determined adversary with comparable resources, is essentially hopeless.

To facilitate discussion we shall now define two terms that have come to be applied to strategic forces and to their uses. By "damage limitation" we mean the prevention of damage to industry and population in a nuclear war or the reduction of such damage to below the levels that might be expected without the use of certain damage-limiting measures or systems. Antiaircraft or ABM defenses of cities would be categorized as being damage-limiting systems. The use of civil defense measures such as population shelters or evacuation of threatened cities would be regarded as damage-limiting measures. So would be attempts to limit the adversary's ability to inflict damage by preemptively attacking any component of his offensive strategic forces. By "assured destruction" we mean the destruction with high confidence of the adversary's society. Measures to achieve such destruction, or systems that might be used for the purpose, would be characterized as assured-destruction measures or systems. They include the use of offensive missiles and bombers against civilian targets, as distinguished from strictly military targets.

With these definitions we recast our earlier statement about the relative roles of offensive and defensive strategic weapons to assert: *In the superpower confrontation any attempt to build significant damage-limiting capabilities can be offset by changes in the adversary's assured-destruction capabilities.* To take a specific example, attempts to limit and reduce the damage to American society by deploying ABM defenses (including appropriate civil defense measures) can be offset by qualitative and quantitative improvements in the adversary's offensive capabilities at a cost to him certainly no greater than the cost of the damage-limiting measures taken. What is more, we believe that by and large such responses will occur, in spite of the fact that realistic security considerations do not necessarily require a response. Even a very large-scale and technically sophisticated American ABM system could not be counted on to prevent totally unacceptable destruction in the U.S. by a Russian attack—even by an attack launched in retaliation after the Russian forces had already been preemptively struck. Such an American ABM system would in no way make our strategic forces more useful as political instruments, and hence no Russian response would really be required to preserve the effectiveness of the U.S.S.R.'s assured-destruction forces. Because of fear, conservatism and uncertainty, however, it seems a foregone conclusion that a fully compensating buildup in Russian strength would follow.

There may, of course, be circumstances in which damage-limiting efforts will be effective. Each of the superpowers would temporarily be able to maintain a strategic posture that might greatly limit the damage to it in a conflict with a lesser nuclear power such as China. This will be particularly true if a preemptive, or "counterforce," attack against the lesser power's strategic nuclear forces is not excluded.

Moreover, if a nuclear exchange between the two superpowers should ever occur, parts of the strategic forces in being at that time probably would be used for active defense or in attacks on the strategic forces of the opponent. Thus they would be used in a damage-limiting role. Their effect would not be great, however, simply because the overkill capacity of each superpower's assured-destruction capabilities is so enormous. Both superpowers almost certainly now have the ability to destroy at least half of the adversary's population and three-quarters of his industrial capacity in spite of any damage-limiting measures that might be undertaken by the other. This situation has come about as a result of two factors. A strategic doctrine has developed, at least in the U.S., that has called for the maintenance of a very great assured-destruction capability under all conceivable circumstances. The doctrine has been one that could be easily implemented simply because thermonuclear weapons and strategic delivery systems are cheap in terms of the damage they can inflict on civilian targets.

This tremendous buildup of offensive forces means that the effectiveness of the last weapons used in destroying another society (in fact, the effectiveness of something like the last 90 percent of all weapons used) would be relatively small, since those already expended would have left so little to destroy. The amount of life and property saved by damage-limiting efforts would be dwarfed by the amount destroyed by weapons whose delivery could not be prevented.

We believe this situation will not change significantly in the near future. Any realistic approach to limitations on strategic armaments in the near future must almost certainly be in the context of the maintenance of very great assured-destruction capabilities. Agreements that would embody quite different strategic balances might result if any of several changes were to occur: technological breakthroughs that would lead to the dominance of the defense over the offense, the development of a high degree of trust between the U.S. and the U.S.S.R., the willingness of both nations to accept intrusive inspection, or an increased appreciation that strategic forces designed to inflict much lower damage levels would also serve effectively as a deterrent. We do not see any of these changes as short-term possibilities.

Because the assured-destruction, or damage-inflicting, capabilities of the two superpowers are so large and so varied, the present strategic balance is remarkably insensitive to either qualitative or quantitative changes in strategic forces. Even major changes in force levels, including the neutralization of entire systems (for example all bomber aircraft), would not be likely to have major effects on the damage levels one would expect each of the superpowers to suffer in a nuclear war. Worldwide radioactive fallout might be reduced significantly, but as far as the superpowers are concerned, cross-targeting with other systems would ensure that all major population and industrial centers would continue to be in jeopardy. When considered in the framework of the virtually certain collapse of an entire society, changes of a few percent in fatalities, which is all one might expect with foreseeable changes in strategic-force levels, are not likely to affect political decisions. Although it may have been correct some years ago to characterize the balance of terror as a "delicate" one, it is not so today, nor is it likely to be so in the foreseeable future. It will not be easily upset. Opponents of the Safeguard ABM decision have argued with some effect (although obviously not with complete success) that the U.S. deterrent was most unlikely to be in jeopardy at any time in the near future simply because of its diversity and because of the improbability of the U.S.S.R.'s being able to develop damage-limiting capabilities and tactics that would effectively neutralize all the deterrent's components.

We have argued so far that one general premise on whose acceptance a successful SALT outcome depends is

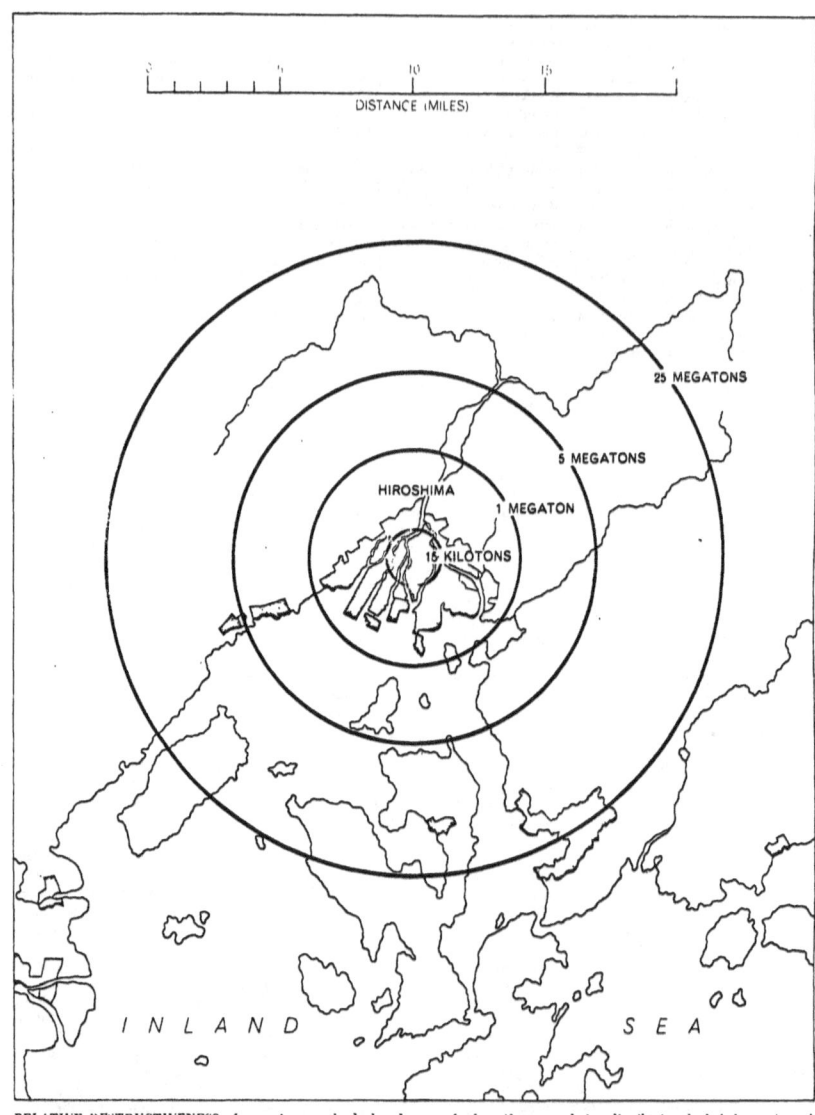

RELATIVE DESTRUCTIVENESS of several currently deployed thermonuclear weapons is illustrated here in relation to the damage caused by the nuclear bomb that was exploded over Hiroshima on May 8, 1945. The colored circles superposed on the map denote each weapon's "lethal area": the area within which the number of survivors equals the number of fatalities outside the circle. For a perfectly uniform population distribution the lethal area times the population density gives the total number of people killed in the explosion. At present most of the strategic warheads deployed by the U.S. and the U.S.S.R. are in the megaton range or larger. Even after MIRVing all the strategic warheads on both sides will exceed the estimated 15-kiloton explosive yield of the Hiroshima bomb.

that the offense will continue to dominate the defense for the foreseeable future. A second technical generalization that may be equally important is: *The uncertainty about the effectiveness of damage-limiting capabilities will be considerably greater than about assured-destruction capabilities.* This statement can be supported by a number of arguments. First, the characteristics of the target against which assured-destruction capabilities will be known with some precision and will change only slowly with time. On the other hand, the characteristics of the systems (and the environment) against which damage-limiting capabilities would operate (adversary's warheads, delivery vehicles and launch facilities) will be generally less well known and more susceptible to rapid variation, both in quality and in number, at the option of the adversary. Second, some of the damage-limiting systems (such as ABM defenses, antiaircraft defenses and under some circumstances antisubmarine warfare, or ASW, systems) must function at the time chosen by the adversary for his offensive, whereas for assured destruction there is a much bigger "time window" during which performance will be acceptable. The effectiveness of submarine-launched missiles in destroying cities will not depend much on the instant of launch. Third, damage limitation generally will involve the use of more intimately coupled systems (for example the radars, computers and missiles of an ABM system), inviting the possibility of "catastrophic" technical failures. All these factors tend to make the advance estimates of the effectiveness of assured-destruction systems far more reliable than estimates of damage-limiting systems.

The inherent uncertainty in effectiveness that characterizes the performance of damage-limiting systems has been of profound importance in the Russian-American strategic-arms race. Each side has reacted to the possible development, or even the possible development, by the other of damage-limiting capabilities by greatly strengthening its offensive forces—to the point of overreaction because of the conservative assumption that the adversary's damage-limiting forces will be far more effective than they are in fact likely to be. For example, the uncertainty about the possible deployment and effectiveness of a large-scale Russian ABM defense has provided the primary rationale for the U.S. decision to introduce MIRV's into both land-based and sea-based missile forces, the net effect being a severalfold increase in the number of warheads these forces will be able to deliver. Barring unforeseeable technical developments, we must expect that the great uncertainty that characterizes the performance of damage-limiting systems will continue, and we must base our approach to SALT on that assumption.

If one accepts the judgments we have made about the relative effectiveness of defense and offense, about the insensitivity of assured-destruction capability to changes in force levels and about the uncertainty that characterizes damage-limiting efforts, one is led to some possibly useful generalizations about the forthcoming substantive phase of SALT. First, the level of damage that each of the superpowers can inflict on the other is not likely to be altered significantly in the near future. Measures that might possibly be agreed on could change the level of damage that each side could inflict on the other by at most

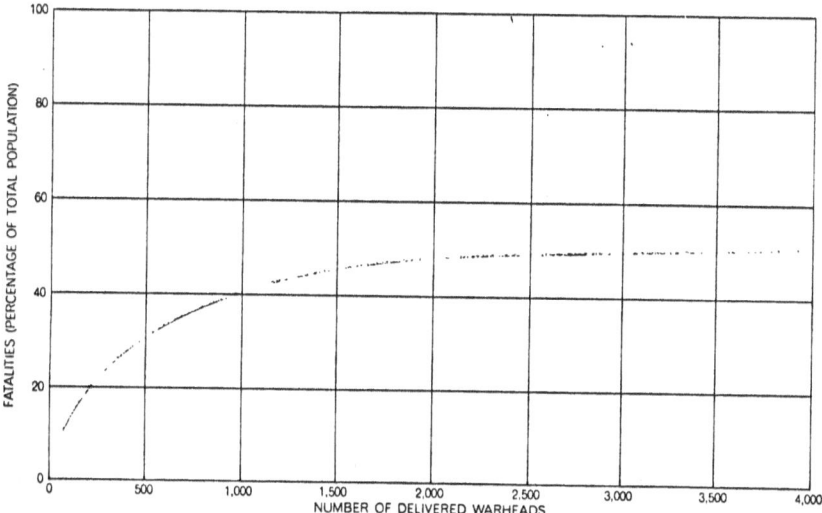

FUTILITY of seeking to mitigate the consequences of a full-scale nuclear exchange between the two superpowers by negotiating modest reductions in strategic-force levels or by resorting to moderately effective "damage-limiting" measures is illustrated in this graph, in which the expected fatalities in the U.S.S.R. are plotted as a function of the number of U.S. megaton-range warheads delivered. The solid curve indicates the immediate, easily calculable fatalities; the shading represents the fact that the total fatalities would probably be much larger. In either case, because of the very large number of deployed weapons, the effects of small changes in the total of delivered weapons would be negligible. The expected effects of a Russian attack against the U.S. would be similar.

a few percent. Therefore the problem of the reduction in damage in the event of war should probably be given low priority as a short-term negotiation objective. More realistic objectives of the negotiations could be to lower the level of tension between the superpowers and so reduce the probability of nuclear war.

Second, apart from possible worldwide fallout effects and domestic political considerations, neither side need be much concerned about the possibility of modest, or even substantial, expansions in the strategic offensive forces of the other side, nor about precise limitations on those forces, as long as the other side does not have a damage-limiting capability. Because of the large overkill capacities discussed above, even large increases in strategic forces will have little military effect.

Third, measures to constrain the introduction or improvement of damage-limiting systems, particularly those whose performance is expected to be highly uncertain, merit high priority. The introduction or improvement of damage-limiting capabilities by either side is likely to result, as we have noted, in an excessive reaction by the other. Because of the insensitivity of the strategic balance to modest changes in force levels, a move toward the development of a narrowly circumscribed damage-limiting capability by one side could in principle be tolerated without undue concern by the other. Such a move might be perceived, however, as an indicator of the adversary's intent to develop an across-the-board damage-limiting capability. (Witness Secretary of Defense Laird's public reaction to a possible Soviet SS-9 MIRV capability.) This, coupled with the fact that a development of damage-limiting capabilities can be offset rather quickly and cheaply, virtually ensures a reaction. The overall effect of such an action-reaction cycle on the ability of each side to inflict damage on the other is likely to be small, but the expenditures of both sides on strategic armaments are likely to be much increased, as will be the tensions between them.

Fourth, owing to the large uncertainty that characterizes the effectiveness of damage-limiting systems and tactics, the two superpowers will face a very troublesome dilemma if, on the one hand, they try to develop effective damage-limiting capabilities with respect to emerging nuclear powers and, on the other, they attempt to limit the strategic-arms race between themselves. With a few exceptions, such as a deployment of Russian intermediate-range ballistic missiles (IRBM's) in Siberia, the measures that could have long-term effectiveness against a third country's nuclear strength would appear to the other superpower to foreshadow an ... m its own assured-destruction, ... ent, capability. This creates an authentic problem of conflicting desires. We would hope that in efforts to deal with this problem the usefulness of damage-limiting capabilities with respect to the lesser nuclear powers would not be overrated. Although such damage-limiting capabilities probably would be effective in reducing damage in the event that a lesser power attempted a nuclear attack against one of the superpowers, we question whether either superpower would ever be willing to take action against a lesser power on the assumption that damage-limiting efforts would be 100 percent effective, that is, on the assumption that "damage denial" with respect to a lesser power could be achieved. Considering one's inability to have high confidence in the effectiveness of damage-limiting measures, and considering the effects of even a single thermonuclear weapon on a large American or Russian city, we doubt that efforts to develop damage-limiting capabilities with respect to the smaller powers would materially increase the options the superpowers would have available for dealing with these powers.

With this background in mind one would be in a good position to evaluate the relative desirability of limiting various strategic systems if each were unambiguously useful only for damage limitation or assured destruction. Unfortunately many existing or prospective strategic systems may play several roles, a factor that greatly complicates the problem.

Of all the ambiguous developments now under way none is more troublesome than MIRV. The development of a MIRV capability may facilitate the maintenance of an assured-destruction capability by providing high assurance that ABM defenses of industry and population can be penetrated. Given sufficient accuracy, reliability and yield, however, MIRV's may also make it possible for a small number of missiles to destroy a larger number of fixed offensive facilities, even if they are "hardened" against the effects of nuclear weapons.

Although the effectiveness of a given missile force in a damage-limiting pre-emptive attack against an adversary's intercontinental ballistic missile (ICBM) force might be much increased through the use of such MIRV's, it does not necessarily follow that the deployment of the MIRV's would make such a strike more likely. As we have noted, in the context of a confrontation between superpowers such an attack would surely be irrational, no matter how severe the crisis, simply because no responsible political leader could ever have high confidence in the effectiveness of the attack and in the effectiveness of the other damage-limiting measures that would be required to keep the damage from a retaliatory response down to acceptable levels. Although MIRV's are not likely to have much actual effect on the willingness or ability of nations to use strategic nuclear forces to attain political objectives, we must accept the fact that arms policies will, to a substantial degree, be based on the assumption that they might be so used.

Beyond that, there is the problem of the impact of MIRV's on events if a crisis should ever escalate to the point where limited numbers of nuclear weapons will have been employed by the superpowers against each other. At some point in the process of escalation it is likely that one or both powers would initiate counterforce attacks against the other's remaining offensive forces. Such an attack would probably come earlier if one or both sides had counterforce-effective MIRV's than if neither did.

Because of what we regard as unwarranted, but nevertheless real, concern about MIRV's being used in a preemptive counterforce attack, and because of more legitimate concern that once a thermonuclear exchange has begun MIRV's may make further escalation more likely, MIRV development may well have a critical impact on the outcome of SALT, and for that matter on the force levels of the two sides independent of the talks. It is generally, although not universally, accepted that the tests of MIRV's have not yet gone far enough for one to have confidence that their reliability and accuracy would be sufficient to assure their effectiveness in a counterforce role against hardened ICBM's. On the other hand, the MIRV principle is now demonstrated, and the expectation is common that with perhaps the second generation of such systems, if not with the first, MIRV's will be effective as counterforce weapons.

If no constraints are put on the development of MIRV's, it is likely that each superpower will go ahead with such development and (in the case of the U.S. at least) an early deployment program. This will be regarded as particularly urgent if ABM deployment continues, or even if there continues to be evidence of significant research and development that might later lead to ABM deployment. Assuming that MIRV programs do continue, each superpower will perceive in the other's deployment a possible threat to its fixed-base ICBM's and will react to counter that threat. The U.S. has already begun to do so in deciding to go ahead with an active ABM defense of Minuteman sites: the Safeguard program. Acceleration in the U.S.S.R.'s missile-launching submarine program and a possible mobile-ICBM program are plausible reactions to the U.S. MIRV programs.

We anticipate that in the absence of agreements the technological race will go much further. It seems likely that the arguments to "do something" about the vulnerability of fixed ICBM's will increase in tempo and will carry the day in both the U.S. and the U.S.S.R. Superhardening alone will be perceived to be a losing game, considering how easily any moves in that direction could be offset by further improvements in missile accuracy. A defense of the Safeguard type will probably also be judged to be a losing proposition. A very heavy defense with components specifically optimized for the defense of hardened ICBM's might be one response. There is likely to be even further reliance on mobile systems: missile-launching submarines, new strategic bombers and, in the case of the U.S.S.R., probably mobile ICBM's. It is conceivable that fixed ICBM's may be given up altogether, although the arguments we have advanced against the acceptability of attacking them preemptively would still be valid.

It is also likely in the absence of agreements that one or the other of the superpowers will deploy ABM systems that will provide more extensive and effective defense of population and industry than either the present Russian defenses around Moscow or the projected Phase II of Safeguard. Defense against a Chinese missile capability may be the rationale, but it is to be expected that the other superpower will respond to any such deployment both by emulation and by increasing its strategic offensive capabilities.

Whereas the strategic-forces budget of the U.S. now amounts to about $9 billion per year (excluding some rather large items for nuclear warheads, research and development, command and control, communications and intelligence activities), outlays for strategic systems could well double by the mid-1970's. Continuing large expenditures on strategic systems are probably also to be expected in the U.S.S.R.

As we have stated, there appears to be no basis for expecting SALT to lead to significant reductions in the assured-destruction capabilities of the superpowers. Therefore other objectives must command our attention. The most important objective is of course to reduce the probability that a thermonuclear exchange will ever take place.

The major factors affecting that probability are likely not to be simply technical but to be largely political. They involve the degree of tension that will exist between the superpowers based on international political considerations, on domestic politics in each country and in an important sense on the strategic-arms race itself. We believe that in contrast to some previous eras, when the motivations for continuing arms races were largely political and economic conflicts, the strategic-arms race now has a life of

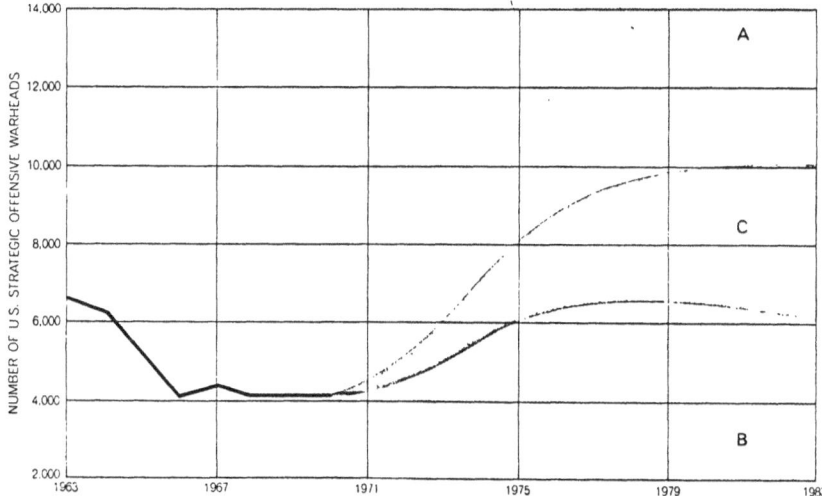

PROJECTED EFFECTS associated with three possible outcomes of the strategic-arms-limitation talks are expressed in the graphs on these two pages in terms of the number of U.S. strategic offensive warheads (left) and the U.S. budget for strategic forces (right). With no agreement (A) the number of weapons and the strategic-forces budget are likely to grow with no obvious limit. A SALT agreement that included a prohibition on the development and deployment of MIRV's (B) could lead to stability in strategic forces and a reduction in the budget to a level required to maintain them. With an agreement that did not constrain MIRV's (C) there would certainly be an increase in the strategic-forces budget for a few years as the composition of these forces changed, probably accompanied by the replacement of some fixed-base offensive missiles by mobile systems (either land-based or sea-based) or possibly by its own. For instance, the strategic-weapons programs of each superpower are more dependent on the programs of the other than on the levels of tension between the two countries. If this race can be attenuated, it would have a number of effects that would result in a diminution of tensions and hence in a reduction in the risk of war. That is perhaps the major reason for the urgency of a serious SALT effort. Keeping budgets for strategic forces at low levels is desirable in its own right in that significant resources, both financial and intellectual, will be freed for more constructive purposes. More important, in the U.S. lower military budgets will diminish the role of what President Eisenhower termed the military-industrial complex: those who have a propensity for, and in some cases obviously a vested interest in, the acquisition of more armaments and in exciting and maintaining an often unwarranted attitude of alarm and suspicion regarding an adversary's intentions. Lower military budgets in the U.S.S.R. would almost certainly have a similar desirable effect.

A poorly designed agreement could of course prove to be a vehicle for increasing suspicion and tension. Venturing into the realm of unprovable value judgments, however, we assert that it is not beyond the wit of man to design agreements that would result in there being less objective cause for concern than if the strategic-arms race continues unabated. In general, it would seem that any understanding that slowed the rate of development and change of strategic systems would have an effect in the right direction.

Beyond affecting the probability of a nuclear exchange's beginning, one would like to see strategic forces structured so that there would be at least some possibility that, if an exchange started, it would not have to run its course. A necessary but of course not sufficient condition for this is that there be no particular advantage to be gained from precipitate launch of more nuclear weapons after a few have been dispatched. By this criterion vulnerable ICBM's would seem to be the quintessence of undesirability. If both sides have them, each will recognize that if they are withheld, they may be destroyed.

Whether or not MIRV development and deployment will be controlled may not be a question for the SALT negotiators to consider, because of the inability of one side or the other to decide in a timely fashion the position it wishes to take on the issue. The rate of MIRV development is so rapid that the question may thus be settled before the substantive phase of the talks is well advanced. If such development is still in doubt, however, either because the talks get to such substantive issues very quickly or because of a moratorium on MIRV testing, MIRV limitation should be an issue of the highest priority.

The arguments for preventing deployment of MIRV's advanced enough to be effective counterforce weapons are persuasive. They have been made at great length elsewhere (for example in public hearings before committees of the Senate and the House of Representatives). We simply summarize here by pointing out that if MIRV deployment is prevented, it may be possible to freeze the strategic balance at something approximating its present level. Most of the incentive to defend hardened ICBM's or to replace them with mobile systems will

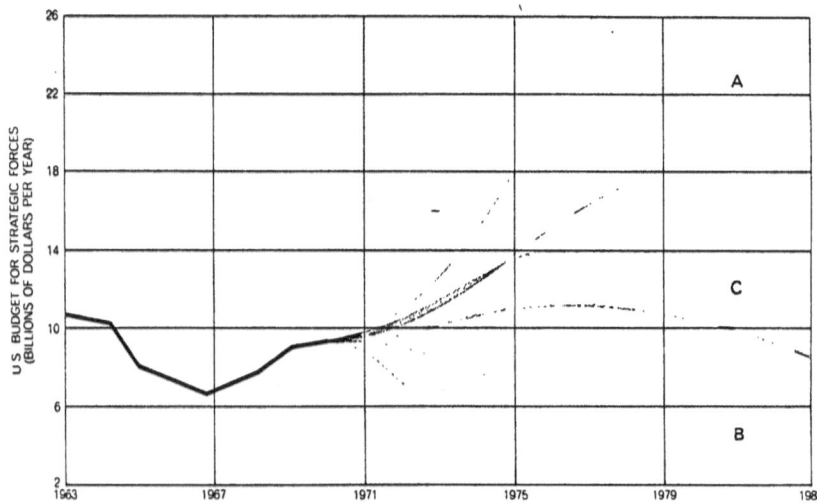

"superhardening" and heavy specialized ABM defense of missile sites. Assuming under case C that a large-scale ABM defense of population is prohibited, there would be little military rationale for either side to acquire large additional numbers of offensive warheads. Nonetheless, the numbers might increase significantly with the implementation of present plans to deploy MIRV's. Future Russian strategic-forces levels would probably display similar trends, but budget projections would differ somewhat. The Russian budget for strategic weapons is possibly at an unprecedentedly high level now, considering the present rapid rate of growth in their strategic systems. Thus in case B the drop in the strategic-forces budget for the U.S.S.R. might be sharper than for the U.S., and in the two other cases there would be a less pronounced increase. Estimates are in constant-value 1969 dollars.

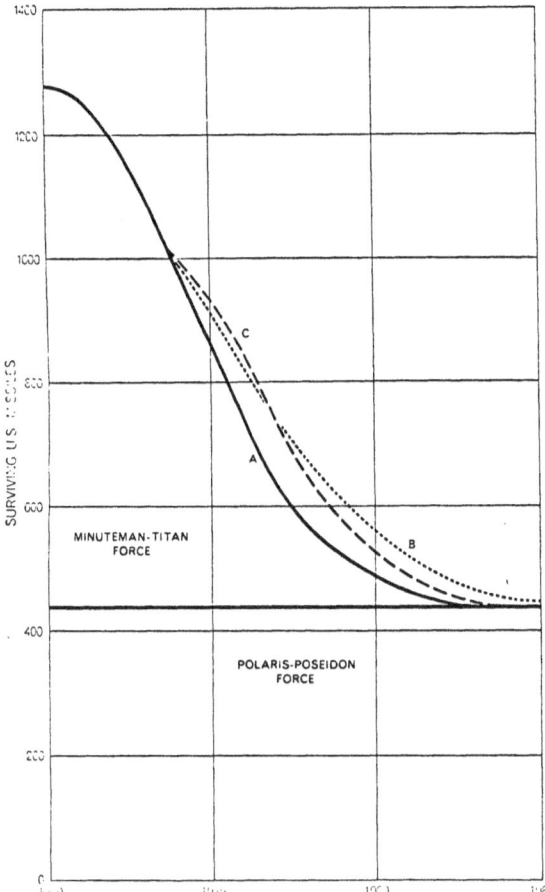

DIMINISHING UTILITY of fixed-base intercontinental ballistic missiles (ICBM's) as a component of the U.S. "assured-destruction" forces would result from further development and deployment of MIRV's, even in the event of a SALT agreement that freezes the number of missiles on both sides. In preparing this graph it was assumed that in a preemptive, or counterforce, strike against the U.S. the U.S.S.R. would target its SS-9 missile force (estimated to be frozen at 280 missiles) at the U.S. Minuteman-Titan force. The numbers of surviving U.S. ICBM's are based on the assumption that each SS-9 will carry one 25-megaton warhead in 1970, three five-megaton warheads in 1975, nine 500-kiloton warheads in 1980 and 25 50-kiloton warheads in 1985; delivery accuracies are assumed to improve by a factor of two every five years. Curve A assumes that no additional measures are taken to protect the already "hardened" U.S. ICBM force. Curve B assumes that the blast resistance of the ICBM sites is improved by "superhardening" so that by 1972 they can withstand three times the overpressure sustainable in 1970. Curve C assumes full operational capability (and a generous estimate of performance) of the Safeguard ABM system by 1978. It is apparent that neither superhardening nor active defense (unless many times more effective than Safeguard) is likely to extend the period of invulnerability for U.S. ICBM's by very much. (The number of surviving submarine-launched missiles is based on the assumption that a third of the Polaris-Poseidon force is destroyed in port by the Russian preemptive attack.)

have been reduced, if not eliminated.

The arguments for continuing MIRV testing and then deployment because MIRV's may someday be required to penetrate an adversary's ABM defenses are not convincing. There is little doubt that currently designed U.S. MIRV's could be deployed on a time scale short compared with that required for deployment of any significant Russian ABM defenses. Accordingly there is no need for any MIRV deployment pending firm evidence that the U.S.S.R. is beginning the construction of such defenses. And there is no need for further research and development tests unless a counterforce capability is intended. For similar reasons the U.S.S.R. should also abstain from further multiple-warhead tests and deployment, which it can do at no great risk to its security.

Essential to the survival of an agreement not to test MIRV's would be a prohibition of large-scale ABM deployment. If ABM systems were deployed, the pressures to deploy MIRV's and to test them frequently in order to maintain confidence in their reliability would be overwhelming. Furthermore, there would undoubtedly be great domestic pressures to develop and test more sophisticated penetration aids. Under such circumstances neither side could have any confidence that the other was not developing counterforce-effective MIRV's. An ABM freeze would be a logically required companion measure to any agreement prohibiting MIRV's.

Assuming that ABM deployment and MIRV testing are both frozen, the other important component of a strategic-arms-limitation agreement would be an understanding to maintain something like parity in ICBM-force levels by freezing these levels or preferably reducing them, and if necessary permitting replacement of fixed-base ICBM's by mobile systems whose levels could be verified by unilateral means. In the absence of such a measure there would be the possibility of one side's gaining such a superiority in missile strength that, with improved accuracies and even without MIRV's, would enable it to knock out a large fraction of its adversary's forces by delivering a counterforce attack against them. The reasons for concern about such a possibility have been identified above: the probability of arms-race escalation and the reduction in whatever small chance there may be of a nuclear exchange's being terminated short of running its suicidal course.

If the development of MIRV's that are perceived by the adversary to have counterforce capability cannot be prevented (and we are pessimistic about preventing it), the relative importance of some of the measures discussed above will be changed materially. A prohibition on large-scale ABM deployment would still be desirable, but it would be less important; it would not in this case prevent the MIRV genie from escaping the bottle. Moreover, continuing development and deployment of MIRV's would make a large-scale ABM defense unattractive simply on cost-effectiveness grounds.

A provision permitting the replacement of fixed ICBM's by mobile systems would seem virtually unavoidable because of concern about the vulnerability of the ICBM's to counterforce attack. Indeed, in the interest of stabilizing arms at low levels, and to minimize concern about damage-limiting strikes, agreements could probably include measures that would enhance the viability of mobile systems. An area of agreement that would seem to merit most serious consideration would be prohibition on certain improvements in antisubmarine-warfare capabilities. Actually the possibility of breakthroughs in antisubmarine warfare is extremely remote. It is probable that through noise reduction, extension of missile range and other techniques the gap between ASW capability and the capability of the missile-launching submarine to escape detection and destruction will widen rather than narrow. Yet it seems likely from recent debate in the U.S. that the present American leadership, and presumably the leadership of the U.S.S.R. as well, would be reluctant to rely solely on a missile-launching submarine force for deterrence, given the possibility of further ASW development by its adversary. Constraints on ASW such as a limitation on the number of hunter-killer submarines would increase the acceptability to both sides of relying more heavily on missile-launching submarines for deterrence.

Similar arguments might be made for limitations on or curtailment of air defense. Such moves would seem less realistic on three counts. First, compliance with limitations on air-defense capabilities could probably not be verified with unilateral procedures as well as could limitations on ASW systems, or for that matter on ABM systems. Intelligence on short-range antiaircraft systems is likely to be poorer than on hunter-killer submarines, specialized ASW aircraft or large-sized components of ABM systems. Second, the overlap between tactical and strategic antiaircraft capabilities is considerable, and neither superpower is likely to be willing to greatly reduce tactical antiaircraft capabilities in the context of SALT. ASW capabilities (except for destroyers) would, on the other hand, have little role other than attack against an adversary's missile-launching submarines. This is far truer now than it was a few years ago because the realization is more widespread that a major war involving large antishipping campaigns is extremely unlikely. Third, neither the U.S. nor the U.S.S.R. is likely to have enough confidence in bombers to rely much on them in a missile age even if air defenses are constrained, whereas both superpowers obviously are prepared to rely heavily on submarine-launched missiles.

Finally, if counterforce-effective MIRV's were a reality, and if as a consequence both sides were to place reliance very largely on mobile systems, additional offensive weapons on one side could not be used effectively to limit the other side's ability to retaliate. Considering this fact and the fact that since strategic-force levels are already at least an order of magnitude larger than is rationally required for deterrence, there would be little incentive for either side to acquire additional offensive capabilities. Also in this situation it would hardly matter if either side were to introduce new assured-destruction systems such as, for example, small mobile ICBM's that could not be easily counted.

Even this incomplete discussion shows that the strategic balance between the superpowers is likely to be very different depending on whether or not MIRV development and ABM deployment are allowed to continue. Both possibilities will have a serious impact on future strategic postures, but with respect to ABM deployment nothing much is going to happen overnight. Dealing with the issue of MIRV development, although perhaps no more important, is far more urgent. That is why it is the watershed issue for SALT. If counterforce-effective MIRV's (and large-scale ABM deployment) can be stopped, the present strategic balance of force levels may endure for some time. If such MIRV's are deployed, the balance will unavoidably change in qualitative ways. How large an escalation in the arms race will result will depend on whether agreement to constrain or cut back other strategic systems could still be negotiated.

We have attempted here to present an objective analysis of the prospects for various agreements to limit strategic armaments. In so doing we are aware that many of our readers will be dismayed that our discussion has been in the context of each superpower's preserving the capability of destroying the other. This has been so not because we ourselves favor the continuing retention of huge stocks of thermonuclear weapons but because we have tried to be realistic. The distrust that exists between the U.S. and the U.S.S.R. will induce both to preserve the capability of destroying the other; such a capability, as we have noted, is unfortunately easier to attain than an effective defense of one's own society, whether or not there are agreements on strategic armaments. Both superpowers will preserve this capability because they see it as the only effective deterrent to the war that neither wants or could win.

The most that can reasonably be expected of the forthcoming talks is a move toward a strategic balance where (1) uncertainties about the adversary are reduced and with them some of the tensions; (2) each side can inflict a level of damage on the other sufficient to destroy its society but neither feels a need to maintain a great overkill capability as a hedge against possible damage-limiting efforts by the other; (3) there will be an improved chance that a thermonuclear exchange, should one begin, would be terminated short of running its course, and (4) the levels of expenditure on strategic armaments are lower, so that larger fractions of the resources available to each society can be used for more constructive endeavors.

We believe that the realization of these objectives would be a tremendous accomplishment and one that is possible without the solution of the deep-seated political problems of the Russian-American confrontation. To go further will require dealing with those problems. We do not believe, however, that the superpowers can afford to delay attacking the strategic-arms race while trying to solve political differences. Regrettably the situation with respect to technical developments (MIRV's, ABM defenses and nuclear proliferation), and quite possibly with respect to domestic politics as well, will probably make strategic-arms-limitation negotiations less likely to be successful several years hence than now. Time is of the essence, and we write with a feeling of urgency. Although our tone is pessimistic, we do not despair. We are convinced that latent public support for an agreement could be exploited by effective political leadership on both sides to reverse the trends we have lived with for two decades.

DEFENSE DEPARTMENT COMMENTS ON THE JOINT MORATORIUM

Senator GORE. I will also put in the record a copy of a letter from the Director of Defense Research and Engineering, Dr. John S. Foster, Jr., addressed to Senator Brooke, dated August 30, 1969.
(The letter follows.)

DIRECTOR OF DEFENSE RESEARCH AND ENGINEERING,
Washington, D.C., August 30, 1969.

Hon. EDWARD W. BROOKE,
U. S. Senate,
Washington, D.C.

DEAR SENATOR BROOKE: The Secretary of Defense has asked me to reply to your letter of July 20, regarding a joint moratorium on MIRV testing. We have been aware of your feelings in the matter and also of the considerable extent of press comment to the general effect of those samples you enclosed with your letter.

I should mention at the outset that there is no intrinsic objection on the part of the Department of Defense to a joint MIRV test moratorium, provided that appropriate collateral provisions are also implemented. In fact, a joint moratorium is one of the options we are considering as a candidate for the Strategic Arms Limitation Talks agenda.

There are, however, several points which I believe need be made:

(a) Our development of MIRV is, in essence, a reaction on our part to Soviet ABM activity, including those elements which we feel certain to be ABM and those which we believe to be oriented toward aircraft defense but which may be capable of short term conversation to ABM capability, or perhaps even now possess some ABM capability. Faced with these Soviet defense measures, our deterrent capability could erode seriously without a countering move on our part. Our counter, as you are aware, is our MIRV program. I emphasize the point that its purpose is to preserve our deterrent from degradation in the face of Soviet ABM possibilities.

(b) On the other hand, as we are able to understand the Soviet MIRV, if it truly is a MIRV, it appears designed as a weapon against our land-based missile force and, thus, also is a Soviet move which degrades our deterrent. Their MIRV, therefore, falls in the category of a potential "first-strike" weapon.

I should emphasize here a significant point. Our own MIRV systems are not efficient against missile silos; they are designed for, and intended for use against defended urban/industrial type targets. They are not "first-strike" weapons.

In view of the above, I am sure you will understand the point I mentioned earlier about collateral provisions. Since we are reacting essentially to Soviet ABM activity, any moratorium must also include suitable provisions for restriction of Soviet ABM capability. We do not consider the Soviet MIRV and our MIRV as symmetrical weapons. Even if they did not have the SS-9 triplet, we would need our MIRV as a counter to their ABM.

Another facet to be considered is that of verification of adherence to a MIRV test moratorium, should one be agreed upon. So far, we in the Department of Defense have been unable to determine any reliable method, using national means only, for verifying with certainty Soviet adherence to a ban. As perhaps you are aware, there has been intensive study on this particular point. Your letter states that you believe it possible to devise adequate means to monitor a test limitation. I should be happy, at your convenience, to explore your views on the subject.

Nevertheless, in view of our inability in Department of Defense to devise any certain verification means, it seems to us that we must then restrict or control other items at the same time a MIRV moratorium is entered into. These others would include such things as penetration aids, maneuvering RVs, and multiple RVs. All such matters must be considered in negotiations leading to a joint MIRV test moratorium.

I do not believe we will, in the terms of your letter, "fall captive to a sense of inevitability regarding the advance of MIRV technology" in preparing for the SALT talks. And, I repeat, the Department of Defense has no intrinsic objection to a joint moratorium. We do feel, however, in order to safeguard properly the security of the United States, the matter must be approached with the above thoughts in mind. We are doing so in our preparation for the proposed Strategic Arms Limitation Talks.

Sincerely,

JOHN S. FOSTER, Jr.

Senator GORE. The hearing is concluded.

(Whereupon, at 5:15 p.m., the subcommittee was adjourned, subject to the call of the Chair.)

ABM, MIRV, SALT, AND THE NUCLEAR ARMS RACE

The Arms Race: Past, Present and Future

WEDNESDAY, APRIL 8, 1970

UNITED STATES SENATE,
SUBCOMMITTEE ON ARMS CONTROL,
INTERNATIONAL LAW AND ORGANIZATION
OF THE COMMITTEE ON FOREIGN RELATIONS,
Washington, D.C.

The subcommittee met, pursuant to notice, at 10:30 a.m., in room 4221, New Senate Office Building, Senator Clifford Case presiding.

Present: Senators Case, Gore (chairman of the subcommittee), Fulbright (chairman of the full committee), Cooper, and Javits.

OPENING STATEMENT

Senator CASE. The subcommittee will be in order.

I have to announce that unfortunately Senator Gore, chairman of the subcommittee, is held up on his way back to Washington by transportation trouble. He expects to be here this morning, but asked that we go ahead in his absence; and so I would like, if I might, to put a statement in the record that he would have made if he were here, a purely formal statement about the hearings.

(The statement referred to follows.)

UNITED STATES SENATE COMMITTEE ON FOREIGN RELATIONS, SUBCOMMITTEE ON ARMS CONTROL, INTERNATIONAL LAW AND ORGANIZATION, OPENING STATEMENT BY SENATOR GORE, CHAIRMAN, SUBCOMMITTEE ON ARMS CONTROL, INTERNATIONAL LAW AND ORGANIZATION, APRIL 8, 1970.

The Subcommittee on Arms Control, International Law and Organization continues today a series of hearings on ABM, MIRV, SALT and the Nuclear Arms Race. Our hearings began on February 2 when Gerard C. Smith, Director of the Arms Control and Disarmament Agency, briefed the Subcommittee in classified executive session on the Strategic Arms Limitation Talks. On March 2, the Director of the Central Intelligence Agency, Richard Helms, briefed the Subcommittee on the strategic threat, again in executive classified session.

The first public hearing of the Subcommittee was held on March 16 when Senator Brooke and Dr. Marshall Shulman, Director of the Russian Institute at Columbia University, testified on Senate Resolution 211. Dr. Shulman's testimony dealt, in part, with Soviet decision-making in regard to the Strategic Arms Limitation Talks and the relationship of the talks to our long-term relations with the Soviet Union.

Our subject today is "The Arms Race: Past, Present and Future." Our witnesses are the Honorable McGeorge Bundy, President of the Ford Foundation and former Assistant to the President for National Security Affairs; and Dr. Herbert York, Dean of the Graduate School, the University of California at San Diego and former Director of Defense Research and Engineering.

Surely, there can be few men in America more qualified to talk about the past, present and future of the arms race than Mr. Bundy and Dr. York, and we are most grateful to them for their willingness to be with us this morning.

They are appearing at a most opportune time. The Armed Services Committee has before it draft legislation which would expand Safeguard. And the pending business before the Senate is Senate Resolution 211 which has, as its purpose, an interim freeze on the further deployment of all offensive and defensive strategic nuclear weapons systems. I am sure that the testimony we will hear today will be most useful in connection with debate today and tomorrow on S. Res. 211.

Senator CASE. I have just a very brief comment that I wanted to make myself, which I can do now.

If there are any further comments by any members of the subcommittee, we will hear them and then go ahead.

PURPOSE OF COMMITTEE HEARINGS

Our hearings, as I see them, are for the purpose of trying to get information and not trying to develop for the public a viewpoint that we have already established as our own. But I think this is a very serious exercise about what is perhaps the most serious matter that we face in this decade: Our whole strategic arms program and our international relations as affected by it and as affecting it.

QUESTIONS TO BE EXPLORED

Last year, Administration officials emphasized that Safeguard expansion was based in their minds primarily on its importance as a defense of our missile sites and the Senate, as I guess we all know or remember, almost defeated Safeguard.

Since that time it has appeared that the Senate's questioning of the value of and importance and necessity of Safeguard for that purpose has been justified. One of the most important questions here is, I think, whether this is correct and whether Safeguard is important, necessary, and effective for the purpose of defending our missile sites.

The second justification, of course, is what has been termed very loosely the Chinese threat. Nobody has ever made clear as to what was meant by it. It has a variety of meanings, I think, depending upon the context in which it is used and who is using it.

Is this important? Is it necessary? Is it useful? Is it counterproductive? These are other questions we want to raise this time.

Why do we need a special defense against the Chinese nuclear threat? Why is not the deterrent on which we have to rely and do rely with respect to Soviet Russia equally effective against the Chinese?

If we need something special, will Safeguard provide it? Is it not true that Safeguard will not give us a defense against a Chinese threat against our populations until it has completed not one, two, three, five, six, but all its stages; that is, the whole number of sites? Is this a fact? If so, since it is not planned to be in place to its full extent until something like 1978, what about the Chinese threat between the time the Chinese acquire nuclear capability several years before that time and the time these defenses are in place? These are the questions.

The last justification last year, as I recall it, was that Safeguard was useful and necessary against a stray missile that might be shot off by accident, the saving of x number of American lives was in itself a justification for this elaborate apparatus. The question was never gone into very fully last year because the concentration was on the first of the three rationales, and I think this is a matter we want to explore fully this year and get an answer, if we can.

The witnesses we have before us, and those who are coming, are very well equipped to advise us as to whether Safeguard will work against missiles fired at us accidentally; whether a high degree of automaticity of response will not be required for a system which will accomplish this; and whether the automaticity will completely eliminate any control by the President of the United States over the discharge of nuclear weapons. Those three basic rationales must be fully tested. They certainly have never been established so far as most of us are concerned by the evidence so far.

The fourth not very explicitly stated justification has been mentioned privately in recent weeks, namely, that, leaving everything else aside, Safeguard is necessary and its expansion is required in order to give us a bargaining counter in the SALT talks. This isn't ever made very explicit, just what kind of a bargaining counter is talked about, and I think we ought to explore that, find it sound or find it completely unsound.

I do not by the questions that I have raised in any way mean to indicate that my mind is so completely closed on these matters that reasonable presentations may not change them.

I obviously have indicated some skepticism in the past which I retain now, but it is not, believe me, anything that cannot be changed if the evidence is such as to justify change. I am sure this applies to the whole committee.

I am sorry I have taken so long. Mr. Chairman, you, as ranking member, should have been allowed to speak first.

Senator FULBRIGHT. No, I am ready for the witnesses to proceed. I came here to hear them. I have nothing to say at this time.

Senator CASE. I thank you.

Senator, do you have anything?

Senator COOPER. No.

COMMENDATION OF THE WITNESSES

Senator CASE. On behalf of the committee and the subcommittee and in his absence, the Chairman, I want to express the satisfaction we all feel at being able to persuade two such eminent gentlemen as we have before us to come before us, and again to assure you that whatever you say will be received by all of us with minds that are open, however persuasive to education and with full respect for the qualifications, particular qualifications, that each of you brings to us.

I understand that Dr. York planned to make his statement first, followed by Dr. Bundy, and that then we may have questions, if that is satisfactory.

Dr. York.

(The biographical sketch of Dr. York follows.)

BIOGRAPHY OF DR. HERBERT YORK; DEAN OF THE GRADUATE SCHOOL, THE UNIVERSITY OF CALIFORNIA AT SAN DIEGO, SAN DIEGO, CALIF.

Born: November 24, 1921, Rochester, New York
Education: University of Rochester, B.A., 1942; M.S. 1943; University of California, Berkeley, Ph. D., 1960; Case Institute of Technology, D. Sc. (hon.), 1960; University of San Diego, LLD (hon.), 1964.
Experience:
  1943–58: Member research and teaching staffs of Lawrence Radiation Laboratory, University of California, Livermore.
  1952–58: Director of Above.
  1957–58: Member of the President's Scientific Advisory Committee.
  1958: Research administrator of Institute for Defense Analyses, Washington, now trustee.
  1953–61: Director of Defense Research and Engineering, Department of Defense, Washington, D.C., 1961–64: Chancellor of University of California at San Diego, La Jolla, California, now professor.
  1953–61: Director of Defense Research and Engineering, Department of Defense, Washington, D.C.
  1961–64: Chancellor of University of California at San Diego, La Jolla, California, now professor.
  1964–67; Member of the President's Scientific Advisory Committee (Vice Chairman 1965–66); Consultant, government and industry; Trustee Aerospace Corporation, El Segundo, California.
  1968– : Dean of the Graduate School, the University of California at San Diego.
Awards and Memberships:
  Recipient Ernest Orlando Lawrence Memorial Award of AEC, 1962.
  Member of American Physics Society, International Academy of Astronautics, Phi Beta Kappa, Sigma Xi.
Research and Publications:
  Research and publications in application of atomic energy to national defense, elementary particles, high energy physics, nuclear weapons and power defense research.

STATEMENT OF DR. HERBERT YORK, DEAN OF THE GRADUATE SCHOOL, UNIVERSITY OF CALIFORNIA AT SAN DIEGO

Dr. YORK. Shall I proceed, Mr. Chairman? Mr. Chairman, and members of the committee, I appreciate very much having the privilege of appearing before your committee at this particular crucial moment. I plan to discuss the ABM (antiballistic missile) and the MIRV (multiple independently-targetable reentry vehicle) and their relationship to each other and to the arms race as a whole. I should like to begin by first describing how we got where we are, and then speculating a bit on where we're going to be if the current attempts to halt the arms race fail. I will also present my views on how the current ABM and MIRV developments and deployment affect the prospects for a successful outcome to the SALT talks.

U.S. DEVELOPMENT OF ABM AND MIRV

In 1955, about a year after the United States started development of its first intercontinental ballistic missile, the Army asked the Bell Telephone Laboratories to make a study of the feasibility of an antiballistic missile. The problem was then thought of as being simply how to hit a "bullet with a bullet," or more accurately, how to intercept large simple incoming warheads one at a time. The Bell Laboratories concluded that the technological state of the art in radar, electronic computing, nuclear explosives, and rocketry had reached a point such that it was indeed feasible to build an ABM with that simple objective. As a result, the Nike Zeus project was started late in 1956.

Very soon after, it was recognized that the defense problem might well be complicated by various hypothetical penetration aids available to the offense. The office of the Secretary of Defense set up a committee to review the matter. In early 1958, this committee pointed out the feasibility of greatly complicating the missile defense problem by using decoys, chaff, tank fragments, reduced radar reflectivity, nuclear blackout and last, but by no means least, multiple warheads.

At first, the designers of our offensive missiles did not take missile defense very seriously. By 1960, however, technical progress in our own Nike Zeus program, plus accumulating evidence of a major Soviet effort in the ABM field, forced the developers of our ICBM's (intercontinental ballistic missile) and Polaris missiles to take this possibility into account. These weapons designers accepted the challenge, and they initiated a number of programs to exploit the possibilities enumerated above. Thus began the technological contest between missile defense and missile offense which continues to the present and which was discussed before this committee in considerable detail last year.

For our purposes here today, the most important result of this contest was the emergence of the multiple warhead idea as the most promising of all the various "penetration aid" concepts. At first, the idea involved a shotgun technique in which a group of warheads plus some lightweight decoys were to be launched along several different paths all leading to a common target area. But shortly after, methods for aiming each of the individual warheads at separate targets were invented. The reasons for this extension of the original idea were: (1) It provided additional flexibility for the offense, (2) it made the defense problem still harder, and (3) it was more complicated and expensive, and thus provided the weapons engineers and scientists with a still better means of displaying their technological virtuosity. This extension of the original idea is, of course, the now well-known MIRV, an acronym standing for multiple independently targetable reentry vehicles. It is, I think, most important to note that these early developments of MIRV and ABM were not primarily the result of any careful operations analysis of the problem or anything which might be described as a provocation by the other side. Rather, they were largely the result of a continuously reciprocating process consisting of a technological challenge put out by the designers of our own defense and accepted by the designers of our own offense, then followed by a similar challenge/response sequence in the reverse direction. In this fashion, our ABM development program made very substantial progress during the early sixties.

CONCURRENT SOVIET PROGRESS

Concurrent with this internal contest, the Soviets were making progress on their own. As early as 1962, Premier Khrushchev and Defense Minister Malinovsky boasted about how they had solved the missile defense problem. By 1965, Soviet progress in development and deployment of an ABM had proceeded to the point where we felt compelled to react. As a result, we decided to deploy MIRV as the one certain means of assuring penetration of Soviet defenses and thus maintaining the credibility of our deterrent.

RESULT OF UNITED STATES-SOVIET ACTION AND REACTION CYCLE

What was the result of this cycle of action and reaction? Last year, in the course of the national ABM debate, it was said that the Soviets had deployed a total of about 70 ABM interceptors, all of them around Moscow. This year it was announced that the United States was going ahead with its plans to deploy MIRV's on our Minuteman and on our sub-launched Poseidon missiles. Using figures generated by this committee last year, we see that the result of this U.S. reaction will be a net increase of around 5,000 in the number of warheads aimed at Russia. If every one of those Soviet interceptors was successful in the event of an attack (and I have substantial doubt that they would be), they could cope with just 70 of those additional 5,000 warheads. The deployment of the Moscow ABM must rank as one of the history's most counter-productive moves. It also shows more clearly than any speculative analysis how, despite its defensive nature, the ABM can be a powerfully accelerating element in the nuclear arms race.

But that's not the whole story. The Russians have proceeded with a multiple warhead development of their own. Their program apparently is a number of years behind ours. It was probably stimulated by our program, and their technologists probably used the same justifications for it that ours did. The device they are currently testing is the payload package for the large SS-9 missile. It is said to contain three separate warheads of five megatons each. The present device may not be a true MIRV, but there is no doubt they could develop one soon.

After making a number of estimates and projections concerning the accuracy, the reliability, and the current deployment and rate of buildup of such SS-9 missiles, our defense officials concluded last year that the threat posed by this Soviet MIRV required us to deploy the Safeguard ABM system to defend our Minuteman force. We thus see that the whole process has made one full turn around the spiral: Soviet ABM led to U.S. MIRV; U.S. MIRV led to Soviet MIRV; Soviet MIRV leads to U.S. ABM.

DIFFERENCES IN UNITED STATES AND SOVIET MIRV'S

Last year, some of those who spoke in favor of the Safeguard System described the Soviet MIRV development as being especially dangerous and foreboding because it seemed to them that its only rational purpose was to destroy our Minutemen before they could be launched. They further speculated that if this were so, the Soviet MIRV indicated preparation for a possible preemptive strike against us. These same people argued, by contrast, that our own MIRV development was clearly benign, since its main purpose was to maintain the credibility of our deterrent in the face of a hypothetical extensive Soviet ABM, and that, in any event, our MIRV was clearly not a missile killer.

The main argument in support of this supposed difference between the purposes of the United States and Soviet MIRVs involves the large difference in their explosive power. The Soviet SS–9 MIRV is said to have an estimated yield of 5 megatons. This yield is 25 times the yield usually quoted for one of the individual warheads in the U.S. Minuteman MIRV; it is 100 times as large as the common estimate of a single Poseidon MIRV warhead. These large differences in yield are doubtless real, and they are important, but they are not by any means the whole story. The killing power of a warhead against a hard target, such as a missile silo, depends much more critically on accuracy than on yield. In fact, a factor of three in accuracy makes up for a factor of 25 in yield, and a factor of 4.6 in accuracy makes up for a factor of 100 in yield. To be more specific, a Minuteman MIRV warhead having a yield of 200 kilotons and an accuracy, or CEP (circular error probable), of about one-eighth of a nautical mile has a 95 percent chance of destroying a so-called "300 p.s.i." target (which is a typical estimate of the strength or hardness of a missile silo). Similarly, a Poseidon MIRV warhead having a yield of 50 kilotons and an accuracy of about 1/16 of a mile has the same probability of destroying a missile silo. And what are the prospects for attaining such accuracies: The accuracy of real operational missiles is classified, but in last year's debates, a figure of about one-fourth of a mile for U.S. accuracies was commonly used. That is quite different from one-eighth or one-sixteenth of a mile, but what is the record of progress in improving accuracy? In 1944, the German V–2 missile, which used a primitive version of the same kind of guidance system as the present Minuteman and Poseidon, achieved an accuracy of about 4 miles in a range of about 200 miles. Ten years later, when the decision to build the U.S. ICBM was made, an accuracy of 5 miles in a range of 5,000 miles was estimated as both possible and sufficient. That was an improvement of twentyfold in the ratio of accuracy to range. Now we talk about one-fourth of a mile at the same range, so in an additional 15 years, we have achieved another factor of 20. Altogether, that makes an improvement of four-hundred fold in only 25 years. Any conservative Russian planner considering these figures would have to conclude that in a relatively short time U.S. technology could improve missile accuracy by another factor of two or four and thus convert not only the Minuteman MIRV but even the Poseidon MIRV into a missile silo destroyer.

UNITED STATES-SOVIET REACTIONS TO ABM AND MIRV

We have seen that the SS–9 MIRV is causing our Defense Department to fear for the viability of our deterrent and to react strongly to it for that reason. In the present international context, and in the absence of any real progress in arms control, the Soviets must be expected to react to our MIRV in some similarly fear-inspired way.

ABM and MIRV are thus inseparable; each one requires and inspires the other. Separately or in combination, they create uncertainty in each of the nuclear powers about the capability and even the intentions of the other. These uncertainties eventually lead in turn to fear, overreaction, and further increases in the number and types of all kinds of weapons, defensive as well as offensive.

What about the future? In the absence of international arms control agreements, what can we expect? Predictions are, of course, very uncertain, but one can single out some likely possibilities.

LAUNCH ON WARNING DOCTRINE

The ABM is a low confidence system. The expressions of confidence in the system made by those who supported it last year are bound to give way to a more realistic appraisal by the time the system is deployed. When that happens, the defense establishment will turn in accordance with the precepts of "worst plausible case" analysis to other methods of insuring the survival of the Minuteman. Of the various possibilities, the surest, quickest, and the cheapest, is simply to adopt the launch on warning doctrine. This doctrine involves, first: detecting that a launch of enemy missiles has occurred; second: analyzing the information in order to determine whether the launch endangers our missile forces; and, third: if it does, launching our missiles toward their targets before the incoming warheads can catch them in their silos and destroy them. This method of coping with the problem has been in people's minds since the beginning of the missile program.

In the early fifties, we anticipated that the early warning systems then foreseen would provide about 15 minutes' notice before enemy warheads landed. For that reason, the original Atlas was designed to be launched within less than 15 minutes after receipt of orders to do so. One of the major reasons in the early sixties for switching to the Titan II, with its storable propellants, and the Minuteman with its solid propellants, was that the time from the "go signal" to the actual launch could be made still shorter.

AUTONOMOUS ASPECTS OF LAUNCH ON WARNING SYSTEMS

Many of the people who have proposed this solution to the problem are thoughtful and moderate, but even so, I find this resolution of the dilemma to be completely unsatisfactory. The time in which the decision to launch must be made varies from just a few minutes up to perhaps 20 minutes, depending on the nature of the attack, and the details of our warning system, communication system, and our command and control system. This time is so short that the decision to launch our missiles must be made either by a computer, by a preprogramed President, or by some preprogramed delegate of the President. There will be no time to stop and think about what the signals mean or to check to see whether they might somehow be false alarms. The decision will have to be made on the basis of electronic signals electronically analyzed, in accordance with a plan worked out long before by apolitical analysts in an antiseptic and unreal atmosphere. In effect, not even the President, let alone the Congress, would really be a party to the ultimate decision to end civilization.

If launching our missiles on electronic warning does not seem so bad, then consider the situation the other way around. Our current technical developments, specifically greater accuracy and reliability of missiles, MIRV and ABM are pushing the Russians in the same direction. Further, in their case a far larger fraction of the deterrent is provided by fixed land-based forces than in ours, and so they have an even greater need to find a truly reliable means of protecting their deterrent from a preemptive attack by us. If we continue with our MIRV developments, and thus force the Soviets to go to a launch on warning system, can we rely on them to invent and institute adequate controls? Do they have the necessary level of sophistication to solve the contradiction inherent in the need for a hair trigger (so that their system will respond in time) and a stiff trigger (so they won't fire accidentally)? How good are their computers at recognizing false alarms? How good is the command and control system for the Polaris-type submarine fleet they are now rapidly, if belatedly, building? Will it be "fail-safe?"

It cannot be emphasized too strongly that unfavorable answers to these questions about their capability will mean diminished national security for us. Yet there is no way for us to assure favorable answers to them. The only way we can avoid the danger to our security inherent in these questions is by eliminating the need to ask them. Strategic weapons systems on both sides must be designed so that no premium is put on a preemptive attack, and so that neither side is forced to adopt the kind of "hair trigger" epitomized in the "launch on warning" concept.

Fortunately for use, the Soviets have also expressed concern about this problem. In words very similar to those used before this committee last spring, Foreign Minister Gromyko last summer said, "[There] is another matter that cannot be ignored * * * It is linked to a considerable extent to the fact that the command and control systems for arms are becoming increasingly autonomous. * * * from the people who create them * * * The human brain is no longer assessing at sufficient speed the results of the multitude of instruments. The decisions made by man depend in the last analysis on the conclusions provided by computers. Governments must do everything possible to be able to determine the development of events and not to find themselves in the role of captive of events."

INCREASE IN MILITARY POWER AND DECREASE IN NATIONAL SECURITY

The nuclear arms race has led to a situation that is at once absurd and poses a dilemma. Ever since the end of World War II, the military power of the United States has been steadily increasing, while at the same time our national security has been rapidly and inexorably decreasing. The same thing is happening to the Soviet Union.

At the end of World War II, the United States was still invulnerable to a direct attack by a foreign power. In 1949, the development of the atomic bomb by the Soviet Union ended that ideal state of affairs, perhaps forever.

By the early 1950's, the U.S.S.R., on the basis of its own unilateral decision to accept the inevitable retaliation, could have launched an attack on the United States with bombers carrying fission bombs. Most of these bombers would have penetrated our defense and the American casualties could have numbered in the tens of millions.

During the late fifties and early sixties first thermonuclear bombs and then intercontinental missiles became part of the equation. As a result, by 1970, the U.S.S.R., again on the basis of its own unilateral decision to accept the inevitable retaliation, could launch an attack that could produce 100 million or more American casualties.

This steady decrease in national security does not result from inaction on the part of responsible U.S. military and civilian authorities. It is the inevitable consequence of the arms race and the systematic exploitation of the fruits of modern science and technology by the United States and the U.S.S.R. Our attempts to deploy bomber defenses during the fifties and sixties did not substantially modify this picture, and ABM deployment will, I believe, have an even smaller direct impact on the number of casualties we might suffer in a future attack.

Nearly everyone now recognizes the futility of the arms race, and nearly everyone now realizes that still more of the same baroque military technology is not going to provide a solution to the dilemma of the steady decrease in our national security that has accompanied the increase in our military power. The SALT talks are one hopeful result of the widening recognition of the absolute necessity of finding some other approach to the problem, and finding it soon.

EFFECT OF ABM AND MIRV ON SALT

So, how do ABM (and MIRV) affect these talks? We must consider both of these elements of the arms race since they are really inseparable. ABM automatically leads to MIRV, and vice versa. There are at least two major effects.

First of all, ABM has both a multiplying and a rachet effect on the arms race; its deployment produces a stepwise, irreversible increase in the number of offensive missiles required. It does not matter whether it is Chinese-oriented or Soviet-oriented. Consider a Chinese-oriented ABM. People who propose such imagine the Chinese blackmailing us with just a few (50-100) ICBM's by threatening to destroy some small but vital part of the United States. Since the defensive coverage of an ABM interceptor is small compared to the dimensions of the United States, since Hawaii and Alaska must also be defended, and since the offense in this special and peculiar case would concentrate all of its missiles on just one small area of the United States, we would need many times as many ABM's as the Chinese have missiles. If they have no penetration aids, we might get by with only 24 times as many interceptors as they have missiles; however, if they do have good decoys or multiple warheads, a cautious U.S. defense planner would call for a great many more. Thus, a really serious Chinese-oriented ABM system requires many thousands of U.S. ABM interceptors. Now reverse this and ask what the Russians would have to do in the face of such a supposedly Chinese-oriented U.S. ABM deployment. In their case we do not imagine them as merely blackmailing us by threatening to destroy a few cities. Rather, we imagine them as trying to deter us, as we try to deter them.

According to the current fashion in strategic analysis, in order to achieve deterrence it is necessary to have an offensive force which, after weathering a surprise attack against it, can still retaliate and destroy a large fraction of the enemy population and industrial base; and as much of his offensive forces as may still remain in silos and on bases. In order for the Soviets to be able to do that, they must be able to penetrate all parts of our ABM shield with whatever force they might have left after a first attack by us. And to guarantee that outcome, a conservative Soviet planner would have to call for many more total Soviet offensive warheads than there were total U.S. interceptors. Thus, an ABM designed to cope with blackmail by 50–100 Chinese missiles, can produce a multiplying and a rachet effect requiring a total Soviet warhead inventory much larger than the more than 1,000 they even now possess. Clearly, in such an event we cannot hope to achieve any meaningful strategic arms limitation.

A second way in which ABM and MIRV affect the possibility of a successful outcome of the SALT talks is through the uncertainties they introduce into the strategic equation. The main uncertainty connected with ABM is the one that has been so persistently raised here: How well will it work? The main uncertainty connected with MIRV has to do with the impossibility of knowing how many warheads were actually poised for launch. As is well-known, we are fairly confident about our ability to know how many missiles they have, but as others have pointed out, it is quite another matter to know how many MIRV warheads each missile carries.

At present, then, each of us is fairly confident in his predictions about the results of a hypothetical nuclear exchange, and each is confident of possessing an adequate force to deter the other. With ABM and MIRV, this confidence will be greatly weakened, and neither of us will be sure of what we could do to the other, and what they could do to us. Unfortunately, experience has clearly shown that such gross uncertainties produce an atmosphere in which arms control agreements are practically impossible. For example, explosions combined with wild speculations about the kinds of developments which might flow from a secret series of underground tests have inhibited any progress toward eliminating such tests, and thus achieving a complete nuclear test ban. In the same way, the uncertainties inevitably associated with ABM and MIRV will lead us into a similar morass, and no progress will be possible in the extremely vital area of strategic arms limitations.

NECESSITY FOR HOLDING PRESENT STRATEGIC BALANCE

In summary: The steady progress of the arms race has led to an equally steady and seemingly inexorable decrease in our national security and safety. Today, the strategic balance is such that strategic arms limitation agreements, which could bring an end to the nuclear arms race, seem possible. ABM and MIRV threaten to upset this balance in a way which will make such agreements impossible, or at least extremely difficult. ABM and MIRV are inseparable; each inspires and requires the other. They must be stopped before it is too late if we are to avoid another increase in the magnitude of the nuclear holocaust we all face.

We must do everything possible to insure a positive income to the SALT talks. The interim freeze on the deployment of offensive and defensive strategic weapons, now being considered by the Senate, is one such move.

Thank you, Mr. Chairman.

Senator CASE. Thank you, Dr. York.
Dr. Bundy.
(The biographical sketch of Mr. McGeorge Bundy follows.)

BIOGRAPHY OF MCGEORGE BUNDY, PRESIDENT OF THE FORD FOUNDATION, 320 EAST 43D STREET, NEW YORK, N.Y.

McGeorge Bundy was born in Boston, Massachusetts, March 30, 1919, son of Harvey Hollister and Katharine Lawrence (Putnam) Bundy. He received his preparatory education at the Dexter School, Brookline, Massachusetts, and the Groton (Massachusetts) School and was graduated A.B. in 1940 from Yale University. In the following year he became a Junior Fellow at Harvard University.

Mr. Bundy entered the U.S. Army as a Private in 1942 and was advanced through grades to the rank of Captain prior to his discharge in 1946, participating in Operation Husky, the invasion of Sicily, and Operation Overlord, the invasion of France.

Following the war he served during 1946-48 as Assistant to Henry L. Stimson, who was readying the manuscript of the book, "On Active Service In Peace and War" (1948), of which Mr. Bundy was co-author.

Early in 1948 Mr Bundy served as a consultant to the programs division of the Economic Cooperation Administration, which administered the Marshall Plan. In September, 1948, he served as research analyst for foreign policy on a committee recruited by the Republican presidential candidate, Thomas E. Dewey. He then served as a political analyst for the Council on Foreign Relations, New York City, in a study of the Marshall Plan.

In 1949 Mr. Bundy returned to Harvard University as visiting lecturer in government. He was advanced to Associate Professor in 1951 and to Professor of Government in 1954, maintaining the latter position until 1961. He also was Dean of the Faculty of Arts and Sciences at Harvard University from 1953 to 1961.

In December, 1960, Mr. Bundy was appointed by President-elect John F. Kennedy to the post of Special Assistant to the President for National Security Affairs. In this capacity Mr. Bundy served as a staff officer on foreign and defense policy for Presidents Kennedy and Johnson until March 1, 1966 when he became President of the Ford Foundation.

Mr. Bundy is editor of "Pattern of Responsibility" (1952), and the author of "The Strength of Government" (1968). Honorary LL.D. degrees have been conferred upon him by Brown University, Harvard University, Oberlin College, Hofstra College, the University of Notre Dame, Brandeis University, and Boston University, and an honorary L.H.D. degree by Yale University. Mr. Bundy is a member of Phi Beta Kappa, the American Political Science Association, and the Council on Foreign Relations.

Traveling and playing tennis are his principal avocations.

Mr. Bundy was married at Beverly Farms, Massachusetts, June 10, 1950, to Mary B. Lothrop of Boston, Massachusetts. They have four sons, Stephen, Andrew, William and James.

STATEMENT OF McGEORGE BUNDY, PRESIDENT, THE FORD FOUNDATION

Mr. BUNDY. Mr. Chairman and members of the committee, I am happy to accept your invitation to testify on the arms race, and I am particularly happy to appear in company with Dr. York. I would like to associate myself strongly with his basic argument.

STOPPING STRATEGIC ARMS RACE

My broad view of the arms race was stated last October in an article in Foreign Affairs, and to save the time of the committee I would like, with your permission, to offer that article for the record instead of repeating it.

Senator CASE. Without objection, that will be done.

(The article referred to follows.)

TO CAP THE VOLCANO
By McGeorge Bundy

Reprinted From

FOREIGN AFFAIRS
AN AMERICAN QUARTERLY REVIEW

OCTOBER 1969

TO CAP THE VOLCANO

By McGeorge Bundy

THE summer of 1969 has seen men on the moon and almost half the American Senate voting against a defense decision supported by two Presidents. In the summer pride of the moon landing it is not pleasant to turn the mind back to the terrible topic of nuclear danger. Yet the splendid technical achievement of Apollo contains its own reminder that similar skills applied with similar single-mindedness have now led the two greatest powers of our generation into an arms race totally unprecedented in size and danger.

The next year or two offer to the United States and the Soviet Union what may be the best chance yet to limit their extravagant contest in strategic weapons. We Americans may not understand this opportunity very well, and our friends in Russia may not understand it either. That weakness of understanding, together with the transcendent importance of the subject, is an excuse for one more effort to put some light on it. I shall begin with a review of the ABM debate and then go on to consider some larger political questions which that debate did not address—questions which may grow in importance as strategic arms limitation talks (SALT for short) get started.

II

The debate on ABM deployment was remarkable less for its content than for the simple fact that it happened. The level of argument was high. In analytical force the Administration's supporters were less persuasive than its opponents. There were some excessive claims on both sides, but the overstatements of some Administration spokesmen, although not the President, offered particularly easy targets. What held a slim majority, in the end, was the traditional and powerful argument that in matters of this sort—especially with international negotiations in the offing—the sober recommendation of the President is entitled to the benefit of doubt. Both the case against the ABM and the case for supporting the President are likely to be at least as strong in the future as they have been this past summer, and the task of reconciling them is an important element in the work ahead.

Yet the central significance of this debate is less in the competing arguments than in an underlying agreement which pervades the hundreds of pages of the *Congressional Record*—an agreement that the arms race is taking a new and highly unsatisfactory turn. Senators disagreed on the remedy, and what happens so often in hard debates happened again in this one: the case against a given line of action was easier to make than the case for an alternative. Those who opposed ABM deployment were fearful that American action would increase the world's danger; those who favored deployment found the same result in lack of action. But there were no voices to suggest that the continuing race is either safe or easy.

One heavy element in the argument of opponents was cost. Here the Administration encountered an unanticipated and widespread reaction against defense costs of all sorts, and still more against the seeming financial irresponsibility of the massive defense machine. The one amendment which carried as the debate concluded was a requirement for better financial accounting from the Pentagon. Efforts to emphasize the limited costs of initial ABM deployment were painfully reminiscent of earlier Pentagon underestimates, and opponents were able to remind the Senate of such high-cost and low-yield enterprises as the massive air defense program of the 1950s. On the evidence before the Senate it seems highly believable that a fully developed ABM system might cost much nearer 50 billion than 10. Yet cost alone was probably not the central issue for most Senators.

The central issue was danger. The supporters of the ABM had in mind the one-sided danger of an emerging Soviet strength, to which they ascribed the deeply alarming characteristic of a capability to knock out the American deterrent. If this argument had been persuasive to opposing Senators, they could hardly have voted as they did, because there is no significant sentiment in the Congress or in the country for acceptance of the notion that any other state should ever have—or even seem to have—the capacity to make a nuclear attack on the United States without receiving a devastating reply. It is no cause for complaint that the Defense Department in the nuclear age must address itself to this question, and no cause for surprise that military men put this question first.

What is now open for argument is whether this basic question is being asked in the right way. Certainly the Senators who voted against ABM did not think so. To them it was not the Soviet menace which was now most severe; it was the arms race itself. Quite aside from the prospect of a new order of cost, the technological implications of ABM and other new systems were seen as profoundly destabilizing. While questions can be asked about this analysis too, there is much force in the case that stands in the record. These new systems, whether designed for defense or for penetration, do appear to share one highly disturbing characteristic: no one seems to know just what they will and will not be able to do, and no one will ever know with certainty unless there comes a dreadful day of actual use.

This uncertainty is multiple. Each side is unsure of what its own systems can do, and is still less sure of the quality of the other side's systems. There is a tendency to place a high value on the effectiveness of a system when winning support for its adoption. But when it is in hand, the prudent military course is to place a minimum value on its effectiveness, precisely in order to plan against the worst possible future case. The ABM debate, like previous debates, found the Pentagon casting doubts upon the effectiveness of the very systems whose value it had most praised in earlier years. This was not disingenuous; it was a natural product of the rhythm of technological contest.

It is still worse when one estimates what the adversary has or can have. Just as Soviet deployment of primitive defensive missiles around Moscow played a major role some years ago in turning us toward the new system of penetration called MIRV, so our own plans for an ABM force, carefully limited though they have been in different ways by different Presidents, must have important meaning for Soviet military planners. As they must see it, maybe our system will stay small, and maybe it is as ineffective as its critics claim—but maybe not.

It is not clear just how far the technological uncertainties of the next stage are more destabilizing than those of the last twenty years. On this point opinions have differed. Certainly it will be much harder to be sure about the number and quality of multiple warheads than about the number and size of fixed missile sites. But much depends upon highly sophisticated and subtle techniques of observation and analysis about which no outsider can be dogmatic. The first half of the 1960s saw an extraordinary increase in the capacity of each side to know the strategic strength of the other, and it is not likely that the technological revolution of intelligence is at an end. Unfortunately there is a long and growing distance between what the intelligence analyst knows and what is immediately apparent to his political superiors. In the great case of the missiles in Cuba, it was the persuasive conviction of the experts and not the naked appearance of the first photographs which was immediately conclusive to President Kennedy on October 16. If he had not learned to know and trust these experts, he might well have doubted their story. This problem may be more acute today.

If the danger of uncertainty and imperfect communication exists in the small circle of those who have full and current knowledge of the evidence, it is reasonable to suppose that the distance from that evidence to public understanding and confidence may be greater still. Moreover, at best, technical intelligence can show us only what exists and not what may be intended. The best example here may be our own Sentinel/Safeguard ABM system. The new Administration did not change the basic characteristics of that system when it changed its name, but there is a wide difference between the declared purposes of Secretary McNamara and those of Secretary Laird. Which one should a Soviet planner believe? The right answer may be "both," but if so, one's sympathy for such a planner must increase.

At the edges of the Senate debate, and more visibly in other public comment, another danger could be seen—that of polarization. Some of those supporting the Administration seemed to set no limit upon the number, cost and variety of desirable nuclear weapons systems. To such men the nuclear superiority—or even supremacy—of the United States was an absolute requirement. At the other extreme, and clearly growing in their importance, were those to whom any nuclear weapons system—and *a fortiori* any new one—must be bad. Ironically, to both sets of extremists the real relation between our power and that of the Soviet Union was irrelevant. Both were proceeding on the assumption that nuclear danger could somehow be handled by the United States alone. In so far as they considered Soviet behavior at all, it was only to assume it into conformity with their own preferences.

We have had sharp differences at the fringes of opinion throughout the nuclear age, but the debate of 1969 suggests that if the arms race does continue to expand, both fringes may grow sharply in strength. A rapidly expanding nuclear budget would probably require much more tub-thumping than we have seen this year, and the predictable response would be an increasing rejection of the whole notion of nuclear deterrence. Such a division would be very different from the sober debate we have just come through, and its consequences for nuclear safety could be grave. In Western Europe, for example, there is not yet any substitute for a stable, reliable and defensive American nuclear presence. Throughout the last twenty years the decisive military element in the safety of that part of the world has been the nuclear strength and commitment of the United States. That dependence has been uncomfortable but inescapable. One element in its acceptability has been the generally sober and responsible behavior of the United States in nuclear matters. If that sobriety and responsibility should be called in question, either by increasing nuclear militarism or increasing rejection of all nuclear weapons, or both, then the relations within the Atlantic Alliance could be shaken, and the temptation for Soviet adventure increased.

It is a long way from the wonder of Apollo 11 to this morass of division, doubt and danger. Yet both are products of technology and teamwork. Why should the technology and teamwork which can electrify mankind in one context spread so much fear and confusion in another? The most obvious answer is of course that modern weapons are instruments of totally inhuman destructive power, but for our present purposes there is a different and perhaps a more enlightening answer. The race to the moon is like a game of golf—each player is responsible for his own performance alone—and in the case of Apollo the last stages of the course were played out in an atmosphere comfortably free of competition. But the arms race is like a boxing match: what each contestant does depends as much on his opponent as on himself. It is this fact of interlocking behavior which decisively separates decisions on nuclear weapons systems from decisions on reaching the moon. In a boxing match and in the nuclear arms race a defense may be imperfect and yet seem necessary; a threat may be uncertain and yet seem compelling. So the very technological capability which can be used to insure complete reliability on the way to the moon becomes a force for uncertainty and terror. In their dependence on technology and teamwork the two undertakings are brothers, but the environments in which they live and interact are almost wholly opposite.

The endangering effect of technological gamesmanship is a subject on which others have spoken with the authority of close experience, and I cannot do better than to refer the interested reader to a paper by Dr. Herbert York in the August issue of *Scientific American*. Writing primarily from experience gained as Director of Defense Research and Engineering in the Eisenhower Administration, Dr. York reaches the conclusion that if there is to be any escape at all from the rapid crescendo of strategic cost and uncertainty, it must be through political and not technological decisions. I find this conclusion compelling, and the remainder of this paper is addressed to the present political situation and the prospects for such escape.

III

The first characteristic of the political scene is the dominant role of two nuclear powers. The nuclear age has other dangers which we cannot afford to neglect; there is persistent importance in controlling our own systems, for example, and also in preventing nuclear proliferation. But the heart of the matter in 1969 is in the relationship between the Soviet Union and the United States. Throughout the nuclear age the two superpowers have made their strategic nuclear decisions almost exclusively in relation to one another, and the prospect of escalation makes this lonely interdependence more apparent than ever. No one is suggesting the early appearance of ABMs or MIRVs in any other countries. Whatever adjustment either power may wish to make because of its awareness of nuclear weapons in the hands of third parties, this element in the problem is marginal in comparison to the nuclear arsenals of the two great powers.

The dominance of the two-power relationship does not make it simple. The debate this summer sufficiently illustrates the complexity of decision-making in the United States. We have groups with special interests in and out of uniform, and on both sides of the question. What we tend to forget is that there are competing interests and attitudes in the Soviet Union too. There is evidence of at least four such forces. The first, and undoubtedly still the most important, is that of the party apparatus. Both doctrine and history confirm the importance of this element, and some of its characteristics are painfully familiar: conspiratorial suspicion of all non-communists and most non-Russians, massive preoccupation with the protection of power positions already occupied, practical concern for whatever crisis is most immediately dangerous to itself. A second major force is that of the managers and planners. Where these men are not military, we may expect them to have a heavy concern for the husbanding of scarce resources and the limitation of defense budgets. They may well be better placed in this respect than Americans with similar concerns who too casually assume that what is saved on weapons will automatically be spent on the cities. A third element is the military, and to put it mildly there is no reason to suppose that they are less powerful than our own defense establishment, although like our own military men they appear to have important differences among themselves on the priorities of different weapons systems. Finally, there are scientists and intellectuals. Though their views are better known in the West than they are to most of their countrymen, they clearly constitute a force for reconciliation. They operate on a sufferance which expands and contracts at the will of the party apparatus, and in the last year they have come under renewed restraints.

Sometime in the first half of 1968, the Soviet Government did reach the conclusion that it would be sensible to open a negotiation with the United States on strategic weapons. This decision in and of itself does not tell us much. The Soviet purpose in negotiation with non-communist powers is not always benign, and Soviet alertness for a one-sided advantage is proverbial. (There is no reason for resentment; in another context similar behavior is praised as Yankee shrewdness.) If one may extrapolate from the American experience, it seems likely that different elements in the Soviet Government may have had different reasons for urging or accepting negotiations of this sort. But at a minimum it must have been the judgment of the Soviet Government that the opening of negotiations might lead to an improvement in terms of Soviet interest and offered no unacceptable risks. A similar judgment had long been held by the Johnson Administration in Washington, and this spring the Nixon Administration has reaffirmed it. So both sides seem ready, at least in principle, for a major negotiation.

The prospect of negotiation is not in itself a prospect of progress. Under the pressure of world opinion the great powers have been discussing nuclear arms control in different forums and in different ways for a generation. During the ABM debate, one Senator extracted from the Arms Control and Disarmament Agency the interesting statistic that there have been more than 1500 arms-control meetings between American and Soviet negotiators. The vast majority of these meetings have been fruitless, and with the single exception of the Limited Nuclear Test Ban Treaty, neither of the great powers has accepted any significant restriction on its own capabilities. Both the Soviet Union and the United States have grown expert in the plausible presentation of proposals which they know in advance will be unacceptable to the other side. Even in minor matters each faces a complex task in framing a position which does not produce unacceptable opposition from internal interests. Neither one can wholly separate the nuclear problem from other questions. So discussions have been delayed at one time or another, by one side or the other, because of trouble in Berlin, Viet Nam or Czechoslovakia. In midsummer there seemed to be still another pause, this time in Moscow.

It seems reasonable to expect, therefore, that even without further delay in the opening of strategic arms talks there will be a wide distance between the parties at the outset. The first formal position of the Soviet Union may not go much beyond the enigmatic formulas in the Soviet memorandum of July 1, 1968. That memorandum did express readiness to discuss limitations of strategic delivery systems, and it also addressed itself to many other elements of the nuclear problem, but it is little more than a set of topic headings—hardly even an agenda. The initial American position, in turn, may well be more forthcoming in appearance than in reality. One may guess that there will be emphasis on inspection and verification, and there may also be an initial resistance to any possibility of an unpoliced moratorium on the development or deployment of new systems. Yet the slim progress we have made in the last twenty years has been possible only when we have skirted the issue of agreed international inspection, and it seems most unlikely that the particular weapons systems which are now in the offing can be restricted without some such initial device as a moratorium. If the last positions of the two great states are not different from their first ones, therefore, little will come of these negotiations, and there will be no successful transfer of the problem from technology to politics. Indeed, if the discussions are like those which have occurred in most of the 1500 earlier meetings, they will merely transfer to the language of diplomacy the differences of the technological contest itself. So we shall not meet the challenge of Dr. York's conclusion merely by moving from the nuclear laboratory to the conference table. If we are to escape from technology to politics, we must do something more.

IV

The neglected truth about the present strategic arms race between the United States and the Soviet Union is that in terms of international political behavior that race has now become almost completely irrelevant. The new weapons systems which are being developed by each of the two great powers will provide neither protection nor opportunity in any serious political sense. Politically the strategic nuclear arms race is in a stalemate. It has been this way since the first deliverable hydrogen weapons were exploded, and it will be this way for as far ahead as we can see, even if future developments should be much more heavily one-sided than anything now in prospect. This proposition does not square with the complex measurements of comparative advantage which dominated the ABM debate, but I think it can be supported both by logic and by history.

In light of the certain prospect of retaliation there has been literally no chance at all that any sane political authority, in either the United States or the Soviet Union, would consciously choose to start a nuclear war. This proposition is true for the past, the present and the foreseeable future. For sane men on both sides the balance of terror is overwhelmingly persuasive. Given the worst calculations of the most pessimistic American advocate of new weapons systems, there is no prospect at all that the Soviet Government could attack the United States without incurring an overwhelming risk of destruction vastly greater than anyone but a madman would choose to accept. Conversely, even the most cold-blooded of American planners has always understood, at least since 1954, that the concept of a strategic first strike by the United States is wholly unacceptable because of the prospect of Soviet retaliation.

There is an enormous gulf between what political leaders

really think about nuclear weapons and what is assumed in complex calculations of relative "advantage" in simulated strategic warfare. Think-tank analysts can set levels of "acceptable" damage well up in the tens of millions of lives. They can assume that the loss of dozens of great cities is somehow a real choice for sane men. They are in an unreal world. In the real world of real political leaders—whether here or in the Soviet Union—a decision that would bring even one hydrogen bomb on one city of one's own country would be recognized in advance as a catastrophic blunder; ten bombs on ten cities would be a disaster beyond history; and a hundred bombs on a hundred cities are unthinkable. Yet this unthinkable level of human incineration is the least that could be expected by either side in response to any first strike in the next ten years, *no matter what happens to weapons systems in the meantime.* Even the worst case hypothesized in the ABM debate leaves at least this much room for reply. In sane politics, therefore, there is no level of superiority which will make a strategic first strike between the two great states anything but an act of utter folly.

My argument evidently rests upon an assumption of sanity. It does not protect against madness. But neither is there any protection against the madman in close calculations of "assured survivable destruction capability." Indeed it may be easier for a madman to understand the simple horror of *any* exchange between the superpowers than to be persuaded by intricate calculations of residual "advantage" after the world as we know it is destroyed.

What we have somehow forgotten, in the expanding megatonage of the age of missiles, is that already fifteen years ago we were scorpions in a bottle, able to sting each other only at the price of death. Yet what either side had then was insignificant in comparison to what both sides have now. Moreover, we have somehow let the necessary comparisons of one weapons system with another delude us into a belief that these calculations of cost-effectiveness are also calculations of real advantage. Certainly when we determine that a certain level of deterrent strength is needed (a calculation which has always been generous in both our countries), it makes very good sense to do our best to pick the systems that will do the job most economically, and it follows that close comparative analysis is well worthwhile. But the fact that Minuteman is better in these terms than the

B-70—or Poseidon better than Polaris—does not tell us anything about the real value, politically, of any one system, or of all our systems together. Their one purpose is deterrence. They must not do less, and they cannot do more.

Thus the basic consequence of considering this matter politically and not technically is the conclusion that beyond a point long since passed the escalation of the strategic nuclear race makes no sense for either the Soviet Union or the United States. Nothing in the national interest, the ideology or the personal political position of any leader in either country can be advanced by any strategic nuclear exchange. No weapons systems now in sight for either side can change that fact. It follows that in political, as distinct from technical, terms we have all been wrong to talk of nuclear superiority. President Nixon was surely right when he changed the terms of the discussion from "superiority" to "sufficiency." Sufficiency is what we both have now, in ample measure, and no superiority worth having can be achieved. It is sometimes argued that in the past nuclear superiority—ours over the Soviet Union or that of the Soviet Union over Western Europe—has had a decisive influence on events. I find this a very doubtful proposition. This is not the place for a close reëxamination of relevant crises like Suez, Berlin and Cuba, but my own belief is that in none of the three has the nuclear "superiority" of any major power been decisive. In all three cases the risk of escalation has certainly been an element in the problem, and in all three, in different ways, that risk has been a deterrent to action. But in all three cases, questions of will and purpose have been more important than questions of nuclear numbers. In none of the three cases, I feel confident, would the final result have been different if the relative strategic positions of the Soviet Union and the United States had been reversed. A stalemate is a stalemate either way around.

Since it is vital to avoid misunderstanding, let me emphasize here that in asserting the preëminence of the political judgment on the use and non-use of nuclear weapons I am not at all downgrading the importance of technical proficiency in the deterrent forces we do decide to maintain. It seems to me wholly plain that a credible strategic nuclear deterrent is indispensable to the peace, and for that reason no task is more clearly indispensable than that of maintaining and protecting such a force. There is a great distance between a belief in strategic stalemate and any suggestion that we should proceed to unilateral disarmament. We have bought and paid for parity, and we must not lose it. So it will be as true in a future of stable balance as it has been in the past of presumed supremacy that the men who stand guard over our strategic forces are men who place us all in their debt.

But it is one thing for military men to maintain our deterrent force with vigilant skill, and it is quite another for anyone to assume that their necessary contingency plans have any serious interest for political leaders. The object of political men—quite rightly—is that these weapons should never be used. I have watched two Presidents working on strategic contingency plans, and what interested them most was simply to make sure that none of these awful events would occur. Political leaders, whether here or in Russia, are cut from a very different mold than strategic planners. They see cities and people as part of what they are trying to help—not as targets. They live with the daily struggle to make a little progress—to build things—to grow things—to lift the quality of life a little—and to win honor, and even popularity, by such achievements. The deterrent that might not please a planner is more than deterrent enough for them. And that is why the deterrent does work, even at a distance, as in Berlin. *Maybe* the American nuclear commitment is not as firm as it seems—but what sane Soviet leader wants to put the whole Soviet society in the scales to find out?

It is also important to distinguish the nuclear sufficiency of the superpowers from the very different level of deterrent strength which has been sought by such a leader as General de Gaulle. French theorists have sometimes argued as if a very small number of thermonuclear weapons would be a sure and permanent deterrent. Most American analysts, in my view correctly, have been skeptical of this thesis. The armaments of the middle-level nuclear powers are indeed vulnerable to an obliterating first strike, and that situation may not entirely disappear even if they shift to seaborne missiles. But several orders of magnitude, and as many orders of complexity, separate the difficulties of an attack on such a force from those of a preëmptive attack on either the Soviet Union or the United States. The nuclear sufficiency of the superpowers is as far removed from the deterrent capacity of the *force de frappe* as the Great Pyramid from a molehill.

V

At this point in the analysis our effort to move from technology to politics may seem encouraging, but now we must take account of a much less cheerful aspect of the matter. The politics of the analysis so far is the politics of international relations—of what one state or another will actually do on the world stage. This analysis points plainly to the advantages of limiting the strategic arms race, since it tells us that the existing parity between the superpowers is all that they can hope to use internationally, and since no one in any society wants to pay tens of billions for nothing.

Unfortunately we have not exhausted the politics of strategic weapons. Along with this crude but powerful international politics of common sense goes the politics of consensus and consent within each superpower. Presidents and Politburos may know in their hearts that the only thing they want from strategic weapons is never to have to use them; in their public postures they have felt it necessary to claim more. They may not themselves be persuaded by the refined calculations of the nuclear gamesmen—but they do not find it prudent to expose them for the political irrelevance they are. The public in both countries has been allowed by its leaders to believe that somewhere in ever-growing strength there is safety, and that it still means something to be "ahead." The politics of internal decision-making has not been squared with the reality of international stalemate.

In consequence, the internal politics of the strategic arms race has remained the prisoner of its technology. The ABM debate showed a shift from an earlier emphasis on American "superiority" toward the question whether somehow now the Russians might move "ahead"—but there were only a few voices raised to support the notion that within very broad limits no one now can have a lead worth having. That may be the necessary premise of international political behavior; it is not yet the possible premise of national political debate. Internally, in both countries, the present premise of the debate leads remorselessly toward escalation. In both countries, moreover, this framework of argument is powerfully sustained by the force which Americans have been taught to call "the military-industrial complex." Since the opponents of escalation refuse to contest the basic political premise, they are driven back to technology; those who oppose the ABM tend to argue that it may not work technically—not that it is irrelevant politically. And while excellent answers were made to the Pentagon suggestion that the Russians might be "going for a first strike," there were few to suggest that the necessary assumption of any such scenario must be that the Soviet Government had gone suicidally mad.

What appears in our ABM debate appears also in Soviet behavior. The Russians continue to spend much too much money on large weapons which do them no good and whose only real effect is to frighten us into further efforts of our own. We can afford it better than they can, of course, and in terms of economic cold warfare there has always been a certain spurious attractiveness about trapping the Russians into a constantly accelerating competition. Fortunately, that particular brand of nonsense has never been anyone's official policy, and the tenor of the ABM debate suggests that it may be permanently out of fashion. But the fact that we are not trying to induce this sort of Soviet folly does not make it less real, or less foolish. In every international crisis of the last fifteen years Soviet leaders have shown their understanding that the strategic balance requires mutual restraint between the superpowers. But in their weapons decisions they have been as heedlessly and unproductively excessive as we.

There is a curious and distressing paradox in all this. The same political leaders who know these terrible weapons must never be used and who do not run the foolish risks of nuclear gamesmanship abroad still do not hesitate to authorize system after system. The usual resolution of the paradox is to describe the decision to build as an "insurance policy." But the argument is unsatisfying; the gap between what the political leader orders and what he can do with it is too great. I know of no escape from the conclusion that both in his sensible abhorrence of nuclear conflict and his persistent attachment to still more weapons systems the political leader is reflecting his constituency. The fault is less in our leaders than in ourselves.

VI

On the surface, this analysis suggests a dim future for the SALT talks. If our domestic debates are necessarily carried forward in terms of technological pros and cons, what chance is there that we can base an international negotiation on the cruder, simpler and less demanding realities of international political choice? If there is a real danger that this or that concession or limitation may affect the technological balance, if the technological balance has continuing importance in domestic political debate, and if suspicion and wariness on our side are easily outmatched on the other, then indeed the prospect seems unpromising.

But is the analysis complete? Not necessarily. The SALT talks carry with them not only the requirement of formal opening positions, but two much more promising and important opportunities. The first is the chance for all concerned to reaffirm the need of mankind for greater safety from the risk of nuclear disaster. The same American public opinion which gives general support to any responsible recommendation for a new weapons system has also steadily supported the struggle to stop the arms race. Some hard-boiled gamesmen have never liked the nuclear test ban treaty, but the American people have overruled them, and not one voice was heard in the recent Senate debate to reopen that national decision. So the SALT talks provide a major occasion for the mobilization of that part of our opinion which feels the essential futility of escalating the strategic arms race. And if, as is likely, many of us are divided against ourselves, believing things which do not really fit together, then the SALT talks and the discussion around them may help to clear our heads. What is true of Americans is likely to be true also of many in the Soviet Union. And what is still more plain is that a straightforward disbelief in the wisdom of the race in strategic weapons can be observed among those who are not Russians or Americans. I am not thinking here of those who have preached unilateral disarmament but rather of those who have always understood the need of each of the two great states for its own nuclear defense. The difference between one level of unspeakable disaster and another has never been interesting to sensible statesmen in third countries, and we may expect them to give persistent encouragement to those who may seek to move the SALT talks from technology to political reality.

A second opportunity of the SALT talks is the chance they should give for informal and often private communication. Each of the two great governments knows more about these matters than it has yet said in public statements. Each has an intense interest in learning more about the real thoughts of the other. If sophisticated understanding of the interlocking implications of weapons systems has come earlier and cut deeper in the United States, still there has been about the Soviet approach to these matters a certain rough realism which is not to be underrated. It seems at least possible that realism and sophistication could now converge toward the conclusion that enough is enough. As they explore each other's thoughts, moreover, the negotiators will have the chance to make it clear to one another that many forms of secrecy are self-defeating and, as the boxers get to know each other better, they may understand that all they can have is a draw, so that threats of a technical knockout are of no help to anyone. In any event, the presence in one place of American and Soviet officials in substantial numbers and interesting varieties should give an excellent opportunity for patient exploration of such possibilities. In this context there is a special reason for hope in the apparent present readiness of the Soviet Government for businesslike discussion of just such issues of mutual concern.

Neither public encouragement nor private conversation will produce agreement by themselves. Our analysis has already indicated what a long distance there is between the current posture of intense technological competition and the desired result of mutual recognition of a stable political reality. To put the proposition quite simply, each great power must move from a zealous concern for its own advantage to a sober acceptance of parity. Both the intellectual and the practical consequences of such movement are grave, and obviously there are interests and attitudes in both countries to which the shift will be unwelcome, at least at first. Moreover, a movement of this kind is not likely to come by negotiation and diplomatic agreement alone. Somewhere along the line—perhaps quite early—it will be important for one power and then for both to take practical steps in this same direction. In the much simpler case of the Test Ban Treaty, there was an informal moratorium, a temporary breach in the moratorium, and then a conclusion by both governments that a treaty should be signed. It is worth remembering that the Soviet Government had two sets of atmospheric tests after breaking the moratorium, against one for the United States. But what is most significant about that "imbalance" is that it was regarded as acceptable both by President Kennedy and by the Senate. It seems likely that major progress in the SALT talks will require a similar American broadmindedness at one point or another. We are still "ahead," and we may also be closer to a national recognition that such a lead means nothing. Our process of government does not impose a requirement of fear and suspicion that is remotely like that imposed by the Soviet party apparatus. We now have a fully developed public debate which will not die down, and since that debate is inevitable, prudent leadership will seek to take account of it. And finally, we can take the lead in practical steps for the simple and persuasive reason that even without agreement some such steps are in our own best interest.

Yet it would be a great mistake for Soviet negotiators to suppose that the Americans are likely to embark on a continuous course of unilateral strategic disarmament. Opinion in our country will never be separated from an observant concern with what the Soviet Union is doing, and neither international nor domestic political concerns could justify any American government in seeming to accept a wholly one-sided policy of limitation. I hope the logic of the argument I have put forward is strong, but logic alone will not permanently sustain a national policy of unilateral limitation. It will take two to cap the volcano of strategic competition.

Since it is evident that the negotiators will have much to do, we can take comfort in the fact that there is one major area in which there is no reason for them to have unmanageable problems—the area of their relations with their various allies. In the Soviet case the point is obvious: the Soviet Government has never shown any interest in sharing its nuclear responsibilities with other members of the Warsaw Pact, and the troubles of recent years make any such move less likely than ever. The situation in NATO is more complex, but its meaning for strategic arms talks is not different. While it is true that the presence of American men and nuclear weapons on the ground in Europe is still today a necessary element in the security of the West, it is also true that this decisive protection is unaffected one way or the other by the question of strategic arms control. The strength of the American guarantee will be neither increased nor decreased by acceptance of parity, and the level of American commitment in Europe is not a proper topic for bargaining in the SALT talks. It was never the American superiority in nuclear weapons that was decisive in protecting Europe; it was simply the high probability that any large-scale use of force against a NATO country would set loose a chain of events that could lead to nuclear war. For reasons we have already discussed, any war between serious nuclear powers would be as bad to "win" as to "lose," so that relative numbers of weapons have never been decisive in the credibility of the American deterrent in Europe. That deterrent has been made credible, ever since the first Soviet nuclear explosion, by two quite simple things: first, the American conviction, expressed again last winter by Mr. Nixon, that the safety of Europe runs with our own, and second, the confirmation of that conviction by the stationing of wholly persuasive numbers of American men and American nuclear weapons in Europe. Nothing in that conviction or its confirmation need be modified in the slightest by an agreement to keep the balance of strategic power both stable in shape and limited in size.

VII

One cannot end any discussion of this somber subject without thinking about the burden that it places on the President of the United States. The debate in the Senate has been healthy, and the prospect of more debate is encouraging, but in the end the President does have a special and personal responsibility here, and it may well be that the President's need for understanding support is greater now than at any time in the nuclear age. That seems a lot to say if we look back at the decisions that four Presidents have faced. But if our analysis is right, it has fallen to Mr. Nixon to come to terms with the politics of parity—and to do it in a time when angry men at both edges of the argument would like nothing better than to pick a fight right through him.

In this situation Mr. Nixon himself has in the main been careful. Like many of the rest of us, he has a past on this subject, and he has been trained by his particular experiences to give the benefit of the doubt to those who urge the need for action to sustain our strength. Yet his own arguments have been restrained, and according to informal but authoritative reports from Europe he has been eloquent in reminding friends abroad that strategic parity is now both inescapable and acceptable.

It seems at least possible, then, that if the President is hesitant about arms limitation, it is less because of any misplaced faith in the will-of-the-wisp of "superiority" than because he does not yet see any solid political base, here at home, for relatively low-keyed, low-cost parity. His majority for ABM was small—but should he trade it in for nothing? Those who wish he had decided the ABM question differently have an obligation to examine that question.

My own answer is that the President does indeed have a claim on the help of those who seek strategic arms limitation, just as they have a claim on him. He and he alone can manage the process of negotiation, and in the end any agreement he may reach will have to have the confident support of the American people. No one is going to help that kind of negotiation or increase the chance of that kind of agreement by assuming that the President should be pushed around by noisy public pressure. It has been entirely reasonable for believers in arms control to place themselves where their own best judgment led them in the debate on the ABM, but as the SALT talks begin the President has a necessary claim to trust.

This Presidential claim need not be extended to a blanket advance endorsement of any sentence that any American delegate may utter. The very primacy of the President himself in these matters requires a certain freedom to help him out by complaining of his subordinates. The long distance we have to go is not likely to be covered at one bound, or even in a straight line. There are men with strong opinions around Mr. Nixon; some of them have said arguable things on this subject already, and on the long journey from here to a sensible bargain there will be many occasions for objection. By the same token, the partisans of arms control will not all be right all the time. The position which they must avoid is that of a self-righteousness which offers the President only sermons and never support. Presidents, like other men, have a limited tolerance for counsel unaccompanied by help.

What one may hope for from the President, in return, is that he will indeed maintain the continuous review of our strategic position which he announced on March 14 along with his first ABM decision, and also that he may be willing to look again at the doctrine which found its way into his Colorado speech— a doctrine according to which arms races do not make conflict, but the other way around. That doctrine is not so much wrong as incomplete. It is quite true that the differences between nations are the ultimate source of their military arrangements, but it is also true that arms races can develop a life of their own, and that nuclear arms races have a menace of their own. The American and British navies were still in a foolish arms race with each other as late as 1930. The current race has become a wildly irrelevant technical competition which brings no help to statesmen, and sooner or later the true statesman must say so. Indeed the arms race between the United States and the Soviet Union may well be unique in history and in politics, as it is certainly unique in technology. The notion that its escalation is politically dangerous is somehow plausible to nearly all of us, even when we choose to think it is all the other fellow's fault. It is well worth our while to consider the converse proposition: if we can slow it down, or perhaps even turn it back, will that not perhaps help us both—even help us *all*—politically?

As a nation we cannot afford a great division on these issues, and we must look especially to the President to hold us together. Throughout the nuclear age we have expected our Presidents to show not only prudent concern for defense, but also strong personal leadership on the hard road away from nuclear danger. Every President so far has found himself more and more caught up in the effort for arms control as he has lived with the nuclear realities. Mr. Nixon's chance comes early in his term, and his predecessors might well be envious if on this subject they had not all been forced to move far beyond personal pride.

I believe that the American people know in their bones that nuclear weapons are different, and I believe they will support the President in decisions based on that difference. In particular I believe he will find solid support for the kind of reassessment that could lead to a decision that the United States, on its own, will take a small step away from the nuclear arms race. That small step too could be a giant leap for mankind.

Mr. BUNDY. Its principal conclusion was simply that the strategic arms race between the United States and the Soviet Union has gone too far, threatens to go further, and should be stopped by an early agreement between these two great powers. Since then SALT has begun in a businesslike way, and our Government is now considering what its position will be as the talks resume in Vienna next week.

SENATE RESOLUTION 211 AS BEST NEXT STEP IN ARMS LIMITATION

My own strong belief is that the best next step for the United States in this field is to follow the course proposed in Senate Resolution 211. That resolution first states the sense of the Senate that prompt negotiations be urgently pursued between the two great powers, and on this point I think there is little or no disagreement among Americans. The second part of the resolution expresses the sense of the Senate that we should now propose an immediate suspension by both sides "of further deployment of all offensive and defensive nuclear strategic weapons systems." An excellent basic argument in favor of this resolution is developed in the report submitted by Senator Fulbright, and I will not waste your time by repeating it. Let me rather offer 10 brief comments on the significance of your committee's position.

UNITED STATES-SOVIET MUTUAL SUSPENSION OF STRATEGIC SYSTEMS

1. I assume that in passing Senate Resolution 211, the Senate will be urging the President to propose to the Soviet Union the mutual suspension of these deployments for some reasonable term during which further progress could be made toward a definite agreement. There are some who suppose that "moratorium" implies a form of permanent self-entanglement, but as I understand it no such self-entanglement is either necessary or intended.

2. I strongly support the statement in the committee report that an agreed suspension of deployment of strategic systems will necessarily imply a suspension also of tests—as well as deployment—of such emerging systems as MIRV. The committee report makes the correct connection between the Soviet SS-9 and the American MIRV. This connection goes both ways. Just as the Soviets must limit SS-9 if they wish to stop MIRV, so I believe that if we are to get any early limit on SS-9 deployment, we ourselves must place MIRV on the bargaining table.

U.S. SHOULD TAKE INITIATIVE BY LIMITED SUSPENSION

3. I believe that there will not be much progress in SALT until the U.S. Government is prepared to make a specific proposal. I think the odds are heavy that it will prove wise and right for us to move first. Your committee has heard the sensitive and preceptive testimony of Prof. Marshall Shulman on Soviet attitudes toward arms negotiation. I share his view that Soviet wariness is at least equal to our own. Our experience, understanding, and present strength make it right for us to take the initiative.

4. Specifically, I believe that as a part of any proposal for an agreed moratorium the United States should take a first step by announcing a suspension of its own deployment of ABM and MIRV for a limited

time. Such a time could and should be relatively brief, and its extension could and should depend upon the promptness and seriousness of Soviet response. There might be some marginal inconvenience for our defense organization in such a suspension, and our already overwhelming strategic war plans might need marginal revision if specific planned deployments are delayed—but there is no real or present danger in such a limited suspension, and if we want results in SALT, we should try it. How long such a trial should be, and precisely what it should include, are matters I do not attempt to cover, since I think it would be unwise for a private citizen to try to define the exact length and direction of any first step. My point is simply that we should begin by an action as well as a proposal.

5. This belief rests not on any sentimental notion that we must be more virtuous than the Russians, but rather upon the deep conviction that effective limitation and reduction of the strategic arms race is an objective deeply in our own national interest as well as the interest of all mankind. It is wholly false for reasons which Dr. York has spelled out with great clarity, to suppose that the national security is always served by adding strategic weapons and never by their limitation. In the world of the 1970's the truth is more nearly the opposite. We have more than enough strategic weapons today. The addition of new systems which will inevitably produce further Soviet systems is not the road to safety for anyone in this country.

WEAPONS SYSTEMS AS BARGAINING COUNTER AT SALT

6. We should be especially on guard, I think, against the notion that it is useful to press the development or deployment of any given weapons system because of its value as a bargaining counter for SALT. It is quite true that if we get nowhere in SALT and if Soviet strategic expansion continues, we shall have to take careful stock of our own needs. But there is no evidence at all that pressing the deployment of systems we do not yet need is likely to have a constructive effect on Soviet behavior in SALT. There are times and topics for toughness with Moscow, but SALT in April is not one of them, and many of those who urge this tactic are men who do not want SALT to succeed. It will be very hard to get a good agreement even if we do only what we have to do in our own weapons development. It will probably be impossible if we provide unnecessary ammunition to Soviet weapon lovers by pressing our own deployments relentlessly throughout the talks.

ARGUMENTS AGAINST DELAY IN WEAPONS SYSTEMS

7. In moving toward effective limitation of the arms race, we shall need to be alert and skeptical against distractions and diversions from those whose special interests may be threatened. The history of arms negotiation includes many examples of efforts by the partisans of particular weapons systems to prevent any agreement at all. During the negotiations before the Limited Test Ban Treaty, for example, it was suggested that the Soviets might obtain some decisive advantage by secret nuclear tests conducted behind the sun or by the construction of underground holes so big that the very existence of a test could not be detected. These arguments now rest properly

in the dustbin of dead fantasy. But now new dangers are depicted in the effort to justify a refusal to limit or delay our own new weapons system. Such arguments should be subjected to most meticulous and skeptical analysis, and in such study the role of the Congress is of high importance.

DOCTRINES OF STRATEGIC SUPERIORITY OR SUFFICIENCY

8. There is a particular danger in the uncritical acceptance of doctrines of strategic superiority—or even sufficiency—which may be used by zealous men in support of their own preferred weapons. This is as true of the Eisenhower administration's belief in "prevailing" in a general war as it is of later doctrines of "assured destruction" and "damage limitation." All of these forms of words can be used to justify excessive expenditure on unnecessary strategic systems. At present there are four new criteria of strategic sufficiency, but the Administration has not told us what they are. According to press reports, these criteria include "assured destruction," "hostage equality," "crisis stability" and "third country protection." If the Administration and the Congress are not alert and watchful, criteria like these can be protective umbrellas for unchecked strategic expansionism. They can also be roadblocks in the way of arms limitation. They deserve public discussion. My own conviction is that the realities of strategic nuclear weapons are not subject to control by such verbal formulae. In the language of Justice Holmes, I believe that criteria like these tend to be spiders' webs inadequate to control the dominant facts.

UNITED STATES SOVIET FUNDAMENTAL PARITY

9. The main proposition which we need to understand in order to limit the dangers of the nuclear age is that enough is enough. The Soviet Union and the United States have long since reached and passed that point. Each is now able to do totally unacceptable damage to the other, no matter how a nuclear catastrophe might begin. Sane political leaders on both sides know this reality for what it is. It is of course possible that some still unknown technological development might genuinely disrupt this fundamental parity, but there is no evidence whatever that any such development is likely in the present decade of the seventies. So we have enough, and more than enough, and we are on the edge of a most unstabilizing and dangerous escalation. Now is the time to stop.

PRESIDENTIAL DECISION ON ARMS CONTROL

10. And finally, your committee report recognizes what I would like to emphasize in closing: that while citizens can comment and the Senate can advise, only the President can decide. It will take negotiation to reach agreement, and the official position of the Government of the United States can be stated to the Soviet Union only by our President and his authorized agents. The President must choose the timing and the shape of any initiative he takes; in the end his leadership is what will decide. As he considers the possible choices and deliberates on decisions which have not yet been made, as far as we

know, the President is entitled to the thoughtful advice of the Senate, and in this field, where the weight of bureaucratic influence has historically been heavily on the side of arms as against arms control, such advice can be of particular value to him. The easy course is always to avoid decisions; politically the argument for weapons is easy, and the argument for acts of restraint is hard. A President who wants to take the lead needs all the help he can get. The Senate can give such help, and in this situation it is obviously the duty of citizens to respond to the Senate's request for their honest views. I have stated mine, and I will be glad to try to answer your questions.

COMMENDATION OF WITNESSES

Senator CASE. Thank you very much.
Before I ask Chairman Fulbright to proceed with questioning, I just want to remark that the value of this testimony is almost without measure. Two men with the experience and background that the two witnesses have brought to us this morning, can and do make contributions in this area that we need to have very much indeed.
To have a witness who is the former Assistant to the President of the United States for National Security Affairs, and a witness who was former Director of Defense Engineering and Research is not only a privilege but an opportunity for this committee, the Senate and the country to acquire knowledge of these matters that couldn't be gained in any other way.
Senator JAVITS. Mr. Chairman would the Chair allow me to associate myself with those views. I may not be able to stay for the questioning.
Senator CASE. Yes indeed. Thank you.
Mr. Chairman, would you like to ask questions?
Senator FULBRIGHT. Mr. Chairman, I would like to associate myself with the sentiments expressed by the Senator from New Jersey. Both of these gentlemen have a very fine reputation for their knowledge and sophistication in the field of government, and particularly in this field. I think they are doing a great service at great inconvenience to themselves. I know any time you express yourself publicly you are subject to criticism by someone, and this is a very controversial area.
I think the last part of your statement, Mr. Bundy, is especially appropriate because, as you have said, it is so true that it is much easier to avoid decisions. It is much easier just to go along as we have been going, and no one will notice it much until we reach a catastrophe. If you change the status quo in any respect, especially with regard to limitation of weapons you are bound to be criticized.

REQUEST FOR REFERRAL OF SENATE RESOLUTION 211 TO ARMED SERVICES COMMITTEE

I am glad you said what you did about the Senate. This committee, at least in having reported out resolution 211, has at least taken a first step.
I may say, and perhaps you would like to comment on it, that yesterday afternoon the Armed Services Committee chairman requested that this be referred to his committee for exercise of concurrent jurisdiction. He didn't question the jurisdiction of this committee. That

isn't the right way to put it. This committee clearly has jurisdiction, but the Armed Services Committee has an interest in it. We have recognized this before and my own position is that it would be a good thing to have it referred with the provision that it be reported back not later than the 14th, and under a unanimous consent agreement that it be voted on on the 18th. That is the only condition under which I would recommend that it be referred.

OPPOSITION TO ARMS LIMITATION AGREEMENTS WITH RUSSIANS

However, I think it is a good idea for that committee to express itself because I believe there is opposition to any kind of an agreement on limitation of arms with the Russians. There is a considerable body of opinion in this country that does not believe in any kind of agreement with any Communists.

I don't think I am overstating it. At least I see articles and statements such as this.

Do either of you disagree with that? You are aware of such sentiment; aren't you?

Mr. BUNDY. Mr. Chairman, everyone knows there is sentiment of that kind. The point that can be made the other way, and I think it is important to make, is that when there is leadership and energy in pursuing agreements and when they are prudently negotiated, there historically has been strong support in the Senate and in the country. This is true of the Limited Test Ban Treaty and, of course, in the Nonproliferation Treaty.

Senator FULBRIGHT. I think that is correct, and I think the majority of the country and the Senate wish to proceed in this direction. Both of you have given excellent reasons why it should.

I think your statements are very good indeed. I believe the Senate will pass that resolution, given an opportunity. I am quite sure they will pass it if it comes to a vote. And I think hopefully it will pass before the SALT talks begin.

FOUR NEW CRITERIA OF STRATEGIC SUFFICIENCY

Both of you have raised some very interesting questions. One matter that I particularly want to note is your reference that at present there are four new criteria of strategic sufficiency. The Administration has not told us what they are. I wonder if you can tell us why that has not been elaborated, and describe in more detail what these criteria are?

Mr. BUNDY. I really don't know myself, Mr. Chairman, why they have not been put out. The President's message to the Congress on the general condition of our foreign affairs says that there are four criteria, and says that they constitute a substantial intellectual improvement in our understanding of these matters. I believe that we would all gain from sharing in a discussion of what these criteria mean.

My best understanding of what they may be is stated just after my first reference to the criteria and is based on press reports.

My worry about this kind of criterion is that when you state it in a formal National Security Council (NSC) document or otherwise as a Presidential directive, the people down the line who are working on their particular concerns can take any one of the criteria, and argue that it constitutes a binding reason for doing whatever it is that they would like to do. If you read the testimony of the Secretary of Defense on the Chinese defense aspect of ABM, I think it is possible to guess that what has happened there is that a criterion like this one of third-country protection has been taken rather uncritically as a basic justification for a system whose limitations, even from this point of view, Dr. York has already described. The criteria, as I read them, do not include explicitly what, it seems to me, should always be in any criteria for strategic weapons systems; namely, what are their consequences on the planning and behavior of others, and the real danger of ABM, as Dr. York has said, is that it seems very hard to imagine any Soviet planner—Chinese planner, for that matter—who would not adjust and increase his own strategic planning in the light of a continuing deployment of ABM.

So that one way of putting my point is that when taken alone, criteria of this kind can reinforce bureaucratic inertia unless they are carefully managed and controlled by persons who do not have a specific bureaucratic interest.

CRITICISM OF POLICY IS NOT CRITICISM OF MILITARY

Let me emphasize, if I may, I am in no sense critical of military men for doing their job. It is their job to think about and to advance their case for a particular defense system. Of course the job of a government as a whole is to determine what a given weapons system will do to the overall national safety and that kind of thinking—Dr. York can say more about this than I because he has lived through it right in the engineroom—that kind of thinking is harder to get and has to be fought for.

Senator FULBRIGHT. You are quite right on this last. I know there is a tendency for military men to take personally criticism of a policy for which they are not responsible. For example, some have identified criticism of the policy in Southeast Asia as an attack upon the military. It is in no sense intended that way, and it is the same with these weapons systems. To want to restrain the proliferation of these strategic weapons is in no way a criticism of the military even though they have a different function. Yet they tend to take this as a criticism of them and of the military. As a consequence they react in a very serious way. The Naval Institute recently gave a quite substantial prize for an essay outlining this very problem, as to how they have to come to the defense of the Constitution against internal enemies.

DENIAL OF INFORMATION ON CRITERIA OF STRATEGIC SUFFICIENCY

I wrote a letter to the Director of the Arms Control and Disarmament Agency on March 26, asking about these criteria. I received no answer. We have orally been told that the letter will not be answered, that for some reason or other these criteria are considered to be classified and we are not to be told what they mean. I don't quite understand why. I think you have given very persuasive reasons as to why they should be explained.

POSSIBILITY OF RUSSIANS ATTACKING UNITED STATES AND VICE VERSA

Mr. Bundy, I like particularly your statement that we should take the initiative. I strongly agree with this because it is in our interest and not because we are interested in anyone else.

You made reference to Mr. Shulman. To me you are not a specialist in a particular field, but what I would call a generalist. With your background, could you say anything about the probabilities or the circumstances that would inspire an attack? What is it that is going on in the world that makes us so nervous about the Russians attacking us and vice versa? What is your feeling, in a general way, about the human relations aspect of the problem? It has often bothered me. Why are we so certain if given the slightest opportunity one or the other would immediately attack to destroy the other? There seems to be an assumption always present.

Mr. BUNDY. There are, I think, two elements of a possibly useful comment on that.

I think myself that since the autumn of 1962 we have had no international tension which makes the question of war of any sort, much less strategic war between us and the Soviet Union, either probable or inevitable. Indeed, I am inclined to the belief that the intense experience of real danger, which we did then go through in both Governments, had an inoculating effect that I hope will be lasting; and I believe that the overall posture of our relations with the Soviet Union now makes it reasonable to hope for the kind of progress that comes step by step and case by case, although there are obviously serious difficulties in our relations in many parts of the world.

CONSIDERATION OF STRATEGIC WEAPONS QUESTIONS IN TERMS OF CAPABILITY

On the other hand, it is right, I think, to consider these strategic weapons questions not only in terms of intention or likelihood, but also in terms of capability. I think if we were in a position in which it could be plausibly argued to Soviet political leaders that a single, bold strategic campaign would eliminate the United States at "acceptable" cost to the Soviet Union, this would be dangerous not because I think even then it would be likely but because it could encourage a kind of adventurism which we have seen in the past in some cases on the part of Soviet leaders.

Senator FULBRIGHT. Do you mean with nuclear weapons though?

Mr. BUNDY. I don't think that in the first instance, but I think the question of capability does have to be considered.

But my own view is that when you consider that question of capability, and the question of inescapable loss, and you put yourself in the position of the Soviet political leader who might be dreaming, Stalin at his worst, of some very dangerous act, and you think of the questions he would ask of the Soviet defense planner, and you look at the American forces that are in existence and the difficulties of putting them out of action by any kind of first strike or combination of first strikes, my belief is that as far as one can see for now and for the foreseeable future this is not an argument I would wish to have to make if I were a Soviet military planner. Nor would I find this argument persuasive if I were a Soviet military-political leader, because the actual costs of a nuclear holocaust or at least the danger of such cost would be so high that there is just nothing we know about the history of the Soviet view of building a civilization and starting a new socialist society and all which would lead us to believe that there is any chance at all that they would find it attractive.

It is a fact that we all have these enormous systems. We have three strategic systems in the United States, each of which, in the eyes of defense planners themselves, is sufficient to deter, and no one of which in the present time range is vulnerable to preemptive attack.

Now, you can get a good argument and I think it is a tough question, as to why we should have three independent strategic systems and whether this isn't in itself a kind of overkill. The bureaucratic reasons why we like to have strategic bombers and still another Air Force system and a system for the Navy and now a defense system for the Army, these are fairly clear and one doesn't need to spell them out.

But the balance of power arguments are not that persuasive. Therefore, while I think there is a need to measure capabilities as well as intentions, I believe the capabilities on both sides are now overwhelming.

Senator FULBRIGHT. Overwhelming.

CONCEPT OF U.S. STRATEGIC FIRST STRIKE

You made reference to your article in the October issue of Foreign Affairs. You wrote in that article and I quote, "Conversely, even the most cold-blooded of American planners has always understood, at least since 1954, that the concept of a strategic first strike by the United States is wholly unacceptable because of the prospect of Soviet retaliation."

Do you recall that?

Mr. BUNDY. Yes, sir.

Senator FULBRIGHT. In light of that comment, how do you explain the fact that our Air Force Manual, 101, entitled "United States Air Force Basic Doctrine," and dated August 14, 1964, contains a section 3-11 entitled "First Strike Considerations," which states among other things and I quote:

Since we cannot preclude contingencies in which the United States may be the first to initiate the limited use of strategic force, our force posture and general war plans must consider the requirement for both first and second strike operations.

Mr. BUNDY. Well, perhaps my statement was excessive, Senator Fulbright. My own experience in my years in Washington was that when you came right down to the hard-boiled business of whether people really thought that making a first strike made sense, whether they were in or out of uniform, they did not find that an attractive choice.

Senator FULBRIGHT. I agree with you, but I think this kind of statement is a great obstacle to successful SALT talks. It would strike me that it would be. How can anyone take us very seriously when we have this as basic doctrine for our Air Force or for our Government? This troubles me.

PROSPECTS FOR SUCCESS AT SALT

Once or twice in your statement you said, "And many of those who urge this tactic are men who do not want SALT to succeed." That being so how do you feel about it? I believe Dr. York also suggested this. Do you think there is a good prospect of SALT succeeding? Do you think so, Dr. York?

Dr. YORK. I don't really know. I hope so. As to what the prospects are, the probabilities of success, I must say, I simply don't know. I would, however, strongly emphasize, as has Dr. Bundy, that they are much higher now than they will shortly be. Whatever the prospects now are, they are going down.

Senator FULBRIGHT. They are getting worse?

Dr. YORK. The introduction of ABM and MIRV and other technological improvements in things like accuracy and reliability that we don't talk about so much because they are not quite so easy to get a hold of, and because they are not quite so glamorous, progress in those areas is greatly reducing the prospect for successful SALT talks, whatever they may now be.

Senator FULBRIGHT. Would you agree that Resolution 211 is not irrelevant to the SALT talks?

Dr. YORK. It is very much relevant; I think that the time is so late that firm measures, strong measures, to come to grips with the problem as quickly as possible are essential.

Senator FULBRIGHT. I want to congratulate both of you on excellent statements. There are many other things to develop, but the chairman and others have come in and I will have to desist for the moment. I yield the floor.

Senator CASE. I yield the chairmanship to our chairman and we are very glad indeed he was able to get here as early and he was.

Senator FULBRIGHT. It is a great mystery to me that we can contemplate an ABM or going to the moon and we can't have an efficient transport service to get the chairman here or make an elevator work. You are a great physicist, Dr. York. I never have understood the mystery of why we can't do that.

Senator GORE. It was not the fault of the airline. I walked out on the ramp and there were two planes, both marked Washington, waiting for me. I was diverting some of my attention to some constituents. It was after I discovered that I was on a plane headed for Washington, but with three stops, that I looked out and the other plane was taking off. I took the wrong plane. [Laughter.]

Senator CASE. There is not much you can do about a man who will do that. [Laughter.]

EFFECT OF COMPUTER AGE ON SALT

Senator GORE. This does raise an interesting question in this computer age of the possibility of the wrong button.

Dr. YORK. Computers make far fewer mistakes than human beings do, but they make much larger ones when they do.

Senator GORE. How does that apply to the SALT talks?

Dr. YORK. Well——

Mr. BUNDY. Let me try that. I think it applies very pertinently and very importantly, Senator Gore, because one of the things that is going to make it hard for us to make the decision to take a lead in these talks is a kind of process of calculation, in which it is assumed that computers can whir and decisions can be made and that one can walk around these terrifying weapons in a mechanical way, in ways that Dr. York spells out in his testimony.

Now, political leaders don't approach these weapons that way. At least in my experience.

When you seriously think about whether you want to use these weapons, what you conclude is that you don't, and you really do not make a habit in your own mind of thinking that your strategic power is much of a bargaining counter in the real business of international affairs. The margin of safety, in fact, is much larger than mechanical or computation-minded considerations would lead you to think on both sides and, therefore, the arguments against limitation are much weaker than they sometimes appear in technological discussions.

Beyond that is Dr. York's concern, stated so clearly in his testimony, that certain kinds of systems produce uncertainty, and I fear that both ABM and MIRV have this characteristic, which could lead people to conclude that they cannot trust the judgment of statesmen, and must move to the judgment of machines and with him, I think that would be most dangerous.

U.S. EXECUTIVE DECISIONMAKING PROCESS

Senator GORE. You referred to the view of political leaders with respect to nuclear weaponry, and I notice in your statement that you say, "There is no real or present danger in such a limited suspension."

According to published reports the Advisory Committee to the President, which is composed of eminent civilians, it has unanimously recommended a vigorous approach toward the SALT talks. The rumors about Washington are that the military has unanimously made a contrary recommendation.

Since you have been intimate in the decisionmaking processes, how does our decisionmaking process really operate? I am not asking you to forecast what the President of the United States may decide in this case, but to explain to us just how it works when we have such a conflicting recommendation to the President.

Mr. BUNDY. There are, of course, different ways of arranging the internal management of the decisionmaking process, and there has been extensive revision of that process in the last year, and I think I should leave it to the Administration, which has made statements on it, to describe how it now goes about this process.

But when all is said and done, and this is, I think, the point that I would emphasize, when you get presentations couched in their own terms from advisers with strongly held specific points of view, there is no substitute for the President standing back and deciding this matter, and this kind of matter is preeminently of this sort in terms of the overall national interest and the responsibility of the President for all aspects of the problem. The risk and the hazard is that because of the weight, the simple weight, of the numbers of men and dollars engaged in advancing the case for a particular military system, there will be inadequate analysis of the limitations that may exist in those arguments for a military action, and I do not know exactly how these matters are considered in the current Administration.

I do know that in any administration the final responsibility for making a judgment, which requires a wider spectrum of considerations, rests with the President, and that, I suppose, is why the Constitution has given to the senior political officer the clear-cut authority also of Commander in Chief.

I would like to emphasize, Mr. Chairman, a point that came home to me many times when I was in Washington, that when a President makes his decision there is, I think, no part of the Government, certainly at its top echelons, which will give him a more disciplined response than the military services. This is not a matter in which, if the President decides to take the lead, he will have, in my judgment, any fundamental difficulty with his military commanders.

I remember very well, for example, what seems to me to have been the critical Presidential decision with respect to the limited test ban treaty, a decision taken by President Kennedy alone in the spring of 1963, the decision not to have another series of atmospheric tests merely because Khrushchev had had two and we had only had one after the moratorium ended. That decision was taken by the President quite alone, announced by him as a Presidential decision in the famous speech at American University, and never questioned within the executive branch because it was his right, indeed his duty, to make that kind of decision.

Senator CASE. Would the Senator yield for an intervention here?
Senator GORE. Yes.

TIMING OF SENATE PARTICIPATION IN DECISIONMAKING PROCESS

Senator CASE. Doesn't this mean that if the Senate and the country are to have any kind of voice in any decision based upon adequate information, when the matter is a military one or has high military content, that they have to be asked to consider the matter and given a chance to before the President makes up his mind, for if we wait until afterward then we are not going to get from the military a completely objective and comprehensive judgment on their part? Do you understand what I am getting at, sir?

Mr. BUNDY. I think I do but I am not sure that what I have to say meets your point head on.

My own view is, I guess, that the right and obligation of the Senate to express its views, to inform itself and to register its advice on matters of this importance, is so deeply imbedded in the Constitution, indeed in the very nature of democratic process, that I don't see how there can be argument about it.

It is equally clear that a decision on a negotiating posture belongs to the President under the Constitution. But the need for consultation and communication in a case in which any serious agreement would require the consent of the Senate, seems to me just self-evident.

Senator CASE. Yes. But on this question of timing, your point just made was that after the President made up his mind and told the military what it was, they went along. Now this, it seems to me, inevitably means that after that point is reached we are not going to get, nor is the country going to get, any independent view from the military as to the wisdom from the military standpoint of that decision. So hadn't we better be consulted before the President makes up his mind and tells the military what his decision is? What should we do if we are going to get competent comprehensive military advice?

Mr. BUNDY. I think that it is true that the discipline of the executive branch is such, that once the President has made a decision, what the Senate is likely to hear, at least from most members of the executive branch, is defense of the President's decision. It is in the nature of things.

Senator CASE. And you made that rather clear before in respect of the military.

Mr. BUNDY. I don't criticize that. I think it has to be that way.

Senator CASE. No, I am not criticizing it either, but in our problem of relationship with the executive and fulfillment of our role without trying to overstep——

Mr. BUNDY. The time to influence those fellows is before they have made up their minds; that is right.

Senator CASE. That is to say when you say those fellows——

Mr. BUNDY. All of them.

Senator CASE. Including the President of the United States. Thank you very much, Mr. Chairman.

EXECUTIVE AND LEGISLATIVE RESPONSIBILITY IN DECISIONMAKING PROCESS

Senator GORE. This, it seems, brings us to the role of public opinion and the role of the elected representatives of the people in this particular situation.

If appropriations are required, as in the case of ABM deployment, then the legislative branch certainly has a decisionmaking power that is effective, the power of the purse being peculiarly that of the legislative branch.

Whether or not to take the initiative, as you referred to it, with respect to policy in an international conference is a decision peculiarly belonging to the President.

As you have said, ultimately the activation of a decision that may lead to an agreement involves the Senate, but the important decision now is peculiarly one of the President. All of us are sympathetic with the very enormous burdens of the Presidency. One of the purposes of this hearing is to build a body of public information so that the Senate and the American people will be able to reach reasoned judgment. As Senator Case has pointed out, the sooner both the Senate and the American people are able to reach such a judgment, based upon a body of responsible information, the better the chances are that the process of public opinion in our democracy may have a way of reaching the White House itself. This is, as I say, the purpose of this hearing, so far as the SALT talks are concerned.

ABM is in a different category.

Would you comment on that?

Mr. BUNDY. Well, perhaps I can comment this way. Starting from the premise we share that the responsibility for actually making a choice of negotiating position and a negotiating proposal is and must be Presidential by nature—I believe it is strongly to the advantage of the President and of those working with him not only to have the benefit of advice and of public discussion but to reach out for it.

It is the very loneliness and heaviness of the responsibilities which bear on the President that accentuate the importance, it seems to me, of his having access to and curiosity about the currents of opinion and of analysis and thought and of concern in the country as a whole, and not just what comes through the official channels of the executive branch.

There is a danger of a kind of windowless internal communication in the way in which the executive branch thinks about its own problems, and airing questions and being eager to participate in or at least to listen to that kind of discussion is, I believe, a great advantage to any administration.

Senator GORE. Might he in some way, perhaps, minimize or mitigate the danger that all Presidents face of becoming isolated and the victim of his immediate advisers?

Mr. BUNDY. Well, I am not going to go into the business of suggesting that the immediate advisers of Presidents are unsatisfactory people, Senator Gore.

(Laughter.)

Senator GORE. I did not mean to imply that either in the past or present.

Mr. BUNDY. I hope that hasn't always been so.

(Laughter.)

Senator GORE. I didn't mean to imply that at all.

Senator CASE. They are hard as nails and they are sharp as this and that. You know the characterization of them.

POSSIBILITY OF VERIFYING A MORATORIUM

Senator GORE. Dr. York, I would like to solicit from you an observation on the possibility of verifying a moratorium.

Dr. YORK. Well, there are many elements of a moratorium, and there are various degrees of possibility involved in verifying those elements, and there is also the length of the moratorium, so there is no simple answer. But we have seen in these discussions last year, and I am sure you will see it again this year, that there are statements made as statements of fact about what the current Russian deployment is, what the rate of new deployment is, what they are doing in the way of developing MIRV's or MRV's (multiple reentry vehicle), what they are doing in the way of building submarines and deploying them, and you will also see that those who oppose some of our Government's plans and policies don't disagree with those facts. And many of the persons who opposed the Administration's actions in the ABM matter are persons who are also privy to the information.

I offer this only as evidence that there is a great deal of confidence now about what they are doing in terms of numbers, in terms of rates of change of those numbers, and in terms even of qualitative factors like where do they stand in accuracy, where do they stand in the development of a MRV, and so forth.

Of course, some uncertainties have also been expressed but I think the most striking thing of all of this is how sure everyone is of just what these facts are.

In other words, we have a pretty good verification system going right now with regard to what they are doing and what they have done, and we can expect that to continue.

The details of the verification system, as we all know, are of course, a very highly classified matter but the results have been brought before this committee, and it is clear that we know a great deal already, and that it ought to be possible to continue to keep track of what is going on, at least for a fixed moratorium period. I don't know whether it is a satisfactory answer or not.

VERIFICATION OF MORATORIUM ON TESTING

Senator GORE. Let me put it a little differently from a layman's standpoint.

If we have the sophisticated detection and evaluation apparatus to which you have referred to estimate accuracy and performance, the volume, the speed, and the range of tests, would it not be easier for that apparatus to determine the absence of such tests than to determine the measurements of such tests?

Dr. YORK. Yes. Generally speaking, there are things which are easier and there are things which are harder to monitor. In particular, tests are relatively easy, production is difficult, deployment is again relatively easy, but the original research may be difficult.

A moratorium on tests would be much easier to monitor than a prohibition on let us say, improvements of accuracy beyond such and such a point. I think that is inherent in what you are saying, and I believe that is right. So elimination of tests would be much easier to monitor than to get right into those tests and monitor the prohibition of certain specific kinds of improvements.

Senator CASE. You are talking about, among other things, at least certainly MIRV testing?

Dr. YORK. Yes, MIRV testing would be included under that. One might even put in a proviso on a temporary basis that if any testing which was needed for reliance purposes or for allowing the troops to have some kind of practice firings, then such tests might be limited to the Pacific area, rather than being conducted in areas where it was harder to keep track of them.

VERIFICATION OF DEPLOYMENT

Senator GORE. Would you comment upon the problems of verification with respect to actual deployment?

Dr. YORK. The deployment of a large missile requires a fairly extensive operation, the building of the silo and so forth, and it is just during that phase that it is most easy to keep track of what is going on.

Once missiles are deployed, then it becomes difficult to tell just what kind of payload they carry, and it becomes difficult to determine whether changes in the payload are being made. In other words, it is easy to know that they have deployed SS-9's; it is even easy to know that they are getting ready to deploy some more. It is hard to know whether those have single warheads or multiple warheads.

Senator GORE. Then, as I understand your statement, verification of actual deployment is considerably less difficult than several other aspects.

Dr. YORK. Yes. The difficult things to keep track of are at the laboratory research phase. It is relatively easy to keep track of what is going on during the test phase; it is again difficult to keep track of it during the production phase, and then it is easier again during the development phase.

Senator CASE. Thank you very much.

First, may I ask two questions Senator Javits asked that I ask on his behalf.

He had to leave for another obligation which he could not avoid. First to Mr. Bundy:

ADMINISTRATION'S APPARENT RELUCTANCE TO PUT FORWARD MUTUAL MORATORIUM

There seems to be a preponderance of opinion among those outside the executive branch that a mutual moratorium is both desirable and feasible. This morning, it is reported that a Presidential Advisory Commission has so recommended. I think reference was made already to that.

Having been both an insider and now an outsider, although I may say personally that someone like you is never an outsider concerned with this question, do you believe that the apparent reluctance of the Administration to put forward a mutual moratorium can be explained by their possession of information not available to those outside the inner circles of government or does this reluctance simply reflect a congenital cautious bias on the part of officials formally charged with national security responsibility?

Mr. BUNDY. I don't think that I ought to speculate—I don't have the evidence on which to speculate about the current thinking of the executive branch, whether indeed it is reluctant. There are press reports which suggest that the matter is now being reviewed again, and that these questions are being discussed right now in the National Security Council.

Senator CASE. In the Security Council?

Mr. BUNDY. Or elsewhere in the government.

I think it is unlikely that there is evidence different from the basic evidence presented to the Congress in different ways by the President in his own report, the Secretary of State, the Secretary of Defense in their various reports.

It is certainly true that Soviet development and deployment has continued, and it is quite true that if no agreement is possible in the next months and years, these deployments would have consequences even within the very broad sense of sufficiency and enoughness that I have tried to describe earlier.

AVAILABILITY OF EVIDENCE FOR JUDGMENT ON MORATORIUM

I have much doubt, however, that there is any persuasive evidence that is not, in essence, available to the Members of Congress as they make their own judgment, and I would be very puzzled to know what kind of evidence that could be, because in its nature it could only be something that the Soviet Union or the Chinese are doing, and the fact that we know it, and that we have ways of trying to find out about it except in some extraordinary case of an espionage penetration by an individual, would not create a reason for us to hold back on a description of what they are doing.

We have spent years trying to describe, on the basis of the kinds of intelligence effort which Dr. York was discussing, the state of the strategic arms race and I think it is a quite proper conclusion that it is to everyone's interest that this matter should be opened, so much so that much of the best Soviet thinking on this subject, even about Soviet weapons systems, by nonmilitary Soviet people, is based on American sources. This is a real service which we provide to people who are not Soviet weaponeers.

Moreover, the considerations with which we are now working as we think about the strategic arms balance have to do with things that may or may not happen several years from now. So it is very unlikely that they would relate to some particular piece of intelligence information about some particular hazard or attitude or personal position or something else of that sort which it might be necessary to keep secret.

My own feeling, derived from the years when I was a consumer of the work of the intelligence community, is that Dr. York has, if anything, underestimated the capacity of our intelligence community to put together a very wide range of the kinds of information, some technological, some economic, some relating to systems, some relating to specific bits of evidence, and to frame a responsible and broadly accurate account of the real situation in the strategic arms posture of the Soviet Union and indeed of the Chinese. So I rather doubt there is inside information of a decisive sort.

Senator CASE. I am very glad to have that, and I know that the subcommittee and the full committee will be glad to have that testimony, too. It is in accord, I think, with my own judgment and my own observation as a member of the committee.

For example, we received a highly sensitive top secret briefing by CIA Director Helms on March 2 about the strategic threat, and I am convinced that, broadly speaking, there is no real secret information that warrants any blind acceptance by the Senate, by the public, of doctrine from on high—if we concede that there is any on high in respect of the public or of the Senate. My own experience, too, has led me to think that any claim that we must go along because of secret information which can't be made public should be viewed with great skepticism, and I take it—

Mr. BUNDY. I share that view.

Senator CASE. It is just another way of saying what you already have said so well.

Is this your judgment, too, Dr. York?

Dr. YORK. Oh, yes.

Senator CASE. Dr. York, the second question Senator Javits asked me to ask for him is directed to you:

ARGUMENT FOR DAMAGE LIMITATION CAPABILITY AGAINST SOVIET ATTACK

Would you give your view of the chief argument used in favor of ABM by the Joint Chiefs of Staff; namely, that we need a damage limitation capability against a hypothetical Soviet attack. The Joint

Chiefs say this is the best way to preserve the post-Cuba power environment, that is our nuclear superiority and that it is necessary as a deterrent. Would you have any comment on that?

Dr. YORK. Well, the best comment would be, I suppose, a few-sentence summary of what has been said by a great many people over this period of time. In the first place, the deterrent consists of three components. The SS-9 and its MIRV really threatens immediately only one of those. Second, there was the view, which I share, that the time scale that was suggested for this threat, namely, that it would become real in 1975, is probably exaggerated. But third and most important if there really is a danger to that particular element of the deterrent (to the Minuteman) then the ABM approach, and specifically the Safeguard ABM, is a low confidence way of reinstating the credibility of the deterrent.

Senator CASE. May I just pursue that directly with you now because it was one of the broad questions, of course, that we want to get as complete information on as we can from experts.

CAPABILITY OF ABM TO DEFEND MINUTEMAN

Put in layman's language this isn't going to work very well, this precise system, as a defense of our Minuteman.

Dr. YORK. It is a low confidence way of trying to defend the Minuteman. ABM in general is a low confidence way. The Safeguard ABM, within the general class of ABM, is a still lower confidence way of doing it.

Senator CASE. And there are better ways, of course?

Dr. YORK. There are surer ways, ways that one would have more confidence in.

Senator CASE. So this, in your judgment, this is at least a waste of money?

Dr. YORK. Yes, sir.

Senator CASE. Beyond that is it a deterrent, if I may use that word in this context, to our finding a better way?

Dr. YORK. Yes, it is. But worse than that, it is a stimulant to the arms race, and——

Senator CASE. That is another point.

Dr. YORK. Yes.

Senator CASE. But this will affirmatively deter us, in your judgment, from seeking a better way to defend our Minuteman?

Dr. YORK. It does, although one sees in this year's statements by Defense authorities that their confidence is also shaken in Safeguard as a way of preserving the deterrent. We find the statement that it may be necessary to find other ways. We also find hints of a recognition of the fact that silo-based missiles may be obsolescent.

Senator GORE. One almost reaches a conclusion if they weren't stuck with it they would think of something else.

Dr. YORK. If we were starting over, I think that would be true.

Mr. BUNDY. But let it be said, Mr. Chairman, if I may, that Dr. York had his share of responsibility. The administration that came in in 1961 had its share of responsibility for Minuteman deployment. The fact that it may be obsolescent now is not a reason for not having done it then, and it is just that kind of danger that once we have done something we will think up reasons for continuing to do it, that, it seems to me, we need to be alert to.

One of the principal justifications of many of our weapon systems is that they exist.

FULL DEPLOYMENT OF SAFEGUARD DOUBTED

Senator CASE. Would either of you comment on the suggestion that this system is never going to be built in fact and fully deployed?

Dr. YORK. That the Safeguard is never going to be built?

Senator CASE. Yes.

Dr. YORK. I do doubt that the system which we now describe as Safeguard——

Senator CASE. That is what we are talking about.

Dr. YORK (continuing). Will ever be fully built. The reason I doubt it is that the weaknesses that have been brought out about it will be widely recognized and that, in fact, the system, will not be built.

WHAT IS THE COMMUNIST CHINESE THREAT?

Senator CASE. Mr. Bundy, would you tell us, and I will ask you this, too, if you will, Dr. York, what is the Chinese threat?

May I just lead up to this thing: Please tell me why wasn't the Chinese threat perceived until Secretary McNamara perceived it and then why did he perceive it and what is it?

Senator GORE. Then he disperceived it.

Senator CASE. That we will ask him.

Mr. BUNDY. Yes, I think that would be better.

Senator GORE. He did say in a public speech that he perceived it. What is it?

Mr. BUNDY. Well, the Chinese threat is a phenomenon with which I don't have any direct familiarity from my time inside the Government. The first Chinese nuclear explosion occurred just at the end of 1964, and the question of weapons changes in the United States against an anticipated Chinese nuclear threat was not urgent when I left the Government in early 1966. So what I can give you are only my own personal thoughts about it from reading about it, testimony about it and comments about it.

I believe that there is certainly a fractional importance to the notion that the Chinese will have some intercontinental missiles. The date for that, incidentally, seems to have slipped, by the testimony from the Department of Defense at least a year, so that the urgency of this can hardly be greater than it was a year ago, since we have done more and our intelligence estimate of what they can do has gone back a year.

Senator CASE. That they would have these missiles has been obvious to all of us for many years.

Mr. BUNDY. Exactly so.

Now, the difficulty with it is, first, that it seems to me essentially a marginal matter compared to the impact of things we do under the rubric of the arms race with the Soviet Union, so I think it is a lesser problem.

I also think it very dangerous to assume that what the designers of a system urge upon you as its capability is something that you would in fact rely on 5 or 10 years from now in actual crisis. It seems to me extremely unlikely that in a crisis which engaged the United States and China any American Government 10 years from now would say, "ABM means they can't hit us," because systems don't work that way. They don't have this kind of foolproof errorlessness. We constantly read of small sporting aircraft coming in under the air defense system of the United States, and the notion that military men would be able to say to a President in the late 1970's. "There will be no Chinese missile detonated on American territory," and that a President would believe it seems to me fanciful.

It is quite understandable that in looking at a proposal and hearing a briefing one would say, "This is going to be a marvelous defense," but it is a different thing to believe it in a moment of crisis.

Beyond that I very much doubt that it will be practicable to have the kind of total nuclear guarantee to Asian nations vis-a-vis the Chinese that is sometimes suggested by some advocates of the Chinese defense position. It seems to me that the relationship between our nuclear power and the development of events in Asia is a much subtler affair than that. That has been plain in differing ways in the moments of crisis that we have had in the years since the Korean war in Asia, and so I have grave doubt on political grounds that the Chinese defense theory is in fact an important justification for an ABM deployment.

Senator CASE. Either from the standpoint of their own aggression against the United States or the subtle and involved problems in regard to our providing a nuclear shield or what not for nations of Asia?

Mr. BUNDY. I think, in addition, you will have witnesses better able to talk to this point than I.

COMMUNIST CHINESE USE OF MISSILE CAPABILITY

In addition I think the kind of picture of the Chinese ways of using a missile capability for political advantage or a threat to the United States, that that kind of picture which appears in Pentagon testimony primarily does not, in fact, correspond to what we know about Chinese behavior in international military and political matters, but that is a separate subject relating to intentions rather than capabilities.

Senator CASE. Our own judgment is that there is not all that difference between the Russians and the Chinese.

Mr. BUNDY. Well, there are many differences between the Russians and the Chinese.

Senator CASE. Many indeed, but I mean in regard to a threat.

Mr. BUNDY. But I don't believe that it is a good justification—I have never thought it was, and I have heard no argument that makes it a better justification now than it was a year ago. In fact, I think the reverse is the case.

Senator CASE. You mentioned the Pentagon. It has made a point that the Chinese are inherently better able to use this as a threat than we because our concentrations of population are so great that we are highly vulnerable to a few weapons as opposed to the dispersal of populations in China.

Mr. BUNDY. There is that kind of difference but the difference between stockpile sizes is so overwhelming the other way that it seems to me not a very important or impressive argument.

Senator CASE. Is it not also true that while the populations in China are dispersed there is a great concentration of military and and manufacturing and industrial capacity so that with a relatively small number of weapons this might be eliminated and China, in effect, brought back to a very primitive society?

Mr. BUNDY. I am not an expert on the question of hypothetical targetry of mainland China, Senator Case, but I do believe it extremely unlikely that the Chinese, either for political or strategic reasons, whether in terms of intention or capability, whether in terms of behavior or of expected result, would behave in the way in which some Pentagon planners choose to believe that they would behave in order to justify the ABM.

Senator CASE. Thank you, sir.

Dr. York, would you have any comment on this whole situation?

CREDIBILITY OF COMMUNIST CHINESE THREAT

Dr. YORK. I agree with everything that Dr. Bundy has said. I don't regard the Chinese threat as credible. Those who have talked about it put it in terms of blackmail, where they threaten to hold some important part of the United States as hostage for some kind of an act, threatened or otherwise. Since that can be any part of the United States, as I remarked in my prepared testimony, if we take that seriously, we have to be ready to protect the entire United States against it. And that means we have to have a great many more interceptors than they have offensive missiles even if they have no decoys, no multiple warheads or, anything else. If they do have even a few of those then the whole thing escalates greatly again.

Senator CASE. And it is true, isn't it, that the timetable that has been proposed so far for completion of the whole system of ABM defense would put it in place over the country as a whole not until several years after the Chinese are expected to have the capacity?

Dr. YORK. Oh, yes. The Safeguard deployments we were talking about last year and appear to be talking about this year are virtually irrelevant as far as the so-called Chinese threat is concerned.

Senator CASE. In other words, there would be a long period of several years in which this system would not protect against any threat from China?

Dr. YORK. Yes, several is probably an understatement. I think it is 5 years or more.

Senator GORE. Mr. Chairman, could I ask one question?

Senator CASE. Please.

INFLUENCE OF TECHNOLOGICAL SIDE OF THE ARMS RACE

Senator GORE. Dr. York, I have now had a chance to look over your statement and in two places I find intriguing language. You say that such weapons were "more complicated and expensive and thus provided the weapons engineers and scientists with a still better means of displaying their technological virtuosity."

Then you also say that MIRV and ABM "were not primarily the result of any careful operations analysis of the problem or anything which might be described as 'provocation' by the other side, but, as I understand it, you say they were rather the result of responding to technological challenge.

Does this mean we are just trying to find out what we can do?

Dr. York. It is a way of saying that to a very high degree the technological side of the arms race does have a life of its own. In that same speech by Robert McNamara that was alluded to a moment ago in which he talked about the Chinese threat, he also used that phrase that the arms race seems to have a mad momentum of its own.

That is not to say that is the whole picture, but to a large degree the technological side of the arms race does proceed from internal stimuli. New ideas are taken up, regarded as a challenge, developed, and sold to the weapons buyers.

Ultimately the deployment of these things does, of course, depend on decisions made in the executive branch and legislative branch, but even then often the developments in the technological world reach a point where the decisions that can feasibly be made really are relatively narrow compared to the totality of all possible decisions.

Senator Gore. The scientific community is not the only place where precedent and commitment play a part. In political life we find there is a great value placed upon consistency of position. One Senator finally broke out and said to the world that consistency was the hobgoblin of small minds. A lot of us cheered, but we didn't follow the example. Consistency is considered to be a political virtue and, I suppose it is considered a virtue in the scientific community. Once we go to the moon, we must keep going to the moon to show that we could. Now we don't know how to quit.

Senator Case. Everything in moderation is the rule.

Senator Gore. I am not sure.

[Laughter.]

Senator Gore. Surely though in so deadly and dangerous a field as the nuclear armaments race we don't have to continue the race just to prove that we can. It seems to me that is about what you are saying.

Dr. York. Well I think, it is a fact that it does have a life of its own to a very high degree. We should bear that in mind in considering what to do both with respect to what weapons to buy and what steps to take in arms control and otherwise.

Senator Gore. Thank you, Mr. Chairman.

JUSTIFICATION OF DEFENSE AGAINST STRAY WEAPONS

Senator Case. Dr. York, I did want to ask you for your comment upon the third justification that we have commonly been given, that is to say, defense against a stray weapon. I wonder if you would mind making that comment in a short statement for the record at this point, because I do want to give Senator Cooper a chance to ask questions. We may come back to it before we have to leave for the Carswell vote, but Senator Cooper has been most patient, and I wish that you would go ahead.

(The information referred to follows.)

Safeguard and the "Accidental" Attack

One of the justifications given for the Safeguard System is that it would be able to cope with an "accidental" attack by a single missile. It has never been made clear just what Safeguard proponents have in mind in the way of such an accident, and so it is in truth almost impossible to assess the usefulness of Safeguard in this case, but even so, some comments may be worthwhile.

In many cases, and from the narrowest technical point of view, such an "accidental" single missile attack is easier to deal with than the purposeful multi-missile attack usually considered. Many of the penetration aids and techniques that are most effective in a purposeful attack would not be involved. For example, the attack would presumably not be massive enough after atmospheric sorting to saturate the radars, the computer, or the available supply of ready missiles. Similarly, the problem of the defense radar not being able to see through the blackout produced by an earlier precursor attack would be absent.

This means that, in principle, an accidental attack by a single "Chinese" or other unsophisticated missile against any part of the country defended by Spartans could be readily contained, and an accidental attack by a single Soviet or other sophisticated missile against those parts of the country defended by Sprints could probably be contained. On the other hand, it should be emphasized that according to current plans, no major cities (except Washington) are to be defended by Sprints, and therefore a single Soviet missile, accompanied by the kind of penetration aids that are effective against Spartans, would, if "accidentally" launched at an American city, succeed in destroying it.

But even the favorable cases above depend on the interceptors actually rereiving a "launch" order. And this in turn depends not only on successful detection of the "accidental" missile, but also on the correct functioning of the command and control system. If it is true, as we have been repeatedly assured, that an ABM can be launched only by order of the "highest authority," then the accidental case is precisely the one where the command and control system is most likely to fail. An accident, by definition, is a "bolt from the blue," and would not normally be preceded by a threat or an escalation in tension which would probably precede a deliberate attack and which would serve to alert the system. The "accidental launch" case is precisely the one wherein the problem posed by the inherent "hair trigger/stiff trigger" contradiction is most difficult.

Senator COOPER. I haven't been able to be here all the time.

Senator CASE. But you have been most patient while you were away, too, because you are a patient man. [Laughter.]

PENTAGON 10-YEAR SYSTEMS COST

Senator COOPER. I would like to ask Dr. York a question. Here in the Senate we have had great difficulty in getting an estimate of the costs of the ABM system. From your experience in the Pentagon, and your knowledge, could you describe for the committee how the Pentagon makes its so-called 10-year systems cost?

Dr. YORK. Well——

COST OF FULLY DEVELOPED SAFEGUARD SYSTEM

Senator COOPER. Also could you make an estimate of what we now know as the total Safeguard system fully deployed would cost?

Dr. YORK. I am not sure that I can do a good job on either of those questions, Senator Cooper. But as to the one about what the full Safeguard would cost, the answer to that has to depend on what people really mean for Safeguard to do. Do they mean that it should protect the entire country against blackmail by a small Chinese threat? That would require something very much bigger than what has been discussed so far. Do they mean to protect the entire Minuteman force against a Russian threat and do they mean to keep upgrading the Safeguard as the Russians, in turn, change their—react to the ABM itself?

I think estimates of $50 billion are entirely reasonable for the cost of a system which would accomplish those two objectives, that is, for a system that looks like it would defend the Minuteman against a preemptive Soviet attack and, at the same time, defend the entire United States against blackmail or, for that matter, against the accidental launch which could go anywhere.

If half the United States is defended, this accidental launch that Senator Case refers to has a 50–50 chance of ending up in the part that is not defended. So the extensive system that will accomplish these three objectives will probably cost a minimum of $50 billion. Those are estimates which have been made before, and which I think are reasonable.

SUGGESTED PROCEDURE FOR DEVELOPING BEST ABM SYSTEM

Senator COOPER. You know, because you yourself have participated in these hearings and studies, but there has been much doubt cast upon the capability of the Safeguard ABM and other proposals for a more effective ABM system and other systems have been made. On the basis of your experience of directing large-scale research projects at the Lawrence Radiation Laboratory and as a key administrator in the Pentagon, if you were given the task of developing the best ABM this country could produce, how would you proceed?

Dr. YORK. I am not sure how to answer that. My first answer is seek out the best advice one can get. But you may mean perhaps how would I design the system. I don't think that the present Safeguard system, which really is the Sentinel system, very little changed so far as engineering is concerned but considerably changed as far as goals are concerned, is the right way to do it. If one wants to defend against the Chinese blackmail, then some components of the Safeguard system might be a reasonable way to do it.

The Spartan missile and Perimeter Acquisition Radars (PAR) may be the way to handle a Chinese blackmail threat but there has been expressed considerable opinion that the other part of the system, the Multiple Site Radars (MSR's) and the Sprints (the MSR's in particular) are not the correct way to build a so-called dedicated hard point defense system. If that is what you really want to do and that is all you want to do, then many persons whose judgment I take very seriously have said that that is not the right way to do it. What we are doing now is not the right way to do it.

Senator COOPER. I believe you have testified in the past that the intercontinental ballistic missile systems will become obsolete in a few years.

Dr. YORK. The silo-based version will.

MISSILE SYSTEMS WHICH WOULD BEST PROTECT UNITED STATES

Senator COOPER. We hope the SALT talks will not fail, but if they should fail, what would you recommend as a system or systems which would best protect the security of this country?

Dr. YORK. Well, there are a number of possibilities and the Defense Department is seriously considering that very problem. That is essentially what they refer to when they talk about rebasing studies. The emphasis on rebasing arises from their own doubts about the long-range viability of a system like Minuteman, a land-based system protected in silos.

It is hard to say what is best, but among the possibilities surely is something like what they refer to as the undersea long-range missile system (ULMS). It is also possible that some kind of air-based system might work out to be a substitute. There are also mobile land-based systems. I would hesitate to say which one is best. I have myself generally favored the sea-based system, in large part for the rather general reason that it does not draw fire on the continental United States.

If deterrent fails and there is an attack, there is some value in having that take place some place else than on the continental United States, and these land-based systems, including mobile land-based systems, would draw fire in the event that deterrence failed.

CONSEQUENCES OF SOVIET NUCLEAR ATTACK ON THE UNITED STATES

Senator COOPER. Again, looking at a situation in which the SALT talks have not prevailed, if Safeguard should be deployed and performed at 100-percent reliability, what would be the effect of a full-scale Soviet nuclear attack upon the United States? What would be the result? What would the devastation of the country be like?

I ask this question because I have emphasized my own conviction, and I am sure there are others here, that the greatest thing that could happen for our security would be the success of the SALT talks. But can you visualize and tell us what the consequences of a Soviet attack on this country, on land-based missiles, would be? Considering fallout and other things.

Dr. YORK. We have always talked about this as if it were machines versus machines and we have forgotten the inhabitants of both countries will be there as bystanders. If the attack was a preemptive attack focused entirely on the Minuteman, one has to assume it wouldn't be made unless the Russians assumed they could get through either by overwhelming the ABM or by exhausting it, or by confusing it in some way, and an attack on the Minuteman force would mean that attacking weapons would be burst on the ground which is the worst possible situation from the point of view of producing local fallout.

We should assume in that case that there are at least a thousand of them, because that is how many Minuteman there are, and I think one would assume that they are several megatons each. We now talk about five megatons for the SS-9 MIRV warhead, so something like 5,000 megatons would be exploded on the ground in the United States if there were an attack focused just on Minuteman.

Now, one megaton produces lethal fallout over an area whose size and shape depends on the weather. It depends on the winds, which way they are blowing, how hard they are blowing, but roughly speaking, you get about 1,000 square miles of lethal fallout from one megaton. So these 5,000 megatons would give, if they were all placed just right, up to 5 million square miles of lethal fallout which is larger than the area of the United States. Now, that wouldn't happen because the explosions would be concentrated on our bases. Rather, the area which was bathed in lethal fallout would be smaller than the whole area of the United States but the fallout within the area would be more intense than "merely" lethal.

With the bases where they are (Malmstrom, Grand Forks, and Whiteman), that means that it is the northeast United States that would most likely get all this fallout. If the wind was very light at all altitudes it might only cover Milwaukee, Chicago, Detroit, Toledo, St. Louis and so on. If the winds were very strong at any altitude on up to 100,000 feet, then the fallout could reach the east coast, covering New York, Boston, Philadelphia, Washington.

It is hard to estimate exactly what would happen, because that, in turn, depends on what people will really do. Some of them could save themselves by getting deep in their basements, but certainly many would be killed, and many others would be sick as a result of the immediate fallout. Others, probably an equal number, would die from secondary effects, that is from the breakdown of communications, the breakdown of power, the breakdown of water supply, or, in short, the general breakdown of civilization. So I suppose somewhere up to 50 million Americans would be killed as an indirect result of an attack on the Minuteman.

In the case of Canada, the proportionate trouble is probably greater because the great majority of Canadians live in southeast Canada, and that is precisely where the fallout from Grand Forks and Malmstrom would most likely go. So numerically it would be a smaller number but a larger fraction of the Canadian population that would be caught in this attack on the Minuteman.

Now, you only have to add a few more which are deliberately aimed at cities to bring the fatalities up to a hundred million or 120 million.

EFFECT OF NUCLEAR ATTACK ON SOVIET UNION

Senator COOPER. I think you are correct in saying that sometimes we think about these matters chiefly in terms of reliability and effectiveness of one system against the systems of the Soviet system. I would assume something of the same sort would happen in the Soviet Union.

Dr. YORK. Yes. There again, where the fallout would go would depend on where their missiles are with respect to their population. If it were just an attack on the missiles and if the missiles are mostly in Siberia then the prevailing winds would usually take it further into Siberia. It might not be quite so bad in that case. But again it only takes a few more aimed specifically at population targets to bring the figures in their case also up to a hundred million or 120 million.

Senator COOPER. All of this argues, I am sure you would agree, that the most important thing we can focus our attention on is the success of the SALT talks.

Dr. YORK. It is the only way to get the thing turned around so that these figures become fantasy.

Senator COOPER. I have a question for Mr. Bundy, and you perhaps have answered this, too.

WITNESS'S VIEWS ON DEVELOPMENT AND HALT OF NUCLEAR ARMAMENTS

As National Security Adviser to Presidents Kennedy and Johnson until 1966 you were one of the principal advisers to the President, on the decisions to deploy 1,000 Minuteman and I assume to go ahead with MIRV and not to deploy ABM.

In the period 1961 the United States developed, put great effort into the development of these nuclear armaments, and now 10 years later you are advocating a halt to nuclear weapons deployment. You probably have answered this in your statement and if you have not elaborate on it.

Mr. BUNDY. No, I think I have not.

Senator COOPER. What has changed you in the last 10 years and what has changed your mind?

Mr. BUNDY. I don't think really I have changed my mind. It happens, Senator, that I have been concerned in one way or another with this question of the nuclear arms race since 1946 when I was working with Secretary Stimson who had so much to do with the first atomic bombs, and I have felt throughout that time that there was no substitute for arms control in the long run.

The particular case of Minuteman in the early 1960's and indeed before that was a case in which it did appear, and I think correctly, that the Minuteman system was a much more reliable and a much less provocative system in the arms race balance of that time than other alternatives, such as the B-70, and indeed some of the existing systems.

My own view throughout the time I was in Washington was that it would be better to do a little less, if you asked my personal view, and my view of ABM through the time I was here, was that the ABM system was not needed.

The development of MIRV seemed to me a quite different kind of issue and I don't recall that this development was seriously a matter of trouble or concern outside the Pentagon under Mr. MacNamara's leadership. Those of us outside the Pentagon had, and I personally had, the highest respect for and confidence in Mr. MacNamara's abilities.

The situation now, however, is that, instead of having a weapon like Minuteman as it was in the early sixties, and is today and will be for some years to come, we are talking about the problem of an enormous qualitative and quantitative difference some five years from now. With MIRV we are not talking about what Minuteman is today—a secure weapon appropriate for deterrence and retaliation and not particularly in fact not practically, designed as a first-strike weapon in terms of magnitude. The original Minuteman system was a different thing from the breed of systems now being considered; systems which have the ratchet effect on the arms race that Dr. York referred to. I am not saying the Minuteman didn't have some of that sort of effect but it seemed a lesser one than these new systems seem to have.

IMPORTANCE AND DIFFICULTY OF AGREEMENT AT SALT

However, we have a moment here, both in terms of the present state of technological and weapons parity and in terms of the political possibilities, which gives us the best chance that we have had at any time, I think, since 1945, to try to achieve a general strategic limitation. That is a target of such enormous importance that it seems to me overriding.

I should add that I think it is very hard to get. I am very sure that your committee understands, and I think it is terribly important for all of us to understand that SALT is not an easy process and that an agreement with an adversary as wary and secretive as the Soviet Union is a hard thing to get in the best of circumstances. This is the most complex agreement we have tried for. But because of the alternatives described with such eloquence by Dr. York throughout the morning, it is just tremendously important to try, and I believe myself critically important for us to take the first step, to take it fairly soon, and this is why I so strongly support the central provisions of S. Res. 211.

Senator GORE. Would you yield? I want to say that that is an eloquent statement and I concur in it thoroughly.

Senator CASE. May I just ask one follow-up question to that?

Senator COOPER. Yes.

WOULD SENATE ADOPTION OF SENATE RESOLUTION 211 BE HELPFUL?

Senator CASE. You have repeated now what you said in your statement, in brief, that you do support the substance of that resolution. Do you believe that its adoption by the Senate would be helpful? Now, that is a slightly different question, and maybe you think it is not fair, but where are we going to go to get answers to questions like this involving the operation of the executive branch of the Government and what not if we don't go to people who have had experience with it?

Senator GORE. To be specific, is it helpful to make the veiws and sentiments of the Senate felt with respect to this decision which is peculiarly the province of the President in directing these negotiations.

Mr. BUNDY. There are difficulties in that point as I am sure you are aware.

Senator CASE. Surely.

Mr. BUNDY. I want to say, if I may go back for a minute, that in speaking to this question of Presidential responsibilities and still more the responsibilities of the Presidential staff, I really am very far from being critical of those who now have that responsibility as they face this decision. Indeed my own impression is that the President's staff have worked very hard to inform themselves and to consult widely beyond the mere bureaucratic channels.

There is a problem for the President in a negotiation as to whether he wants his hand played for him or to seem to have it played for him whether by editorials in leading newspapers, by comments from distinguished professors and *a fortiori* by advice from the Senate, which is so critical to the total democratic process.

I don't think it would be proper for me to respond in any conclusive way, and my instincts and training are those of a man who has studied the work of and worked in the executive branch. I can only put it this way, I think, Senator Case: If I were in the executive branch now, feeling as I do, and having the convictions that I have about what needs to be done, I would welcome this resolution and welcome a Senate vote on it.

Senator CASE. Thank you very much. Thank you, Senator.

Do you have any further questions?

COMMUNICATION BETWEEN PRESIDENT AND SCIENTIFIC COMMUNITY

Senator COOPER. One other question: From your experience as an adviser to the President, do you believe that questions like we are now considering, ABM, MIRV, or proposals to freeze the existing offensive and defensive systems, that the President has or should have the best advice, but does he get the advice of the scientists who know more about the systems and the effect of these systems than anyone else?

Mr. BUNDY. Perhaps my most useful way of commenting on that is to say that one of the things I admired most about President Kennedy was his intense and insistent concern to discuss these terrifying questions directly with the scientific men and the military men of differing views who knew most about them. I remember long discussions, sometimes in small groups, sometimes face to face, that the President had with men of very different views, and we all know that the scientific fraternity is not monolithic on this subject. I do believe that the degree of understanding which he developed with respect to the arguments, his experience after considering what he was advised before the first series of underground tests and what actually happened in that set of underground tests, his sense of the degree of reality and unreality of particular kinds of arguments, gave him great personal mastery, as the years passed, of a very difficult subject, and I doubt if this could have been done without this kind of personal exchange.

Senator COOPER. Of course your answer is that it would be that kind of exchange which should continue between the President and the scientific community now?

Mr. BUNDY. The President has, of source, access to the scientific community. I am not personally familiar with the ways and means by which that communication goes on. I do know that the White House staff have been in close communication with a number of leading scientists of varied views.

CLARIFICATION OF RELATIONSHIP BETWEEN PRESIDENT AND MILITARY

Senator CASE. Mr. Bundy, we had a discussion a little bit earlier about the relation between the military and the President and the military and Congress and it has been suggested that that may have left an impression that it was your judgment that the military were a rather exclusive possession of the President of the United States. I assume that you mean nothing of that sort at all.

Mr. BUNDY. The President is the Commander in Chief. Senator Gore pointed out just a few minutes afterward that the power of the purse and all the attendant authority belongs primarily to the Congress, so it seems to me we are working with a system of separation of powers. But I welcome the chance to accept that view.

CONGRESSIONAL RIGHT TO MILITARY INFORMATION

Senator CASE. My purpose in that discussion was to elicit information as to how we could most usefully perform our role and get the maximum amount of military information in order to do that properly, and it is still my major concern. It wasn't intended to be an academic discussion of who was the big shot or who was the boss——

Mr. BUNDY. I understand.

Senator CASE (continuing). That kind of thing, but it is obvious that you believe in performing our roles in regard to advice and consent, and in regard to furnishing the sinews of war and in regard to our specific obligations to provide for the common defense and what not in the Constitution, that we have the right to complete military information if we can get it.

Mr. BUNDY. Yes, sir; I feel that very strongly, and I believe, just to emphasize this, that the number of things which are real secrets is always very much smaller than any large institution likes to admit.

Senator CASE. Our time is up. We could go on for hours, but it would be imposing on you if we were able to do it. I just want to express for myself and I know for the Chairman our deep gratitude to you for coming and giving us on this occasion the information and advice that you have been so generous with in the past and which we couldn't do without.

ANNOUNCEMENT OF NEXT HEARING

The Chairman has asked me to announce that the hearings of the subcommittee will continue tomorrow morning at 10 o'clock. The subject then will be the ABM and U.S. relations with China. Our witnesses will be Dr. A. Doak Barnett, senior fellow of the Brookings Institution, and Dr. Alice Hsieh of the Rand Corp.

The hearing will not be held in this room but in the Caucus Room, room 318 of the Old Senate Office Building.

Thank you very much.

The subcommittee will be adjourned.

(Whereupon, at 12:55 p.m. the subcommittee recessed to reconvene at 10 a.m., Thursday, April 9, 1970.)

ABM, MIRV, SALT, AND THE NUCLEAR ARMS RACE

The ABM and U.S. Relations With China

THURSDAY, APRIL 9, 1970

UNITED STATES SENATE,
SUBCOMMITTEE ON ARMS CONTROL,
INTERNATIONAL LAW AND ORGANIZATION
OF THE COMMITTEE ON FOREIGN RELATIONS,
Washington, D.C.

The subcommittee met, pursuant to recess, at 10 a.m., in room 4221, New Senate Office Building, Senator Albert Gore (chairman of the subcommittee) presiding.

Present: Senators Gore, Fulbright (chairman of the full committee), Aiken, Case and Cooper.

OPENING STATEMENT

Senator GORE. The Subcommittee on Arms Control, International Law and Organization continues today a series of hearings on ABM, MIRV, SALT and the nuclear arms race.

Our hearings began on February 2 when Gerard C. Smith, Director of the Arms Control and Disarmament Agency, briefed the subcommittee in classified executive session on the strategic arms limitation talks. On March 2, the Director of the Central Intelligence Agency, Richard Helms, briefed the subcommittee on the strategic threat, again in executive classified session.

The first public hearing in this series was held on March 16 when Senator Brooke and Dr. Marshall Shulman, Director of the Russian Institute at Columbia University, testified on Senate Resolution 211. Dr. Shulman's testimony dealt, in part, with Soviet decisionmaking in regard to the strategic arms limitation talks and the relationship of the talks to our long-term relations with the Soviet Union.

The second public hearing was held yesterday when our witnesses were the Honorable McGeorge Bundy, president of the Ford Foundation and former Assistant to the President for National Security Affairs, and Dr. Herbert York, dean of the graduate school, the University of California at San Diego and former Director of Defense Research and Engineering.

The subject for today's hearing is the ABM and U.S. relations with China.

Our witnesses are Mr. A. Doak Barnett, senior fellow, the Brookings Institution, and Mrs. Alice Hsieh, of the Institute for Defense Analyses, two distinguished and well-known authorities on China.

We are pleased to have each of you with us today, but the committee particularly welcomes the diversity of your appearance, Mrs. Hsieh. We will give you lady's preference; you may go first.

STATEMENT OF MRS. ALICE LANGLEY HSIEH, INSTITUTE FOR DEFENSE ANALYSES

Mrs. HSIEH. Mr. Chairman, and members of the committee, I am complimented by your invitation to present my views on China's military policies and their implications for U.S. ABM deployment and Sino-United States relations.

The views expressed in this statement, as well as any made in response to questions, are my own. They should not be interpreted as reflecting the views of the Institute for Defense Analyses or any of its governmental or private research sponsors.

I might add that I am going to summarize briefly the longer statement which has been distributed to you and which I would like——

Senator GORE. The committee would like to have your full statement appear in the record.

Mrs. HSIEH. Yes; thank you, sir.

Some of you may be familiar with the testimony I gave before the Subcommittee on Military Applications of the Joint Committee on Atomic Energy in November 1967 on the same general subject. Because certain points I made then are worth underlining and may be even more valid today than they were in 1967, I shall quickly summarize them before proceeding to more recent developments which throw further light on the question before us today. My analysis of China's military strategy indicates that China, far from conforming to the image of a militarily reckless, adventurous regime, has in pursuit of its long-term foreign policy objectives (great power status, hegemony in Asia, removal of U.S. power and influence from the Western Pacific) followed military policies which have been characterized by a considerable degree of caution—policies particularly noted for their low-risk nature.

China's recognition of the implications of nuclear warfare, of its vulnerability to nuclear attack, of its military inferiority to the United States (and for that matter to the Soviet Union), of its inability to count on Soviet military backing in support of its external objectives, and, increasingly, of its suspicions of Soviet intentions toward China are strongly reflected in Peking's intention to avoid any military initiatives that might lead to a direct confrontation with U.S. forces, conventional or nuclear.

Today I want to focus my discussion on several recent crisis situations and trends in international politics and their implications for China's strategy; namely, the war in Vietnam; the Sino-Soviet border conflict; the effect of the wider discussion in Japan of Asian security issues, particularly the growing, though still limited, Japanese interest in the indigenous development of nuclear weapons; the significance of the September 1969 underground detonation for China's nuclear development and capabilities; and the reaction of Peking to certain developments in U.S. security policy in Asia, for example, the Guam or Nixon doctrine. I shall then turn to Peking's likely use of its evolving nuclear-missile capability and conclude my discussion with the implications of the deployment by the United States of a China-oriented ABM system for China's strategy and Sino-United States relations.

PEKING'S ATTITUDE TOWARD VIETNAM WAR

Contrary to the general impression that the Chinese were masterminding the operations of Hanoi and the National Liberation Front (NLF) or that certain professionally oriented officers within the People's Liberation Army (PLA), for example, Lo Jui-ch'ing, then chief of the general staff, were advocating more militant action in Vietnam, close analysis of Peking's attitude toward the war in Vietnam indicates that even Peking's verbal bellicosity in support on Hanoi declined in early 1965 as the Chinese became increasingly concerned that the United States might extend the bombing of North Vietnam to the mainland of China. The debate that took place within the Peking leadership during 1965 was not a debate over whether or not China should intervene overtly in the war in Vietnam (that is, aside from the provision of construction troops, equipment, and technical assistance), but a debate on how best to defend China in the event of a U.S. air attack. Mao Tse-tung and Lin Piao probably did not agree with the emphasis that Lo wanted to give to beefing up China's conventional air defense and his possible preference to downgrade the Sino-Soviet dispute in order to create the framework within which Peking could request a revival of shipments of conventional defensive equipment from Moscow. Nevertheless, Lo no doubt expressed the view of the Peking leadership in general when in his May 10, 1965 article he asserted:

"Our principle is: We will not attack unless we are attacked, if we are attacked we will certainly counterattack * * *."

This assertion reinforced earlier indications that China's support and aid to Hanoi would fall short of overt participation in combat operations. In fact, Lo's statement evidenced a further retrenchment and conditioning of China's commitment to Hanoi. Only a direct attack on China would invoke overt intervention.

I emphasize this quotation because it is indicative of a highly defensive stance on China's part. Identical phraseology was to be used in the course of this past year when the situation on the Sino-Soviet border was so tense that many observers were predicting a major war in the imminent future.

But before turning to the Sino-Soviet question, I think we should ask ourselves what lessons, in terms of strategy, the Chinese may have learned from the war in Vietnam. Vietnam has not necessarily confirmed the Chinese in their oft-repeated description of the United States as a "paper tiger." It has indeed confirmed the Chinese in their estimate that where a people have the will to make revolution and can appeal to weaknesses and instability in an existing regime, wars of national liberation have a good chance of success. It has also demonstrated to the Chinese the limits of conventional bombing of a nation that is still highly underdeveloped. But the unwillingness of the Chinese to take on the United States, or during this past year the Soviets, indicates that Peking is aware that the effects of conventional bombing may not be as limited to a country which, though still largely underdeveloped, does possess key military targets, in particular nuclear production facilities and important industrial, communication and transportation centers. If this is true for conventional bombing, it is bound to be all the more true for Peking's recognition of the implication of a nuclear attack.

SINO-SOVIET BORDER CONFLICT

The situation on the Sino-Soviet border which was brought dramatically to public attention with the military incidents of March 2 and 15 on Chen Pao (Damansky) Island in the Ussuri River provides a further opportunity to analyze the so-called adventurism and recklessness of the Peking regime. Difficulties along the Sino-Soviet border, whether in the area of Manchuria, Mongolia, or Sinkiang, appear to date from 1959 and parallel the growing tension in Sino-Soviet relations since that time. As the situation between Peking and Moscow became more tense in the early sixties, the Soviets in the 1965–66 period began to strengthen their military forces along the border. Chinese troop deployments remained largely unchanged and what moves did take place in the 1966–69 period could be attributed as readily to considerations of internal security as to those related to national defense. However, with enhanced Soviet troop strength, resulting in more intensive patrolling, and tensions arising from the cultural revolution, the probability of larger scale clashes involving more men and equipment increased.

This is not the place to indulge in an analysis of the two March incidents.

The question before us today is the strategic/tactical parameters of the border issue, i.e. the reactions of the Chinese and the Russians on the military or military threat levels. These parameters were established early in the game. Despite their usual verbal bellicosity, the Chinese took steps 2 days after the first incident, on March 4, to state their strategic defensive posture when they revived the formula—this time in relation to the Soviet Union: "We will not attack unless we are attacked." This formula, so reminiscent of Peking's statements in 1965 with regard to Vietnam, underlines China's defensive stance vis-a-vis the Soviet Union and demonstrates its awareness of its vulnerability to a Soviet attack and its unwillingness to take risks which might result in a confrontation with the Soviet Union.

POSSIBLE JAPANESE NUCLEAR CAPABILITY

The foregoing examples briefly outline the nature of China's military policies and strategy during the past five and a half years, that is, since the detonation of its first nuclear device. A crucial element in China's military thinking, and one which has frequently been ignored, is China's reaction to the possibility of Japan developing its own nuclear capability within the next decade. To what extent Japan is not ruling out its nuclear option remains a controversial issue among observers of the Japanese political/military scene.

During the past 5 years, for a number of reasons the debate on security issues in Japan has widened. A far larger number of Japanese appear prepared to support "made-in-Japan nuclears" than is usually credited. Polls of Japanese public opinion during the second half of 1968 and the first half of 1969 indicate a rising public interest in a Japanese nuclear capability.

To date, the Japanese Government has taken a position opposing Japan's development or possession of nuclear weapons. The latest disclaimer was that made by the recently appointed director general of the Defense Agency, Minister Yasuhiro Nakasone, who on March 5, reversed his earlier position supporting the indigenous development of nuclear weapons when he declared that "Japan should not, now or in the future, build its own nuclear weapons."

Particularly since the U.S.-Japan joint communique of November 1969 on the reversion of Okinawa, the Chinese have on several occasions referred to the possibility of Japan developing its own nuclear weapons. These charges have usually been in the context of Japan reviving military aggression in Asia as an instrument of the United States or as an independent power and of harboring designs on Taiwan, South Korea, and Indochina. This harder line toward Japan indicates a growing sensitivity on the part of Peking to Japan's growing role in Asia and internationally.

However brief the foregoing discussion, the key question is: what does this mean for China's strategy? Any strengthening of Japan militarily, particularly as far as nuclear weapons are concerned, whether in conjunction with the United States or on a Gaullist basis, would be bound to make China even more cautious in its military policies, if such can be the case. China might pickup some political benefits, for a nuclear armed Japan would revive suspicions of Japan's intentions in the area. This might be offset, however, by the fact that many of the countries of Asia look toward the highly industrialized Japan for economic assistance. Moreover, Australia and India might ask whether or not it was necessary to follow Japan's example. China could then exist in a highly brittle political/military environment. The Chinese could be confronted with still another nuclear power on its periphery and a competitor for leadership in Asia. The present balance of power in the area might be further complicated to China's disadvantage. Thus, a Japanese regional nuclear capability deployed and operated either independently of the United States or in conjunction with the U.S. strategic capability may well have the effect of limiting China's political/psychological use of its emerging nuclear capability, let alone any overt military use. China could well be confronted with diminishing returns from its development of a nuclear-missile capability.

Some observers have argued that because of this, the nuclearization of Japan would be in the interests of both Japan and the United States. The best answer to such a proposition were the reasons given by Minister Nakasone on March 5 as to why Japan should not build its own nuclear weapons. These reasons included such factors as the triangular stalemate developing between the United States, the Soviet Union, and Communist China, the cost of such an endeavor, and the inability of Japan to achieve an effective second strike capability.

CHINA'S NUCLEAR MIX

Another factor that must be taken into account before projecting the way in which China is likely to use its emerging nuclear missile capability is the type of nuclear mix the Chinese may be envisaging. Considerable controversy exists as to whether the Chinese will give priority to an Intercontinental Ballistic Missile (ICBM) or to a Medium Range Ballistic Missile (MRBM) capability, and when I refer to an MRBM capability it is a 1,500-mile range capability. As I have noted on several occasions in the past, my own evaluation, based primarily on an analysis of political considerations, has been that the

Chinese are likely to give emphasis to the deployment of an operational MRBM system, a regional capability, though this does not necessarily rule out their testing and development of a token ICBM or submarine launched missile capability.

Since coming to this conclusion, a new ingredient has entered the picture—the detonation by China of its first underground nuclear device on September 28, 1969. The two more plausible explanations for an underground test at that time appear to be (1) that the Chinese are interested in setting up controlled experiments whereby they can more effectively analyze nuclear design information as well as the physical effects of a detonation, and (2) that the Chinese are interested in denying debris and other technical intelligence material to both Western and Soviet analysts because they are beginning to test tactical nuclear weapons designed for battlefield use. These explanations are not mutually exclusive and may well be mutually reinforcing. The objectives of conducting a controlled experiment for the purpose of more effectively analyzing nuclear design material fall within the general pattern of their tests to date, that is, the development of a 3-megaton device reduced in size so as to be usable as a warhead on a medium-range (1,500-mile) or and intercontinental range ballistic missle.

The more controversial explanation—but the one toward which I, for reasons to be given, lean—is that the Chinese may be experimenting not only with reducing the size of the device but also with minimizing the amount of fissionable material in the device, with plutonium the key element, in order to develop a tactical nuclear weapons capability, that is, weapons that could initially be carried by a fighter or fighter-bomber.

The tactical nuclear weapon thesis has generally been downgraded by Western analysts in the belief that the Chinese were more likely to go for the bigger bang, that is the 3-megaton thermonuclear warhead designed for an ICBM.

Yet Chinese military literature contains continuing hints of an interest in tactical nuclear weapons. The *Kung-tso Tung-hsun* (*KTTH*) material, better known as the *Bulletin of Activities of the People's Liberation Army*, has a number of references to the use of low-yield nuclear weapons by the Chinese.

The context of this material tends to suggest that as early as 1961 the Chinese were considering the battlefield use of nuclear weapons. When read in context Chinese directives would appear to be referring to land-type warfare. This provides us with clues as to why the Chinese may be interested at an earlier date than usually credited in including tactical nuclear weapons in their nuclear arsenal. The Chinese, despite the improbability from a U.S. point of view (though not necessarily from a Soviet), remain the captive of the concept of invasion by enemy ground forces for the purpose of control and occupation followed by a surprise nuclear attack. Tactical nuclear weapons delivered by aircraft might well be regarded by the Chinese as an important attack weapon against troop concentrations, landing operations, etc. Likewise, the one area in East Asia where the use by the United States of battlefield nuclear weapons can be considered with any degree of plausibility is Korea. The Chinese might believe that the mere possession of battlefield nuclear weapons on their part could act as a deterrent to a U.S. use of such weapons in the event of a crisis situation, or that at least their possession by the Chinese would lead such countries as Japan to place pressures on the United States to deny itself the use of tactical nuclear weapons. And now with the tension along the border with the Soviet Union the Chinese may see further deterrent advantages in the possession of battlefield nuclears.

PEKING'S REACTION TO NIXON DOCTRINE

I want to turn now to Peking's reaction to the Nixon doctrine.
This doctrine first enunciated by President Nixon on July 25, 1969 in a press interview on Guam, can be interpreted as saying that the United States will rely on the self-effort of Asian countries to resolve their political, economic, and social problems.
Senator GORE. Could I ask you a question about that?
Mrs. HSIEH. Yes, sir.

COMPATABILITY OF NIXON DOCTRINE WITH VIETNAMIZATION

Senator GORE. In asking this question I don't wish to criticize the Nixon doctrine, but I must say that I have felt that the Nixon doctrine, when applied to Laos and Cambodia, was incompatible with the policy of Vietnamization for South Vietnam. Believing that the war in Southeast Asia, whether it be in Laos or Cambodia or Vietnam, is essentially the same war, I have felt that the Nixon doctrine, which you have just described, was contradictory in assigning to the Cambodians and the Laotians the responsibility for their own defense, while in an adjoining little country pledging U.S. troops to remain and continue the war under the formula described as Vietnamization. That operates as an open invitation for the movement of North Vietnamese troops into Laos and Cambodia, thus outflanking the U.S. position in South Vietnam.
I state my apprehension. Perhaps I should not have stated mine before I inquired of yours, but I wanted to explain to you why I interrupted your statement, in the light of your recognized competence in this field, to ask you to give the committee the benefit of your views in this regard.
Mrs. HSIEH. Well, I wanted to mention this question of the ambiguity and indeterminacy of the so-called Nixon doctrine. Particularly from the point of view of the Chinese, this lack of clarity and this ambiguity leaves a number of questions open.
Senator GORE. I didn't hear the last part.
Mrs. HSIEH. The Nixon doctrine leaves a number of questions open as to how it will be interpreted by, let us say, the Chinese or by the North Vietnamese.
Senator GORE. Will you give us the benefit of your views?
Mrs. HSIEH. I am getting to it.
Senator GORE. O.K.
Mrs. HSIEH. Not Cambodia and Laos in particular but from the Chinese point of view and perhaps from there we could then go on to that of the North Vietnamese. I think the North Vietnamese interpretation might differ somewhat from that of Chinese.
Senator GORE. Fine.

COMMUNIST CHINESE INTERPRETATION OF THE NIXON DOCTRINE

Mrs. HSIEH. I was remarking that the Nixon doctrine can be interpreted as saying that the United States will increasingly consider it the responsibility of Asian countries to meet the threat of conventional aggression on their own and that the United States will remain prepared to counter a nuclear threat or attack by a nuclear power. It remains unclear where and under what circumstances the United States would be prepared to counter conventional aggression by a nuclear power.

Contrary to what might have been one's initial impression, the Chinese have not interpreted the Nixon doctrine as the beginning of U.S. disengagement from the area. To some extent the Chinese appear to have read the Nixon doctrine as increasing U.S. reliance on the use of nuclear weapons. At the same time there is the implication in their comments that U.S. options, in particular the use of nuclear weapons, in responding to a broad spectrum of threats, are now more limited. Equally important, the Chinese have interpreted the Nixon doctrine, especially after the November 20 joint U.S.-Japan communique on the reversion of Okinawa, as an attempt by the United States to turn Japan into the instrument of U.S. aggression in Asia.

The first assessment, that is, increased U.S. reliance on the use of nuclears, could lead the Chinese to believe that the United States was giving up certain of its flexibility in responding to Chinese or Chinese-inspired aggression in Asia. The Chinese could also calculate that the United States would be reluctant to use nuclear weapons in response to any but the most serious type of overt aggression in the area. Or the Chinese might believe that if the United States were confronted with the choice between a nuclear respose or no response, it might opt for the latter reason, that is, no response. While these calculations might lead the Chinese to believe that both the political-military value of China's nuclear missile capability and the role of China's conventional forces had been enhanced, such a conclusion might well be recognized by the Chinese, who do not rule out irrationality in U.S. behavior, as opening the way to serious miscalculation of U.S. intentions on their part. In fact, the ambiguity that characterizes certain aspects of the new doctrine would appear to argue in favor of caution on China's part.

The introduction of the Japan equation into Chinese strategic thinking, as already noted, underlines the political/military use of China's nuclear missile capability, a use with perhaps diminishing returns.

In sum, a more accurate assessment of China's interpretation of the Nixon doctrine and whether it regards the shifts in U.S. Asian policy as opportunities to be exploited or as increasing pressures on China will only be found in Chinese responses to concrete U.S. actions in the area in the future. Meanwhile, to the best of my analysis, China is not likely to be incautious in testing the underlying intent of the Nixon doctrine.

Before I go on would you want to raise—does that answer the question?

NIXON DOCTRINE AND VIETNAMIZATION

Senator GORE. I would say to the Chairman of the full committee that I had asked this scholar on U.S.-Chinese relations, who had just made reference to the Nixon doctrine, to examine the possible incompatibility of the Nixon doctrine, as applied to Laos and Cambodia, with the policy of Vietnamization in South Vietnam. Mrs. Hsieh, are you ready at this point to discuss this?

Mrs. HSIEH. The policy of Vietnamization and the steps taken in Laos and Cambodia were taken prior to the enunciation of the—the first enunciation of the Nixon doctrine was in July of last year. I see certain inconsistencies, as you have suggested, but in general both the policy of Vietnamization and our policy in Laos and Cambodia appear consistent with the Nixon doctrine.

NORTH VIETNAMESE INTERPRETATION OF NIXON DOCTRINE

Senator GORE. You told us how you think China interprets the Nixon doctrine and the dependence upon nuclear weapons, I believe in the President's words, to add credibility to our policy in Asia.

How does North Vietnam, in your view, interpret this policy?

Mrs. HSIEH. It would be my interpretation that North Vietnam might see this as a greater opportunity to exploit the situation in Cambodia and in Laos, that they would possibly or probably anticipate less of a reaction on the part of the United States to moves there.

Senator GORE. They would anticipate less reaction on the ground?

Mrs. HSIEH. Yes. And in the air. This would be backed up by their interpretation of U.S. public opinion.

Senator GORE. Do I gather from this that you think the North Vietnamese do not think it likely that the United States would use nuclear weapons to add credibility to its policy in Laos and Cambodia?

Mrs. HSIEH. Decidedly, yes, sir.

Senator AIKEN. That they would not?

May I ask a question?

COMMUNIST CHINESE INTERPRETATION OF PRESENT U.S. POLICIES

I noticed you say that the Nixon doctrine was received with mixed reaction in China. Was there any indication that the Chinese preferred the Johnson doctrine? Did they think the Nixon doctrine was an improvement over the previous doctrine?

Mrs. HSIEH. Yes, I would say from their point of view they might view the Nixon doctrine as providing the United States with less flexibility in responding to the spectrum of possible problems that could arise in Asia. Under the Johnson doctrine, in their view, there was a greater reliance on the use of conventional forces and the maintenance of conventional forces in the area.

The Chinese appear to have read the Nixon doctrine as implying a greater reliance on the use of nuclear weapons.

Senator AIKEN. Do you think the Nixon doctrine offers a little more hope for Asia?

Mrs. HSIEH. Of less U.S. involvement.

Senator AIKEN. Of less U.S. involvement?

Mrs. HSIEH. Yes.

Senator AIKEN. Can you tell us what the reaction has been to the withdrawal of 118,000 American troops from South Vietnam? Has that been favorable or don't they believe it?

Mrs. HSIEH. It has been described by the Chinese as a two-faced policy on the part of the United States. They assert that at the same time that we are withdrawing forces we are supporting the Vietnamization of the war. They have, at least in their public statements, not viewed this as a particular gain.

Senator AIKEN. Do they consider Vietnamization to be the maintenance of the government of South Vietnam by itself?

Mrs. HSIEH. Yes.

Senator AIKEN. Is it that they do not believe in two Vietnams?

Mrs. HSIEH. They are against any strengthening of the government of South Vietnam. They are opposed, of course, to the continued partition of Vietnam, although their objectives in Vietnam are to some extent slightly different from those of Hanoi. Hanoi sees the situation in Vietnam as an immediate problem of reunification. China looks at the situation in a much longer term context—as a step toward the eventual removal of the U.S. presence from the area of continental Asia. This has brought about some of the differences that we know have existed in policy as between Peking and Hanoi.

Senator AIKEN. Speaking of military and economic influence, do they have the same feeling about Japan and other countries or do you think that their attitude is directed primarily to the United States or Russia?

Mrs. HSIEH. No, I would say at this point the Chinese consider the Soviet Union their No. 1 enemy, the United States No. 2, and increasingly they are becoming concerned about Japan.

Senator AIKEN. Have you had any reaction to the resumption of meetings between U.S. and Chinese representatives in Warsaw or the slight relaxation in trade restrictions with China?

Mrs. HSIEH. Not openly. But one has a feeling that there may be groups within—I mention this somewhere in my statement—that there may possibly be a group within the Peking leadership that is searching for a new way of dealing with the United States, however tentative and experimental. That is one of the questions I wanted to discuss in terms of this anti-China ABM deployment—that this could possibly prejudice the efforts of such a group, if such a group exists. However, there is no evidence that such a group exists.

Senator AIKEN. We have small groups in the United States that differ with various policies. I expect every country has the same. Of course, the desire for expansion of trade exists in all countries, and China has possibly a most bountiful future if the cost of production continues to go up in the rest of the world and in the United States as it has in recent years.

Mrs. HSIEH. The best estimate of their reaction is the fact that they have not openly attacked these moves on our part. They have remained silent, which is a hopeful factor, regarding the relaxation of the trade and the travel restrictions. There was also a change in their public treatment of the ABM deployment decision as of last March and what they said about the more recent decision. I will go on into that.

Senator AIKEN. That is all for now.

PEKING'S LIKELY USE OF EVOLVING NUCLEAR MISSILE CAPABILITY

Mrs. HSIEH. Then I shall turn to a very brief description of Peking's likely use of its evolving nuclear missile capability.

While it remains impossible to predict with any degree of certainty the long-term future, my analysis of China's military doctrine and behavior to date has given me no reason to believe that when China is in possession of a nuclear delivery capability, it will be more prepared than at present to engage in a high-risk military policy.

Whatever the priority the Chinese give to their nuclear-missile program, they will still have to live with the vast military/technological gap that will continue to exist between China on the one hand and the United States on the other, and for that matter the Soviet Union. At least two factors characterize the U.S. deterrent posture, that is, a posture that would both deter overt Chinese military action and prevent Chinese miscalculation: (1) Its massive military superiority to the Chinese (and China's awareness of this superiority), and (2) U.S. preparedness to make the risk of any overt Chinese military operations extremely high and the communication of this preparedness to Peking, as much by the deployment of certain weapon systems in the areas as by declaratory policy. Time does not permit an extensive discussion of the components of a U.S. deterrent posture, but it is my conclusion that the Chinese are more sensitive to weapon systems deployed in the region than any number of Minutemen in silos in the continental United States.

The latter could always be viewed by Peking as designed primarily for an attack against the Soviet Union. Moreover, the Chinese could also calculate, or miscalculate, that the United States might be reluctant to threaten the use of, or use, such a weapon system as the Minuteman because it could lead to misinterpretation on the part of the Soviet Union. Consequently, there is the need to decouple the Chinese and Soviet threats. Such weapon systems as sea- and land-based aircraft, the 7th Fleet, and the Polaris-Poseidon system offer, in my view, the preferred deterrent to the Chinese.

Let me briefly say that I do not see any real improvement in Sino-Soviet relations in the foreseeable future. Nor do I see after the death of Mao any reduction of Chinese caution in its military policies.

Consequently, in attempting to project China's future military behavior, to suggest a Chinese first strike or threat of such strike against one or a few U.S. cities in the absence of an ABM defense at a time when China may possess something like 10 to 25 ICBM's—should it opt to develop even that many—is like suggesting a willingness on the part of the Chinese leadership to commit national suicide. So long as the United States remains prepared to make the risks of overt Chinese military operations extremely high, the Chinese are likely to avoid military initiatives that might invite massive U.S. nuclear retaliatory strikes against the mainland. Rather, in accordance with China's preferred foreign policy style, the Chinese are likely to make a low-risk and subtle use of their nuclear capability along political-military and propaganda lines with a view to achieving the following objectives:

1. The enhancement of China's international political stature.
2. In the event of an evolving crises situation, the deterrence of a U.S. attack on the China mainland, as well as the imposition of restraints on U.S. military policies in the area.
3. The undermining of the U.S.-Asian alliance and security arrangements.
4. The inhibition of Asian nations' self-defense efforts.
5. The fostering of internal instability and, where chances of success appear high, national liberation movements.
6. The enhancement of the role of China's conventional forces.

PROBABLE USE OF NUCLEAR MISSILE CAPABILITY BY PEKING

Any token capability to threaten the U.S. homeland, or even test firing of a Chinese ICBM, will, of course, have political and prestige payoffs. The Chinese may also hope that, when in possession of a token or even limited ICBM capability, they could in the course of an evolving crisis situation create just the type of uncertainty in the United States that some observers have referred to in discussing the uses of a Chinese ICBM—that is, an uncertainty which would lead the United States to limit its military responses, particularly any consideration of the use of nuclear weapons. But if such should prove the case, it is an uncertainty which we will have created for ourselves by attributing to the Chinese a degree of recklessness and adventurism which does not in fact exist.

By means of a regional capability, the Chinese may hope to create a similar uncertainty as to U.S. intentions among U.S. allies and friendly neutrals in the area, to exploit Asian fear of involvement in a nuclear war, and concern that any U.S. confrontation with a nuclear-armed China would escalate into a nuclear, if not general, war. Peking might calculate that fear on these various scores would lead Asian nations to assert pressures on the United States to avoid any confrontation with China—conventional or nuclear. It is thus quite indirectly that Peking would hope to make gains. An overt nuclear threat to a U.S. ally or friendly neutral would represent such a high-risk undertaking that the Chinese are likely to avoid its use.

The Chinese may also see a nuclear capability, particularly a capability designed for battlefield use, as enhancing the role of their conventional forces, first, as a deterrent to invasion and, secondly, as a means of deterring a U.S. introduction of tactical nuclears should a conflict break out, for example, on the Korean Peninsula.

In sum, from my analysis of China's past and current Chinese military doctrine and policies, I would conclude that China is unlikely to adopt incautious military initiatives in its use of a nuclear delivery capability whether of an intercontinental or regional character. At one time it looked as though a nuclear-armed China, because of the instabilities present in many parts of Asia, would be likely to find ample opportunity to advance toward her long-term objectives in Asia through reliance on the political-military and propaganda uses of forces. Today

I am not so sure that it will find even these political payoffs from the possession of a nuclear-missile capability. Because of Soviet suspicion of a nuclear armed China and Japan's possible development of her own nuclear capability, China's nuclear-missile development may prove to have diminishing returns. China may discover that there is little merit in being a second- or third-rate nuclear power—that the problems such a status invites may well offset even the political advantages.

EFFECT OF U.S. DEVELOPMENT OF COMMUNIST CHINA-ORIENTED ABM

It would thus appear from the foregoing that the deployment of an anti-China ABM system by the United States is irrelevant to the type of strategy China is likely to pursue when in possession of a nuclear-missile capability. Nevertheless, the question must be asked: Should the United States deploy a China-oriented ABM system, what effect would this have on China's policies, in particular its relations with the United States?

In contrast with Peking's reaction in March 1969 to the President's decision to deploy the Safeguard system, the Chinese, probably because of the revival of Government-to-Government talks in Warsaw, failed to report the President's January 30 announcement that the United States would initiate phase II of the Safeguard program as a defense against China's growing nuclear-missile capability. In commenting on the President's foreign policy report to Congress, Peking also ignored the President's reference to the ABM and the China "threat," but Peking at the same time boasted that the President "had to admit China's growing strength and her tremendous influence in the world" and his expressions of "apprehensions over the fact that 'China has acquired thermonuclear weapons' and thus broken the U.S. and Soviet nuclear monopoly." Thus, the United States gives not only prestige but also credibility to a threat which is still far from materializing—at least in the eyes of less sophisticated Asians. At the same time deployment of a China-oriented ABM reinforces Peking's image of the United States as basically hostile to China. To what extent is another matter.

However, any reinforcement of Peking's paranoia regarding the West, particularly when the justification is subject to serious challenge, is completely inconsistent with other moves on the part of the United States to reduce tensions with China. U.S. gestures regarding trade, exchange of scholars, and newspapermen, could be seriously prejudiced. Nor can we rule out the possibility that there may, as I suggested just a few minutes ago, elements within the Chinese leadership that might be searching for some new relationship with the United States, however tentative and experimental. If such should prove to be the case their efforts would be undermined by new indications of U.S. hostility.

On the scientific-technological side, the Chinese could, as some observers have suggested, give priority to the development of penetration aids. Quite aside from China's technological capability to pursue such a development, it is necessary to ask what this would gain for them. If we accept the premise that I have been stressing that the Chinese are unlikely to be reckless in their use of a nuclear missile capability, pen aids simply do not gain anything for them.

Another possibility and a far more likely one is that U.S. deployment of an anti-China ABM system will reinforce the priority the Chinese are likely to give to the development and operational deployment of MRBM's and on the political-military use of a regional capability.

An equally important effect could be that on the Japanese. In addition to Chinese recklessness and miscalculation, the deployment of a China-oriented ABM has been justified on the grounds of the confidence such deployment would instill in U.S. allies, such as Japan, that the United States would come to Japan's assistance if subjected to Chinese blackmail. Contrary to this thesis the very opposite has in some instances turned out to be the case. There has been some suggestion in Japan that such deployment by the United States would mean that the United States would respond to Chinese aggressive moves only if the U.S. homeland were threatened. The Japanese may also believe that as a consequence of U.S. ABM deployment their country has become a lightning rod so far as Chinese nuclears are concerned. This concern, this worry, combined with a questioning of U.S. reliability has on occasion led some Japanese to raise the possibility of a regional ABM system and again on occasion been used to rationalize Japan's indigenous development of nuclear weapons.

The Chinese could also interpret the U.S. deployment of a China-oriented ABM, particularly if agreement were reached with the Soviet Union in the course of the SALT talks on a level of ABM deployment which would be China oriented, as a further example of U.S.-Soviet collusion against China.

NECESSITY FOR DEPLOYMENT OF COMMUNIST CHINA-ORIENTED ABM QUESTIONED

In conclusion, I do not believe the deployment by the United States of a China-oriented ABM is necessary. Arguments based on China's projected recklessness when in possession of a limited nuclear-missile capability, China's possible miscalculation of U.S. intentions or because our friends in Asia are likely to feel more confident of U.S. support if the U.S. homeland is defended against a theoretical Chinese attack do not stand up under close analysis. In turn, I would take the position that with time the possible payoffs that China will gain from a nuclear-missile capability are diminishing, even the political-military payoffs from which I believed they at some time expected some dividends. I also believe that revival of the China "threat" as a key reason for ABM deployment by the United States is likely to create more problems than it resolves. It will not only prejudice any attempt on the part of the United States to enter into some type of understanding with Peking, it could reinforce charges of U.S. collusion with the Soviet Union. Moreover, it might lead other countries in the area to give a higher credence to China's nuclear-missile capability than it merits, to question U.S. reliability, to stimulate demands for a regional ABM system, and to encourage those governments capable of doing so to opt for their own development of nuclear weapons.

Forgive me for being so long.

(Mrs. Hsieh's complete prepared statement follows.)

133

CHINA'S NUCLEAR STRATEGY AND A U.S. ANTI-CHINA ABM

(Statement before the Subcommittee on Arms Control, International Law and Organization of the Foreign Relations Committee of the U.S. Senate, April 9, 1970, Alice Langley Hsieh, Institute for Defense Analyses)

Mr. Chairman, members of the committee. I am complimented by your invitation to present my views on China's military policies and their implications for U.S. ABM deployment. The views expressed in this statement, as well as any made in response to questions, are my own. They should not be interpreted as reflecting the views of the Institute for Defense Analyses or any of its governmental or private research sponsors.

Some of you may be familiar with the testimony I gave before the Subcommittee on Military Applications of the Joint Committee on Atomic Energy in November 1967 on the same general subject. Because certain points I made then are worth underlining and may be even more valid today than they were in 1967, I shall quickly summarize them before proceeding to more recent developments which throw further light on the question before us today. My analysis of China's military strategy indicates that China, far from conforming to the image of a militarily reckless, adventurous regime, has in pursuit of its long-term foreign policy objectives (great power status, hegemony in Asia, removal of U.S. power and influence from the Western Pacific) followed military policies which have been characterized by a considerable degree of caution—policies particularly noted for their low-risk nature. These policies reflect a realistic assessment of the military situation and the careful calculation of risks.

China's recognition of the implications of nuclear warfare, of its vulnerability to nuclear attack, of its military inferiority to the United States (and for that matter to the Soviet Union), of its inability to count on Soviet military backing in support of its external objectives, and increasingly, of its suspicions of Soviet intentions toward China are strongly reflected in Peking's intention to avoid any military initiatives that might lead to a direct confrontation with U.S. forces, conventional or nuclear. This does not mean that in the case of an evolving crisis situation China may not believe its vital interests, in particular its own security or the preservation of neighboring Communist regimes (as in the case of Korea in 1950), so directly affected that she will avoid a confrontation with the United States at any cost. Nor does it rule out a possible miscalculation of U.S. intentions under similar circumstances. It does mean that where the initiative remains with Peking, China's preferred strategy will be a low-risk one.

Today I want to focus my discussion on several recent crisis situations and trends in international politics and their implications for China's strategy; namely, the war in Vietnam; the Sino-Soviet border conflict; the effect of the wider discussion in Japan of Asian security issues, particularly the growing, though still limited, Japanese interest in the indigenous development of nuclear weapons; the significance of the September 1969 underground detonation for China's nuclear developments and capabilities; and the reaction of Peking to recent developments in U.S. security policy in Asia, e.g. the Guam or Nixon doctrine. I shall then turn to Peking's likely use of its evolving nuclear-missile capability and conclude my discussion with the implications of the deployment by the United States of a China-oriented ABM system for China's strategy and Sino-U.S. relations.

THE WAR IN VIETNAM

Contrary to the general impression that the Chinese were masterminding the operations of Hanoi and the NFL or that certain professionally-oriented officers within the PLA, for example Lo Jui-ch'ing, then Chief of the General Staff, were advocating more militant action in Vietnam, close analysis of Peking's attitude toward the war in Vietnam indicates that even Peking's verbal bellicosity in support of Hanoi declined in early 1965 as the Chinese became increasingly concerned that the United States might extend the bombing of North Vietnam to the mainland of China. The debate that took place within the Peking leadership during 1965 was not a debate over whether or not China should intervene overtly in the war in Vietnam (that is, aside from the provision of construction troops, equipment, and technical assistance), but a debate on how best to defend China in the event of a U.S. air attack. This debate on defense in turn may well have reflected still another level of differences and one which has persisted within the Peking leadership since the end of the Korean war, that is, whether priority should be accorded economic and scientific/technological development as a basis for a future national defense posture or whether priority should be given to "quick fix" type of improvements in defensive capabilities. Mao Tse-tung and Lin Piao probably did not agree with the emphasis that Lo wanted to give to beefing up China's conventional air defense and his possible preference to downgrade the Sino-Soviet dispute in order to create the framework within which Peking could request a revival of shipments of conventional defensive equipment from Moscow. Nevertheless, Lo no doubt expressed the view of the Peking leadership in general when in his May 10, 1965 article he asserted: "Our principle is: We will not attack unless we are attacked, if we are attacked we will certainly counterattack. . . ."

This assertion reinforced earlier indications that China's support and aid to Hanoi would fall short of overt participation in combat operations. In fact, Lo's statement evidenced a further retrenchment and conditioning of China's commitment to Hanoi. Only a *direct attack on China* would invoke overt intervention.

I emphasize this quotation because it is indicative of a highly defensive stance on China's part. Identical phraseology was to be used in the course of this past year when the situation on the Sino-Soviet border was so tense that many observers were predicting a major war in the imminent future.

But before turning to the Sino-Soviet question, I think we should ask ourselves what lessons, in terms of strategy, the Chinese may have learned from the war in Vietnam. Vietnam has not necessarily confirmed the Chinese in their oft-repeated description of the United States as a "paper tiger." It has indeed confirmed the Chinese in their estimate that where a people have the will to make revolution and can appeal to weaknesses and instability in an existing regime, wars of national liberation have a good chance of success. It has also demonstrated to the Chinese the limits of conventional bombing of a nation that is still highly underdeveloped. But the unwillingness of the Chinese to take on the United States, or during this past year the Soviets, indicates that Peking is aware that the effects of conventional bombing may not be as limited to a country which, though still largely underdeveloped, does possess key military targets, in particular nuclear production facilities and important industrial, communication, and transportation centers. If this is true for conventional bombing, it is bound to be all the more true for Peking's recognition of the implication of a nuclear attack. Moreover, while North Vietnam had a backup support area in mainland China, Peking no longer possesses a similar rear guard in the Soviet Union.

THE SINO-SOVIET BORDER CONFLICT

The situation on the Sino-Soviet border which was brought dramatically to public attention with the military incidents of March 2 and 15 on Chen Pao (Damansky) Island in the Ussuri River provides a further opportunity to analyze the so-called adventurism and recklessness of the Peking regime. Difficulties along the Sino-Soviet border, whether in the area of Manchuria, Mongolia, or Sinkiang, appear to date from 1959 and parallel the growing tension in Sino-Soviet relations since that time, if not earlier. As the situation between Peking and Moscow became more tense in the early sixties, the Soviets in the 1965-1966 period began to strengthen their military forces along the border. Chinese troop deployments remained largely unchanged and what moves did take place in the 1966-1969 period could be attributed as readily to considerations of internal security as to those related to national defense. However, with enhanced Soviet troop strength, resulting in more intensive patrolling, and tensions arising from the Cultural Revolution, the probability of larger scale clashes involving more men and equipment increased.

This is not the place to indulge in an analysis of the two March incidents. However, on balance it would appear that the initial March incident was Chinese initiated, while the second incident represented a demonstration of Soviet military muscle and warning to the Chinese.

The question here is the strategic/tactical parameters of the border issue, i.e. the reactions of the Chinese and the Russians on the military or military threat levels. These parameters were established early in the game. Despite their usual verbal bellicosity, the Chinese took steps two days after the first incident, on March 4, to state their strategic defensive posture when they revived the formula— this time in relation to the Soviet Union: "We will not attack unless we are attacked." This formula, so remininiscent of Peking's statements on 1965 with regard to

Vietnam, underlines China's defensive stance vis-a-vis the Soviet Union demonstrates its awareness of its vulnerability to a Soviet attack and its unwillingness to take risks which might result in a confrontation with the Soviet Union.

This defensive stance represented a genuine concern within the Chinese leadership with regard to Soviet intentions, for even before the March 15 incident the Soviet Union was making pointed reference to Soviet strategic rocket forces in the Far East. This type of threat warning was to continue throughout the summer with reported Soviet sounding out of the East European Communist governments with regard to a possible preemptive strike against China's nuclear facilities. Peking's concern, its defensive stance, the non-threatening deployment of Chinese troops was to some degree contradicted by continuing minor Chinese provocations along the Soviet border between March and September. In the sense the Chinese were reversing their usual formula: "Despise the enemy strategically; respect him tactically." Now the Chinese were respecting the enemy strategically, but in a number of minor ways despising him tactically. To what extent the contradiction in Chinese behavior was the result of differences within the Peking leadership is an open question. Logic would appear to argue that differences were bound to exist given the continued presence of professionally oriented officers in the leadership, as differences may have existed later over the course of the negotiations with the Soviets.

In any event, despite the reading of Mao quotations from the Chinese side of the border, Peking took a number of steps to cool the situation and agreed to renew border negotiations with the Russians in October 1969. Thus, the Sino-Soviet dispute of the past year further underlines China's defensive strategy, her willingness, within limits, to engage in low level provocations, but at the same time her unwillingness to become involved in a direct confrontation with the Soviet Union.

THE JAPAN EQUATION

The foregoing examples briefly outline the nature of China's military policies and strategy during the past five and a half years, that is, since the detonation of its first nuclear device. I would like to turn now to those factors which may throw further light on Peking's future use of its nuclear power. A crucial element in China's military thinking, and one which has frequently been ignored, is China's reaction to the possibility of Japan developing its own nuclear capability within the next decade. To what extent Japan is not ruling out its nuclear option remains a controversial issue among observers of the Japanese political/military scene.

During the past five years, for a number of reasons—the Chinese nuclear detonations, the non-proliferation treaty, the U.S. announcement in September 1967 of its intention to deploy a light ABM system on grounds of the China threat—the debate on security issues in Japan has widened. A far larger number of Japanese appear prepared to support "made-in-Japan nuclears" than is usually credited. Polls of Japanese public opinion during the second half of 1968 and the first half of 1969 indicate a rising public interest in a Japanese nuclear capability.[1] Time does not permit an extensive discussion of the various, though limited, groups that support or the reasons they support "made-in-Japan nuclears." Among some of the reasons cited are: the reemergent role of nationalism; the acquisition of political leverage on the United States, a greater voice in decision-making in the Far East, and a position more independent of the United States; and the neutral/nuclear syndrome that characterizes the attitude of many young people of college age.

To date, the Japanese Government has taken a position opposing Japan's development or possession of nuclear weapons. The latest disclaimer was that made by the recently appointed Director General of the Defense Agency, Yasuhiro Nakasone, who on March 5 reversed his earlier position supporting the indigenous development of nuclear weapons when he declared that "Japan should not, now or in the future, build its own nuclear weapons."

Particularly since the U.S.-Japan joint communique of November 1969 on the reversion of Okinawa, the Chinese have on several occasions referred to the possibility of Japan developing its own nuclear weapons. These charges have usually been in the context of Japan reviving military aggression in Asia as an instrument of the United States or as an independent power and of harboring designs on

---

[1] In the fall of 1968, 20-25 percent of the respondents in three public opinion polls supported the indigenous development of nuclear weapons. In a poll conducted in the spring of 1969, 45 percent of the respondents believed that Japan should either immediately (2 percent), in the near future (16 percent), or eventually (27 percent) arm itself with nuclear weapons.

Taiwan, South Korea, and Indochina. This harder line toward Japan indicates a growing sensitivity on the part of Peking to Japan's growing role in Asia and internationally. The Chinese must be aware that should Japan opt for the indigenous development of nuclear weapons, it could, because of its industrial/technological base, do so at a rapid pace.

However brief the foregoing discussion, the key question is: what does this mean for China's strategy? Any strengthening of Japan militarily, particularly as far as nuclear weapons are concerned, whether in conjunction with the United States or on a Gaullist basis, would be bound to make China even more cautious in its military policies, if such can be the case. China might pick up some political benefits, for a nuclear armed Japan would revive suspicions of Japan's intentions in the area. This might be offset, however, by the fact that many of the countries of Asia look toward the highly industrialized Japan for economic assistance. Moreover, Australia and India might ask whether or not it was necessary to follow Japan's example. China could then exist in a highly brittle political/military environment. The Chinese could be confronted with still another nuclear power on its periphery and a competitor for leadership in Asia. The present balance of power might be further complicated to China's disadvantage. Any attempt on the part of Peking to pressure Japan politically as a means of restricting U.S. or joint U.S.-Japan policies in the area in the event of crisis situations involving, for example, Korea or Taiwan, could conceivably lead to Chinese miscalculation and unpredictable consequences. Thus, a Japanese regional nuclear capability deployed and operated either independently of the United States or in conjunction with the U.S. strategic capability may well have the effect of limiting China's political/psychological use of its emerging nuclear capability, let alone any overt military use. China could well be confronted with diminishing returns from its development of a nuclear-missile capability.

Some observers have argued that because of this, the nuclearization of Japan would be in the interest of both Japan and the United States. The best answer to such a proposition were the reasons given by Minister Nakasone on March 5 as to why Japan should not build its own nuclear weapons: the "triangular stalemate" developing between the United States, the Soviet Union and Communist China; the increase in defense costs at the expense of expenditures for education and technological advancement or social security; the effect of such a decision on the national consensus; and the inability of Japan to achieve an effective second strike capability.

CHINA'S NUCLEAR MIX

Another factor that must be taken into account before projecting the way in which China is likely to use its emerging nuclear missile capability is the type of nuclear mix the Chinese may be envisaging. Considerable controversy exists as to whether the Chinese will give priority to an ICBM or to an MRBM capability. As I have noted on several occasions, my own evaluation, based primarily on an analysis of political considerations, has been that the Chinese are likely to give emphasis to the deployment of an operational MRBM system, though this does not necessarily rule out their testing and development of a token ICBM or submarine launched missile capability.

Since coming to this conclusion, a new ingredient has entered the picture—the detonation by China of its first underground nuclear device on September 28, 1969. The two more plausible explanations for an underground test at that time appear to be 1) that the Chinese are interested in setting up controlled experiments whereby they can more effectively analyze nuclear design information as well as the physical effects of a detonation, and 2) that the Chinese are interested in denying debris and other technical intelligence material to both Western and Soviet analysts because they are beginning to test tactical nuclear weapons designed for battlefield use. These explanations are not mutually exclusive and may well be mutually reinforcing. The objectives of conducting a controlled experiment for the purpose of more effectively analyzing nuclear design material, as well as the physical effects of a detonation, fall within the general pattern of their tests to date, i.e., the development of a three-megaton device reduced in size so as to be usable as a warhead on a medium-range (1500 mile) or an intercontinental range ballistic missile.

The more controversial explanation—but the one toward which I, for reasons to be given, lean—is that the Chinese may be experimenting not only with reducing the size of the device but also with minimizing the amount of fissionable material in the device with plutonium the key element, in order to develop a tactical nuclear weapons capability, that is weapons that could initially be carried by a fighter or fighter-bomber. This explanation is supported on several grounds. First, that of timing. Timing plays no important role insofar as the test was tied to R&D in the reduction of the size of the warhead. On the other hand, timing would play an important international political role were the test designed to develop tactical nuclear weapons. The Chinese may well have considered it imperative to deny debris or technical intelligence to Western and Soviet observers at this time. They may believe that positive indicators—as would be the case were the test to be carried out above the ground—that they were experimenting with fission (plutonium) weapons would be regarded as provocative by the United States in the light of the situation in Vietnam and even more so by the Soviet Union in view of the tension on the border.

The tactical nuclear weapon thesis has generally been downgraded by Western analysts in the belief that the Chinese were more likely to go for the bigger bang, i.e., the three-megaton thermonuclear warhead designed for an ICBM. Or the development of tactical nuclear weapons has been regarded as a long-term follow-on to the megaton warhead.

Yet Chinese military literature contains continuing hints of an interest in tactical nuclear weapons. The best evidence to date was that which was made available in the *Kung-tso Tung-hsun* (*KTTH*) material, better known as the *Bulletin of Activities of the People's Liberation Army*, during the first half of 1961. It is interesting to note that the 1961 documentation made no reference to the use of large-yield nuclear weapons by the Chinese, though it referred specifically to the future use of tactical nuclear weapons. Tactical training directives emphasized the use of advanced weapons and defense against such weapons. Units above the regiment level were to be instructed not only in defense but also in the principles of using atomic and chemical weapons, and even in methods of exploiting the results of Chinese-initiated surprise attacks with atomic and chemical weapons.

The context as well as the substance of the *KTTH* material tends to suggest that as early as 1961 the Chinese were considering the battlefield use of nuclear weapons. When read in context Chinese directives would appear to be referring to land-type warfare. This provides us with clues as to why the Chinese may be interested at an earlier date than usually credited in including tactical nuclear weapons in their nuclear arsenal. The Chinese, despite the improbability from a U.S. point of view (though not necessarily from a Soviet), remain the captive of the concept of invasion by enemy ground forces for the purpose of control and occupation following a surprise nuclear attack. Tactical nuclear weapons delivered by aircraft might well be regarded by the Chinese as an important attack weapon against troop concentrations, landing operations, etc. Similarly, the one area in East Asia where the use by the United States of battlefield nuclear weapons can be considered with any degree of plausibility is Korea. The Chinese might believe that the mere possession of battlefield nuclear weapons on their part could act as a deterrent to a U.S. use of such weapons in the event of a crisis situation, or that at least their possession by the Chinese would lead such countries as Japan to place pressures on the United States to deny itself the use of tactical nuclear weapons. And now with the tension along the border with the Soviet Union the Chinese may see further deterrent advantages in the possession of battlefield nuclears. The threat of their use, or their first use, is an entirely different matter, for such action would leave the Chinese open to the risk of escalation to higher levels of warfare they would not want to contemplate. But as a backup for conventional action—and the Chinese have shown no intention of downgrading their conventional forces despite their nuclear development—the possession of tactical nuclear weapons could have important payoffs for the Chinese, particularly insofar as it complicated military decisionmaking within the U.S. and Soviet Governments.

THE NIXON DOCTRINE

The Nixon doctrine has met with mixed reaction from Peking. The doctrine, first enunciated by President Nixon on July 25, 1969 in a press interview on Guam, can be interpreted as saying that the United States will rely in the self-effort of Asian countries to resolve their political, economic, and social problems; that the United States will increasingly consider it the responsibility of Asian countries to meet the threat of conventional aggression; and that the United States will remain prepared to counter a nuclear threat or attack by a nuclear power. It remains unclear where and under what circumstances the United States would be prepared to counter conventional aggression by a nuclear power.

Contrary to what might have been one's initial impression, the Chinese have not interpreted the Nixon doctrine as the beginning of U.S. disengagement from the area. To some extent the Chinese appear to have read the Nixon doctrine as increasing U.S. reliance on the use of nuclear weapons. At the same time there is the implication in their comments that U.S. options, in particular the use of nuclear weapons, in responding to a broad spectrum of threats, are now more limited. Equally important, the Chinese have interpreted the Nixon doctrine, especially after the November 20 joint U.S.-Japan communique on the reversion of Okinawa, as an attempt by the United States to turn Japan into the instrument of U.S. aggression in Asia.

The first assessment, that is, increased U.S. reliance on the use of nuclears, could lead the Chinese to believe that the United States had given up certain of its flexibility in responding to Chinese or Chinese-inspired aggression in Asia. The Chinese could also calculate that the United States would be reluctant to use nuclear weapons in response to any but the most serious type of overt aggression in the area. Or the Chinese might believe that if the United States were confronted with the choice between a nuclear response or no response, it might opt for the latter. While these calculations might lead the Chinese to believe that both the political/military value of China's nuclear missile capability and the role of China's conventional forces had been enhanced, such a conclusion might well be recognized by the Chinese, who do not rule out irrationality in U.S. behavior, as opening the way to serious miscalculation of U.S. intentions on their part. In fact, the ambiguity that characterizes certain aspects of the new doctrine would appear to argue in favor of caution on China's part.

The introduction of the Japan equation into Chinese strategic thinking, as already noted, underlines the political/military use of China's nuclear missile capability, a use with perhaps diminishing returns.

In sum, a more accurate assessment of China's interpretation of the Nixon doctrine and whether it regards the shifts in U.S. Asian policy as opportunities to be exploited or as increasing pressures on China will only be found in Chinese responses to concrete U.S. actions in the area in the future. Meanwhile, China is not likely to be incautious in testing the underlying intent of the Nixon doctrine.

PEKING'S USE OF ITS EVOLVING NUCLEAR MISSILE CAPABILITY

The foregoing updating of factors which may influence China's present military thinking has been necessary in order to establish a basis for projecting China's future use of a nuclear-missile capability, whether intercontinental or regional. While it remains impossible to predict with any degree of certainty the long-term future, my analysis of China's military doctrine and behavior to date has given me no reason to believe that when China is in possession of a nuclear delivery capability, it will be more prepared than at present to engage in a high-risk military policy.

Whatever the priority the Chinese give to their nuclear-missile program, they will still have to live with the vast military/technological gap that will continue to exist between China on the one hand and the United States on the other, and for that matter the Soviet Union. At least two factors characterize the U.S. deterrent posture, that is, a posture that would both deter overt Chinese military action and prevent Chinese miscalculation: 1) Its massive military superiority to the Chinese (and China's awareness of this superiority), and 2) U.S. preparedness to make the risk of any overt Chinese military operations extremely high and the communication of this preparedness to Peking, as much by the deployment of certain weapon systems as by declaratory policy. Time does not permit an extensive discussion of the components of a U.S. deterrent posture but it is my conclusion that the Chinese are more sensitive to weapon systems deployed in the region than any number of Minutemen in silos in the Continental United States. The latter could always be viewed by Peking as designed primarily for an attack against the Soviet Union. Moreover, the Chinese could also calculate, or miscalculate, that the United States might be reluctant to threaten the use of, or use, such a weapon system as the Minuteman because it could lead to misinterpretation on the part of the Soviet Union. Consequently, there is the need to decouple the Chinese and Soviet threats. Such weapon systems as sea- and land-based aircraft, the Seventh Fleet, and the Polaris-Poseidon system offer, in my view, the preferred deterrent to the Chinese.

Furthermore, any real improvement in Sino-Soviet relations appears unlikely in the foreseeable future. And even if such an improvement were to materialize, the relationship could hardly be any better than that which existed in the mid-fifties—a relationship which fell short of supporting China's external military objectives, as was so amply demonstrated at the time of Quemoy 1958.

Nor does the death of Mao suggest any basic change in the cautious nature of China's military policies. Well before his death the leadership in China appears to be returning to the control of technocratic-professional types. China today gives every evidence of being under the control of the military and the military have demonstrated in the past their caution and defense mindedness. And as China develops an ever-increasing vested interest in its modernization and industrialization it will be all the more likely to shun the risk of devastating retaliation.

Consequently, in attempting to project China's future military behavior, to suggest a Chinese first strike or threat of such strike against one or a few U.S. cities in the absence of an ABM defense at a time when China may possess something like 10 to 25 ICBMs—should it opt to develop that many—is like suggesting a willingness on the part of the Chinese leadership to commit national suicide. So long as the United States remains prepared to make the risks of overt Chinese military operations extremely high, the Chinese are likely to avoid military initiatives that might invite massive U.S. nuclear retaliatory strikes against the mainland. Rather, in accordance with China's preferred foreign policy style, the Chinese are likely to make a low-risk and subtle use of their nuclear capability along political-military and propaganda lines with a view to achieving the following objectives:

1. The enhancement of China's international political stature.
2. In the event of an evolving crisis situation, the deterrence of a U.S. attack on the China mainland, as well as the imposition of restraints on U.S. military policies in the area.
3. The undermining of the U.S.-Asian alliance and security arrangements.
4. The inhibition of Asian nations' self-defense efforts.
5. The fostering of internal instability and, where chances of success appear high, national liberation movements.
6. The enhancement of the role of China's conventional forces.

Any token capability to threaten the U.S. homeland, or even test firing of a Chinese ICBM, will, of course, have political and prestige payoffs. The Chinese may also hope that, when in possession of a token or even limited ICBM capability, they could in the course of an evolving crisis situation create just the type of uncertainty in the United States that some observers have referred to in discussing the uses of a Chinese ICBM—that is, an uncertainty which would lead the United States to limit its military responses, particularly any consideration of the use of nuclear weapons. But if such should prove the case, it is an uncertainty which we will have created for ourselves by attributing to the Chinese a degree of recklessness and adventurism which does not in fact exist. The Chinese may also hope by way of an ICBM capability to cast doubt on the reliability of the United States in the minds of friendly Asians.

By means of a regional capability, the Chinese may hope to create a similar uncertainty as to U.S. intentions among U.S. allies and friendly neutrals in the area, to exploit Asian fear of involvement in a nuclear war, and concern that any U.S. confrontation with a nuclear-armed China would escalate into a nuclear, if not general, war. Peking might calculate that fear on these various scores would lead Asian nations to assert pressures on the United States to avoid any confrontations with China—conventional or nuclear. It is thus quite indirectly that Peking would hope to make gains. An overt nuclear threat to a U.S. ally or friendly neutral would represent such a high-risk indertaking that the Chinese are likely to avoid its use.

The Chinese may also see a nuclear capability, particularly a capability designed for battlefield use, as enhancing the role of their conventional forces, first, as a deterrent to invasion and, secondly, as a means of deterring a U.S. introduction of tactical nuclears should a conflict break out, for example, on the Korean Peninsula.[1]

In sum, from my analysis of China's past and current Chinese military doctrine and policies, I would conclude that China is unlikely to adopt incautious

---

[1] The Chinese position on arms control has carefully avoided any reference to the reduction of conventional forces, specifically ruling out arrangements that might include such forces.

military initiatives in its use of a nuclear delivery capability whether of an intercontinental or regional character. At one time it looked as though a nuclear-armed China, because of the instabilities present in many parts of Asia, would be likely to find ample opportunity to advance toward her long-term objectives in Asia through reliance on the political-military and propaganda uses of forces. Today I am not so sure that it will find even these political payoffs from the possession of a nuclear-missile capability. Because of Soviet suspicion of a nuclear armed China and Japan's possible development of her own nuclear capability, China's nuclear-missile development may prove to have diminishing returns. China may discover that there is little merit in being a second- or a third-rate nuclear power—that the problems such a status invites may well offset even the political advantages.

IMPLICATIONS OF A CHINA-ORIENTED ABM FOR SINO-U.S. RELATIONS

It would thus appear from the foregoing that the deployment of an anti-China ABM system by the United States is irrelevant to the type of strategy China is likely to pursue when in possession of a nuclear-missile capability. Nevertheless, the question must be asked: should the United States deploy a China-oriented system, what effect would this have on China's policies, in particular its relations with the United States?

In contrast with Peking's reaction in March 1969 to the President's decision to deploy the Safeguard system, the Chinese, probably because of the revival of government-to-government talks in Warsaw, failed to report the President's January 30 announcement that the United States would initiate Phase II of the Safeguard program as a defense against China's growing nuclear-missile capability. In commenting on the President's foreign policy report to Congress, Peking also ignored the President's reference to the ABM and the China "threat." However, the NCNA statement boasted that the President "had to admit China's growing strength and her tremendous influence in the world" and his expressions of "apprehensions over the fact that 'China has acquired thermonuclear weapons' and thus broken the U.S. and Soviet nuclear monopoly." Thus the United States gives not only prestige but also credibility to a threat which is still far from materializing—at least in the eyes of less sophisticated Asians. At the same time deployment of a China oriented ABM reinforces Peking's image of the United States as basically hostile to China. To what extent is another matter.[2] However, any reinforcement of Peking's paranoia regarding the West, particularly when the justification is subject to serious challenge, is completely inconsistent with other moves on the part of the United States to reduce tensions with China. U.S. gestures regarding trade, exchange of scholars and newspapermen, could be seriously prejudiced. Nor can we rule out the possibility that there may be elements within the Chinese leadership that might be searching for some new relationship with the United States, however tentative and experimental. If such should prove to be the case their efforts would be undermined by new indications of U.S. hostility.

On the scientific/technological side, the Chinese could, as some observers have suggested, give priority to the development of penetration aids. Quite aside from China's technological capability to pursue such a development, it is necessary to ask what this would gain for them. If we accept the premise that I have been stressing that the Chinese are unlikely to be reckless in their use of a nuclear missile capability, pen aids simply do not gain anything for them.

Another possibility and a far more likely one is that U.S. deployment of an anti-China ABM system will reinforce the priority the Chinese are likely to give to the development and operational deployment of MRBM's and on the political/military use of a regional capability.

An equally important effect could be that on the Japanese. In addition to Chinese recklessness and miscalculation, the deployment of a China-oriented ABM has been justified on the grounds of the confidence such deployment would instill in U.S. allies, such as Japan, that the United States would come to Japan's assistance if subjected to Chinese blackmail. Contrary to this thesis the very opposite has in some instances turned out to be the case. There has been some suggestion in Japan that such deployment by the United States would mean that the United States would respond to Chinese aggressive moves only if the U.S. homeland were threatened. The Japanese may also believe that as a consequence

---

[2] The deployment of an anti-China ABM system may not make as much difference to the Chinese as one might at first glance suspect. Other issues such as Taiwan, U.S. bases, and weapon deployments in the area, U.S.-Japan relations, and so forth may play a far greater role in contributing to China's image of a hostile United States.

of U.S. ABM deployment their country has become a lightning rod so far as Chinese nuclears are concerned. This concern combined with a questioning of U.S. reliability has on occasion led some Japanese to raise the possibility of a regional ABM system and again on occasion been used to rationalize Japan's indigenous development of nuclear weapons.

The Chinese could also interpret the U.S. deployment of a China-oriented ABM, particularly if agreement were reached with the Soviet Union in the course of the SALT talks on a level of ABM deployment which would be China-oriented, as a further example of U.S.-Soviet collusion against China.

CONCLUSION

In conclusion, I do not believe the deployment by the United States of a China-oriented ABM is necessary. Arguments based on China's projected recklessness when in possession of a limited nuclear-missile capability, China's possible miscalculation of U.S. intentions or because our friends in Asia are likely to feel more confident of U.S. support if the U.S. homeland is defended against a theoretical Chinese attack do not stand up under close analysis. In turn, I would take the position that with time the possible payoff's that China will gain from a nuclear-missile capability are diminishing, even the political-military payoffs from which I believed they at some time expected some dividends. I also believe that revival of the China "threat" as a key reason for ABM deployment by the United States is likely to create more problems than it resolves. It will not only prejudice any attempt on the part of the United States to enter into some type of understanding with Peking, it could reinforce charges of U.S. collusion with the Soviet Union. Moreover, it might lead other countries in the area to give a higher credence to China's nuclear-missile capability than it merits, to question U.S. reliability, to stimulate demands for a regional ABM system, and to encourage those governments capable of doing so to opt for their own development of nuclear weapons.

Senator GORE. Would you like to put some questions to Mrs. Hsieh before we hear Mr. Barnett?

Senator FULBRIGHT. If I might, I would like to ask one or two.

COMMUNIST CHINESE VISAS

I have one question that does not grow out of your statement so much as my curiosity. Have the Chinese given any visas at all to any Americans to your knowledge in the last 3 or 4 years?

Mrs. HSIEH. Not to my knowledge, sir. I believe the last time Edgar Snow applied for a visa he was denied one.

Senator FULBRIGHT. I had heard that. I wondered if you knew about it. No one has been granted one?

Mrs. HSIEH. No, there has been no reciprocal reaction on China's part unfortunately.

COMMUNIST CHINESE ATTITUDE TOWARD SOUTHEAST ASIA

Senator FULBRIGHT. Do you think the Chinese feel that Vietnamization means a permanent client state of the U.S. in South Vietnam?

Mrs. HSIEH. Yes, sir.

Senator FULBRIGHT. What is the attitude of the Chinese toward a genuin neutralization of Indochina, assuming that that was done in such a way as to be credible? Would they like it or not if it could be done?

Mrs. HSIEH. I think we have to make a distinction between Chinese objectives and North Vietnamese objectives.

I think—and here I would want to say that there are other people who have followed more closely the political aspects of the China-Southeast Asian relationship than I have—the Chinese would be satisfied with a neutral Southeast Asia with a pro-China foreign policy, the type of relationship that existed at one time with Burma and Cambodia. I don't think they have any intention, let us say, of wanting to invade and directly to control Indochina.

I remember a statement made by Chou En-Lai a number of years ago. I believe it was in 1964 or 1965, in which he said, in answer to a question as to whether the Chinese wanted to invade and occupy Southeast Asia—forgive me for using this language but it represents about the best translation—that the Chinese would have to have holes in their heads to want to invade and control Southeast Asia.

Senator FULBRIGHT. It seems to me that is a very appropriate expression. We know lots of people with holes in their heads. It is not unusual expression. [Laughter.]

There is a story that, I think at the Cairo meeting, President Roosevelt inquired of Chiang Kai-shek if he didn't wish to take Vietnam, or something to this effect, and he said no, that they weren't Chinese. Did you ever hear such a story?

Mrs. HSIEH. I never heard that, sir, but Southeast Asians are regarded by the Chinese—whether Nationalist or Communist—as third- or fourth-class Chinese.

Senator FULBRIGHT. They weren't qualified to be first-class, full-fledged Chinese and they didn't wish to incorporate them. They might, as you say, have good relations.

CHINESE SENSE OF SUPERIORITY

Isn't it surprising how much of the ancient attitude of being the central empire of the world has survived? It surprises me.

Mrs. HSIEH. No, this is very typical——

Senator FULBRIGHT. It has survived, hasn't it?

Mrs. HSIEH. Yes.

Senator FULBRIGHT. In spite of all their difficulties?

Mrs. HSIEH. Yes, and the traditional Chinese superiority complex also survives.

Senator FULBRIGHT. How do they reconcile that to their sad state? Beginning with the opium wars and their inability to hold their own even in a most primitive way, how do they reconcile this superiority with their own situation?

Mrs. HSIEH. Well, you may be interested in one statement that I found very intriguing. After their first detonation of a nuclear device in October 1964, Chou En-Lai made a very revealing statement. He said in effect that, "This achievement on our part wipes out a hundred years of humiliation."

Senator FULBRIGHT. I don't see that it does, particularly in view of the fact that the primitive Americans have already many more of them. They haven't accomplished so much.

Mrs. HSIEH. Well, they are the first Asian power to develop nuclear weapons.

Senator FULBRIGHT. I don't know. This is an attitude that I find in other areas, but it is always unexplicable to me. I don't understand how people maintain this attitude of superiority. I just wondered how they do it.

EFFECT OF U.S. PRESENCE ON COMMUNIST CHINA

You have said you do not believe they have any intention of overrunning their neighbors.

Mrs. HSIEH. Yes, sir.

Senator FULBRIGHT. Does it make any difference whether we are present militarily in one of their neighbors?

Mrs. HSIEH. I don't think it makes a difference if we are militarily present in some of the areas provided we maintain a U.S. presence in the region. That is why I supported the maintenance of a U.S. deterrent posture in the western Pacific; that we retain a capability to act should the Chinese prove not to be as peace loving as some people have suggested.

Senator FULBRIGHT. I don't wish to suggest they are peace loving. I don't think anybody is particularly peace loving. It is whether it is in their own interests, whether they recognize their own interests or not. I think the great difficulty with this country is not whether it is peace loving. It is the difficulty of recognizing what is in our own best interests. It is in their own interests, not their Christian humility or peace-loving nature. Do you think they are peace loving or not?

Mrs. HSIEH. As I have mentioned the Chinese are very cautious in their military policies. I think they would think more than twice about any action that would lead to a confrontation with the United States in the western Pacific in view of the type of weapons system deployments there, the 7th Fleet, et cetera.

EFFECT OF U.S. WITHDRAWAL FROM SOUTH KOREA

Senator FULBRIGHT. I was leading to another question.

Does it make any difference in the attitude of the Chinese whether we maintain troops in South Korea? To put it another way if you would like, if we withdrew them would they overrun South Korea or participate——

Mrs. HSIEH. Not if we were prepared to move very rapidly back into South Korea, and that would mean the maintenance of deployments in the area.

But this raises a very interesting question, sir, whether we would have the capability to operate rapidly on a conventional basis or whether we would be confronted with only one type of response, a nuclear response.

Senator CASE. Mr. Chairman, may I just press that question?

Senator FULBRIGHT. Yes.

Senator CASE. They wouldn't if we were able to respond quickly from outside. Would they if we were not able to respond quickly from outside?

Mrs. HSIEH. If we were not able to respond quickly from outside, the possibility would then exist that the North Koreans, supported perhaps by the Chinese, might be willing to take higher risks than otherwise.

Senator FULBRIGHT. As a matter of fact, the North Koreans are only about half as many as the South Koreans. Without Chinese support and encouragement, there would be little likelihood they would overrun South Korea, would there?

Mrs. HSIEH. Yes, but they have a considerable military capability which has been provided by the Soviet Union.

Senator FULBRIGHT. Do you mean to say that this small Communist state, one-half as large as the great democracy of South Korea, is a more effective, forceful community and can overrun South Korea?

Mrs. HSIEH. In such contingency it is usually assumed that the North Koreans would not be acting alone.

COMMUNIST CHINESE INTEREST IN NORTH KOREAN TAKEOVER

Senator FULBRIGHT. I was assuming without China.

Of course, with China's full support they would. Could you explain why it is in the interest of China to have North Korea overrun South Korea. What good does that do China?

Mrs. HSIEH. It establishes the reunification of Korea under Communist jurisdiction. It poses a greater problem and possible threat to Japan. The Korean peninsula dominated by the Communists would again constitute the dagger poised at the heart of Japan. A unified Korea under a pro-Peking Korean domination would be very much in China's interest.

Senator FULBRIGHT. It would?

Mrs. HSIEH. Yes.

Senator FULBRIGHT. How would she benefit by it? Is it just the ideological idea of having a Communist state?

Mrs. HSIEH. It would eliminate the possibility of a renewal of conflict reoccurring on the Korean peninsula in which the Chinese might become involved. The situation would have been resolved satisfactorily to their advantage. It would also be easier for China to intimidate Japan.

I think the more important, the more interesting problem there today is the relationship between China and the Soviet Union. I think it is very possible, quite aside from our own posture in the area, that this very basic conflict that exists between China and the Soviet Union is a restraining factor on either one or the other supporting a North Korean move against South Korea.

Senator FULBRIGHT. I would think so.

U.S. INTEREST IN SOUTH KOREA

Do you think it is of vital importance to the United States own interests whether the present government or a different government rules South Korea?

Mrs. HSIEH. Yes, sir; I believe there have been such considerable advances made in South Korea during the last 6 years, since about 1964, that we have a continued interest in seeing the maintenance of a free, viable government in South Korea.

Senator FULBRIGHT. I wish you would outline for me clearly and simply the interest of the United States. The people of the United States are overwhelmed with domestic problems. How does what happens in South Korea benefit the ordinary citizen of the United States? This is what I am unable to make plain to my constituents.

Mrs. HSIEH. It is in part an interest that derives from our interest in Japan. Japan is the key country so far as I am concerned, the key country of Asia.

Senator FULBRIGHT. The key to what?

Mrs. HSIEH. The key country of Asia. The second——

Senator FULBRIGHT. I think that is all interesting. The Japanese are doing very well. How does the idea that Japan is a key country affect my constituents in Arkansas? I am trying to relate it to the people of this country and not to some ideological conception. How would you relate it if you were talking to a group in my home town? Would you impress upon them the importance of South Korea?

Mrs. HSIEH. A reunited Korea under Communist jurisdiction would pose a much greater threat to the type of Japan that we would hope to continue to see in the area. It would, on one hand, intimidate the Japanese and possibly cause them to move toward the Communist camp.

Senator FULBRIGHT. In what respect? Do you mean they would send their textiles there instead of to South Carolina?

Mrs. HSIEH. No, politically.

Senator FULBRIGHT. How would you say that affects the people of my State? What difference would it make to them whether the Japanese thought more kindly of the Chinese or less kindly? How would it affect their fortunes and their lives?

Mrs. HSIEH. I think if we were to fail to maintain a reasonably good relationship with Japan, this would be the beginning of a policy of complete U.S. disengagement from the Western Pacific. I think it is in the interest of your constituents that the United States maintains a presence and an interest in the Western Pacific and thus contributes to the maintenance of stability in the area.

Senator FULBRIGHT. Then you feel it is inconsistent for Japan to have good relations with us and the Chinese at the same time?

Mrs. HSIEH. Within limits they may well be able to. I don't know if the Chinese would be satisfied with such a situation. Moreover, the Japanese are developing a much greater economic interest in Taiwan in contrast with several years ago. It may become increasingly difficult for the Japanese to work out their relationship with mainland China because of this growing economic interest in Taiwan. Taiwan is an area for Japanese investment. It provides Japan with cheap labor, the products of which go into the domestic market in Japan.

Senator FULBRIGHT. Do you think it is in our interest to enable Japan to cultivate the market in Taiwan?

Do you agree with this, Mr. Barnett, while Madam Hsieh thinks of this?

STATEMENT OF A. DOAK BARNETT, SENIOR FELLOW, THE BROOKINGS INSTITUTION

Mr. BARNETT. I would agree that we do have an interest in minimizing the chance of increased instability and tension in Northeast Asia, and I believe that if anything dramatic happened on the Korean Peninsula, if there were a takeover by the North of the South, it might do any of several things. It might stimulate the Japanese to go nuclear, for example, and a confrontation between a nuclear Japan and a nuclear China would not be in the interests of stability and peace in that area. What happens in Korea is important.

LIKELIHOOD OF WAR IN KOREA

But in my view, there is not a very high likelihood of a war in Korea. It seems to me that what has been evolving in that part of the world is a very complex interrelationship between four powers, and I think the Japanese interest in Korea, which has increased, plus the Soviet restraints on China, make it unlikely that the Chinese will commit themselves to back a North Korean attack on the South, which means that it is unlikely that the North will feel that it can undertake military action against the South.

So I am not really alarmed, as many South Koreans are. They are quite uneasy about the North's intentions because Pyongyang is very bellicose verbally. But I would say, nevertheless that what happens in that part of the world should be of very great interest to your constituents, because war in that part of the world would inevitably affect the United States' interests, it seems to me.

U.S. INTEREST IN KOREA

Senator FULBRIGHT. It is amazing how only a few years ago it didn't seem to be so important to our constituents. Suddenly it has become vitally important to the extent that it is bankrupting our country to carry out this policy. It amazes me that we got along without our having to be there, and suddenly we have to be all over the world. Every place is now strategic to every expert in the particular area, wherever it may be.

Mr. BARNETT. I would say if one looks at the history of the last 50 to 75 years, Korea is not just "another place," in strategic terms.

Senator CASE. It might have been better if we had been interested earlier.

Mr. BARNETT. If we had been interested in Korea earlier, it is conceivable that we might have affected the way things developed in Asia in the first half of this century. Korea is an extraordinarily strategic area where the interests of the Soviet Union, Japan, and China have clashed, and it has been an area where developments in the past have led to war.

Now, I am not arguing that the U.S. has to make a huge investment or maintain a huge presence in Korea. I think this is a different issue.

Senator FULBRIGHT. That is the issue to which I am coming.

Mr. BARNETT. We are now maintaining what?

Senator FULBRIGHT. 50,000.

Mr. BARNETT. Well, I think it is possible that over time we may be able to reduce this number.

Senator FULBRIGHT. I think we put over $7 billion in economic assistance into South Korea. This isn't counting the very substantial cost to us of the support of our own troops. If this were the only one of these little client states we had, perhaps we could take it, but it is one after another to more or less of a degree. We put almost the same amount, I think, into Taiwan.

Mr. BARNETT. I personally do not think there are many places, certainly not a great many places, that seem to have as strategic and important a position in relation to wider areas and the larger problems.

Senator FULBRIGHT. I find it difficult to convey to people the great importance to us of the fortunes and the kind of government in a particular geographical area. It is still hard for me to say whether Korea should be divided. I have my preferences. We would all like to have it run very much like our country, I suppose, but I don't see that there is a great fundamental significance that warrants the bankruptcy of our own country, which is virtually what we have now.

Mr. BARNETT. Senator, I don't think one has to argue that we have to determine exactly the type of government that exists in a country like Korea.

Senator FULBRIGHT. What is it that is so important? What difference does it make finally when you get down to it, whether South Korea rules North or North rules South? These are two small areas 10,000 miles away.

What difference does it make to the ordinary people here if South and North Korea are merged, if they are separated, or if they are ruled by Mr. X or Mr. Y?

Mr. BARNETT. If Japan, China, and the Soviet Union were indifferent to who rules Korea, and if what happened in Korea were not likely to have very great consequences involving those three powers, then I would say that probably our interest would be substantially less.

Senator FULBRIGHT. Why doesn't Japan look after Korea? Japan is quite able if it is all that important to her. If it is a dagger at her heart, why doesn't she protect it?

Mr. BARNETT. I would not want Japan to remilitarize.

U.S. FOREIGN SPENDING QUESTIONED

Senator FULBRIGHT. Therefore, we are going to be the only great military power. Who is going to pay for it? The Japanese are not a bit anxious to pay for our military power.

Mrs. HSIEH. Sir, I think we should consider very carefully how far we would want Japan to assume the complete responsibility for the security of free Asia. I believe this question of the reunification of Korea could greatly enhance the very limited movement now in Japan toward an indigenous development of nuclear weapons. I do not see an indigenous development of nuclear weapons on Japan's part as either in the interest of the United States or Japan or as contributing to peace and stability in the area. I think it would so complicate the picture in the Western Pacific that we might be drawn into a much more unpredictable situation than we are in today.

Senator FULBRIGHT. Can't almost the same kind of argument be made about Germany, where we have more than 300,000 troops?

Mrs. HSIEH. Yes, sir.

Senator FULBRIGHT. Therefore, we will be expected to maintain the same kind of situation in Germany. This goes on indefinitely. We have substantial forces in Turkey, and we have substantial forces in Spain, and we have substantial forces in Okinawa. Therefore, this is the only way. Everyone apparently has given up all hope whatever in even thinking of making the United Nations work or any alternative to the United States maintaining troops at every trouble spot in the world, and there are plenty of them.

Did it ever occur to you that the South Koreans would not want us to vacate regardless of what happens because they are the recipients of enormous amounts of taxpayers' money from this country every year? This year there was a special effort made. There was $160 million, I think, in the regular budget and the House of Representatives by an extraordinary move, without approval of the Bureau of the Budget or the Administration, added $50 million more. This is $200 million for a country that is quite small. Wouldn't the last thing they want be for us to believe that they could exist on their own? It is against their interests to give the slightest encouragement to us to withdraw.

Mrs. HSIEH. But the visible effects of this type of economic assistance and the increased stability there is unimaginable to anyone who saw Korea even 6 years ago.

Senator FULBRIGHT. What good does that do the people in Arkansas who pay the bills? This is what you seem to completely forget. This is not an experiment in a laboratory.

Mrs. HSIEH. Let me make another point.

You suggested that it might be advisable to turn over the defense of these areas to another country, Germany on the European side, Japan in Asia. However, it may well be cheaper in the long run for us to maintain the responsibility in these areas than to turn them over to proxies which may have rather different interests and objectives than our own. I think this would be of a definite concern to your constituents.

REASONS FOR U.S. MILITARY PRESENCE

Senator CASE. Mr. Chairman, may I just interject here because I think you have gone to the heart of the most sophisticated defense of kind of proliferation of our power all over the world. And I am not prepared to say it is the wrong position. But it is perfectly true, as you suggest, that what we have done, and what our policy now is (and it may be right), is to maintain American troops all over the world, not to fight but to keep things in status quo and pacified, and this really is deeply believed by many students of this problem.

Senator FULBRIGHT. I know.

Senator CASE. Your idea may be right, and I am willing to be persuaded, but I do think we ought to recognize it as just this: We are not there as aggressors in any sense. We are there in the effort to maintain those balances of power and those tensions in status quo more or less to prevent a worse situation.

Senator FULBRIGHT. We don't know what would happen actually if we withdrew from Korea. The South Koreans do everything possible to persuade us it would be disastrous if we withdrew because they don't want to give up the money.

Senator CASE. That is, I think, a relatively marginal point.

Senator FULBRIGHT. It is not very nice to call attention to these matters in public, but it is a fact. It is a fact of life and we have given it and you know it. It is income-tax-paying time next week and it is very important.

Senator CASE. Mr. Chairman, I don't disagree but I do say if there is a basic fundamental reason for us being there, the fact some crooks, some cheap chiselers made some money on us is relatively unimportant.

Senator GORE. Let me make a small contribution and state the ne plus ultra in which the U.S. security is involved—as to which of the brother Princes Souvanna Phouma or Souphanouvong sit on the Laotian throne.

Senator FULBRIGHT. One is a Communist and one is an autocrat. You take your choice.

Senator GORE. Wasn't Souvanna Phouma recommended by the Soviet?

Senator FULBRIGHT. He was. We call him a Communist, but he is now our Communist, whatever he is. [Laughter.]

DOMESTIC EFFECT OF U.S. MILITARY SPENDING

I won't prolong it any more, but I will, in answer to you, say that if it is true that someone has to play this role, I submit it has to be an international obligation. The United States is going broke. We spent all yesterday afternoon on a pay raise that cost something like $4 billion. What does this do? It only adds to the inflation which caused the pay raise. We are in a vicious circle of going broke by raising wages. Costs go up and then the costs go up more because we raise wages. You know that. This is what is happening. We have the highest rate of inflation we have ever experienced, I believe, unless it may have been as high in the Civil War, which is not a very good criterion.

I think we are a disintegrating society unless we can do something about this kind of problem. Every expert feels that his particular area is the strategic area. If someone who is in Latin America testifies here, he will tell you what happens in the Dominican Republic is just as critical as what happens in Korea.

If it is West Germany or East Germany or Berlin, it is just as critical to the welfare of the world and our people ought to be delighted to spend unlimited amounts to support troops in West Germany and anywhere else.

Senator GORE. May I suggest that Professor Barnett give his testimony and then we will have a free-for-all.

Senator CASE. It seems to me, and I am not again questioning you, but would it be fair to describe our chairman's position as espousing the benign neglect which had been advocated in other quarters?

Senator GORE. I will sit back and let you aim that at him.

Would you proceed, Dr. Barnett?

Mr. BARNETT. Mr. Chairman——

Senator GORE. Senator Cooper.

EFFECT OF KOREA ON JAPANESE NUCLEAR DEVELOPMENT

Senator COOPER. I have been listening. First on this issue we have been talking about, South Korea in its relations with Japan; of course we have a large volume of trade with Japan, isn't that correct?

Mrs. HSIEH. Yes.

Senator COOPER. Further, I think in the Nonproliferation Treaty everyone discussed the position of Japan, and I think it is considered that it was important that Japan sign the treaty, and that Japan should not become a nuclear power.

Are you saying that if we were not in South Korea, with an effective force the danger of South Korea being taken over by the North Koreans and therefore being under the influence of the Soviets and China, would make it more probable that Japan would begin to develop nuclear weapons in the belief that it was necessary to protect itself.

Mrs. HSIEH. Yes, sir. May I add that some Japanese already favor the indigenous development of nuclear weapons. In these polls that I referred to in late 1968, 20 to 25 percent of the Japanese questioned believed Japan should arm itself with nuclear weapons. Though the number is still very limited, the trend is not always recognized here in this country.

There was a poll in early 1969, just about a year ago, where in all 48 percent of the Japanese polled favored Japan's development of nuclear weapons, but only about 2 percent said immediately nuclear weapons, 20 percent said in the near future, and the rest said eventually. But in one or another time span 48 percent came out as more or less favoring a Japanese nuclear capability.

Now, I think if something were to happen, such as the reunification of Korea under Communist auspices combined with a reduction of the U.S. presence in the area this would push Japan more rapidly toward a decision in favor of nuclears.

There are other factors—political factors—which could reinforce this development: prestige, leverage on the Americans in the area, a greater role in decisionmaking in East Asia, et cetera.

But I think a new situation on the Korean Peninsula would be a basic military factor which would drive them toward a nuclear capability, and as I have said, I have very grave reservations if this would be in the interest of either the United States or Japan.

COMMUNIST CHINESE ACTIVITY IN BURMA, TIBET AND INDIA

Senator COOPER. Just one other question.

I think you would argue that China is essentially defensive minded?

Mrs. HSIEH. Yes, sir.

Senator COOPER. How would you reconcile that statement with Chinese activity in Burma, the fact that it took over Tibet shortly after it had agreed that Tibet should remain as it was, and also the invasion of the Indian border?

Mrs. HSIEH. Tibet has always been considered by the Chinese as Chinese territory, and whether it were the Chinese Communists or the Chinese Nationalists they would have reasserted their control over Tibet.

With respect to Burma, it is a very low-risk type of military infiltration, exploiting internal instabilities within the area. It is not a high-level or high risk type of aggression which is what I have been talking about.

On the Sino-Indian border it was again a very low-risk type of operation. The Chinese objective was to establish control over the Aksai Chin Road in order to assure communications between Tibet and Sinkiang. The situation developed to the extent it did because the Indians had not been up there for a number of years. The Chinese began to move in; they built the road; the Indians discovered the road; the Indians started to patrol in the area and established posts behind Chinese lines; the patrols met and fought.

But the Chinese as soon as they had fairly well reasserted and established their position in the area, then pulled back and settled for the control of the Aksai Chin area.

If they went further than they had anticipated I would say it was not because of their intentions at the time—despite all those reports about the Chinese going into Assam, et cetera—it was because of the momentum that had been developed and also because of the then weakness of the Indian military. The Indians were in no position to put up any effective resistence against the Chinese. Momentum developed, and the Chinese just went until their logistic support failed. Then they pulled back to the Aksai Chin area. This is, of course, an overly simplistic description of the 1962 Sino-Indian border conflict.

Senator COOPER. I won't continue this questioning now because I know we want to hear Dr. Barnett.

Nationalist China has the same views as Communist China had toward these territories, but I must say for myself I can't accept the statement that China is always defensive minded in view of the fact that it has made these incursions into territories claimed by other countries. It is a fact they did these things, and they invaded Tibet and India after they had promised through, you remember, Bandung and later agreements they would not do so.

It seems to me taking over Tibet is somewhat similar to the claims of the Soviets in invading Czechoslovakia.

Senator GORE. Mrs. Hsieh, you have been a very delightful witness. We now have had an hour and a half of, shall I say, a slightly heavy diet. Before hearing Professor Barnett, the Chair wishes to declare a 5-minute recess.

*　　*　　*　　*　　*　　*　　*

Senator GORE. The recess is terminated.

Professor Barnett.

Mr. BARNETT. Mr. Chairman and members of the subcommittee, let me, too, begin by saying that I am very grateful for this opportunity to meet and discuss with you a number of questions relating to arms control, focusing on the ABM and the SALT talks and their specific relevance to the problem of United States-China relations.

I would like to make two quick preliminary comments about my statement.

First, the views I will express today are purely my own and do not in any way represent views of the Brookings Institution which does not itself take any stands on policy issues.

Secondly, since I have very recently written an article—appearing in the current issue of Foreign Affairs—which summarizes many of my views on questions we are considering today, I am taking the liberty of drawing material from that article for the purposes of the statement I am now presenting to you.

We are now, in my view, at a rather critical juncture in the evolution both of our policy toward China and our policy regarding arms control.

PROSPECTS FOR UNITED STATES-MAINLAND CHINA RELATIONS

For the first time in several years, there now appears to be at least a limited basis for hope that movement can take place in our relations with mainland China, movement which may reduce tensions and increase contacts between us. The current Warsaw talks will help to determine whether some progress is possible, or whether the freeze of the last two decades will continue.

Senator FULBRIGHT. Mr. Chairman, I don't want to interrupt, but in view of what has been said in the previous exchange, I don't see that there is any reason to hope for a change.

Mr. BARNETT. A change in United States-China relations?

Senator FULBRIGHT. Yes, you say there is a limited basis for hope that movement can take place. I thought everything we said a moment ago would indicate there is none.

Mr. BARNETT. I would disagree with that. My opinion was not asked on that issue.

Senator FULBRIGHT. I thought I did ask your opinion about it. Maybe I didn't ask it at the right time.

Mr. BARNETT. Would you like me to respond to that and state why I think there is some hope for movement?

Senator FULBRIGHT. Yes, if you wish to.

Mr. BARNETT. Yes. It seems to me, as one looks at China, that starting about 1965 it went into a period of extreme introspection and isolation. It cut most of its diplomatic relationships abroad. It adopted a very militant verbal posture, but in effect abandoned any real foreign policy. As you may know, it had only one ambassador abroad at the height of this cultural revolution period.

As the cultural revolution began to draw to a close, at the end of 1969, and as the Sino-Soviet conflict began to increase in intensity, at the beginning of 1969, there is good reason to believe—and there are numerous hints and bits of evidence—that the Chinese began not only to look outward again but to reassess what their general policies should be.

Now, I think it is very significant that they agreed to come to Warsaw to meet after a 2-year hiatus, despite the posture they had adopted earlier. I think this is related to changes that are taking place in China, in the Foreign Ministry and in the hierarchy of the leadership in China. I think it is also related to the change in the overall balance in Asia, as they have perceived it. The Soviet Union is now regarded as the major threat. They now see, as I would also see, a much more complicated four-power balance evolving. They not only have come to Warsaw, they have, in small ways, given indication that they may be reconsidering their policies towards us. How far——

Senator FULBRIGHT. Do you think they might allow a few Americans to enter their country in the near future?

Mr. BARNETT. I think this is certainly within the realm of possibility, in the next year or 18 months. My own guess would be that it would be very possible, within the next year or 18 months, for a few businessmen, for example, to be allowed——

Senator FULBRIGHT. Or journalists or anyone like that?

Mr. BARNETT. I think this is possible.

Senator FULBRIGHT. Or scholars?

Mr. BARNETT. This small sign of movement on their side makes it a very important period, because this is the first period, I would say, not only for the last 3 or 4 years but for a longer period than that, in which there has been any reason for thinking that there is any chance of the Chinese being more flexible.

Senator FULBRIGHT. When was Edgar Snow refused a visa?

Mr. BARNETT. I don't know.

Senator FULBRIGHT. I read that in the paper somewhere. I forget when. I think he had been refused a visa

I didn't want to divert you. I was looking for some, if there were any, hope and I wondered why you thought there was. Go ahead.

UNITED STATES-RUSSIAN ARMS CONTROL NEGOTIATIONS

Mr. BARNETT. At the same time I believe that the arms control negotiations which we and the Russians have initiated are clearly the most important ones in the postwar period. We are about to meet again in Vienna at a time when both sides are poised to deploy new weapons systems—in our case, ABM's and MIRV's—if no agreements to forego such systems can be reached. Decisions made in the period immediately ahead by Washington and Moscow individually, and by both at the SALT talks, will determine, therefore, whether the United States-Soviet arms race will accelerate or slow down in the years immediately ahead. These decisions will also—and this is one of the major points I wish to make today—have a very significant impact on the prospects for improved United States-China relations. The evolving triangular relationship among the United States, Soviet Union, and China is now such that any action by one or two of the three inevitably affects the others.

ADMINISTRATION'S MAINLAND CHINA POLICY

Let me proceed with my assignment and start by saying that I believe the Nixon administration is to be commended for the new general approach it has adopted in our overall China policy. In his February 18 report to Congress on foreign policy, the President stated that we do not now wish to "isolate" mainland China but rather hope that in time it will "be ready to reenter the international community," that we look forward to a "more normal and constructive relationship" with the Peking regime, that "the principles underlying our relations with China are similar to those governing our policies towards the U.S.S.R."—if we carried that out there would be a great many changes—and the February 18 statement also said that we will "take what steps we can toward improved practical relations" with Peking.

In my view this is a very sound and very encouraging approach. Moreover, the limited steps we have taken recently to implement this approach—namely, the liberalizing of passport and travel regulations and the reduction of trade restrictions—are highly desirable and deserve strong support. The Administration should now be urged to continue making further and more substantial steps along these same lines—for example—a step it could take rapidly—by removing all restrictions on nonstrategic trade with mainland China.

DEVELOPMENT OF ANTI-COMMUNIST CHINESE ABM SYSTEM

However, having said this, I must immediately go on to say that, in my view, the deployment of an anti-Chinese ABM area defense would be extremely undesirable and would, in fact, run directly counter to, and tend to undercut, the basic objectives that underlie our new overall China policy.

Deployment of an anti-Chinese ABM system would be both unwise and unsound, I believe, for a number of reasons. Let me summarize these briefly now, and then proceed to elaborate on some of them at greater length.

(1) The ABM is not necessary for the defense of the United States against any foreseeable "Chinese threat." For the indefinite future the United States will continue to have overwhelming nuclear superiority in relation to China, and there is every reason to believe that our superiority will operate effectively to deter the Chinese from any offensive nuclear actions or threats. It is not necessary, therefore, to try to achieve a total damage denial capability by building ABM's.

(2) If the United States insists on building an anti-Chinese ABM system, Peking will probably interpret this to mean (whatever Washington says to try to convince it otherwise) that we are determined to maintain an unrestricted capability of making "first strike" threats against China, and that we insist on denying China the ability to acquire even a limited, defensive "second strike" capability. There is every reason to believe that this would tend to reinforce Peking's worst instincts in interpreting our motives and would work against the possibility of improving our relations.

(3) China's present opposition to all international arms control agreements is rooted, in part at least, in its basic sense of vulnerability and nuclear weakness. Peking obviously has been, and still is, fearful of threats by the superpowers and of United States-Soviet "collusion" directed against China. Until China achieves a minimal defensive deterrent itself, this situation is likely to continue. However, once the Chinese do acquire a limited "second strike" capability, it is at least conceivable that leaders in Peking may at that point be more inclined than at present to consider the advantages of arms control agreements in terms of their own interests. If so, the chances of inducing China to participate in arms control may increase at that point. An anti-Chinese ABM will probably work to postpone that day.

(4) For these and other reasons, the United States should itself forego building an anti-Chinese ABM area defense system, and in addition should attempt, at the SALT talks, to reach agreement with the Soviet Union that neither we nor they will build such systems. If, in the absence of such agreement, either or both proceed to deploy anti-Chinese systems, this will tend to reinforce Peking's fear of anti-Chinese collusion between Washington and Moscow, which at the least would complicate, and could well seriously set back, in my view, the prospects for improving U.S. relations with China.

Let me now elaborate on some of these points, starting with a few comments on Chinese motivations, nuclear capabilities, and foreign policy behavior, and how one should view the "Chinese threat."

COMMUNIST CHINESE POSTURE IN BIG POWER RELATIONS

There is no doubt, I believe, that ever since 1949 the Chinese Communist regime, in its relations with the superpowers, has felt very vulnerable to external pressures and possible attack by one or both of the major nuclear powers. Particularly since the late 1950's—following the Sino-Soviet split and the start of United States-Soviet collaboration in the arms control field—Peking has felt itself to be, in a sense, "encircled" by the two superpowers. It is still, in a fundamental sense, weak and knows it; its basic posture in big power relations is, therefore, of necessity defensive.

One of China's basic aims has been, and still is, to acquire at least a minimal nuclear deterrent to improve its ability to deal with the United States and Soviet Union. Its hope is to achieve a position less unequal than in the past, and to strengthen its bargaining position and leverage in relations with the big powers. Above all, its aim is to deter attack against China and reduce China's vulnerability to external pressure. This, in my view, is the basic military-strategic motivation behind its nuclear program.

PROGRESS OF COMMUNIST CHINESE NUCLEAR PROGRAM

Without attempting to summarize in detail the progress of China's nuclear program, let me say that while its technological progress has been impressive in many respects, its actual nuclear capabilities are very limited and will remain so for a long time to come because of the relative weakness of China's resource base.

By the middle or latter 1970's China will, at best, have accumulated perhaps 15 to 40 operational ICBM's plus 100 to 200 MRBM's and a limited number of other bombs deliverable by aircraft. (The most recent Defense Department extimates suggest that by 1975 China may have 10 to 25 ICBM's and 80 to 100 MRBM's.)

To provide a crude basis of comparison, today the United States and the Soviet Union each has over 1,000 ICBM's, plus many thousands of other nuclear weapons deliverable by a variety of sophisticated systems including missiles, airplanes, and submarines.

Projections of China's nuclear capabilities through the 1970's make several things clear. There is no possibility that in the foreseeable future Peking can aspire to parity with the United States and the Soviet Union in the nuclear field. The Chinese cannot come close to achieving a "first strike" capability against either of the superpowers. Under any conceivable circumstances, in the event of a Chinese attack, Washington or Moscow could retaliate massively. The question is whether—and if so, when, and with what consequences, China may be able to acquire a limited, defensive "second strike" capability which will serve as a minimal deterrent for China—that is, a capacity, if subjected to United States or Soviet nuclear attack, to retaliate and hit at least some targets in the attacking country or, in the United States case, possibly American forces in the Pacific or bases in allied countries. To date, it has yet to achieve this.

COMMUNIST CHINESE ACQUISITION OF "SECOND STRIKE" CAPABILITY

If the United States and Soviet Union forego building anti-Chinese ABM systems, they will, in effect, be accepting the fact that by the latter 1970's, China will have acquired a small, defensive "second strike" capability.

What risks or costs would this involve? It would require acceptance of the fact that the United States and the Soviet Union cannot with impunity consider or threaten nuclear "first strikes" against China. One can question, however, whether this would involve high costs. The arguments and inhibitions against considering nuclear "first strikes" in most conceivable situations are already very great. (Conceivably, this may be less true for the Soviet Union than for the United States, as the vague hints about a possible preemptive strike in 1969 suggest, but even Moscow must feel strong inhibitions about initiating a nuclear "first strike.") Moreover, in most limited conflicts in Asia, nuclear weapons are likely to be almost irrelevant.

The possibility that key nonnuclear powers such as Japan, India, and Australia might feel more vulnerable and threatened cannot be ignored. If this impelled them to embark on independent nuclear programs, the cost in relation to U.S. aims (including the desire to prevent proliferation) would be substantial. Yet, as long as such countries have confidence in the U.S. commitment to defend them against nuclear threats, and as long as it is clear that American nuclear superiority in relation to China is such that any offensive nuclear threats by Peking would not really be credible, there is no reason why China's acquisition of a minimal deterrent should basically alter the position or the views of such countries.

It is sometimes argued that if the United States maintains a "first strike" capability against China and builds invulnerable defenses, presumably by developing ABM's, the Japanese are likely to have greater confidence in our defense pledges. I believe that it is much more likely, however, that if the United States focuses on such a defense strategy, rather than relying on the continued applicability of mutual deterrence, the Japanese may conclude that the United States, in a crisis situation, might concern itself only with its own defense and abandon interest in allies not protected by such defenses.

The fact is that not only have the Chinese to date resisted whatever temptation they may have felt to engage in "bomb rattling," it is difficult to see how, from their position of nuclear inferiority, they will have any significant capacity for credible "nuclear blackmail" in the foreseeable future. Peking's cautious emphasis, to date, on defense as its sole aim in developing nuclear weapons suggests that Chinese leaders may already realize this.

Some might fear that once the Chinese believe they have acquired a credible deterrent, they might tend to become more aggressive in areas such as Southeast Asia, feeling that they could take more risks in nonnuclear or subnuclear situations, involving conventional weapons, because they would be less vulnerable to nuclear counterthreats. Whether one considers this to be a significant risk depends very much on one's general assessment of China's foreign policy goals, strategy, and behavior.

COMMUNIST CHINESE MILITARY POSTURE

If one views China as a power committed to broad territorial aggression and expansionism by military means, willing to take large risks, and prone to irrational action (that is, inclined to commit aggression withour regard for possible consequences), there would be cause for major concern. However, among specialists on Chinese affairs, both in and out of the U.S. Government, there appears to be a fairly broad consensus that analysis of China's behavior and doctrine over the past two decades does not support this view. In general, this consensus, which I believe is sound, maintains that:

Although China encourages revolutionaries abroad, it is not committed to broad territorial expansionism. Among its national goals is the recovery of certain areas that it considers to be lost territories, but even in regard to these territories its inclination is to pursue long-term, low-risk policies, not broad military expansionism.

It appears to be predisposed to keep Chinese military forces within China's boundaries, and it seems likely to continue doing so, except in cases where it feels Chinese security—or that of a Communist buffer state on its periphery—is seriously threatened (as it did in Korea).

Its primary stress, both in the structure of its conventional military forces and the doctrine governing their use, is on defense rather than offense.

It cannot and does not ignore the possible risks and costs of large-scale conventional war, even when nuclear weapons are not involved, and it places a high priority on the desirability of avoiding large-scale war of any sort with the major powers.

It is strongly predisposed, in general, to low-cost, low-risk policies. While it clearly encourages and supports, as I said, revolutionary struggles in other countries, such support does not include Chinese manpower on any significant scale. Even Maoist doctrine insists that all revolutionaries must be "self-reliant," and should depend primarily on indigenous resources; it opposes the use of Chinese forces to fight other revolutionaries' battles for them.

China has used pressure and probes against its neighbors for a variety of purposes, but in doing so its use of force has generally been carefully calculated, limited, and controlled.

Senator GORE. Why is it, then, Professor, that there is such a widespread feeling that China is an aggressive military power?

Mr. BARNETT. I think in part it is a literal interpretation—it is not even a literal interpretation—it is a misinterpretation of China's verbal militancy, and the general Chinese posture; China is verbally militant, and it calls for world revolution saying the whole world should go Communist.

I think it also derives, in part, from the fact that there have been a variety of situations on the Chinese periphery in which the Chinese have been militarily involved over the last 20 years. I could go through an inventory of them, the way Mrs. Hsieh did, and give my own view about them. I think in the case of Korea, I think the Chinese intervened when they thought that there was both a threat to the existence of the North Korean regime, one of the two Communist buffers on its periphery, and a potential threat to Manchuria, and the best studies that I have seen of the Korean war, analyzing how the Chinese became involved suggest that these were their motivations. They came into the war very late. There is good evidence to suggest that they did not plan to come in at the time the Korean war started.

The offshore islands crises, that we have been involved in, are ones which have also helped to create this image of a dangerous China, in the American view, but in both of these cases, if one studies them carefully, the Chinese were extremely cautious and prudent in what they did. In both cases they did no more than shell these islands from the mainland.

WHO IS COMMUNIST CHINA?

Senator CASE. Would the Senator permit me to intervene?

Since the Chairman raised this question, would you give us your idea of what China is? You speak of China doing this, China doing that and thinking this and thinking that, and being conservative in action or bellicose in words. Who is China?

Mr. BARNETT. Who is China?

Senator CASE. What continuity is there or what continuity can be expected in policy, in behavior?

Mr. BARNETT. That is not an easy question to answer.

Senator CASE. It has been very puzzling to me, and you have said China is this and China is that. I just wonder what you mean.

Mr. BARNETT. It is a very legitimate question because to the extent that by using the term "China" one implies that it is a totally monolithic country, with a totally monolithic leadership, one is not correct.

It is true that we had the impression, up until, I would say, the mid-sixties, that China had an extraordinarily unified leadership; one did not see a great deal of evidence, on the surface, of important policy differences, or differences in outlook, or differences in revolutionary ethos. The evidence that has come out in the last 5 years clearly indicates that there are wide differences within the Chinese leadership, as there is in the leadership of most countries.

Crudely speaking, I would say that, on the one hand, there is a group around Mao, the "Maoists," who have a commitment to a particular kind of revolutionary ethos that Mao has been promoting; it would take quite a while to try to go into this in any detail.

On the other hand, it seems to me, a very large segment of the leadership has, I would say, been more realistic, more pragmatic, and more inclined to adapt to changing conditions as they see them.

I don't believe that in terms of what we can know, or can guess, about their outlook, however, that either of these groups has adopted positions that one would call reckless, in any sense.

Senator CASE. Of course, that answers the question from our point of view.

Mr. BARNETT. So far as I know, there has been no evidence that either of these groups has been pushing for a more expansionist or a more aggressive external policy.

FUTURE COMMUNIST CHINESE POLICIES

Senator CASE. Nor is there any evidence that you have seen that this should be reasonably expected in the future?

Mr. BARNETT. I would not expect it in the future.

Senator CASE. No matter what internal——

Mr. BARNETT. Not "no matter what." One needs to be cautious about predicting the future, to some extent, in any situation in any country.

All I would say is that, on the basis of what we know about the forces at work in China and the existing situation—the context of the general situation as it affects China—I would not expect any of these would work to push China toward more extreme foreign policies.

Senator CASE. We have been anticipating the possibility, for example, of a reunited Korea and a more aggressive Chinese policy against Japan——

Mr. BARNETT. Might lead Japan to decide to "go nuclear." But the forces we see affecting China lead in just the opposite direction. The forces within and without that are affecting China are forces that have weakened China. They have great problems domestically which make them more preoccupied with internal problems than they have been in the past, and I would expect this to be true for a considerable period of time. Externally, they feel a greater sense of encirclement and threat; I suspect they feel the need for greater independence of maneuver and action than they have felt in the past. So both of these overall developments, changes in their relations with the big powers and political developments within China, have imposed new constraints on the Chinese.

COULD WEAKNESS PROMOTE CHINESE COMMUNIST AGGRESSIVENESS?

Senator CASE. Isn't it though, in the case of Japan, where at least we are suggesting the possibility that a period of greater anxiety on their part would lead them to aggressive behavior, and why shouldn't this reaction come from a weakened China?

Mr. BARNETT. I doubt if Mrs. Hsieh—I cannot speak for her—if she was saying she feared renewed Japanese aggression.

Senator CASE. No, I think there is no intention.

Mr. BARNETT. My own view would be that the Japanese might conclude that, for defensive reasons, they would have to remilitarize and to develop nuclear weapons. But the consequences of this, affecting their relations with China, with the smaller countries in Southeast Asia, and in the longrun even with us, would alter Japan's position, alter its relationships. I think it would increase tensions in that area, and increase the likelihood that there would be a dangerous interaction between China and Japan over a period of years.

I would not suggest that the Japanese are on the verge of considering embarking on a new period of military expansionism.

Senator CASE. I was not suggesting that either, although I must admit I did make a mental leap, perhaps incorrectly, from going nuclear to increased militarization and reversion to something that we had known before, as a result of this leaving its present policy of non-militarization and civilian control and a high degree of democracy.

Mr. BARNETT. If Japan remilitarizes and goes nuclear it will be because of a sense of insecurity in Japan; because of a belief that this is necessary for the defense of Japan. But it would increase the sense of insecurity in China. A remilitarized and nuclear-armed Japan would arouse very deep historical memories and anxieties in the Chinese.

Senator CASE. My question is again why, if increased insecurity in Japan leads it to go nuclear, shouldn't the same thing happen in China?

Mr. BARNETT. I am not clear on what "the same thing" would be, in your mind.

Senator CASE. Really I am not trying to quibble at all, but to go to the general point that you thought China was not likely to be aggressive but rather to have a sense of weakness or what not, and, therefore, not engage in adventures outside. Isn't it precisely when you are timid and insecure or weak that you are tempted to take those actions in the way of rearmament and the things that follow from that, that lead you to be less stable in your international relations?

Mr. BARNETT. This hypothetical course of events is what we are talking about. A remilitarized, nuclear Japan would increase the pressures in China to keep on investing the maximum amount of resources in the Chinese military buildup. It would reinforce such pressures in China.

But I would be very dubious that it would lead the Chinese leadership, any conceivable Chinese leadership in the next few years, to feel that they would have to lash out and could take the increased risks that would then exist.

Senator CASE. Thank you, Mr. Chairman. I am sorry to have interrupted.

Senator GORE. Senator Cooper?

COMMUNIST CHINESE ACTIVITIES IN INDIA AND TIBET

Senator COOPER. I would repeat the question I asked earlier. How would you explain Chinese action in India, Burma?

Mr. BARNETT. Right. Often as occasions——

Senator COOPER. The border clashes with the Soviet Union.

Mr. BARNETT. In the case of India, I think an examination of the facts suggests that this was a case where the claims of these two countries to territory made it very hard for even an objective outside observer, to say nothing of the two parties immediately involved, to have a clear picture of the situation. One could say there was a well-based claim on either side.

In other words, the action that took place in the Indian border affair was over territory for which there is a legitimate basis for dispute, regarding territorial claims.

The Chinese did not go into territory which they, from their point of view, considered Indian. That is one point I would make.

I would also say— and I am not trying to paint the picture of Peking as being a totally benign power, because it does have ambitions; it is willing to use pressures on its neighbors. I think China hoped by its pressure on India to achieve some fairly broad political goals. It wanted to discredit the Indian Government, to some extent. I think this whole affair did, actually, reduce India's international prestige and status.

China's hope was also to set at work forces that would be disruptive in India. I do not think it has had much success in doing this, but it had some impact.

There never was any evidence, however, at any point, that the Chinese prepared for or thought in terms of using their military forces to go in and take a large piece of Indian territory.

Senator COOPER. May I interrupt to say, of course, I understand that China claimed this territory rightfully belonged to China, and in its relationship with Tibet it wanted to show it.

But why, when they had good relations or assuming good relations with both Tibet and India, why it would use force instead of attempting to negotiate.

Mr. BARNETT. I think that is a legitimate question, and I personally think the Chinese leadership was foolish, in terms of their long-range objectives, even though I think they achieved some short-range objectives they were interested in in that case.

WISDOM OF COMMUNIST CHINESE POLICIES QUESTIONED

If you are asking me whether I, as an outsider, could make a judgment about Chinese policies, whether they have been wise, my responses would be quite different. I frankly think that since the end of the Bandung period, since about 1957 or 1958, when China switched from a policy which I think in the longrun would have been much more to China's interest, to the kind of policy they pursued after 1957–58, Peking's policies have not effectively promoted China's interest; they have actually reduced China's international influence. These policies have not supported its long-term interests, in my view as an outsider.

I think it is quite possible, however, that at some point leadership that is now emerging in China, or the post-Mao leadership, might switch back in the direction of a policy which would be, in essence, like the Bandung policy. Such a policy might downgrade revolutionary objectives, relatively speaking, and put considerable stress on the development of normalized diplomatic, economic, and other relationships with other countries.

China made quite a bit of progress abroad during the Bandung period. I would certainly not, myself, say it has been wise in the kind of militant posture it has adopted in the interim decade.

Senator CASE. You do not say, by any means, that the United States should develop its own policy and pursue it on the assumption that another country will act in its own best interests?

Mr. BARNETT. No, I do not think China has, in actual fact been acting in its own best interests. But I think it is important to have a realistic view of the type and degree of threat it poses. In my view, one should not tailor one's policy on the basis of an expectation that the Chinese are thinking in terms of, or are likely to embark on, major military expansionism.

COMMUNIST CHINESE TERITORIAL CLAIMS

Senator COOPER. I have another question. I believe it is correct that China claims that most of the territory now under Soviet control was acquired by the Soviets or Russia rather from China by so-called unequal treaties.

Now, take into consideration this action in India where they claimed the boundary was set by the British in another treaty. You consider then that China will continue to dispute the Soviet Union and have even possible border clashes because it takes the position that the territories were acquired by unequal treaties?

Mr. BARNETT. I do not believe that China in a literal sense claims these territories. The Russians have interpreted some Chinese statements to mean this and have, to a degree, convinced themselves that China does have irridentist objectives in the Russian Far East and Soviet Central Asia. But the Chinese have never specifically claimed such territories. Mao has made some statements which do have lurking implications of possible Chinese claims regarding these territories—of all territories that they lost in the past through "unequal treaties."

It is quite clear, I think that these statements were a form of political warfare on the part of China against the Soviet Union, in response to what they felt was Soviet pressure on China. There have been much more concrete statements, in connection with the negotiations now going on in Peking, that suggest the Chinese are quite prepared, in the long run, to accept the present boundaries with minor adjustments. There is no basis for believing—and I do not think the Russians ought to believe China has vast claims. But I think clearly the Russians have been disturbed. Deep apprehensions and historical memories have been aroused as a result of the border clashes.

The border clashes may well continue for some time. The relationships between these two countries are likely to be quite tense. But in terms of real territorial issues, I think they would only involve minor adjustments. If the overall relationships between these two countries moderated, the border problem in and of itself would not be insoluble, in my view. And to repeat, I do not believe there is any real evidence that the Chinese literally have large territorial claims against the Soviet Union.

COMMUNIST CHINA'S OBJECTIVES IN SOUTHEAST ASIA

Senator COOPER. Just one question. Can you state what you consider are Communist China's aims toward Southeast Asia? That includes Vietnam, Cambodia, Laos, Thailand.

Mr. BARNETT. Like many very important questions, it is a difficult question because, among other things, I think one has to try to differentiate between what the Chinese would like to see, in the best of all possible worlds, what they think maybe they can achieve over a long period of time, what they would like to achieve in shorter periods of time, and what they are willing to live with; these are all probably different.

I think that in the best of all possible worlds the Chinese would like to see Southeast Asia as an area in which the Western and external powers had no presence and no significant influence whatsoever, and in which the regimes throughout the area were—under the best of all possible conditions—Communist regimes. But in my opinion she does not really expect this, so she would like at least to see regimes which would be extremely friendly toward and oriented toward Peking.

I do not believe that the Chinese want, or at least think in terms of, direct Chinese control, or incorporating any of this area territorially into China.

What I have described, however, is an objective one would classify as being an extremely longrun objective, under conditions that would be ideal from the Chinese point of view.

I think that more realistically they hope that over time—and I do not think that they look on this in terms of a very short time span—there will be a reduction of the Western presence and influence in the area, and a gradual trend in the direction of regimes that are more friendly to China and do not have any American presence.

In the short run, I think China is willing to live with situations much less desirable from its viewpoint even than that.

The question was raised earlier as to whether the Chinese might be interested in neutralization, let us say, of the Indochina states. There is no firm evidence upon which one can judge. My own feeling would be that under certain conditions the Chinese might well be very interested in this, if the conditions were such that North Vietnam would go along with it. I think the real pressures in that area come from North Vietnam, not from China. The Chinese in the middle 1950's were moving toward accepting a compromise in the area, and I could theoretically envisage a situation in the future where the Chinese would be quite happy with some compromise situations far, far short of the long term goal of an area with the West totally out and the local regimes all extremely pro-Chinese.

COMMUNIST CHINESE PARTICIPATION IN POLITICAL SETTLEMENT OF VIETNAM WAR

Senator COOPER. Do you believe it is possible to bring about the end of the war in Vietnam without a political settlement in which Communist China participated?

Mr. BARNETT. My own view is that it is very unlikely. I have increasingly moved, myself, toward to the view that we ought to strive very hard for a political settlement that covers all three of the Indochinese states; in the process we will have to be prepared to make some important political compromises that go further than any we have been willing to make so far.

I think the recent French proposal is one that we should take very seriously; we should see if it can be moved along and pursued in any way I certainly think that if there is any attempt at an international settlement, a political settlement, for these areas, for it to have any meaning over the long run the Chinese would have to be included.

Senator COOPER. It is my view as well.

NEUTRALIZATION OF INDOCHINA

Senator CASE. Can I pursue that? You speak of neutralization. This means some kind of status quo would be guaranteed by some kind of power, and that any machinery that was created would have to have the force to enforce it. Is this a possibility? Can you conceive of any establishment being created that would be satisfactory to any of us, if not just all of us, that would also have the authority to act not only to enforce neutrality but also assume a real decisionmaking capacity? It is something to think about, because neutralization is something that is terribly appealing. Everybody wants it. But how do you get it if you cannot even have a United Nations operation? The chairman talked earlier about the United Nations.

Mr. BARNETT. I suppose there are many different definitions one could use.

Senator CASE. I just wonder what conception you have.

Mr. BARNETT. There are many different concepts one could have of what a neutral Indochina area would be. Mine would be very limited, I think. I think if there were an internationally agreed upon political settlement in which it was agreed that the external powers did not maintain any forces in the area——

Senator CASE. Any what?

Mr. BARNETT. Any forces in the area. The crucial question in the whole area, I think, relates to North Vietnam's relations to the other three areas. What limits would North Vietnam be willing to accept, in that context, regarding its forces in South Vietnam, Laos, and Cambodia. I do not have the answer to that, but I would think the search for a political settlement would have to be one in which there were limits placed on the extent to which North Vietnam could have its forces in the other area.

I would not think that any internationally agreed upon formula for "neutralization," and I am not sure that I particularly like that word——

Senator. CASE. No, I do not either.

Mr. BARNETT. I do not think that it could hope to create a mechanism that could preserve the status quo forever in that area, that it could guarantee that the existing governments in that area would be preserved for the indefinite future.

I take a rather pessimistic view of that particular area of Southeast Asia. I would stress, though, that I think the Indochina states are a special, and in many respects unique, problem within Southeast Asia, and I do not think that the other countries of Southeast Asia face comparable problems, nor do I believe that, even if very undesirable developments were now to take place over a period of time in the three IndoChinese states, this would inevitably mean that similar developments would necessarily take place then in Thailand or elsewhere.

If one thinks in terms of a political settlement, one has to have rather limited objectives that may be possible to achieve.

Senator CASE. I think it is terribly useful to bring this out because most people when they think of neutralization and a settlement think of something that would go on indefinitely and will have some enforcing instrument that will see that people live up to their agreements, and that are not violent changes within a foreseeable time. This is not at all what you mean or what you think is possible, I take it.

Mr. BARNETT. That would be fine, if it were feasible, I do not see it would be very feasible.

Senator CASE. You do not think it would be possible, so it is not what you mean when you assent to something that you would like a better word for than neutralization.

Mr. BARNETT. Yes. One has to be realistic in facing up to the special problems of that area, and by that I do not mean Asia, I mean the Indochina states, and I reiterate I think that they pose a very special problem. One must realize that all of the options we face are undesirable, in varying ways and degrees.

POLITICAL SETTLEMENT IN INDOCHINA

Senator CASE. What you really mean then, I take it, and I do not mean by putting it this way to say I do not agree with you, is that you should leave these people to work out their own salvation.

Mr. BARNETT. Essentially to work toward a situation where the political forces in those areas are going to determine the future in the long run.

I do not think that we have shown a capability to determine for the long run what the specific political situation in those particular areas is going to be.

Senator CASE. And we should face the reality, as you see it, that it is impossible to work out a situation here which will prevent that from happening.

Mr. BARNETT. Obviously, it would be in our interests if there would be peace in the area, and moderate non-Communist governments. But I think it has now been demonstrated that our capacity to insure that this will be the outcome is extremely limited. We have to accept that there may be outcomes that are much less desirable

Senator CASE. You do not feel that there are any commitments, to use a terribly overworked misused word, on our part which prevent us from letting this happen?

Mr. BARNETT. On the contrary. It seems to me that, getting back to the Guam doctrine, the Nixon doctrine, which was raised earlier, although it is not an operational doctrine, it is a statement of objectives. If we were to translate these stated objectives, over a period of time—and I do not think it can be done all of a sudden but must be done over time—into an operational policy, this would call for making sure that we do not get involved with American troops in Laos and Cambodia, for example, and that we work steadily toward the withdrawal of American troops from South Vietnam. If one accepts this as a desirable direction of policy, one has to think in terms of trying to get the best possible—which may not be terribly good from our point of view but the best possible—political settlement. Ideally it would be desirable to have some kind of international approval, and international involvement in it if this is possible.

Senator CASE. Yes. But you do not put any real faith in it being very strong of that nature.

Mr. BARNETT. I am not optimistic; I tend to be pessimistic.

PROSPECTS FOR NIXON DOCTRINE

Senator GORE. You say the Nixon doctrine is not an operational policy.

As I understand it, it is an operational policy insofar as Laos and Cambodia are concerned.

Mr. BARNETT. That remains to be seen. I hope that proves to be the case, but I think the decisions that we make over the next few months will demonstrate whether they are applying it in that situation or not.

I would say: so far so good, in many respects. The evidence suggests that the Administration is resisting what might have been, a few years ago, a much stronger impulse to get immediately involved with American forces.

Senator GORE. What keeps me a little nervous is that I remember how often former President Johnson said, "We seek no wider war," but the war was widening every day.

Mr. BARNETT. What will make the Nixon doctrine operational or not are some very concrete decisions, and I too am uneasy when this kind of fluid situation develops, because inevitably there will be some pressures for participation with American forces. So I share that uneasiness. But I think whether or not we make the Guam doctrine operational will depend on whether we can keep the situation under control, can exercise restraint, and can pursue policies consistent with the principles laid down in the Guam doctrine.

COMPATIBILITY OF NIXON DOCTRINE WITH VIETNAMIZATION

Senator GORE. You heard my expression of doubt to Mrs. Hsieh that the Nixon doctrine and the policy of Vietnamization were compatible. Would you comment on that?

Senator COOPER. Did you say compatible or incompatible?

Senator GORE. I said incompatible. I said I doubt that they are compatible.

Mr. BARNETT. I am not sure. I would suppose if, in fact, we proceed step by step, with reasonable speed, to withdraw American forces from South Vietnam, and that if in the process Vietnamization has helped the South Vietnamese genuinely to have a capacity to carry the burden of their own defense against the Vietcong and North Vietnamese, I would think that, in a sense, this would be very much within the framework of, and compatible with, the concepts of the Nixon doctrine.

I think, however, that a great many people are extremely doubtful that it will move down this road and be successful and, hence, feel that it is unwise to put all of our eggs in that basket and rely only on Vietnamization. We probably are going to have to conclude some kind of a political settlement, somewhere along the road, whether it is at Paris or at some other kind of international forum.

I, therefore, do not think that, in theory, if we went down the road of Vietnamization and got out, and Vietnam then continued on its own to cope with its own problems, that this would be inconsistent with the Guam doctrine.

Senator CASE. You are not against that happening.

Mr. BARNETT. I am not against that happening at all; I am all for it. I have a considerable amount of skepticism as to whether, in fact, things can proceed in this fashion and whether such a policy can be successful.

Senator GORE. In other words, if Vietnamization is successful to the end that the United States disengages militarily from South Vietnam, and South Vietnam succeeds in developing the ability to preserve its own integrity, then you would say the incompatibility does not appear.

Mr. BARNETT. I would say it would be both desirable and compatible with the Guam doctrine. But I doubt that this would be possible.

Senator GORE. Let me state what gives rise to my apprehension. In President Nixon's first speech to the American people on Vietnam on May 14, he based his policy upon a negotiated settlement and mutual withdrawal of foreign troops from South Vietnam. Three times in that one speech he denounced unilateral withdrawal.

About 3 weeks later at Midway a policy of unilateral withdrawal was announced. Since then there have been, as I believe Senator Aiken said, a hundred and some thousand troops withdrawn or that number of U.S. troops there reduced.

Meanwhile there are constant reports of stepped-up infiltration by North Vietnamese into South Vietnam. Since then we have been told by President Nixon that 67,000 North Vietnamese troops have infiltrated or moved into Laos. I have forgotten the number in Cambodia.

Senator COOPER. 25,000.

Senator GORE. I thought it was 40,000. Some several thousand have moved into Cambodia.

With unilateral withdrawal on the part of the United States unmatched by any withdrawal of North Vietnamese, but rather accompanied by an increased infiltration into South Vietnam, into the demilitarized zone, into Laos, and then into Cambodia, all of which seems to almost surround and flank American and South Vietnamese positions, I wonder if, in fact, Vietnamization can succeed with this kind of overwhelming flanking operation. Perhaps I should not use overwhelming. It may not be overwhelming. Do I make my point?

Mr. BARNETT. Yes; you do make your point, and I think a great many people have doubts about its potential success unless there is some kind of a political settlement. I tend to share this feeling.

THREE CHOICES OF UNITED STATES IN VIETNAM WAR

Senator GORE. If I may go one step further, I am to the conclusion that I have had for a long, long while, that in this desperate and tragic and needless war, there are three choices:

We could fight to win a military victory. President Johnson ruled that out when he ceased bombing North Vietnam. He never quite said so, but that was implicit in the policy.

In President Nixon's speech of May 14 he specifically, and I use the exact language, "ruled out." He said "We have ruled out settlement on the battlefield."

Winning a victory seems to be out. Perhaps it has been out all the while and I am not questioning the wisdom of that.

Second is a compromise peace, a political settlement of the war. It is not just South Vietnam, but, as you said a moment ago, in the Indo-China area, which seems to me to be one war. The priority of a negotiated settlement seems to have been downgraded. Indeed, without a top diplomatic representative in Paris, it has become a rather unnoticed sideshow.

This leaves the third choice, which is to continue. Frankly, I consider Vietnamization a semantic cover for continuing the war. Maybe it will succeed. Since it is the only policy we have, I hope it will, but it seems to me the most stupid policy of all to send American boys up and down Hamburger Hill with no hope of either winning or ending this tragic war.

Excuse me, Senator Cooper.

Mr. BARNETT. Mr. Chairman, just one thing. I wondered if you wanted me to finish this or shall I insert it in the record? I would be glad to discuss these questions.

Senator GORE. Let us hear from Senator Cooper.

Senator COOPER. I am sorry I must go, but I would like to say before I go I think the witnesses, both of them, have provided us with helpful material on the effect of ABM deployment upon China based upon their deep knowledge of this area. We are indeed grateful to both of you.

CONSISTENCY OF U.S. POLICIES IN SOUTHEAST ASIA

I would just like to say this about Vietnam policy. I think it is consistent with the Guam doctrine, that there are no U.S. troops in Cambodia. I think it would have been better if the Administration had withdrawn the troops it has in Laos, which the former administration put in Laos. Our operations there are consistent with what the President said.

I think, with all deference to Senator Gore, and I think also in deference to Senator Fulbright's speech the other day, they were talking about something entirely different. I believe our forces may be flanked and threatened, in Laos and Cambodia, but I think that is an entirely different thing from saying that the policy of the Guam doctrine does not apply to the policy there.

What you leave unanswered there is if our own troops are endangered there are two possible courses among others: One is to put more troops in, which I believe the President will not do, or just withdraw summarily.

POLITICAL SETTLEMENT OF VIETNAM WAR

Senator GORE. I wish a political settlement. I thought political settlement was it from the beginning.

Senator COOPER. I think a political settlement is what we are all striving for.

Senator CASE. But you cannot have a political settlement that does not reflect the power situation on the ground, can you?

Mr. BARNETT. I do not think anyone can be confident that a political settlement is possible, but I do not myself think that we are going as far as we ought to go in really exploring that as a possibility.

I would agree with your statement that in the balance between stress on Vietnamization and stress on the search for a political settlement, the balance seems to have swung almost wholly toward hope and faith in Vietnamization. I personally think we ought to upgrade our representation in Paris, we ought to reexamine our position in terms of what is an acceptable minimal political settlement as far as we are concerned, and we should press to see if a political settlement is possible.

Senator GORE. I agree with that completely. If Vietnamization is the only policy we have, then I hope it succeeds, of course. However, I am very disturbed that negotiation has lost its priority. I hope the President would dispatch no less a diplomat than the Secretary of State himself to Paris to revive and rejuvenate the hopes for a peaceful settlement.

Won't you finish your statement?

VIETNAMIZATION POLICY AS WITHDRAWAL

Senator CASE. May I just make one further statement. There is one alternative to what has been suggested. I think you were suggesting that this was a semantic cover for military—a search for military victory.

It is equally possible that it may be a semantic cover for withdrawal.

Senator GORE. If the latter be true then it is a rearguard action without hope of success, and we have lost over 40,000 American casualties since Vietnamization began.

How many men must we cripple and maim? At midnight the other night a distraught mother from Tennessee called me. Her son hadn't been killed, she said, but he had lost both legs and an arm.

This is a horrible price we are paying.

Senator CASE. It is a horrible price, indeed, but it is possible that a country as vast as ours cannot immediately turn and just disengage without some kind of covering mechanism, and I am not at all sure that that is not what Vietnamization is practically designed to do.

Senator GORE. Mr. Barnett, you came here to educate us. Do you feel a sense of enlightenment?

Mr. BARNETT. I would like to say a few more things from my statement, if I might.

Senator GORE. It will be included in the record.

FUTURE COMMUNIST CHINESE FOREIGN POLICY

Mr. BARNETT. In crisis situations, China has tended to act with considerable prudence and caution, and repeatedly it has moved to check escalation when there has appeared to be a serious risk of major conflict.

There is, of course, no absolute guarantee that these patterns of behavior, which seem to have characterized Chinese actions over the past two decades, will persist in the future. Nevertheless, there is a remarkably broad consensus among China specialists that they are likely to continue. In fact, there is a fairly widely held view—a view that I share—that post-Mao leaders are likely to be more pragmatic and realistic than Mao, and subject to even greater internal as well as external constraints.

As a result of the internal disruptions caused by the cultural revolution in China during the past 4 years, the Peking regime has clearly been weakened in some respects. Consequently, there are now new constraints, in fact if not in theory, on Chinese policy, which will certainly affect its strategies abroad.

Moreover, as a result of the steady deterioration of Sino-Soviet relations in the 1960's, the "Russian threat" appears to have replaced the "U.S. threat" as Peking's major foreign policy preoccupation, and this seems to have impelled the Chinese leadership to consider new options and strategies, to reduce China's present isolation and vulnerability and explore new opportunities for maneuver and flexibility.

It is at least plausible to believe, therefore, that future Chinese leaders may downgrade the importance of revolutionary aims (not ending, but possibly deemphasizing, Chinese act vity in this field) and upgrade the importance of state-to-state relationships and more conventional political and economic instruments of policy. There is remarkably little support among China specialists for the idea that China is now, or is likely to be in the future, prone to act in an irrational or highly reckless manner, which it would certainly be doing if it were to ignore the continuing fact of its nuclear inferiority, and its vulnerability to both conventional and nuclear retaliation, even if, and when, it acquires a minimal deterrent.

COMMUNIST CHINESE NUCLEAR AND ARMS CONTROL POLICIES

If these judgments are correct, there are strong reasons to assume that once China achieves a nuclear deterrent it can be expected, in a basic sense, to act much as the other nuclear powers have, and to be constrained, as they are, by the realities of nuclear deterrence. There is little basis for arguing that the United States, or Soviet Union, can feel secure vis-a-vis China only if they have a total damage denial capability and an unquestionable ability to threaten China with a "first strike". To argue this is to argue, in effect, that the United States and the Soviet Union can only feel secure under conditions that guarantee that the Chinese will continue to feel highly insecure.

As I stated earlier, if the United States operates on other assumptions and proceeds to build an anti-Chinese ABM, this will not only tend to strengthen Chinese suspicions that we are determined to maintain a potentially threatening "first strike" capability against China and to deny China even a minimal defensive "second strike" capability, it will also tend to postpone the day when China may be willing to consider participating in international arms control agreements.

Fundamental change in China's posture on strategic and nuclear arms control issues will not be easy for Peking to make, under any circumstances, because of China's basic weakness relative to the two superpowers. However, if one asks when and under what conditions a more flexible and pragmatic leadership in China might be inclined to change its posture on arms control, and even begin to see arms control measures as in the interest of China as well as of the other powers, the answer would seem to be the following: When China is convinced that its own nuclear development has reached a stage where it has at least a minimal credible nuclear deterrent—that is, some kind of defensive "second strike" retaliatory capacity—so that it will be able to deal with the United States and Soviet Union on terms less unequal than at present.

It is not easy to define when this point will be reached. But it will doubtless be reached eventually, whether or not we build an anti-Chinese ABM. It is almost certain that in time the Chinese will have acquired a sufficient nuclear capability so that no one could be sure whether, if China were subjected to a "first strike," it could not mount a significant retaliatory strike, at least against allies or forces in the Pacific if not against the United States itself.

Whenever the Chinese, and we, are convinced that China has acquired some sort of limited "second strike" capability, the possibility that Peking may reconsider its present blanket opposition to arms control may increase, for a variety of reasons. The realization that pursuit of parity is a will-o-the-wisp is likely over time to begin to sink in, in China. Moreover, once China has acquired any sort of credible deterrent, some Chinese leaders may conclude that it is more feasible to try to reduce the gap between China and the superpowers through agreements limiting (or reducing) United States and Soviet capabilities than by trying to catch up in a hopeless race. And, as the cost of deterrence goes up (it inevitably must, as China gets involved in more sophisticated hardware), and as the competition for resources in China increases (between those stressing economic development and those emphasizing defense), there may be greater pressures within China, on economic grounds, to limit investment in strategic arms development.

The construction of anti-Chinese ABM systems would be likely, therefore, to postpone the day when there may be some realistic hope of including China in international arms control. It would tend to raise the level of nuclear development which Peking's leaders will consider essential as a minimum goal. And in general it will tend to make more remote the possibility of establishing a more normal and constructive relationship with China and the possibility of inducing Peking to reenter the international community—which are now our stated, and in my opinion, eminently sensible, goals.

SUGGESTED UNITED STATES-SOVIET POLICIES CONCERNING ANTI-CHINESE ABM SYSTEM

What does all of this suggest regarding the decisions we should make and the policies we should pursue regarding an anti-Chinese ABM system—both in our own consideration of the problem and in discussions with the Russians at Vienna?

I strongly believe we should clearly decide that, in terms of our broad national interests and aims, we should not build an anti-Chinese ABM system, because it conflicts with the main thrust of our new China policy and is unnecessary for our defense—wholly apart from other possible reasons. The cost of such a system would certainly be its disfavor, too, but clearly the costs would be tolerable if it were essential in terms of our defense and foreign policy goals. The point is that it is not only unessential, but would tend to be damaging in terms of our overall objectives.

We should not only make this decision ourselves; we should also in the SALT talks attempt to reach agreement with the Soviets on this issue, so that both we and they will forego traveling this road. This would be desirable in relation both to our aims regarding China and our desire to check the United States-Soviet arms race.

Both the United States and the Soviet Union must concern themselves, more than they have in the past, not only with the problem of strategic stability in their bilateral relations but also with the task of inducing China, over time, to improve relations in general and, eventually, to participate in arms control efforts and accomodate more fully than it has to date to the requirements of the nuclear age. Neither need fear that the Chinese will be able to achieve a "first strike" capability, or approach nuclear parity, in the foreseeable future. Nor should they consider China's eventual acquisition of a minimal deterrent to be a special danger. While it is true that China's acquisition of a credible deterrent will improve Peking's defensive capabilities, it will not significantly alter the overall nuclear balance. Moreover, China can be expected, as I have said, to act much as other nuclear powers have, and to be constrained, as others are, by the realities of mutual deterrence. Equally important, when China achieves a credible deterrent, Peking's leaders may be more inclined than at present to reassess their strategic policies and consider the value of arms control.

The hope should be that Moscow as well as Washington will see the importance of this. But even if Moscow does not, the United States in shaping its own strategic and arms control policies, should take the "China problem," as well as the problem of United States-Soviet bilateral relations, fully into account.

Thank you.

COMMENDATION OF WITNESSES

Senator GORE. Since the Senate is now debating the Brooke resolution, I really have no choice but to express the deepest appreciation to both of you for your very learned discussion. You have been very helpful. I won't apologize for our interventions because the purpose of the hearing is to stimulate and promote public discussion and understanding. Thank you very much.

Mr. BARNETT. Thank you.

ARGUMENTS FOR DEPLOYMENT OF ANTI-CHINESE ABM SYSTEM

Senator CASE. May I ask a question of Mr. Barnett?

You have discussed several things that our Chinese deterrent won't do, won't accomplish.

What is your understanding of the reason those who urge this as a defense against Chinese nuclear attack do in fact urge it? Why is it urged? Why did McNamara urge it? What did he say was the reason why he urged it, and what is the reason that this Administration is urging it?

I do not understand, frankly, what they want to do, either one of them.

Mr. BARNETT. I wish I understood more fully. If you do not understand I will join you and say that I do not fully understand.

Senator CASE. I just wondered because——

Mr. BARNETT. I think underlying some people's position is a very vague kind of fear of the possibility of irrational action on the Chinese part, which I do not think is a valid one.

Senator CASE. I would agree fully if that is what is the reason.

Mr. BARNETT. In one of Mr. McNamara's speeches, for example, a very elaborate kind of situation was considered, in which the Chinese might have a fear of an initial first strike by the United States, and then be stimulated to make an earlier first strike themselves before all of their nuclear weapons were destroyed.

Senator CASE. Which would be suicidal.

Mr. BARNETT. Which, to me, is not in the realm of reality. I just cannot conceive of that kind of irrationality. But I do not have the full answer to your question.

Senator CASE. Well, thank you very much. I do not either. Do you Mrs. Hsieh?

Mrs. HSIEH. I was going to say my own impression at times has been that the China rationale has been used as a gimmick. On occasion I have called the work I have done on China and the ABM "the weapon system in search of a rationale." Rather than disturb or increase tensions with the Soviet Union the China rationale has been pulled out and then on the basis of that we develop an elaborate case of Chinese recklessness, adventurism, etc.

I think, on the other hand, there is the desire on the part of some people to maintain the momentum in the research and development o˙ the ABM. I think this possibility came out in the course of the hearings of a year ago, either in March or in May. In order to avoid using another rationale the Chinese rationale appeared to be a sort of a low-cost one without anyone thinking of all the implications that Professor Barnett and I have tried to bring out today.

Mr. BARNETT. Can I add one thing? I have been impressed that in the most recent statements great stress has been put on the argument that the ABM is necessary to maintain the credibility of our general policies in Asia, the implication being that if we did not build the ABM countries like Japan would lose their faith in us.

I am not convinced by that argument at all, as I tried to say earlier; on the contrary, to the extent that one can make a judgment on this, I am inclined to think that it would have the opposite effect.

Mrs. HSIEH. Yes.

Senator GORE. One justification for the deployment of ABM, as I understood the President, was to preserve the integrity of the Nixon doctrine in Southeast Asia.

That can do nothing but lead to a return of the old policy of massive retaliation or the threat to do so with nuclear weapons. It has not worked in Laos and Cambodia and, in my view, cannot work in these small situations.

Our country, in my view, will never unloose a nuclear war to preserve the credibility of a policy with respect to a small country in Southeast Asia.

UNACCEPTABILITY OF U.S. NUCLEAR ATTACK ON COMMUNIST CHINA

Senator CASE. Because we did not use nuclear weapons when we had a monopoly, it would seem to me incredible (if that is what is in mind), that China will be afraid that we will use them. And it seems to me incredible that any one of a number of countries will not regard our protection as a real protection unless America is invulnerable to an irrational attack. In other words, that is another way of saying the same thing, isn't that true, and I would say anything as irrational as that which would involve the destruction of China (because even though we might not be able to kill every single person in China because of the remoteness and vastness of the area, we certainly could deal them a terrible blow) which would be regarded as unacceptable, I take it.

Do you agree that a nuclear attack on China would be thoroughly unacceptable?

Mr. BARNETT. I would certainly hope so, and I believe so.

Mrs. HSIEH. Yes, very definitely so to the Chinese.

Senator CASE. By the Chinese. You do not believe there is anything to this point that if they only lose 300 or 400 million people China would still have some left?

Mrs. HSIEH. This is a myth that has grown over the years.

Mr. BARNETT. Apparently promoted by the Soviets, I might add.

Mrs. HSIEH. Mao is reported to have said at one time "We can lose 200 million people and we will still be a big country; we can lose 400 million people and we will still be a big country," I would argue Mao is the first one to realize, yes, China would be a big country, but it would be a big country minus all its modernization, all its industrial facilities, and so forth.

Senator CASE. Thank you very much.

ANNOUNCEMENT OF NEXT HEARING

Senator GORE. The next hearing in this series will be held on April 13, at which time Dr. Panofsky and Dr. Scoville will be the witnesses.

(Whereupon, at 12:50 p.m., the committee adjourned, to reconvene Monday, April 13, 1970, at 10 a.m.)

ABM, MIRV, SALT, AND THE NUCLEAR ARMS RACE

Safeguard, ABM, and SALT

MONDAY, APRIL 13, 1970

United States Senate,
Subcommittee on Arms Control,
International Law and Organization
of the Committee on Foreign Relations,
Washington, D.C.

The subcommittee met, pursuant to recess, at 10:05 a.m., in room 4221, New Senate Office Building, Senator Albert Gore (chairman of the subcommittee) presiding.

Present: Senators Gore, Fulbright (chairman of the full committee), Symington, Case, Aiken, and Cooper.

OPENING STATEMENT

Senator GORE. The subcommittee will come to order.

The subcommittee on Arms Control, International Law and Organization continues today hearings on the interrelated subjects of ABM, MIRV, SALT, and the nuclear arms race. Our witnesses today are Dr. Wolfgang K. H. Panofsky, director of the Stanford Linear Accelerator Center, and Dr. Herbert Scoville, Jr., of the Carnegie Endowment for International Peace and former Assistant Director of the Arms Control and Disarmament Agency.

Dr. Panofsky's subject is "Safeguard, ABM, and SALT." Last year Dr. Panofsky put his great technical knowledge and experience at the service of the subcommittee and did as much as anyone to educate the subcommittee and other Members of the Senate and the general public on the technical deficiencies of the Safeguard ABM system and the inconsistencies and contradictions in the rationale advanced for beginning deployment of the system. We are grateful to him for agreeing to continue that process of education today.

Dr. Scoville will address the problem of verification as it relates to limiting strategic arms, a subject of obvious importance, which perhaps has not been sufficiently explored in public. Last week the Senate adopted Senate Resolution 211 resolving that it was the sense of the Senate that the President should propose to the Soviet Government an immediate suspension by both the United States and the Soviet Union of the further deployment of all offensive and defensive nuclear strategic weapons systems, this mutual suspension to be "subject to national verification or such other measures of observation and inspection as may be appropriate." Verification is thus a key element in such a mutual suspension of the further deployment of strategic weapons systems, as indeed it is in any strategic arms limitation agreement. We are indeed fortunate to have a witness, as knowledgeable as Dr. Scoville on the subject, willing and able to talk to us.

I should add that on Wednesday afternoon the subcommittee will meet in executive session with witnesses from the Central Intelligence Agency to discuss certain aspects of verification that cannot be discussed in an open forum.

We seek to bring before the subcommittee in these hearings those witnesses best qualified to represent the opposing views on the various related questions of strategic weapons systems and arms limitations. We had hoped at this point in our hearing to receive testimony from the Secretary of Defense and the Director of Defense Development Research and Engineering in behalf of the Safeguard system in the context of the coming strategic arms talks. While the Department of Defense did not agree to provide witnesses at this time, I am pleased, nevertheless, that Secretary Laird has now agreed to appear before the subcommittee at a later date.

Pending his appearance we shall have to rely on earlier statements by the President, Secretary Laird, and Dr. John Foster for an understanding of the Administration's position. I asked our witnesses this morning to take into account previous Administration testimony in preparing their remarks. They are extremely well qualified to comment on the Administration's positions and I look forward to hearing their testimony, just as I look forward to the possible subsequent appearances of the Secretary of Defense and his subordinates on behalf of the Administration.

PROSPECTS FOR SALT

Before you proceed with your general statement, would you share with the subcommittee your general views with respect to the prospects at Vienna?

STATEMENT OF DR. WOLFGANG K. H. PANOFSKY, DIRECTOR, STANFORD LINEAR ACCELERATOR CENTER, STANFORD UNIVERSITY

Dr. PANOFSKY. Senator, I am generally optimistic that we will make progress. I hope very much that SALT will actually mark the end of the rapid growth of armaments on both sides and may even pave the way for future reductions, but at the present time there is such a large gap between us in communication, and in the understanding of one another's principles, that we have to be quite guarded in our optimism, at least as to hoping for their rapid development.

WORLD SECURITY INTERESTS ARE SERVED BY NUCLEAR ARMS CONTROL

Senator GORE. Some people, Doctor, are inclined to think that those of us who have pressed for a conference may not be as concerned with the security of our country and the threat to the Western World as others who have expressed doubts about the conference. I know this does not describe your attitude in many behind-closed-doors sessions where I have heard you speak of the necessity for the greatest of caution. Would you state that publicly?

Dr. PANOFSKY. I am very much concerned indeed with the security of the United States and also that of the world. But I am deeply convinced that more security can be had at a lower level of armament than at the high level of armament which we now have. So I strongly believe that security and high-level armaments do not go together, and I believe that the Soviet Union and ourselves have a common overriding interest, despite all the other differences which separate us: to preserve their security and our security the strategic arms race should be stopped—it is for this reason that I have some optimism.

Senator GORE. To put it in a little different way, you would agree, as I understand it, that in your view the greatest amount of security for the United States, for the Soviet Union, and for mankind would flow from a control of nuclear armaments rather than an increase in armaments.

Dr. PANOFSKY. Yes, sir; that is my view.

Senator GORE. Will you proceed with your statement?

Dr. PANOFSKY. Thank you very much.

Last year I had the opportunity of discussing the phase I ABM deployment decision before this committee, and I very much appreciate the privilege of appearing before you again this year.

Again to avoid any misunderstanding, let me say that I am testifying before you as an individual scientist who has been involved in defense matters in general and ABM in particular for a long period of time since 1955. I have been participating in various advisory roles since that time.

I would like to divide this testimony into two parts, with your permission, a general outline and a more detailed discussion.

PRESIDENT'S OBJECTIVES IN PROCEEDING WITH SAFEGUARD

Last year, during his press conference of March 14, 1969, the President gave three reasons for wishing to go forward with phase I of the Safeguard System:

(a) Protection of the land-based deterrent (Minuteman and SAC air fields).

(b) Protection against an accidentally launched missile: and

(c) A thin area defense against small nuclear powers, and presumably he meant mainland China.

In connection with announcing his deployment decision, the President emphasized several additional points last year. Among these were:

(a) He did not wish the ABM deployment to threaten the Soviet deterrent against U.S. attack. For this reason he specifically ruled out deployment of ABM in the role of defense of U.S. cities against Soviet attack; in contrast a defense dedicated solely to defending Minuteman silos does not threaten the Soviet deterrent.

(b) The deployment decision should not endanger the chance of success of the forthcoming SALT talks.

As I testified last year, I welcomed the President's statement that he did not wish to endanger SALT and that he did not wish to escalate the arms race further by endangering the Soviet deterrent, thus forcing the Soviet Union toward further increases of its own offensive weapons. However, I am opposed to the phase I deployment as actually carried out by the Department of Defense and to the proposed Safeguard expansion. In my opinion, these steps do not meet the President's objectives as stated in many essential respects as summarized here:

(a) The Safeguard system does very little, if anything, to protect the Minuteman force—better protection could be achieved at a lower cost on a comparable or shorter time scale;

(b) The President stated in his press conference of January 31, 1970, that he had been assured that the system would provide a "virtually infallible" defense against ICBM attack from China. Safeguard does not fit this description, nor does technology permit construction of a dependable ABM shield over the entire country;

(c) A national policy requiring a highly effective ABM defense against mainland China implies an ever-growing deployment of city defense ABM's, which would threaten the Soviet deterrent in direct contrast to the President's stated objectives; and

(d) An expanded ABM deployment, as now proposed, in particular considering its stated objective as being an anti-China defense, seriously interferes with the flexibility the President will have in negotiating an acceptable ABM level with the Soviet Union at the SALT talks.

The President promised that this program will be reviewed annually from the point of view of:

(a) Technical development:
(b) An expanded evolution of the threat; and
(c) The diplomatic context, including any talks on arms limitation.

JUSTIFICATION FOR EXPANDED ABM DEPLOYMENT QUESTIONED

Where, then, is the new experience on which the decision to expand ABM deployment now was to be based? There also have been no production of radars or missiles; the contract to develop the first site for future technical use was awarded by the Army just 2 weeks ago. The date at which equipment can be received at the sites has slipped by almost 1 year. None of the technical results in the ongoing development work have made Safeguard look better. On the contrary, several factors exist which tend to degrade the expected performance of Safeguard: The ability of the PAR, perimeter acquisition radar, to function in the presence of nuclear explosions is highly dubious, and the computer severely limits the performance of the system in handling large attacks: also, costs have risen substantially.

Where is the new threat justifying ABM expansion? The Soviet threat against Minuteman has indeed been growing, but it is just in defending Minuteman against growing threats that Safeguard is now admitted to be uneconomical and ineffective. As a "hedge" to counter the Soviet threat we can develop a system specifically designed to protect Minuteman on a time scale at least as fast as that of Safeguard, and at much lower cost. Estimates of a Chinese ICBM intercontinental ballistic missile threat have been slipping farther into the future; yet we are now reemphasizing the anti-China mission of Safeguard.

What is the diplomatic context to justify expansion of Safeguard now? The agreed level of ABM deployment which might arise from the SALT talks will control more than any other single factor the total level of strategic armament at which we might be able to freeze the weaponry of the world as a result of SALT. Authorization to expand Safeguard with emphasis on its anti-China mission would thus endanger the success of SALT, since the negotiability with the Soviets to reduce ABM levels is limited by such a decision. The argument for an expensive but technically ineffective expansion of Safeguard in order to "negotiate from a position of strength" has little merit: Although the Soviets have greater total explosive power than we do in their nuclear arsenal, we have numerical superiority of 3 to 1 in nuclear warheads, and U.S. MIRV's (Multiple Independently Targetable Reentry Vehicle) are ready for deployment.

Senator GORE. How much more strength would we need to negotiate from a position of strength?

Dr. PANOFSKY. This is of course a matter of political judgment. My personal view is that at present no further increases in numbers of warheads, or in ABM deployment are needed to negotiate from a position of strength. I think this is an unequaled opportunity to negotiate from a position where both sides can feel with confidence they have a secure deterrent.

The sequence of events between last year's Safeguard and this year's request for expansion gives little confidence that we are embarking on an "orderly, phased" deployment, carefully tailored to changing circumstances. I feel that this is the time to push toward a halt in the nuclear arms spiral—a race which has cast a shadow over the history of our time.

Senator GORE. I take it you would agree with the thrust of the resolution the Senate passed?

Dr. PANOFSKY. Yes, I think that the attempt to start negotiating from a temporary freeze in strategic weapons is well worth trying, but I also do believe if that was unsuccessful this is not a reason to be pessimistic about the main negotiations. I think it is well worth trying to go in that direction first.

PROTECTION OF MINUTEMAN

Let me go into somewhat more detail first in discussing the value of Safeguard in protecting the Minuteman.

During the past year the Soviet threat against the Minuteman force, due to growth of the numbers of Soviet SS-9 missiles of high explosive power, and owing to the recognized technical possibility of improved accuracy of Soviet missiles, has increased at approximately the rate forecast by Secretary Laird last year. However, a threat against Minuteman is not synonymous with a first strike capability against the United States, let alone a first strike threat against the United States, and does certainly not demonstrate a first strike intent. In last year's testimony it was conclusively demonstrated that a first strike against the United States would have to envisage a simultaneous attack against the American Minuteman force, the SAC (Strategic Air Command) bomber fleet, and the Polaris-Poseidon fleet on a time scale which is technically infeasible because of existing U.S.

early warning capabilities. I note that under current policies each of these U.S. forces is designed to be able to inflict enormous damage on the Soviet Union and on Mainland China; even after absorbing a first strike the level of damage the United States could inflict would be such that the society of the attacker would be unlikely to survive.

Nevertheless, in view of the reality of the emerging threat against Minuteman it might be prudent to consider a number of alternatives to improve the U.S. deterrent, such as:

(a) ABM defense of the Minuteman force against missile attack. This is the subject of discussion here;

(b) Phase-out of the land-based deterrent force and relying for deterrence entirely on an airborne bomber force and an improved or amplified submarine force;

(c) Increase in the hardness of the Minuteman force or improvement of its chance for survival under attack through increased mobility; and

(d) Increase in the number of Minuteman silos at a rate sufficent to stay ahead of the Soviet threat.

But the best alternative is limitation of the threat by freezing the numbers of Soviet missiles as a result of the SALT talks, possibly preceded by an agreed temporary moratorium during the talks.

Naturally, the last alternative is the most attractive one from the point of view of the peace of the world; thus nothing should be done to endanger the success of SALT.

Secretary Laird has testified that he considers this year's request for military authorization—which includes expansion of the Safeguard system at a cost of $1.45 billion of new obligational authority—to be a holding operation in order to avoid the difficult decisions this year among the alternate options listed. He maintained that defense of the Minuteman silos is a nonthreatening hedge to lengthen the period of time over which Minuteman might be expected to survive. With this conclusion I agree, as I also agreed with the President's stated objective to protect Minuteman last year. However, during last year's hearings, many witnesses—and I among them—introduced several technical criticisms which have never been answered satisfactorily by the Defense Department on the role of Safeguard in Minuteman defense. The dominant points of these criticisms were: The Safeguard system provides only a single, very expensive—about $200 million—radar for each Minuteman complex and only a very small, still classified, number of Sprint missiles to protect the Minuteman silos and the radar. If, therefore, the radar were to malfunction, or be destroyed by enemy attack, then the whole system collapses. Attack on the radar is an attractive enemy tactic, since the Missile Site Radar (MSR) is much "softer", that is vulnerable, than the missile silos it defends.

Defense of an entire Minuteman complex by a single MSR radar contradicts the fundamental philosophy of the Minuteman system: The value of Minuteman as a deterrent is based on the survival, separate survival, of each silo, independent of any other silo which might be destroyed. The single radar on which the entire defense depends is thus the Achilles heel of the entire system and a substantial part of the defense has to be dedicated to protecting this radar, that is, to "defending the defense."

SAFEGUARD SPECIFICATIONS AND OBJECTIVES

Senator CASE. Dr. Panofsky, will you just permit this brief intervention? Have you seen the contract for the building of this system? Do you know what the specifications are and what the system is supposed to do?

Dr. PANOFSKY. I have not seen the contract, sir.

Senator CASE. This is not for technical purposes, but what I am trying to get at is what it is that the system as contracted for is supposed to accomplish.

Dr. PANOFSKY. I have just been exposed to the three stated objectives of the President; namely, protection of Minuteman, protection against accidental launch and the "thin" defense protection against China. But I have not seen the detailed numerical specifications.

Senator CASE. Would it not be a good thing for us to see what these are, to see what it is that we are asking the manufacturer to accomplish?

Dr. PANOFSKY. I am rather sure that a detailed quantitative description as to what it is to accomplish may not exist in detail. For instance, I refer to the fact that the complexity of the computer has limited the magnitude of the threat which can be handled. I believe that at the present moment there is no firm specification as to how large a threat is to be handled by Safeguard. I think that this is still to be determined as a result of the ongoing development.

Senator CASE. Well, in other words, we are beginning to build something we don't know what for?

Dr. PANOFSKY. We know what for, but we don't know how much it will accomplish in relation to the stated objective. It is a quantitative uncertainty. Qualitatively the objectives have been stated, but we keep changing the emphasis among the objectives, and we keep changing the estimates, how much quantitatively can be accomplished.

Senator CASE. Well, this is the heart of the matter, isn't it?

Dr. PANOFSKY. That is right. In my view——

Senator CASE. If you are going to have protection, you are going to have protection. You are not going to take two jumps from the ferry to the slip which is not quite enough.

Dr. PANOFSKY. That is right. In my view, the quantitative aspect as to how much protection for Minuteman we are actually buying is the crux of the matter. And my view is that we are buying very, very little at a very large cost.

Senator CASE. Thank you.

U.S. RETALIATORY OFFENSIVE CAPACITY

Senator GORE. To put it in layman's language, Doctor, as I understand your testimony thus far, you are not saying that Minuteman in fixed silos constitute only a small part of our retaliatory offensive capacity, are you?

Dr. PANOFSKY. No, I am not quite saying that. I am saying it constitutes a substantial part of our retaliatory capacity, but that Minuteman, Polaris and the SAC bombers are each truly formidable retaliatory forces and I also agree that in time the Minuteman force will be threatened if the Soviet build-up continues. What I am saying is that Safeguard does essentially nothing in protecting it.

Senator GORE. Of course. A thousand Minuteman nuclear missiles should not be described in any context as small.

Dr. PANOFSKY. That is right.

Senator GORE. I agree, but compared to the total number of nuclear force loadings that we have, 1,000 is some fraction of the total.

Dr. PANOFSKY. That is correct. I will introduce into the testimony later the chart which Secretary Laird included in his budget presentation to the Senate last month which documents what you say, namely, that as of September 1, 1969, the United States has over 4,000 nuclear strategic weapons in its deliverable arsenal.

VULNERABILITY OF MINUTEMEN AND ABM'S

Senator GORE. Then, secondly, as I understand your statement, you make the point that the stationary characteristic of the Minutemen in silos renders them more vulnerable to attack than, let us say, missiles on submarines?

Dr. PANOFSKY. Yes, that is correct. The nature of the threat against Minuteman is the fact that they are stationary; therefore, with increased accuracy and increased explosive power of enemy missiles they are becoming exposed.

Senator GORE. And thirdly, you make the point that ABM defensive missiles, which are supposed to defend the Minuteman, are more vulnerable than the Minuteman and, therefore, we would have to defend the defensive ABM's.

Dr. PANOFSKY. Yes. I am saying that the radar is more vulnerable than the missiles it defends and, therefore, it itself will be an attractive target and, therefore, we have to dedicate a fair fraction of the defensive missiles to defend the defending radar.

Senator GORE. So, the ABM is a defense of the most vulnerable strategic weapon and the ABM then is still more vulnerable and the radar of the ABM is still more vulnerable?

Dr. PANOFSKY. Yes; that is correct.

Senator GORE. So we really are dealing with an Achilles heel.

Dr. PANOFSKY. That is the central point. We are buying very little. If one calculates for various models of attack how many extra missiles the enemy would have to have to defeat Minuteman with Safeguard or without, you get only really minute differences in what he would need.

Senator GORE. Thank you very much.

NECESSITY OF "DEDICATED" DEFENSE FOR MINUTEMAN

Dr. PANOFSKY. Now this criticism is aggravated by a second objection never answered by the Defense Department. The Soviet SS-11 missiles (which now exist in much larger quantities than the SS-9's) are at present of sufficient accuracy and explosive power to destroy the missile site radar, although they do not endanger the Minuteman silos. Thus, in effect a Safeguard defense to protect Minuteman against the SS-9 could be totally negated by the Soviets even if the system were deployed today.

During the last year it has become clear beyond a reasonable doubt that if the defense of Minuteman were the only, or even the principal function of Safeguard, its deployment clearly could not be justified.

Not only is the number of Minuteman silos saved by the Safeguard negligible, but it is also clear that if the attempt were made to increase the protection offered by Safeguard by increasing the numbers of missiles and radars using the Safeguard technology, then such an undertaking would be enormously expensive. Specifically, the cost per silo defended would be many times the cost of each Minuteman saved and the defense cost would also exceed the cost of the enemy missiles which could be intercepted with confidence.

These criticisms have now been tacitly agreed to this year by the Defense Department. Secretary Laird——

Senator GORE. What do you mean by tacitly?

Dr. PANOFSKY. Implicitly would be the more correct way of saying it.

Senator GORE. All right.

Dr. PANOFSKY. Have been implicitly agreed to by the Defense Department.

Secretary Laird in his statement on February 20, 1970, before the Joint Session of the Armed Services and Appropriations Committees of the Senate, proposed:

> If, in the future, the defense of Minuteman has to be expanded, new and smaller additional radars placed in Minuteman fields would be less costly than the Safeguard Missile Site Radar (MSR) because they would not have to cover such large areas. For this reason we will pursue a program to determine the optimum radar for such a defense and begin the development of this radar and associated components in fiscal year 1971.

Similarly, the Secretary of the Air Force stated before the Senate Armed Services Committee in March 1970:

> If the Soviets continue to increase the threat (against Minuteman) it may prove most cost effective to rely on a broader list of defensive measures * * * *close hardpoint defense*, hardening and multi-basing as examples. * * *

The Deputy Secretary of Defense recently testified to the House Committee on Armed Services:

> For example, we have under consideration a new, smaller, less expensive radar and data processor aimed specifically at close-in defense of Minuteman * * *.

May I quote in contrast the statement of the Secretary last year, on April 16, 1969, in which he said that he saw "no feasible substitute for Safeguard."

The Secretary of Defense has now proposed an additional appropriation of $158 million for these new development programs, intended to protect Minuteman by techniques better than Safeguard. This is an admission of the validity of the technical criticisms voiced last year: Those witnesses opposing Safeguard deployment maintained that a more effective and less expensive way to defend Minuteman would clearly be a system which employed smaller radars rather than a large, vulnerable one. The Defense Department now recognizes belatedly that any hope of a reasonably effective defense of Minuteman would require the development and deployment of a system of defense against incoming missiles which is specifically "dedicated" to defense of hardened Minuteman silos, rather than being a general purpose development such as the Safeguard adaptation of the former Sentinel and Nike-X systems, which were primarily designed as city defense ABM systems.

DO WE HAVE TIME TO DEVELOP BETTER MINUTEMAN DEFENSE?

A frequent "criticism of the critics" voiced last year was, "Assuming you are right, that Safeguard is technically very poorly suited to defending Minuteman, but considering the evolving threat, can we afford to wait to develop a better system specifically designed for defending Minuteman?" The answer to that question is, "Yes, we can." The total schedule for deploying the Safeguard Phase I defense is not controlled by providing the hardware—that is, the missile and radars—but is paced by the unprecedented complexity of the computer and the associated programing which is required to control the system.

Last year Secretary Packard testified that the data processing job was a large one and this year DOD witnesses testified that progress was "satisfactory." What they did not state was that the programing task not only controls the level of threat which can be handled, but also paces the entire deployment schedule. Therefore, "doing the job right" will not delay the time at which Minuteman could be defended, and may in fact shorten it.

IMPAIRMENT OF PAR RADAR BY PROXIMITY OF NUCLEAR EXPLOSIONS

Last year critics expressed concern that the performance of the PAR radar would be impaired by the proximity of nuclear explosions. This year Dr. Foster testified on February 24, 1970: "We have encountered no serious problems in engineering the PAR." What he did not state is that the concern of the critics is more than justified: Nuclear bursts degrade the expected performance of the PAR to such an extent that there now is great doubt that the PAR can contribute to the defense of Minuteman at all, and that furthermore its role in area coverage is seriously impaired. I consider this a "serious engineering problem."

Senator CASE. How much of this is a quote? Is that just an error?

Dr. PANOFSKY. I am referring back to Dr. Foster's testimony, Senator Case——

Senator CASE. I see.

Dr. PANOFSKY. I am fundamentally expressing disagreement with the statement of Dr. Foster.

Senator CASE. May I ask you, because of the importance of this point, what is your statement based upon, what evidence?

Dr. PANOFSKY. I am afraid I cannot discuss this in open session.

Senator CASE. But you are satisfied it is factually true?

Dr. PANOFSKY. I am satisfied with its correctness.

Senator FULBRIGHT. Dr. Panofsky, it looks to me in a way that Dr. Foster deliberately misled the committee.

Dr. PANOFSKY. Well, I am saying that my definition of what an engineering problem is and Dr. Foster's definition are different.

Senator CASE. You would not try to quibble, either of you, about the use of engineering as opposed to some other kind of aspect, would you?

Dr. PANOFSKY. I believe what Dr. Foster referred to was that they have not encountered serious problems in the actual putting together of the hardware of the PAR. But he did not include in his statement the evaluation of performance of the device.

Senator FULBRIGHT. Have you ever discussed this matter with Dr. Foster?

Dr. PANOFSKY. Not personally; no, sir.

Senator FULBRIGHT. Why not?

Dr. PANOFSKY. There hasn't been a logical opportunity.

Senator FULBRIGHT. They are not very anxious for outside advice, I take it.

Dr. PANOFSKY. No; I believe this particular matter has been brought to Dr. Foster's attention.

Senator FULBRIGHT. If what you say is true, it is a deliberate misrepresentation on their part. I am not raising any question. You certainly should know. I think it is a deliberate misrepresentation, misleading of the Congress and the country in an effort to promote the ABM.

Dr. PANOFSKY. As I said before, his statement describes no serious engineering problem to the PAR, and I believe he did not include in his statement some of the changing revisions of the effectiveness of the PAR. I was being deliberate in the words which I chose here when I said there is great doubt that the PAR can contribute to the defense of Minuteman at all. However, its contribution to area defense, the anti-China mission, does remain substantial.

Senator FULBRIGHT. I don't see how any reasonable person could say that a nuclear burst in the vicinity of a PAR is not one of the engineering problems that has to be overcome. It is a problem which engineering must overcome. I don't see how any reasonable person could say otherwise and, therefore, if what you say is correct, I think he is deliberately misleading the committee and the country.

Senator COOPER. Can I ask a question there?

Senator GORE. Senator Cooper.

Senator COOPER. By "nuclear burst" do you mean the defensive ABM or the incoming enemy weapon?

Dr. PANOFSKY. Both, sir. The problems which are involved here would be irrespective as to whether you are talking about defensive or offensive bursts.

EXPECTATIONS FOR SAFEGUARD

Senator CASE. This is the kind of thing I was trying to get at before when I asked what the expectations for this system were. It is one thing to say that A, B, C, and D will be done, and the contractor can get his money when those things are done, but it isn't the same to say this is going to protect Minuteman or protect against a Chinese threat or protect against a stray missile coming in by mistake. The whole problem has to be included, it seems to me, if we are going to evaluate the performance and usefulness of the system; is that correct?

Dr. PANOFSKY. Yes; I agree it would be good if there was a numerical expectation which says very specifically we could stop so many incoming missiles with so and so much confidence, and it would be good to have that. However, as the development has proceeded some of the estimates of effectiveness have indeed been moving around.

Senator CASE. I was just trying to get at what the situation was in that regard.

Senator GORE. Senator Cooper, did you have a question?

SAFEGUARD'S READINESS FOR DEPLOYMENT

Senator COOPER. I don't want to interrupt his testimony now but we recall all last year, we recall that there had been argument, repeated again and again by the Administration, that the system was ready to deploy. At some point I wish you would tell us what, if anything, is ready to be deployed.

Dr. PANOFSKY. Well, I testified in the first part of my statement——

Senator COOPER. Yes.

Dr. PANOFSKY (continuing). That at this moment the contract to begin work on the first site has just been let 2 weeks ago but not as yet on the second site authorized last year; there has been no actual production, so at present the progress, which was testified to by the Defense Department witnesses, was primarily progress in the development work, not actual production.

LIMITS OF SAFEGUARD PROTECTION OF MINUTEMAN

Let me summarize, the totality of all these technical facts amount to only one thing: Even if Safeguard functions perfectly it offers significant protection to Minuteman only over a very narrow band of threats; if the threat continues to grow as rapidly as it is at present, Safeguard is obsolete before deployed; if the threat levels off, Safeguard is not needed. If one combines this fact with the likelihood of catastrophic failure of the single radar and computer controling the system, and the fact that a less failure prone and more effective system to defend Minuteman can be produced on the same time scale for less money, Safeguard looks like a very poor use of the shrinking defense dollar indeed.

Senator SYMINGTON. Mr. Chairman, may I ask a question?

Senator GORE. Senator Symington.

SECRECY SURROUNDING PAR AND NUCLEAR BURSTS

Senator SYMINGTON. Dr. Panofsky, I will defer questions until my time comes, but would ask this question at this time. The chairman asked you about the details of the PAR and the nuclear bursts, and the ultimate degradation of the performance of that vital link in this overall operation. You say you cannot answer it in open session, but then you say it is a matter of general knowledge.

It is becoming increasingly clear to me over the years that one of the chief reasons we are in deep trouble economically, as well as perhaps physically because of overcommitment, is all the secrecy that surrounds the entire nuclear picture in this Government; not giving out information that every American wants to know about and so many other people already know about. I think this has resulted in the wasting of billions of dollars, and I have been in a position to watch it. I also believe this secrecy may be getting us into something which might be called a trap.

With those premises, if it is a matter of general knowledge, why can't you discuss it before the American people and this committee? Those were your own words.

Dr. PANOFSKY. What is a matter of general knowledge is the qualitative nature of these problems. What is not a matter of general knowledge is the detailed numerical analysis which indicates how serious these problems might be, and I have to abide by the classification rules as anybody else regarding the nature of these calculations.

Senator SYMINGTON. I don't mean to labor it, but what you are saying is that people in the Soviet, people say like Dr. Kapitza, would know as much about this as we do. They never tell their people anything they don't want to, but as I understand our system, we are supposed to give our people all facts on a matter of general knowledge that does not help the enemy. So why is there this constant refusal to disclose to the American people what everybody else knows in the world except those who have the misfortune to live under a totalitarian form of government. Of course, the leaders of those countries know about it.

Dr. PANOFSKY. I am sure that the Soviets know about the general nature of these problems but I am also not sure that they have been able to analyze and compute in detail as to how serious quantitatively these problems are.

I am not saying this as an excuse to hold these things as tight as they are being held, but I would not take it for granted that the Soviets do know these specific results to the extent that we do.

Senator SYMINGTON. If you say you do not think this information should be released, that would satisfy me. Is that what you are saying?

Dr. PANOFSKY. No; I am not saying that. I believe that a statement, the information should be released which indicates at least qualitatively the seriousness of these problems—rather than trying to avoid the issue.

Senator SYMINGTON. Thank you.

Dr. PANOFSKY. Shall I continue, Senator?

Senator GORE. Yes, please.

DEFENSE OF MINUTEMAN DOES NOT JUSTIFY SAFEGUARD

Dr. PANOFSKY. Now let me turn to the second mission of the Safeguard defense; namely, the defense against Chinese ICBM's, and let me start again with the statement that there is now general agreement that the mission of defending Minuteman alone cannot justify Safeguard Phase I deployment, let alone deployment of an amplified Safeguard system.

Senator GORE. When you say general agreement, to whom do you refer?

Dr. PANOFSKY. I believe in this statement I am referring to the defense community in general. I would rather not elaborate on specific individuals.

Senator GORE. All right.

Dr. PANOFSKY. Therefore, the principal justification for continuing deployment has been the multiple-purpose nature of the system because the purpose emphasized last year; namely, defending Minuteman, has really not stood up to the technical criticism; this is really what I am saying.

Senator GORE. If I understand, you are saying that the justification given for the deployment of phase I a year ago is now deficient?

Dr. PANOFSKY. If concern about the survival of Minuteman was the only concern, then it is now, I believe, generally agreed in the defense community that a different system; namely, one which is specifically dedicated toward defending Minuteman and is not a potential city defense would be cheaper and could be gotten ready on a faster time scale.

Senator GORE. Therefore, we now must justify it within the context of the Chinese threat?

Dr. PANOFSKY. Yes; that is correct, that is what I am coming to.

Senator GORE. All right.

SAFEGUARD AS CITY DEFENSE

Dr. PANOFSKY. Therefore, the principal motive for wishing to go forward has again become the role of the system in defense of cities. It was this role which was deemphasized in the testimony of Department of Defense witnesses last year; for example, the Deputy Secretary of Defense testified before this committee on March 26, 1969:

> I must say that I am very pleased to know that you and I have come to the same conclusion on this matter—that an ABM defense of our cities makes no sense and that it is the kind of thing that does lead to escalation of the arms race. That is one of the first conclusions I came to after getting into the study of this matter. That is why I have recommended a different course—the course of protecting our retaliatory capability rather than protecting our cities.

However, the President put city defense again into primary focus as an anti-Chinese defense during his press conference of January 31 of this year. This shifting role of Safeguard was described by Senator Gore last year by the words "a defense looking for a mission;" we now find that such a multiple role system is very poorly suited for the defense of Minuteman and is also of little value in offering total protection against a possible Chinese threat, and I will discuss this point now.

SAFEGUARD AS PROTECTION AGAINST COMMUNIST CHINESE THREAT

Although there has been progress in the development of Chinese nuclear devices, our projections of a Chinese ICBM capability have continuously slipped in time. We expected that the Chinese would undertake an experimental launch of an ICBM in 1967—as was recently mentioned by Secretary Laird—but now the expectation of such an event has slipped to 1970, a shift of 3 years. What is therefore the new urgency for an anti-ICBM defense against China?

The President, in his press conference of January 31, 1970, indicated that he had been assured that Safeguard would provide a "virtually infallible" defense to provide a "credible foreign policy in the Pacific areas." Presumably under such an umbrella the United States can use its nuclear power to respond to Communist moves without exposing its population.

Senator GORE. Can you explain how that would apply to Cambodia and Laos just now?

Dr. PANOFSKY. I have no comment on that, sir.

I will not enter into the controversial question whether the threat by the United States of a nuclear massive retaliation against unacceptable Communist moves is a wise or moral policy in Asia; I only would like to point out that for this role Safeguard is subject to many valid technical objections. The thin area defense proposed is very fallible indeed for many reasons. Among these are:

(a) Any system as complex as an ABM and which can never be tested is subject to many sources of failure—human or technical.

(b) Since the PAR radar is required for complete area coverage the nuclear environment produced both by explosions of the defensive Spartan missile and the incoming missile can interfere with proper functioning in many ways.

(c) Since each interceptor will never have perfect reliability there is always a good chance of the enemy's attack leaking through.

(d) The area defense against China is of no value at all until one has completed the full deployment of all planned sites, since otherwise it can be bypassed by ICBM attack against uncovered areas. Hawaii and Alaska are not covered by Safeguard.

(e) Many mechanical devices designed to penetrate ABM defenses and which can be added to ICBM's with relative ease are well known. These could be adopted by the Chinese at their option to confuse and thus defeat the radar.

(f) Should the Chinese really plan or threaten a suicidal attack against the United States they would have means other than an ICBM to deliver a nuclear explosion to the U.S. homeland, for instance by smuggling in a bomb.

Secretary Packard, in his testimony to the Committee on Armed Services of the U.S. House of Representatives, agreed that "Relatively simple devices like tank fragments have a limited ability to deceive a sophisticated defense system like Safeguard." I would go beyond this by stating that the Safeguard area defense can definitely be defeated by tactics as simple as tank fragmentation (the United States did this in its Atlas program in the late fifties!), as well as other simple penetration devices such as balloons. It is well known from more than a decade of experience that defeating the defense by presenting many confusing objects outside the atmosphere is no longer a technological challenge.

TANK FRAGMENTATION

Senator FULBRIGHT. What is tank fragmentation?

Dr. PANOFSKY. If you blow up the tank which propels the reentry vehicle into space, then it blows apart and forms several independent targets which in the vacuum move with the same or approximately the same speed as the main vehicle.

Senator FULBRIGHT. I see.

Dr. PANOFSKY. And therefore the radar can't tell which is which until the fragments enter the atmosphere.

Senator GORE. But scattered over many miles of space.

Dr. PANOFSKY. It can be scattered over many miles of space depending on how much explosive power is used initially to spread them apart. And we did this, as I mentioned, in the late 1950's.

In his testimony, Secretary Packard tried to minimize the threat of such Chinese moves by pointing out that the Chinese would have to construct range instrumentation to monitor whether the tank has actually exploded and would have to possess detailed knowledge of the characteristics of Safeguard. Since the President was proposing protection in "perhaps 10 years from now" it is clear that the Chinese are fully capable of providing such simple radar instrumentation once they have successfully mastered the technology of ICBM development itself.

RANGE INSTRUMENTATION MONITORING OF TANK EXPLOSION

Senator CASE. Would you mind explaining that for one who really does not understand technical things very well? What is range instrumentation? Why is it necessary to monitor whether the tank explodes?

Dr. PANOFSKY. They have to monitor it. What Secretary Packard was referring to was the following: If the Chinese would use this tactic of blowing up the tank, then they would have to have some instrumentation to find out whether they had been successful, since this blow up occurs beyond the visible range they would have to have some radars to look at the sky to see whether they had been successful, since this blow up occurs beyond the visible range they would have to have some radars to look at the sky to see whether the tank had in fact blown up the way it was supposed to.

Senator CASE. Why is that necessary for this purpose?

Dr. PANOFSKY. If they wanted to use that technique for penetration of U.S. defenses, then presumably they should test it; in order to test it they have to find out whether it did in fact work.

Senator CASE. You mean this is testing, this isn't operating it?

Dr. PANOFSKY. Testing, not operation.

Senator CASE. I am sorry. Thank you, Doctor.

Dr. PANOFSKY. My feeling is that since we are talking about 10 years from now and it takes a simple kind of radar to do this, and therefore I feel there is little substance to this particular point raised by the Secretary.

INADEQUACY OF SAFEGUARD PROTECTION AGAINST COMMUNIST CHINESE

Considering this combination of facts it is clear that an area defense system such as Safeguard can never be expected to achieve total protection. Defeating Safeguard, if desired by the Chinese, would, of course, require additional effort, but it is an effort which they are clearly capable of undertaking. The only hope would be that the Chinese would not choose to adopt measures to defeat Safeguard, or would fail to remedy some essential defect of their ICBM's.

I am impressed how tortured the argument of the DOD witnesses has become: In order to justify Safeguard as a defense against Soviet missiles and to justify immediate deployment of MIRV against suspected clandestine Soviet ABM defenses, we are giving the Soviets credit for a degree of performance and reliability of their military systems which we could not dream of achieving ourselves: on the other hand, when talking about an infallible defense against China we are assuming that even a decade from now the Chinese could not achieve results we accomplished more than 10 years ago.

The serious inadequacy of the area defense against China will, of course, become apparent to us as time goes on. As a result pressure will mount to add progressively to the thin defense to make it more and more effective against the conjectured threat from mainland China. This means that once the United States has adopted the policy that it needs a complete shield against China the stage is set for an ever-expanding but never fully effective ABM system at enormous cost. My point is here that I am more concerned about the policy than the actual implementation.

TECHNOLOGICAL ARMS RACE WITH CHINA

It is this last conclusion, namely, that adoption of an anti-Chinese ABM policy leads us to a technological arms race with China, which gives rise to the most serious concern: Pressures will rise to have each area of the country covered by a thicker defense so that each center of population can be protected against the total Chinese ICBM force. But the very existence of a growing U.S. city ABM system, however dubious its performance, would lead the conservative Soviet planners to conclude that their deterrence against U.S. first strike nuclear attack is threatened: Therefore the Soviets will press for expansion of their offensive weapons. Conversely, the U.S. conservative planners, being well aware of the technical deficiencies of Safeguard, are ignoring the protection it may offer in their strategic force planning. It was for this reason that last year President Nixon in his March 14, 1969, press conference ruled out a substantial city defense ABM; he agreed that such a move would be escalatory and hence undesirable. This year this position appears reversed through the emphasis on defense against China, although in the intervening year no developments have created a new urgency to deploy an anti-Chinese ABM.

RELATION OF ABM TO SALT

I would now like to turn to my most important topic, namely, the relation of the ABM to SALT.

In the previous sections I have demonstrated that Safeguard is ineffective in defending Minuteman, and is incapable of providing a tight umbrella over the United States to defend reliably against ICBM attacks which mainland China might be able to launch late this decade. Despite the clear technical limitations of Safeguard as an anti-Chinese defense the very fact that the President has stated such a defense to be a U.S. policy objective creates a danger to the success of SALT. Fortunately, the President has emphasized, in particular in his more recent statements, that he considers ABM levels fully negotiable in the forthcoming SALT talks. I hope that the President can justify to the American people giving away in negotiation with the Soviets a system which he is now persuading the American people is a defense we need against Communist China.

UNITED STATES-SOVIET STRATEGIC OFFENSIVE FORCES

While emphasizing the negotiability of ABM deployment the President and DOD witnesses urge an expanded Safeguard system now, in spite of the obvious technical inadequacies, in order to be in a position of negotiating from strength at SALT. The expressed fear is that since the Soviet strategic forces are growing in numbers, while the $7 billion U.S. strategic budget is only buying qualitative improvements, the Soviets will not feel under sufficient military pressure to negotiate a limitation of strategic arms under terms acceptable to the United States. But are we really negotiating from weakness? Quite apart from MIRV deployment, the status of United States versus

Soviet intercontinental strategic offensive forces (as presented on February 20, 1970, by Secretary Laird) is given in the following table which I have posted here on this chart.

(The table referred to follows.)

UNITED STATES VERSUS SOVIET INTERCONTINENTAL STRATEGIC OFFENSIVE FORCES

	Sept 1, 1968—		Sept 1, 1969—	
	United States	Soviet	United States	Soviet
ICBM launchers	1,054	900	1,054	1,060
SLBM launchers	656	45	656	110
Total launchers	1,710	945	1,710	1,170
Intercontinental bombers	646	150	581	140–145
Total force loadings: Weapons	4,200	1,100	4,200	1,350

This, Mr. Chairman, is an exact copy of the chart which Secretary Laird introduced February 20 in his testimony before the appropriate Senate committees.

Now, on this chart you see that the total number of deliverable warheads as of September 1969 is 4,200 on the side of the United States, and 1,350 on the side of the Soviets.

This belies the fact that the United States is in an inferior position. At present the United States is clearly ahead by a large factor in the total number of deliverable nuclear warheads while the Soviets are ahead in terms of the total explosive power of their weapons.

Senator GORE. Doctor, what would be total force loadings a year or two years from now, if we proceed with this program?

Dr. PANOFSKY. If the Soviets continue at their present deployment rate, it is estimated that the SS-9 force will grow roughly 50 per year or so, and then the SS-11 will also continue to increase and so will the submarines.

You can see that the Soviets have been gaining by 350 warheads through the last year and that rate may continue or not.

Senator GORE. While we have the capacity of destroying the Soviet Union many times over and they have the capacity of destroying the United States several times over, should we and they seek greater security by being able to destroy each other many more times?

Dr. PANOFSKY. That is, I think, a very valid question.

RESCHEDULING OF WITNESSES

Senator GORE. With this interruption, let me ask the indulgence of the commitee. Dr. Panofsky has given us such a comprehensive statement. It is now 11 o'clock and all of us will want to question him. If it would be agreeable with you, Dr. Scoville, would you be so accommodating to the committee as to postpone your testimony until tomorrow so we can deal more fully with Dr. Panofsky today?

Dr. SCOVILLE. Yes, sir.

Senator GORE. The committee would appreciate it. This is particularly helpful to us because Dr. Carl Kaysen had a misfortune yesterday. He is in the hospital and is unable to appear tomorrow, so we will have a full go at you tomorrow, and at Dr. Fisher.

Then, the day is yours, Doctor.

NUMBERS BUILDUP IF UNITED STATES DEPLOYS MIRVS

If I may, with this little added leeway, ask one other question with respect to this projection: If the United States continues with MIRV deployment, will we not soon reach the level of 10,000 warheads?

Dr. PANOFSKY. Yes, this is correct. I believe last year in testimony here, your own charts presented the numbers buildup if MIRV's would be deployed.

As you know, the multiplicity of the MIRV's and Poseidon were such that these numbers would go up enormously.

RELATIVE IMPORTANCE OF NUMBERS AND EXPLOSIVE POWER

However, as you know, there is a steady debate going on of what is more important, numbers or explosive power. I testified here that the United States is ahead in numbers of independent warheads which can be delivered, and the Soviets are ahead in terms of total megatonnage, in terms of total explosive power. So whenever there is a debate between the groups who would like to put a limit to the arms race now and those who would like to build up the forces further by saying we should negotiate from strength, the two groups are generally talking about different subjects.

Many military people are frequently talking about the inequality in explosive power, where the Soviets are ahead, and I am talking here. using Mr. Laird's chart, about the number of independent deliverable warheads.

Now, I maintain when you are talking about a deterrent role what counts is the number of warheads, not the total explosive power; if a city is destroyed by several nuclear weapons, the total damage to a city doesn't change very much whether you use weapons carrying one megaton or five megatons or a half-megaton of explosive power.

Senator GORE. Or 50.

Doctor, put this into context: Even the smallest of the anticipated MIRV warheads would be several times as powerful as the weapon that destroyed Hiroshima?

Dr. PANOFSKY. That is correct, sir.

Senator GORE. Would it be 50 times as powerful?

Dr. PANOFSKY. No, sir; the smallest one would not be 50 times but would be several times. The smallest one of the planned MIRV's on our part would be larger than the Hiroshima and Nagasaki bombs by a substantial factor but not 50 times. I can assure you, those who have seen the recently released movie on the damage to Hiroshima and Nagasaki will agree that it does not matter very much.

Senator GORE. Whatever the factor of greater magnitude, if it is large enough to destroy a city, that would seem large enough to accomplish the purpose, if the purpose is to destroy a city?

Dr. PANOFSKY. Yes.

Senator FULBRIGHT. Very good logic. [Laughter.]

IMPORTANCE OF ACCURACY

Senator CASE. When you speak of those two factors, particularly from the standpoint of capability against a Minuteman force, then accuracy is something that is terribly important; is that not correct?

Dr. PANOFSKY. This is correct. The effectiveness of an attack against the Minuteman force depends on a combination of accuracy and explosive power. The higher the accuracy the less explosive power you need. The Soviets in the SS-9 have a very much larger explosive power than the American Minuteman. Therefore, the Minuteman would need a very much higher accuracy to be a threat against the Soviet SS-9 than the SS-9 needs to be a threat against Minuteman.

Senator GORE. May I suggest you proceed and come to SALT?

SOVIET TEST OF LARGEST NUCLEAR WEAPON

Senator SYMINGTON. Mr. Chairman, as long as we got into the details of this, and based on the largest drop in the Arctic, isn't it true that the Soviets have dropped a nuclear weapon which is perhaps a thousand times stronger than the Hiroshima bomb?

Dr. PANOFSKY. A thousand times stronger than Hiroshima? It is well known the Soviets have conducted a test which is the largest one which anyone has tested. However, it has also been said in public testimony that the reason we have not gone to the extremely high megatonnages is not because of our inability to do so but because of our conviction, which I share, that this is not a useful military objective.

UNITED STATES-SOVIET STRATEGIC NUCLEAR POWER

So let me continue. The chart there belies the fact that the United States is in an inferior position. At present the United States is clearly ahead by a large factor in the total number of deliverable nuclear warheads while the Soviets are ahead in terms of the total explosive power of their weapons. Under current circumstances neither side could deliver a first strike against the other without exposing itself to a retaliatory blow of such enormous magnitude as to endanger the very survival of the society of the attacker. However, the Soviets appear to be racing ahead to achieve a nuclear "war fighting" capability and the United States has already acquired nuclear strategic armaments greatly in excess of those required for deterrent purposes only. What better time could there be for both sides to attempt to freeze strategic armaments near current levels rather than escalating the arms race further by trying to negotiate "from a position strength?"

EFFECT OF EXPANDED SAFEGUARD ON SALT

Once the Congress approves an expanded Safeguard under the announced policy to give full protection against Chinese ICBM's it will be difficult for the U.S. negotiators to propose ABM levels below those authorized at home. In turn the Soviets will find it impossible to agree to ABM levels on their own below those proposed by the United States. I note that current Soviet ABM deployment levels consist of only the few interceptors and associated radars deployed around Moscow. The expanded Safeguard system now before the Congress involves many more interceptor missiles than those deployed around Moscow and is technically much more advanced. An ABM freeze agreed at SALT at a level no lower than that of the expanded Safeguard system would thus permit and in fact encourage the Soviets to further expand and improve their ABM systems.

If the agreed ABM levels are high then both sides will insist on higher levels, both qualitatively and quantitatively, of offensive arms in order to retain their deterrent against the other country. Thus the level of ABM defenses which may be agreed on at SALT ultimately will control the limit which one has any hope of imposing on both the offensive and defensive strategic weapons of the two nations. This is my conclusion here, namely, that the level of ABM is the most controlling element of any of the items under negotiations at the SALT talks.

IMPORTANCE OF AGREED ABM DEPLOYMENT LEVEL AT SALT

The level of ABM deployment which will be agreed on at SALT is even more critical than the question of prohibition on MIRV testing and deployment and the associated questions of verification of such a MIRV ban. A highly accurate MIRV, if deployed, can only threaten the fixed land-based deterrent of the other side; for example, the multiple nuclear warheads of the SS-9's may endanger our Minuteman, and Soviet fears that upgrading and accuracy of the U.S. Poseidon and Minuteman III MIRV's may endanger the Soviet land-based missile silos are well justified. In contrast, ABM's threaten to intercept ballistic missiles from wherever they are launched—land or sea—and therefore will raise doubts on the effectiveness of the entire deterrent missile force of each country.

Senator COOPER. Can I ask a question there, Mr. Chairman?

Senator GORE. Yes, Senator Cooper.

Senator COOPER. The last sentence in the paragraph you just read assumes that if either side had an effective ABM system then there would be greater likelihood of a fear of first strike.

Dr. PANOFSKY. That is correct: what I am saying here is that the question of the level of city ABM is fundamentally a more important issue in relation to SALT than the question of MIRV. Despite the fact that recently the MIRV question has been more in public debate because of the imminence of deployment I would like to say that whether ABM is actually effective or not, the worry about the possible generation of an effective ABM will raise doubts about the effectiveness of the deterrent power of each side; therefore fears of a first strike will be generated.

Senator COOPER. You have been arguing that the Safeguard ABM system will not be effective. Does your statement contradict what you have been saying?

Dr. PANOFSKY. This question refers to the reason why I believe that Safeguard or any city protective system is escalatory. The conservative planner on the opposing side, the Soviet side, tells his Government he cannot afford to believe that our ABM won't work, therefore he has to build up his own offensive forces. But our conservative military planners are already ignoring in their forward planning the protection which Safeguard offers to us. It is just this uncertainty whether it will work or not work which is another ingredient in the widening gap between conservative estimates on the two sides.

The terms of the SALT treaty setting a level of ABM at agreed numbers of interceptors or radars other than at "zero" would be difficult to police: It is much easier to assure compliance with provisions which prohibit a weapons system entirely than with a specific limit on the number of weapons. Once both sides have agreed to ABM levels as high as those of the advance phases of Safeguard, then the fears of clandestine upgrading of the Soviet ABM system into an even larger system sufficient to endanger the U.S. deterrent will gain in substance. Once radars as sophisticated as the Safeguard MSR are extensively deployed around the Soviet Union, and once other components of a legal ABM system are widely deployed, then clandestine upgrading using some of the existing parts of the air defense system would be harder to prevent. I therefore foresee a real danger that if the agreed levels of ABM deployment at SALT turn out to be no lower than that of the expanded Safeguard, then in turn we will be unable to accept a freeze on the quantity of our offensive missiles or a ban on MIRV deployment and testing.

Specifically, the objections to a moratorium on MIRV deployment, or a prohibition of MIRV under SALT voiced by Department of Defense witnesses in the past, have been based on the assertion that MIRVs' are required to penetrate Soviet ABM. While I conclude that such statements have no technical validity at present, they may become valid if increases of ABM in the Soviet Union are permitted or in fact encouraged at SALT. It is this chain of events which leads to the conclusion that the decision to expand Safeguard now is a clear danger to the entire success of the SALT talks, both in regard to limiting strategic offensive and defensive missiles.

ARMS RACE ESCALATION BY ABM

With your permission I would like to summarize my conclusion: There can no longer be any question that ABM has escalated and will continue to escalate the nuclear arms race; let me review some recent history. I note that Dr. York has done some of this before you in earlier testimony. The history is as follows: The suspected deployment of ABM by the Soviets has given the incentive for U.S. development of the MIRV, deployment of multiple warheads by the Soviets has given last year's justification for the U.S. deployment decision on Safeguard, the possible expanding role of Safeguard in protecting our cities will give rise to Soviet fears of being able to maintain their deterrent against us, the possibility of improving the accuracy of American MIRV's with which we are trying to counter Soviet ABM's appears to threaten Soviet missile silos, et cetera. In short, starting from the concern about ABM deployment, the world is embarking on the next large step of the arms race. It seems to me, Mr. Chairman, that in view of this history I do not see how anyone can maintain that ABM is not an ingredient of the arms race. The world has now strategic nuclear armament sufficient to destroy life as we know it on both the European and North American continents and in fact to endanger survival of the entire human race. The various arguments in which contrived situations are created to justify even further expansion of this enormous arsenal in the name of security must be weighed against the resulting ever-increasing danger of accident and inadvertent escalation into nuclear war.

CONTROL OF ARMS RACE BY SALT

SALT extends the hope to freeze nuclear strategic arms at their present levels which are already vastly in excess of those required to maintain a strategic balance between the two super powers; SALT may even extend hope for reduction from those levels in the future. I have presented technical evidence that the actual Safeguard deployment contracts sharply with the justification stated by the President, that the anti-Chinese rationale for Safeguard impedes the negotiability of ABM levels at SALT, and that any level of ABM other than a very minimal one will endanger seriously the success of SALT in achieving meaningful arms limitation. I urge that the Congress express its intent to bring the arms race under control through successful SALT negotiation by rejecting any expansion of the Safeguard ABM system at this critical time.

Thank you, Mr. Chairman.

Senator GORE. Thank you very much, Doctor.

Senator Fulbright.

Senator FULBRIGHT. Dr. Panofsky, your statement today recalls your appearance last year when you gave one of the most penerating and persuasive arguments at that time against the then proposed Safeguard.

After a year's contemplation, of course, your statement this year I think is even more persuasive. All through your testimony and the discussion and debates about Safeguard and the proliferation of the arms race is a certain kind of absurdity which continues to appall me. I can't quite grasp why people who are supposed to be rational people engage in this kind of activity.

CONSERVATIVE PLANNERS

Do you have any reflections upon it? You referred to conservative planners. I can't imagine who would be a conservative planner. Would you call a man like Dr. Foster a conservative planner?

Dr. PANOFSKY. I would, yes, in the sense in which I used the word in my testimony.

Senator FULBRIGHT. You used the word conservative in a very special sense. What do you mean by a conservative planner?

Dr. PANOFSKY. I mean here conservative from the narrow military point of view, namely, where you identify security with confidence in being able to prevail in a purely military sense.

Senator FULBRIGHT. It seems to me if anything isn't conservative of resources or life or anything, it is this kind of planning. It is as wildly romantic a kind of madness as I have ever heard.

I hate to use that word, but I always thought the word conservative was a very respectable political term. I hate to see it distorted in this specialized manner. [Laughter.]

Don't you think you can think of a better word, perhaps these mad planners who have no idea? [Laughter.]

Dr. PANOFSKY. I should use in all my statements the term defense conservative.

Senator FULBRIGHT. That is right. With reference to the latter part of your statement, I can hardly imagine why we have gotten into this situation and why we proceed with it. One reason, of course, why the Congress has been deceived, of which you already have given an example, is the secrecy with which these things are surrounded, the fear with which so many of these programs are associated. I couldn't begin to improve upon your statement on the level at which it is given, but the political circumstances that surround this whole controversy are more in our area.

There has been recently, as you know, a very vigorous attack upon the media in this country which is still reasonably, in my view, free. Yet it has, I think, intimidated them. I don't blame them. Many of them continue to express themselves and I think it is the only possible way for our democratic system to function. Many of these media have on their own obtained material which has been helpful to some in the Senate and in this committee. There is one example of the other kind of media in my view which is in no way intimidated and which is supported by many of these "conservative" elements that you mention in the political sense. One of them in particular has come to my attention because it pays special attention to me and others on this committee. It has very great circulation. I hear it on the radio. I think it has hundreds of radio outlets and many different publications. It is supported by some of the richest and most generous contributors such as Mr. Patrick Frawley, and he is simply a symbol of that group of people who support this kind of activity. One of his principal publications is called "The Twin Circle." I read this morning an example of how they approach the effete snobs. Certainly this is not an example of either the effete snob or the intellectual and this is not the one that is intimidated. In fact, they have been encouraged and are encouraged by the attacks upon what I would consider legitimate publications. Let me read you this in view of your testimony. This is a recent, April 5, publication.

The April 5 issue of "Twin Circle," the National Catholic Press, contains a column by the editor, Father Lyons, commenting on a meeting of the Freedom Study Center in Boston, Virginia, which is apparently run by the American Security Council. It says that a Dr. Judd was the first of several expert professors lecturing to a group of 25, including the writer.

The writer, I assume, is Father Lyons. He is said to be a Catholic priest and he is the one who speaks on the radio every morning in thousands of places or hundreds of places over the country.

The next speaker, Col. Ray Sleeper, U.S. Air Force (retired), is described as one of the best informed men we have on Soviet military technology. Col. Sleeper pointed out that the U.S.S.R. has the best air defense the world has even seen, that it has almost twice as many bombers as the United States, that it has more ICBM's and more sub-launched ballistic missiles. He said it now has 3,000 nuclear missiles, whereas we have only 1,710, that the U.S.S.R. is far ahead of us in civil defense, and they can put nuclear bombs into orbit which could destroy much of our country with just 3 minutes' warning.

I will not put the whole article in the record. It is too long. That is the principal part, which is so clearly pertinent to what you have testified to this morning.

This goes to a great many people in this country under the auspices of a Catholic priest and a former Member of Congress.

THE AMERICAN SECURITY COUNCIL

The American Security Council is made up of some of the most wellknown, former admirals and generals, among others. I will read you a few of the names to give you an idea of those who are responsible for this kind of information being taken throughout this country and undeterred by any allegations that they are effete snobs. These are the real people; this is the silent majority to whom this is addressed.

The staff of the council consists of men who are particularly qualified in cold war strategy and research. They include Robert Galvin, chairman of Motorola, Patrick Frawley, chairman of Eversharp;

I believe he is with Technicolor too and a patron of many public people.

Clifford Hood, former president of the American Bar Association; Gen. Thomas Power, former head of the Strategic Air Command; Gen. Albert Wedemeyer, chief of U.S. strategists, World War II; Dr. Charles Malik, former president of United Nations Security Council; Dr. Edward Teller, the nuclear scientist;

I believe we have heard of him before.

Dr. Stefan Possony, of the Hoover Institution on War, Revolution and Peace; Dr. Anthony Bouscaran, formerly of the National War College; Dr. Gerhart Niemeyer of Notre Dame; Dr. Anthony Kubek of the University of Dallas; Dr. Walter Judd, the Far Eastern expert.

PROBLEM OF TRANSLATING WITNESS' STATEMENT INTO POLITICAL ACTION

The problem is this: You give a statement like this which, it seems to me, is absolutely unanswerable. Yet this ABM has the most powerful support, and I think the origin of much of this support is that the people are frightened.

This kind of thing will at least raise doubts and I have heard many of the leading Members of this Congress say, "Whenever I am in doubt I always come down on the side of security," which means more weapons.

We went through this fight last year and we lost by a narrow margin. I don't know how to emphasize or make more appealing the reasoning of your statement. I think it is absolutely unanswerable, but if the newspapers and television use your statement, particularly that part which contests the present party line, they expose themselves to retaliation. You can see this is a very difficult problem. Translating the wisdom of your statement into political action is the most difficult problem of the present day, I think.

Do you have any ideas about that?

Dr. PANOFSKY. No, sir; that is not my domain.

Senator FULBRIGHT. It ought to be. As brilliant as you obviously are from your testimony on ABM, I would think you could understand the political problem. Is it more difficult than the ABM?

"DEDICATED" DEFENSE FOR MINUTEMAN

Dr. PANOFSKY. I would like to point out for the record again that I am not against the defense of Minuteman. I feel fundamentally that most statements on ABM which the President has made—other than the statements which he made in the January 31 of this year's press conference about China—I would support. I am testifying in opposition to the implementation of the policy decisions which the President has announced.

I believe that the correct way to implement those policies is to develop a "dedicated" defense which does not have a city defense potential, and the quotations which I gave from the Defense Department witnesses, I believe, make it quite clear that this opinion which I am giving here is shared by a substantial faction within the Defense Department: technically, the right answers to defending Minuteman is to develop many small radars and corresponding missiles.

MUTUAL FREEZE AND THEN SALT

Senator FULBRIGHT. But in your statement you gave five different approaches. I thought the last one you very clearly made was the best one and the only one that you thought had real hope for the future. That was limitation of the threat by freezing and then SALT talks, freezing the present level and not proceeding. Isn't that your position?

Dr. PANOFSKY. Certainly, this is my position of the preferred situation. I am, however, realistic enough to recognize that it takes two to play and the SALT talks may or may not be successful. I earnestly hope they will be, and I feel the highest priority item right now is not to do anything which endangers them and I believe the Safeguard decision *does* endanger them. But I also feel we have to be prepared for the eventuality of the SALT talks failing. So we cannot assume that the best solution is necessarily going to materialize.

Senator FULBRIGHT. You seem to have very little confidence in the SALT talks.

Dr. PANOFSKY. No, sir; as I said before, "guarded optimism" is probably the best description of my expectations and, I feel that eventually this is where the hope must lie.

Senator FULBRIGHT. That is what I gathered from your statement. I think the only logical conclusion from it is that the only hope is some kind of agreement.

Dr. PANOFSKY. On limiting both offensive and defensive weapons.

SUPPORT FOR WEAPONS SYSTEMS

Senator FULBRIGHT. These other changes are only matters of an interim effect. What bothers me is the persistence and tenacity of those in support of weapons systems. I didn't used to subscribe much to the theory of people having such a deep interest in the economic aspects of arms sales. Never having had a factory in my State or a constituent who participated in it, I used to downgrade that. While there were a few, I never thought it was really as significant as it now appears.

In your statement, you say that last year the Department of Defense said it makes no sense. This year they come right back and propose what they said last year made no sense. This raises very serious doubts about the sincerity of these people. This is a game in which you just move the checkers. At appropriations time, just before they want the money, they move the checkers in the best way to scare the people and to get the money. This is the way it leaves it. This is the absurdity, the senseless, the inability to make any rational judgment about it, as if they were all mad.

IMPORTANCE OF SALT

I recently received in a letter this paragraph with which I will end. I don't want to take up too much time. I think it is pertinent to the SALT talks. Before I do I want to say that the other day when Chancellor Brandt was visiting the committee, he gave the greatest importance to the SALT talks. It was all in accord, I would say, with your conclusion, that there are so many other things that cannot go forward that ought to go forward in behalf of a more rational world. In that respect you and he agree to its primary significance, and I think that you have rendered a very great service in emphasizing that.

U.S. PURSUIT OF POLICIES NOT IN THEIR INTEREST

This paragraph had reference not only to ABM's but also such activities as we are now engaged in in Indochina. The writer says:

> If I were a Russian I would be terrified by the Americans, not because they are malevolent but because of their collective propensity to pursue policies over a long period against their own interests.

It seems to me this applies to the arms race, because it is against our interests to escalate the arms race. Yet your own testimony with regard to the shifting bases seems to me for ABM to indicate that it is clearly intended and it will result in the escalation of the arms race. It is against our interests.

That is all, Mr. Chairman, unless you wish to comment, Dr. Panofsky.

Dr. PANOFSKY. No.

Senator GORE. Senator Case.

Senator CASE. Thank you, Mr. Chairman.

I join in the appreciation that has already been expressed to you for your contribution this morning as well as your help many times over the last period of several years in which I have been actively involved in this whole matter.

POLICY OF IMPENETRABLE DEFENSE AGAINST COMMUNIST CHINA

At the risk of repetition, and I don't think that repetition is a bad thing, may I summarize what I understand your overall views to be on this: As far as general policy goes you support the President's statements except that one which he made in his press conference about the infallibility of the system against the Chinese threat.

Dr. PANOFSKY. That is partially correct. I support the President's stated objective of defending the deterrent. The only policy statement which I felt I would like to take exception to is the statement that we have a policy of providing an impenetrable defense against China. I consider that particular policy to be, very unfortunate because it impedes the negotiability of the level of ABM at SALT. I have some concern that the President will find it difficult on the one hand to try to convince the American people that ABM is needed now as a defense against China while he then negotiates with the Soviets to give it away. I think that this is not an entirely consistent position; and I also feel the need for a China defense is very unpersuasive. Therefore it is the anti-China policy objective I do not agree with. But the policy objective of defending our deterrent I do agree with.

"DEDICATED" DEFENSE OF U.S. DETERRENT

Senator CASE. Now, as to the defense of the deterrents, last year and again this year you have made it very clear you think there are cheaper ways to do this, and ways that are more effective than Safeguard.

Dr. PANOFSKY. I agree with that! What I consider even more important, is the need to develop a "dedicated" defense; namely, a defense system which is specifically dedicated to defending Minuteman and which does not even potentially have a capability of defending cities; such a system would remove that ambiguity which would be escalatory vis-a-vis the Russians which is now contained in Safeguard.

Senator CASE. So that both from the standpoint of its primary purpose, that is, the defense of Minuteman, and the avoidance of complications in regard to Russia's fear that we might be trying to defend our cities, you would strongly urge, you have and you now do urge, the development of another sort of defense.

Dr. PANOFSKY. Yes. This is correct, and I was trying to imply by quoting the Defense Department sources that such developments are now being considered entirely feasible within the Defense Department while last year there was considerable doubt that that was a feasible solution, so this is really a major shift in DOD approach.

Senator CASE. A great deal of money you point out is being asked for now for that specific purpose?

Dr. PANOFSKY. That is correct.

Senator CASE. So much for the defense of Minuteman by Safeguard.

PAR PERFORMANCE IN DEFENSE AGAINST COMMUNIST CHINA

Now, as to the matter of effectiveness of Safeguard as a defense against the so-called Chinese threat, that is a different question from a desirability of having such a specific defense against a presumed Chinese threat. You point out this time, this year, that the effectiveness in the face of nuclear bursts of the PAR radar, which is essential to this area defense, is seriously open to question. Is that correct?

Dr. PANOFSKY. This is correct, if there are multiple attacks.

Again this is a subject—I am sorry to come back to this—which I cannot discuss in detail, but if one is worrying about stopping a single Chinese missile, then this particular technical limitation would not be pertinent. It is the problem that, if a defense is required against a multiple attack involving about 20 Chinese missiles—that is the number the President used, of Chinese missiles—then the combination of offensive and defensive bursts would change the whole environment through which the radar has to operate to such an extent that there is considerable doubt as to effectiveness, as to whether this PAR could do this job. To stop a single Chinese——

Senator CASE. In other words, the scientific point is that this doubt does not exist probably in the case of a single shot but if there were several at one time the doubt would be very serious?

Dr. PANOFSKY. That is correct. At some level of numbers of attackers you would get these problems of disturbance of the PAR performance.

Senator CASE. And certainly you gave a figure of 20 as to which this would be applicable.

Dr. PANOFSKY. Something like that.

Senator CASE. Or less than that?

Dr. PANOFSKY. It depends on how it is done.

Senator CASE. And this is well within the capability of the Chinese?

Dr. PANOFSKY. As Senator Cooper pointed out not only the offensive but the defensive missiles give you trouble. This is a problem which we create ourselves which the Chinese don't even have to induce necessarily, although they could tailor their tactics to its existence. However, my main point here is that the whole concept of an infallible defense, a tight umbrella, makes no sense. I think it is very dangerous for the Chief Executive to assume that he can ever operate with impunity under a tight umbrella of this kind. Even if there were no specific technical objection, one could never have confidence in such protection. You can't test it in any actual situation, you have problems about its readiness. At any given moment you never know what the reliability really is. So all of these sort of intangible problems exist quite apart from the hard technical fact that the Chinese have options which if they so wish they can develop for purposes of penetrating the defense.

Senator CASE. I think you have made this very clear.

EFFECT OF DETONATION OF U.S. SPRINTS AND SPARTANS

The other day Dr. York gave a rather terrifying picture of the devastation to our country if the Soviet Union attacked our missile sites and their missiles exploded on the ground. Could you tell us what the likely effect on the ground would be, on our people, buildings, crops, and so forth if they did attack us and we repelled their attack with ABM's?

In other words, what effect would the detonation of our own Sprints and Spartans have on us?

Dr. PANOFSKY. I do not believe that the detonation of our own Sprints and Spartans give rise to very much of a problem in the way of fallout because they are high-altitude explosions, and the Spartans have relatively little fallout associated with them.

I think that, although I agree completely with what Dr. York said about the enormous devastation of the actual ground impact getting through and the fallout coming from that, I do not agree with some of the criticisms of the ABM system which is often made which imply that the defensive missiles in themselves would be a substantial health hazard.

EFFECT OF GROUND EXPLOSION OF SOVIET MISSILES

Senator CASE. But you do agree with Dr. York as to the effect of the Soviet missiles exploded on the ground?

Dr. PANOFSKY. I have not read his detailed numbers but I do agree that Soviet missiles on the ground would clearly give a large amount of fallout even though the missile sites are located rather far from cities.

EFFECT OF ATTACK ON SAC BASES

Senator CASE. I wonder if you would develop a little bit more the position as far as nuclear environment goes?

I am not sure I understand exactly what that means but in relation to our strategic bombers, I guess my question is if our bomber bases come under attack from sea-launched missiles and the warning is therefore very short and many of our bombers are on the ground and we have an ABM to defend them and if the Sprints are going off in the air and maybe an incoming missile or two is exploding, what would the effect of these nuclear explosions be on the bombers themselves, on their ability to take off and fly missions?

Dr. PANOFSKY. I am not familiar with this problem in detail, Senator Case. There are some problems with dust and the fallout produced. However, I believe that defensive Sprint missiles, a doctrine can be developed in which our bombers can take off even after Sprints have gone off.

I think there has been some confusion about this problem. If sea-launched missiles attack our SAC (Strategic Air Command) airplane bases, only a very short time of warning in order to have that scenario which you indicated to me to be true, presumably the Minuteman bases have not been attacked yet by enemy missiles because their flight time is 30 minutes. Therefore, if our SAC bases were actually attacked without any warning, it follows from that that our ICBM sites are still fully operational. How the Soviets could ever consider such a thing is beyond my belief, because if they were to attack the bombers and not the ICBM's they would be exposed to 1,000 ICBM's, so that whole time sequence simply is not credible. That is one point.

The other point is that the Air Force is undertaking an extra effort to simply disperse some of the airfields to alternate sites; this is a much more straightforward way of protecting SAC to have alternate runways to take off from rather than to go in for an ABM kind of system.

CONTINUANCE OF SAFEGUARD RESEARCH AND DEVELOPMENT

Senator CASE. Going back now to the use of Safeguard or its value or importance as far as defense of our missile sites goes, based upon your showing there and the Defense Department's picture on the strength of the Soviet Union and the Safeguard, do you think it detrimental to our security if further deployment of Safeguard beyond phase I were not undertaken now but research and development were continued?

Dr. PANOFSKY. No, I do not. I believe if the construction and deployment phase of Safeguard were terminated but if research and development, particularly research and development leading toward a dedicated hard point defense was continued, that would not be detrimental to our security.

Senator CASE. I think that is all at this time, Mr. Chairman.

Senator GORE. Senator Symington.

Senator SYMINGTON. Thank you.

EFFECT OF EXPANDED ABM ON SALT

In your statement you discuss your belief that an expanded ABM system, by which presumably you mean the Safeguard, would damage the SALT talks. You are pretty well convinced of that?

Dr. PANOFSKY. Yes, I am convinced of that. I recognize this is a political judgment, not a technical one; I am considering two contravening arguments. The Administration's argument that the Safeguard deployment helps the SALT talks is based on the negotiation from strength rationale. The argument that it would hurt the SALT talks is based on the rationale given here, that emphasizing the anti-China role of ABM will impede the negotiability which the negotiators would have in working with the Soviets toward arms limitation or reduction. I recognize that those two arguments are political and they contravene one another.

DIFFERENCE IN VIEWS ON ABM AND SALT

Senator SYMINGTON. I have known Dr. Teller a long time, and Dr. Brown, and Dr. York, and Dr. Foster. They are all four nuclear physicists and all four former heads of the Livermore Laboratories. I am sure they are all good Americans, but your testimony worries me because I am sure you are a good American, too. How do you think this all developed to a point where you and Dr. Foster are in such complete disagreement.

Dr. PANOFSKY. Well, this is a very hard thing to say. I think that, I come back to the defense conservative argument that Dr. Foster approaches most of his proposals from what I like to call the worst case analysis position, namely, he always assumes if the Soviets have a technical capability of being able to do something then they will, in fact, do it and it is prudent for us to be able to counter that by purely technical military means. Such an approach to me is a prescription for the arms race and it is that approach which is the cause for the problems in which we find ourselves to be in.

Senator SYMINGTON. With great respect, I can't follow that as an answer to my question. For example, you yourself bring us this fascinating chart, which shows not only that we are ahead of the Soviets, but that we are far ahead of them in strategic offensive forces.

Dr. PANOFSKY. This, incidentally, is Mr. Laird's chart given in his testimony.

Senator SYMINGTON. Presumably Dr. Foster has access to that chart.

Dr. PANOFSKY. He made it, I guess.

Senator SYMINGTON. If that chart is true, it would be much to our interest to work out a mutual agreement on the control of arms in the SALT talks.

Dr. PANOFSKY. I agree.

Senator SYMINGTON. But how can you correlate your agreement with sincerity on the part of our SALT talk negotiators, some of whom were leaders in the pro-ABM fight. If they really want to see the SALT talks succeed, why do they do what you say is a dangerous thing to do from the standpoint of their success, namely, proceed with the Safeguard system?

Dr. PANOFSKY. Well, I think—let me answer your two statements in a different way.

Senator SYMINGTON. I am trying to understand. I just cannot coordinate based on these figures you present and say Secretary Laird presented. I cannot but conclude this is the right time to get ahead with the SALT talks. If that is true, in as much as we all agree the control of nuclear weapons is a logical step so as to prevent destruction of civilization, how can these people be for doing what you say is against success at the SALT talks.

Dr. PANOFSKY. I believe that some of the proponents who are saying we should go ahead with Safeguard now in order to negotiate from a position of strength are sincere in believing that the Soviets would respond favorably to such a tactic. Their argument is based— I am representing their views and I am sure you will get their testimony here later—on not comparing the status of missiles, but the rates of buildup. Now, you see, we have been relatively static while the Soviets have been building up at a certain rate. The argument given is that unless we build something, even if it isn't very good, that this gives some urgency to the Soviets, in terms of time, to reach a rapid conclusion at the SALT talks, while at the present moment if the Soviets keep building up while we are static then the longer the talks last then the worse relatively our position would become.

I don't believe this. I believe, for instance, that the very fact that we are ahead in MIRV technology and we are ready for deployment while the Soviets are not give us several other intangible advantages which are not given on this chart.

UNITED STATES-U.S.S.R. STRATEGIC WEAPONS STRENGTH

Another point which I should like to point out—and I should not be the one to speak for Dr. Foster, but I believe one of his reasons why he would not identify this chart with clear evidence that we are ahead is his worry about defenses. In order to have these missile be useful from the military point of view they have to be launched and they have to penetrate.

Now, it is true that the air defense system of the Soviet Union is many times larger than that of the United States. Therefore, even though we have clear superiority in the numbers of intercontinental bombers, as an example here, 581 as compared to 140 to 145, that he would raise the question, and with a considerable amount of substance, as to what fraction of those would get through Soviet defenses.

Senator SYMINGTON. But if you wipe out our ICBM launchers entirely, we are still well ahead of the Soviet Union.

Dr. PANOFSKY. That is correct. We are substantially ahead in SLBM (Submarine-launched Missile) launchers.

Senator SYMINGTON. That is right. If you take out some bombers and all our ICBM, you are still way ahead if you put in the Poseidons; correct?

Dr. PANOFSKY. I agree with this.

Senator SYMINGTON. If you agree with it, and it sure seems logical to me, then why doesn't Dr. Foster agree with it?

Dr. PANOFSKY. Because—again I should not speak for him——

Senator SYMINGTON. Why not?

Dr. PANOFSKY. But I have heard the argument often enough——

Senator SYMINGTON. He has certainly told us that you have been wrong.

Dr. PANOFSKY (continuing). You cannot rely on a single system because there may be hidden unknown deficiencies in it and, therefore, that is a dangerous thing. There may be deficiencies known to the Soviets and not to us and, therefore, that is a dangerous posture to find yourself in.

DIFFERENCE IN VIEWS ON SAFEGUARD

Senator SYMINGTON. Now you state, speaking of deficiencies, "The totality of all these technical facts amounts to one thing: Even if Safeguard functions perfectly it offers significant protection to Minuteman only over a very narrow band of threats; if the threat continues to grow as rapidly as it is at present, Safeguard is obsolete before deployed; if the threat levels off, Safeguard is not needed. If one combines this fact with the likelihood of catastrophic failure of the single radar and computer controlling the system, and the fact that a less failure prone and more effective system can be produced on the same time scale for less money, Safeguard looks like a very poor use of the shrinking defense dollar indeed."

Aren't those opinions and facts available to everybody, including the people in the Pentagon?

Dr. PANOFSKY. I believe so, sir. I think, as I said before, that if the defense of Minuteman was the only designated purpose of Safeguard, and not its growth potentially into a city defense, which was not a requirement, then it is my view that there would be little difference in opinion about this statement.

Senator GORE. Before the Senator asks another question, would you suggest, in view of this line of questioning, that the subcommittee ought to invite Dr. Foster to appear in public session?

Senator SYMINGTON. I would, Mr. Chairman, being in the unfortunate dual position of listening as a member of the Armed Services Committee to Dr. Foster's testimony, and then as a member of this committee to the testimony of people like Dr. Panofsky.

Dr. PANOFSKY. Well, I think the difference here comes from two sources. One is that the question of abandoning the concept of a city defense is one which is not generally accepted in the Defense Department. My presentation was centered around the fact whether Safeguard is worth buying if defense of Minuteman was its objective, and my conclusion to that is no. That conclusion is based on straight technical reasoning, and is incontrovertible.

But the main reason why Dr. Foster and other members of the Defense Department would like to proceed anyway is in order to preserve the option of a city defense which is counter to the President's statement of the objectives of Safeguard: He would like to maintain the option of a thick city defense and I know many other Defense Department members would like to keep that door open, and the question is how much of a price we are willing to pay to keep that door open.

SOVIET INTERPRETATION OF U.S. ANTI-CHINESE DEFENSE

Senator SYMINGTON. The price, all these prices are high indeed, and could destroy the country in another way. You quote Deputy Secretary of Defense Packard. He is a hope of mine because he is a practical engineer. Apparently he would like to get some hardware instead of theoretical arguments, which is very costly but doesn't result in hardware. I have been hopeful about some of the things I have heard Secretary Packard was doing. You know as well as I, there is nobody farther away from a production line than a theoretical scientist with a lot of preconceived opinions. As quoted in your statement, could he have been talking there about city defense against Soviets.

Dr. PANOFSKY. Yes. He was talking there about city defense against the Soviets.

Senator SYMINGTON. Doesn't that then make it somewhat inapplicable to the next observation about the President's statement about anti-Chinese defense? Do you see what I am getting at?

Dr. PANOFSKY. Yes; I see what you are getting at.

My point is the following. My point is that the Soviets have no way of knowing whether a given defense which is labeled anti-Chinese is anti-Chinese or anti-Soviet. It is the same system. So what my concern is, that although Mr. Packard has agreed that anti-Soviet defense is not a useful concept, the statement of policy that we need a defense, an impenetrable defense, an infallible defense, against China will inexorably lead to a thick defense. A thin defense will soon be recognized to be fallible and, therefore, the pressures will continue to mount to remove its deficiencies which are clearly there, and as soon as you start doing that then the distinction which you, Senator Symington, made between the anti-Soviet and anti-Chinese defense is going to go away. Therefore, the statement of national policy that anti-China ABM is needed is to me a more dangerous thing than the actual hardware which admittedly doesn't give much of a defense.

Senator SYMINGTON. Thank you.

Senator GORE. Senator Cooper.

1969 DEFENSE DEPARTMENT ARGUMENT FOR SAFEGUARD

Senator COOPER. I would like to pursue for a minute the question that Senator Symington was asking about the reason for the difference between the views which you hold and the views held by the Defense Department.

Last year, during the debate, all of us tried to analyze the different positions taken by the Defense Department, and their reasons, their very tenacious effort to hold onto this system.

I may make it too simple but it seems to me they pressed two points. First, there was a real threat, the development of the SS-9's. They said, I believe correctly, that if it reached the point of 400 SS-9's with three MIRV's, 1,200 warheads in all—with accuracy these could destroy our ICBM force.

Then low trajectory missiles would destroy our bombers; they could also attack our submarines, they said. They made a real threat appear to be developing against our submarines, which would develop, they said, about 1975.

Then the argument of timelag came in, that it was necessary to commence this system, and I am not now talking about whether it is a good system or not, but it was necessary to commence this system, the best that you had, so that by 1975 you would have whatever value it had. It seems to me the threat, plus the timelag, impressed most of those who supported this system.

INCREASE IN ATTRACTION TOWARD FIRST STRIKE

I read in the New York Times yesterday the article by Anthony Lewis—I guess you did too—in which the Institute for Strategic Studies provides information about our relative strengths. It shows the Soviet Union having 1,880 warheads rather than 1,350. And it goes on to say with the movement into new systems that this will increase the relative attraction for a first strike surprise attack. For example, the report says:

> Area defense ABM systems, in as far as they might be thought to defend civilian population effectively against a major retaliatory attack, could tend to loosen the restraints of deterrence.

Is it correct that you are saying that the United States and the Soviet Union have reached a point where there is now a relatively stable deterrent, but if we move into these other systems would you say there is a danger of the attraction of a first strike attack?

Dr. PANOFSKY. Yes. I believe that at present the situation is entirely stable. I believe that the advent of MIRV's or at least accurate MIRV's and of city ABM defense decreases stability and increases the attraction toward a first strike. This is precisely why this is the right time for the SALT talks.

PROPOSED MUTUAL WEAPONS SUSPENSION

Senator COOPER. Now, the Senate adopted a resolution which gave at least the sense of the Senate that at the commencement of talks, the United States should propose mutual suspension of deployment of both defensive and offensive systems. We asked Ambassador Smith about his views about this and he said there were complexities about it, there would be difficulties about it, and I read in the papers that one of the difficulties might be trying to agree upon the length of the moratorium. If we did not set a precise time limitation, it would be taken advantage of. But in your view are there substantial complexities which would make such a proposal unreasonable?

Dr. PANOFSKY. I don't believe it is unreasonable; the only reservations I have are the following: I can think of many reasons why the Soviets would not agree to a moratorium. Therefore, rather than protracting or delaying the SALT talks in order to get the moratorium, the details of the moratorium going, I think one should therefore not give it overriding priority.

I don't believe one should take the position, in my personal view, that a moratorium is a necessary condition in order to get on with the SALT talks. I think from our past experience with the Soviets, they would like to be rather concrete and specific in terms of the negotiated results. Therefore, there may be as many problems and stumbling blocks raised in trying to negotiate a mutually agreed moratorium as there might be in the treaty itself and, therefore, the matter would be delayed. So I am in favor of making an attempt to get a mutually agreed moratorium going accompanying the first phase of the SALT talks, but I do not believe one should interpret the matter so strongly that we would be unwilling to go forward with the SALT talks unless within a relatively short time agreement is reached on a moratorium.

RESEARCH AND DEVELOPMENT DURING SAFEGUARD DEPLOYMENT

Senator COOPER. I think we were told even if the Safeguard system should not turn out to be effective, that we should proceed with it because during the deployment, the R. & D. (research and development) would continue and modifications could be made as needed to provide a more effective system. Do you consider that a good argument?

Dr. PANOFSKY. No. I have always considered that argument to be a particularly poor one because deployment is not R. & D. Deployment is a very inflexible situation. On our presently deployed strategic systems, even to make a relatively minor modification is always a matter of 2 years or something of that kind.

I do not believe a deployed system is the way to learn fundamental performance. There are several reasons for that. First, you can't test as well. We can't fire into the deployed sites. We can fire into Kwajalein, which is an R. & D. site.

Second, the actual deployed sites will be under management of routine Army forces; deployment has to be combined with troop training using standardized manuals, and so forth, because personnel keep being rotated. Therefore, all the procedures have to be worked out to be independent of the detailed skill and training of the personnel because they are rotated. You, therefore, actually have available less flexibility, after deploying military systems. That is the actual experience of anyone having anything to do with the military. Once a deployment decision has been made then the ability to retrofit changes is very, very much more tedious than the ability to make changes in a developmental system.

ABM DEPLOYMENT ON TWO SITES FOR TESTING COMMUNICATIONS

Senator COOPER. What about the claim made that it would be good to proceed with the two sites for purposes of testing communications.

Dr. PANOFSKY. Yes, there is some validity to that, I mean there is some validity to say that. I guess you might call it the human experiment of having a defense system and trying to have it integrated into the overall command and control system is an experience which is rather difficult to attain in any other way. It is well known that once systems have been put onsite lots of bugs have to be worked out in the way of communication. I think there is some validity to that argument. I don't know what strength it has.

For one thing, I would also like to say that the communication problem is very much worsened by the nature of this system. If there was a system which is uniquely dedicated to defending Minuteman so that a given radar belongs to a small number of Minuteman, then that becomes a small integrated complex which can be managed in a more autonomous way than Safeguard. Therefore, there is no need for as much communication and complexity as there is with Safeguard. To some extent the communication problem is a self-created problem because of the nature of the Safeguard system.

EFFECTIVENESS OF SAFEGUARD IN DEFENDING MINUTEMAN

Senator COOPER. I know you said last year that a more effective ABM can be built than Safeguard. You say the Safeguard system just won't work as far as the protection of the Minuteman is concerned.

Dr. Panofsky. I said even if it works perfectly it will only save a very small number of Minuteman, and the value of what it saves, the number of Minuteman, their cost, is a small fraction of the cost of the system which we are buying for protection, so I am saying even if it works perfectly, which many doubt, and I just don't know, you are buying very, very little in protecting the deterrent.

I am fundamentally in favor of protecting the deterrent. I also am in favor of using whatever part of the budget which Congress dedicates to defense to buy the maximum defense, and we are precisely not doing that in defending Minuteman with Safeguard.

Senator Cooper. You are saying at the present the way we are moving now, our ABM is on the wrong course. If we are going to have an ABM system, work should be shifted to another system altogether.

Dr. Panofsky. That would implement the President's stated policy.

Senator Gore. May I ask a question. Doctor, one fundamental purpose of these hearings as an example of participatory democracy is to build a body of information by which the public as well as the Senate can reach a judgment. Now I would like to ask you a few simple questions in layman's terms.

As I understand it you are saying that the radar that is planned is more vulnerable than the Minuteman missiles which the ABM is supposedly designed to protect.

Dr. Panofsky. That is correct.

Senator Gore. Then you say, however, that even if the ABM worked perfectly, only a few Minuteman would be protected.

Dr. Panofsky. Yes. That is correct, and the reason is that there are only very few interceptor Sprint missiles deployed around each site and, therefore, even if everything worked perfectly you can simply exhaust the ammunition which the defense has.

PROTECTION PROVIDED BY PHASE II OF SAFEGUARD

Senator Gore. Would Phase II of Safeguard, the deployment of which would, in your view, threaten the success of SALT talks—if deployed and working perfectly, protect only one Minuteman missile site?

Dr. Panofsky. No, I did not say that, sir.

Senator Gore. I am asking you.

Dr. Panofsky. There are several Phase II of course, varieties.

Senator Gore. I am speaking now of the expansion that has——

Dr. Panofsky. One additional one, yes.

Senator Gore. One additional one.

Dr. Panofsky. The expanded system now before the Congress would altogether protect three sites, namely, the two authorized last year and the one additional one.

Senator Gore. I am speaking now about the one additional one.

Dr. Panofsky. That is the one in Missouri.

Senator Gore. The one in Missouri. Is the number of Minutemen at that site classified?

Dr. Panofsky. I think it probably is, I am sorry to say. It is also classified how many interceptors are being provided in the Secretary's proposal.

Senator Gore. I think I know how many are there, but I was fearful that the figure was classified. At least it is an extremely——

Dr. PANOFSKY. But it is a comparable number. The Missouri site is a site which had a comparable number of Minuteman as the Dakota and Nebraska sites.

Senator GORE. Without dealing in classifications, is it somewhere on the order, of between five and 15 missiles.

Dr. PANOFSKY. No, no. The number of Minuteman at each of these sites is on the order of 200.

Senator GORE. How many ABM?

Dr. PANOFSKY. How many ABM interceptor missiles?

Senator GORE. Yes.

Dr. PANOFSKY. That number is classified. I would rather not discuss it.

Senator GORE. We will have to leave this particular point because it can't be developed. The point I am trying to make is that this expansion of one additional ABM deployment would provide protection, if it worked perfectly, for only one Minuteman field in Missouri.

Dr. PANOFSKY. One additional one, that is correct.

Senator GORE. You say that, if attacked, the radar is far more vulnerable and therefore might not work at all.

Dr. PANOFSKY. That is correct.

Let me be specific to avoid confusion here.

The new deployment for which the Executive asked an additional obligational authority of $1.58 billion does several things: It activities a new site in Missouri. It increases somewhat the number of Sprint missiles at the other sites and it starts doing survey and general site exploration of further sites so that the money is distributed for these various additional purposes. However, if you actually analyze against this expanded model how many Minuteman can be saved by the defense, the number still comes out to be very small.

Senator GORE. Very small.

NEED FOR AND OBSOLENCE OF SAFEGUARD

Yet you say that if the threat is stabilized then ABM, even if perfected and even if it would work, would not be needed.

Dr. PANOFSKY. If it is stabilized the way it is now, then Minuteman is not at risk now. I mean you have to take the projections of the increasing number of SS-9's into account.

Senator GORE. I understand.

Dr. PANOFSKY. Increased accuracy, further testing and development of the multiple warhead, all these things have to occur.

Senator GORE. I understand, but the simple statement is, as you have said to us, that if the situation is stabilized, if the threat is stabilized, under present conditions ABM is not needed.

Dr. PANOFSKY. Right.

Senator GORE. You also said if the threat continues to grow, then it is obsolete.

Dr. PANOFSKY. What I am saying is it will be very rapidly overtaken. I mean if the threat keeps going then if at a given point in time we are in danger without Safeguard, then if we did have Safeguard we would be in danger in a very short time thereafter.

Senator GORE. I understand that. But you are now giving details. Your conclusion is that if the threat continues then ABM would be obsolete.

Dr. PANOFSKY. That is right. If the threat continues then Safeguard will be—if the threat continues at the same rate at which it is growing now then Safeguard would be—overtaken and therefore be obsolete before it is ever deployed.

Senator GORE. I understand. I am trying to get this in terms that I can use in explaining it to my own people and in terms that other people can read and understand.

Here is something, the deployment of which, in your view, threatens the success of the SALT talks. Yet it is supposed to protect the most vulnerable of our retaliatory weapons. And the ABM is even more vulnerable than the Minuteman because the radar is more vulnerable than the ABM missile. Yet if it is needed, it is obsolete. Nevertheless, we must spend billions of dollars on it and threaten the success of the SALT talks.

Dr. PANOFSKY. That is essentially the summary of what I am trying to say.

Senator GORE. Thank you.

Senator CASE.

INCREASING SAFEGUARD TO MEET INCREASED OFFENSE

Senator CASE. In that connection, it has been argued that while the presently conceived Safeguard does admittedly only protect against a certain level of attack, if that, if the offense is increased so can the Safeguard be increased. What is your comment on that?

Dr. PANOFSKY. Yes, this is technically possible. That is definitely correct. I mean we can engage in a Safeguard versus SS-9 race. But the costs are the dominant factor. There is overwhelming evidence if we used the Safeguard technology to keep up with the Russians then this would be just enormously expensive. It is not an accident that for the present price tag we protect so few of the Minuteman, only a small fraction of the 200 which I recited. The reason for that is cost. We would like to, and I am sure the Defense Department would like to, buy more protection than we are buying.

Cost is therefore another argument for pushing forward, in my view, with the development of the cheaper small radars because by this means—and this has been shown by analysis—keeping up with the Soviet buildup is economically a much more defensible proposition than keeping up Safeguard radar and the Safeguard technology. The cost of using the Safeguard technology is very much higher per unit Minuteman silo defended than the dedicated technology which I was talking about.

COST OF SECOND MISSILE SITE RADAR

Senator CASE. It has been suggested that the softness and vulnerability of the MSR radar can be relatively easily minimized by adding a second one.

Dr. PANOFSKY. Yes, that is about another $200 million.

Senator CASE. Would it be that much more. Would it be, say $40 million?

Dr. PANOFSKY. Probably not. It depends, in detail on how you do it. The $40 million is the cost of just the hardware, and the $200 million is the cost of the hardware, plus the total military environment, site development, power and personnel support and so forth which have to be provided.

Senator CASE. Which would be involved in any such expansion.

Dr. PANOFSKY. Which would be needed, but maybe not quite as much so. That would be a matter of detail.

Senator CASE. But it would be very expensive still.

Dr. PANOFSKY. That has been looked at and it is perfectly feasible just to build more and more, but if you do that you are simply on very weak ground economically and time-wise, both.

Senator CASE. May I have one more question, Mr. Chairman?

Senator GORE. Yes.

LIMITATIONS AND VULNERABILITY OF SAFEGUARD

Senator CASE. You mentioned in your testimony the statement by Secretary Packard about relatively simple devices having limited ability to deceive a sophisticated defense system like Safeguard—relatively simple devices like tank fragments.

I take it that this means really that Safeguard has a limited ability to handle more than single incoming warheads.

Dr. PANOFSKY. It has a limited capability of handling more than single or few incoming warheads on an area-wide basis. But in addition to that it is vulnerable to relatively straightforward tactics of defeating it even with one missile; this tank business is a technique which Secretary Packard identified as one which we ourselves are familiar with, and he said that this gave a limited capability to defeat it. What I am saying is this is true. He is acknowledging it. But I am also saying we are talking about defense 10 years from now and you have to give the Chinese some credit for being able to advance in 10 years.

The essence of my statement here is, that it always perturbed me that in order to justify these systems we make the Russians 10 feet tall and the Chinese 2 feet tall. In order to have a rationale for building the ABM system we are giving the Russians an enormous amount of credit for the maximum they can possibly do, but in preparing for something which China might be doing, we are claiming we will have an infallible defense by denying them even relatively straightforward technological things at their command.

Senator CASE. You have discussed the effectiveness and the value of Safeguard as a defense of our Minuteman. You dealt with its usefulness and limits on it, in regard to the so-called Chinese threat.

SAFEGUARD AS PROTECTION AGAINST ACCIDENT

The third justification is the additional launch or the mad colonel or whatever you want to call it.

Dr. PANOFSKY. Yes.

Senator CASE. Have you got any comment about its application in such circumstances.

Dr. PANOFSKY. Yes.

Here the function of Safeguard for the protection against accident there, has a certain amount of validity; how much validity is a matter of judgment.

If there were a Safeguard system, and if it worked perfectly, and if the nature of the accident were such that only one or two, a small number of missiles, came over, and if the nature of the accident was such that the accident did not also automatically dispense such penetration aids which the opponents might have, then you would indeed have some protection.

My worry about the accident argument is a rather profound one. I did not wish to put it into my prepared statement because the statement was already quite long. In order to be prepared against an accident, then the readiness of the system has to be very high, it has to be sitting on a hair trigger. It is my feeling that in order to give the ABM any capability against accident the President would have to predelegate the authority to fire nuclear weapons; clearly in an accidental situation the time involved would be so short that there would be no practical way to react with anything but an almost automatic response. Therefore, I am raising the question whether the probability of an accident by the defensive system wouldn't be also an appreciable factor if we have to switch to a hair trigger doctrine rather than a more controlled type of response; we would not take our warning system, for instance, seriously if only a single ICBM, emerged from the Soviet Union. It is very doubtful that such an isolated warning would form a basis of decisionmaking under current circumstances. Therefore, to be prepared against single accidental attacks the degree of automatic readiness of the system would have to be quite a bit higher than for the other announced functions of the Safeguard system.

Senator CASE. You couldn't have a system that was automatic for such purposes and still require a rational decision by the President in other circumstances?

Dr. PANOFSKY. Well, I suppose one could have a system programed to be hair triggered to intercept a minor attack but not a major one, but even that kind of hair trigger would mean that you are setting off nuclear explosions in an automatic way which may give rise to many other problems.

Senator CASE. Well, on that, just what other problems would there be. After all, this is a stray missile coming over, there are no international complications against shooting it down, are there?

Dr. PANOFSKY. Well, for one thing you would violate the Nuclear Test Ban.

Senator CASE. I should expect that is true.

Dr. PANOFSKY. So if you would launch an interceptor missile and there was in fact nothing there, and you set it off, this is a clear violation and we would owe an explanation as to where and how it occurred. I am sure if the Soviets did that we would be very perturbed and would accuse them of deceptive testing practices and so forth. So I think there probably would be complications.

Senator CASE. Yes. Well, thank you, Mr. Chairman.

SAFEGUARD SYSTEM'S COMPUTER

Senator GORE. You have raised so many questions about its workability. For instance you say "the computer severely limits the performance of the system in handling large attacks."

I won't go into why this is true because I accept your statement, but you raise these questions about its workability, the vulnerability of the radar, the reliability of the computer system. Actually the radar and computer are largely the same as those designed for the old Sentinel system, are they not?

Dr. PANOFSKY. The radars are essentially the same. The computer is not. There is a lot of new work in it. When I referred here to the computer I am sure you know that in making a computer work, you need two things, you need the hardware——

Senator GORE. I don't know. You tell us.

Dr. PANOFSKY. You need both the electronics, the actual boxes full of gear, and then you have to do a large amount of programing. It means you have to design the instructions by which the computer can identify the incoming object, compute its tracks and then generate the commands for the interceptor, do all these things.

Senator GORE. Including accidents?

Dr. PANOFSKY. Including the accidents, including the different directions and so forth and so forth, and it turns out to be that task, what is called the software task, turns out to be a very time consuming one and, of course, very, very difficult because you have to prethink all these logical alternatives in which attacks can go on, and it is that task of writing the programs which I referred to in my statement, which controls both the actual deployment schedule and which limits the magnitude of the threat which can be handled. It is an essentially enormous task to preprogram, preinstruct this device so that in the very short time of an engagement it can do all these things which it is supposed to do.

Senator GORE. Doctor, you have been an engaging instructor.

UNITED STATES-SOVIET REACTIONS TO EACH OTHER'S ABM

Senator COOPER. I would like to ask this one question: You emphasize that the continued deployment of Safeguard would have an adverse effect on SALT talks and you gave reasons for this view.

Now, if out of the Safeguard system that is not any good, and if the Galosh system in Moscow is not any good, why should anyone of us bother with it. We were accused last year of a kind of double talk saying it wasn't any good and yet saying it will have an influence on the SALT talks. What about that question?

Dr. PANOFSKY. The answer to that question is similar to the reply to the questions raised by Senator Fulbright about the "defense conservative" and "offense conservative" attitudes of the military on both sides. The point is that we are worrying about the Soviet's ABM, whether it is good or bad. We are deploying MIRV because of the Soviet ABM even though we really think it isn't much good. But we are worrying about it, so to be "conservative" we are saying we need MIRV, or the Defense Department is saying that they need MIRV.

We here are saying that Safeguard is not useful in any major way to protect Minuteman, but the Soviet in looking at it will say if it is not useful for that purpose, then what are the Americans doing, why are they making this design compromise? The reason we are making the design compromise is because we want to have the option of quickly going into the city defense mode. So the problem is that we are not designing a "dedicated" defense, a defense especially designed for Minuteman, but one which the Soviets can fear grow fairly rapidly in defending the cities. Considering that the Soviets also always worry about their reaction time, this would give the Soviets cause for concern even though right now Safeguard has a limited capability. This is the dichotomy: We are saying rationally that we don't think it gives much protection, but the Soviets are saying it may grow into some protection; similarly, when we are talking about the Soviet ABM we are saying we don't think it is much good, but it may become good so we had better buy MIRV. It is just this kind of double thinking by which the arms race becomes accelerated through these arguments.

Senator GORE. Doctor, the committee is indebted to you. I think the country is, and we appreciate your presence.

The committee will stand adjourned until 10 tomorrow when we will hear Dr. Scoville.

(Whereupon, at 12:35 p.m., the subcommittee was adjourned, to reconvene at 10 a.m., Tuesday, April 14, 1970.)

ABM, MIRV, SALT, AND THE NUCLEAR ARMS RACE

ABM, MIRV, SALT, and Verification

TUESDAY, APRIL 14, 1970

UNITED STATES SENATE,
SUBCOMMITTEE ON ARMS CONTROL,
INTERNATIONAL LAW AND ORGANIZATION
OF THE COMMITTEE ON FOREIGN RELATIONS,
Washington, D.C.

The subcommittee met, pursuant to recess, at 10:10 a.m., in room 4221, New Senate Office Building, Senator Albert Gore (chairman of the subcommittee) presiding.

Present: Senators Gore, Fulbright (chairman of the full committee), Case, Cooper, and Javits.

OPENING STATEMENT

Senator GORE. The Subcommittee on Arms Control, International Law and Organization continues today hearings on the interrelated subjects of ABM, MIRV, SALT and the nuclear arms race.

Our witnesses today are Dr. Herbert Scoville, Jr., of the Carnegie Endowment for International Peace, former assistant director for science and technology of the Arms Control and Disarmament Agency, and Mr. Adrian S. Fisher, dean of the Georgetown University Law School and former deputy director of the Arms Control and Disarmament Agency.

Dr. Carl Kaysen, director of the Institute for Advanced Study at Princeton, and former Deputy Special Assistant to the President for National Security Affairs, was to testify today, but he unfortunately had an accident over the weekend and cannot be with us. We wish him a speedy recovery.

Dr. Scoville was kind enough to agree to delay his testimony until today so that the subcommittee could spend the entire morning yesterday questioning Dr. Panofsky.

Mr. Fisher will testify on ABM, MIRV, and the SALT talks. The appropriateness of his subject is obvious. The SALT talks will open in Vienna the day after tomorrow, talks that are perhaps as important as any negotiations in which the United States has been involved in the past 25 years.

Dr. Scoville will address the problem of verification as it relates to limiting strategic arms, a subject which has perhaps not been sufficiently explored in public. Last week the Senate adopted Senate Resolution 211 resolving that it was the sense of the Senate that the President should propose to the Soviet Government an immediate suspension by both the United States and the Soviet Union of the further deployment of all offensive and defensive nuclear strategic weapons systems, this mutual suspension to be "subject to national verification or such other measures of observation and inspection as may be appropriate." Verification is thus a key element in such a mutual suspension of the further deployment of strategic weapons systems, as indeed it is in any strategic arms limitation agreement. We are indeed fortunate to have a witness as knowledgeable as Dr. Scoville on the subject and one who is willing and able to talk to us.

I should add that on Wednesday afternoon the subcommittee will meet in executive session with witnesses from the Central Intelligence Agency to discuss certain aspects of verification that cannot be discussed in open forum.

Dr. Scoville, because we kept you waiting all morning yesterday, I think you have earned the right to go first. With your permission, Professor Fisher.

Mr. FISHER. I certainly have no objection to that.
Senator FULBRIGHT. He is now Dean Fisher. Be careful.
Senator GORE. Oh, yes.
You may proceed, Dr. Scoville.

STATEMENT OF DR. HERBERT SCOVILLE, JR., CARNEGIE ENDOWMENT FOR INTERNATIONAL PEACE

Dr. SCOVILLE. Thank you.

Mr. Chairman, it is a great pleasure to accept your invitation to come before this committee again this time as a private citizen after having met with your committee for many years as a member of the Government.

In this connection, I should like to emphasize that any statements I may make here today are my own personal views and do not necessarily reflect those of the Carnegie Endowment for International Peace for whom I am now working part time. Furthermore, I would like to make it clear that I have not had access to classified Government documents or positions for the forthcoming strategic arms limitation talks (SALT), and so what I say should not in any way be construed as describing the views of any member of the Government on this subject.

VERIFICATION AND ARMS LIMITATION AGREEMENTS

I have been asked and am particularly pleased to be able to present to you my thoughts on the subject of verification since this has been and is, a key problem in achieving arms control. Any limitations on strategic arms, whether they be by formal agreement or occur as a result of mutual understanding, must be able to be verified to provide confidence that violations which would endanger security are not occurring. Unless this confidence exists, any agreement will be dangerous, unstable, and probably of short duration.

Verification has been a stumbling block in negotiating almost all arms control agreements since World War II. The closed society in the Soviet Union has always fed fears in this country that the Soviets might use an arms control agreement to restrict a U.S. weapons program while allowing the Russians to continue their program clandestinely to the point of achieving a military advantage.

A classic and perhaps overemphasized example of this problem has been in the negotiation of a comprehensive test ban treaty. The United States has always feared that the Soviets could derive significant military gains by underground tests which could not be distinguished from earthquakes and has sought inspections to clarify the nature of the seismic events. The Soviet Union resisted this desire as a threat to their society, and as a consequence no agreement on banning underground nuclear tests has yet been achieved.

U.S. CAUTION IN ARMS LIMITATION NEGOTIATIONS

Senator GORE. I would like to cite this, Doctor, as an example of the caution with which our Government has moved. I mention this again today because so often in the public mind those who urge agreement on arms limitation are regarded as insufficiently cautious about national security.

I was one of those who insisted that we could not include underground tests in the limited test ban treaty for the very reason that the Soviets would not agree to on-site inspection. This was the position of President Kennedy, and it was the position of the Government of the United States at that time.

As the record now stands, we may have been overly cautious, but I am not yet prepared to reach that conclusion. I interrupt only to emphasize the caution with which the United States has moved and with which it must move because the stakes are so very, very great.

Dr. SCOVILLE. Let me say I concur completely with what you say, and actually I, Mr. Fisher and others have spent quite a lot of time trying to get research programs going so that one can improve the verification procedures and, therefore, reduce the need for these on-site inspections which are so difficult to negotiate.

ARMS LIMITATION VERIFICATION PROCEDURES

In evaluating the adequacy of any verification procedures, it is important to emphasize that it is not necessary to be able to detect every possible violation but only to have the ability to detect those which could significantly affect U.S. security. If a nation believes that there is a risk of the violation being discovered, it is unlikely that it would take that risk unless the violation provided a significant gain. Cheating on an ICBM launcher freeze by secretly building a dozen or even a hundred missile silos makes no sense when both nations already have more than a thousand missiles.

Any arms limitation together with its means of verification should also be designed to avoid continual alarms that violations were occurring, since if these occurred frequently the value of the agreement would be greatly reduced. Fears of minor infractions of the agreement should not be allowed to become a source of major international incidents. This can be avoided as much by proper phrasing of the agreement as by the mechanics of verification itself. In general, arms limitation verification procedures are divided into two categories. The first are known in the jargon as national or unilateral verification techniques which do not require any agreements for inspection within the boundaries of another nation. The second category are termed "on-site inspections" in which a nation would agree to allow nationals of another country to inspect within its territories to determine whether a violation had occurred. Intermediate to these two categories would be those situations in which both sides agreed to conduct their operations so as to facilitate verification by national means.

Only in the case of the Antarctic Treaty has the Soviet Union allowed the use of onsite inspections to verify compliance with the treaty. At one time Chairman Khrushchev agreed in principle to three onsite inspections per year within the Soviet Union to monitor a comprehensive test ban treaty, but at that time the United States did not believe three a sufficiently large number. Since then the Soviet Union has withdrawn that offer. All other arms control agreements which have been negotiated have relied primarily on national means of verification. The limited test ban treaty is monitored by such national systems, and all countries have a high degree of confidence that significant violations are not occurring. The same is true of the undertaking in the outer space treaty not to place nuclear weapons in orbit around the earth. General Wheeler in testifying in support of that obligation said he favored reliance on national means since he did not believe that the Soviet Union could, without U.S. knowledge, violate this provision so as to obtain a significant military advantage.

Senator GORE. I would like to interject there, too, that we do not depend entirely upon so-called national identification and inspection and information because in the case of an atmospheric burst we have our own monitoring devices and sources of information. It would be very difficult indeed for atmospheric tests to be made that would escape attention and the knowledge of the United States.

Dr. SCOVILLE. These are the kind of techniques that I am including under national means.

Senator GORE. Yes.

Dr. SCOVILLE. That is right.

LIMITED TEST BAN TREATY

In this connection it is interesting to consider briefly the history of the Limited Test Ban Treaty. This treaty is verified by highly sophisticated scientific national techniques, and I believe that all countries have a high confidence that any significant violation of this treaty could be detected. Nevertheless on several occasions since the treaty came into effect, radioactive material from underground tests has been detected outside the boundaries of the country in which the tests were held. This could be considered a technical violation since the treaty bans tests which cause radioactive debris to be present outside the territorial limits of the state under whose control the explosion is conducted. While these occasions have resulted in exchanges of notes and requests for explanation both the United States and the Soviet Governments have recognized that the events did not threaten either nation's security nor did they significantly increase the health hazards throughout the world. As a consequence neither nation has made a major international incident out of these possible technical infractions. However, it is an example of where the wording of the treaty may have been sufficiently ambiguous as to permit a difference of views as to whether a violation had occurred even though the verification procedures were quite satisfactory. Such ambiguities in treaty language should be avoided to the maximum extent possible, without, however, at the same time incorporating so many technical details that the treaty could become inoperable as a result of unforeseen scientific developments.

UNILATERAL NATIONAL SECURITY PLANNING

Verification is not limited to arms control agreements but is also an important factor in our everyday unilateral national security planning. Decisions that are made on ICBM force levels, on whether to deploy an ABM, or on whether to develop MIRV's or other penetration aids to overcome a Soviet ABM are all based on the best information nationally available on Soviet armament programs. In such day-to-day unilateral planning it is not enough just to know that a missile has been deployed. One must also know the characteristics of that missile and have some basis for estimating the quantity and the timing of the total deployment program. Thus, the information required for unilateral planning is much more difficult to obtain than that required to monitor an arms limitation agreement where information that a single missile launcher had been added to the force would all that might be required in order to verify that a freeze was not being abided by.

A good example of where it would be much easier to verify satisfactorily an arms control agreement than the size of the force for unilateral planning would be in the area of mobile ICBM's. If, as a result of SALT, it were agreed that mobile ICBM's would be totally banned, then the ability to detect the deployment of even a single such missile would be sufficient to verify whether the agreement was being abided by. It would not be necessary to count precisely the number of mobile missiles deployed, which might be very difficult unless one had instantaneous observation of the entire Soviet Union to avoid confusion if the missiles were moved from one place to another between observations. On the other hand in order to determine for our unilateral force planning whether a Soviet mobile ICBM force, which had not been restricted by an agreement, posed a threat, one would need to know the size of such a force. This might be very difficult to accomplish with suitable reliability.

MOBILE LAND-BASED ICBM MISSILE

Senator GORE. Could I ask you to describe briefly a mobile land-based ICBM missile?

Dr. SCOVILLE. Well, a mobile land-based ICBM might be an ICBM which was placed on a railroad car and moved up and down the railroad tracks from one location to another on some unknown schedule, and fired from an unknown point so that it could not be targeted by the opposing force. It also might be a missile on a large wheeled vehicle which followed the roads. In other words, it has no fixed launching point and, therefore, is invulnerable to a first strike or at least much less vulnerable to a first strike.

Senator GORE. Could it not have many launching points if a harder foundation were needed than an ordinary roadbed at various intervals along the roadway? The bed of the railroad could be hardened into very thick concrete.

Dr. SCOVILLE. Well, you could have hardened sites along the railroad track. I think this would be rather difficult. I am sure it would be terribly expensive so the cost of the whole installation would certainly go up.

On the other hand, there have been proposals made for having I guess what you might call a mobile hardened ICBM force in which, you excavated the interior of a large mountain and had a number of railroad tracks either going around in a circle within the mountain with maybe eight or 10 different launch points. The other side would never know which launch point you were going to use. This is one of the sort of wild far-out ideas for a future ICBM force. I hate to think of the expense of such a system. I am sure it is the easiest way to protect your force.

EFFECT OF SS-9 DEPLOYMENT ON ABM AND MINUTEMEN

Senator GORE. You were kind enough to be with us throughout Dr. Panofsky's testimony yesterday. In the course of his testimony he concluded that unless the threat increased deployment of an ABM would not be needed.

On the other hand, if the SS-9 threat were significantly increased then stationary Minutemen would become obsolete. So unless some agreement can be reached in the SALT talks the United States may be forced to look to mobility, both at sea and on land.

Dr. SCOVILLE. I think that is correct. I might say it isn't only Dr. Panofsky who made that statement. Secretary Laird himself made that statement in the Foster statement.

Senator GORE. When did he make that statement?

Dr. SCOVILLE. It is in this book. Fiscal year 1971 Defense Program and Budget.

Senator GORE. That is this year. He didn't make that statement last year?

Dr. SCOVILLE. No, he didn't make that statement last year.

Senator GORE. All right. Go ahead.

Dr. SCOVILLE. This example raises another point——

Senator GORE. Do you have that testimony marked so you can cite it? Would you mind reading it?

Dr. SCOVILLE. Let us see, I can give you the page. It is on page 48 of the Fiscal Year 1971 Defense Program and Budget.

Senator GORE. Is it long?

Dr. SCOVILLE. Well, it is a half page.

Senator GORE. I don't mean the whole statement but that particular point.

Dr. SCOVILLE. He cites three cases analyzing where the Safeguard might be useful in defending Minuteman. Case a is: "That the Soviets do not increase deployment of SS-9 and SS-11; do not develop a MIRV for the SS-9 and do not improve ICBM accuracy. Under these circumstances there is no need for a defense of the Minuteman force."

Senator GORE. That is the situation now?

Dr. SCOVILLE. That is the situation now.

Senator GORE. So as of now——

Dr. SCOVILLE. That is the first case Dr. Panofsky was talking about.

Now, the second case, which is b, "that the Soviets stopped building ICBM's beyond those now operational or started; they do not develop a MIRV for the SS-9, but they do improve the accuracy of their entire ICBM force. Under these circumstances the force could constitute a threat to the Minuteman force, and Safeguard would be quite effective against that threat."

That is the case where it would be effective, according to Secretary Laird.

Then there is case c "that the Soviets deploy a MIRV on the SS-9, improve their ICBM accuracy and do not stop building ICBM's at this time but continue building them at their present rate. We would then be faced in the mid-1970's with a threat which is much too large to be handled by the level of defense envisioned in the Safeguard system without substantial improvement and modification.

Senator GORE. That would seem to amount to concurrence with Dr. Panofsky's conclusions.

Dr. SCOVILLE. Right.

Senator GORE. Does not case a, however, depend upon the Soviets stopping where they are while the United States proceeded with MIRV?

Dr. SCOVILLE. No, I don't believe it does.

Senator GORE. You don't think so?

Dr. SCOVILLE. No.

Senator GORE. Thank you.

EVALUATION OF RELATIVE RISK

Dr. SCOVILLE. This example raises another point which should be kept in mind in evaluating the adequacy of verification capabilities for any arms control agreement. First one must always evaluate the relative risk from a possible violation against the risk which might exist if no arms control agreement were achieved. For example, the risk of an undetected Soviet violation of a ban on mobile ICBM's which the United States has no plans to deploy would be far less than the risk of no agreement which allowed the Soviets to build up a force of undeterminable size and characteristics. Further when programs are proceeding without any restrictions, information on the nature of new developments and deployments can often be confusing and misleading and consequently produce less than optimal unilateral U.S. weapons decisions.

PRESENT SIZE OF SURVIVABLE STRATEGIC FORCES SIMPLIFIES VERIFICATION

Finally, adequate verification of limitations on strategic arms is greatly simplified at this time by the fact that both sides now have such large forces of survivable strategic weapons that any clandestine program in violation of a treaty would have to be very great before it could threaten our national security. Not only are the numbers large, but there are also several different types of systems available in our assured destruction force, that is, submarine launched missiles, hardened land-based missiles, and intercontinental bombers, so that a sudden unexpected threat to one system will not jeopardize the entire second-strike force. Deterrence can be maintained by both sides despite large changes, either qualitative or quantitative, in the force structure of either side. For example, although the Soviets have more than trebled their missile force in the last 5 years they are still a long way from being able to prevent the United States from inflicting widespread and unacceptable devastation on the Soviet Union in a retaliatory attack. Even if in the highly unlikely event that the Soviets succeeded in secretly developing a MIRVed missile force which could destroy all U.S. land-based missiles, the United States would still have a force of 41 Polaris submarines each with 16 missiles, only a small fraction of which would be required to devastate the Soviet Union.

This was, however, not the case in 1960 when the deterrent force relied almost entirely on vulnerable bombers and had only a few or no ICBM's. Then, even a small increment to these missile forces would have had very significant military consequences. Likewise we are much better off technically to verify by national means the size and characteristics of the opposing strategic forces than in the fifties. While it is not appropriate for me to discuss our technical capabilities in an open hearing, I am sure it is no secret that our capabilities have improved markedly in the last 10 years.

I am sure you will get more information on this when you hear the CIA. Had they not so improved it would not have been possible for Secretaries McNamara, Clifford, and Laird to report year after year with high confidence on the size of the Soviet ICBM force, submarine force, and ABM's.

ARMS LIMITATION AGREEMENTS SHOULD BE DESIGNED TO FACILITATE VERIFICATION

Any nation which attempts to violate any arms limitation agreement on a scale sufficient to obtain a significant military advantage will run some risk of being detected. Defection by disillusioned personnel or disclosure of the violation by an agent can never be ruled out for even the most secret program. However, such sources of information are unreliable and cannot be counted on by the United States when its vital security interests are at stake. Therefore since verification capabilities vary greatly for different phases of the weapons development cycle, arms limitation agreements should be designed to emphasize those phases which are at the same time easy to monitor and critical to security.

Research and development, while still in the laboratory phase, could rarely be reliably detected either by any type of national observation system or by any acceptable onsite inspection scheme. Thus it is only when the development reaches the testing phase that strategic weapons programs become observable and provide opportunities to verify restrictions on development of new systems. Before most offensive missile systems can be reliably deployed, they require extensive tests at long range so that they can be monitored beyond the borders of the testing nation. The United States has been able to observe Soviet ICBM tests consistently since their program began in 1957. Not only have successive Secretaries of Defense reported on the number of missile firings but in many cases on the characteristics of the weapons being developed. While defensive interceptor missiles do not travel such long distances, the high-powered radars which track the incoming warhead and guide the interceptors emit radio waves which can often be discernible at remote locations. Since much testing is relatively easily verifiable, it is frequently a good point in the weapons cycle to start applying limitations.

The production of strategic weapons is again more difficult to observe. Many components can be produced in small buildings and even a complete missile could be assembled in structures which might not be easily identifiable. National means of verification might locate many suspicious structures, and frequent on-site inspections might be required to provide sufficient confidence that violations of a ban on production were not occurring. For ABM systems it would be even more difficult since the missiles are smaller and the electronic components for the radars would be indistinguishable from those required for other purposes until they were finally assembled in the deployed radar. The one exception would be the production of missile launching submarines which employ for their construction large and fairly easily identifiable shipyard facilities.

Finally, looking at the last stage in the weapon cycle—deployment. It is easy to observe deployment and determine changes in the number of operationally deployed systems. To simplify the verification it is usually best to have a complete ban or to freeze the number at existing levels rather than agreeing on a fixed number of items. After a freeze has been achieved, then the levels can be reduced by agreed numbers.

It is often not so easy to determine the characteristics of the systems deployed, since many of these are independent of the external configuration of the hardware. Once missiles with certain capabilities were demonstrated and proven in testing and particularly if troop training were observed, one must assume that they could be deployed. However, it will frequently be impossible to know how many have been incorporated in the force and what will be their real operational capability. It would, for example, be difficult to verify with high confidence whether a new type of missile was being substituted for an existing one or whether improvements were being made to existing systems. Therefore, limitations on deployment should emphasize numbers of weapons rather than weapon characteristics.

In order to evaluate the ability to verify deployment limitations, it is necessary to look at each individual strategic weapons system. For the purpose of discussion today I have concentrated on those systems which would be most critical in a freeze on strategic offensive and defensive weapons.

VERIFICATION OF LAND-BASED ICBM's

Fixed land-based ICBM's require extensive launch site construction in order to provide the necessary hardening to make them resistant to blast from a nuclear explosion. This construction requires many months, and therefore ample time is available to permit its detection. In presenting his fiscal year 1971 Defense program, Secretary Laird has reported with great precision the numbers of such Soviet launchers, both operational and their rate of construction, each year since 1966. While in theory it might be possible to build clandestinely at great cost in time and money a few additional launchers using elaborate camouflage techniques, such a violation would have no effect on U.S. security since they would be an insignificant addition to the already large existing forces of more than a thousand ICBM's on both sides. Therefore, a limitation on numbers of ICBM launchers could be adequately verified by national means without the need for any supplementary procedures.

Mobile land-based missiles would be more difficult to monitor, but even these require logistic support which would be difficult to conceal. This would be particularly true in the Soviet Union, where the road system is limited and the rail system well known. However, if large numbers were already deployed, it might be hard to obtain a reliable count of the number of such missiles since the missiles might be moved between observations. If deployment were nonexistent or small at the time the agreement was reached, then a large new deployment would become apparent. Therefore, a total ban on deployment of such systems would be preferable, since the detection of even one would constitute a violation. This country has not developed or deployed any mobile ICBM's, and there are no reliable reports of Soviet deployment of either mobile ICBM's or IRBM's (Intermediate Range Ballistic Missiles), although the Russians have displayed missiles in the Moscow parade which they claim to be such. It is highly unlikely that the Soviets could secretly deploy the many hundreds of mobile ICBM's which would be required to affect the present strategic balance, but the sooner a ban took effect the easier the verification.

VERIFICATION OF SUBMARINE-LAUNCHED BALLISTIC MISSILES (SLBMS)

Submarines which have large numbers of long-range missiles and which can operate for protracted periods at long distances from their home ports require large and distinctive facilities for their construction. Secretary Laird has reported in his fiscal year 1971 Defense program that the Soviets can accommodate 12 complete hulls at two different shipyards. After the submarines are launched they require many months for fitting out, during all of which they are subject to observation. To have a reliable operational capability they must be shaken down and cruise in the open oceans. Secretary Laird, like his predecessors, has on several occasions reported with confidence the numbers of existing Soviet submarine-launched missiles. Again, for the Soviets to increase their present relatively small, but rapidly growing, SLBM force without U.S. knowledge to a point where it could significantly affect U.S. security would not seem possible. Therefore a ban on construction of new ballistic missile submarines could be verified by national means.

VERIFICATION OF MIRV'S AND MRV'S

So far I have addressed only the numbers of missiles or their launching platforms; the number of nuclear warheads within a given missile is another thing. Since a single large warhead can be replaced, without changing the external configuration of the missile, by several smaller warheads either with or without a capability to be individually targeted (MIRV's or MRV's), it is hard to visualize how the United States could verify by national means whether a deployed missile has or has not multiple warheads. In fact even onsite inspection to make this determination would be difficult. It would require the right to inspect any deployed missile including those on submarines, on sufficiently short notice to prevent substitution of the reentry vehicle. The inspection would require access into the interior of the reentry vehicle or at very least, the use at close range of some scientific technique, such as X-rays, to determine the number of warheads present. Such inspection would almost certainly not be acceptable to the U.S.S.R. If the Soviets required similar inspection to verify that the United States was not secretly deploying MIRV's, it is doubtful that the United States could accept it.

Therefore, if MIRV's are to be controlled, every effort should be made to limit testing as well as deployment. At the present time, neither the United States nor the U.S.S.R. have fully developed and tested a MIRV system with sufficient accuracy and reliability to provide a first strike capability. The Soviets began testing MRV's on the SS-9 in August 1968, and President Nixon in the summer of 1969 stated that the "footprint" of the Russian MRV indicates that they may happen to fall in a pattern comparable to the area covered by a complex of three Minuteman sites. However, Dr. John Foster, Director, Defense Research and Engineering, has stated on February 24, 1970, that the Soviets "have not demonstrated to us the flexibility necessary to target each warhead at a different Minuteman silo." All Minuteman sites do not have the same spacing so that the Soviets would require the ability to vary the footprint reliably and accurately if they were to have a capability to wipe out the entire Minuteman force.

The United States started a 2-year program to test first generation MIRV's for the Poseidon and Minuteman III missiles also in August 1968, and Department of Defense officials have announced that the Minuteman III will begin to be fielded in June 1970 and the Poseidon become operational in January 1971. While U.S. officials have emphasized that the accuracy-yield combination of these first MIRV's will not be sufficient to provide a first strike counterforce capability, the Soviets may nevertheless be concerned that the first U.S. systems might have such a capability. Fortunately, the Soviets should be able to satisfy themselves that the United States was not deploying MIRV's in violation of a ban on deployment since it is hard to conceive how the United States, with its open society, could place MIRV's in a large part of its force without detection. Certainly we should not prejudge the decision for the Soviets and conclude that controls on MIRV's are unverifiable because the U.S. program has proceeded too far. There is still time, but maybe only a little, to prevent deployment of MIRV's if a ban on testing and development can be achieved soon.

What are the opportunities for the United States to verify a ban on MIRV and MRV testing? (MRV testing would probably also have to be banned to be confident that these were not confused with MIRV's.) Since the type of MIRV which could threaten the fixed land-based missile force is one which has a very high capability for destroying hardened ICBM sites, that is, a reliable MIRV with high accuracy and high yield. I believe verification is possible. In order to achieve such a capability it will be necessary to test at full range and at as near operational conditions as possible. Such tests can be monitored to determine the number of reentry vehicles. No nation would replace existing reliable missiles and consider initiating a nuclear war with a missile which had only been partially tested. Planners would demand high confidence on the reliability and accuracy of the full system before risking national suicide by carrying out a first strike.

Tests in which only one of the multiple warheads was allowed to separate would be useful for development but not satisfactory for proving out the complete system. Such tests would in any case probably raise suspicions. Likewise, simulated tests in space or, as has been suggested in analogy to the proposal for evading the Nuclear Test Ban Treaty, "tests behind the moon" would be equally unsatisfactory. Elaborate schemes for clandestine testing will undoubtedly be put forward, as they were in the case of nuclear weapons testing, but even with much simpler system than MIRV's, military planners like to see full operational testing before undertaking deployment. For example, even more than 5 years after development testing has been completed on the Polaris A3 MRV system, the military are claiming that additional firings of the complete system are essential to maintain confidence in its operational capability. Based on past experience the Soviet military are even more stringent than the United States, in their requirements for full operational testing. It is most unlikely that the Soviets could without U.S. knowledge violate a MIRV–MRV test ban to the extent that they would be in a position to deploy a MIRV system which would be sufficiently reliable and accurate to threaten to destroy the entire Minuteman force.

VERIFICATION OF LONG-RANGE BOMBERS

The Soviets have no known present program for deploying a new truly intercontinental bomber. If they were to undertake such a deployment in violation of a ban it is almost certain that the force would be detected before it had reached a significant size. Bombers are not easy to conceal, and U.S. authorities have known with confidence and publicly reported the size of the Soviet bomber force since the mid-fifties. Suggestions have been made that they would masquerade such a force under the guise of supersonic transports which could be rapidly converted to bombers. Both Generals LeMay and Power have frequently emphasized that a bomber force which does not train and carry out realistic simulated operations is of almost no value. It is inconceivable that the Soviets could secretly create an operationally capable bomber force which could provide any serious additional threat to U.S. security.

VERIFICATION OF ABM'S

Finally, going to strategic defensive systems, I shall concentrate on ABM's, since they pose the most serious potential threat to our confidence in our strategic deterrent forces and since they are the defensive system of most interest in any strategic arms limitation agreement. In 1966 Secretary McNamara publicly announced that we had clear evidence that the Soviets were building an ABM system around Moscow, and the progress of this system has been reported on since at regular intervals. Secretary Laird has recently reported that a number of the complexes in this system were only brought to operational status this past year. Furthermore both Secretaries Clifford and Laird were even able to report that the deployment had been reduced in scope from that originally planned and that on the other hand the Soviets are continuing to press forward with R. & D. (research and development) on a more advanced system. Secretary Laird also referred to large Soviet phased array radars for initial tracking and warning. I am confident, and these statements are a public substantiation, that we are now capable of verifying a freeze on the deployment of ABM systems and that any significant violation could be detected well in advance of their becoming operational.

ABM's to cope with the sophisticated type threat of which the United States is capable are complicated and large systems. They require large radars which have a high visibility, have a long leadtime for construction and which, furthermore, must radiate energy continuously if they are to be of any value. In addition, an ABM system requires large numbers of high performance defensive missiles if it is not to be saturated. Extensive training exercises must be carried out to develop operational competence. All these factors greatly facilitate the verification of a freeze on ABM's. If, however, the limitation did not ban a nationwide net of large radars similar to the U.S. PAR's (perimeter acquisition radars) and MSR's (missile site radars) and keep the number of missiles to low levels, then verification would be much more difficult since additional defensive missiles could be secretly produced and then rapidly deployed. Once ABM radars with nationwide coverage are in place it will be much harder to verify any ABM limitations. The existing vulnerable early warning radars (HENHOUSE) deployed on the periphery of the U.S.S.R. do not themselves serve this purpose and would have to be backed up by other advanced radars nearer the ABM launchers.

A serious problem in the ABM area could be the confusion between systems designed for defense against aircraft with those designed for defense against ballistic missiles if the former were not controlled. For example, during the early construction period there was some doubt as to whether the so-called Tallinn air defense system was for ABM purposes or not. However, as deployment proceeded, it became more and more clear that it was for defense against aircraft.

Nevertheless, fears still exist that the Tallinn or other air defense systems might be upgraded to provide an ABM capability without our knowledge. In evaluating this risk it is important to realize that any air defense system may have some limited capability to shoot down an incoming missile.

DIFFICULTIES IN UPGRADING TALLINN SYSTEM

Senator GORE. Doctor, if they did undertake to upgrade the Tallinn system to have an anti-ballistic missile capability, would they not likely run into the same technological problems that the United States has faced in trying to convert the Sentinel system to the Safeguard system?

Dr. SCOVILLE. They would have an even more difficult problem. I think a closer analogy is that we haven't at all seriously considered upgrading our Nike-Hercules to an ABM system. Although this could be done an awful lot cheaper than building Safeguard its value would be very low. Yet we are assuming that the Soviets, or at least those who think this is a real risk, are assuming the Soviets can do this so as to have an effective system in a clandestine program which we could not detect. It would be very difficult to have a system with a high capability.

POSSIBLE SOVIET PROPOSAL FOR DEPLOYMENT MORATORIUM

Senator GORE. Since I interrupted, I note in the paper this morning a press report from London speculating on the possibility that the Soviets might offer in Vienna a temporary freeze or moratorium upon deployment. I have no notion at all as to the authenticity of the report, but if it turns out that the U.S. Government declined to take the advice of the U.S. Senate but the Soviet Government did, it would be an interesting development to comment upon. Would it not?

Dr. SCOVILLE. It certainly would. I hope the U.S. Government would take the advice first.

Senator GORE. Do you think this might be a case of guilt by association.

Dr. SCOVILLE. I hope not. Just because you have the right idea and somebody else picks it up is not necessarily to make it bad.

Senator GORE. You may proceed.

ABM VERIFICATION

Dr. SCOVILLE. However, to be a threat to a retaliatory attack of which the United States is capable and thereby rode the deterrent it must have an extremely high capability. Its radars must be able to handle rapidly large numbers of incoming targets and must also be defended. The missiles must have a high acceleration to avoid the necessity of committing the defense before the radar has determined the nature of the incoming objects. President Nixon has stated when the Safeguard decision was first made that the heaviest defense system considered, an ABM system designed to protect cities from a Soviet type threat, could not prevent a catastrophic level of U.S. fatalities. Clearly a Soviet system to cope with the even larger U.S. threat cannot be built by clandestinely upgrading existing air defense systems. New or large numbers of greatly improved radars, new missiles, new command and control systems and new radar defenses would be required if the Soviet anti-aircraft systems were to be turned into even a partially effective ABM. Extensive troop training would be needed to develop operational effectiveness. Such a program would undoubtedly be detected with plenty of lead time to incorporate counter measures to permit penetration of such a system. The United States already has developed and tested MIRV's capable of penetrating an ABM system, and these could be deployed in an emergency much more rapidly than a Soviet ABM.

Thus it would appear that limitations on ABM's to low or zero levels can be adequately verified by national means. While some fears might arise about the upgrading of Soviet defense systems, it is believed that the risk to our security from such a secret program would be less than if there were no limitations on ABM's. It would be preferable to ban ABM's or restrict them to very low levels, since in these instances radar deployments could be limited and thus facilitate verification.

BROAD FREEZE ON OFFENSIVE AND DEFENSIVE STRATEGIC WEAPONS RECOMMENDED

Finally I should like to point out that a broad freeze on offensive and defensive strategic weapons is easier to verify so as to maintain security than a ban on only one of the systems.

For example, if ICBM launchers, MIRV's and ABM's were all frozen at their current status a nation would have to succeed in violating without being detected in at least two of these areas before security could be jeopardized. In such a freeze a clandestine MIRV program for the SS-9 would not threaten the U.S. deterrent since the Soviets would be precluded from building more SS-9's or ABM's and the United States would still have an assured destruction capability in weapons which could not be destroyed by the Soviet MIRV's on its existing SS-9's. If only MIRV's were banned, then in time a clandestine MIRV program together with permitted ABM and SS-9 deployments could be perceived as threatening the U.S. deterrent.

In summary: Quantitative limitations on the deployment of key strategic weapons systems can be adequately verified by national means.

Limitations on the testing of all multiple reentry vehicles can be adequately verified by national means and, if MIRV's are to be controlled, should be sought immediately together with a ban on MIRV deployment. It is not yet too late to achieve such limitations since MIRV systems which are sufficiently reliable and accurate to threaten hardened ICBM sites are not yet fully tested and deployable and since secret deployment of MIRV's by the United States is not possible.

ABM deployment limitations at zero or low levels of defensive missiles and particularly radars can also be verified. Any upgrading of existing air defense systems which could escape detection would not provide an ABM capability which could seriously degrade the U.S. deterrent.

ARMS LIMITATION AGREEMENT NOW WOULD INCREASE SECURITY

In light of existing national verification capabilities, the large numbers of weapons on each side, and the insensitivity of each side's deterrent to relatively large force changes, I am confident that an agreement can be designed which would significantly limit strategic armaments and in fact increase real security.

Senator GORE. That last statement is a very reassuring one. Of course security is what we must have, and you conclude, as Dr. Panofsky did yesterday, that an agreement limiting nuclear arms would provide more not less security.

Dr. SCOVILLE. I certainly do. I think we are in a position right now where there is really a high degree of stability on both sides and the risk to either side is minimal. Continuing the arms race is likely to decrease that stability and increase the risk that nuclear war will break out.

Senator GORE. If a high degree of stability exists, as you have described, does that not constitute an optimum condition and circumstance in which to obtain an agreement?

Dr. SCOVILLE. I think it does. It is just an ideal time right now to have an agreement. I don't think we have ever been in as good a position, as we have in the last year or so. In the early sixties we were not in that position because with rather low force levels of missiles and particularly unhardened missile systems there was considerable risk that initiating nuclear war might possibly provide some advantage. At the present stage there is just no advantage in initiating nuclear war and the risks are overwhelming.

On the other hand, with the forthcoming deployment of MIRV's and ABM's, then the incentives or the advantages of going first increase, and this is not the type of situation that I like to look forward to.

PRESENT U.S. DETERRENT POWER

Senator GORE. In connection with this degree of stability that exists, is it not an undeniable fact that a greater number of land and sea based retaliatory missiles, offensive missiles, are possessed by the United States at this time.

Dr. SCOVILLE. We have a very large force of missiles which are capable of retaliating even after the most extensive Soviet first strike that anybody can imagine.

Senator GORE. In other words, you think that our power of deterrence is ample when measured beside the Soviet capability even if they struck first?

Dr. SCOVILLE. I certainly do.

Senator GORE. That being the case, I take it you support strongly the resolution that the Senate passed?

Dr. SCOVILLE. I do indeed.

U.S. POSITION IN EVENT OF SOVIET PROPOSAL TO FREEZE DEPLOYMENT

Senator GORE. From your experience in the Government, would you assume that the Administration has prepared a position in the event the Soviets do, in fact, seize the initiative and propose a freeze on the deployment of both defensive and offensive missiles?

Dr. SCOVILLE. I would certainly hope so. Certainly in my experience in the Government, one prepared all types of contingency positions in the event that the Soviet might suggest various things, and I am sure Mr. Fisher could amplify on that even more than I can because he has prepared a lot of alternatives.

Senator GORE. He is from my State. I made that mistake this morning. Let us call him dean from now on.

Dean Fisher, would you comment on that?

STATEMENT OF ADRIAN S. FISHER, DEAN, GEORGETOWN UNIVERSITY LAW SCHOOL

Mr. FISHER. I would certainly hope they would have a variety of alternatives against the, in my mind, happy conditions if the Soviets came up with that type of offer that the papers report that they may be considering.

Senator GORE. Would you be so optimistic as to think that it just may be they may have such a plan and that our Government might have a plan in case the Soviets might be about to seize the initiative?

Mr. FISHER. Well, I would certainly hope so, and since I am an optimist by disposition, I would hope that they would take advantage of an opportunity which, as I agree with Dr. Scoville, exists now, a rare combination of strategic and political factors exist, it is really a time and tide that may come just once and an opportunity that if not seized may never come again.

I would hate to think that we would be doomed again, in the words of the bard, to spend the rest of our lives in the shadows and miseries because we didn't take this opportunity.

POSSIBLE OBJECTIONS TO INTERIM FREEZE ON STRATEGIC WEAPONS

Senator CASE. Mr. Chairman, on that point, it seems that perhaps you and we have been looking at this too much from one side or with one view in mind. The more we consider and talk with each other the more difficult it is to understand how there could be any rational view except that which accepts the desirability of an interim freeze on all weapons.

Would you please explain so that we might have some better understanding what objections there may be because it is obvious that up to now there has been reluctance on the part of our Government to take this position.

Mr. FISHER. Well——

Senator GORE. If you will answer this question, then I am going to ask you to read your statement and we will question both of you.

Mr. FISHER. Yes. Well, allowing myself to be put in this position which is a hard thing to do and I do not agree with this position, and I will deal with it in this statement, but I can imagine someone saying we have to have a complete ban on everything and since the Soviets apparently are continuing to deploy SS-9's, and since they may be continuing to build subs, we have to continue to do the things we are doing and we have to do them very quickly.

Now, as I will get into in my statement insofar as that relates to the deployment of MIRV's inside of 2 months, I think that is a program of doubtful merit, and certainly extremely doubtful timing.

Senator CASE. Mr. Chairman, then I think I will withdraw the question now unless you want to continue because it might be more effectively discussed after your statement has been presented.

Senator GORE. Will you proceed with your statement.

Mr. FISHER. Thank you, Mr. Chairman.

SUGGESTED ACTIONS FOR SUCCESS IN IMPLEMENTING SENATE RESOLUTION 211

In view of the action that the Senate has taken on Thursday, April 9, on the Senate resolution, Mr. Chairman, I thought it might be useful if I directed my remarks primarily to two actions which I believe should be taken in the light of the hard realities of international negotiations, if the sense of the Senate expressed in that resolution is to have a reasonable chance of success.

Senate Resolution 211 expresses the sense of the Senate that prompt negotiations between the United States of America and the U.S.S.R. to seek agreed limitations on both offensive and defensive strategic weapons should be urgently pursued. I certainly agree with that. Senate Resolution 211 expresses the sense of the Senate that the President should propose to the Government of the U.S.S.R. an immediate suspension by the United States and by the U.S.S.R. of the further deployment of all offensive and defensive nuclear strategic weapons systems, subject to national verification or such other measures of observation and inspection as may be appropriate. And I believe Dr. Scoville's recent testimony gave rather eloquent evidence that national verification is appropriate and satisfactory.

Now, the two actions which I believe should be taken to give the program outlined in Senate Resolution 211 a fair chance of coming into being are:

First, a deferral by at least 6 months of the impending deployment by the United States of the multiple independently targetable reentry vehicles and, second, a postponement of any action looking toward the authorization or implementation of the proposed modified Phase II Safeguard system.

Now, these actions, Mr. Chairman, are necessary to preserve the opportunity that we now have, an opportunity created by a rare coincidence of both favorable political and strategic considerations which provide a real but perhaps fleeting opportunity for an agreement between the United States and the U.S.S.R. to halt the arms race in both the quantity and quality of weapons, and then hopefully to diminish the threat to mankind posed by existing weapons.

EFFECT OF INTRODUCING MIRV'S INTO NUCLEAR RELATIONSHIP

Now, dealing first with the problems posed by the MIRV's, introduction into the present nuclear relationship would have the initial effect of substantially increasing the number of deliverable nuclear warheads available to each side. The increased number might not be increased in yield, in fact in total deliverable yield might even be a little less, but they would be where there would be a thousand, there might be 1,500 or 2,000, or 3,000 of land-based, and the same would be true as far as the Soviets. The total nuclear confrontation in terms of number of nuclear warheads aimed at each other would be drastically increased on each side.

This is bad enough——

Senator GORE. With no more security for either side, but rather more insecurity?

Mr. FISHER. I think insecurity, Mr. Chairman.

Senator GORE. At least we could kill each other more quickly and multitudinously.

Mr. FISHER. Yes, we would have spared ourselves the luxury of overkilling some people but spread it out by just one time killing more. I mean this sounds terribly crude the way I state it, but reading these force postures and the estimates that have been made from time to time about the number of people killed in the event of all-out nuclear exchange, these are just straight-out fatalities in the first bang, not people who die from famine or starvation or epidemics, the other horsemen of the Apocalypse. You talk about 180 million on one side, 80 million, circumstances will change a hundred million, a hundred million. We have read these figures so many times we sort of get to be a little fascinated with them, sort of like a bird by a snake. So even the total increase in number of deliverable warheads I am not sure increases our security but decreases it.

EFFECT OF INCREASE IN MIRV ACCURACY

But the MIRV problem takes on a new dimension, Mr. Chairman, particularly in its land-based configuration, as the missile accuracy increases.

When these accuracies increase, of this MIRV, which I explain to my friends who sometimes get confused by the acronym gap, the difference between MRV's and MIRV's, one of them is a shotgun, the MRV, and the MIRV has the effect of a shotgun in which the pellets are aimed at individual directions. But when this happens it may become possible for one side, if it strikes first with missiles armed with MIRV's, to take out more than one missile site on the opposing side.

Now, the obverse of this quite frightening coin is that each side may find that unless it strikes first, the MIRVed missiles on the other side may be able to substantially eliminate its own land-based ICBM force with the other side still having substantial ICBM forces left in reserve.

Now, of course, as long as we have sea-based forces that are under the surface, the deterrent may still exist but I think we will all agree that a situation in which both sides have substantial land-based forces which may be wiped out by the other unless a first strike is—unless they are used in a first strike, is not a healthy situation. It isn't a situation anywhere near as safe as the present balance is. Dangerous though our present balance may be, at least it is controllable. If you were in a situation in which the temptation is to say, well, unless you strike first your system is going to be useless, the situation is much more tense.

I will read this from a responsible journalist who I will—he is writing about the Helsinski talks in the December 19, 1969, issue of the Washington Post, and he makes this comment:

"The MIRV warheads on the Minuteman missiles will not matter much either if the SS-9's can take all those missiles out in one blow."

Now, that is a responsible columnist writing in a morning paper of general circulation for which I used to work, and which I think of very highly but if that sort of discussion is, "Well, our missiles won't be any good if they can take them out with one blow," you can imagine a Soviet opposite number saying the same thing, and this isn't a terribly—it was an argument in favor of ABM's in this particular case but the argument is the same.

So I think we can all agree that if we continue to develop the MIRV's, and as the accuracies are increased at least as far as in their land-based configuration are concerned, the situation gets much less stable than a situation where the MIRV's are not in yet.

Senator GORE. At this point, Dean, this relative stability, of which both you and Dr. Scoville speak, is threatened by the Soviet development and deployment of the SS-9 and by U.S. deployment of MIRV's and the ABM.

U.S. IMMINENT DEPLOYMENT OF MIRV'S

Mr. FISHER. Well, I think the present chances of proceeding along the line outlined by the second operative paragraph of Senate Resolution 211 is threatened most immediately as of right now by the U.S. imminent deployment of MIRV's.

In Mr. Seaman's statement he said, "After a number of delays and stretch-outs we will start fielding the Minuteman III in June."

Now, since the testing program was originally scheduled to be completed in June of this year, I am not quite sure what delays and stretch-outs he is talking about. It doesn't give the impression to me of a delayed or stretched out program. It gives the impression to me of a program which in relationship to his initial schedule is so close as to be almost miraculous.

Senator GORE. You know when that statement was made, a further statement was issued. I don't know to whom it was attributed. It said that there had been a slip-up and that this announcement was not intended. I inquired of the Defense Department, and—some 2 days later—I was informed that it had been a cleared statement.

Mr. FISHER. Well, Mr. Chairman, I can't speak to the question of whether it was intended or not. I know it was made and it has not been denied.

Senator GORE. I was told by the Defense Department that it was a cleared statement.

Mr. FISHER. Well, Mr. Chairman, according to this statement, we are in the process apparently of completing a test series of MIRV's, a series which began in September of 1968, and no one who was in the Government during that period can shirk the responsibility. The test period did begin in September of 1968, and which was scheduled for completion in June of this year. And according to the statement we are going to start deploying in June of this year. And I have been advised, not advised, I read in the paper which I gather is true, we have similar plans with respect to putting Poseidon in the Polaris submarines in either the latter part of this year or the early part of 1971.

Now, the deployment of the first MIRV's would represent a real setback, Mr. Chairman, in our effort to control the arms race. It would make a situation which is already dangerous enough, because of our testing MIRV's up to the point of deployment, far more dangerous.

Now, I know this committee is well aware of the difficulties in verifying by physical inspection a restriction on MIRV deployment once MIRV's have been tested up to a point where they are ready to be deployed.

The preamble to Senate Resolution 211 makes this point quite clear and Dr. Scoville's testimony made it clear also.

From this I know it has been argued and one might argue that we have already passed the point of no return, so to speak, in view of the completion of the test series, a series begun in September of 1968, up to the point of being ready for deployment.

U.S. MIRV'S LACK COUNTERFORCE CAPABILITY

Now, two factors, I think, may have prevented us from having passed this point. The first factor is that we have not pressed our tests to the point where our MIRV's have a counterforce capability. We apparently pressed the tests to the point where they are ready to be deployed, but we apparently have not pressed them to the point that they would be thought of as a counterforce weapon.

Senator GORE. Explain that. What do you mean by that?

Mr. FISHER. Well, for our MIRV's to be a counterforce weapon they have to have a very, very high accuracy, because we don't—our Minuteman III, if MIRV has reasonably small yields, one may describe a yield roughly 10 times Hiroshima as reasonably small, you have to put it down the proverbial pickle barrel so to speak.

Senator GORE. Can't we find some term other than small?

Mr. FISHER. I tried to put a verbal quotation mark around it, Mr. Chairman. It is hard for me to describe something as 10 times Hiroshima as small, but in view of the——

Senator CASE. The question is its relation to accuracy.

Mr. FISHER. Accuracy. We have not yet gotten the accuracy, at least we testified to that effect. The Secretary, the Chief of Staff of the Air Force last year in testifying in support of his appropriation said, "We have a program we are pushing to increase the yield of our warheads, and decrease the circular error of probability so that we will have a hard target killer which we do not have in the inventory at the present time."

Senator COOPER. May I interrupt here for a minute?

Mr. FISHER. We do not have a counterforce capability. I don't believe, at least we have testified to that effect.

Senator CASE. You mean with such accuracy that the Soviets could consider that it might be used for a first strike?

Mr. FISHER. Yes.

INCONCEIVABILITY OF U.S. FIRST STRIKE

Well, I personally can't conceive of the U.S. system, thank goodness, pushing the button either. But I am not sure they have quite the same confidence in us that I have. It is what it does to them in terms of their own thinking, Senator. For my own part the notion of the President suddenly authorizing a first nuclear sort of kill capability I find utterly inconceivable.

Senator FULBRIGHT. Why do you say that when you know the Air Force has been examining the possibility of first-strike capability since 1964? Why do you say it is inconceivable?

Mr. FISHER. I think the President is still Commander in Chief and while there are certain things which I would differ with the Presidents on, including the incumbent, I have confidence in him as a rational man.

Senator FULBRIGHT. Are you familiar with the Air Force Manual 1-1 entitled "Air Force Basic Doctrine"? Are you familiar with that manual?

Mr. FISHER. I think in about 1946 I decided to stop reading Air Force manuals.

Senator FULBRIGHT. Maybe that is why you have this "inconceivable" attitude. If you haven't kept up with what goes on in the Pentagon, I can imagine it. You are thinking about civilized, imaginary countries. Aren't you?

Mr. FISHER. I still have confidence in the President as Commander in Chief of the United States, sir.

Senator FULBRIGHT. If you haven't read it, it is in the Air Force Manual, dated August 14, 1964. It is right interesting that the foreward is signed by a very well known man named Curtis LeMay, General, U.S. Air Force, Chief of Staff. The fact that you don't know about it really shocks me, but I think it ought to be in the record. It says: "This manual contains U.S. Air Force basic doctrine for employing aerospace forces to support U.S. objectives in peace and war. It provides the ultimate reference authority for this employment and thus serves as a basis for all other Air Force manuals dealing with aerospace operations."

I don't quite know what these dashes mean but on page 3-5 and the subsection is 3-11, it says, "First strike consideration." This is a quote: "Since we cannot preclude contingencies in which the United States may be the first to initiate the limited use of strategic force, our force posture and general war plans must consider the requirement for both first- and second-strike operations."

For you to say, "I don't think they will do it" or that "We surely are not so foolish," is one thing, but to say it is inconceivable, it seems to me you overstate the case considerably.

Mr. FISHER. Perhaps, Mr. Chairman, but I had confidence in the President of the United States, the President then, not to permit this to happen, and I have confidence in the President of the United States, the President now.

Senator FULBRIGHT. So it is all up to the President. If he thinks it is all right, it is OK with you. If not, it is OK with you.

Mr. FISHER. No, sir; I put it the other way around. I have confidence that all past Presidents and the incumbent President will not do an act of national destruction which this would involve, and now——

Senator FULBRIGHT. You think, therefore, that going into Vietnam was very much in the interest of this country. A President wouldn't possibly do something against the interests of this country.

Mr. FISHER. Well, I am always reminded in answer to that question, sir, when I was in the Government I was dealing with the Nonproliferation Treaty and strategic arms race, I didn't have to deal with Vietnam, and when one talked with me about it, I said, "Don't tell me your troubles; I have enough troubles of my own," so I was not in position to deal with it and I wouldn't want to comment about Vietnam.

Senator FULBRIGHT. I know, but you make such generalized statements that you trust the President's judgment that there is no reason in having a Senate or Congress.

LACK OF CONGRESSIONAL BRIEFING ON SALT TALKS

By the way, there is a statement in this morning's paper. This is a usually reliable reporter—not always. The other day I understand he made a mistake, but this morning it is reported that the Administration's negotiating position was wrapped in considerable secrecy. It is a quote from The New York Times of this morning, April 14. "In contrast with past practices the Administration made no attempt to brief congressional committees or the press on what to expect as the talks enter the negotiating phase. The U.S. delegation, headed by Gerald C. Smith, Director of the Arms Control and Disarmament Agency, will stop first in Brussels to brief the North Atlantic Treaty allies on the American position before proceeding to Vienna."

It really doesn't sit very well with me that he is going over there to brief the Ambassador from Greece about our plans in Vienna. How in the world do you think you can justify it? You have just come out of this Agency. What in the world is going on? Are they taking the attitude that this has nothing to do with the Senate, that they trust the President to make whatever judgment is to be made?

Mr. FISHER. Mr. Chairman——

Senator FULBRIGHT. You are Dean now.

Mr. FISHER. I can only comment that I believe that during the period that I was Deputy Director of the Agency I was no stranger to this committee as far as the question of briefing it in advance is concerned.

Senator FULBRIGHT. They refused to brief us. When was the other time you asked them?

Senator GORE. It was before they went to Helsinki.

SOVIET VIEW OF U.S. DEVELOPMENT OF PREEMPTIVE STRIKE CAPABILITY

Senator FULBRIGHT. Now they refuse to brief us on this and it is all a great secret. Then you say you trust the President, any President, apparently, and therefore that this first strike couldn't happen. Of course, it can happen.

Mr. FISHER. Well, Mr. Chairman, in order to qualify that, I was saying in response to Senator Cooper's question that I don't consider, notwithstanding Air Force manuals, the possibility of a preemptive strike a realistic possibility. I do not, however, preclude the fact that the development of a capability that makes that possible, particularly when you have manuals like you have read, and I thought that I was given an even more damning indication from the Soviet point of view, of a statement that we are pressing a program to get a hard target kill capability when the Soviets read that that makes the first factor that I said, that is a growing force, more control over MIRV's, somewhat more fragile than I would like to have it.

Senator GORE. I might ask, since the chairman of the full committee is from Arkansas and the chairman of the subcommittee is from Tennessee, if the Administration might be discriminating against the South? [Laughter.]

Mr. FISHER. But in answer to the question, if I can get back to the one Senator Cooper asked me, I have been appearing before Senator Cooper since 1947 and I always hope I give him an honest answer to the question he puts to me, what I think is, I don't think it is a realistic probability but I am not sure the Soviets think that and I think the testimony that I just read, which was not in my prepared statement, by the Chief of the Air Force saying they were pushing the program to get a hard target killer is not something calculated to increase their confidence that we are not going to push something to get a hard target killer with the possibility some day we will use it.

LACK OF U.S. MIRV COUNTERFORCE CAPABILITY

So, as I said, two factors might have prevented us from going over the edge not being able to control MIRV's any longer is that we have not got a counterforce capability. I think it is a fragile factor because they may not believe it. They think it is only a temporary factor, and they can read public testimony of responsible officials to say that we are going to try to get one, and that is one of the reasons that I think the proposal in this Senate Resolution 211 on a mutual MIRV test restriction is terribly important.

But I do not think in terms of immediacy, Mr. Chairman, and the chairman of the full committee, I appear as an apologist for executive power, I don't think it is really what I had in mind. There is a somewhat more serious problem.

UNITED STATES HAS NOT YET DEPLOYED MIRV

The second factor, which is also fragile, is that we have not yet deployed any MIRV's, and here again I will be subject to a soft impeachment of being too trusting, but it is my view that if the President were to announce that he was going to defer deployment of MIRV's that anyone with any knowledge of the way the U.S. Government operates could have high confidence, and I change my statement there—my original prepared statement said reasonable confidence—I would say high confidence, that the U.S. Government couldn't take any action inconsistent with this announcement without either the press, our colleagues of the Fourth Estate or the Congress or both, finding out about it, and a good deal of hell being raised about it. In other words, I am not—this isn't the complaint of an ex-negotiator what a terrible thing it is to work in an open society, I think it is a great thing, but it is a fact of life.

I think any rational Soviet planner, I am sure there are Soviet planners and I am sure there are arguments——

Senator FULBRIGHT. If it is so open, why aren't they willing to brief this committee? That isn't very open between the executive and the Senate these days.

Mr. FISHER. Well, I again don't want to appear as apologist for the executive branch, but what I am saying is not intended to either be critical or apologetic with respect to the executive. It is just a fact of life if we had made a public announcement we are not going to defer any MIRV's I don't believe——

Senator CASE. Deploy them?

Mr. FISHER. Deploy, I beg your pardon, Senator Case.

Senator FULBRIGHT. I didn't think anybody was raising the question of whether you can trust them when they made that commitment. They made no such commitment.

Mr. FISHER. Well, my problem is that if we were to start a little MIRV deployment in June, and that is presently planned, then we wouldn't have a black or white situation. The issue would then be considerably fuzzed.

Senator FULBRIGHT. We are not arguing with you there. This committee approves of that position.

Mr. FISHER. Well, I am urging the fact that this committee should be aware that we are just about to cross a bridge in less than 8 weeks in which the ability to have a black or white situation, MIRV deployment or no MIRV deployment, will disappear.

Senator GORE. To put it another way, aren't you saying that this stability to which you and Dr. Scoville have referred will be shaken?

Mr. FISHER. I think it will be shaken very badly because I think it is quite a different situation from the point of view of a Soviet planner. When they are saying the United States has deployed—the United States has said it will not deploy MIRV's, we are confident they cannot take any action inconsistent with that without it being known. That situation exists today.

If we go ahead with deploying MIRV's the question will be how many will they deploy, will they deploy a little less than a hundred, as The Washington Post of Monday indicated, how good are they, then you get a situation where you have a clear yes or no will become a very cloudy situation.

HOW CAN CONGRESS INFLUENCE THE PRESIDENT?

Senator GORE. Dean, if Senator Fulbright will let me interrupt, we agree.

Senator FULBRIGHT. The Senate agrees with it by 72 to 6.

Senator GORE. Seventy-two to six. You come to us as recently a distinguished Ambassador, our negotiator with the Soviets, a high-ranking and honored member of the executive branch. How do the elected representatives of the people bring their collective judgments, so overwhelmingly reached, to bear and to be influential with the President who has the peculiar responsibility for directing negotiations?

Mr. FISHER. Well, if the Senate, it is the sense of the Senate in this substantial vote last Thursday, is that the planned deployment of MIRV's, now planned for less than 8 weeks away apparently, would be the destruction of an opportunity I am not sure that the generalized language of Senate Resolution 211 makes it that clear. It says——

Senator FULBRIGHT. You don't? What do you think it means?

PROPOSED MUTUAL FREEZE ON STRATEGIC WEAPONS

Mr. FISHER. Well, Senate Resolution 211, I would hope you would make it clear that it does mean that. I can hear an apologist for the Administration, and I am not saying it critically, saying that "unless you are prepared to have negotiations that include all, unless we have been able to negotiate an interim agreement that includes the testing of MIRV's, the deployment of all MIRV's, no new deployment of land-based missiles, no construction of ABM's and no new starts on subs, until we can get that entire ball of wax," which we are very unlikely to do, between now and the middle of June, "Let's go ahead with the MIRV's."

Senator FULBRIGHT. I can't follow that at all. The Russians are reported to see the good sense of it. The Senator from Kentucky made a most persuasive argument that this is a simpler way than picking out one. For example, I think it was yesterday we heard Mr. Panofsky. If I understood him, he thinks ABM is more threatening than the MIRV, that it is a more unsettling element. So you get these differences.

I think the virtue of the Senator from Kentucky's view is, is that you take all of them, and this is simply a temporary freeze pending negotiations. What is so difficult about that?

Mr. FISHER. Well, Mr. Chairman, I think the time——

Senator FULBRIGHT. Why is it difficult?

Mr. FISHER (continuing). I think the time schedule is desperately tight. The notion of negotiating——

Senator FULBRIGHT. Certainly it is tight. That is why we went this route.

Mr. FISHER. But the notion of negotiating an interim freeze that includes all strategic systems between now and sometime in June——

Senator FULBRIGHT. It ought not to take a week. I mean this is supposed to be done. I don't know why you are so complicated. You have been in that Agency too long.

Mr. FISHER. I have been out of it.

Senator FULBRIGHT. I meant to say you haven't been out long enough.

Senator CASE. Mr. Chairman, isn't this the fact, we are not talking about negotiating an agreement, really we are talking about de facto stopping.

Senator FULBRIGHT. Exactly. This isn't a long negotiation. You might call it simply a declaration of intent that both of them make in the beginning pending a negotiation.

Senator COOPER. Mr. Chairman, I have been waiting patiently here.

Senator FULBRIGHT. Well, it is your resolution we are talking about. We could talk about it better than you can, but go ahead. I yield to you.

Senator COOPER. I will be brief.

Senator FULBRIGHT. You don't have to.

SHORTNESS OF TIME TO NEGOTIATE MUTUAL FREEZE

Senator COOPER. I disagree with you, Mr. Chairman, I think Mr. Fisher has made his position clear. He is simply saying he agrees with this resolution, it should come into effect. What he is saying, I believe, is that the short time between now and July 1 when our negotiating team will be talking together with the Soviet negotiating people they might not be able to agree upon a freeze, isn't that correct? You are hoping that we will not further complicate the situation by starting deployment of MIRV on July 1.

Mr. FISHER. That is correct, Senator Cooper.

If it were possible to come to a complete freeze called for in the second operative paragraph between now and the 1st of July and that would preclude our development of MIRV's, I would throw my hat in the air and cheer. What I am saying——

Senator FULBRIGHT. That is what the report says and it is certainly one of the clear intentions.

Mr. FISHER. But if it is not possible, if it is not possible, if the 1st of July comes and goes and we have not worked out that arrangement, the fact that we then make dealing with the MIRV situation infinitely more difficult by starting the deployment, I would consider to be a tragedy of the first magnitude.

Senator COOPER. I understand.

I must say in the discussion of the resolution in the committee and on the floor, it was understood that it did include stopping the testing and deployment of a MIRV, too. And it has been said in the debate, publicly; I must say it has been communicated to the President, too.

Senator FULBRIGHT. Senator, if you will yield to me, in the discussion of this, we considered this resolution not as an invitation to negotiate. It was really a proposal to agree in the beginning preliminary to negotiation.

Senator COOPER. I agree with you wholly.

Senator FULBRIGHT. That was the purpose of it and it was never contemplated it was going to drag out for weeks and weeks as it used to at Geneva. This is one part of it. The other might take a long time.

Senator COOPER. We agree wholly that a freeze was meant to be proposed, at the beginning. He is simply saying, as I understand it, if you can't reach that agreement before July 1 your chances of any agreement on arms control would be endangered by the deployment of MIRV.

Mr. FISHER. That is correct, and I further say that I think it would be a mistake to put to the Soviets the following proposition: "We have between now and the first of July to both stop testing MIRV's, stop deploying any intercontinental missile, stop building any subs or any building of ABM's, and unless we have that by the first of July we are going to start the MIRV's," and the cat will be out of the bag. I think that will be a mistake and I think that will be a danger that will happen, and I think if that would happen it would be a great tragedy.

Again, Mr. Chairman, if the Soviets were to come in and say, "OK, we will do it," then we would then——

Senator FULBRIGHT. Do you think we will do it?

Mr. FISHER. I would certainly hope so.

Senator FULBRIGHT. I didn't ask you if you hope so. Do you think we will? Do you have any reason to think we will?

Mr. FISHER. I think that question of what the Government is going to do had better be addressed to somebody else.

RELEVANCE OF SENATE RESOLUTION 211 TO SALT

Senator FULBRIGHT. You can say you don't know if you want to. I have seen nothing to indicate what their attitude is because the Executive says this resolution was irrelevant. I am not sure what that meant, but he said it was irrelevant to the SALT talks.

Mr. FISHER. With that I would dissent.

A similar resolution introduced by the Senate was, in 1963, was, very helpful in the negotiation of the test ban where I was Mr. Harriman's deputy.

The Pastore resolution passed by the Senate was very, very helpful in the negotiation of the Nonproliferation Treaty where I was then, because of Mr. Foster's illness, was the U.S. representative at the final stage.

I think this resolution is quite relevant. I think the one thing that I think the Senate ought to make very clear is whether or not in the short time frame made possible by the current, I use the term "impending," it has sort of an impending doom phrase to it but impending MIRV deployment, whether during that period we can have a reciprocal halt across the board that it would be a great tragedy if a MIRV deployment sometime in June, as Secretary Seamans had indicated, were permitted to destroy an opportunity and, in my judgment, it would destroy the opportunity.

Senator FULBRIGHT. This is a sense of the Senate resolution. There is absolutely nothing to prevent the Administration from agreeing on MIRV alone. It isn't all or nothing. This is the sense of the Senate that this is a better way. The President has already dismissed it as irrelevant. There is nothing in it to prevent him from tomorrow morning saying we will stop MIRV alone and think of what to do on the other.

Mr. FISHER. I am not being critical of it.

Senator FULBRIGHT. You are being critical of it.

Mr. FISHER. If I may, Mr. Chairman, I am pointing out that unless certain steps are taken by the Administration——

Senator FULBRIGHT. There is nothing to prevent them from taking any step they want.

Mr. FISHER. And that step includes a deferral, an announced deferral, now really of the deployment of the presently planned deployment of MIRV's, I think the resolution stands a very good chance of being rendered——

Senator FULBRIGHT. You don't think they would hold the President in contempt if he did that tomorrow morning, do you?

Mr. FISHER. No, of course not.

U.S. ATTITUDE TOWARD STRATEGIC ARMS MORATORIUM

Senator FULBRIGHT. We wouldn't do a thing. In Mr. Finney's article he says: "In view of the technical as well as political objections raised by Administration officials to such a moratorium approach, it seems doubtful that the Administration would respond favorably to a Soviet initiative in that direction." He has reason to believe that even if the Soviets propose it, we wouldn't do it.

Senator COOPER. Who wrote that?

Senator FULBRIGHT. Mr. John Finney of The New York Times. He is sometimes right. He admits it.

Mr. FISHER. I have no method of checking on the accuracy of Mr. Finney's statement.

Senator FULBRIGHT. I am asking if you have any view of your own about it. Do you have any reason to believe that they are going there with any real determination to do anything about it or not? You know all these people personally.

Mr. FISHER. Well, I think——

Senator FULBRIGHT. You are free of the Government shackles. You ought not to be so cautious now as you used to be.

Mr. FISHER. Well, put it this way, I think if the Soviets were to make such a proposal it would be in the U.S. interests to accept it. The people there, the people who are representing the U.S. Government, in my judgment are rational people, with the interests of the security of the country in mind.

Senator FULBRIGHT. Did you say the security?

U.S. DETERMINATION TO DEPLOY MIRV

Mr. FISHER. I think so, yes, I think it is the long-range security we are looking for. My own concern is there seems to be, and this again, this Administration doesn't speak with one voice any more than the last Administration did or anyone does, there seems to be almost an apparent determination to get these MIRV's deployed, and if I were looking at it from the Soviet point of view, I would have the impression that there seems to be a drive to get these things into the ground which will take them out of the negotiations, because once we put them in the ground, as I indicated, the negotiations don't become a "Have you deployed or haven't you," it is how many, how good, and a very murky area which makes dealing with it in a verified arms agreement almost impossible. That is the one factor which frightens me because there seems to be almost a determination, at least from the Soviet point of view, to get these MIRV's deployed and get that out of the negotiation and that seems to me to be a very dangerous thing.

Now, why that is so, I do not know. I have never heard a really good explanation of the present necessity for MIRV's. It was originally justified on the ground it was necessary to prevent—to saturate the Tallinn system which was then thought to have an ABM capability. We all believe the Tallinn system does not have an ABM capability but the drive to get the MIRV's in the ground still goes on. To that extent I can't give you a rational explanation.

Senator FULBRIGHT. Is it really different from a drive to get the ABM's underway? In view of the fight last year, you know all about it. Now it comes back again in a different form, and with a rationale that was abandoned last year. It seems to me not very different. This is just part of the drive of everyone in this field to get anything to which they put their minds.

Mr. FISHER. Well, I think I said about as much as I know about MIRV's.

REQUEST FOR MODIFIED PHASE II OF SAFEGUARD

Let me talk about what I think about the request for modified phase II of the Safeguard system.

Senator GORE. We can do something about this.

Mr. FISHER. At this stage of the game perhaps out of my excessive caution——

Senator FULBRIGHT. We can if we have the votes.

Mr. FISHER (continuing). I don't think I would like to reargue the elements that went into the 50-to-50 vote last year. That action has been taken and whether it will help or hurt is a matter for history to decide.

But I don't see what possible U.S. interest is advanced by now proceeding with either the approval of the authorization of modified phase II.

I am aware of the argument, Mr. Chairman, that it is necessary to go ahead with authorizing the proposed modified Phase II Safeguard item in order to strengthen our bargaining position in Geneva. I don't believe that is persuasive. As a practical matter, authorizing armaments so that they can be included in a disarmament program soon reaches the point of diminishing returns and that point may well have been reached, passed, well passed, with the approval of phase I. If both sides were to play this game of proceeding with further weapon systems to strengthen their hands in negotiations you would have a gigantic buildup, just so you would have something in the SALT talks and far from being a help to peace they would be a greater threat to the world. It would be an excuse for both sides to build up now, each saying, "I hate to do it but I have to do it so I have something to bargain with in Vienna."

In particular, looking at the problem from the Soviet point of view, going ahead with the modified Phase II Safeguard system so soon after phase I had been made a separate program would clearly belie the implications of the separation, that there was going to be a deliberate consideration before you went any further, and I think you give the Soviets the impression that the United States was determined to push the ABM system to a finish come what may, to take that out of negotiations, so I feel exactly the same about the phase II of the ABM as I do about the MIRV.

I think timewise I feel—I am one of 200 million citizens, I think— the country is more in a time bind on the MIRV than they are on the

ABM problem primarily because I think it is going to be some time, and I stand corrected by Dr. Scoville, whether the radars, which are the critical elements in phase I, will actually be constructed and because the modified phase II is currently—nothing can be done about it until it is authorized, and so that seems to me to be at least more controllable.

MIRV DEPLOYMENT LACKING MUTUAL FREEZE

With respect to the MIRV deployment, I feel that we are in a desperate situation, because there is at least the danger, you may say, Mr. Chairman, Chairman Fulbright, chairman of the full committee, that the Administration should be able to do this in a week, I don't know whether they could or not. If they could and were able to do it and that would take the MIRV problem out of it I would, as I said, throw my hat in the air and cheer.

On the other hand, if they were not able to do it and were going ahead and deploying the MIRV's with all that involves would be one of the most classic examples of cutting our nose off to spite our face that I could possibly imagine, and I am suggesting—and I am not suggesting that this 211 requires it but one action under 211 might say that, "O. K. Soviets, you have got just one chance now to the first of June or July you have got to agree to an across the board and if you have not agreed, mutually acted, across the board to stop all deployments, if we haven't agreed on that, the MIRV's are out of the bag."

Senator FULBRIGHT. They don't have to say that. They are perfectly free to take any one or part of it. There is nothing legal about that resolution. It is good advice, that is all.

Mr. FISHER. I would like to use your considerable persuasive powers, Mr. Chairman, to indicate that, and there are others here that are equally persuasive, for goodness sakes put some reason into the MIRV deployment. Why are we doing it? I haven't heard any good answer yet.

DELAYING MIRV DEPLOYMENT DURING SALT

Senator CASE. Aren't you saying just in addition to what we have done, then, as a condition to the accomplishment of what we have urged in this resolution, this specific thing should also be done?

Mr. FISHER. Yes.

Senator CASE. And now so that we have a longer time to accomplish the other, that is all you are saying?

Mr. FISHER. That is all I am saying. The MIRV thing there should be a delay of it and particularly since I know of no reason why it is time critical in any sense of the word other than some contracts apparently that they will have to go ahead and do it and just go ahead and do it like the old War Production Board cartoon, "No reason for it, it is just our policy" I mean I am not trying to be facetious about this. But it seems to me we have a real danger and I consider that in view of the fact, as I said in my statement, of the relatively fragile factors that will make the Soviets think that they can check on our MIRV deployment.

IS IT TOO LATE FOR MORATORIUM?

Senator CASE. This is, I think, the crucial question really. Is it too late right now?

Mr. FISHER. I don't think so.

Senator CASE. I suggested last year that we immediately stop, not ask the Soviet to agree to stop, but that we stop and keep stopped as long as they didn't deploy or didn't continue testing. Nobody paid any attention to this one. And time has run on and on and on and at that time we were told we were almost at the point of no return. What we really need now, and what the President needs and the country needs, are some assurances that it is still not too late.

Mr. FISHER. Well, Mr. Chairman, I believe that our colleagues in the Fourth Estate and our colleagues in the Congress can probably effectively verify from the Soviet point of view, from the nice hard-boiled view of the person in the Kremlin saying he doesn't trust us, saying he couldn't trust this statement. I can imagine our saying the same thing if the Soviets made a similar statement for them saying, "I think we can because we know even with the capitalist warmongers they really couldn't get away with deploying when they said they weren't going to," because someone in the Fourth Estate or someone in the Congress would blow the whistle on them, forgive my slang. I think that situation will cease to exist when the deployment is begun and the question then is not is there deployment because we all agree there has been, but how much, how good, how many.

U.S. DEPLOYMENT OF MIRV

Senator CASE. Isn't it fair to ask why do we still speculate about this thing. Why don't we try it and find out what the Russians will do?

Mr. FISHER. I agree with you. But try it and give it a reasonable period of time for negotiations.

At the risk of serving, my past time serving operations, having spent too much time in Geneva and not having been out of the agency long enough, I have a feeling that 6 weeks is a little short, 6 months seems to me a little more realistic, and that is one of the things I would urge that you——

Senator FULBRIGHT. Then you would say it is hopeless.

Senator CASE. Mr. Chairman, at this time maybe it would be appropriate to ask to be inserted in the record a statement made by the American assembly, under the guidance of the dean, on this specific point with these specific recommendations.

Senator GORE. Without objection.

(The statement follows.)

THE AMERICAN ASSEMBLY,
COLUMBIA UNIVERSITY,
New York, N.Y.

THE AMERICAN ASSEMBLY ON ARMS LIMITATION

These pages contain the views of a group of Americans who met March 31–April 2, 1970, at Arden House, Harriman, New York, to consider the outlook for arms limitation. The meeting was held with immediate and timely reference to the Strategic Arms Limitation Talks, scheduled to resume in Vienna, April 16.

Reference was also made to the broader problem of slowing down the arms race and to the effect of military expenditures on national resources.

The meeting was held under the auspices of The American Assembly of Columbia University, which regularly convenes for the purpose of focusing attention on issues of public importance. The recommendations of this Assembly were adopted in the plenary session of April 2, after two previous days of discussions as a committee of the whole. (Because of the urgency of the topic, standard American Assembly procedures were modified somewhat for the occasion, and the number of participants was reduced accordingly. Many had taken part in earlier American Assembly programs on arms: Arms Control, 1960, and Nuclear Weapons, 1966.)

Adrian S. Fisher, dean of the Georgetown Law School and former deputy director of the U.S. Arms Control and Disarmament Agency, prepared a background paper as the basis of discussion.

As a non-partisan educational institution The American Assembly takes no official stand on the opinions herein, which belong to the participants in their private capacities. They represented themselves and not necessarily the institutions or persons with whom they are associated.

CLIFFORD C. NELSON,
President, the American Assembly.

FINAL REPORT OF THE AMERICAN ASSEMBLY ON ARMS LIMITATION—1970

At the close of their discussion the participants in The American Assembly on Arms Limitation—1970 reviewed as a group the following statement. Although it represents general agreement, no one was asked to sign it, and it should not be assumed that every participant necessarily subscribes to every recommendation.

We call upon the President of the United States to propose to the Soviet Union, on a reciprocal basis, an immediate interim halt in the deployment of strategic offensive and defensive weapons and of tests of multiple warheads. To give this proposal a chance of success, we ask the President to defer for six months the impending deployment of Multiple Independently Targetable Re-Entry Vehicles (MIRVs).

The Strategic Arms Limitation Talks are resuming in Vienna at a time when mankind has a unique opportunity to end the nuclear arms race. At present there exists a roughly equal and relatively stable nuclear balance between the U.S. and the U.S.S.R. A rare coincidence of favorable political and strategic conditions provides a real but fleeting opportunity for agreement between the U.S. and the U.S.S.R. to halt the arms race in both quality and quality of weapons, and then to diminish the threat to mankind posed by existing weapons. Whether agreement can be reached we do not know, but wisdom and common sense require every plausible effort to exploit the present promise.

This opportunity will be put in jeopardy if the U.S. soon deploys Multiple Independently Targetable Re-Entry Vehicles (MIRVs), or proceeds with plans for a modified Phase II Safeguard Anti-Ballistic Missile System (ABM), or if the Soviet Union extensively tests large ICBMs (SS-9) with multiple warheads (which may not themselves be independently targetable but may well be steps in the development of a Soviet multiple independently targetable delivery system).

The introduction of MIRVs into the present nuclear relationship would have the initial effect of substantially increasing the number of deliverable nuclear warheads available to each side. MIRV program will take on new dimensions as missile accuracy increases. When this occurs, it becomes possible for one side *if it strikes first* with missiles armed with MIRVs to take out more than one missile site with a single attacking missile. The obverse of this frightening coin is that each side may fear that, *unless it strikes first*, the MIRVed missiles of the other side may be able substantially to eliminate its own land-based ICBM force, with the other side still having substantial ICBM force left in reserve.

New and worrisome uncertainties would enter into the strategic calculations. For example, Secretary Laird has testified that 420 Soviet SS-9s with three warheads of five megatons each and an accuracy of one quarter of a mile could eliminate all but 50 of our Minutemen. Similar calculations by the Soviet Union would show that if the U.S. were to MIRV its Minutemen with three warheads, with yields approximating a quarter of a megaton each and having an accuracy of one-tenth of a mile, it could be using 580 Minutemen, eliminate all but 70 or so of the Soviet missile force.

Whatever their validity such calculations make it clear that both sides would feel more secure if neither one had a MIRV. The U.S. plan to *deploy* MIRVed Minuteman III in June of this year, within two months after the beginning of the talks, may well close the door on this possibility. Although the generation of MIRVs which would be deployed would not be capable of a first strike, this step would cast serious doubts on our seriousness in pursuing SALT. This would present the U.S.S.R. with a *fait accompli*. One of the most important things that the SALT talks could accomplish is to prevent the deployment of MIRVs. This opportunity should not be lost.

We in the American Assembly therefore call on the President to postpone this deployment for six months. Such deployment at this time would not contribute to our security. Far from improving our bargaining strength at SALT proceeding with that deployment would make negotiations more difficult, and would invite the Soviet Union in turn to present us with *faits accomplis*. No harm can result to our strategic posture by such delay, which will involve only a handful of land-based missiles in a MIRV program that is already being widely questioned as unnecessary, wasteful, and certainly premature, since the large Soviet ABM program it was designed to penetrate does not exist.

We also suggest that current U.S. and Soviet testing of multiple warheads complicates the political and strategic climate on which these negotiations depend. We urge mutual restraint in this regard.

We also urge postponement in implementing the proposed modified Phase II of the Safeguard System. The argument that going ahead with this program would strengthen our bargaining position at Vienna is not persuasive; authorizing armaments so that they can be included in a disarmament program soon reaches the point of diminishing returns. If both sides play this game, SALT will result in an increase in the arms race. Going ahead with modified Phase II Safeguards so soon after Phase I had been made a separate program would belie the promise of deliberate consideration upon which that separation was in part based. It would more likely give the Soviets the impression that the U.S. was determined to push the complete Safeguards program to a finish, come what may. This would make success in SALT less rather than more likely.

These measures of restraint will give our negotiators a chance. But the negotiation of a treaty at the SALT talks will be difficult and complex and may take years. To keep the present opportunity from eroding during this period, an interim halt is necessary to prevent any substantial changes in the rough strategic balance which now makes such an agreement possible.

We therefore urge the President of the United States to propose to the Soviet Union, *on a reciprocal basis*, an immediate two-year suspension of the deployment of strategic offensive and defensive weapons and of the tests of multiple warheads. Specifically we propose that during this two-year period interim halt there would be:

1. No testing of any multiple warheads, whether MRV or MIRV;
2. No deployment of multiple warheads;
3. No new deployment of land-based intercontinental ballistic missiles;
4. No construction of Anti-Ballistic Missile radars or deployment of anti-ballistic missile interceptors;
5. No new "starts" on constructing submarines for launching ballistic missiles.

In such an interim agreement we see no necessity for limits on air defenses or on new bomber construction because developments in these areas do not carry an immediate potential for upsetting the present strategic balance.

The short term of the agreement and its comprehensive quality would simplify the requirement for inspection. From the standpoint of the U.S. security, compliance with these provisions can be adequately determined by national means of verification. In particular, the halt in Soviet buildup of ICBMs and SLBMs, including the SS-9, could be verified. With regard to the restrictions on multiple warhead testing, however, to enhance confidence during the interim halt, an understanding that missile tests will be preannounced and restricted to designated areas may be desirable.

The restraints that we propose and an agreed interim halt would create an environment of stability and mutual confidence. In such an improved climate more lasting agreements, taking account of new technological and political developments, could be achieved.

We have not attempted to blueprint the details of a more permanent agreement; planning for it should take account of what is learned during the interim halt. Some of the major issues which would need to be taken into account during the negotiations of a treaty are:

1. *ABM levels.* A key question appears to be whether some level of ABMs is necessary for the U.S. in light of the developing Chinese nuclear capability. We believe that an area ABM is not vital to protecting U.S. interests in Asia and that we should be prepared to accept a mutually agreed zero ABM level if it improves the prospects for obtaining an effective agreement with the Soviet Union. Without an ABM, deterrence is as effective against China as against others; and a Safeguard system designed for area defense against the Chinese may, in the eyes of Soviet planners, pose a threat to their deterrent.

2. *Control on Missile Testing.* A ban on MIRVs would require a prohibition on all multiple warhead tests and limits on a number and location of all missile tests. We believe that such controls would be feasible and desirable.

3. *Reduction.* We believe that the U.S. should seek agreement on reduction in numbers of strategic systems. In particular the U.S. should consider proposing the phasing out of fixed land-based missiles which will become increasingly vulnerable even if MIRVs are banned.

Depending on how these and related issues are resolved, a whole range of agreements is possible. One type of agreement which most of us would favor would seek to freeze the existing situation by banning MIRVs and ABMs. A second type would concentrate on banning ABMs and phasing out fixed land-based missiles if it does not prove possible to ban MIRVs. A third type would focus on freezing numbers of offensive missiles and limiting ABMs if it is not possible to ban MIRVs and if the judgment is reached that an area ABM against China is needed. On our current understanding of the issues most of us favored the first type of agreement.

We believe that the initiatives and agreements we propose will enhance U.S. security by improving the prospects for peace. These efforts can also lead to the wise and prudent use of our national resources. The expenditures thus avoided would amount to at least several billion dollars a year in the short run and much more in the long run if the U.S. and the U.S.S.R. enter into a new and costlier phase of the arms race. The SALT talks, and the clearer assessment of our real security requirements which may result from those talks, may prevent these expenditures. More of our resources can then be devoted to human needs, both at home and abroad. This is an important aspect of our national security. Unless urgent social needs are met, our national security may be progressively undermined, not by external threats but by failure to meet internal and justifiable social needs.

The negotiation of a treaty to end the arms race will involve many complex technical details. But the overriding considerations are not technical; they are deeply political. They required a fresh and clear reassessment of the fundamentals of U.S. security.

We must recognize that it is at least as dangerous to focus on "worst cases" as it is to overlook significant threats to our deterrent. If one proceeds from the most pessimistic view of U.S. capabilities, and the most generous view of the Soviet capabilities, one arrives at a U.S. second-strike posture that may look to the Soviets so much like a first-strike posture that they will be inclined to increase their own forces, thereby continuing the arms race and increasing the danger of nuclear war. In fact, the proper test for the adequacy of U.S. nuclear retaliatory power is not the U.S. worst estimate of its effectiveness, but the Soviet estimates of the damage it would suffer in a nuclear exchange. That estimate will not be based on assumptions that take the Soviet performance at its best possible level and the U.S. performance at its worst. If we arm against a "parade of imaginary horribles" on the part of an adversary, the adversary will do the same, and we will have devised a sure prescription for a dangerous and wasteful arms race.

We have made this mistake in the past, from a misdirected sense of caution. In the interests of our own security we must not make this mistake again. We must end the nuclear arms race.

PARTICIPANTS IN THE AMERICAN ASSEMBLY ON ARMS LIMITATION—1970

Adrian S. Fisher, Dean, Georgetown University Law School (discussion leader and director of drafting).
Alexander, Archibald S., Bernardsville, N.Y.
Bader, William B., New York.

Bloomfield, Lincoln P., Center for International Studies, Massachusetts Institute of Technology.
Brown, Courtney C., Editor, Columbia Journal of World Business.
Daniloff, Nicholas, United Press International, Washington, D.C.
Dudman, Richard, St. Louis *Post Dispatch*, Washington, D.C.
Finkelstein, Lawrence S., Center for International Affairs, Harvard University.
Fischer, Benjamin B., Harriman Scholar, Columbia University.
Halperin, Morton H., The Brookings Institution, Washington, D.C.
Henkin, Louis, Hamilton Fish Professor of International Law & Diplomacy, Columbia University.
Herzfeld, Charles M., Technical Director, Defense-Space Group, ITT, Nutley, New Jersey.
Knorr, Klaus, Center for International Studies, Princeton University.
Manton, Thomas B., United Church of Christ, New York.
McDermott, Rev. Patrick P., S.J., Assistant Director, Division of World Justice & Peace, United States Catholic Conference, Washington, D.C.
Fitzgerald, Ernest, Businessmen's Educational Fund, Washington, D.C.
Gulick, Lewis, The Associated Press, Washington, D.C.
Paffrath, Leslie, President, The Johnson Foundation, Racine.
Palfrey, John G., Professor of Law, Columbia University.
Parrent, Rev. Allan, Department of International Affairs, National Council of Churches, Washington, D.C.
Persinger, Mrs. Richard, Chairman, Committee on Public Affairs, National Board of the Y.W.C.A., New York.
Posvar, Wesley W., Chancellor, University of Pittsburgh.
Rathjens, George W., Professor of Political Science, Massachusetts Institute of Technology.
Scoville, Herbert, Jr., Carnegie Endowment for International Peace, Washington, D.C.
Shulman, Marshall D., Director, The Russian Institute, Columbia University.
Stone, Jeremy J., International Affairs Fellow, Council on Foreign Relations, New York.
Stuhler, Barbara, Associate Director, Minnesota World Affairs Council, Minneapolis.
Yarmolinsky, Adam, Professor of Law, Harvard University.

1969 ABM DEBATE

Senator FULBRIGHT. The Senator from New Jersey of course is quite right. It was last summer that the original Brooke resolution was introduced and the Senator from New Jersey had much to say about it. One reason they didn't proceed with it at that time is that the ABM was up and it was thought the committee and the Senate could do something positive. They would be more likely to do it than if they tried to handle both and it would interfere with the action on the ABM. It wasn't because they were not interested in MIRV. It was a deliberate choice of what could be done and what was possible and we still have what is possible to accomplish at this time. I don't see how you feel that the resolution in any way prejudices an agreement not to go forward with MIRV. I mean just because it would——

Mr. FISHER. Mr. Chairman, if I gave you that impression——

Senator FULBRIGHT. The ABM may be not as crucial that way, but it is very expensive and some of us would like to stop the waste of money that is going on in this area.

Mr. FISHER. I agree with that and I do not want to give the impression that I view the Senate resolution as counterproductive in this regard.

Senator FULBRIGHT. Well, you do.

CESSATION OF MIRV DEPLOYMENT NECESSARY TO OBJECTIVE OF S. RES. 211

Mr. FISHER. I believe I didn't make myself clear, Mr. Chairman. What I intended to convey was the fact and I think that unless there was a cessation of MIRV deployment, the objectives of the resolution will be made infinitely less likely of realization.

Senator FULBRIGHT. Well, I concur.

Mr. FISHER. And that an announcement of the deferment of the MIRV deployment would, on the other hand, give the objectives of the resolution a fighting chance.

Senator FULBRIGHT. I wouldn't quarrel with that. I think it would be a great thing if they would announce it very soon.

Mr. FISHER. But I say, I would put it rather the other way around. I would hope that the Administration could see its way clear to make such an announcement as good faith cooperation with the objectives of the Senate Resolution 211 because unless they do, or if they present it to the Soviets, maybe the Soviets will come up with a proposal. That would make it an entirely different ball game but if we were to present them with a situation in which we say: "You have 6 weeks to stop everything and barring that we are going to make it impossible by starting our MIRV deployment," I think that would make the compliance or cooperation with the objectives impossible.

U.S. RESPONSE TO POSSIBLE SOVIET-PROPOSED FREEZE

Senator FULBRIGHT. Let me ask you a hypothetical question. You have been there. Supposing the Soviets do come up with a proposal as indicated in the report the Senator from Tennessee discussed. What do you think the American response would be?

Mr. FISHER. Well, my guess is the American response in the first instance at least would be to cable back to Washington.

Senator FULBRIGHT. Why would it take 6 weeks or 6 months, supposing they did? This is the sort of situation I meant. Obviously it couldn't be done quickly unless the Soviets agree, but I don't see why if the Soviets made the proposal, it should take us more than a week to resolve our doubts to go along with it as a preliminary matter.

Mr. FISHER. I would hope you would be correct.

On the other hand we only have an unidentified news source they are going to make this proposal, and at the risk of sounding defensive, Mr. Chairman, my statement was prepared before I had—compliance with this request of this committee was before I had—access to this New York Times report.

Senator FULBRIGHT. I have no reason to believe we would agree to that because of the attitude which has been expressed not only in this piece, but the newspaper report of the attitude of our Government, of its extreme caution and that no broad agreements are to be made. In the previous article in The New York Times by the same writer, Mr. Finney stated that he interpreted at least the report of the McCloy Commission to be in agreement on a moratorium. This is what I had in mind for a moment when I said he corrected it. He said that they did not interpret it that way. It is all very secret. They haven't given it to us, but someone had interpreted it not to be an across-the-board moratorium that they were recommending at the moment. So there was a little difference in the interpretation there.

However, generally speaking, its thrust would seem to be a moratorium at some time but not at the beginning.

EFFECT OF EXCESS CAUTION ON ARMS RACE

Mr. FISHER. Mr. Chairman, on this one perhaps this is just getting it off my chest, but a word about caution on this.

I guess we are all for caution, but it seems to be possible that we should recognize that being cautious and focusing on the so-called worst cases can be just as dangerous to us as overlooking significant threats.

If we took every conceivable doubt about our capabilities and put it on the low side and every conceivable doubt about the Soviet capabilities and put it on the completely high side in order to correct the imbalance, we have talked ourselves to where we would have a posture so big that the Soviets looking at it from the opposite point of view would think we were trying to create a first strike. So you can in the name of caution, misdirected caution, talk yourself into a position of extreme danger, each side piously saying, "We have got to be cautious here and we have got to react," and as a result escalating the arms race and I would hate to see——

Senator GORE. Isn't that precisely what we have already done and are about to do again?

Mr. FISHER. Yes; and I would hate to see us do it again, and since we are using this as a form of caution which, if I may use an Air Force parallel, is very much like the mother of the Air Force cadet who told her son to be cautious, if he had to fly please fly low and slow. [Laughter.]

Senator CASE. Mr. Chairman, may I go to one point.

Senator FULBRIGHT. Let me put one point. You remind me of how often I have heard it said in the last few years, "Whenever in doubt in these matters I always resolve that doubt on the side of security and more weapons."

Mr. FISHER. Well, you can by doing that, talk yourself into a very dangerous position.

Senator FULBRIGHT. We are in a dangerous position as a result of that kind of talk.

DEFERMENT OF MIRV LACKING IMMEDIATE MUTUAL FREEZE

Senator CASE. Dean, is it possible you are saying a little bit more than has come out yet? Is it possible that you may have in mind that, for their own purposes, the Soviets may not be quite satisfied at the present level of deployment of SS-9's, not quite satisfied at the deployment of their submarines and might want a little more time to do this, but still be willing to stop at a level below danger to us and which would be useful for us to agree to and therefore they may not be willing to stop right this minute in the deployment of all strategic weapons? Aren't you saying that they might be willing to stop at a time at which it would still be useful to us to agree to this, and that you want to avoid putting everything together and passing the point of no return on the one thing where a point of no return is imminent? That is your point, isn't it?

Mr. FISHER. That is correct, stated much better than I have stated it.

Senator CASE. I don't think so at all. It is desirable to keep this possibility open, and I agree with you.

Senator GORE. Senator Cooper.

Senator COOPER. I can only repeat what I said a while ago. In passing the resolution, and during its consideration, it was understood by the Foreign Relations Committee and in the debate in the Senate that it included the stopping of, suspension of, tests and the deployment of MIRV.

On the other side—you haven't talked about that yet—the resolution included also suspension of the deployment of SS-9's which is a matter of concern to our country. You would agree with that?

Mr. FISHER. Yes, sir; I would. But as I replied to Senator Case's question, if we were not able to work out stoppage of SS-9's in the next 6 weeks, I don't think that our reaction should be, "OK, we will deploy MIRV's," because there we would have passed the point of no return that would not have been passed by—for another month or so of SS-9 deployment at the current Soviet rate and the current level.

So I would not like us to say to the Soviets, "Unless we can mutually restrain everything and have that put into effect between now and the first of July, we are going to take a step which is irreversible," and that is the step caused by the deployment of MIRV's.

Senator COOPER. I understood the position clearly. Your chief argument is if we can't reach an immediate agreement about a freeze that we should not endanger either the possibility of a freeze or negotiations about the deployment of MIRV by deferring testing and deployment of MIRV, for at least a reasonable time to see if it is possible to get an agreement.

Just for the record, I would like to say——

Senator CASE. I am the temporary chairman. You go right ahead. You have the floor.

U.S. NEGOTIATING POSITION

Senator COOPER. I would like to say since there was much discussion about our briefing, that there was accurate and comprehensive briefing of the committee after Helsinki, about what had occurred there, and what was proposed and what courses they might take in the present negotiations. We have also had briefings from the Secretary of State and Ambassador Smith. I would not say the briefings were detailed about their plans, but covered their general purposes.

Also you were talking about this Air Force Manual citation. You were making the point whether the Air Force doctrine existed or not, or if any such statement had ever been made, the fact that we proceed with the task of making very accurate MIRV's would reach in fact a position of a first strike capability. Isn't that correct?

Mr. FISHER. Yes, sir. And I think, if I were a Soviet, I would be more inclined to read recent testimony before the Appropriations Committees as to what the projected plans were than Air Force manuals of 1964, vintage of 1964. So I consider——

Senator COOPER. It was also asked if the negotiating team would actually consider a freeze. I don't know what their present plans are, but the fact is that it was discussed by Ambassador Smith when he gave me the information and that they certainly would consider it. This is the impression I got. Whether they will do it I don't know.

Mr. FISHER. I am sure they will consider it and I am sure Ambassador Smith is an intelligent, patriotic man.

Senator COOPER. Senator Case and I, 2 months ago, made this proposal to the Executive. It was finally embodied in the resolution. Since that time we have made definite proposals to the President that all of these steps which you have discussed be taken. There has been no response yet, but I know the various steps that you have suggested to make clear the purpose of the resolution have been made.

Mr. FISHER. Well, Mr. Chairman, Senator Cooper, the only point I really wanted to make is that for the purpose of the resolution to be carried out or to have a reasonable chance of having it carried out, we should avoid two things: One, we should avoid appearing to put the Soviets in a position that unless they mutually stop everything in 6 weeks we will go ahead with the MIRV. They will interpret that as a fait accompli, presenting it to them as a fait accompli in that time frame. They would say, "You have got 6 weeks. If you don't do it we will go ahead with MIRVs," that is a take it or leave it really, and they would consider that a fait accompli and I think the temptation would present us with other faits accompli.

Now, the final thing is that——

SOVIET REACTION TO PUBLIC U.S. PROPOSAL ON MIRV

Senator COOPER. I would like to ask one more question. With all your experience in negotiating with the Soviets, if this proposal should be made by the President through his ambassador, should those proposals be made by the team at the beginning of talks or by a public proposal by the President? Would there be some danger that a public proposal might be termed propaganda by the Russians?

Mr. FISHER. Well, you know they vary, Senator Cooper. A proposal that got the test ban negotiations started was quite public. It was made at American University by President Kennedy.

Senator COOPER. Yes.

Mr. FISHER. And I don't think an indication of restraint in the planned deployment of MIRV's or an indication that it perhaps was premature to press for a decision on phase II would hurt if it were made publicly.

On the other hand, I think much more detailed than that, I think the public would probably be—the Soviets, they are for ultimately now open agreements but on the whole privately negotiated. As Mr. Kuznetsov said in a stage whisper when we were all discussing a step in the Nonproliferation Treaty in the Security Council Chamber with people in the audience and tourists one Sunday afternoon, "It's very simple. We are engaged in a secret conspiracy openly arrived at."

But they, on the whole, prefer private discussions but I don't think the public indication of restraint in the MIRV deployment and/or backing off a little bit on Safeguard's Phase II, modified phase II, would hurt it if made publicly, if it was made in the same tone as the American University speech. It could be.

SOVIET REACTION TO U.S. UNILATERAL WEAPONS SUSPENSION

Senator CASE. Would you think that in our negotiations with the Russians either our suspension, even for a short time, unilateral suspension of deployment of MIRV, or on all weapons, would be regarded by the Soviets as a sign of weakness?

Mr. FISHER. I don't think so. I think a little bit the other way around.

I think they are probably as concerned, as really I am, about this apparent drive to get the MIRV thing in the ground and out of the negotiating table.

I think they would regard that as a fact—you know some of those people still believe the references to the military-industrial complex running the complex. I realize it is a misquotation of the speech of our then President who said he was concerned to prevent it from happening. But some of them think it has happened and if the President says, "Look, we are not just madly determined to deploy MIRV's come what may, we are prepared to allow reasonable time for negotiation," provided the general sense of the negotiation was in the, was along the lines of the, first two operative, the two operative paragraphs of Senate Resolution 211, I don't think that would be considered a sign of weakness at all. I think that would be interpreted by the people that would like an agreement in the Soviet Union to be an indication that the President was serious about it and had gotten some of his own military people under control, and that people that might be reading Air Force manuals in the Soviet Union with perhaps less skepticism than one of the oldest flight status captains in the entire history of the Air Force; namely, me. Those people who don't read it with skepticism are aware of the authority of the Commander in Chief—I think would be heartened. I think they would realize that the President was serious about the situation and was in control of the situation completely.

U.S. OBJECTIVES IN ARMS NEGOTIATION

Senator CASE. Would that be because they, as we—I say you and we, I think the Administration—feel that the only basis for arms limitation is to preserve a mutual parity. Is that first of all a correct statement?

Mr. FISHER. I think it is correct. Parity has become inside the Government sort of a fighting word.

Senator CASE. I mean only the preservation of a situation in which the deterrent is available to both sides.

Mr. FISHER. Well, I would describe it, sir, as a rough balance.

Senator CASE. A rough balance, and what we are trying to do are two things: Preserve the rough balance within a limited, and it is to be hoped, eventually a reduced scale of armaments on both sides.

Mr. FISHER. Right. But the first activity is to keep the balance from imbalance.

Senator CASE. Keep the balance in balance and, of course, that is the reason for the Senate's adoption, of the committee resolution as proposed by Senator Cooper.

HORSE TRADING ELEMENTS IN ARMS NEGOTIATION

The last thing is that an arms limitation and negotiation is a horse trading operation. Is that right, except in the sense of small details?

Mr. FISHER. It has certain elements of a horse trade in it, but if it becomes a horse trade, treated as a horse trade, from the point of view of building up chips to bargain with it can be terribly counterproductive. Everyone can authorize everything in sight just so they can have something to bargain with at Vienna. And it can be an incentive to the beginning of an arms race, rather than a basis for turning it down and I would hate to see that happen in this situation. And that is the reason I said, sir, that the argument that you can authorize an armament program to have something to bargain with is an argument that hits the point of diminishing returns.

Senator CASE. Does it have any returns at all?

Mr. FISHER. Not very many although once we have decided to get rid of an arms system our ability—and made that known to the Soviets, our ability—to bargain some equivalent reduction on their part is rather limited. When we were——

Senator CASE. You are not going to do this unless they do?

Mr. FISHER. Well, no, we authorized the basic phasing out of the B-47 and although the B-47 is a somewhat better airplane than the Soviet, what is it—Soviet Badger, our suggestion that we destroyed some B-47's, why didn't they do something for some Bears didn't get anywhere because they said, "You would get rid of the B-47 anyhow."

The Soviets are still traders, there are some elements of horse trade in it but there are very distinct limits and the limits are really bigger—if one looks at it as really who is going to try to outsmart the other one, it is not going to last very long in any event.

DEFERMENT OF ABM AND MIRV

What it is is institutionalizing a rough balance, Senator Case, with the recognition—it is my concern, as I say, that the MIRV's may throw that out. I am equally concerned that the ABM's may throw that out, but the reason I put more emphasis on the MIRV than ABM is the ABM that is authorized is not as time critical as the MIRV and the AMB that has been requested is up to you gentlemen to decide whether to authorize it. The MIRV has already been authorized and is about to happen and that is the reason for my concern and, as you stated it earlier—and I wouldn't want to repeat it—a feeling that we shouldn't let it happen until we have had a reasonable period to talk out the whole business. And I don't consider between now and July 1 necessarily such a period. I certainly wouldn't recommend any one putting it to the Soviets on that basis.

Senator COOPER. Have you finished your statement?

Mr. FISHER. I think by interpolation I got most of it in in answer to questions.

Senator COOPER. Shall we agree then that it will be printed as you have made it for the sake of the record?

Mr. FISHER. Yes.

(The statement follows.)

STATEMENT OF ADRIAN S. FISHER BEFORE THE SENATE FOREIGN RELATIONS COMMITTEE, APRIL 14, 1970, WITH RESPECT TO THE CURRENT STRATEGIC ARMS LIMITATION TALKS

In view of the action taken on Thursday, April 9, 1970, on Senate Resolution 211, I believe it will be useful if I direct my remarks primarily to two actions which should be taken, in light of the realities of international negotiations, if the sense of the Senate expressed in that Resolution is to have a chance of success. Senate Resolution 211 expresses the sense of the Senate that prompt negotiations between the United States of America and the U.S.S.R. to seek agreed limitations on both offensive and defensive strategic weapons should be urgently pursued. It also expresses the sense of the Senate that the President should propose to the Government of the U.S.S.R. an immediate suspension by the United States and by the U.S.S.R. of the further deployment of all offensive and defensive nuclear strategic weapons systems, subject to national verification or such other measures of observation and inspection as may be appropriate.

ACTIONS IN SUPPORT OF S. RES. 211

The two actions which I believe should be taken to give the program outlined in this Resolution a fair chance of coming into being are: *First*, a deferral, by at least six months, of the impending deployment by the U.S. of Multiple Independently Targetable Reentry Vehicles; and *Second*, a postponement of any action looking toward the implementation of the proposed modified Phase II Safeguard System.

These actions are necessary to preserve the rare coincidence of favorable political and strategic conditions, which provides a real but fleeting opportunity for agreement between the U.S. and the U.S.S.R. to halt the arms race in both quantity and quality of weapons, and then to diminish the threat to mankind posed by existing weapons.

EFFECT OF MIRV DEPLOYMENT

Dealing first with the problems posed by MIRV's, their introduction into the present nuclear relationship would have the initial effect of substantially increasing the number of deliverable nuclear warheads available to each side. The MIRV program will take on new dimensions, particularly in its land based configuration, as missile accuracy increases. When this occurs, it becomes possible for one side *if it strikes first* with missiles armed with MIRV's to take out more than one missile site with a single attacking missile. The obverse of this frightening coin is that each side may fear that, *unless it strikes first*, the MIRVed missiles of the other side may be able substantially to eliminate its own land-based ICBM force, with the other side still having substantial ICBM force left in reserve.

We are apparently now in the process of completing a test series of MIRV's a series which began in September of 1968 and which are scheduled for completion in June of this year. According to the testimony of the Secretary of the Air Force, we are now scheduled to start deploying the MIRV's in the form of the Minuteman III, in June of this year. It has been indicated that we have similar plans with respect to the Poseidon in the latter part of 1970 or early 1971. This deployment of the first MIRV's represents a real setback in our efforts to control the arms race. It would make a situation, which is already dangerous enough because of our testing MIRV's up to the point of deployment, far more dangerous.

Now I know this Committee is well aware of the difficulties in verifying by physical inspection a restriction on MIRV deployment once MIRV's have been tested up to a point that they are ready to be deployed. The preamble to S. Resolution 211 makes this point quite clear.

From this one might argue that we have already passed the point of no-return in view of the completion of our test series up to the point of being ready for deployment. Two factors may prevent us from having passed this point. One is that we have not pressed our tests to the point where our MIRV's have a counterforce capability. This is a fragile factor because the Soviets may or may not believe this to be the case. The second is that we have not yet deployed any MIRV's and, if the President were to announce that he had deferred deployment of the MIRV's, anyone with any knowledge of the way the U.S. Government operates could have reasonable confidence that we could take no action inconsistent with this announcement without either our press or our Congress finding out about it. The issue will be a clear one—black or white—no deployment or some. As a practical matter, clandestine deployment on our part would be impossible.

On the other hand, once we deploy some MIRV's, this clear situation becomes a murky one. The question then becomes not are we deploying MIRV's, but how many, and of what kind. Has the deployment been limited to less than a hundred, as intimated in yesterday's story in The Washington Post, or is it even less, or perhaps, substantially more? All of these are questions that will have to be dealt with in the arms control contest and these are questions on which we could not expect the Soviets to take an unverified promise. We certainly would not if the situation were reversed.

POSTPONEMENT OF MIRV

Now, how should this be dealt with? One suggestion might be that the MIRV deployment should be considered a part of the immediate suspension of the deployment of all offensive and defensive strategic weapons recommended by the second operative paragraph of S. Res. 211. This will be a very far-reaching proposal. In addition to dealing with the question of testing of multiple warheads, whether MRV or MIRV's, it will have to cover at least the following elements:
1. No deployment of multiple warheads;
2. No new deployment of land-based intercontinental ballistic missiles;
3. No construction of Anti-Ballistic Missile radars or deployment of anti-ballistic missile interceptors;
4. No new "starts" on constructing submarines for launching ballistic missiles.

The talks are beginning on April 16. Our MIRV deployment is scheduled for June. Taking the position that we will allow the Soviet Union approximately two months to negotiate a suspension of this scope and that, if we are not able to accomplish this result in this time, we will make the MIRV problem immensely more difficult by proceeding with our MIRV deployment, would certainly be interpreted by them as presenting them with such a tight deadline that it was, in effect, a fait accompli.

This is a step that would cast serious doubts on our seriousness in pursuing the SALT talks in the first place. It would leave them the impression that we were determined to press home the MIRV issue and get them deployed, come what may, so that would not be an issue which could be dealt with in the Strategic Arms Limitation Talks.

One of the most important things that the SALT talks could accomplish is to prevent the deployment of MIRV's. This opportunity should not be lost. It is for this reason that I respectfully submit that the sense of the Senate, expressed in S. Res. 211, will not be given a reasonable chance of success unless the planned deployment of the MIRV's is postponed for a reasonable period, say for example six months, and an announcement to this effect made by high authority.

We could take such a step without any disadvantage to our security. Beginning the deployment of MIRV's in June of this year, far from improving our bargaining strength at SALT, would make the negotiations more difficult, and would invite the Soviet Union in turn to present us with a fait accompli. I find it difficult to see how any harm can result to our strategic posture by such a delay, which would involve only a handful of land-based missiles and the MIRV program that is already being widely questioned as unnecessary, wasteful and certainly premature, since the large Soviet ABM program it was designed to penetrate does not exist.

DELAY IN AUTHORIZING MODIFIED PHASE II OF SAFEGUARD

With respect to Modified Phase II of the Safeguards System, I do not intend to reargue the elements that went into the decision on Phase I. That action has been taken and whether it will help or hurt the objectives of S. Res. 211 only history can decide. But I do not see what interests of U.S. security are advanced by requesting approval of Modified Phase II.

I am aware of the argument that it is necessary to go ahead with authorizing the proposed Modified Phase II Safeguard System in order to strengthen our bargaining position in Vienna. I do not believe that this is a persuasive argument. Authorizing armaments so that they can be included in a disarmament program soon reaches the point of diminishing returns.

If both sides were to play this game, the Strategic Arms Limitation Talks, far from resulting in a decrease in the arms race, would serve as an excuse for both sides to build up their strategic armaments, both offensive and defensive, substantially each saying that they have to have something to deal with at Vienna. And in particular, from the Soviet point of view, going ahead and authorizing a modified Phase II Safeguard System so soon after Phase I had been made a separate program would belie the implication of deliberate consideration which the separation of the Safeguard System into Phase I and Phase II would seem to imply. It would clearly give the Soviets the impression that the U.S. was determined to push the complete Safeguards program to a finish, come what may. This, in my judgment, would make success in SALT less, rather than more, likely. It is for that reason that I think the Senate should recognize that in passing S. Res. 211, it was expressing a hope that would not have much chance of fruition unless a decision is made to delay the authorization of the proposed Modified Phase II of the Safeguards System, as well as to defer, for at least six months, the impending deployment of the Multiple Independently Targetable Reentry Vehicles.

Senator CASE. If there is anything further you wanted to say before final questions you can go ahead about it.

Mr. FISHER. I do not believe so, Senator. I think I have said just about all I know, so that at that stage of the game it is probably wise for me to be quiet.

Senator CASE. Senator Cooper, have you any questions?

Senator COOPER. I have two or three questions.

MILITARY CONTINGENCY PLANNING

We were talking about the Air Force manual. I will ask you, is it not correct that the military usually provides for every contingency that they can think about? It is rather unfortunate that this was printed in the Air Force manual, but I think it is the task, is it not, of the military to consider all contingencies. If they did not do that they would not be doing their job.

I know and you know from your own experience and service that that is the job of the military.

I would like to ask Dr. Scoville two or three questions.

VERIFICATION OF MOBILE ICBM DEPLOYMENT

You said it would be very difficult to verify, to discover whether or not the mobile ICBM's have been deployed.

Dr. SCOVILLE. I did not say quite that. What I said was that it might be very difficult to get an accurate count of the number of mobile missiles because since they can move between one observation and another you are never quite sure whether you are counting the same missile twice or whether it was there the day before you looked and not when you got around to look; you might miscount rather badly.

On the other hand, I think you can verify a ban on mobile missiles quite satisfactorily because then even spotting a few missiles would be enough to know that a violation had occurred, and I do not think there is a major risk to our security from a limitation on mobile ICBM's.

Senator COOPER. It has been suggested several times that the Soviets have already begun or are beginning to deploy mobile ICBM's. Do you have any information on whether or not that is correct?

Dr. SCOVILLE. Well, I think I stated, and probably this is something you should really ask the CIA representatives when they come—but

I think I stated that I know of no reliable reports that they have actually started deployment of mobile ICBM's or IRBM's.

Senator COOPER. Apparently we have no information that they have reached such a stage where it would be difficult to verify them.

Dr. SCOVILLE. I do not think they are at the stage now where it would be difficult to verify, but maybe 2 or 3 years from now it would be more difficult.

SOVIET MISSILE CAPACITY

Senator COOPER. The Soviets have tested multiple warheads. We do not know for certain whether they have tested MIRV or MRV, but assuming they have tested and are satisfied with their tests, and then go into production, you said at that stage it would be very difficult to detect what is happening during the production stage.

Would it be possible, do you think, for the Soviets to have reached a stage either by testing where they could produce and then change the characteristics of their missiles, by putting MRV in, Dr. Scoville?

Dr. SCOVILLE. Well, I do not think they have got to the stage where they can deploy a MRV or MIRV system which could threaten our Minuteman force, and I think the Defense Department agrees with that conclusion now; I do not think they did some time back.

Dr. Foster, in his recent testimony—I have forgotten the exact date, but in February—flatly stated that they had not demonstrated a capability to be able to deploy multiple warheads of the kind that you need to be able, to knock out the Minuteman sites. So technically I think we are still fortunate that one can still have a ban on MIRV testing, and that ban adequately verify as well that the Soviets are not actually deploying missiles with multiple warheads which could threaten the Minuteman force.

Senator COOPER. My next question is somewhat similar. It has been said also that the Soviets have been testing new antimissile missiles. Is there information that they could change the characteristics of the Galosh system around Moscow, Tallinn, and also the many, many air defense systems scattered around Russia?

Dr. SCOVILLE. I certainly believe technically that they have the capacity of making the so-called Moscow system better than it presently is, and also building ABM systems throughout the rest of their country. In other words, they have been carrying out an active research and development program to try to improve the existing system.

On the other hand, I feel quite strongly that we would be able to detect such deployment or upgrading well in advance of the time in which it would provide any real threat to our deterrent force.

RECOMMENDED LEVEL OF U.S. ABMS

Senator COOPER. You said it would be better to have a zero level of ABM rather than to go ahead with any ABM's. I thought there might be some contradiction there.

Were you suggesting zero ABM or perhaps limited ABM?

Dr. SCOVILLE. Well, I think what I tried to say was zero or low levels of ABM. In other words, if you have an ABM with, say, only 100 launchers, and maybe a couple of large radars to support those

100 launchers, then it is rather difficult to expand that system rapidly without its being detected into a system which would be large enough to really threaten our deterrence.

On the other hand, if you had a system with, say, 1,000 missiles and particularly with maybe six to a dozen large radars which provided nationwide coverage (the radars are the really critical factor here) then it might be possible to rather rapidly expand that system— and you might not know it was being expanded—by just adding more missiles on a rather short time scale. Such a system with a nationwide net of large radars could, at least, give us concern as to whether our deterrent was still viable.

FRACTIONAL ORBIT BOMBARDMENT SYSTEM

Senator COOPER. You allude also to the fact that General Wheeler did testify before the committee that he preferred national inspection in this field. Do you consider that FOBS is a dangerous factor in our discussion of relative strength of the United States and the Soviet Union?

Dr. SCOVILLE. The FOBS, in a sense, is really another form of ICBM which gives you the option of firing it around the South Pole or on a depressed northern trajectory and which reduces the warning time.

However, you have to sacrifice accuracy and yield and, therefore, FOBS is available for surprise attack only against relatively soft targets and does not in any way threaten our deterrent force. It is just not a counter-force type of weapon.

Senator COOPER. It could only be used against soft targets.

Dr. SCOVILLE. It can only be useful against soft targets.

Senator COOPER. So it really does not affect the deterrent.

Dr. SCOVILLE. Except in one possible case, and that is the FOBS might be a useful weapon against bombers on the ground in that the warning time of a FOBS attack would probably not be sufficient to let the bombers get up into the air, so it could take out that part of the deterrent, but it cannot affect a missile force in any way.

Senator COOPER. I was always rather interested in the statement by Mr. McNamara that it was not any violation of the Outer Space Treaty.

Dr. SCOVILLE. Well, I think there are two reasons at least why I consider, without being a lawyer, why FOBS was not a violation of the Outer Space Treaty.

First and foremost, it forbids the placing of nuclear weapons in orbit around the earth. I think there is every reason to believe there were no nuclear weapons involved in the test firing of the FOBS.

I think it is most unlikely that the Soviets would have put a nuclear weapon in a missile which was then going to land on their own territory. That is a little risky.

Second, the space treaty really was aimed at weapons being placed in orbit, being stationed in orbit on a continuing basis, and not aimed at another form of ICBM with a different trajectory. So I do not think, for both of these reasons, that the Soviet program on FOBS should be considered a violation of the treaty. I believe I should remind you that the testing of even a true orbital bombardment system is not banned provided no nuclear warhead were involved.

Senator COOPER. That is all.

DISTINGUISHING BETWEEN REAL AND DUMMY MISSILE SILOS

Senator CASE. Dr. Scoville, can satellites distinguish between real missile silos and dummy missile silos?

Dr. SCOVILLE. Well, I think it is certainly possible to build a dummy silo which might be difficult to differentiate from a real silo.

On the other hand, I think this would be a rather expensive proposition. It is an alternative means of making a land-based, a fixed land-based force, survive a little bit longer in that it does provide more targets.

On the other hand, the expense of providing these extra targets without having any weapons in them is probably high, and I think, marginal utility. It is the same sort of a problem you face with MIRV's and penetration aids.

You could have a system to penetrate an ABM in which you had three reentry vehicles, only one of which had a nuclear warhead in it. This would confuse the defense.

On the other hand, if you are going to go to the expense of bringing in a reentry vehicle which looks like a warhead, you might just as well put a warhead in it, and that is why people went to MIRV's as being the most certain system for penetrating an ABM.

Senator CASE. From the standpoint of any agreement you would have to count dummy silos just as——

Dr. SCOVILLE. Yes; you would have to count a dummy silo just like any other.

PROTECTION AGAINST ACCIDENTAL LAUNCH

Senator CASE. Dean, as you know, one of the justifications offered for Safeguard was the protection it would provide against an accidental launch or the mad colonel aberration.

Dr. Panofsky testified yesterday on the technical aspects of that argument. I wonder if in this connection you would give me your view as to what safeguards we have that insure that we won't launch missiles accidentally, and what safeguards the Soviets have, and whether you think we ought to exchange information with the Soviets on how to protect against both sides against an accidental launch. Have you any views on that?

Mr. FISHER. Well, the latter, I think, would be a good idea. I have not analyzed our command and control system of our national command and control systems in any detail. I have only done this in the context of the weapons stationed in Europe in connection with the Nonproliferation Treaty, and I am satisfied there that it takes an order by a U.S. general coming down from the Commander in Chief to send off a tactical nuclear weapon.

The one problem about exchanging information is all of these command and control structures are a tradeoff, to use the jargon, between safety and not having it so safe if you ever had to use it it wouldn't work, and there probably would be some resistance by the people involved not to tell a potential adversary what our reaction time is.

On the other hand, my own view is that command and control is probably a better way to deal with the problem of accidental launch than the highly expensive ABM, and some discussion on command and control at some place I think would be useful.

Senator CASE. Have you any comments, Dr. Scoville?

Dr. SCOVILLE. Could I comment just a little bit on the safety problem?

Senator CASE. Please.

Dr. SCOVILLE. The problem of developing the Safeguard system so that you are able to handle accidental launches is that the command and control has to be such that it will react to a single unknown coming in and it has to be able to react rapidly. In this case it seems to me it is virtually impossible to leave the order to fire in the hands of the President. For the communication to get from the field to the President and back in a situation of where there is only a single vehicle coming is extremely difficult, and the President might not—you just cannot guarantee him—as being available.

Secondly, the President won't have any information on which to act in the case of an accidental launch, so he really is not in a better position than the man in the field to make the decision. He would have to take the man's word for it as to whether it was a likely missile or not. The problem you have with all kinds of radars and computer systems, of which the ABM certainly has many, is that radars do occasionally observe false targets. It is unlikely that the radars would see hundreds of false targets simultaneously as might occur in an actual Soviet attack, but a single false target is likely to show up quite frequently. I personally do not look forward with a great deal of pleasure to every time a single unknown shows up on the radar or in the computer system that we start firing a multimegaton warhead up into the upper atmosphere.

Senator CASE. Why not? Why is it a very serious matter? Please describe that.

Dr. SCOVILLE. Among other things, I think it never will be done twice. The phenomena which occur following a multimegaton burst at high altitude are very striking and are observable for hundreds of miles. They probably won't produce casualties in terms of deaths, but the optical effects are quite serious. If you happened to be looking directly at the burst, particularly if it was nighttime, you might get burns to your eyes. Certainly if you were a pilot in a plane, you might have a little difficulty seeing your instruments for the next 4 or 5 hours and you would have rough time coming back.

Senator CASE. What degree, if any, of fallout would there be?

Dr. SCOVILLE. There would not be any fallout.

Senator CASE. That is not a problem.

Dr. SCOVILLE. That is not a problem.

ABORT SYSTEMS

Senator CASE. Would either of you comment, or both of you, on the matter of abort systems. At one time, I think a great many Americans, including many members of the committee, thought that we had the capacity to destroy our own weapons after they were launched. This is not so.

Dr. SCOVILLE. I am afraid I cannot comment——
Senator CASE. Is this a means of limiting dangers of accidental launch, if this is a serious matter?
Dr. SCOVILLE. I am sure you could design such a system. I do not know anything about whether such systems exist other than I think Secretary Laird last year made a statement that it did not exist, but I am not positive about that.
Senator CASE. He said first that they did and then he corrected that statement.
Dr. SCOVILLE. Then corrected himself.
I can see it is certainly technically possible to do it, but there are also certain objections to doing it which would certainly be voiced by the military. As soon as you design into a system a method of aborting it, you always worry that somehow or other that will increase the likelihood that the system won't work when you want it to work, or that the opposition may learn what that signal is and that might be their ABM.
Senator CASE. And trigger it.
Have you any comment on that?
Mr. FISHER. No.

VERIFICATION OF COMPREHENSIVE ARMS LIMITATION AGREEMENT

Senator CASE. There was an article in yesterday's Post by Chalmers Roberts who wrote that the SALT negotiators are leaving for Vienna with cautious instructions for a limited proposal on how to curb the arms race in strategic nuclear weapons.
He says that there are two basic reasons for this cautious approach: The difficult problem of verifying a comprehensive agreement that would necessarily include accounting for all new multiple warheads; the American independently targetable type known as MIRV, and the Soviet version known as MRV.
What difficult problem is involved in verifying a comprehensive agreement that would necessarily include accounting for all multiple warheads? Dr. Scoville, have you any comment you would like to make?
Dr. SCOVILLE. I won't say it is easy but I do not feel it is too difficult. I tried to make it rather clear in my prepared statement that I believe verification can be adequate to protect our security.
I furthermore believe, as I think I mentioned at the end, that a comprehensive agreement or at least a fairly broad agreement is probably easier to verify than one which tackles only a single system. The risks from a violation are probably less when you have a broad agreement because it is necessary to violate two or three times or in two or three different areas to have any real security advantage. So I do not agree with the view that a comprehensive agreement is more difficult to verify.
On the other hand, I do not mean by that that verification is automatically perfect, but I think it can be adequately verified, using national means.
Senator CASE. Mr. Roberts also reported in the same story that as recently as last week a high Administration panel on verification was still arguing about new factors then being introduced. Exactly what

these new factors were was not made clear. But officials involved are not convinced that testing of MIRV's could be adequately monitored to prevent cheating. That, I think, is just a report of fact. You do not have any comment on that, do you?

Dr. SCOVILLE. I do not have any knowledge of what goes on in these discussions. I can only—and I am sure Mr. Fisher can, too—hark back to somewhat similar discussions in connection with the test ban, and the rather great lengths that certain of the opponents went to in order to conceive of ways in which the Soviets might test and ways in which we might not be able to observe them. An example of testing behind the moon, I think, is a good example. I think that our security is enhanced by trying to halt the arms race and the risks from not halting it are far greater than the risk of the Soviets testing MIRV's behind the moon or some similar program.

Senator CASE. You have any further comment on it?

RISK OF VERIFICATION MEASURED AGAINST RISK OF ARMS RACE

Mr. FISHER. Well, yes; just to indicate that any verification system, particularly relying on national capabilities, as it does, it is possible to say it is not foolproof. It is the easiest thing in the world to get up and say "It is not foolproof. It is too risky for me. I am for U.S. security and, therefore, don't do it."

But that overlooks the fact that that measures the risks against another set of risks which are the set of risks that are involved in going on with the arms race, and I would think that the necessary comparative in every person who comes up saying how easy it is to test a MIRV in a suborbital trajectory, is the danger to that greater than the danger to an unrestricted arms race which would be made necessary if you decided not to go ahead with attempts to halt it because of the concerns over this type of cheating, and if just one side of the coin is looked at, it always gives you this "You can't be too careful" type syndrome in which, if you are being very, very cautious, you put yourself in a position of great danger, it seems to me a danger that we always have to be concerned about.

MONITORING A BROAD WEAPONS BAN

Senator CASE. Dean, do you have any comment on Dr. Scoville's point, as I understand it, that an overall ban would be considerably, in many respects, easier to monitor than a ban on individual weapons systems?

Mr. FISHER. I just agree with him. I agree with the reasons that he gave, Senator Case.

Dr. SCOVILLE. Could I just comment, when I say an overall ban, I think, perhaps, one should say a broad ban.

Senator CASE. I meant a broad ban.

Dr. SCOVILLE. I can conceive of things that you can put into an overall ban that might be hard to verify.

EFFECTS OF IMPROVING ACCURACY AND INCREASING YIELD

Senator CASE. The weekend press carried a lot of stories reporting on the strategic survey, 1969, published by the Institute of Strategic

Studies. For example, a story in The Washington Post by Alfred Friendly on April 12, said the survey argued that one reason talks in Vienna are so important is because of the possibility that the deterrent relationship between the Soviet Union and the United States may be upset by the increasingly efficient defense provided by the ABM system and the accurate warheads on offensive missiles. And the study's report added that the effects of improving accuracy are dramatically greater than the effects of increasing yield.

Would you agree that the effects of improving accuracy are greater than the effects of increasing yield?

Dr. SCOVILLE. Yes, indeed. You gain an awful lot more by increasing the accuracy than you do by increasing the yield.

Senator CASE. It is true, is it not, that we have stressed the increase in accuracy over the increase in yield in our own weapons development?

Dr. SCOVILLE. That is true.

Senator CASE. Does our concentration on accuracy suggest that we are going for a first strike? Could the Soviets so conclude?

Dr. SCOVILLE. I think the Soviets could look at it that way. I hope that is not the case.

Senator CASE. Is it part of the long-range possibility, though, involved in the instability of increasing development of our weapons and increasing perfection?

Dr. SCOVILLE. It certainly is.

Mr. FISHER. In this connection, Senator, I referred to a statement the Air Force made that, "We have a program we are pushing to increase the yield of our warheads and decrease the circular error or probability so that we will have a hard target killer which we do not have in the inventory at the present time."

That is saying, in effect, that the current MIRV does not have a counterforce capability, but we are pushing a program that will give it one, and I consider that—I am not being critical of the General, but it is a fact that the Soviet Union will read that just like I did.

Senator CASE. Thank you.

SATELLITE RECONNAISSANCE OF SOVIET RADAR

I have, I think, just one more question suggested by our staff in relation to an item in the Newsweek magazine, its Periscope column this week. It says:

> Pentagon analysts of spy-satellite reconnaissance photographs are paying special attention to radars around Soviet air-defense bases. They are on the look out for any signs that the regular Russian aircraft-tracking radars are being converted to the big radars needed to track intercontinental ballistic missiles. Such conversion would indicate that the Soviets could be switching their far-flung antiaircraft missile sites to anti-ballistic-missile defenses. This in turn would serve to support the contention of some U.S. defense analysts that the Soviet Union is escalating the missile race—and that the United States must counter this with its own elaborate ABM system plus multiple warheads to penetrate Soviet ABM defenses.

I know you have discussed this, perhaps, two or three times in different ways, but I just wanted to have you comment on this particular version of the point.

Haven't satellite reconnaissance photographs always paid close attention to radars around Soviet air defense bases for this very reason?

Dr. SCOVILLE. Certainly watching radar deployment is a key to being able to determine the other side's ABM capability, and I would certainly hope that that is what we were doing. I am sure we have, and I am sure it is the basis for a lot of the statements that have been made by others. Secretary Laird mentioned these large radars in his recent posture statement, the large Soviet radars.

Senator CASE. Do you know of any signs that regular Russian aircraft tracking radars are being converted to the kind of radars which would be needed to track ICBM's?

Dr. SCOVILLE. I do not know of any such information. You should ask the CIA.

Senator CASE. Of course, if there are not, in fact, those things, there is not much use in putting out the story.

Dr. SCOVILLE. I do not blame the story which said they had observed it. I think it only said they are looking for it. On the other hand, I can agree with you that the purpose of the story was to leave the implication that it might be occurring.

Senator CASE. Exactly so. And the effect of any such journalistic operation—and I am not talking about the Newsweek side of this thing because they are obviously reporting something that was told to them—like putting out a story of this sort which may or may not have any basis in fact or in actual development, but is just a speculation that something might happen, is a somewhat favorite way of creating the impression that it is happening. Is that not so?

Dr. SCOVILLE. I think that is true.

Senator CASE. Senator Cooper, do you have any further questions?

Senator COOPER. One, and I promise it is the last one.

EFFECTIVENESS OF ONSITE INSPECTION

I would like to ask Dr. Scoville: There are many people who say we have to have onsite inspection. Would you describe the limitations on onsite inspection so far as the effectiveness is concerned?

Dr. SCOVILLE. Well, very briefly, if you look at the major things, uncertainties that we would have to verify in a strategic arms control situation, it is not too easy to find examples where onsite inspection would provide very much better information than you already can get through national means.

On the other hand, there are cases where onsite inspection would probably add to our confidence that the agreement was being abided by.

I could, perhaps quote two examples, one which is, perhaps, not onsite inspection, but is that category that I classed in between onsite inspection and national means: It has been proposed that each site after giving advance notice, carry out its missile tests over predesignated ranges which could be observed from outside the country. This would certainly make life easier in terms of verification. I personally do not believe it is essential, but I think it would certainly add to the confidence that an agreement banning MIRV tests was being abided.

Senator COOPER. That would not be a true case of onsite inspection.

Dr. SCOVILLE. That would not be a true case. An example of more true onsite inspection might be the case where you were worried that a given air defense radar, or let us say air defense system, was, in fact, being upgraded to have an ABM capability.

An onsite inspection of the site that you were worried about might provide information which would give greater confidence that it was not being so upgraded. Again I do not think it is necessary but it might be useful.

Senator COOPER. Even if you do not get onsite inspection it is better to have a freeze, limitation and control, and to rely upon national observation than to go on with further deployments.

Dr. SCOVILLE. Yes.

Senator COOPER. That is all.

Senator CASE. The subcommittee is most grateful to both of you for your testimony, and we appreciate all that you have done.

We will be adjourned until next week when an announcement of the witnesses and dates will later be made.

(Whereupon, at 12:45 p.m., the subcommittee adjourned, subject to the call of the Chair.)

ABM, MIRV, SALT, AND THE NUCLEAR ARMS RACE
Safeguard Phase 2, SALT, and Southeast Asia

MONDAY, MAY 18, 1970

UNITED STATES SENATE,
SUBCOMMITTEE ON ARMS CONTROL,
INTERNATIONAL LAW AND ORGANIZATION
OF THE COMMITTEE ON FOREIGN RELATIONS,
Washington, D.C.

The subcommittee met, pursuant to recess, at 2:35 p.m., in room 4221, New Senate Office Building, Senator Gore (chairman of the subcommittee) presiding.

Present: Senators Gore, Fulbright (chairman of the full committee), Church, Symington, Aiken, Case, and Cooper.

Senator GORE. The subcommittee will come to order.

OPENING STATEMENT

On behalf of the subcommittee, I wish to welcome the Honorable Secretary of Defense, former Congressman Mel Laird, with whom it was my pleasure to serve for a long while.

We have been looking forward to this occasion since early March when our invitation to testify was first extended. We will be most interested to hear what you have to say in support of Safeguard Phase II and to have your views on its relationship to the present Strategic Arms Limitation Talks in Vienna.

Last year when President Nixon announced his decision to seek funds for Safeguard Phase II, he noted that one of the criteria for proceeding with Phase II would be experience gained in the course of the coming year with the initial Phase I installations at Grand Forks and Malmstrom. As it happens, the contracts for these two sites have only recently been let. Nevertheless, the President has requested authorization for Safeguard Phase II.

Perhaps in your statement today you will explain to the subcommittee the Administration's basis for recommending the next phase of Safeguard in the absence of any operational experience with Phase I.

In this connection, the President has referred to the necessity of a "virtually infallible" defense against the Communist Chinese ICBM threat. At the same time, we have been told that the Safeguard system is negotiable in the context of the SALT talks. We would be interested to learn whether to date there is any indication of Soviet interest in negotiating an ABM limitation. If such a negotiation should present itself, how could we avail ourselves of it in view of the emphasis which the Administration has placed on the construction of a "virtually infallible" Chinese ABM?

Finally, we are concerned about the burgeoning costs of the Safeguard system. If the system were indeed vital to our defense, I take it we could and would bear its costs. On the other hand if it is negotiable as we have been told, then how can it be justified and what priorities do we set in its use?

In addition, if you do not mind, I have just learned that your Department has in a public statement indicated that the U.S. advisers did, in fact, accompany South Vietnamese land forces on an invasion into Laos. Perhaps you would be willing to give us a statement on that.

You have been so kind as to furnish the subcommittee with a copy of your statement. The entire statement will be inserted in the record of the hearings, and the subcommittee would be pleased to have you proceed as you so desire, either with the full context or, if you would be willing, with an abbreviation of your preprinted statement.

Mr. Secretary.

STATEMENT OF HON. MELVIN R. LAIRD, SECRETARY OF DEFENSE; ACCOMPANIED BY ADM. THOMAS H. MOORER, CHAIRMAN, JOINT CHIEFS OF STAFF; AND DR. JOHN S. FOSTER, DIRECTOR OF DEFENSE RESEARCH AND ENGINEERING

Secretary LAIRD. Mr. Chairman and members of the committee, Dr. Foster, Admiral Moorer, and I appreciate the opportunity to appear before this committee to discuss the important strategic arms limitation talks (SALT) which we are conducting with the Soviet Union and the relationship of U.S. strategic force programs to these talks.

President Nixon in his report to the Congress on U.S. foreign policy for the 1970's, characterized these talks as "the most important arms control negotiations that this country has ever entered."

I want to emphasize that I, as Secretary of Defense, and our military leadership, hope that SALT will be successful.

PURPOSE OF SALT

As you know, the purpose of SALT is to determine whether it is possible to find an agreement—acceptable both to the United States and to the Soviet Union—which can improve the security of both countries, reduce the likelihood that nuclear war will occur, and reduce the portion of our national resources devoted to strategic weapons.

We believe that it is possible to reach a historic agreement with the Soviet Union on the limitation of strategic arms. We believe such an agreement should be acceptable to the Soviet Union provided the Soviets do, in fact, share our objective of deterrence.

Senator GORE. Share our objectives?

Secretary LAIRD. Share our objective of deterrence.

Senator GORE. Do you mean if they concur in a similar strategy of deterrence?

Secretary LAIRD. Yes, deterrence. Our objective in the strategic area is to achieve deterrence, and this is an important premise that we must make in order to have success in the strategic arms limitation talks——

Senator GORE. Would you mind if I asked a corollary question there?

SOVIET EFFORTS TO APPROACH PARITY IN ATTACK CAPABILITY

I noticed in your prepared statement, which I have had the pleasure of reading, that you place considerable emphasis on the fact that while the United States has not been increasing its tonnage, so to speak, in the last 4 or 5 years, the Soviets have.

In view of the fact that we consider that we had a sufficiency, to use President Nixon's word, for the purposes of deterrence, what is the criticalness of the Soviets' undertaking to more or less catch up and approach parity with the United States in attack capability?

Secretary LAIRD. Are you talking about the period of the mid-1970's or the decade of the 1970's, or the present, Mr. Chairman?

Senator GORE. I am talking about the previous period.

Secretary LAIRD. At the present time, Mr. Chairman, I have no concern about the sufficiency of our deterrent or of the program which we have proposed to the Congress, which was outlined in the Defense Report I presented in February. I believe it adequately protects the United States during the time period which the budget covers, that is, fiscal year 1971.

I do, however, have some concern about the momentum of the Soviet strategic program. If that momentum continues it will be necessary for this country to make some very difficult, tough decisions after this transitional year, and that is the time period to which I am addressing my remarks today, I want to make it very clear that we will have a sufficiency of strategic power during the time period, for which this budget, and the programs outlined in it, is submitted.

MOMENTUM OF SOVIET STRATEGIC PROGRAM

Senator GORE. Do I correctly understand you then to say that you are not particularly concerned or at least alarmed at the efforts which the Soviets have made heretofore in approaching parity with the United States, but you think that the momentum of its multiplication may carry forward into the future in a manner which might endanger our deterrent position?

Secretary LAIRD. That is correct, Mr. Chairman.

When I testified before this committee about 1 year ago, I presented certain projections to the committee. I realize that I was questioned about those projections at that time, but they have turned out to be conservative projections. We can take the submarine-launched ballistic missile program of the Soviet Union, or we can take the SS-9 ICBM's. If we were to look at the figures I gave a year ago, I estimated in May of last year that the Soviet Union had approximately 230 SS-9's operational or under construction. Today that estimate has been increased rather markedly, and that the Soviet Union has some 280 operational or under construction at this time.

Last year when I testified before this committee, I discussed the number of Polaris-type submarines that the Soviet Union was going forward with. We now find that the Soviet Union completed approximately eight of the Polaris-type submarines during the last year or so. The number of Polaris-type submarines in being or under construction at the present time is about 25. Since we are not now building any more ballistic missile submarines, this construction rate would put the Soviet Union in a position, where, with the momentum that they have they could equal or exceed our force by 1974-75. This contrasts to the projection I used last year that the Soviets could attain such a force by 1975-77. And as the chairman of this committee knows full well, should we embark upon a submarine construction program as a follow-on to the Polaris/Poseidon-type submarine, the earliest date that we could have the follow-on submarines in our fleet—just one—of them would be 1978. Being a member of the Joint Atomic Energy Committee, I am sure you are familiar with those leadtimes, the number of months from the time when we initiate a program until the time when the first submarine can become operational.

In my statement, I made clear that this momentum of Soviet programs, and the time frame of the mid-1970's, is important as far as the United States is concerned. We have not made any changes in our force level for strategic offensive missile launchers since 1965.

UNITED STATES HAS SLOWED DOWN

The only thing that we have done is to slow down some of our programs. We have slowed down the ABM program from the one that was approved by the Congress. The multiple independently targeted reentry vehicle (MIRV) program has been slowed down since it was approved by the Congress as far as deployment rates are concerned

The point I wish to make is that the United States has not in any way escalated the arms race. The decisions which have been approved by the Congress, if they had been carried out in accordance with the timetables originally given to the Congress, would have involved more rapid deployment not only of ABM's but also of the so-called MIRV vehicles.

IMPORTANCE OF SOVIET MOMENTUM TO FUTURE U.S. STRATEGIC SUFFICIENCY

The point that I wish to make is that the momentum of the Soviets in this time period of 1970 to 1975 is very important in determining whether we will have a sufficiency of strategic forces, and my concern is with that particular time period. That is why I believe the SALT talks are so important. In this transitional year, fiscal year 1971, I believe that we are adequately protected with this budget but I think some hard, tough decisions do face America if we are not successful in the strategic arms limitation talks.

Senator GORE. Mr. Secretary, I think you have made explicit in your answer to my question what I sought to emphasize. You have cooperated in emphasizing that your concern does not go to the sufficiency of our deterrent forces with the balance which roughly prevails today. You are concerned with the results if the momentum now underway in the Soviet Union is carried forward into the mid-1970 period.

Secretary LAIRD. That is a difficult thing for us to assess at this time. We have only the history of the past 4 or 5 years to go on, and in my statement I have tried to make it clear that our estimates have been on the conservative side.

Senator GORE. I believe it is true now, is it not, that the present force level of Soviet SS-9's, without multiple independently targeted warheads, does not, in fact, pose a serious threat to our present Minuteman force?

Secretary LAIRD. The present level today?

Senator GORE. Yes.

Secretary LAIRD. It poses a threat but it would not have the capability of wiping out our Minuteman force as of today—you are correct.

Senator GORE. To bring this colloquy to a close so that you may proceed, what we are really talking about is your concern and this committee's concern, the concern of the whole country and the Congress over the future. As of now our power and force of deterrence is sufficient.

Secretary LAIRD. That is correct, but I don't want to limit our discussion of the rapid Soviet buildup to the SS-9's, Mr. Chairman. Many people do that because the SS-9 is such a dramatic weapon, since it has such a large warhead and is capable of carrying three reentry vehicles of up to 5 megatons each. But I do not want people to get the idea that we should not be concerned about the Polaris-type submarines being deployed by the Soviet Union, because this force will have a capability to destroy a part of our deterrent force, such as our bomber bases, and that is sometimes overlooked. The rapid buildup of this Polaris-type submarine fleet is something that does concern me when we discuss the possibility of our having a sufficiency of strategic forces in the decade of the 1970's.

Senator GORE. When you were an extremely able member of the House committee and I was serving on the Joint Committee on Atomic Energy, we had some cooperation in the field of developing our own nuclear submarine fleet, so I am well aware of what you say. Will you proceed with your statement?

Secretary LAIRD. Mr. Chairman and members of the committee, it is my responsibility as Secretary of Defense to recommend those programs that are deemed appropriate for preserving our national security and the safety of our people.

RATIONALE UNDERLYING PROPOSED STRATEGIC PROGRAMS

In formulating these recommendations and in presenting our programs to Congress, we have outlined the rationale underlying the strategic programs proposed in the fiscal year 1971 budget.

As I noted in my Defense Report to the Congress and have reiterated elsewhere, we believe that today we do have sufficient forces for deterrence. However, we are very much disturbed by what we have observed about the character and rate of buildup of Soviet strategic forces. Thus, our concern is not about today or even next year. Our concern is about what the future may bring.

What the facts show, Mr. Chairman is that the Soviet Union in the past 5 years, has multiplied its strategic offensive missile launchers from around 300 to about 1,500 a fivefold increase. In the heavy bomber area, the Soviets still have about the same number that they had in 1965—200, of which 50 are configured as tankers.

The United States, by contrast, has made no increase in the force level that was established around 1965 for strategic offensive missile launchers—1,710—and has actually reduced its heavy bomber force in this period by more than 200—from 780 to about 550.

In terms of total force megatonnage, the Soviet Union achieved a fourfold increase during this period. In contrast, the United States has reduced its total force megatonnage by more than 40 percent.

We are concerned about the future because of the momentum in this Soviet buildup. The rapid Soviet buildup in the past 5 years has reached the point where there is reason to wonder what the Soviet goal is. It also raises a serious question in our minds about the future adequacy of our forces. Advances in Soviet deployments and technology could threaten the survivability of our ICBM's and bombers.

Our concern is based on the fact that our restraint in weapons deployments during the past 5 years, and the Soviet buildup in that same period have led to a current situation where we are, in essence, at a crossover point in the strategic balance. What gives this concern urgency is the momentum behind Soviet deployments and developments in major strategic systems that could carry them well beyond the crossover point in a short period of time, unless we take major offsetting actions.

In planning our forces, we also must recognize that the recent launching of a satellite has reinforced our judgment on the potential capability of Communist China's ICBM technology.

In considering whether our forces will be adequate, we cannot assume—no matter how high our hopes—that a SALT agreement will be reached, nor can we know what its provisions might be.

At the same time, we also want to insure that we do not complicate SALT by our own actions.

As President Nixon has said, all U.S. systems are subject to negotiation. But it is even more important for all of us to keep in mind the fact that we do not yet have an agreement that preserves our security.

The problem is simple to formulate, but difficult to solve: we must keep open options that would be appropriate either if an agreement is reached, or if there is no agreement at all. In other words, we must preserve flexibility on strategic programs for any possible outcome:

1. For those programs that will still be required even if there is an agreement.

2. For those programs which we would need relatively soon if agreement is not reached, recognizing that we can stop or modify these programs if agreement is reached.

3. For the research necessary for programs that we might need in the future, regardless of the outcome of SALT.

We have been guided by these considerations in formulating our programs for the forthcoming year.

Most of the recent discussion has focused on our recommendations to proceed during these talks with additional minimal deployment of the Safeguard anti-ballistic-missile program as well as the deployment of the multiple independently targeted reentry vehicles (MIRV's) for Minuteman and Polaris which were previously approved and funded by the Congress.

There are two overriding reasons for our recommending these programs. One concerns the preservation of our deterrent. The other involves our negotiating position in Vienna. Let me say a few words about this latter issue first.

DEFERMENT OF SAFEGUARD AND MIRV DURING SALT

Much argument has been put forward that we should stop the previously scheduled MIRV deployments and defer additional Safeguard deployment at this time, in order to enhance the prospects for a successful agreement.

I do not find this proposal inconsistent with the spirit of strategic arms limitation—but I do believe that it is inconsistent with the purpose of the arms limitation talks, which is to sit down at the table with the Soviet Union and work out an agreement that provides essential security and is acceptable to both sides.

Were we to forgo deployment of the programs deemed necessary for the preservation of our deterrent posture in the absence of a SALT agreement, I believe we would convey to the Soviets the impression that their strategic buildup is tolerable when, in fact, it is a matter of great and growing concern. It would suggest to them that we are prepared to postpone unilaterally and indefinitely these programs, while they continue their deployments with the momentum I have just described.

Senator GORE. Why do you add indefinitely? I don't know that that would necessarily follow.

Secretary LAIRD. Well, I think that that is the conclusion that would be reached if such a unilateral action were taken by the United States before any agreement is reached and before substantial discussions were entered into in the SALT talks, because the other side is not doing that.

Senator GORE. That is a rather long time.

Secretary LAIRD. It could be, Mr. Chairman.

Senator GORE. OK.

Secretary LAIRD. Such a course of action could also encourage the Soviet Union to maintain, and perhaps even accelerate, the pace of those programs. It is apparent that our restraint in not going beyond the level of missile launchers decided upon 5 years ago has not caused the tempo of Soviet strategic deployments to slacken.

It is essential to the conclusion of a mutually acceptable and meaningful agreement that the Soviets be willing to constrain the offensive deployments that could threaten our deterrent. If we were to refrain now from moving to protect our deterrent, the Soviet Union would have achieved a one-sided arms control limitation without agreeing to any constraints on its own forces. I believe that such a prospect would be a most serious reverse incentive to the Soviet Union to negotiate a meaningful agreement.

It has been suggested that, as an alternative, we should propose to the Soviet Union an immediate cessation of MIRV testing and a halt to the deployment of MIRV's and other strategic systems. Virtually everyone endorsing this view has agreed that adequate verification should be provided. But I would point out that this proposal raises such complex questions that negotiating it could be as complicated as the negotiation of a durable and comprehensive agreement.

PRESERVATION OF U.S. STRATEGIC OPTIONS

Turning now to the second reason for proceeding with the modified Safeguard program and the deployment of MIRV's, some have argued that the United States and the Soviet Union both possess an adequate deterrent today. I agree. But I should point out that weapons in inventory which can survive and penetrate today would not necessarily have that capability 5 or 7 years from now. We must insure that these forces cannot ever be eroded to the point where there would be a serious doubt about our capability to retaliate effectively after a surprise attack. In other words, we must guarantee the survival of sufficient forces—under all foreseeable conditions—so that the Soviet Union knows it would be a grave mistake to attack the United States, today or in the future.

I believe there are two ways to achieve such a guarantee, through negotiations and through appropriate force planning and deployments. We are pursuing both paths. Naturally there is a close relationship between the two. I do not believe any of you would view a strategic arms agreement that would place the United States at a disadvantage as acceptable to our security.

The same reasoning is applicable to our strategic programs. As I noted, we must base our planning on the situation that we perceive, since we do not have an arms agreement. Naturally, we have no way of knowing conclusively that the projections of future Soviet strategic weapons deployments which we must consider will, in fact, become a reality. But the momentum that they have established makes it imperative that we preserve our strategic options. The programs that we have recommended and are recommending are designed to preserve the availability of necessary options.

Let me review the two important programs which have received emphasis in the current debate over strategic armaments— Safeguard and MIRV.

UNITED STATES-SOVIET SECURITY INTERESTS AT SALT

Senator GORE. I hesitate to interrupt you. You expressed the view that this committee and the Senate generally would not wish to ratify an agreement which put the United States at a disadvantage. Would you not say that you would not expect the Soviets to conclude an agreement which in their view placed them at a disadvantage?

Secretary LAIRD. I think I made that clear in the earlier part of our dialog and in my prepared statement. This is one of the matters that must be negotiated at the conference table, and I assume that the Soviet Union and the United States would both have this as one of their major objectives.

Senator GORE. A mutual objective.

Secretary LAIRD. The reason that I refer to your committee is that the agreement would be ratified here in the U.S. Senate. I don't believe that this committee or any committee in the Congress, although it would be the Foreign Relations Committee that would have the responsibility, would ratify any kind of an agreement that put the United States at a disadvantage as far as the security of our country is concerned, and I am sure that this would be the case.

Senator GORE. As one member of the committee, I thoroughly agree with you. This is one reason why I believe the committee has felt it so propitious that the strategic arms limitation conference began and why we were so pleased that President Nixon finally succeeded in the initiation of the conference. We had hoped that the delay in deployment of ABM would facilitate the conclusion of an agreement. Obviously, as you have just stated, that is not your view. This is a matter of judgment and disagreement.

Secretary LAIRD. I am talking about unilateral delay as far as the United States is concerned, Mr. Chairman, in view of the fact that the Soviet Union is going forward not only with the ABM, a strategic defensive weapon system, but also with their strategic offensive weapons. So I am referring to a unilateral action on the part of the United States before the matter gets into the serious negotiating stage.

The President of the United States has made it clear that all matters are subject to negotiation as far as SALT is concerned, and I believe that that statement of the President sets forth very clearly the position of our negotiators as they proceed in Vienna.

Senator GORE. Just as this cannot be considered by the United States alone and is a matter of mutuality, I don't think weaponry alone can be considered. The Soviet movement into the Middle East, an ominous development, the building up of their fleet in the Mediterranean, the widening of the war in Southeast Asia on our part, all seem to me to have a bearing.

SOUTH VIETNAMESE—UNITED STATES ACTIVITIES IN LAOS

Would you mind in this context stating to the committee whether or not South Vietnamese ground forces have invaded the boundaries of Laos?

Secretary LAIRD. Mr. Chairman, I will be glad to respond to that. Do you wish me to respond to that question now or at the conclusion of my statement?

Senator GORE. If you please, will you do it now?

Secretary LAIRD. There have been no changes as far as the use of American ground forces in Laos is concerned. There are no penetrations of Laos by U.S. ground combat forces except for what has existed over a period of time. I referred to this a year ago last March, when I had a press conference in Danang. At that time I alluded to the fact that during the A Shau Valley campaign American forces had crossed the Laotian border for a short period as a matter of protective reaction. They were engaged with the enemy, and there had been an incursion into Laos along a highway area in connection with activities of a United States-Vietnamese mission in the A Shau Valley. Our forces in South Vietnam have had that particular authority.

I noted with some interest a report from the Foreign Minister of South Vietnam. I have asked the State Department to provide me the text of the statement which he is said by some members of the press to have been made in connection with the Asian conference. I have not had the text of that statement presented to me. I have the reports made by some of the news services, and by several news columnists, but I want to make it very clear before this committee that there has been no change in our operating rules or rules of engagement as far as the Laotian border is concerned.

Senator GORE. To your knowledge, have the forces of South Vietnam penetrated Laotian territory?

Secretary LAIRD. The forces of South Vietnam have penetrated Laotian territory in the same manner that I outlined as far as U.S. forces are concerned. I have no new knowledge of any penetration other than under protective reaction, which has been used very little as far as Allied forces are concerned on the Ho Chi Minh Trail. There have been no changes in the rules of engagement on the Laotian border. Certainly there have been no changes for the last 6 or 8 months.

Senator GORE. "Protective reaction" is a term of military art which——

Secretary LAIRD. I would like to claim credit for that term, Mr. Chairman, or discredit for it, because it was first used by me at the time of the A Shau Valley campaign. As much as I would like to give military commanders credit for that term, that term happened to be used by a civilian.

Senator GORE. I have always had great respect for your inventive genius. [Laughter.]

HAVE SOUTH VIETNAMESE ENTERED LAOS IN LAST MONTH?

To your knowledge, have the forces of South Vietnam gone into Laos within the last month?

Secretary LAIRD. Not to any substantial degree and not in violation of the rules of operation that have been in existence all during this period of time. Now there may have been protective reaction——

Senator GORE. Excuse me, I didn't ask about any violation.

Secretary LAIRD. The important thing is—the important thing to bear in mind is—that a force engaged in combat or carrying out an operation in the border area quite possibly could have crossed the border when it was engaged in combat. It is necessary, from time to time, as far as the South Vietnamese are concerned, to do that, but I want it made very clear that there has been no change. Their mission is not a ground combat mission or a search-and-destroy mission or anything like that. Their activities are in connection with either a battle that is being carried on at a particular time or the air interdiction campaign or rescue missions that may be carried out on the Ho Chi Minh Trail.

The important thing is, Mr. Chairman, that there has been no change since I outlined this policy to this committee and to the Armed Services Committee in connection with the amendment which the Congress adopted on the 1970 appropriations bill covering funds for the Department of Defense.

I have been one who has been insistent all along that we live up to this particular amendment, and the rules of operations that were in existence at the time this amendment was adopted are the same rules that are being followed today. I think it is most important that we all understand that.

I come from the Congress, and I respect the Congress as a coequal branch of our Government particularly when it comes to the question of funding. This has been a matter which I have watched very carefully, and I can assure you that there have been no changes since I outlined the rules of engagement in detail in a classified meeting before the Armed Services Committee and discussed them in closed session with this particular committee.

RULES OF ENGAGEMENT FOR LAOS

Senator GORE. I am sure that the American people would appreciate hearing you, to the extent that you can do so in public, describe the rules of engagement and, second, whether the rules of engagement are applicable equally and in the same way to U.S. forces and South Vietnamese forces.

Secretary LAIRD. As far as the rules of engagement for Laos are concerned, I would have to paraphrase them. I do not believe it would serve any useful purpose for us to lay on the record the specifics of the rules of engagement. We have never done that before, and I am sure that this committee would not want that done.

Senator GORE. I said insofar as you can.

Secretary LAIRD. The rules of engagement so far as South Vietnamese and U.S. forces located along the border with Laos are concerned are still the same and as you know in the last 12 months we have cut down as far as the U.S. forces are concerned, in I Corps and II Corps so there is a much lesser involvement of Americans along the border area than there was a year ago when I testified. This policy is tied to the protection of the forces that are engaged with the enemy in those areas, and the protection of the friendly forces is the overriding consideration in applying the rules of engagement, which are very specific in this area. There has been no change.

PUBLIC CONCERN OVER WIDENING OF WAR IN INDOCHINA

Senator GORE. I ask these questions in some detail, Mr. Secretary, because I think many of us have been surprised at the extent to which the American people have been shocked by the widening of the war in Indochina. I have been concerned about delivery of mail from my Memphis office to the Washington office. I sent a staff member down to the post office in this building this morning with a complaint. She came back and said the mail is stacked up in the halls and they are a week behind delivering to the offices of Senators. This is mail generated by the Cambodian invasion, and this is why I bring this up. I would hope that you could assure the American people that no further widening of the war has occurred, particularly in view of the fact that the Congress passed an amendment to forbid the use of taxpayers' funds for a ground invasion of Laos.

Secretary LAIRD. I hope that this assurance satisfies you, Mr. Chairman, as well as this committee.

Senator GORE. Let me ask one or two further questions before reaching that conclusion.

AMENDMENT TO 1970 DEFENSE APPROPRIATIONS BILL CONCERNING LAOS

Do you think that the amendment that now is the law prevents the United States from sending ground combat troops into Laos?

Secretary LAIRD. Mr. Chairman, I do not care to get into the constitutional question which is involved. I can only tell you that as far as the Department of Defense is concerned, we have been following the amendment enacted by the Congress, and there has been no change in our operation in Laos concerning the operating rules or any movement of American or South Vietnamese ground combat forces into Laos. We are living under the terms of that amendment, and we have abided by it throughout this particular fiscal year.

Senator GORE. Do you think it prohibits the use of ground troops in Laos?

Secretary LAIRD. The language of the amendment does prohibit by its terms the introduction of American ground combat forces into Laos assigned to that particular mission of combat.

Now, the point I wish to make is that we made that very clear at the time the amendment was enacted. My comments were requested at that time, and I can assure you that there has been no change since I made clear my views last year.

Senator GORE. You know, of course, that a somewhat similar amendment is pending and, therefore, I ask this question about the amendment to which you have just referred, which the President signed, I believe, upon your recommendation. Is that correct?

Secretary LAIRD. That is correct

Senator GORE. Has this amendment endangered the lives of U.S. soldiers in Vietnam?

Secretary LAIRD. Mr. Chairman, this amendment has not endangered the lives of American soldiers in Vietnam because this Congress, in its wisdom, and the executive branch in its wisdom, made it very clear that the application of this amendment would not interfere with the protection of Americans serving in Vietnam.

AMENDMENT CONCERNING CAMBODIA

Senator GORE. If this amendment, when applied to Laos, has not endangered American lives, how can it be said that a similar amendment applied to Cambodia would endanger American lives?

Secretary LAIRD. Well, Mr. Chairman, I am glad to discuss this whole question of the various amendments and types of language that can be applied by the legislative branch. I do feel, however, that the Department of Defense is not the proper department to which the legal aspect of such an amendment should be addressed. That would more properly be addressed to the Department of Justice. As far as the international political effects of such amendments are concerned, I believe that that is more properly addressed to the Department of State. Since I have been Secretary of Defense I have stayed away from getting involved in matters that are properly addressed to other departments, particularly as far as the Department of State is concerned. I can well understand the interest of the legislative branch in the whole question of limitations. I believe that the legislative branch has had a lengthy record in the area of writing limitations. As far as the legal question——

Senator GORE. You had some experience in that regard.

Secretary LAIRD. In connection with prohibitions?

Senator GORE. Yes.

Secretary LAIRD. I think that that is a different question, and I don't believe that the executive branch should necessarily be the advocate of limitation language. I think this is a matter that needs to be worked out very carefully and considered very thoroughly by the Congress and certainly by all in the executive branch.

PROTECTIVE REACTION

Senator GORE. The term that you used, protective reaction, does not include attempts to destroy sanctuaries and supplies. Is that correct?

Secretary LAIRD. As far as sanctuaries and supplies are concerned, American ground combat forces are not used for that purpose in Laos. Protective reaction has not been used for that purpose as far as the Laotian operations are concerned. The protective reaction in Laos to which I am referring has to do with our air interdiction campaign, the rescue of survivors, and also with ongoing combat operations within South Vietnam.

U.S. MILITARY ADVISERS AND SUPPORT FORCES ACCOMPANYING SOUTH VIETNAMESE

Senator GORE. Should the South Vietnamese forces make an attack upon the territory of Laos for the purpose of destroying a sanctuary, would either the U.S. military advisers accompanying such forces or military support forces accompanying and assisting such an attack be in violation of the amendment of last year?

Secretary LAIRD. It would certainly not be in accordance with the spirit of the amendment which was passed by the Congress last year.

Now the question about violations involves a legal question. I do not believe that I am a competent witness on the constitutional or legal interpretation that is involved. It is my understanding the State Department and Justice Department have researched that in some detail, and so when you talk about violations with me as Secretary of Defense, I think it should be in terms of the spirit of the amendment rather than the legal context of the amendment, because I would not wish to get into a constitutional discussion with this committee.

I do not believe that I am the proper witness to handle that question adequately with you today.

RULES OF ENGAGEMENT CONCERNING CAMBODIA AND LAOS

Senator GORE. Before yielding to Senator Fulbright, I wish you would clarify the distinction, if any, between rules of engagement as applied to Cambodia and Laos.

Secretary LAIRD. There is some difference in the manner in which we have used the rules of engagement because of the limitation which we do have on current defense funding. The limitation enacted by the Congress applies to Laos and Thailand, and there are some differences because of the limitation which the Congress has placed upon our funds for fiscal year 1970.

(Secretary Laird's full statement follows.)

STATEMENT OF SECRETARY OF DEFENSE MELVIN R. LAIRD

Mr. Chairman and Members of the Committee: Dr. Foster and I appreciate the opportunity to appear before this Committee to discuss the important Strategic Arms Limitation Talks (SALT) which we are conducting with the Soviet Union and the relationship of United States strategic force programs to these talks.

President Nixon, in his report to the Congress on U.S. Foreign Policy for the 1970's, characterized these talks as "the most important arms control negotiations his country has ever entered."

I want to emphasize that I, as Secretary of Defense, and our military leadership hope that SALT will be successful.

As you know, the purpose of SALT is to determine whether it is possible to find an agreement—acceptable both to the Soviet Union and to the United States—which can improve the security of both countries, reduce the liklihood that nuclear war will occur, and reduce the portion of our national resources devoted to strategic weapons. We believe that it is possible to reach a historic agreement with the Soviet Union on the limitation of strategic arms. We believe such an agreement should be acceptable to the Soviet Union provided the Soviets do, in fact, share our objective of deterrence.

It is my responsibility as Secretary of Defense to recommend those programs that are deemed appropriate for preserving national security. In formulating these recommendations and in presenting our programs to Congress, we have outlined the rationale underlying the strategic programs proposed in the FY 1971 budget.

As I noted in my Defense Report, and have reiterated elsewhere, we believe that today we do have sufficient forces for deterrence. However, we are very much disturbed by what we have observed about the character and rate of buildup of Soviet strategic forces. Thus, our concern is not about today, or even next year. Our concern is about what the future may bring.

What the facts show, Mr. Chairman, is that the Soviet Union in the past five years, has multiplied its strategic offensive missile launchers from around 300 to about 1,500, a five-fold increase. In the heavy bomber area, the Soviets still have about the same number that they had in 1965—200, of which 50 are configured as tankers.

The United States, by contrast, has made no increase in the force level that was established around 1965 for strategic offensive missile launchers—1710—and has actually reduced its heavy bomber force in this period by more than 200—from 780 to about 550.

In terms of total force megatonnage, the Soviet Union achieved a four-fold increase during this period. In contrast, the United States has reduced its total force megatonnage by more than 40%.

We are concerned about the future because of the momentum in this Soviet buildup. The rapid Soviet buildup in the past five years has reached the point where there is reason to wonder what the Soviet goal is. It also raises a serious question in our minds about the future adequacy of our forces. Advances in Soviet deployments and technology could threaten the survivability of our ICBMs and bombers.

Our concern is based on the fact that our restraint in weapons deployments during the past five years, and the Soviet buildup in that same period have led to a current situation where we are, in essence, at a crossover point in the strategic balance. What gives this concern urgency is the momentum behind Soviet deployments and developments in major strategic systems that could carry them well beyond the crossover point in a short period of time, unless we take major offsetting actions.

In planning our forces, we also must recognize that the recent launching of a satellite has reinforced our judgment on the potential capability of Communist China's ICBM technology.

In considering whether our forces will be adequate, we cannot asssume—no matter how high our hopes—that a SALT agreement will be reached, nor can we know what its provisions might be.

At the same time, we also want to insure that we do not complicate SALT by our own actions.

As President Nixon has said, all U.S. systems are subject to negotiation. But it is even more important for all of us to keep in mind the fact that we do not yet have an agreement that preserves our security.

The problem is simple to formulate, but difficult to solve: we must keep open options that would be appropriate either if an agreement is reached, or if there is no agreement at all. In other words, we must preserve flexibility on strategic programs for any possible outcome:

(1) For those programs that will still be required even if there is an agreement.

(2) For those programs which we would need relatively soon if agreement is not reached, recognizing that we can stop or modify these programs if agreement is reached. And—

(3) For the research necessary for programs that we might need in the future, regardless of the outcome of SALT.

We have been guided by these considerations in formulating our programs for the forthcoming year.

Most of the recent discussion has focused on our recommendations to proceed during these talks with additional minimal deployment of the SAFEGUARD Anti-Ballistic Missile program as well as deployment of the Multiple Independently-targetable Re-entry Vehicles (MIRVs) for MINUTEMAN and POLARIS which were previously approved and funded by the Congress.

There are two overriding reasons for our recommending these programs. One concerns the preservation of our deterrent. The other involves our negotiation position in Vienna. Let me say a few words about this latter issue first.

Much argument has been put forward that we should stop the previously-scheduled MIRV deployments and defer additional SAFEGUARD deployment at this time, in order to enhance the prospects for a successful agreement.

I do not find this proposal inconsistent with the *spirit* of strategic arms limitation—but I do believe that it is inconsistent with the *purpose* of the arms limitation *talks*, which is to sit down at the table with the Soviet Union and work out an agreement that provides essential security and is acceptable to both sides.

Were we to forego deployment of the programs deemed necessary for the preservation of our deterrent posture in the absence of a SALT agreement, I believe we would convey to the Soviets the impression that their strategic buildup is tolerable—when, in fact, it is a matter of great and growing concern. It would suggest to them that we are prepared to postpone unilaterally and indefinitely these programs, while they continue their deployments with the momentum I have just described.

Such a course of action could also encourage the Soviet Union to maintain, and perhaps even accelerate, the pace of those programs. It is apparent that our restraint in not going beyond the level of missile launchers decided upon five years ago has not caused the tempo of Soviet strategic deployments to slacken.

It is essential to the conclusion of a mutually acceptable and meaningful agreement that the Soviets be willing to constrain the offensive deployments that could threaten our deterrent. If we were to refrain now from moving to protect our deterrent, the Soviet Union would have achieved a one-sided arms control limitation without agreeing to any constraints on its own forces. I believe that such a prospect would be a most serious reverse incentive to the Soviets to negotiate a meaningful agreement.

It has been suggested that, as an alternative, we should propose to the Soviet Union an immediate cessation of MIRV testing and a halt to the deployment of MIRVs and other strategic systems. Virtually everyone endorsing this view has agreed that adequate verification should be provided. But I would point out that this proposal raises such complex questions that negotiating it could be as complicated as the negotiation of a durable and comprehensive agreement.

Turning now to the second reason for proceeding with the modified SAFEGUARD program and the deployment of MIRVs, some have argued that the United States and the Soviet Union both possess an adequate deterrent today. I agree. But I should point out that weapons in inventory which can survive and penetrate today would not necessarily have that capability five or seven years from now. We must ensure that these forces cannot ever be eroded to the point where there would be serious doubt about our capability to retaliate effectively after a surprise attack. In other words, we must guarantee the survival of sufficient forces—under all foreseeable conditions—so that the Soviet Union knows it would be a grave mistake to attack the United States, today or in the future.

I believe there are two ways to achieve such a guarantee, through negotiations, and through appropriate force planning and deployments. We are pursuing both paths. Naturally, there is a close relationship between the two. I do not believe any of you would view a strategic arms agreement that would place the United States at a disadvantage as acceptable to our security.

The same reasoning is applicable to our strategic programs. As I noted, we must base our planning on the situation that we perceive, since we do not have an arms agreement. Naturally, we have no way of knowing conclusively that the projections of future Soviet strategic weapons deployments which we must consider will, in fact, become a reality. But the momentum they have established makes it imperative that we preserve our strategic options. The programs that we have recommended and are recommending are designed to preserve the availability of necessary options.

Let me review the two important programs which have received emphasis in the current debate over strategic armaments—SAFEGUARD and MIRV.

In this transitional budget year, the modified Phase 2 SAFEGUARD program is the only additional step we are recommending to preserve the survivability of our land-based deterrent. We chose this course in order to avoid the necessity this year of either adding to our offensive potential, or taking other steps which would complicate the problems of arms control. The suggestions made last year that we either increase our offensive forces or assume a posture of "launch-on-warning" are examples in the first case of the hard and difficult decisions the Fiscal Year 1971 program is designed to postpone, and, in the second case, of a situation which no President would want to face as the only course of action available in an impending crisis.

SAFEGUARD is not provocative to the Soviet Union. It does not threaten the Soviets' offensive forces in any way if their objective is deterrence. It clearly does not provide a heavy defense of our cities.

SAFEGUARD is designed to provide us the options to fulfill any or all of several objectives, including: to preserve the survivability of our land-based deterrent forces, to defend against the potential ICBM threat from China, and to defend against accidental launches from any source.

If there is a SALT agreement, it could be consistent with the deployment of SAFEGUARD.

If a SALT agreement precluded any ABM's, then we could halt the deployment or dismantle the SAFEGUARD components. If we did, we would have to regard SAFEGUARD as money well spent, since it may have encouraged agreement at SALT. In any case, its continuation today is necessary insurance that we must have.

This is true because if there is no SALT agreement and we did not have the SAFEGUARD deployment or some other offsetting action underway, we would have lost the lead time necessary to counter effectively the growing Soviet threat to our land-based deterrent forces.

Turning now to the other strategic program of importance, we are continuing the previously approved program of deploying MIRV's for POSEIDON and MINUTEMAN for two reasons:

1. To make sure that an adequate deterrent survives in the face of the increasing vulnerability of MINUTEMAN and bombers to the Soviet strategic threat.

2. To insure that our surviving retaliatory forces can penetrate Soviet defenses in the future.

In designing our MIRV programs we could have chosen to use our technology to develop a very major increase in our hard target kill capability, thus giving the Soviet Union grounds for anxiety about whether our intentions included preparation for a major counterforce capability. We have not followed this path but have instead used the technology to enhance our ability to penetrate Soviet ABM defenses and to cover soft retaliatory targets with fewer surviving U.S. missiles. Thus, our scheduled MIRV deployment is designed to preserve our deterrent in the least threatening way in the face of growing Soviet offensive and defensive capabilities.

If we did not plan on actions to offset the expanding threat—I would, as Secretary of Defense, have to face the possibility that, in the mid-to-late 1970's, we might no longer be able to rely on either the Bomber or MINUTEMAN force to survive a surprise attack. In such a situation, without MIRV, we would be left with only the POLARIS deterrent force in our strategic arsenal for high-confidence retaliatory purposes.

Many people overlook the fact that a very large percentage of our retaliatory power (measured in terms of both warheads and megatons) is carried by our bombers and land-based missile forces. As I noted in the Defense Report, we have some 4200 strategic nuclear weapons in our strategic force today. Only about 15% of those weapons are carried by the POLARIS SLBM force, while about 60% of them are carried by our bombers and 25% by our ICBM's.

If we permit our ICBM and bomber forces to become highly vulnerable to a surprise attack by the mid-to-late 1970's, we would be faced with the prospect of relying on the submarines at sea and on alert—carrying even less than 15% of our strategic weapons—for retaliation with high confidence.

We are fully confident that the SLBM force at sea is invulnerable to surprise attack today and should remain so for the next five to seven years and hopefully longer. But is that fraction of the force which is at sea and on alert enough—is that posture sufficient—to insure that the Soviet Union would be deterred? I do not believe that we can afford to take this kind of a risk with our national security. The MIRV deployments provide an essential increase in targeting flexibility to offset the growing vulnerability of our land-based retaliatory forces, which is one of the major reasons for continuing these previously scheduled MIRV deployments.

Compounding this problem is the Soviet Union's activities in the anti-ballistic missile field. In order to be confident in our deterrent, we must insure not only that enough retaliatory weapons are left after a Soviet first strike, but also that they are able to reach their target. An extensive ABM capability on the part of the Soviet Union could greatly reduce our confidence in our penetration capability.

By the mid-to-late 1970's Soviet strategic air defenses and missile defenses could be quite formidable. In addition to the extensive air defense capability they already possess, the Soviets are pursuing a vigorous anti-ballistic missile research and development program designed to improve the present operational system or to develop substantially better second-generation ABM components.

You all know that with regard to ABM defenses, long-lead items are the acquisition and tracking radars. For a decade now, the Soviets have been deploying a system of such radars. As I noted in my Defense Report, "The Soviets probably have a number of these early warning radars either operating or under construction, and as such are expanding their surveillance coverage to include most of the areas that are of concern to them." In addition to the Moscow ABM system, the Soviets have deployed a very extensive, sophisticated air defense system across the approaches to Western Russia. We cannot rule out the possibility that the Soviets have given or will give this system, called the SA-5 or TALLINN system, an ABM role. We believe such a role is technically feasible for this system. This is a problem of particular concern because of the extent of the TALLINN deployment—over 1,000 interceptor missile launchers.

Turning now to possible arms limitation agreements, if a SALT agreement were concluded which banned MIRVs, we would, of course, be prepared to honor it. I think we can all agree that such an agreement would have to include acceptable verification provisions.

If no SALT agreement were reached, and we do not deploy MIRVs on schedule, we will have lost the lead times necessary to counter potential Soviet defenses and the future threats to the survivability of our offensive forces.

To summarize, Mr. Chairman, I would like to note that, in the past fifteen months:

We have not accelerated the planned deployment of offensive systems, but have actually slowed it down.

We have slowed down the previously approved ABM deployment plan, keyed it to the emerging threat, and reoriented this system to provide more timely protection for our land-based deterrent forces.

In short, Mr. Chairman, as I pointed out in my Defense Report, we are seeking every opportunity to enhance the possibility of achieving an agreement and avoid exacerbating the arms race—by deferring decisions, taking minimal steps, and deliberately accepting some increased risk. We could have recommended a considerably expanded strategic forces program for the forthcoming year. I believe there are many who would view such a recommendation as appropriate, in light of the Soviet and Chinese Communist programs.

We have not done so. Neither have we recommended that the United States unilaterally defer or abandon those programs that are deemed appropriate, in the absence of a safeguarded agreement, to preserve our future security.

We strongly believe that the proper place to deliberate these complex issues is at the conference table with the Soviet Union. These talks are in progress. We cannot foresee the outcome, but let me reiterate that we hope for success—for an agreement that preserves our security and permits a continued deferral of those hard choices that we face with regard to new strategic programs.

Mr. Chairman, we are concerned about the momentum evident in the strategic programs of the Soviet Union, and the implications of that momentum for the strategic balance in the future. We are also quite conscious of the Communist Chinese strategic weapons program—and of the recent demonstration of Chinese competence.

These strategic issues are complex, and are not susceptible to simple, easily agreed solutions. We cannot guarantee that our approach is precisely right—that the modest program we are recommending will not be too little or too much for the future. But I believe that it is a responsible program, consistent with our security, and entirely appropriate to preserve our options in this transitional year, pending further developments in the strategic situation.

In summary, let me recall that two of the three principles President Nixon deems essential for peace are strength and a willingness to negotiate. We are serious in searching for a stable and lasting peace. We are serious in our willingness to negotiate. We are negotiating now in Vienna. As the President noted on May 8th, he believes we will be successful in negotiating an agreement.

But we are also serious about maintaining our strength. Without this element, without preserving our strength, there would be no need—no incentive—for the other side to negotiate. And I do not believe that prospect would enhance the possibilities for achieving the durable peace that we all desire. That is why we feel it is essential to continue those programs and options designed to preserve our strength, while at the same time pursuing at the negotiating table our search for an early and effective strategic arms limitation agreement.

Senator GORE. Senator Fulbright.

CONTRAST IN INTEREST IN PUBLIC HEARINGS

Senator FULBRIGHT. Mr. Secretary, I welcome you once more before this committee. Your testimony is always most interesting. I must say it is quite remarkable what a tremendous appeal you have for the television media and the press. They apparently cannot take enough pictures and I am sure every single syllable that you say today will be reported. [Laughter.]

It is a remarkable contrast between the interest in the testimony of today and several hearings we have recently had involving three outstanding business leaders and economists, three very distinguished religious and moral leaders, and General Gavin, one of the most distinguished generals that we have produced in modern days, an adviser of President Eisenhower and General Ridgway. All three hearings didn't attract any attention whatsover. So I congratulate you. If you haven't anything else, you have the attention of the country and the press.

I am unable to evaluate this apparent obsession with the instruments of destruction and death which we are discussing here today with regard to the SALT talks and the indifference to the informed discussion of how and why we might bring the war to an end. I don't know why there is such a lack of interest in the discussions of the other matter.

Anyway it is a remarkable demonstration of your own appeal to the public.

Secretary LAIRD. Well, I will not comment on that.

Senator FULBRIGHT. You are one of the most experienced and distinguished practitioners of the art of politics. How would you explain it, as a politician and not a Secretary of Defense? You used to be up here and shared this same role with us in the hearings. That is one reason I am always very interested in your comments and your points of view on these matters because you haven't yet completely forgotten your experience as a Congressman. Have you?

Secretary LAIRD. No, and I think about it every day. [Laughter.]

Senator FULBRIGHT. I hope with a little nostalgia.

WAS SALT CONSIDERED IN DECISION ON CAMBODIA?

Mr. Secretary, do you believe that the expansion of the war into Cambodia, and apparently into Laos, will affect the talks in Vienna?

Secretary LAIRD. I didn't quite follow that.

Senator FULBRIGHT. Let me put it another way. In making the decision to enter Cambodia, which the Administration did a few days ago, was the effect upon the SALT talks seriously considered and evaluated? The SALT talks——

Secretary LAIRD. Chairman Fulbright, I want you to know that as far as the decisionmaking process, the National Security Council, and the discussion of the President of the United States are concerned, before the decision was made to destroy facilities and supplies in the sanctuary areas in Cambodia occupied by the North Vietnamese, every effort was made to discuss all ramifications of this very important decision. I can assure you that in those discussions, which were very exhaustive, not only the effect upon SALT, the Middle East situation and the importance of maintaining the strategic balance, but also the effect upon the Vietnamization program and upon the possibility of increasing future withdrawals of American forces from Vietnam and reducing American casualties in the latter part of this calendar year, as well as the effect upon American public opinion—all of those matters—were very thoroughly and carefully discussed in many meetings with the President of the United States.

I can assure you that I support the decision of the President of the United States and the Secretary of State supports the decision of the President of the United States. The decisionmaking process was very, I think, well handled, and a complete discussion was held by the President of the United States before this decision was made.

Senator FULBRIGHT. Mr. Secretary, this particular aspect is not new. All throughout the Johnson administration, not once at any meeting that I ever attended did we find that the Administration was in disagreement. They were always unanimous. We never went to a briefing in the Cabinet room, and I am sure you went to them, and heard President Johnson say "the Secretary of State is in agreement but the Secretary of Defense and the CIA disagree." That is utterly meaningless. Of course, you get to that agreement. You have to. I don't criticize you. I am not suggesting you can operate any other way, but that is not what I am getting at. If you are able to say if you did consider the probable effect on the Vienna talks, how did you assess that? Did you believe then that it would have no serious effect upon them? First, did you believe that?

Secretary LAIRD. The overriding concerns which dictated the decision that was made, were, firstly, insuring the success of the Vietnamization program, and, secondly, insuring future withdrawals of American forces from Vietnam, and thirdly, reducing of American casualties.

Now there were many other matters that were discussed.

Senator FULBRIGHT. I don't think that is responsive. I am not able to make my position clear.

Secretary LAIRD. But the decision was based upon those three major considerations. Now there were other considerations, but each time another consideration is discussed, in the minds of some individuals becomes the major consideration. That is why, when you ask about the other things that were discussed in the decisionmaking process, I want to make it very clear that the major considerations were Vietnamization, withdrawals of American forces, and the reduction of American casualties as we went on down the road to secure our objectives in South Vietnam.

POSSIBLE EFFECT ON SALT OF CAMBODIAN ACTIVITIES

Senator FULBRIGHT. That is not what I am asking you about. You know I am not asking you about that. If you don't care to answer it, that is your privilege, but I asked you about the effect on the talks in Vienna. You have set great store by them. I have and others have. In these deliberations, did you believe that this would have no ill effects at all on those talks or that if there were ill effects they would be overweighed by these other considerations?

Secretary LAIRD. Well, first, I do not believe that it will have a substantial effect as far as the SALT talks——

Senator FULBRIGHT. You don't believe it will have.

Secretary LAIRD (continuing). Are concerned. But even if I had reached another conclusion, I believe that the reasons for the move to destroy the sanctuary areas and the facilities would override that concern, but I do not believe it will have an effect upon the SALT talks.

Senator FULBRIGHT. All right.

How do you interpret Premier Kosygin's press conference? It was the first he had held, I believe, in the 5 years since he had been made Premier, wasn't it? He called it apparently for a specific purpose. Do you discount that as being of no consequence?

Secretary LAIRD. No, I do not discount it——

Senator FULBRIGHT. How do you interpret it?

Secretary LAIRD. I do not discount the press conference.

Senator FULBRIGHT. Don't you think it is a serious matter?

Secretary LAIRD. But I believe that the press conference reaction was not the reaction that some had anticipated. I believe that it was restrained comment as far as——

Senator FULBRIGHT. Was it more restrained than you had anticipated or less?

Secretary LAIRD. Well, I was testifying at the time, and——

Senator FULBRIGHT. At the time of what?

Secretary LAIRD. I was asked—before another committee of the Congress, at that time in executive session—to predict what the press conference would cover, and I outlined off the record the press conference at that time in about the same terms that it finally appeared within about 15 or 20 minutes on the ticker.

Senator FULBRIGHT. So you are quite prepared to live with that. You don't think it endangers the success of the talks.

Secretary LAIRD. I do not.

U.S. REACTION TO EXPANSION OF WAR

Senator FULBRIGHT. Was your judgment also vindicated with regard to the reaction here at home; that is, in the Congress and among the population, including young people as well as old? Did you estimate that accurately too?

Secretary LAIRD. I did not estimate that as accurately as perhaps I should have as a politician.

Senator FULBRIGHT. This is your forte.

Secretary LAIRD. I did estimate that there would be certain domestic problems involved with a major decision along this line. But I don't think that anyone could anticipate the situation at Kent State

University or some of the other developments that occurred. So I would be less than frank with you if I said that I anticipated the Kent State University tragedy or the follow-on at several other universities and the other student confrontations that have taken place since the tragedy at Kent State.

Senator FULBRIGHT. They are not all students. As I recall, they were not students in Augusta, Ga. It is both, I think. I wonder how——

Secretary LAIRD. However, I do feel, Senator Fulbright, that the support for the President of the United States is very strong in this country, and I believe there is no question but that currently a majority of the American people support the President of the United States. I support him fully and I am sure a majority of the American people do also.

DISTINCTION BETWEEN SUPPORTING PRESIDENT AND SUPPORTING A POLICY

Senator FULBRIGHT. Mr. Secretary, that is not quite the problem. It is traditional that you support the President if you put it in that term. I think there is a distinction between supporting the President and supporting a specific policy. You don't want us to believe that all the people of the country support every single idea and project and movement of this or any other President. You wouldn't want to say that?

Secretary LAIRD. I believe, however, that a majority of the American people——

Senator FULBRIGHT. You mean Cambodia?

Secretary LAIRD (continuing). Do support the President's desire to destroy the sanctuaries occupied by the North Vietnamese——

Senator FULBRIGHT. His desires are not the question.

Secretary LAIRD (continuing). In Cambodia.

Senator FULBRIGHT. That is not the question at issue. We all support his desires to get the war over, but we question most profoundly the appropriateness of the means he is taking to achieve that end. This is the issue. It is not that we don't support the President or we don't support his desires for peace or his desires for tranquility and health and good will and all of that.

You evade the issue. The issue is are these means that he is taking reasonably designed to achieve those ends upon which we all agree. To say the American people support the President—we all do that. We are trying to help him whether you know it or not. That is what the committee is for. It is its constitutional responsibility to try to find the best means to achieve those agreed-upon goals.

That is all there is.

I believe and all of this committee, I think, believes very profoundly that the SALT talks are a great opportunity and we would be very disturbed to take another line such as invading Cambodia if it endangers the success of the SALT talks.

If I had to weigh those two things in the balance and say that one or the other was more important to the saving of the lives of not only the soldiers now in Vietnam but of all the prospective soldiers and, in fact, all the people in this country, I would certainly come down on the side of the SALT talks against going into the Parrot's Beak or the Fishhook area. I think that these are the very judgments that are at issue. It isn't because we in any way don't support the President as an office and as an official, but certainly it is not only legitimate, it is our duty to question the judgment upon individual means that are taken to achieve our ultimate and our common goals.

I think it is regrettable that the Russians have expressed great dismay. They have stated it has aroused a serious question in their minds about the seriousness of the United States at Vienna. That is about the way Premier Kosygin put it. These people are restrained; they are experienced diplomats. They don't talk as bluntly as some of us do, but I think it is a very serious matter. You say you considered it. You realized that there would be some reaction, but on balance you resolved it in favor of Cambodia.

Now on the Chinese, did——

RESPONSIBILITIES AND INFLUENCE OF SECRETARY OF DEFENSE

Secretary LAIRD. Mr. Chairman, I think that it would be perfectly proper for me to comment as Secretary of Defense——

Senator FULBRIGHT. Yes.

Secretary LAIRD (continuing). On the question which you raise. As Secretary of Defense I have certain responsibilities to the forces assigned in Vietnam, the military forces which are there, and for their protection and the Vietnamization program. I am concerned about the fact that we are embarked upon a very important program to withdraw Americans from that area of the world, and the fact that during the last 12 months we have withdrawn over a hundred thousand and we have announced that 150,000 more will be withdrawn within the next 12-month period. These matters are of major concern to me. Now, it is true that the other foreign policy questions have a very major bearing on certain military decisions. But I think that as Secretary of Defense my primary responsibility must be to the military men who have been assigned in Vietnam, not only the military men who are there but also those who have been taken prisoner. This is my interest and my concern, and my advice might be somewhat different from the advice of, say, the Secretary of State or the Foreign Relations Committee, because as Secretary of Defense I do feel a personal responsibility to the American men assigned to carry on this very important and difficult combat responsibility.

Senator FULBRIGHT. I recognize that you have that relationship, but I am bound to say that on this question of the talks in Vienna you also, in my opinion, are the primary influence. You and your associates were the principal actors, I would say, in the struggle last year on the ABM. I believe that the deployment of the MIRV and the prosecution of the ABM are of first importance to whether or not SALT talks will be successful.

In other words, you are too modest. Your responsibility or your influence is, I think, as great in the success of the SALT talks as in Vietnam.

If you proceed with the MIRV, many people, a lot of them more wise and experienced than I, believe that this will be a very serious blow to the success of the SALT talks.

You can't disassociate yourself from your influence. Here I am talking about what you symbolize in your position, as head of this tremendous Military Establishment with millions of people under you, and some of the most effective, most persuasive advocates of these programs. You undoubtedly have that effect. I mean there is no question about it and I think everybody understands that.

If you don't feel equal responsibility to the success of the SALT talks as you do to the success of the venture into Cambodia, I think we are in a very serious predicament because who else has equal importance or significance to the success of the SALT talks. You are represented there. You have your representatives. That is generals and former generals, and former members of the Defense Department officials are there. In fact I think they predominate and I am not complaining about it. I only point it out that you can't disassociate yourself from the responsibility there.

Secretary LAIRD. We are doing everything we can for the success of SALT. In my statement today I have tried to set that forth as clearly and as concisely as I possibly can.

Senator FULBRIGHT. I gathered from your previous answer that you felt your primary responsibility was the soldiers now in Vietnam, and the responsibility for SALT was of a secondary nature compared to that. I thought you suggested that the Secretary of State may have that responsibility. I mean no reflection upon the Department of State or the Secretary. I think it is just a fact of life. The thing that has attracted most attention is the proposed and up to now, I suppose, continuing deployment or your plans to deploy MIRV and to build ABM. Of course, everyone has to look at his responsibilities in light of his own conscience and his own knowledge, but I think you have the responsibility to make SALT talks succeed or at least not put anything in the way of them. I am very dubious about the venture into Cambodia as well as the deployment of MIRV. Both seem great obstacles to success at SALT. Goodness knows, I hope I am wrong about that.

EFFECT OF ACTIVITIES IN CAMBODIA ON CHINESE

May I ask about the Chinese? Did you consider the probable effect upon the Chinese of the enlargement of the war into Cambodia and how apparently according to the press, into Laos, with or without our ground forces? Has this been thoroughly evaluated?

I think it is a very serious matter.

Secretary LAIRD. Senator, I want to make it very clear that the decisionmaking process was a very thorough one and all of these matters were thoroughly considered.

Senator FULBRIGHT. Is it fair to assume that after thorough consideration you decided that the enlargement of the war will not tempt or provoke, or however one wants to put it, the entry of the Chinese army into this war as they did into the Korean war?

Secretary LAIRD. Senator Fulbright——

Senator FULBRIGHT. Is that the conclusion?

Secretary LAIRD (continuing). The various risks were assessed and the decision was made in favor of destroying the facilities, supplies and sanctuary areas, after these various other factors were weighed.

Senator FULBRIGHT. I think you put it on too narrow a base. You know very well and the press has already stated that Mr. Ky, I think, and Mr. Lon Nol, and various others have made statements in the last few days to the effect that whether or not the Americans stay in Cambodia they are going to stay. They intend to stay, and they are moving, according to the press, into Laos.

They are our clients. They couldn't do any of these things without our money, our supplies, our advice, our weapons and everything else. I wondered what your conclusion is about the Chinese. What worries us is that in the Korean affair the Government was convinced the Chinese wouldn't enter and, of course, they did.

It seems to me it would be a very serious matter if the Chinese decided to enter this war with massive manpower. If a million Chinese should enter the war, I think our men would be exposed to far greater than anything they were exposed to from the Parrot's Beak. Doesn't this concern you?

U.S. INVOLVEMENT IN SANCTUARY AREA

Secretary LAIRD. Mr. Chairman, the operation in the sanctuary area is a very limited operation. The United States will be involved in the destruction of facilities, supplies, logistics support in the time period up through June 30. The President has announced the termination of American involvement as of June 30, of the effort to destroy the sanctuary areas and to uncover the munitions and supplies as well as the facilities in those areas.

We have already started withdrawing Americans from the sanctuary operation.

I can assure you that the dates outlined by the President of the United States will be met by the Department of Defense and by our Armed Forces that are engaged in these operations.

Senator FULBRIGHT. As you know, the Senate is endeavoring to assist him in this determination. We hope to have a vote before the week is over.

Last, and I apologize——

Secretary LAIRD. I would like to make it clear that, whether or not the Senate assists in this area, the timetables established by the President of the United States will be met.

Senator FULBRIGHT. I hope so.

The last question——

CREDIBILITY OF WAR EFFORT IN SOUTHEAST ASIA

Secretary LAIRD. I think it is important, Mr. Chairman, to remind this committee, as I did when I appeared last year on the Vietnamization program, that I fully understood the questions regarding credibility of the war effort in Southeast Asia.

My position has been that if there was one thing I did as Secretary of Defense, it would be to restore the credibility of the Department of Defense as far as our announcements on the war in Southeast Asia are concerned. Every statement, every projection, and every forecast on troop reductions and any other operation in Southeast Asia and Vietnam, has been met.

We will continue to meet those commitments that we have given to the Congress and the American people.

I think it has been important for us to have a public discussion of the operations in Laos, the operations in Cambodia, and the operations in Vietnam. Never before in the history of this conflict in Southeast Asia have the American people had so much information about this conflict, and I think it is important that we give them this information. I also think it is very important that the statements, projections and forecasts which we make, be met, and they will be met.

COMMITTEE WAS NOT CONSULTED ON CAMBODIAN OPERATION

Senator FULBRIGHT. Mr. Secretary, you prompt me to make an observation to set the record straight. I can assure you that this committee hadn't the slightest idea that you were going to move into Cambodia before you did. We certainly weren't consulted in any respect. I think I was present at all the meetings. Unless you surreptitiously spoke to some individual member, no one in the Administration informed us or asked our views or anything else until it was all done and the commitment made.

I don't want the record to show there was a full and free discussion before the fact because there was not.

Secretary LAIRD. Well, Senator Fulbright, as you know and as I know, we have had discussions of the sanctuary problem over a period of time. This is not a problem that was unfamiliar to you or to the members of this committee.

Senator FULBRIGHT. No, but I had no idea you were contemplating invading Cambodia and the sanctuaries. I don't believe anyone did. They can speak for themselves; I will have to speak for myself. True, we knew the sanctuaries had been there for 4 or 5 years and we also know there was no substantial change in the status of the sanctuaries in the last 6 months. Why you suddenly decided to move into them is beyond me, but I don't want to delay. Did you tell any Senator of this ahead of time?

I didn't know anything about it ahead of time. I don't know who you had in mind, but perhaps you did. Did you tell any Senator?

Secretary LAIRD. Mr. Chairman, as far as discussions of this operation with Members of Congress are concerned, of course, we had had discussions before the Armed Services Committee as well as the Appropriations Committee about the sanctuary threat on several occasions. From time to time there have been Members of Congress who have discussed the sanctuary problem and recommended that something be done about it.

I think Senator Gore has made certain statements suggesting that the sanctuary problem is one that exists and that we should hit them. But as far as the operating orders for the operation itself are concerned, this was not a matter that I discussed individually with Members of the Senate.

REACTION AT PARIS PEACE TALKS TO ACTIVITIES IN CAMBODIA

Senator FULBRIGHT. I want to end this by asking one other question. Did you anticipate the reaction at the Paris Peace Talks? Are you perfectly reconciled to accepting the suspension of the Paris Peace Talks as a part of the price for going into Cambodia?

Secretary LAIRD. Every aspect of this decision was discussed in great detail by the National Security Council, the principals——
Senator FULBRIGHT. I understood that.
Secretary LAIRD. The principals in the National Security Council and the President of the United States.
Senator FULBRIGHT. Did you anticipate the talks in Paris would be suspended and say that is another part of the price you were willing to pay?
Secretary LAIRD. I certainly don't want to give you the impression that this matter was not carefully considered. It was.
Senator FULBRIGHT. It was.
Secretary LAIRD. The talks are, however, going forward in Paris.
Senator FULBRIGHT. That is the common understanding, that they are going forward. They are at a complete stalemate and have been for a long time. They are going nowhere.
Secretary LAIRD. They had been for some time, Senator.
Senator FULBRIGHT. They are going nowhere.
Secretary LAIRD. I am, of course, as much interested in the progress of negotiations as anyone. But I would just like to say that as of today there has been no substantial change as far as Paris is concerned.
Senator FULBRIGHT. Surely the report that you believed going into Cambodia would enhance the prospects of negotiated peace at Paris wasn't true, was it? It was reported——
Secretary LAIRD. My primary concern and my recommendations were based upon progress in the Vietnamization program, the possibility of increasing future withdrawals of American forces from Vietnam, and the very solid feel I had that we would be able to reduce American casualties in the third and fourth quarter of this calendar year.
Senator FULBRIGHT. I appreciate your reiterating that sentiment; but that isn't really what I asked you at all. You don't really believe that this invasion in Cambodia will enhance the prospects of the negotiated settlement in Paris, do you?
Secretary LAIRD. Well——
Senator FULBRIGHT. That has been reported.
Secretary LAIRD. I believe that the negotiations in Paris will move forward as soon as the other side decides to go forward and have open and free negotiations there. We have made our position very clear; the President has set it forth on several occasions. If the determination of the United States to pursue the Vietnamization program is thrown into open question, there may be some difficulties in negotiations, but I do not believe Hanoi will misread the determination of the United States.

EXTENT OF QUESTIONING OF WITNESS

Senator FULBRIGHT. I want to close by saying, Mr. Secretary, that I realize you may think it unfair that we expect answers to questions that are not directly and traditionally within the jurisdiction of your department, and there is your attitude that you have reported to other committees, which you consider the appropriate ones, and you didn't think it appropriate to come to this committee. I only want to raise the caveat that——
Secretary LAIRD. Senator Fulbright, I would like to make one thing clear. I enjoy coming before your committee. [Laughter.]

Senator FULBRIGHT. Why do you deprive yourself of this pleasure? Why don't you come more often?

Secretary LAIRD. We had only one difficulty. The only time I couldn't come before this committee was on certain dates when I was asked to come and I had a conflict. But I have talked to you, I have talked to Senator Gore, I have talked to Senator Aiken, and I have talked to Senator Symington. I am delighted to have this opportunity to appear before this distinguished committee, and I do not object to appearing in open session or in any other kind of session. The only problem is that I do appear up here on Capitol Hill more than any other Cabinet officer. As a matter of fact, I spend about twice as much time up here, and there was a conflict on the particular date when Senator Gore first asked me to be here. But I don't want any misunderstanding about this, because I am delighted to be with you today. [Laughter.]

Senator FULBRIGHT. I am delighted too. [Laughter.]

SIZE AND INFLUENCE OF DEFENSE DEPARTMENT

This request was made a long time ago, but I didn't intend to make that point. You say you have been on the Hill more than anyone else. In a sense you fortify the point I was going to make, which is that because of the enormous and unprecedented growth in the size and influence of the Department which you head, the traditional relationship between other agencies and this committee and the Senate has altered. This is a recognition of a fact of life. The fact of life is that the tremendous power in this establishment of this country is under your direction.

Secretary LAIRD. Well, I appreciate your recognition.

Senator FULBRIGHT. The size and scope of the Department of Defense and the Military Establishment simply dwarf the State Department. The State Department wouldn't occupy either financially or otherwise one of the innumerable bureaus that you have in the Department of Defense. It is in recognition of that. We are not seeking to cause you trouble. It is simply that you represent the determining factor in such things as the success of the SALT talks, and whether or not we move into Cambodia or enlarge the war into all of Asia. This is why we are interested in talking to you. We are seeking to play our constitutional role, which is to influence the course of events in this area, and you are the man to talk to. That is the way it looks.

The Defense Department is overwhelmingly the greatest power in this country, barring none. I know of hardly any combination of power that can equal it from the point of view of the resources and manpower it controls. This is the reason why you appear and we expect you to appear. Otherwise we are completely out of touch with the influences which guide this country, and about which, I may say, we are all very apprehensive.

I must say the sentiments of assurance of the stability and tranquility of the country announced within the last few days by such other leading figures as the Attorney General and the Vice President are very disturbing to me. I think there is a misreading of the temper and mood of the country. You being a very successful practitioner of the art of politics are probably much more attuned to the mood of the country than most of your colleagues. Therefore, we expect a lot more of you.

Maybe that is the reason you are so popular up here. [Laughter.]

Thank you very much.

WITNESS' RELATIONSHIP WITH CONGRESS

Secretary LAIRD. Mr. Chairman, I would just want to make it very clear that I am delighted to have the opportunity to be before this committee. I have tried to be as forthcoming and candid with this committee in the last 16 months as I believe any Secretary of Defense has in the history of the Department. I think we have had very good working relationships, and I hope to continue that kind of relationship with this committee. I don't let a few things pass as a witness here because I have learned, having sat on that side of the table, that perhaps I should not challenge certain of your statements such as when you say that the United States has invaded Cambodia. I, of course, don't agree with that. When you say that the United States has widened the war, I don't agree with that. But I understand the difference between being a witness and being a questioner.

As I said the first time I appeared before this committee, I enjoyed asking questions much better than I do answering questions, but I do enjoy being up here on the Hill. I have some 12 committees now that I answer to in the Congress, and I think the relationship that I have tried to maintain with each of those committees has been a good one.

Senator FULBRIGHT. That reflects what I was just saying. You are the man that they all want to hear speak because hopefully we might influence our Government one way or another.

Mr. Kissinger, you know, doesn't come. He doesn't come before the committee.

REPUBLICAN SENATE CONFERENCE

By the way, could I ask if Mr. Kissinger accompanied you to a Republican caucus. If so, why won't he come before this committee? I only heard that.

Secretary LAIRD. Senator Fulbright, I want to make one thing very clear. [Laughter.]

Senator GORE. It is several now.

Secretary LAIRD. In regard to my appearance before the Republican conference, this one thing should be borne in mind in regard to that appearance.

Senator CASE. He was late. [Laughter.]

Secretary LAIRD. I was invited by Mrs. Smith, the very distinguished Senator from Maine, who is chairman of the conference. Mrs. Smith asked me to come, and I told her that I did not make a practice of appearing before partisan groups involving only one party, but that I would do so provided that I could talk with Senator Mansfield. I called the majority leader of the U.S. Senate, and I informed the majority leader that I had such an invitation. I said that I would be glad to appear before the Democratic Senators at any time, but that I had such a request to appear before the Republican Senate conference, and that I would honor that request if he thought it was proper. I have made it a practice since I had been Secretary of Defense to stay away from any partisan meetings. I am a politician and I have a background as a Republican Congressman for some nine terms in the House of Representatives, so I have been very careful in this regard, but I want you to know, Senator Fulbright, as chairman of the Foreign Relations Committee of the U.S. Senate, that I did discuss this matter with the majority leader of the U.S. Senate prior to the acceptance of that invitation.

MR. KISSINGER'S VIEWS ON APPEARING BEFORE COMMITTEE

Senator FULBRIGHT. Did Mr. Kissinger accompany you?
Secretary LAIRD. We appeared at the conference.
Senator FULBRIGHT. He has given me to understand that it is improper for him to come before this committee and I have accepted that. It is more or less no formal declaration of executive privilege, but I think if pushed that is what he would allege. It seems very odd to me that he would go before a partisan caucus and not come before the committee.
Secretary LAIRD. I am sure that Mr. Kissinger would be very happy to appear before a meeting of the Democratic Senators although I have not discussed this with him.
Senator FULBRIGHT. This is not what I am talking about. This is the place for us to conduct business. You come here and I appreciate it. I can reciprocate. You said you like to come. We enjoy having you. I do, speaking for myself, and I agreed with what you said. You are a great artist in sort of going around the question sometimes, but I wouldn't say you mislead me in that sense, not directly at least. It is only because you are cleverer than I. You don't deliberately do it at all. I never said that and I don't think it. But I must say this is the place to do the public's business. I am not interested in your or Mr. Kissinger's appearing before the party caucus. That is a party matter. It seems very unusual to me in view of Mr. Kissinger's effective immunity from coming here, that he would appear before a party caucus because I don't consider this a party matter. As I see it, this war and all the parts about it are entirely nonpartisan. So is the policy about the talks in Vienna or any aspect of it. I see no partisan overtones regarding important matters that involve the life and death of our country.

CHINESE CANCELLATION OF WARSAW TALKS

I was just handed a note that the Chinese have cancelled the talks in Warsaw set for Wednesday. They allege that Cambodia is the reason.
I think you may have misjudged not only the people of this country but also the reaction of the Chinese and the Russians. If you have, I think this is an extremely serious matter.
I am through, Mr. Chairman.

SENATOR GORE'S VIEWS ON SANCTUARY AREAS

Senator GORE. Senator Case, since the Secretary referred to some views I had expressed, I wonder if you would mind.

Mr. Secretary, in some respect you correctly stated the views I have expressed. I think your conclusion was incorrectly stated, if you don't mind my stating it.

Secretary LAIRD. I was referring to the fact that this had been in open discussion.

Senator GORE. Yes. I am referring to your statement with respect to the sanctuaries and the building——

Secretary LAIRD. Which has been an open discussion.

Senator GORE. Yes.

Well, I have warned several times about the developing threat of a counteroffensive. Not that it is important to anyone except me and the people I have the honor in part to represent, I would like to briefly recount the views I have held. When President Nixon made his first speech to the American people on Vietnam war policy on May 14 of last year, he recommended mutual withdrawal of foreign troops from South Vietnam. He indicated a negotiated settlement, possibly a coalition government, and said he would accept neutrality for South Vietnam.

I think the very next day I made a rather lengthy speech in the Senate applauding those particular parts of the President's statement.

Three and a half weeks later, however, he announced Vietnamization, which in no sense embodies mutual withdrawal, but rather a unilateral withdrawal.

I don't recall whether it was the next day, but whenever I could prepare an address, I warned that the inevitable consequences of a unilateral withdrawal of forces by the United States would likely be a buildup of forces by the other side. Only a few days before the President made his last speech in which he said peace was in sight, I warned of the developing threat of flanking operations. I said that the North Vietnamese had infiltrated into South Vietnam a larger number of forces than have been in South Vietnam at any time during the war, that there were larger North Vietnamese forces in Laos and in Cambodia, and that a further unilateral withdrawal of U.S. Forces while the other side was building up and moving into a flanking position from which they could attack did pose a very serious situation.

I reasoned, however, that because this was a narrow peninsula in which three or four little countries are involved, none being very far from any point in the other, this argued not for a widening of the war but for a negotiated settlement.

I have warned about the building up of the sanctuaries, as you have cited, but I believe I recommended the conclusion not that they should be attacked but that the situation argued for a negotiated settlement.

VIETNAMIZATION AND NEGOTIATION

Secretary LAIRD. Senator Gore, I just want to make it clear that Vietnamization does not in any way degrade the opportunity for negotiation. Vietnamization complements negotiation. When I became Secretary of Defense I found that the only program approved by our Government was based upon negotiating the North Vietnamese out of South Vietnam and preparing the South Vietnamese to meet only the Vietcong but not the North Vietnamese threat. I felt that pursuing that avenue as the single course of action as far as our Government was concerned was not the best opportunity for progress.

You perhaps would oppose the unilateral withdrawal which we are carrying out—you call it such. Our withdrawals and force reductions are based upon the progress of the Vietnamization program, and we do not believe a single American should remain in Vietnam any longer than is militarily necessary. I think that as the South Vietnamese improve their military capability, these withdrawals can be justified.

Senator GORE. Mr. Secretary, to the extent that any American is in South Vietnam when he is not needed there, I surely share your view that he should not be kept there. Whether or not there is a viable and reasonable policy is a matter of judgment. It is my judgment that Vietnamization and negotiation are mutually incompatible and mutually contradictory. As I understand it, Vietnamization has as its goal the sustaining of the Thieu-Ky regime in power in Saigon and keeping such forces there as are necessary to maintain them in power.

Secretary LAIRD. But the avenue of negotiation is open at all times.

Senator GORE. On the other hand, it seems to me that the principal issue in the war is the character of the government in Saigon. Unless we are willing to negotiate about that, there really isn't anything to negotiate. It seems to me that a policy which proposes, with whatever forces, for whatever time necessary, to maintain an unpopular military dictatorship in power in Saigon, is contradictory to negotiation which requires, I think, a compromise government, a coalition government in Saigon.

You have stated your view and I have stated mine, and I know of no way we can resolve that here. I don't wish to cut you off. I am just trying to finish by way of apology to Senator Case for occupying so much time, but I don't want to cut you off.

Senator Case.

Senator CASE. Thank you, Mr. Chairman, Mr. Secretary, Admiral Moorer, and Dr. Foster.

We have proceeded along several avenues in our discussion thus far. I would like to go back to the relationship of our strategic program to the SALT talks, which I believe is the central focus of this hearing.

SENATE RESOLUTION 211. PROPOSAL OF MUTUAL SUSPENSION OF NUCLEAR STRATEGIC WEAPONS

Senator Cooper had to leave, but he raised a question about your statement, Mr. Secretary, in which you question the soundness of a unilateral moratorium on ABM's and MIRV's. This statement has been made by Administration people from the President on down to the effect that we don't want unilateral disarmament. I would like to protest the use of this word "unilateral" in connection with proposal for mutual disarmament, especially in connection with the mutual suspension of MIRV and ABM deployment, suggested by the Senate resolution.

I think by implication you again describe those proposals as unilateral——

Secretary LAIRD. I think I made it very clear, Senator Case, that I did not believe this committee or the U.S. Senate would approve any strategic arms agreement that would place the United States at a disadvantage as far as our security is concerned.

Now I do not believe——

Senator CASE. That statement was made by you on a different occasion.

Secretary LAIRD. I do not believe the Senate resolution calls for unilateral action——

Senator CASE. You do not.

Secretary LAIRD. On the part of the United States.

Senator CASE. You said you do not believe it?

Secretary LAIRD. I do not. I believe those who interpret the Senate resolution as calling for a unilateral ban on further ABM deployment, further MIRV deployment, have misread the resolution.

Senator CASE. Well, I appreciate that very much. I know Senator Cooper would, too, because this has been the response that we have received when this has been urged upon the executive branch. I appreciate your making it very clear that you understand that no such thought was in the mind of anybody who voted for it.

I have not been able to get an answer to the question of what harm there would be in proposing a suspension of the deployment of MIRV and ABM pending final agreement at the SALT talks.

Secretary LAIRD. The President has made it very clear that all strategic matters are subject to negotiation as far as the strategic arms limitation talks are concerned.

I do not believe it would serve any useful purpose for me to get into the details of our negotiating positions in the Vienna talks. I can point out, however, that the proposal for a suspension of MIRV deployment would involve some very complex questions for the negotiators. This issue is one that could be more complicated than the negotiation of a comprehensive agreement, and it is a matter that would require considerable negotiation and considerable discussion, and I do not believe that it helps our negotiators in Vienna to be in a position where there is any speculation by me or anyone else in regard to such operations.

Senator CASE. Well, I appreciate your forbearance.

Secretary LAIRD. I have instructed the people in the Department of Defense not to speculate, because I believe that it only hurts the position of our negotiators at this very crucial stage in the discussions that are going forward in Vienna.

Senator CASE. I accept your reluctance as a proper posture for you in these circumstances. I do not accept it as a proper posture for our Government at the negotiating table in Vienna. Unless you wish to make some further comment, we will leave it at that.

S. RES 211

Secretary LAIRD. I think the Senate resolution makes that very clear, Senator Case, and it might be well to put it in the record at this point.

Senator CASE. I would be happy to. It makes it much clearer.

(The resolution follows.)

S. RES. 211

Expressing the sense of the Senate on mutual suspension of further deployment of offensive and defensive nuclear strategic weapons systems by the Union of Soviet Socialist Republics and by the United States.

Whereas the competition to develop and deploy strategic weapons has reached a new and dangerous phase, which threatens to frustrate attempts at negotiating significant arms limitations and to weaken the stability of nuclear deterrence as a barrier to war;

Whereas development of multiple independently targetable reentry vehicles by both the United States and the Soviet Union represents a fundamental and radical challenge to such stability;

Whereas the possibility of agreed controls over strategic forces appears likely to diminish greatly if testing and deployment of multiple independently targetable reentry vehicles proceed;

Whereas a suspension of flight tests of multiple independently targetable reentry vehicles promises to forestall deployment of such provocative weapons; and

Whereas a suspension of such tests could contribute substantially to the success of the strategic arms limitation talks between the United States and the Soviet Union: Now, therefore, be it

Resolved, That it is the sense of the Senate that prompt negotiations between the Governments of the United States of American and of the Union of Soviet Socialist Republics to seek agreed limitations of both offensive and defensive strategic weapons should be urgently pursued; and

Resolved further, That the President should propose to the Government of the Union of Soviet Socialist Republics an immediate suspension by the United States and by the Union of Soviet Socialist Republics of the further deployment of all offensive and defensive nuclear strategic weapons systems, subject to national verification or such other measures of observation and inspection as may be appropriate.

Secretary LAIRD. The importance of our pursuing the course that we presently are pursuing in these negotiations.

Senator CASE. This is a matter for exegesis which I will be very glad to have development of as you proceed.

Secretary LAIRD. The question of national verification and other measures of inspection is raised in the resolution.

Senator CASE. They are mentioned.

Secretary LAIRD. It is very clear in that resolution and I do not believe that what I have said in any way contradicts the Senate resolution.

Senator CASE. No; I don't think so. However, I wouldn't rely on your expression as the strongest support for it.

MUTUAL SUSPENSION PENDING OUTCOME OF SALT

I still don't have an answer as to why our Government should not have taken that position regarding a mutual suspension pending the outcome of negotiations.

Secretary LAIRD. I have quite a discussion of that particular point a little later on in my statement.

Senator CASE. I hope this is in the record even if you do not provide it orally.

Secretary LAIRD. Well, the chairman has very graciously allowed me to put that statement in the record. And I do discuss this in some detail.

Senator CASE. We shall have an opportunity to examine the statement carefully.

CROSSOVER POINTS

In your statement there is a question I wish you would develop which goes to this question of the crossover point.

Secretary LAIRD. The crossover point would be at a different point for different weapons.

Senator CASE. Yes, but what do you mean by crossover points? I take it this is an overall question of strength.

Secretary LAIRD. That is correct.

Senator CASE. Is the crossover point that point at which either country would be able to make a successful first strike?

Secretary LAIRD. First, I think it is important to bear in mind that the crossover point is somewhat different for individual weapons systems.

Senator CASE. Yes, but that is not the question.

Secretary LAIRD. The crossover point has already been reached for ICBM's, and the Soviet Union has crossed over and has acquired a number of land-based ICBM's that is greater than the number which we have.

Now, the crossover point——

Senator CASE. May I just make that clear, also. The Soviet Union has more land-based intercontinental missiles than we now have. Is that your point?

Secretary LAIRD. They also have more megatonnage, and I pointed that out, too, in my statement.

Senator CASE. We know the difference between megatonnage and——

Secretary LAIRD. The crossover point so far as submarines are concerned——

Senator CASE. I am sorry, but what do you mean by crossover point so far as land-based missiles are concerned?

Secretary LAIRD. I am talking about the momentum of the program and the number of missile launchers in being and under construction in the Soviet Union as compared with the number of missile launchers operational in the United States.

Now if you examine this you come to a crossover point as far as numbers are concerned.

Senator CASE. Numbers of missiles?

Secretary LAIRD. Numbers of missile launchers, and if you want to, you can also do it by megatonnage.

Senator CASE. Or warheads.

Secretary LAIRD. Or warheads.

Senator CASE. Or something else.

Secretary LAIRD. That is correct.

Now——

Senator CASE. What you are actually saying——

Secretary LAIRD. What we are talking about is the capability——

Senator CASE. Yes.

Secretary LAIRD. Which is possessed by the Soviet Union. Earlier this afternoon I discussed the crossover point as far as submarine-launched missiles are concerned, and our projection of when that crossover point could be reached.

U.S.-U.S.S.R. FORCE COMPARISON

I have a force comparison, which I will make available to this committee, showing that in the 1974-75 time——

Senator GORE. Could you let us have it in printed form so that we could include it at this point in the record?

Secretary LAIRD. I think we can give you that. It would certainly be on an unclassified basis. I do want it in the unclassified record.

Senator GORE. Yes. Yes.

Secretary LAIRD. We can arrange for that.

Senator GORE. So it makes the question more relevant.

Secretary LAIRD. We will try to arrange it. We are trying to make as much information available as we possibly can.

(The information referred to follows.)

In 1965, the Soviet Union had about 220 launchers for the relatively old-fashioned missiles—SS-6's, SS-7's and SS-8's—somewhat similar to our TITAN. We had 54 TITANs in the inventory at that time.

In 1965, the Soviet Union had no relatively small ICBM launchers comparable to our MINUTEMAN. By 1965, we had 880 MINUTEMAN missiles operational and had established that the total force level for MINUTEMAN would be 1,000 launchers. In the 1965-67 time period, the United States finalized plans to convert a portion of the established MINUTEMAN force to a MIRV MINUTEMAN III configuration.

In 1965, there were no operational launchers for the large Soviet SS-9 missile which, in its single warhead version, an carry up to 25 megatons.

In 1965, neither a depressed trajectory ICBM nor a Fractional Orbital Bombardment System existed in either the Soviet or U.S. inventory.

In 1965, the Soviet Union had about 25 launchers for Submarine Launched Ballistic Missiles (SLBMs) on nuclear submarines, and about 80 more on diesel submarines. Most were designed for surface launch only. The U.S. had 464 SLBM launchers operational on 29 submarines in 1965 and Congress had authorized the last of the 41 nuclear-powered submarines in our POLARIS Force in the previous fiscal year.

In 1965, there was no development underway of a so-called Undersea Long-Range Missile System (ULMS) in the United States and there appeared to be none in the Soviet Union.

Today, these two forces remain essentially the same. So in this category of old-fashioned multi-megaton weapons the Soviets had and still maintain a better than 4-1 advantage.

Today, the Soviet Union has over 800 such launchers operational, and a projected force that could exceed 1,000 launchers within the next two years. These launchers include both the SS-11 and SS-13 missiles. Concurrently, flight testing of an improved SS-11 missile continues. Thus, at present construction rates, the Soviets will achieve parity in MINUTEMAN-type launchers within the next two years or so and could move into a substantial lead in this category by the mid-1970's if they continue to deploy these missiles. The previously scheduled U.S. program to MIRV a substantial part of MINUTEMAN continues in progress.

Today, I can report to you that there are some 220 SS-9's operational with at least 60 more under construction. Testing of an SS-9 multiple reentry vehicle—the triplet version—continues. The U.S. has no counterpart to this program involving large missiles. So, in this area, the Soviets have and will maintain a monopoly.

Today, the Soviets have tested both configurations and could have an operational version already deployed. The United States has developed nothing comparable to these systems.

Today, the Soviets have over 200 operational launchers on nuclear submarines for submerged launch SLBMs and about 70 operational launchers on diesel submarines. In the next two years, the Soviets are expected to have some 400-500 operational launchers on POLARIS-type submarines, and at present construction rates—6-8 submarines a year—could match or exceed the number in the U.S. force by 1974-75. United States POLARIS submarines still number 41 and no increase is projected in current plans. Conversion of our POLARIS submarines to the MIRVed POSEIDON missle is planned, and eight conversions have already been authorized by Congress.

Today, the United States is spending relatively small sums in the research and development area on preliminary investigations of such a system. I can also report to you today that the Soviet Union, on the other hand, already is testing a new, long-range missile for possible Naval use.

In 1965, the Soviet heavy bomber force consisted of slightly over 200 aircraft, about 50 of which were configured as tankers. The U.S. heavy bomber force strength was about 780 in 1965.

In 1965, we estimated that the Soviet Union had a complex of ABM launchers being constructed around Moscow as well as a number of radars under construction which could provide early warning acquisition and tracking functions for ABM use.

Today, the Soviet heavy bomber force is slightly under 200, with about 50 still configured as tankers. U.S. heavy bomber strength has declined to about 550 today.

Today, we believe that 64 Moscow ABM launchers are operational together with sophisticated early warning radars and tracking capabilities. ABM testing for new and/or improved systems continues. Today, the first two SAFEGUARD sites have been authorized, but will not be operational before 1974–75. This modified deployment schedule is considerably behind the schedule Congress had approved in 1967 for the planned SENTINEL area defense, which called for initial capability in 1972, and nation-wide coverage in 1975.

Secretary LAIRD. We run into sort of a cross current in this area. We are sometimes criticized because we make too much information available. We are not making this information available for any reason other than to keep this committee and the American public informed.

Senator GORE. Sometimes we call it by a name other than information.

Excuse me.

Senator CASE. Not at all.

Now, may I paraphrase this? You are now speaking about crossover point in regard to one particular individual type of weapon, is that not correct?

Secretary LAIRD. I am talking about the overall strategic capability, and the overall strategic capability is a combination of all the weapons systems of both the United States and the Soviet Union.

PLANNING FACTORS FOR STRATEGIC SUFFICIENCY

There are certain things that, as a defense planner, one must take into consideration. First, we have to maintain, as far as our deterrent force is concerned, an adequate second strike capability to deter an all-out surprise attack.

Senator CASE. Yes.

Secretary LAIRD. Second, we must see to it that there is no incentive for the Soviet Union to strike the United States first or on a surprise basis in any crisis.

Senator CASE. What is the difference between these two?

Secretary LAIRD. Third, I think it is important in our defense planning to prevent the Soviets from gaining the ability to cause considerably greater destruction than the United States could inflict in any type of nuclear exchange. Fourth, I think it is most important in our defense planning to defend against the major damage which could be caused by small attacks or accidental launches.

Senator CASE. Is that the Chinese deterrent?

Secretary LAIRD. That would be a very good example of it, Senator Case. But I think that all of these criteria must be considered in planning the strategic sufficiency of the United States, and this is the point that I am addressing at that point in my statement.

Senator CASE. What is the difference between your item 1 and your item 2? Item 1 is the possession of an assured second-strike capability, correct?

Secretary LAIRD. Yes.

Senator CASE. What is item 2?

Secretary LAIRD. That we see to it that there is no incentive for the Soviets to strike the United States first in any crisis.

Senator CASE. To me, they seem the same. I want to be sure that I understand you. Is there something that two adds that is not reflected in one?

Secretary LAIRD. I think they are very closely associated with one another. But two applies to the scenario so far as——

Senator CASE. One is that you have it, and two is that the enemy knows you have it.

Secretary LAIRD. That is correct. They are very closely tied together, but I think that one without the other is not as strong as if all four were considered together.

Senator CASE. One alone would not be any deterrent if the enemy did not know you had it.

Secretary LAIRD. That is correct.

Senator CASE. If the Hottentots knew you had it, we would know that we deterred against a first strike by the Hottentots.

Secretary LAIRD. I think it is most important that they understand that we have a sufficient deterrent.

Senator CASE. Certainly.

Secretary LAIRD. I think that in negotiations, as I said earlier this afternoon in answer to a question from the chairman, we must be sure that both sides are building their policy on the basis of deterrence. We are sure that we are.

ASSURED STRIKE CAPABILITY

Senator CASE. And we must be sure also, if we hope to achieve a SALT agreement, that both sides are confident of their ability.

Secretary LAIRD. I made that very clear.

Senator CASE. So this also should be a goal of both sides. I take it, you accept that?

Secretary LAIRD. If deterrence is our principal objective, there is no question about that, and it is the principal objective of the United States.

Senator CASE. So then it is of concern to us that the Russians be satisfied that they have a deterrent against us.

Secretary LAIRD. That is correct. In my opening statement I made that very clear.

Senator CASE. I am not saying that you did not. I am just saying that I think this is one of these first principles that we cannot state too often because we are inclined to get off into side excursions that lead away from these basic principles. An assured strike capability is the core of security for all nations with nuclear capability, is that not true?

Secretary LAIRD. That is correct. I get into that——

Senator CASE. And I grant you you have said it 50 times. I just want you to say it once more.

Secretary LAIRD. Yes, we certainly have the same goal in mind.

PLANNING FACTORS FOR STRATEGIC SUFFICIENCY

Senator CASE. What is No. 3?

Secretary LAIRD. The third point is to prevent the Soviets from gaining the ability to cause considerably greater destruction than the United States could inflict insofar as a nuclear exchange or nuclear war is concerned. I think it is important to take it into consideration when we discuss sufficiency.

Senator CASE. I think perhaps we are going to get into a disagreement here.

Secretary LAIRD. This is tied in with the incentive in the second point that I discussed.

Senator CASE. May I try to restate your proposition?

It is not only important that we have an assured capacity to retaliate by visiting unacceptable damage on the enemy: that is point one.

No. 2 is that this enemy should understand that we have that capacity.

Secretary LAIRD. That is correct.

First, that we have an unquestionable capability to retaliate that will deter a surprise attack, and, second, that there will be no incentive for the enemy, a proposed enemy or any challenger—and I do not like to use names necessarily—we can use names if you want to——

Senator CASE. I did not the last time.

Secretary LAIRD. We have used it both ways here, and I think we are talking about there being no incentive for either the Soviet Union or some other nation to strike the United States first in a crisis.

Senator CASE. What does three add to one and two?

Secretary LAIRD. Well, there is a question of destructive capability. We want to be in a position where we can prevent any would-be aggressor or any nation that would think of the first use of nuclear weapons from having the ability to cause considerably greater destruction than the United States could inflict in retaliation. This is a matter that must be considered as we plan our forces, and in my Defense report to this Congress I outlined some basic points in some detail.

Senator CASE. I must say——

Secretary LAIRD. These are similar to the points I stressed in my Defense report.

Senator CASE. I am generally aware of this, but I still am not quite clear what three adds to one and two.

One is the capacity to visit unacceptable damage on the enemy after receiving a first strike. Now, what is added by three to unacceptable damage?

Secretary LAIRD. Well, I think it should be understood that this is a question of judgment on the part of another nation, and it is just very difficult for one to try to read the intention of the other side.

So, in defense planning one must consider all of these factors, and the factors that I have outlined are the basis for the Defense report which I gave to this Congress in February.

RELATIVE KILL CAPACITY FOR DETERRENT

Senator CASE. Suppose each side has the capacity to kill 100 million people. Would you consider that sufficient?

Secretary LAIRD. Yes, I would.

Senator CASE. Would you think if one side had the capacity to kill 200 million people and the other only 100 million, that the capacity of the country with only 100 million ability would be insufficient?

Secretary LAIRD. Well, these are very "iffy" questions.

Senator CASE. I do not think they are iffy at all. I think they go right to the question of what we are trying to do, and if we get into an arms race that escalates——

Secretary LAIRD. If you hypothetically take a 200-million figure—I would like Dr. Foster to discuss this. We have certain projections along this line. I do not believe that that is a very realistic appraisal. We have appraisals like that, and if you want to discuss them here before this committee——

Senator CASE. I think it is essential.

Secretary LAIRD (continuing). Dr. Foster will talk about it. If you want to take those figures, we would be glad to discuss them.

Senator CASE. I think we should have them.

Secretary LAIRD. I believe that the supposition which you made with these particular trade-offs is not a realistic one.

Senator CASE. I accept that. Let us say 50 and 100.

Secretary LAIRD. I would be glad to give you those figures again which, I think, have been supplied to this committee in the past.

Senator CASE. They may have.

Secretary LAIRD. They are classified, as you know, and I would be glad to supply them again if you do not have them.

Senator CASE. Well, I think it is important that we know, and if they are classified——

Secretary LAIRD. I want to say the supposition which you make is not a realistic one——

Senator CASE. I was just trying to find a starting point for discussion.

Secretary LAIRD. We would be happy to supply that information to you.

Senator CASE. Let me see if we can get to that point by going down a little. How about 50 million as against 100 million lives in each case?

Secretary LAIRD. I would be happy to supply you with an assessment.

Senator CASE. Let us assume this was the relative strength. Would both sides still have a deterrent?

Secretary LAIRD. I would not want to have that great a disparity.

Senator CASE. Pardon?

Secretary LAIRD. I would not want to have that great a disparity.

Senator CASE. You would not want to have that great a disparity. I see.

FOUR SPECIFIC CRITERIA FOR STRATEGIC SUFFICIENCY

Senator GORE. Senator Case, will you yield? Are you referring, Mr. Secretary, to the four specific criteria for strategic sufficiency?

Secretary LAIRD. Pardon?

Senator GORE. Are you referring to the four criteria for strategic sufficiency?

Secretary LAIRD. I am referring to the planning factors I use in my appraisal of what is needed in the strategic area. Are you quoting from the Defense report?

Senator GORE. This is the President's State of the World statement, and I read here:

"We reached general agreement within the Government on four specific criteria for strategic sufficiency."

So far as I know, we have not had those four specific criteria supplied to us. Would you supply them to us?

Secretary LAIRD. No, 1 am not referring specifically to the four criteria of strategic sufficiency. I am referring to factors derived from those criteria that, as a defense planner, one must take into consideration. I will be glad to discuss the other matter with you, but the points that I am using here are the points that are used by me in determining our proposed programs. I believe I discussed our planning factors with this committee last year.

Senator GORE. Could you furnish the committee for its security treatment the specific criteria to which the President referred?

Senator CASE. The Senator from Missouri will have a few questions, and he asked me to allow him to interrupt. I will do so as soon as I finish this one point.

KILL CAPACITY FOR ADEQUATE DETERRENCE

Still, to try to get a little closer to the heart of your thinking on point three, adequate deterrence has been defined as our ability to kill 80 to 200 million of the Soviet population. Secretary McNamara used to talk about 200 to 400 warheads as adequate for that purpose.

Is that still a reasonably accurate measure or definition of the size of the force necessary to deliver that degree of casualties?

Secretary LAIRD. I think Secretary McNamara—and as a Member of Congress I heard his testimony on many occasions—did refer at times to a level of 400 warheads.

He was discussing, of course, warheads that were 1 megaton each, and he was talking about the equivalent megatonnage.

Senator CASE. That is to say, the Minuteman, for example?

Secretary LAIRD. That is correct.

Senator CASE. Or Polaris?

Secretary LAIRD. Well——

Senator CASE. Not Poseidon, of course.

Secretary LAIRD. But the situation does change.

Senator CASE. With the MIRVed weapons.

Secretary LAIRD. Yes.

Senator CASE. Naturally, it does, and we would not have that change unless it were to our interest.

Secretary LAIRD. Well, it does——

Senator CASE. Again, I am not an expert, and I do not want to ask you——

Secretary LAIRD. The MIRV gives us a greater second-strike capability.

Senator CASE. In other words, it would kill more people.

Secretary LAIRD. It gives us a greater capability to penetrate defenses.

Senator CASE. Right.

Secretary LAIRD. And it is a question of penetration——

Senator CASE. Yes.

Secretary LAIRD (continuing). That is involved, rather than anything else.

Senator CASE. Of course.

Secretary LAIRD. As far as megatonnage is concerned, the total missile megatonnage is reduced substantially when the missiles are MIRVed.

Senator CASE. Now, again we are speaking about 400 warheads. I take it that 400 warheads reaching their target would represent an adequate deterrent.

Secretary LAIRD. He was talking about 400 1-megaton-equivalent delivered warheads, so you are talking about——

Senator CASE. Which prevents the multiplication of present warheads by a factor of three to ten, of course, but I still think that perhaps 10 times capacity is adequate. It is the latter with which I am really concerned, and I hope that we can return to it after the Senator from Missouri is finished.

Secretary LAIRD. I would be delighted to talk about this now, Senator.

Senator CASE. Yes.

Secretary LAIRD. Because I think you are talking in somewhat different terms than I am. I am talking about the second-strike retaliatory capability.

Senator CASE. So am I.

Secretary LAIRD. I think that is a much different matter. Secretary McNamara, in the testimony you are referring to, I believe, talked about 400——

Senator CASE. 200 to 400.

Secretary LAIRD (continuing). One megaton equivalent delivered warheads.

Senator CASE. I think it was 200 to 400, but that is all right, I will accept your figure.

Secretary LAIRD. And he was talking about the number of warheads that would reach the target.

Senator CASE. Right.

Secretary LAIRD. And so I think that that should be borne in mind.

Senator CASE. I think it must necessarily be borne in mind, and it is a very proper thing for you to consider, and we must consider it, too.

The question is just——

DEFENSE DEPARTMENT CALCULATIONS CONCERNING FUTURE ADEQUATE DETERRENCE

Secretary LAIRD. We have had new developments which we have to reckon with, whether we like it or not.

The loss of certain retaliatory weapons and the possible loss of, perhaps, certain land-based missiles, and certain aircraft which we are depending on in the time period of the seventies changes our calculations, especially with the increase of Polaris-type submarines on the part of the Soviet Union and the momentum in land-based ICBM's.

But I will be glad to give those calculations to this committee, if you want them. One of the disadvantages of setting forth those calculations in public testimony, I believe, is that it would be just as useful for your committee to consider those calculations in closed testimony or in a classified document rather than to lay on the public record the estimates pertaining to the period of 1972, 1973, 1974, 1975. This is a matter of very grave importance.

Senator CASE. Of course it is.

Secretary LAIRD. But I do not believe it serves our national security or our national interests to make them a part of the public record at this time.

Senator CASE. I would naturally accept your view about this, and we can discuss it when the time comes for consideration of the ABM system.

Secretary LAIRD. It is like discussing whether we would exchange one city for 100 cities. I think that those particular discussions are not necessarily useful. But we do have the calculations worked out, which I will make available to the membership of this committee, if you wish to have them.

Senator CASE. Well, I appreciate that. I would like to pursue this at a further appropriate time, whether this afternoon or later, but the Senator from Missouri has asked that we defer to him because he had several questions. Mr. Chairman, if I may not lose my right to the position of questioning, I will yield to the Senator from Missouri.

Senator SYMINGTON. I appreciate the Senator's courtesy.

Mr. Secretary, I am sorry I missed you at Armed Services. As you know, the date was changed two or three times. Then there was a hearing in the morning, so I was planning to see you in the afternoon, as I was first told you were coming back.

It does not mean that I am not very interested in what you think about these very important subjects.

I was glad to hear you do look forward to appearing before this committee. It is a challenge. I am interested in the dialog you had with the Senator from New Jersey just now, and hope this dialog continues; and perhaps at some time you can come back, because this whole question of relative strategic strength appears to me mighty important, as you know far better than I, from a diplomatic and economic as well as military viewpoint.

KNOWLEDGE OF CAMBODIAN SANCTUARIES

My question would go back, however, to what is going on in Indochina today; and what has been going on in the last few weeks.

I went to Vietnam in the fall of 1965, up to Nha Trang and then west to An Khe, and from there further west to Pleiku; and then in an armed chopper all over the A Shau Valley, where the 1st Cavalry took it pretty bad at that time, if you remember, probably our worst defeat.

In the chopper was a colonel who was in that battle in the valley. He pointed out after an hour of moving up and down close to the

Cambodian border, beyond the Special Forces camps of Duc Co and Pleime, that there was no possible chance the finally defeated enemy, North Vietnamese and Vietcong, could have gone anywhere except across into Cambodia. Therefore, I came back and said it was clear that Cambodia was being used as a sanctuary.

At that time, based on the incomplete amount of facts I had I was in favor of the war, and thought we ought to get on with it. It was costing us so much in lives and treasure, the former being so much more important. I recommended at that time we take out the sanctuaries in Cambodia.

Later on in hearings you know about, though before your time in the Pentagon, we were actually told the names of the units and their locations in Cambodia, North Vietnamese units.

Later on, after receiving more information about what was actually going on in Vietnam I became dubious; and in 1967 decided definitely the game was not worth the candle, especially because of our other costly operations and dangerous positions all around the world. So instead of a policy for getting into Cambodia and taking out the sanctuaries, I was more interested in a policy of getting out of Vietnam, phasing it all out at the earliest possible date.

ATTACK ON CAMBODIAN SANCTUARIES

Therefore, I was glad to hear the President say many months ago he planned to do just that. But we have known for well over 4 years that there were these sanctuaries in Cambodia, yet we did not take this military action until there was a political development; namely, the overthrow of Sihanouk. But it has been presented to the American people that we were taking a military action in response to a military action after we found out there were these heavy sanctuaries in Cambodia. Of course, that just is not true.

Why, therefore, if we were continuing to deescalate, as the President planned, did we have to suddenly turn and attack this country as a process of deescalation, when we did not attack it in the days of escalation?

TROOP WITHDRAWAL

One additional point that has worried me a great deal about this whole operation; although you all have been saying you are going to deescalate the war, and take the troops out, we have not had much success in whatever it is we have been trying to do over there to date. It worried me therefore that you did not, at the same time, say you were going to reduce the amount of geography we were planning to protect, because the number of troops you have per square yard or mile has always been important in any war.

I was hoping you would say, for example, you were turning over to the ARVN more of South Vietnam to adjust to deescalation, instead of continuing to protect all of South Vietnam. You said yourself it would be some time before the South Vietnamese could take over the operation in its entirety. My impression is now that we intend to leave logistic troops and air and sea there indefinitely, more so that we did when the policy of deescalation was first announced.

REPRESENTATION OF U.S. ACTIVITIES IN CAMBODIA AS MILITARY ACTION QUESTIONED

The thrust of my question is, why is the thought given to the people that this is a military reaction to a military action, when it is as clear as light that it is a military reaction to a political action, namely, the overthrow of Sihanouk?

Secretary LAIRD. Senator Symington, earlier this afternoon I addressed this particular question.

Senator SYMINGTON. Mr. Secretary, could you raise your voice a bit?

Secretary LAIRD. Earlier this afternoon I did respond to this question, and I outlined the reasons for the decision to attack and destroy the North Vietnamese sanctuaries in Cambodia.

There is no question but that those sanctuaries did pose a very important threat to the South Vietnamese and to the American troops operating in South Vietnam.

These sanctuaries have been used over a period of time, as you are well aware, and as I was aware as a member of the Defense Appropriations Subcommittee of the House of Representatives.

The situation that developed there did, of course, include the change of government which you outline, but our decision was based upon insuring progress in the Vietnamization program, insuring the continued withdrawal of American troops, and helping to reduce American casualties in the future, particularly as we move into the third and fourth quarter of this calendar year when our force levels will be reduced.

Bearing in mind that those were the primary considerations in the decisionmaking process, it should be pointed out that these sanctuaries were being linked up with the Ho Chi Minh trail as it comes on down through Laos, and linked up in a very elaborate, effective way in Cambodia.

When I testified before the various committees last year, I outlined the fact that most of the supplies that were going into the IV Corps area, and a considerable portion of the supplies going into the III Corps area, were coming through Sihanoukville and through Cambodia.

In the last several months this supply route has been cut off and the supplies have been moving down through a network which was being established from the Ho Chi Minh trail on down through the sanctuary areas.

Senator SYMINGTON. Excuse me, Mr. Secretary, I know all that, have seen pictures of the Trail, the Sihanouk Trail, and have talked about it in Laos as far down as Pak se and Savannakhet, et cetera.

WOULD UNITED STATES HAVE ACTED IF SIHANOUK HADN'T BEEN OVERTHROWN?

All I am asking is, would you have set out against Cambodia in this way if Sihanouk had not been overthrown?

Secretary LAIRD. Well, the question involved here is really one of major importance. I want it to be understood that the primary reason was the protection of American forces in Vietnam.

Senator SYMINGTON. I understand that. But would you have done it if Sihanouk had not been overthrown?

Secretary LAIRD. The protection of American forces was the primary purpose and, as far as the change of government in Cambodia is concerned, the fact that there was no objection on the part of the Cambodian Government, certainly was a consideration.

But although it was a consideration, it was not a primary consideration. The primary consideration was the protection of Americans, and each time you refer to the other considerations that were discussed sometimes it leads people to believe that the primary consideration is being downgraded. I do not want to give that impression to you or to any other member of this committee or to the American public. The primary purpose——

Senator CASE. Will you yield to me?

Secretary LAIRD. The primary purpose is the protection of the American forces in Vietnam.

REACTION OF RUSSIA AND COMMUNIST CHINA

Senator SYMINGTON. Before yielding, you have not answered my question. What worries me about the formulation of our foreign policy in recent years has been the respect we have, and apprehension we have, as to just what the Communists would do in China, or what the Kremlin would do. I personally believe, regardless of party, that over the years much of our foreign policy has not been created in Washington rather in Moscow and Peiping, because of our fear as to what would be the reaction of the two largest Communist countries.

I have heard it discussed by the hour; what would happen in China if we invaded North Vietnam, what the Soviets would think if we moved openly, instead of covertly in Laos, et cetera, et cetera, et cetera.

Therefore, it occurred to me that was the reason we did not take these Cambodian sanctuaries out before which were hurting American boys—let me assure you I am just as interested in protecting them as you are. I know you know that.

Secretary LAIRD. I know you have, Senator Symington, and you made those recommendations so far as North Vietnam and Cambodia are concerned on many occasions, and I heard you make those statements that they should be destroyed.

Senator SYMINGTON. Right. That was years ago, but being true, I believe personally the reason these sanctuaries were not taken out before was because of apprehension of what might happen, apprehension as to what would be the reaction in the capitals of the two big Communist countries.

What now worries me, especially as a result of what has been said recently in the capitals of those two large countries, is the reaction. It looks like we are going to get the same type and character of negative reaction from both Red China and the Soviet Union that we would have if we had moved into Cambodia during the time of Sihanouk. That is what I was leading up to.

I yield to my friend from New Jersey.

Secretary LAIRD. Senator Symington, I want to make it very clear that as the Secretary of Defense, my primary concern is promoting the Vietnamization program and furthering withdrawal of Americans from that area, and protecting the American forces.

Now, as Secretary of Defense, I think I must address those particular questions, and in recommending this action to the President of the United States, those were the overriding considerations that dictated my support.

Senator SYMINGTON. I understand. Senator Case.

TIMING OF SANCTUARY OPERATION

Senator CASE. Of course, we accept the Administration belief that what it did would help save American lives.

What was the difference between the situation on the 20th of April and that on the 30th of April to make it so important in the saving of American lives?

Secretary LAIRD. First, I want it understood that I recommended going into the sanctuary areas prior to the 20th of April.

Senator CASE. When did you do that?

Secretary LAIRD. I approved and recommended the operations which were carried out in the early part of April, of which this committee is certainly aware.

Senator CASE. I am not sure what you mean when you say that this committee is aware of the operations.

Secretary LAIRD. Aware of the operations that were conducted in the sanctuary areas in the early part of April.

Senator CASE. Well, perhaps this committee is; perhaps some members of the committee are. The committee was never advised about this as such, but I am not making a point of that now.

Secretary LAIRD. Well, there were operations, and they were widely reported, in which the South Vietnamese forces made certain incursions into the sanctuaries.

Senator CASE. I understand, I see what you are talking about.

But my point is that we were told——

Secretary LAIRD. I am sure this committee was aware of those operations.

Now, when the situation developed, as I outlined to Senator Symington earlier, of the tie-in between the trail coming down from Laos and the whole complex of sanctuaries in Cambodia—and this development began in the latter part of April—when there was evidence from defectors and other intelligence sources that their forces planned to launch major high points against American forces in order to increase casualties during the month of May, when it became known that there was movement out of the sanctuary areas, this did have an effect upon my recommendation to hit the sanctuary areas and destroy them.

Now, we had ended our combat responsibility as far as the American forces are concerned opposite most of the sanctuary areas.

USE OF U.S. FORCES IN SANCTUARY OPERATION

We do still have a responsibility, however, in the III Corps area, which is opposite the so-called Fishhook area, where we have the 25th Division and the 1st Air Cavalry Division. To move against all of the sanctuary areas at that particular time did require American forces; otherwise a change in very rapid fashion of all of the security responsibilities not only in I, II, III, and IV Corps, but particularly in III Corps, would have been required.

So at that time, in order to carry out the operation in a short period of time, since the weather conditions do dictate the amount of time that we would have in this area—from 3 to 6 weeks—it was felt that the most effective operation could be conducted with the help of U.S. forces in cooperation with South Vietnamese forces.

SECRETARY ROGERS' TESTIMONY ON CAMBODIA

Senator CASE. I want to place in the record, and then I will let Senator Symington ask you a question that Secretary Rogers testified before the committee that we were doing nothing on April 2, and that we were discouraging the South Vietnamese. That is just an example of the information that this committee was getting. It appears that the Secretary did not know what was going on.

Secretary LAIRD. Well, I want to make it clear that you are talking about the first or second of April, I believe——

Senator CASE. The 2nd of April is when he was here and said that.

DATES OF SANCTUARY OPERATIONS IN CAMBODIA

Secretary LAIRD. I want to make it clear that at that particular time I do not think any operations had been——

Senator CASE. The South Vietnamese had been in there then?

Secretary LAIRD. No, I do not believe there had been any major sanctuary operations then. I will give you the date of the first operation for the record.

(The information referred to had not been received as of the date of publication.)

Senator CASE. By American troops.

Secretary LAIRD. No. There were no operations by American troops.

Senator CASE. American advisers.

Secretary LAIRD. There were no operations by any American troops.

Senator CASE. They did not accompany the South Vietnamese?

Secretary LAIRD. Until the 30th of April.

Senator CASE. I see.

Secretary LAIRD. As far as advisers or as far as American combat forces are concerned?

Senator CASE. Or air support.

Secretary LAIRD. I was referring to ground operations, and I think I made it clear, Senator Symington, that I was referring to operations by the South Vietnamese forces.

I think you will find that the American combat forces went in on the 30th day of April, and there were some advisers that went in on the 28th day of April in the so-called Parrot's Beak operation.

I think the number, Admiral Moorer tells me, is 70 who actually went in to Cambodia on the 28th day of April.

EFFECT OF U.S. MILITARY EXPENDITURES ON DOMESTIC ECONOMY

Senator SYMINGTON. Over a year ago, when you first took this position and we talked about it, I predicted you were going to have a problem, because, based on my knowledge and conferences with you in appropriations committees, you were a hawk, but also a hard money man. I hope the fellow who sank that putt on the 18th I saw Saturday, Arnold Palmer, was your partner.

Secretary LAIRD. He was not my partner [laughter]. Bill Rogers was.

Senator SYMINGTON. Well, I am sorry for your sake. [Laughter].

Secretary LAIRD. But it was a great pleasure playing golf with Arnold Palmer.

Senator SYMINGTON. I wish I had had the opportunity; a great fellow.

I am sure you remember that. I said because you were a hard money man, you were going to have a problem.

I had no idea the economy was going to collapse the way it has under these tremendous expenditures abroad. Counting Europe, it is over $100 million a day.

The stock market, I think, registers, at least to some extent, the growing apprehension of the people; but more important, for the first time in our history we have the three witches in the brew together, namely, unprecedentedly high-interest rates, increasing inflation, and growing unemployment.

Five divisions in Europe for a quarter of a century, two divisions in Korea for 20 years next month, all this gigantic expense still going on in Southeast Asia. Don't you sometimes wonder what will happen to our country if the economy really does collapse which it could be in the process of doing. Is the game worth the candle if it does collapse?

We will still have the same land here, and I am sure a lot of patriotic people here like you, but are we going to have the same type of government we had before if the dollar continues to deteriorate to the point where it falls apart. I ask this with seriousness, because of the importance of this fact incident to the creation of the International Monetary Fund as a result of the Bretton Woods Agreement.

Secretary LAIRD. Let me tell you, Senator Symington, what President Nixon and the Nixon administration, and I, as Secretary of Defense, are trying to do with the problem which you outline.

I am well aware of the problem of priorities within our country. I had the opportunity to serve on the Health, Education, and Welfare Appropriations Subcommittee ever since that Department was created. I believe that I was very knowledgeable not only about all of the welfare, education, and health programs, but also about the poverty program and others. As you know I also served on the Defense Appropriations Subcommittee, and I felt that I knew a great deal about those particular programs then, and still do.

DEFENSE DEPARTMENT REDUCTIONS

In the Department of Defense, we are trying to make a contribution to the fight against inflation and to the reordering of our national priorities.

When I came into this Department we were spending over 40 percent of the Federal budget. The fiscal year 1969 and fiscal year 1970 budgets were reduced, based on recommendations that I made to this Congress which were supported by President Nixon in the last session. We have reduced our share again this year, so that we are at the point where DOD outlays represent 34.6 percent of total Federal budget outlays, the smallest share at any time during the last 20 years.

We have gone from 8.7 percent of the gross national product in fiscal year 1969 down to 7 percent in fiscal year 1971.

If you take the fiscal year 1964 budget and compare it with the fiscal year 1971 budget, you will find that in terms of constant dollars, even with the war in Southeast Asia, our expenditures are estimated at only $3.8 billion above the 1964 budget.

Senator SYMINGTON. You have done a good job.

Secretary LAIRD. In addition to that——

Senator SYMINGTON. But what is going to happen?

Secretary LAIRD. In addition to that, Senator Symington, we are reducing civilian employment under the programs that we have set forth to this Congress, as I outlined in my Defense report, by over 130,000 civil service employees of the Federal Government between fiscal year 1969 and fiscal year 1971.

We estimate we are causing reductions of over 600,000 contractor employees of the Department of Defense in the program that I have submitted to this Congress. That estimate is made using a base of 2 million in prime contractor plants, and does not include the subcontractors.

I am concerned about this rapid cutback as far as industry is concerned in the United States, and the effect it will have upon our economy. But I felt that it was necessary for us to make these reductions which affect our industrial base and the employment picture. So there will be a reduction of over 600,000 contractor employees.

In addition to that, we are reducing our military personnel strength between fiscal year 1969 and fiscal year 1971, in the program that I have presented to this Congress and that the President supports, by over 550,000.

So I think that there is an awareness——

U.S. MILITARY SPENDING

Senator SYMINGTON. There is an awareness, but how are we going to stop what is going on. That is what I want to know.

Secretary LAIRD (continuing). In the Department of Defense.

Senator SYMINGTON. All the Federal money we placed around the United States helped at least from the standpoint of creating jobs and commercial business. If you build dams and roads, you have the money working here in this country; but the money that goes into Vietnam never comes back. It is part of our debt that you can never say you owe yourself. The money that goes into Europe, in my opinion, does not come back or very little of it; and you are putting out abroad, money that is gone forever. You cannot ever say, as you do with the rest of our debt, that you owe it to yourself. It is just debt, money that will never come back.

Secretary LAIRD. We are cutting back on that, Senator Symington.

Senator SYMINGTON. People who are considered experts tell me the market is going down further; and inflation is continuing, and regardless of the fine job you have done in cutting expenses, that is the situation.

The best way to cut these gigantic expenditures is to get out of these wars and stop babysitting the world. If we will do that maybe we can bring a readjustment to the financial picture regardless of any cuts that you made in the Defense Department, which, at best, is only a part of the overall pie.

Senator CASE. Mr. Chairman.
Senator FULBRIGHT. Is the Senator through?
Senator SYMINGTON. Yes.
Senator FULBRIGHT. Senator Case.

Senator CASE. I would like to go over this again, because I would like to get it clear in my own mind as to why we went into Cambodia.

WHAT WAS THREAT TO U.S. TROOPS FROM BORDER AREAS?

In explaining this position, both the President and you stress the rapidly growing threat to U.S. troops in South Vietnam from the border areas.

The President said on April 30 that Communist troops in the sanctuaries—and I am quoting—"were building up to launch massive attacks on our forces and those of South Vietnam."

When you spoke on May 12 before the Armed Services Committee, you are quoted as referring to reports that the enemy activity would be stepped up, and I quote now, "from out of the Cambodian sanctuaries into the Delta of South Vietnam," and these are also your words, "information which triggered President Nixon's decision to attack the sanctuaries."

But 2 days later you were reported as saying that you changed your mind about sending in troops when you learned that enemy troops were moving westward, not toward South Vietnam, but away from the border areas. You were quoted as saying that in mid-April, and these are your words, "We found the enemy forces facing in the opposite direction and moving away."

I would like to know whether the enemy troops were massing to threaten us in South Vietnam or whether they were not.

Secretary LAIRD. Well, first, I would like to say that I would like to give you the entire transcript of the discussion——

Senator CASE. I know. But the question is, what are the facts.

Secretary LAIRD (continuing). Of the discussion you are referring to. The facts are, and I have outlined them here this afternoon, that the primary consideration in the decisionmaking was the protection of American forces.

Senator CASE. I know, but that——

Secretary LAIRD. The Vietnamization program.

Senator CASE. Against what?

Secretary LAIRD. But the reason I have to repeat that, Senator Case——

Senator CASE. I understand it has good propaganda value, but I want facts. [Laughter.] Really, I do.

Secretary LAIRD. The important thing, and the reason I have to repeat that is because each time some of the other factors involved are discussed then people say, "You have changed your position." There has been no change in my position, and I want you to understand that.

Senator CASE. I want to know about the North Vietnamese position.

Secretary LAIRD. These were the factors involved that had a contributing influence upon my recommendation to the President of the United States.

The President made it very clear in his statement of the threat to the IV Corps and the III Corps area when this announcement was made. We have very good, solid, clear information regarding the movement of equipment, ammunition and other stores into a position to cause difficulties as far as American Forces and South Vietnamese forces are concerned, and this difficulty was anticipated during the month of May.

As far as the threat within the sanctuary area of Cambodia——

Senator CASE. That is what we are talking about.

Secretary LAIRD (continuing). This is a different situation from the one in South Vietnam.

MILITARY THREAT IN CAMBODIAN SANCTUARY AREAS

It is true that from a military standpoint the threat in Cambodia, as far as the number of forces stationed in the sanctuary areas at the time of the sanctuary attacks, was going down because of the movement of some of the forces in the other direction, That did have an effect upon my decision to recommend to the President the course of action which he followed. The military threat within the Cambodian sanctuaries themselves was reduced by a movement of some of the forces in another direction, reducing the possibility for combat within the sanctuary areas.

Now, that does not refer to any change of mind as far as I am concerned. It has to do with the military threat in the Cambodian sanctuary areas. That is a different matter from the military threat within South Vietnam.

But as a defense planner, it is necessary to take into consideration those military questions that do have an effect upon the level of casualties, because I am interested in keeping American casualties at the lowest possible level.

Senator CASE. Well, Mr. Secretary, that all may be very well——

Secretary LAIRD. I would like you to read that complete transcript, because you are quoting about three sentences.

Senator CASE. Yes. But I happened to be present when these briefings were given by the President, and it was very clear that we were meant to believe that the Communist troops in the sanctuaries were building up to launch massive attacks on our forces and those of South Vietnam, and again you talked about Cambodia——

Secretary LAIRD. That is very true.

Senator CASE (continuing). Out of the Cambodian sanctuaries into the delta, and that is not about III and IV Corps.

Secretary LAIRD. The IV Corps is the delta.

Senator CASE. IV Corps is the delta, of course. Take that back.

Secretary LAIRD. And Cambodia has been the primary source of supply, up until several months ago, of the delta area—that is the IV Corps area—which is the richest area in Vietnam.

Senator CASE. I know all about that. But the question is whether they were building up to launch massive attacks on us from the Cambodian sanctuaries. I do not find any evidence that was a fact.

Secretary LAIRD. Well, I have the evidence.

Senator CASE. Well, it is not clear from what——

Secretary LAIRD. I certainly have made it very clear that we have it, not only from defectors, but also from other intelligence sources. I believe that if you would like to have an intelligence briefing it would be better if the CIA gave you that briefing. But I can assure you that evidence, as far as the threat in South Vietnam is concerned, is solid, firm evidence.

When you talk about the threat in Cambodia, you are talking about a different situation. But I want you to be very clear in your mind——

Senator CASE. Yes.

Secretary LAIRD (continuing). That we have that evidence, and I hope you will listen to a CIA briefing.

Senator CASE. I find this very difficult. The threat is in South Vietnam, not in Cambodia. The threat is in South Vietnam from Cambodia, but not in Cambodia. I honestly do not know what you mean.

Secretary LAIRD. I am sorry you are confused.

Senator CASE. Would you say repeat it in a simpler way? What happened to change the military situation? I do not see specifically what happened in the 2 weeks in April to change the situation.

Secretary LAIRD. You don't really understand?

Senator CASE. Well, if I did——

Secretary LAIRD. Seriously——

Senator CASE. I am serious.

Secretary LAIRD. Well——

Senator CASE. The troops were moving away——

Secretary LAIRD. Senator Case, the situation is much——

Senator CASE. We have known about the sanctuaries, of course.

Secretary LAIRD. The best intelligence information available to our Government indicated that serious high points would be launched by the North Vietnamese and Vietcong during the month of May.

Senator CASE. May I ask you when that became evident to you? Was that after——

Secretary LAIRD. In the latter part of April.

Senator CASE. You did not know this before the middle of April?

Secretary LAIRD. During the latter part of April we had firm intelligence information that high points were contemplated during this particular time.

PLANNING AND PREPARATION FOR SANCTUARY OPERATION

Senator CASE. Was all of the preparation done then between the middle of April and the end of April, all this tremendous amount of planning? We know that is not so. The general who briefed us told us about this going on for months.

Secretary LAIRD. I have not said that.

Senator CASE. This had to be going on for months, did it not?

Secretary LAIRD. It takes a considerable amount of time to bring these supplies into the sanctuary areas, and I am sorry if I implied that it did not. But, as far as the attacks were concerned, the intelligence information on that was developed during the latter part of April, and we also saw the development during the latter part of April of the tie-in with the Ho Chi Minh trail with the sanctuary areas in Cambodia and this was a very important development since the route from Sihanoukville had been shut off.

There is no question in my mind about the adequacy of this intelligence information. Now, if the Senator has serious questions about that——

Senator CASE. No. What I have——

Secretary LAIRD. I believe the CIA would be the proper source to brief the distinguished Senator from New Jersey.

Senator CASE. Would the distinguished former member of the House, and currently distinguished Secretary of Defense, just let me say what my concern is: that this had been in preparation for a long time, many weeks if not many months. I do question whether this was triggered by any recent intelligence information that came into the Government.

As a matter of fact, one of the generals on our side who was helping the Vietnamese plan this operation, explained how well they kept the secret for months while the preparation was going on. There is nothing to be gained by pretending that this was not so.

Senator SYMINGTON. If the Senator will yield, I am on the CIA Subcommittee, have been for a decade, and have no information of this kind. I do not doubt anything you have said, but this is my subcommittee.

Secretary LAIRD. When was the last time you were briefed, Senator?

Senator SYMINGTON. I could not answer that. On the other hand——

Secretary LAIRD. Has it been within the last 2 months; has it been since the 20th of April?

Senator SYMINGTON. Information on this was lacking in every committee I am on, Appropriations, the CIA Subcommittee, Armed Services, Foreign Relations. We knew nothing about this until our troops were in Cambodia.

Secretary LAIRD. I am sure my friend from Missouri was not briefed since the 20th of April.

RESULTS OF CAMBODIAN SANCTUARY OPERATION

Senator SYMINGTON. Well then I am sure that is correct. But getting back to the point of Senator Case, the idea there was a tremendous attack going on; we had no major battles when we got in there; did not find much of the enemy, so typical of the tremendous excursions we made in South Vietnam—without finding the enemy.

I will get a briefing at your suggestion, but I want to make one other point, Mr. Secretary. The best way to support these young men, and the best way to protect them, which you have emphasized time and again this afternoon, is to get them out of Vietnam at the earliest possible date.

Secretary LAIRD. And that is what the——[applause].

Senator FULBRIGHT. It is against the rules of the Senate to demonstrate in these committee hearings.

Secretary LAIRD. That is what the Cambodian operation in these sanctuaries occupied by the North Vietnamese is all about. Senator Symington, I would like to make one other point. This operation was not undertaken to kill people or to come into combat with people. This particular operation was undertaken to destroy facilities, to destroy ammunition, and to destroy weapons, and that is what this operation is all about.

Senator SYMINGTON. How many people did you kill?

Secretary LAIRD. Senator Symington, I can give you the figures from the field, but I have been one of those who has been stressing the amount of ammunition and underground facilities that have been destroyed.

Since I have been Secretary of Defense I have not gotten into the business of body count and killed in action. In connection with the Cambodian operation, I have tried to discuss the millions of rounds of ammunition that have been uncovered, the underground facilities that are being destroyed, the weapons captured, and so forth. These are the objectives of this operation.

If you want me to give you the other figures, I will, and I will have Admiral Moorer give them to you at this time.

Senator SYMINGTON. I do not want to take the time. Please put it in the record.

Secretary LAIRD. Admiral Moorer will give you an up-to-date report on the facilities, the ammunition, and other factors of this operation.

Senator FULBRIGHT. I hope you won't take the time to do it here.

Senator SYMINGTON. Please put it in the record.

Secretary LAIRD. As long as the question has come up, it should be put in the record.

U.S. ACTIVITIES IN SOUTHEAST ASIA

Senator SYMINGTON. You can answer it now, or put it in the record, but for years we have been hearing that we have been successful because 128 Americans have been killed, 100 or 200 South Vietnamese have been killed; 9,860 of the enemy have been killed. The idea apparently was that if we killed enough of these people they would quit. I think that is one of the major mistakes of our getting into this war, and then escalating it; because we are running into nationalism; and are in a guerrilla war.

General Dayan wrote an article. It was published here in the papers in Washington years ago. He said if the North Vietnamese and Vietcong turned to guerrilla warfare, we would never beat them. It seems we do not want to beat them now because we are moving out.

If we really want to get out, it is hard for me to see how we are getting out by invading another country. These are the thoughts which run through my mind. If you want to, please give the figures for the record.

FIGURES ON CAMBODIAN SANCTUARY OPERATION

Secretary LAIRD. Well, Senator Symington, I would be happy to put them in the record. I know that in these congressional hearings, sometimes it is better to yield to the judgment of the committee members, and if it is your judgment that you do not want——

Senator SYMINGTON. Not mine.

Secretary LAIRD. We will be happy to put them in the record at this point.

Senator SYMINGTON. I bow to whatever you want to do, sir.

Secretary LAIRD. We will put them in the record at this point.

(The information follows.)

Military update of Cambodian operations May 18, 1970

Latest cumulative data:

Enemy killed	6,495
Detainees	1,576
Individual weapons captured	9,109
Crew-served weapons captured	1,233
Rice (tons)	3,305
Rice (man months)	145,420
Rockets (each) captured	15,763
Mortar rounds captured	38,879
Small arms ammunition captured	7,238,336
Land and personnel mines captured	1,865
Bunkers destroyed	4,779
Vehicles destroyed or captured	206

Secretary LAIRD. But I think it is important that we understand the number of underground facilities, ammunition, and supplies that have been captured or destroyed. This operation from a tactical standpoint far exceeds the expectations of our military commanders in South Vietnam.

I think it is important that this particular operation not be judged on the day-to-day tactical activities. This type of operation will be judged on its overall strategic success, which has to do with the further reduction of the American presence in Southeast Asia and, particularly, in Vietnam.

Since I have been Secretary of Defense, I have tried to change the debate in America from a debate on why Vietnam, to a debate on why Vietnamization, and I believe there can be a dialog and a debate in this area. As to whether the program that I have recommended to the President, which he supports, for the reduction of the American forces in Vietnam is too fast, as some people seem to think it is, or too slow, as others seem to think it is, I can only say that it is the right program.

WOULD UNITED STATES GO BACK INTO CAMBODIA?

Senator SYMINGTON. If the Communists in Cambodia put the supplies and rice back into Cambodia, would you go back into Cambodia after you come out?

Secretary LAIRD. First, let me reply to that by saying that it will take from 6 to 9 months for that to be done.

In my last visit with General Abrams—and I have a constant exchange with him, but I remember very well on my last visit to Vietnam—he believed that the period through this summer was a critical time period as far as the Vietnamization program was concerned.

The Vietnamization program was started, as you know, at the Midway Conference, and we have increased the size of the South Vietnamese Regular and Regional Forces and Popular Forces at a very rapid rate.

With the training and the leadership problems which they had, we feel we have had success beyond our anticipated goals on all of the military training aspects. We are on schedule on all of the other programs also as far as the military aspects of Vietnamization are concerned.

Should it be necessary in 6 to 8 months to pursue such a program again with respect to Cambodia, I would not announce at this time that it would never be undertaken by the South Vietnamese forces.

But I am willing to state my belief that it would not be necessary for Americans to participate as far as combat responsibilities in Cambodia are concerned.

Senator SYMINGTON. Thank you, Mr. Secretary.

Secretary LAIRD. That is the important thing to bear in mind. I do not believe that to make any other kind of a statement would serve your purposes or my purposes.

Senator SYMINGTON. I agree.

Senator CASE. Mr. Chairman, I just have two or three questions.

Senator FULBRIGHT. It is getting very late, and I would like to clarify one or two things.

Senator CASE. I am almost through.

Senator FULBRIGHT. The Senator has had many questions.

Senator CASE. I had some.

Senator FULBRIGHT. You have had more than all the rest of the committee put together.

Senator CASE. Except the chairman.

Senator FULBRIGHT. Go ahead.

Senator CASE. By that I mean the chairman of the subcommittee.

Senator FULBRIGHT. I wonder if I could ask the witness to make his answers a little shorter.

Senator CASE. Perhaps that is the problem.

Senator FULBRIGHT. His endurance is absolutely unbelievable.

Secretary LAIRD. I will try to answer as many questions as I can with a "Yes" or a "No."

Senator FULBRIGHT. That is right. [Laughter.]

AIR AND LOGISTICS SUPPORT FOR SOUTH VIETNAMESE

Senator CASE. Mr. Secretary, you spoke about not using American troops on another Cambodian exercise similar to this one. You said you would not guarantee that South Vietnamese would not be so used, but that American troops would not.

Suppose South Vietnamese troops do this. Will it be our policy, as the President has announced, that our logistics support and air support will come out with our troops, and will that continue to be our policy if the South Vietnamese go back? Will we give them air and logistics support in that operation?

Secretary LAIRD. This is a question that I cannot answer with a "Yes" or "No," because you have to understand what particular period of time you are talking about in the Vietnamization program.

I am sure the Senator from New Jersey realizes that in phase 1 of the program we turn over the ground combat responsibility to the forces of South Vietnam. The American responsibility for ground combat is presently being reduced.

The programs for air and artillery support are part of phase 2 of the Vietnamization program, but they have already started. We are now turning over at a very rapid rate, a much more rapid rate than was anticipated a year ago, the air support responsibilities in Vietnam.

They have a greater number of pilots in training now than we anticipated a year ago when I briefed this committee. It will not proceed, however, as rapidly as will the turning over of the ground combat responsibilities.

We will be providing some air support for the Vietnamese forces after the ground combat responsibility has been turned over to them.

So, My answer to your question would have to take into consideration the time period to which your anticipated action refers, and where we are in the Vietnamization program with air and artillery support activities.

AIR AND LOGISTICS SUPPORT FOR SANCTUARY OPERATION

Senator CASE. Well, is it still our policy to get out as far as our air support and logistics support and advisers go when we leave at the end of June, even if the South Vietnamese still remain?

Secretary LAIRD. No, we will be maintaining certain logistics support, air support, and artillery support in Vietnam, in phase 2 of the Vietnamization program after the primary combat responsibility has been turned over to the Vietnamese forces.

Senator CASE. I read from the President's press conference: "When we come out our logistics support and air support will come out with the U.S. troops."

Secretary LAIRD. Yes, but you are talking about Vietnam in one breath and Cambodia in the other. The President has made it clear that as far as air support and artillery support in South Vietnam is concerned, that that is not the case. We still will support them. But the President——

Senator CASE. In South Vietnam.

Secretary LAIRD. In South Vietnam.

Senator CASE. I was not talking about that—I was talking about South Vietnamese troops in Cambodia. Will we still give them air and logistics support after we are out?

Secretary LAIRD. As far as air and logistics support are concerned, I think it depends on where we are in the Vietnamization program.

Senator CASE. I am speaking about the end of this June, 1 month and 2 weeks from now.

Secretary LAIRD. That all air support as far as strikes in the sanctuary areas be withdrawn?

Senator CASE. I am referring to what the President was talking about when he said these words, "When we come out our logistics support and air support will come out with them," that is, with our troops.

Secretary LAIRD. Well, Senator Case, I would not recommend to the President that all air operations cease over the sanctuary areas on June 30.

Now, as far as giving close air support to the South Vietnamese forces, I would recommend that we not give close air support in the sanctuary areas to the South Vietnamese forces. But I do not want that confused in any way with other types of air operations in Cambodia, because I would recommend the use of American air power for interdiction in the sanctuary areas after June 30.

Senator CASE. Then I do not really quite understand what the President was talking about.

There is just one further aspect and that is this: on May 13——

Secretary LAIRD. Senator Case, you asked for my recommendation. I would not recommend——

Senator CASE. I understand. I know.

Secretary LAIRD. I would not recommend as a fixed announced position of the U.S. Government that airpower not be used at all in the sanctuary areas after June 30. If that is the impression that the President's statement leaves with you, I regret it, because I would recommend that airpower be used.

Senator CASE. I just want to understand what we are talking about.

Secretary LAIRD. I would only recommend it if it is necessary to use it, of course, Senator Case. But in the event that it is necessary to use it I would so recommend, and I do not want to mislead this committee as far as my recommendation is concerned.

AIR AND LOGISTICS SUPPORT FOR SOUTH VIETNAMESE IN CAMBODIA

Senator CASE. The last question: on May 13, Vice President Ky seemed to be suggesting that South Vietnamese operations were in direct support of the Cambodian Government. He said, "if they, the Cambodians, really need our help we will stay here and fight."

My question is whether air and logistics support of South Vietnamese forces in their achievement of this mission will be supplied, and also our advisers?

Secretary LAIRD. I think the Secretary of State and the White House, in its briefing on Saturday, made it very clear that they would not support that kind of an operation.

Senator CASE. Thank you, Mr. Chairman.

Senator FULBRIGHT. Mr. Secretary, I want to start with one or two questions you can answer yes or no.

REQUEST FOR DR. FOSTER TO APPEAR

Can you relay the request to Dr. Foster to appear before the subcommittee of this committee within the next 2 weeks?

Secretary LAIRD. I would be very happy to do that, Mr. Chairman.

Senator FULBRIGHT. Will you see that he appears?

Secretary LAIRD. I think I can arrange that.

Senator FULBRIGHT. We would like you to come back, too, of course, if you have time.

Secretary LAIRD. I would be delighted to come back.

Senator FULBRIGHT. Senator Gore had to leave for a family matter and he asked me to arrange for Dr. Foster's appearance between the two of you. If Dr. Foster would agree to come before the subcommittee, we would appreciate it.

Secretary LAIRD. I will see, Mr. Chairman, that Dr. Foster is here.

NEWSWEEK REPORT OF CABLE ON CAMBODIA

Senator FULBRIGHT. Here is one. The Washington Post May 18, 1970, has an article which says that Newsweek Magazine carries a report of what the magazine said was a top secret cable sent to General Abrams from the Secretary of Defense here, which, I assume, is you. It reads as follows:

Dear Abe, in light of the controversy over the U.S. move into Cambodia, the American public would be impressed by any of the following evidence of the success of the operation: (1) high-ranking enemy prisoners, (2) major enemy headquarters such as COSVN (the Communist Central Control Office for South Vietnam), (3) large enemy caches * * *

The answer to that is yes or no. Which is it?

Secretary LAIRD. The answer is no. No such cable was sent, and the Washington office of Newsweek called to apologize this morning.

Senator FULBRIGHT. That clears it up and I am glad to give you the opportunity to do that.

Secretary LAIRD. The problem is that it did receive quite a lot of attention before the retraction came through.

Senator FULBRIGHT. You always have the advantage of your comments here. As I said in the beginning, they receive quite a little attention too, so I do not think you need to be as worried as some.

RESERVATION OF TROOP PROTECTION IN VIETNAM

You said earlier that the protection of the troops in Vietnam was reserved in the Laos amendment that was passed last year.

I have had the staff make a search of the record. There is no such discussion, no reservation of any kind, nor allusion to any kind of a reservation. I do not know how you could have gotten the idea that the amendment last year with regard to troops in Laos and Thailand had a reservation that it did not apply to the protection of troops. How could you get——

Secretary LAIRD. There was no question in my mind at any time that the right to protect Americans serving in Vietnam was certainly a very important element of the amendment.

Senator FULBRIGHT. On what do you base it? There was nothing in the debate in the Senate.

Secretary LAIRD. I am sure that it was implied—there has been no change of policy now so far as that is concerned.

Senator FULBRIGHT. I know, Mr. Secretary, but you have developed a novel application of a theory. The theory is all right in a reasonable application, that is to protect the President's right to protect the troops. Now you are expanding it without limit. Apparently he can do anything he likes abroad by alleging that he is protecting the lives of the troops.

Someone said the other day that on that theory you could expand the war to any length, even bombing Peking and Moscow.

Are there any limits at all to the theory that he can protect our troops by moving anywhere in the world that he feels is necessary? This is rather new constitutional law.

Secretary LAIRD. Certainly, there are limits. I am talking about the protection of U.S. forces in combat in South Vietnam. I do not mean to filibuster this question, Mr. Chairman, but I think it is interesting just to take an example of the experiences I have had.

When I was in Vietnam up in the I Corps area back in 1969, when the operation in the A Shau Valley was going on, we had a situation where a route was being used in Laos, and it was necessary for American forces and South Vietnamese forces to use a road that goes into Laos to carry on a military operation that was going on in South Vietnam.

I approved that action on the spot because there would have been, in my mind, considerably more American casualties if it had not been permitted, and I do not believe it was the intent of the House of Representatives or the Senate of the United States to prevent that kind of an operation.

Senator FULBRIGHT. The clear purpose of that, as of the present resolution, is preventing the spread of the war to these adjoining countries. Mr. Cooper and Mr. Church both had that in mind then and they have it in mind now.

They regret they did not include Cambodia in the hope that this might have been a deterrent to this move to enlarge the war into Cambodia, but it was certainly the clear understanding, and the debate will not reveal any reservation of the kind you mention.

There are no U.S. ground combat troops, as I understand it, in the delta. Is that correct?

Secretary LAIRD. That is correct. We have completely Vietnamized the operation in the delta area. We have ground advisers, however, in the delta area, but as far as ground combat responsibilities in the IV Corps area are concerned, they have been turned over to the forces of South Vietnam.

DENIAL OF INFORMATION ON WEAPONS SHIPMENTS TO CAMBODIA

Senator FULBRIGHT. I don't like to have a distinguished member of the Joint Chiefs and an admiral here without asking him something. Admiral Moorer, are you aware of the fact that two of our staff members were in Saigon just a few days ago. They were told that following Joint Chiefs of Staff orders, MACV (Military Assistance Command Vietnam) would not tell them how many of the AK-47's sent to Cambodia were from U.S. stock, how many M-1's and M-2's were sent to Cambodia and from where, and how the M-1's were transported to Cambodia. Are you aware of such an order?

Admiral MOORER. No, sir.

I am aware that they asked the question and that it was referred to Washington.

Senator FULBRIGHT. Are you aware that the Joint Chiefs ordered MACV not to answer those questions?

Admiral MOORER. I am not aware of a direct order to that effect, but rather it was stated they should as the question in Washington.

Senator FULBRIGHT. How about an indirect order? Did you suggest indirectly that they not respond to the committee's inquiries?

Admiral MOORER. No, sir; we have never made any indirect order of that kind.

Senator FULBRIGHT. How do you explain the refusal of MACV to answer their questions about the M-1 and M-2 rifles?

Secretary LAIRD. Could I answer that, Mr. Chairman?

Senator FULBRIGHT. Yes, they were told this was from the JCS orders. You can certainly answer it.

Secretary LAIRD. I believe, Mr. Chairman, it should be pointed out that under the terms of the Foreign Assistance Act determination and authorization under section 503, 505(b)——

Senator FULBRIGHT. We are aware of that. We discussed that at length.

Secretary LAIRD (continuing). Of the Foreign Assistance Act, it requires a Presidential determination.

Senator FULBRIGHT. We are aware of that. Has a Presidential determination been made?

Secretary LAIRD. A Presidential determination must be sent to the Congress within 30 days after its effective date. The President announced on April 30 in his appearance to the Nation that certain supplies would be made available. Such a Presidential determination will be forthcoming to the Congress, and at that time, after the determination has been signed by the President of the United States, that matter will be fully outlined before this committee, but until the actual signing takes place—and it was my understanding that congressional notification has to be within 30 days following the effective date of the President's action—I can assure you that that Presidential determination will be presented to this committee.

Senator FULBRIGHT. This was all over the press. There were statements. The only variations were in the numbers. One report said 1,500. The next day or two it was 2,500, and then I think it went up to all kinds of numbers emanating from Saigon. This would seem to indicate that there was reluctance to communicate with representatives of this committee rather than the press.

Secretary LAIRD. The problem involved here, Mr. Chairman, is that I believe the full Presidential determination should be put before this committee and it will be, and it is just a matter of a day or two.

The time limit runs out shortly and I can assure you that the law will be adhered to as far as the Presidential determination is concerned.

AVAILABILITY OF INFORMATION TO THE COMMITTEE

Senator FULBRIGHT. Is our committee staff going to be met in the field with instructions that no one in the field is to answer questions, that they have to get all their answers here in Washington? Is that going to be the policy of the Defense Department?

Secretary LAIRD. I do not believe that is the policy of the Department of Defense, Mr. Chairman. In regard to this particular Presidential determination, though, I do not believe it is proper——

Senator FULBRIGHT. What is improper about it? You say he has 30 days to make it. According to what you just stated, if he can get under the wire, it will be legal. What is improper about stating it?

Secretary LAIRD. I can assure you that the full amount will be given to this committee. I believe that your committee is better served by having the full presentation made all together rather than on a piecemeal basis.

As I understand it——

Senator FULBRIGHT. I suppose when this war is over, if it is, then you are going to come up and inform us about all that happened.

It completely nullifies the function of the Senate in this whole matter of foreign relations.

Secretary LAIRD. Senator, I was here when this section was put into the Foreign Assistance Act. There was a determination made by the legislative branch of our Government. The procedures are set forth clearly and concisely. They will be followed by the President of the United States and if the Congress wishes to establish other procedures than the 30-day notification, that certainly can be done by the Congress of the United States. But I can assure you that the President is following the Foreign Assistance Act as approved by this committee and the Congress.

Senator FULBRIGHT. When were the first M-2's shipped to Cambodia?

Secretary LAIRD. The first were delivered within a few days after the President made his public announcement on April 30.

Senator FULBRIGHT. None were shipped before?

Secretary LAIRD. Yes, sir; I can give you the dates, and the full information will be presented in the Presidential determination.

Senator FULBRIGHT. By that time it will be obsolete and there will be other things than AK-47's that will be worrying us, but this ties-in. All of these questions tie in to the relationship of the executive and the Senate, in particular as to whether or not you are willing for the Senate to play a part in foreign relations.

Secretary LAIRD. Mr. Chairman, I just want to make it very clear that we are following the provisions of——

Senator FULBRIGHT. That provision does not say you shall not inform the Senate when you do it. It says you eventually will have to make another report. There is nothing in the law that does not require you to tell the Senate when you ship these. As a matter of fact, I could read the law as if we ought to be told before you do it to give us a reasonable interpretation in order to have an opportunity to express our views.

SECRETARY OF STATE'S TESTIMONY ON CAMBODIA

I think that comes back to this matter, which is very confusing to everyone. I want to read what the Secretary of State said on April 23, as reported in The New York Times of the 14th of May.

He (the Secretary) explained publicly for the first time controversial testimony that he had given to a congressional committee on April 23, which has been interpreted as meaning that he opposed the move into Cambodia. According to congressional sources, Mr. Rogers had said, "We recognize that if we escalate and if we get involved in Cambodia with our ground troops that our whole program is defeated."

That is a quote, and I will put the whole article in. This had been used before.

(The article follows.)

ROGERS RULES OUT TROOPS TO DEFEND CAMBODIA REGIME—ALSO BARS U.S. PLANES BUT SAYS AID BY BANGKOK AND SAIGON IS ENCOURAGED—NIXON DOCTRINE CITED—SECRETARY EXPECTS ANXIETIES OVER THE INCURSIONS TO BE EASED BY WITHDRAWALS

(By Peter Grose)

WASHINGTON, May 13.—Secretary of State William P. Rogers said today that the United States would not become "militarily involved" with troop or air support to defend the Cambodian Government, but was encouraging South Vietnam and Thailand to cooperate with Cambodia in meeting Communist threats.

This policy, he said, is the essence of the Nixon doctrine—"Asians cooperating with each other to handle Asian problems."

Since both Thailand and South Vietnam receive large amounts of United States military aid, Mr. Roger's remarks pointed toward the possibility of some long-term arrangements for the United States to aid the Cambodian regime of Lon Nol indirectly even if direct engagement was ruled out.

The Secretary put in a surprise appearance at a routine State Department briefing to make his first detailed public remarks on the two-week-old military sweep of Communist sanctuaries in Cambodia and the subsequent wave of criticism in this country and abroad.

TELLS OF MEETINGS

Describing his meetings in the last week with five delegations of university students and faculty members, Mr. Rogers said: "The moderates were very confused about whether the Government was going to get bogged down in Cambodia."

"I was impressed by their emotional involvement," he said. "It was an emotional involvement based on a reasoning process. They talked of the real issues, asked intelligent questions."

But he expressed confidence that their anxieties would be dissipated as the Cambodian operation was terminated.

"This is not an escalation," he said. "It is not an attempt to win a military victory. If it were, their anxieties would be well founded. But the President has committed himself to limitations of time and distance, and events will answer these anxieties."

Initial foreign reaction has been "reserved or negative," he said, but this, too, is changing as the limits of the operation become clear.

By the end of June, Mr. Rogers stressed, all American troops will be withdrawn from the Cambodian sanctuaries, as will the American personnel accompanying a South Vietnamese flotilla up the Mekong River to a point 21.7 miles inside Cambodia—the limit of penetration imposed by President Nixon.

SEA AND AIR ACTIVITY

The Secretary left the way open, however, for continuing two other actions to curtail Communist operations in Cambodia: patrolling of international waters to prevent supplies from reaching Communist base areas and air activity—which he did not further define—over the jungle border between Cambodia and South Vietnam.

Both of these measures have long predated the move into the sanctuaries, Mr. Rogers said. He would not commit the Administration to terminating them at the same time as the specific maneuver now under way.

"We don't intend to become involved militarily in support of any Cambodian government," the secretary said several times. Under questioning, he explained that by involvement he meant the use of American troops or air support for other national forces.

"I'm talking about United States troops, or air support or something," Mr. Rogers said. "Now, in terms of assistance, military assistance by way of supplies or otherwise, the President has announced that we are going to provide some assistance consistent with the present authority that we have. Obviously any larger program would require Congressional approval. I don't think we have crossed that bridge. We have no present plans to embark on that kind of program."

Elsewhere in his relaxed 35-minute news conference, Mr. Rogers made clear that he included military advisers when he spoke of limitations on engaging American troops in Cambodia.

He said it was probably premature to discuss all the ramifications of the relationship evolving among Cambodia, South Vietnam and Thailand.

DOUBTS THREAT TO PROGRAM

Mr. Rogers acknowledged that South Vietnamese military support for the Lon Nol Government might divert energies from the war in South Vietnam, but he dismissed it as a threat to the Nixon program for transferring combat duties to South Vietnamese forces.

Mr. Rogers reiterated the pledge made yesterday by the Secretary of Defense, Melvin R. Laird, that American troops "will be out of combat in South Vietnam by the middle of 1971."

He explained publicly for the first time controversial testimony that he had given to a Congressional committee on April 23, which has been interpreted as meaning that he opposed the move into Cambodia.

According to Congressional sources, Mr. Rogers had said "we recognize that if he escalate and if we get involved in Cambodia with our ground troops that our whole program is defeated."

POINTS OUT THE CONTEXT

Mr. Rogers did not challenge the accuracy of the quotation, but pointed out that it was in the context of questions about sending United States troops to support the Lon Nol Government.

"I was not referring to the possibility of incursions, of temporary activities," he said. "If I had been able to read over the transcript, I would have made it clear that I meant any 'deep' involvement, involvement of any length."

Mr. Rogers also confirmed that he had discussed the Administration's problems of relating to young people with Walter J. Hickel, Secretary of the Interior, before Mr. Hickel wrote his stern letter to President Nixon last week.

"There was no discussion of any letter or any problems he may have had seeing the President," Mr. Rogers said, "but I agreed with his concern about the attitude of young people, the importance that young people have confidence in their Government and the question of whether we were communicating enough with them."

"Communication is such a fashionable word these days, but I'm not sure that anyone really knows what is meant by the word," he added.

TIME REQUIRED FOR PLANNING CAMBODIAN OPERATION

Senator FULBRIGHT. We had two meetings with the Secretary and one of them was on the 27th of April. There wasn't the slightest indication in that entire hearing that you were contemplating moving our forces into Cambodia. It is perfectly obvious that you had been contemplating this and plans had been made long before that.

Is that not so? You could not possibly mount this kind of operation on 2 days' notice, could you?

Secretary LAIRD. Mr. Chairman, as the decision is concerned, the decision was between the evening of Monday, April 27th, and the morning of Tuesday, April 28th.

Now for the planning figures and planning dates, there are many different dates involved in the planning area, but as far as the decision is concerned, it was on that Monday evening that the decision was finally made.

Senator FULBRIGHT. I don't know what you mean by decision—the go order. It is like sending off the Apollo. They have been working on the Apollo for 5 years. The go order or the decision to go, comes at the last seconds of the count-down because up until that moment they can always say "Don't go," but here is the Secretary of State who comes before this committee, and this prompts me to ask you——

U.S. INVOLVEMENT IN CAMBODIA

Secretary LAIRD. Mr. Chairman, I want to make clear that I agree with the Secretary of State, and I am sure that there was no disagreement in this operation between the Secretary of State and myself. I think he was referring to the use of American forces and American advisors in a Cambodian operation.

Now, the sanctuary areas are really North Vietnamese areas, they were occupied by them, and in an interview in U.S. News & World Report that was conducted prior to the President's speech, I expressed the same feeling as far as Cambodia itself was concerned. But in the same interview I supported and recommended the use of American forces and American advisers in the sanctuary areas.

Senator FULBRIGHT. Mr. Secretary, this kind of semantic gymnastics makes a whole shambles of any possibility of communication. This was Cambodia.

Secretary LAIRD. Mr. Chairman, I made this very clear in my interview in U.S. News & World Report.

Senator FULBRIGHT. You made very clear what you said, but it does not conform with any traditional use of the language. These new terms, the new use of this language makes it impossible to understand.

The Secretary says, "We recognize that if we escalate and if we get involved in Cambodia." He did not say in that area of Cambodia under the influence of the North Vietnamese; he said, "Cambodia."

The line had been recognized for 4 or 5 years. This is why you have already spent a long time discussing these sanctuaries. There is no mystery about that.

The reason you had not done it before was because it was Cambodia.

Secretary LAIRD. Mr. Chairman, the Secretary of State is perfectly capable of taking care of himself, but I do not believe that it is quite fair to use that particular quote when he was talking about a complete overall——

Senator FULBRIGHT. I am only using it by way of background.

Secretary LAIRD. Involvement. The President has set out a very limited objective in the so-called sanctuary areas. We are not going to become involved beyond that. We are going to be out of that area by the 30th of June.

COOPER-CHURCH AMENDMENT

Senator FULBRIGHT. Why do you oppose the Cooper-Church resolution if you are going to be? It is beyond my comprehension if you really mean that.

Secretary LAIRD. Well, I would just like to make one comment in regard to the Cooper-Church amendment. I think it is the thrust of the amendment and the attitude it represents that I have trouble with.

Senator FULBRIGHT. The what?

Secretary LAIRD. The thrust of the amendment and the attitude it represents.

Senator FULBRIGHT. It is certainly consistent with what you just said.

Secretary LAIRD. It does not have a date on it.

Senator FULBRIGHT. Would you prefer we put in "end of June"? Would that make it acceptable to you?

Secretary LAIRD. It certainly would be in support of the President's position with a particular date on it.

Senator FULBRIGHT. You do not think it would be enacted before the end of June, do you?

Secretary LAIRD. Well, I am talking about the thrust of the amendment, Senator.

Senator FULBRIGHT. Yes.

Secretary LAIRD. I am not talking about when it is enacted.

Senator FULBRIGHT. As a matter of fact, it had a date in it and it was taken out at the request of some members. I do not want to get off on that line now. Since you volunteered this, I wondered if you would be willing to accept it.

I cannot for the life of me understand how it is inconsistent with what you just said.

Secretary LAIRD. I want you to know——
Senator FULBRIGHT. I want to explain why I asked you to use Secretary Rogers' testimony.
Secretary LAIRD. This goes to the whole question of our delivering on our pledges as far as Vietnamization is concerned.
Every commitment that has been made has been lived up to by this Administration.

DOES UNITED STATES INTEND TO INVADE ANY OTHER COUNTRY?

Senator FULBRIGHT. This is one thing I am leading up to with this. That was the 23d. On the 27th, we had a hearing and it has been said that we did not ask Secretary Rogers directly, "Are you going into Cambodia with the troops?" The reason we didn't is this previous statement and the fact that no one thought or dreamed that we would be so foolish. So we did not ask him.
Here is a question you can answer yes or no. Are you contemplating now going into any country in the foreseeable future with American forces?
Secretary LAIRD. We have no plans——
Senator FULBRIGHT. I do not want to overlook it.
Secretary LAIRD. We have no plans. [Laughter.]
Senator FULBRIGHT. Admiral, do you know of any plans now to invade any other country in the foresseable future?
Admiral MOORER. I do not, Mr. Chairman.
Senator FULBRIGHT. Good. I regard that as a commitment that as of now that you are not about to, and I would hope that the decision won't be made tomorrow to move into Burma or into Laos. This is what we were accused of being less than careful in asking the Secretary, but I can pledge you my word we had a request for a very large amount of weapons. Our time was taken up by that and it was thoroughly examined. The committee was unanimous in opposition to giving weapons.

EXECUTIVE BRANCH'S CANDOR WITH SENATE ON CAMBODIA QUESTIONED

The record is clear that you had surveyed this, as you said, from every point of view, the effect on the Chinese, upon the Russians, upon the SALT talks, upon everything. I do not know whether or not you did all that in that last 10 minutes. The Secretary is a member of the National Security Council, is he not? If then he participated in this, how in the world, if there is any effort or any desire for frank and open communication, could he come before the committee and not volunteer the knowledge that we were contemplating, not arms so much. This was the matter under discussion, which he discussed at length and seemed very solicitous of our views, while at the very same time you were about to send troops.
That is what is behind this very uncertain relationship and also, I may say, behind a move like the Church-Cooper resolution. I, at least do not believe that we have been treated with candor and with frankness to the degree that our responsibilities under the Constitution justify. I think as a former member of this body you could appreciate that because I cannot say the Secretary refused and deliberately misrepresented it. He just did not represent what was obviously underway.

You agree that you do not have to justify the Secretary, but I am telling you why there is this feeling on the part of the committee and why there is, in my view, the strength of the Cooper-Church resolution. It is not by any means an effort to try to hamstring the President. It is simply a genuine effort to try to assert what we believe to be the direct, clear constitutional responsibility of this committee to be consulted and to have an opportunity to give its advice on these very serious moves which involve the lives of the people.

As a former Member here, you ought to appreciate it. I don't blame people, who have spent their lives in other activities and feel no responsibility up here, for not appreciating that the Senate has a feeling of this character.

Secretary LAIRD. Mr. Chairman, could I respond?

Senator FULBRIGHT. Yes.

Secretary LAIRD. I believe that the relationships which this Administration has had with the various committees to which we have responsibilities have been as candid and as frank as we possibly could make them. We have tried to deliver on every one of the commitments we have made to this committee, to the Armed Services Committees, and to the Congress. We have done this at a time when we are cutting back on the American involvement in Vietnam. Instead of American forces going up in Southeast Asia, American forces have been going down.

Senator FULBRIGHT. Mr. Secretary, it has been bogged down. How do you explain the last thing?

Secretary LAIRD. As far as the language in the amendment is concerned, I hardly think that it would have been the proper position of the executive branch to be presenting limitations as far as Executive power is concerned.

Senator FULBRIGHT. I understand that.

Secretary LAIRD. When I was in the Congress I was involved with placing a few limitations on the executive branch of our Government, but I never expected to receive the support of the Eisenhower administration, the Johnson administration——

Senator FULBRIGHT. I am not asking for your support.

Secretary LAIRD. Of the Kennedy administration.

Senator FULBRIGHT. If you do not care to give it, that is perfectly all right.

Secretary LAIRD. I think the matter is one that can be worked out, but I believe that it should be worked out through the legislative process.

Senator FULBRIGHT. You are a master at obfuscation. I raised the question of the Secretary's coming before this committee and not telling the committee when I think all the circumstances dictated that he should if there were any desire to communicate with the committee in a way that we could play our role. I think he clearly did not do it. Maybe he did not know it.

WAS SECRETARY OF STATE AWARE OF SITUATION?

Do you know whether or not he was aware of what was going on in the Joint Chiefs and with General Abrams? Can you say yes or no? Do you know?

Secretary LAIRD. Of course he was aware.

Senator FULBRIGHT. He was aware.

Secretary LAIRD. But the decision had not been made at that particular time.

Senator FULBRIGHT. It was about to be made, and within the very near future.

I wanted to ask Admiral Moorer one other question.

COMMUNIST CHINESE REACTION TO SANCTUARY OPERATION

When you considered this move, did you believe that the Chinese would break off the talks in Warsaw?

Admiral MOORER. Well, I think there was always a possibility, sir, in evaluating this overall, we did not think that they would.

Senator FULBRIGHT. Do you believe today that China will not enter the war in Indochina if our incursion into Cambodia significantly weakens the North Vietnamese?

Admiral MOORER. Yes, sir; I do not believe that the Chinese will come all the way into Cambodia in force.

Senator FULBRIGHT. What was the Joint Chiefs' belief in Korea just prior to the Chinese entering that war? It was the same, was it not? They did not believe they would. Isn't that so?

Admiral MOORER. I think it was an evaluation made by General MacArthur to that effect, sir.

Senator FULBRIGHT. Do you mean the Joint Chiefs did not enter into it?

Admiral MOORER. I am sure the information was explained and the entire command structure made that evaluation as I recall history.

Senator FULBRIGHT. Why do you think we should have such confidence that your judgment now is any better than it was then about the Chinese? In fact the circumstances are so similar——

Admiral MOORER. Well, sir, I think they are not similar in the sense that at that time the action was geographically located very close to the Chinese border, and there was a very close alliance between the North Koreans and the Chinese. I do not think it is quite a similar situation from a geographic or political point of view.

Senator FULBRIGHT. You say the Chinese would not come all the way into Cambodia. What about Laos? Do you think they might come into Laos?

Admiral MOORER. I think they might cross the northern border of Laos with a few forces if they saw fit to do so, but it is a long way from northern Laos at the Chinese border to Cambodia.

Senator FULBRIGHT. We are in Laos. What do you think our reaction would be if they came into Laos? Would we withdraw?

Admiral MOORER. Well, I think that decision would have to be made at the time.

Senator FULBRIGHT. You undoubtedly have contingency plans to meet such contingencies. Do you not?

Admiral MOORER. Yes, sir; we are continually looking into all possibilities.

Senator FULBRIGHT. That is right.

Admiral MOORER. I think we would be derelict in our duties if we did not.

RISK OF CHINESE COMMUNIST ENTRY INTO WAR

Senator FULBRIGHT. What worries me is the equanimity with which the entry of the Chinese is regarded apparently by both the Secretary and the Joint Chiefs. This doesn't seem to be a matter of concern.

Aren't you worried about it?

Admiral MOORER. Yes, sir; I am worried. I am worried about the entire operation. But I think on balance that it is unlikely that the Chinese would move into Cambodia with combat forces.

Senator FULBRIGHT. Not that you have asked me, but speaking for myself, I think it is a risk that is utterly out of all proportion to any possible gain. I deeply regret either your entry into Cambodia or certainly your impending entry, as it appears from the press, into Laos. My own view would be that if this war continues to escalate in the next few weeks, as it has the last 2 or 3, that they are very likely to come in, for whatever it is worth, because I do not think they have changed very much. They resent the intrusion of Western countries with military forces right up against their frontiers.

Admiral MOORER. Well, Mr. Chairman, I testified that we have no plan for——

Senator FULBRIGHT. No decision has been made.

Admiral MOORER. No plans to do that.

Senator FULBRIGHT. I realize you did.

Secretary LAIRD. Mr. Chairman, as long as they are not using the TV cameras, why don't we turn the lights off?

Senator FULBRIGHT. I broke my sun glasses. I should have been forewarned. Turn off the lights.

Secretary LAIRD. As long as they are not using them, we might as well have a pleasant hour or two this evening. (Laughter.)

Senator FULBRIGHT. If I had thought of this yes-or-no answer earlier, perhaps we would have been through by now. I did not think of it at the time.

Do you have——

Secretary LAIRD. This is kind of like the fourth degree here.

Senator FULBRIGHT. These are easy questions now.

U.S. PLANS CONCERNING CAMBODIA

Do you have plans to retain U.S. forces in Cambodia?

Secretary LAIRD. No.

Admiral MOORER. No, sir.

Senator FULBRIGHT. You have no plans to send U.S. advisers to the Cambodian Government?

Secretary LAIRD. No.

Senator FULBRIGHT. Do you have plans to finance third-country advisers or combat troops to the Cambodian Government?

Secretary LAIRD. The question involving the use of South Vietnamese forces, and their particular support, is a question which has not been completely resolved.

I cannot give you a yes-or-no answer to that particular question as far as I am concerned.

Senator FULBRIGHT. These are the advisers to the Cambodian Government. Do you have any plans for flying combat missions to support the Cambodian Government forces?

Secretary LAIRD. Not to support the Cambodian Government forces, no.

Senator FULBRIGHT. The Church-Cooper resolution deals with that.

Secretary LAIRD. Our particular plans as far as I am concerned would be as they affect our operations in Vietnam.

Senator FULBRIGHT. What is that?

Secretary LAIRD. As they would affect our operations in Vietnam—concerning any air power used in Cambodia.

Senator FULBRIGHT. Using this qualification, you could support the Cambodian Army if you felt that had some relationship to the war in South Vietnam. Is that right? Is that what you are saying?

Secretary LAIRD. I believe the thrust of the amendment refers to air activities whose primary mission is in support of the Cambodian Army, and there are no plans to use air power in that way.

Senator FULBRIGHT. No; I think if the Cambodian Government were induced to support the war in South Vietnam, I think this would be prohibited by that amendment.

The thrust of the amendment is to prevent our involvement in Cambodian affairs. As you know, it is very carefully worded.

Secretary LAIRD. That is correct. There are no plans as long as that is the primary mission, Mr. Chairman.

Senator FULBRIGHT. You have no plans for flying combat missions to support the Cambodian Government's military operations?

Secretary LAIRD. No; but as I testified before the Armed Services Committee, and I want to be very frank with you and the members of this committee, as far as air power in support of our mission in Vietnam is concerned, I would recommend that air power be used in the sanctuary areas if it is needed and necessary in order to protect our Vietnamization program.

Now this is a decision that——

PRESIDENT'S 21-MILE LIMIT

Senator FULBRIGHT. How long is that area or how wide is that area from the South Vietnamese border? Is that the same as the President's 21 miles?

Secretary LAIRD. Yes; the President has established a 21-mile limit.

Senator FULBRIGHT. Do you accept that as a limitation of what you are saying?

Secretary LAIRD. As a defense planner, I do not believe from my point of view that long-term limitations necessarily improve our military effectiveness.

Senator FULBRIGHT. The President said this himself. Did he not? Didn't he say this publicly? I think he used 30 kilometers.

Secretary LAIRD. He used this in regard to ground operations, sir. I think he used 21 miles in his briefing of the congressional leadership and it was reported soon after that briefing that he had placed a limitation and this is correct as far as the ground operations are concerned.

DOES UNITED STATES PAY MERCENARIES TO HELP CAMBODIANS?

Senator FULBRIGHT. Do we have any mercenaries today that we are paying helping the Cambodians?

Secretary LAIRD. That we are paying?

Senator FULBRIGHT. Yes; that we are paying.
Secretary LAIRD. Not to my knowledge——
Senator FULBRIGHT. That is what I meant.
Secretary LAIRD. Mr. Chairman.
Senator FULBRIGHT. That is one of the elements involved in the Cooper-Church resolution. You would know if we had any. Would you not?
Secretary LAIRD. If they were paid by the Department of Defense, I certainly would know, but I know of no mercenaries paid by the U.S. Government.
Senator FULBRIGHT. Government?
Secretary LAIRD. At this time, and I think certainly if they were paid by any Department, we would know it.
Senator FULBRIGHT. That is what I meant.

EFFECT OF SANCTUARY OPERATION ON SALT

Mr. Foster, is it your view that these developments in the recent weeks, the intrusion or whatever you care to call it—What do you prefer to call it, a visit rather than an invasion? You have this fancy word that is too difficult for me to remember. It is some kind of reaction.
Senator CASE. Protective reaction.
Senator FULBRIGHT. You do not mind my saying incursion or intrusion. You do not think this will have any effect on the SALT talks, Mr Foster?
Dr. FOSTER. I have thought about it, Mr. Chairman.
Senator FULBRIGHT. You had not thought about it.
Dr. FOSTER. I have thought about it.
Senator FULBRIGHT. You have?
Dr. FOSTER. Yes. It was my opinion that SALT is of such overriding importance, both to us and I would hope to the Soviet Union, that the U.S. effort with regard to these sanctuaries in Cambodia would not affect those talks.
Senator FULBRIGHT. Then your decision and your own view is that this intrusion into Cambodia and possibly into Laos, which is, as I say, foreshadowed by the reports this morning, will not have an adverse effect on the SALT talks? How do you explain Mr. Kosygin's press conference statement? How do you reconcile your view with Mr. Kosygin's? Do you think your or Mr. Kosygin's view is more likely to reflect the Russian Government's view?
Dr. FOSTER. Mr. Chairman, that transcends my area of responsibility. In that respect, I am just not competent.
Senator FULBRIGHT. I do not know why not. You made a judgment. I assume you advised your superiors that in your opinion this intrusion would not affect the SALT talks.
Dr. FOSTER. No, sir; I was not consulted with regard to this.
Senator FULBRIGHT. You were not consulted?
Dr. FOSTER. No, sir; I was not. I was just stating my personal opinion, I did think about the matter myself and I came to the conclusion that our action in Cambodia would not affect the SALT talks. Now whether Mr. Kosygin spoke from the point of view of giving political support to Communists in the Asian theater or not, I just do not know.

EFFECT OF DEPLOYMENT OF MIRV ON SALT

Senator FULBRIGHT. Has your opinion been requested with regard to the deployment of MIRV? Has anyone consulted you about that?

Dr. FOSTER. Yes, sir.

Senator FULBRIGHT. Have you recommended that it be deployed?

Dr. FOSTER. Yes, sir; I have.

Senator FULBRIGHT. Your judgment is that the deployment of MIRV's will not affect the SALT talks?

Dr. FOSTER. My judgment is, sir, that its effect will be to help the U.S. position in the SALT talks.

Senator FULBRIGHT. Really?

Dr. FOSTER. Yes.

Senator FULBRIGHT. How?

Dr. FOSTER. I believe the United States must do what is necessary for its own security, and at the same time make the greatest effort to honestly and earnestly negotiate with the Soviets for a settlement in regard to strategic armed forces.

INDEPENDENT SCIENTIFIC AGREEMENT WITH WITNESS'S POSITION QUESTIONED

Senator FULBRIGHT. Do you know of any reputable or well-known scientist in your general field, not in the employ of or paid by the Government, such as Dr. Kistiakowsky and Dr. York, who agrees with your position?

Dr. FOSTER. Well, Mr. Chairman, I have not discussed this particular point.

Senator FULBRIGHT. Then the answer is no. You do not know. Is that right?

Dr. FOSTER. Mr. Chairman, if I answer your question with a "no," it implies that no scientist supports my view. The truth of the matter is that I have not asked any of them that question.

Senator FULBRIGHT. All I am asking is if you know them. I realize you do not know everyone in the world, but do you know of anyone, just one of them? You remember the time Mr. Packard mentioned Dr. Panofsky in a similar circumstance and it turned out Dr. Panofsky had some reservations in that case.

Can you name one well-known physicist or scientist in this general area who agrees with your estimate of the effect of the deployment of MIRV on the SALT talks? You can say that yes or no as easily as the Secretary.

Secretary LAIRD. Mr. Chairman, I think the question is one that I am not sure Dr. Foster has even directed to the scientific community because we would not be directing that kind of a question to the scientific community.

We have directed questions to the scientific community on the scientific aspects involved with MIRV. But we have not conducted such a poll that I know of among the scientific community of the effect of MIRV deployment on SALT, and I do not believe that this committee would look with favor on that kind of a polling operation by the Department of Defense. We have been criticized for carrying on some kinds of polling operations, and I do not believe that you would support us in doing so.

Senator FULBRIGHT. Now, now, Mr. Secretary, you know you should not get excited. Just because he is in a tight spot and cannot think of one, you want to divert our attention from it now. [Laughter.]

You know very well that, of course, you do not conduct polls.

Secretary LAIRD. I would hope that you would not expect us to conduct polls on these various questions.

Senator FULBRIGHT. I do not expect you to conduct a poll.

Secretary LAIRD. We are handling our public affairs budget——

Senator FULBRIGHT. Oh, now.

Secretary LAIRD. On a small basis and we had reductions made, and we are continuing to handle this on as effective a basis as we can.

Senator FULBRIGHT. I do not mean polls on this.

Secretary LAIRD. And if the Senator directs us to do polls, I would be glad to give it consideration, but I would also ask you to consider the costs.

Senator FULBRIGHT. I do not request it, nor do I recommend it, but these scientists talk among themselves. They write letters to the editor and they speak up on this subject just like politicians. You do not have to take a poll to know. If there were one who is not in your employ who supported your view, I am sure he would come forward himself.

EFFECT OF MIRV ON SALT IS A POLITICAL JUDGMENT

Secretary LAIRD. I would respect your political judgment on this question more than I would the scientific personnel that we have working in these various areas. I really believe that this is a political judgment.

Senator FULBRIGHT. I do too.

Secretary LAIRD. And I respect your judgment as a politician, and your are a politician. And I believe a political judgment is one that should be discussed by people who have that particular responsibility, listening to all people in the United States. I do not believe it is necessary to single out any one particular group, but rather as politicians, we should listen to all Americans.

Senator FULBRIGHT. Mr. Secretary, you have demonstrated your very deep understanding and you have rescued Mr. Foster from having to answer the question. His reply would have been that this is primarily a political question, and judgment should be made on that basis. Unfortunately in this country, many scientists have been accorded a feeling of infallibility and no matter what they think about their word is accepted, whether it is in their field or not. I was very much impressed in the debates last year in the people cited as authorities on political questions. I agree with you that it is a political question.

POLITICAL CONSEQUENCES OF CAMBODIAN INCURSION

This question of the effect of the incursion into Cambodia is primarily, from my point of view, one of the political consequences, not military.

The other day we heard General Gavin who is uniquely qualified to talk about Southeast Asia. Long before many of the people who are now interested in it, he was interested in it under the direction of President Eisenhower and General Ridgway. He talked about the military. I haven't presumed to say that this did not have some military consequences. I am quite sure it does, no matter how exaggerated the statistics on liberated rice. That is all very well. It has some.

The basic question is the political result, and the effect upon China and Russia, which is primarily, I think, of a political nature. This is the question in which you and the President and others should involve themselves, and, I think, this committee and the Congress. We are all politicians, the Senate, in particular. Perhaps there are statesmen in the House, but in the Senate we are all politicians and I think we have a right and a duty to be involved in it. Fundamentally, what we do not like is that you are ignoring the constitutional role of the Senate. I think this is really the essence of all this debate. We also disagree with your political judgment. I thoroughly disagree with Mr. Foster's judgment, that the intrusion into Cambodia is going to enhance the probabilities of a favorable result in Vienna. I cannot imagine that it would enhance those at all.

Secretary LAIRD. I do not believe that was the question you directed to my distinguished friend and colleague, the Director of Defense Research and Engineering, Mr. Chairman.

Senator FULBRIGHT. I thought he volunteered the answer that his private opinion was that it would improve the chances of——

Secretary LAIRD. The question had to do with the deployment of MIRV and its effect on the SALT talks.

Dr. FOSTER. The Secretary is correct, Mr. Chairman.

Senator FULBRIGHT. The development of MIRV.

Secretary LAIRD. And its effect upon SALT.

Senator FULBRIGHT. That is right. It was the effect of MIRV.

Secretary LAIRD. The question you are propounding is entirely different and takes his answer out of context.

EFFECT OF MIRV ON SALT

Senator FULBRIGHT. I have exactly the same feeling about MIRV. It is a political matter and I believe this view is shared by a great many of my colleagues. I know it is shared by a number of scientists. I think all of the previous scientific advisers of the three previous Presidents have publicly stated their views that the deployment of MIRV would be a step of much greater escalation and that they disapproved of it.

I think they have in public. I have seen a number of letters. Mr. York put one in The New York Times just a day or 2 ago.

Secretary LAIRD. Yes; I have seen their political comments.

Senator FULBRIGHT. You are aware of their views.

Secretary LAIRD. I do not believe that I have seen an assessment on the basis that it would not work, however, from the scientific community.

Senator FULBRIGHT. That MIRV would not work?

Secretary LAIRD. Yes.

Senator FULBRIGHT. Neither have I.

I am talking about its effect on the SALT talks.

Secretary LAIRD. I have seen certain political assessments that they have made.

Senator FULBRIGHT. That is right.

I agree with you, however, that this is primarily the political estimate of its effect. It is also economics. I do not know how you disassociate these differences because, as you know, the country is going broke. The business community is indicating that they are apprehensive about the economics of it. I do not have to tell you about that.

MILEAGE LIMITATION OF SANCTUARY AREAS

This definition of the sanctuary areas is an elusive concept. That is why I wanted to ask you about the extent of it. If you do stop at the 21 miles, and the North Vietnamese create new sanctuaries between 21 and 31 miles, what will you then do? Will you say, "Well, that is no longer Cambodian territory. This is now under the control of North Vietnam and therefore we can bomb it and invade it?" Is that a policy that we can expect?

Secretary LAIRD. The President has made the rules of engagement so far as the use of Americans within Cambodia is concerned. These ground rules of engagement are very clear and very precise.

Senator FULBRIGHT. What are they?

Secretary LAIRD. I do not care to discuss them beyond those parts that the President has made public. But I want you to know that the specific mileage limitation covered in his briefing of the congressional committees is included in the rules of engagement. And these rules of engagement will no longer be applicable after the 30th of June when no American ground forces will be operating in Cambodia.

Senator FULBRIGHT. I thought I read in the paper that the rules of engagement for the South Vietnamese forces were to protect U.S. and free world forces, but they were not to destroy any supplies. That was published the other day.

Do you consider the rules of engagement a secret? Is that supposed to be secret?

Secretary LAIRD. We do not discuss the actual operating orders in public.

Senator FULBRIGHT. I mean as to what you describe as orders not to kill people, but to take supplies and destroy the headquarters. Aren't those rules of engagement?

Secretary LAIRD. Yes.

The primary objectives——

Senator FULBRIGHT. I thought that was what we were discussing.

Secretary LAIRD. The primary objective of this mission is to destroy facilities, ammunition, and supplies. Now the rules under which this mission is being carried out do contain a limitation on the number of miles that U.S. forces can move into Cambodia. The President made the determination to make that public and I can assure you it is being adhered to.

Senator FULBRIGHT. It is 21 miles; is it not?

Secretary LAIRD. Twenty-one miles is approximately correct.

Senator FULBRIGHT. I thought you equivocated about it when I asked you about bombing. Doesn't that limit apply to bombing?

Secretary LAIRD. No; the problem here, sir, is—and I am not trying to hedge on this—that the operating orders are expressed in terms of kilometers, and there is a difference so I say it is approximately 21 miles. I just want to be precise with this committee because in the——

Senator FULBRIGHT. Does that apply to bombing as well as to the troops on the ground?

Secretary LAIRD. That particular operating rule does not.

LIMITATION ON BOMBING

Senator FULBRIGHT. This is what I was trying to get a while ago, but I did not think I got it. What limit is there, if any, upon bombing?

Secretary LAIRD. There is a limitation.

Senator FULBRIGHT. What is it?

Secretary LAIRD. That has not been released, but I will be glad to discuss it with the chairman of the committee.

Senator FULBRIGHT. Do you mean it is still classified? In other words, the combat troops——

Secretary LAIRD. Mr. Chairman, the operating order for the use of airpower is a different operating order than the one for ground forces. I would be glad to discuss that matter with the chairman and the members of the committee in a closed session, but there is a very severe limitation which does apply to the use of airpower.

Now, Mr. Chairman, I do not believe that there has ever been a time when the direct operating orders were put forth in an open congressional hearing in the history of my service in the Congress.

We have done this and discussed this in executive session and I would be pleased to do that at your convenience.

Senator FULBRIGHT. I think you miss the point about these hearings and I am surprised you do. We are not trying to elicit secret testimony about minute operations.

Secretary LAIRD. I know you are not. I am sorry if you misread my reasons for not laying everything out to the enemy. I do not believe that it serves a useful purpose for all information to be laid out on the public record. We spend thousands of dollars to get this kind of information, Mr. Chairman.

Senator FULBRIGHT. Obviously the President volunteered this and his objective was to make this operation acceptable to the public.

Secretary LAIRD. Yes, and he——

Senator FULBRIGHT. I do not know whether you said you weighed it, but I feel there are a lot of members of the Administration who feel there is a substantial and, I think, very deep-seated discontent and apprehension in this country generally. I think that people who dismiss some of these more extreme violent actions as superficial, as having no real roots, are quite wrong in their judgment of the situation. I think that they are merely the tip of iceberg, to use a hackneyed and trite phrase. I think there is a profound malaise in this country. It is the discussion of these subjects and assurance in public that is important. It is not just to tell me. It is not very important that you tell me that you can go 100 miles or 500 miles. That is not important and I am not trying to elicit, nor am I particularly interested in eliciting, any secrets. The President stated this limitation of 21 miles and I was trying to tie it down because it is some degree of assurance that it is all limited there and it fortifies the feeling that we are not in an ever-escalating, endless war. I am afraid your predecessor described it all too well in this week's Life magazine when he called it a formula for a perpetual war. I believe those are his words.

Secretary LAIRD. Mr. Chairman, I would like to state, if you will permit me at this point——

Senator FULBRIGHT. I do not want to harass you. I thought this was all for the public knowledge.

Secretary LAIRD. The operating rules which we are using presently as far as airpower is concerned are in accordance with the fourth section of the Church-Cooper amendment. Would that satisfy you?

Senator FULBRIGHT. This is with respect to the support of Cambodian forces. South Vietnamese forces——

Secretary LAIRD. The airpower is being used in support of allied forces, not Cambodian forces.

Senator FULBRIGHT. That would be tactical air support of South Vietnamese forces.

Secretary LAIRD. That is correct. And I hope that satisfies this committee.

Senator FULBRIGHT. I did not really intend to try to belabor you or even ask about it.

Secretary LAIRD. But as for the actual rules of operation, I do not believe it would serve any useful purpose for us to put them on the table at this time.

REAL CONCERN IS VIETNAM WAR AND ITS EFFECTS

Senator FULBRIGHT. As you know, what really concerns me and many of us is not the way you conduct the war. It is the fact we are in there at all and, I think, its very likely effect upon the SALT talks and upon our relations with China. As bad as they are, at least we were beginning to resume conversations. It is the likely effect upon the Paris peace talks. I mean they were supposed to be peace talks. And of course, it is the effect on our general relations with the rest of the world. There are very few countries other than those immediately involved who have not expressed their disapproval of this measure from the political point of view. Even the meeting at Jakarta involving a number of the Asian countries, I think, ended up not by endorsing our move into Cambodia but recommending that it be taken up by the United Nations. Isn't that about the effect of it?

Secretary LAIRD. That was one of their recommendations, that the views and recommendations of the conference be placed on record with the United Nations. There were certain other recommendations that came out of the conference, however, sir.

Senator FULBRIGHT. What?

Secretary LAIRD. There were other recommendations, too, but that was one of the recommendations.

Senator FULBRIGHT. None were expressing their approval of our enlargement of the war into Cambodia, were they? I do not think they were.

OBJECTIVE OF CAMBODIAN OPERATION

Secretary LAIRD. I would disagree, and I did earlier today, Mr. Chairman, that we are enlarging the war.

Senator FULBRIGHT. Are we visiting in Cambodia? How do you like to describe it other than that long story about sanctuaries.

Secretary LAIRD. We are shortening the war and we are making possible acceleration of the Vietnamization program and increased withdrawals of American personnel from Vietnam. I do not like to make predictions or assumptions, but I believe that the long-term strategic results of the Cambodian operation, in addition to further withdrawals from South Vietnam, will make possible a reduction of American casualties as we move beyond this action.

Senator FULBRIGHT. My only rejoinder to that, Mr. Secretary, is that about two or three times a year, for 5 years, we have heard similar highly optimistic statements made by Mr. McNamara and General Wheeler. General Westmoreland came and addressed a great political meeting of both Houses. You are familiar with those?

Secretary LAIRD. Yes; and you asked me that same question when I was here before, and you did not think we would make our troop reductions, but we have. The first announcement has been met, the second announcement has been met, the third announcement has been met, and the fourth announcement will be met.

Senator FULBRIGHT. This wholly unexpected involvement, which most people call an invasion, whether you would recognize it or not, has altered the situation and there is a profound difference of opinion as to whether it can possibly accomplish your purpose. There are a great many very responsible people who believe the incursion into Cambodia was to disguise the fact that Vietnamization could not work, that it was a completely inappropriate conception. There are a lot of responsible people, not just the chairman of this committee.

Secretary LAIRD. Well, I regret that, Mr. Chairman.

Senator FULBRIGHT. As a matter of fact, your predecessor, in no uncertain terms, in my opinion, takes exactly that view, and he was Secretary of Defense just before you were.

Secretary LAIRD. Yes; and I have great respect and admiration for him. He helped me during the transition period as I assumed this particular office.

Senator FULBRIGHT. Yes.

Secretary LAIRD. I had known him for a great many years, but I believe that we have a sound program to reduce American forces. We are reducing American forces, and during the months prior to the time this Administration took office they were being increased. All I can do is point to the record.

Senator FULBRIGHT. I was recalling the record of this war of your predecessor's to you. The record is a very bad one.

Secretary LAIRD. The record of Mr. Clifford and Mr. McNamara speak for themselves.

Senator FULBRIGHT. Yes.

Secretary LAIRD. I would like to point to the record of the Nixon administration. We can show that we have reduced the American presence, and I cannot see any place you can point to over the past few years where the number of troops in Vietnam or in Southeast Asia was on the decline. It was on the increase ever since the early days of the Kennedy administration.

Senator FULBRIGHT. Well, of course, I think——

Secretary LAIRD. So I am glad to discuss my predecessors' records. They were fine, outstanding men. But I do wish that you would take notice of the record of the present Administration in reducing the American presence in this area of the world. I believe that record speaks much louder than any words that I can say today.

GENERAL GAVIN'S VIEWS ON CAMBODIAN OPERATION

Senator FULBRIGHT. There is one other aspect of it to complete the record. General Gavin is, I think, one of the better authorities when it comes to records because his recommendation to President Eisenhower, is one that time has proved to have been quite correct. He thought the same thing about the military aspects of this intrusion into Cambodia. You see in addition to this——

Secretary LAIRD. I have great respect for General Gavin. I sat on that side of the committee and I quizzed him as a member of the Defense Appropriations Subcommittee. I recently went over some of that testimony and it is very interesting to read, and I realize that people change, change their positions and change their minds. I have done that and I think you have done that and this is quite important.

Senator FULBRIGHT. I was going to end with this thought. You were talking about your record.

DETERIORATION OF DOMESTIC SCENE

In the meantime, with the progress of your so-called Vietnamization, you have seen a dramatic deterioration in the domestic scene all the way from the killing of students to the decline of the stock market. Some people seem to think the stock market is simply a group of gamblers losing their money. This is a very erroneous view. I saw in the paper the other day that the decline that has taken place, I think in the last 12 months, indicates an erosion of some $160 billion of values which Americans thought they had, whereas the total decline in the great depression of the 1930's that almost brought on a revolution in this country was only $50 billion. In the context of this relatively brief period, you have had a three times greater erosion than in the great depression. These are aspects of this situation which create an urgency about this war that no one dreamed of 5 years ago when your predecessors were talking. There was a more leisurely approach to it.

We were so rich that we could afford anything, and there was no great hurry. There were even those who thought we could spend the Russians into bankruptcy. If we would just go all out spending in military and supplies, they would go broke first and change their ways.

Secretary LAIRD. As you know, Senator, when I was a Member of the legislative branch not too long ago——

Senator FULBRIGHT. I am sorry you ever left it.

Secretary LAIRD. I made certain statements that we could reduce the American presence in Vietnam. I made those statements, and I was challenged by the then Secretary of Defense on "Meet the Press" within a very short period of time that it was not possible to do that.

VIETNAMIZATION PROGRAM

I became Secretary of Defense and we started the Vietnamization program under the leadership of President Nixon. We have gone forward with it, and I am sure that the vast majority of the American people support the program to withdraw American forces from Vietnam.

Senator FULBRIGHT. They support the objective. I am not at all sure they support the war in Cambodia and the means being used. As I said in the beginning, we all support the objective.

Secretary LAIRD. This is all part of our overall withdrawal program as far as Southeast Asia is concerned. I do believe that the Vietnamization program has been an important start in these first 15 months that I have had the opportunity to serve the President and the country as Secretary of Defense.

Senator FULBRIGHT. I do not want to have my remark misunderstood. When I said I was sorry you left the Congress, I only meant that we need your talents in the Congress because you are too formidable as a Secretary for us to hold our own when you are down in the Defense Department.

You make it extremely difficult for us because you know so much about how we operate up here, and [laughter] it is a great handicap to us because of your talents.

I did not mean it the way it might have been interpreted.

SCHEDULING OF DR. FOSTER'S APPEARANCE BEFORE THE COMMITTEE

It is understood that in the next 2 weeks we will negotiate with your office or with Mr. Foster directly and he will come before the Gore subcommittee?

Secretary LAIRD. Yes; Mr. Chairman.

Senator FULBRIGHT. I haven't the date at my disposal at the moment. Senator Gore asked me to ask you for that commitment. With that, we will adjourn. You are very patient.

Secretary LAIRD. Thank you, Mr. Chairman.

Senator FULBRIGHT. Thank you very much.

(Whereupon, at 6:45 p.m., the committee adjourned.)

ABM, MIRV, SALT, AND THE NUCLEAR ARMS RACE

THURSDAY, MAY 28, 1970

UNITED STATES SENATE,
SUBCOMMITTEE ON ARMS CONTROL,
INTERNATIONAL LAW AND ORGANIZATION
OF THE COMMITTEE ON FOREIGN RELATIONS,
Washington, D.C.

The subcommittee met, pursuant to recess, at 10:10 a.m., in room 4221, New Senate Office Building, Senator Albert Gore (chairman of the subcommittee) presiding.

Present: Senators Gore, Pell, and Case.

Senator GORE. The subcommittee will come to order.

The Subcommittee on Arms Control, International Law and Organization is meeting today to continue hearings on ABM, MIRV, SALT and the nuclear arms race.

SCHEDULE OF WITNESSES

We will hear testimony from four distinguished witnesses today. Our first witness is the Honorable Joseph S. Clark, a former member of the Committee on Foreign Relations, a member of this subcommittee for 4 years, and now president of the World Federalists.

We are delighted to welcome Senator Clark this morning not only because he is a former colleague, although that would be reason enough, but also because of his long interest and experience in the subject matter of arms control.

Our other three witnesses this morning are all former Presidential science advisers. They are Dr. George P. Kistiakowsky, special assistant to President Eisenhower for science and technology from 1959 to 1961, now professor of chemistry at Harvard University; Dr. Jerome P. Wiesner, science adviser to President Kennedy from 1961 through 1964, now provost of MIT, and Dr. Donald F. Hornig, special assistant to President Johnson for science and technology from 1964 through 1968, vice president of Eastman Kodak Co. until last week, and now president of Brown University.

We thus have with us today three of the four distinguished men who have served as science advisers to the Presidents since that position was first established by President Eisenhower.

The fourth former Presidential adviser, Dr. James R. Killian, was unable to testify this morning, but did testify before this committee last year.

Senator Clark, the committee is very pleased to have you. The Chair directs that your testimony be printed in full in this hearing and invites you to proceed ad lib.

Mr. CLARK. Thank you very much, Mr. Chairman.

STATEMENT OF HON. JOSEPH S. CLARK, PRESIDENT, WORLD FEDERALISTS, U.S.A.

Mr. CLARK. I deeply appreciate your courtesy in permitting me to appear before your subcommittee and also the courtesy of your colleagues, my former colleagues.

If I have any competence in this regard it is perhaps due to the fact that I, with the exception of the Secretary of Defense, am the only witness who appears before you who has ever held elected public office and, perhaps, the politician's approach to these serious problems which you have under consideration is worth mentioning to supplement the testimony of the distinguished scientists and members of, former members of, the executive branch of our Government whom you have already heard.

Since you have been kind enough to place my testimony in the record, I would prefer just to comment on it and believe that I can save the committee some time by hitting the highlights.

WITNESS' REPORT OF APRIL 23, 1970

On April 23 of this year, when I had expected to testify before the subcommittee, I prepared a report to the subcommittee stating my views at that time on the various important issues which are before you. That was sent to all Members of the Senate, including, of course, this subcommittee, and if it has not been put in the record, I would ask to have it put in the record at this time. I don't know whether it was or not.

Senator GORE. It will be included at this point.

(The information follows.)

REPORT OF JOSEPH S. CLARK, PRESIDENT, WORLD FEDERALISTS, U.S.A., CHAIRMAN, COALITION ON NATIONAL PRIORITIES AND MILITARY POLICY

APRIL 23, 1970.

These hearings which you have now recessed for a month were called to consider:

First, the desirability, in light of the responsibilities of this Committee, of the United States deploying additional anti-ballistic missiles;

Second, to consider the desirability of the United States deploying MIRV, or multiple independently-targeted re-entry vehicles;

Third, to consider the impact of SALT—the strategic arms limitation talks—on our country and the Soviet Union, and;

Fourth, the arms race in general.

My views on these subjects are the same now as they were when I was a member of this Subcommittee. They have not changed since I became President of World Federalists, U.S.A., and Chairman of the Coalition on National Priorities and Military Policy.

Succinctly stated, they are:

1. I believe the anti-ballistic missile is ineffective for the purposes for which it is designed—to destroy incoming ballistic missiles targeted on our fixed base Minutemen silos. The so-called Safeguard ABM is neither safe nor does it guard. But worse than that, to continue deployment of the ABM will have a serious and adverse effect on the SALT talks. Finally, the cost—estimates go as high as $50 billion—is money which should go to meet critically urgent human needs here at home. It is pointless to waste money on a gimmick like the ABM, which will not enhance national security, at a time when money is so desperately needed for domestic programs which are currently underfunded. I refer to, among others, feeding hungry Americans, upgrading our educational system, and to improving the environment and ecology.

2. I believe the deployment of the MIRV will inevitably escalate the arms race, quite possibly to a point of no return. It also will have a serious and adverse effect on the SALT talks. With our present superiority over the Russians, it makes no sense at all to deploy MIRV by June of this year as the Secretary of the Air Force has stated we will do. I would hope that this Committee would use its best efforts to see that deployment does not take place. The passage of S. Res. 211 is a useful and significant effort to achieve this result.

3. I believe the success of the SALT talks is essential to the future well being of the United States.

These SALT talks very well could be man's best—and last—chance for peace and the survival of civilization as we know it. All the cliches have come true; we have reached the time of a technological age where, once and for all, as President Kennedy said in 1961, either "Mankind must put an end to war, or war will put an end to mankind."

4. I believe it is essential to not only stabilize the arms race, but also to get on with the task of completing a treaty of general and complete disarmament, which has been in limbo since the assassination of President Kennedy on November 22, 1963.

I point out that the Nuclear Nonproliferation Treaty, in effect since March 5 of this year, is now, as President Nixon then said, "the law of the land." Article VI of that treaty obligates both the United States and the Soviet Union to "undertake to pursue the negotiations in good faith on effective measures relating to cessation of the nuclear arms race at an early date and to nuclear disarmament, and on a treaty on general and complete disarmament under strict and effective international control."

The intent of Article VI is very clear. It binds all signatories to the Nuclear Nonproliferation Treaty, including the United States, to negotiate in good faith to cease the nuclear arms race and to move towards nuclear disarmament and, further, to move in a treaty of general and complete disarmament under strict international control. This is a solemn obligation on the part of the United States of America. I hope we will live up to this obligation.

It is not enough to say, as Director Gerard Smith of ACDA did before the Foreign Relations Committee on March 23, "the prospects for achieving some constraints on strategic arms competition appear somewhat brighter than they have in the past." It's his duty and that of this government to use our best efforts to meet the commitments made by this country in Article VI.

The purport of Senate Resolution 211—passed so positively by this body—is very clear. It recommends to the President, as the sense of the Senate, that we should not deploy any offensive or defensive nuclear weapons pending the discussions with the Russians on SALT. There is not the slightest reason for us to do so except for the purpose of being provocative.

Mr. Smith's March 23 statement to this Committee, "I do not think we ought to stop any evolution of existing programs in anticipation of a SALT agreement," is in my judgment unsound. It is contrary to the reported proposals of his Agency's Advisory Commission, to the proposals of the American Assembly, and to the sense of the Senate Resolution 211 passed just two weeks ago.

We do not need ABM and we do not need MIRV, certainly not until after we can see, as a result of the negotiations this summer and fall, whether or not we can come to an agreement with the Russians to turn the nuclear arms race downward.

It is clear that both of these proposed weapons would be considered by the Russians as menaces threatening their own country. If we go forward with this escalation of the arms race while we purport to be negotiating with the Russians to turn the arms race downward, it would seem clear to me that they would think, and so would any other objective nation-state think, that we were just fooling when we talked about SALT; and that we have no real interest in moving forward to meet the commitments which we undertook under Article VI of the Nuclear Non-proliferation Treaty.

President Nixon, in ratifying that Treaty, said he trusted "that on April 15 the climate for progress in those SALT talks will be good . . ." I cannot believe that administration announcements of plans for ABM and MIRV deployment only a matter of weeks before the talks begin will create such a climate. On the contrary, depolyment of ABM and MIRV can only cloud the climate by adding uncertainty, mistrust, and instability at what is an ideal time for productive arms limitation and reduction agreements, with the Soviet Union and the U.S. both possessing "sufficiency" in strategic nuclear weaponry.

The United States cannot seriously think that the Soviet Union will not react adversely to our deployment of ABM and MIRV while the negotiations are going forward. There is a very influential and hawkish military establishment in the Soviet Union, just as in the United States. In fact, the Russian military has been fighting the SALT talks from the beginning, long before the United States decision on ABM and MIRV, claiming that the United States is preparing for a first strike against the USSR. The Soviet government, with prodding from its military establishment, will now more than ever react by, what Herbert York calls, "erring on the side of military safety," or "worst case analysis."

While the Joint Chiefs of Staff and the Pentagon have argued that ABM and MIRV will be top bargaining cards at SALT, this kind of "bargaining from strength" analysis provokes a similar reaction from the Soviet Union and makes arms control nearly impossible. It is this kind of action-reaction syndrome that time and time again has dashed the hopes for meaningful arms control agreements in the past.

It is a unique twist of logic that claims to be seeking a reduction of arms in secret while, at the same time, proposing an increase in public.

There is little doubt that the uncertainties caused by our deployment of ABM and MIRV seriously jeopardize the SALT talks. Herbert York contends that "in view of most of us who have lived through past attempts at arms control negotiations, such gross uncertainties and the worries that would flow from them, even before being massaged by 'worst case analysts,' would severely inhibit if not entirely prevent further steps toward arms control." What is more, York concludes, "They would instead strongly induce further moves along the arms race spiral."

My concern deepened when the Secretary of Defense, in his well known posture statement, made a deliberate attempt to persuade the Congress to escalate the arms race in several ways. He requested an expansion of ABM, full well knowing that this, in and of itself, will likely push the Russians to a further deployment of the SS9, the SS11, the SS13 to assure the success of a counter attack on our Minutemen missiles should we strike first, thus escalating the arms race on their side. And this despite the fact that, in all likelihood, the most knowledgeable Russians realize that our ABM missiles are really ineffective and would not work if put to the test.

My concern is again increased by the absolute nonsense we have been hearing from Secretary of Defense Laird about the so-called Chinese threat. Both Dr. Alice Hsieh of the Institute for Defense Analysis and A. Doak Barnett of the Brookings Institution have demolished his argument before your Committee. These long time China experts rightly noted that ABM is not needed to defend against China's nuclear threat—neither now nor in the forseeable future. They were in agreement that ABM will only increase Chinese anti-West feeling and paranoia, and encourage a Chinese nuclear build-up in response to what Chinese military leaders might consider is a U.S. move for a first-strike capability against China. All this at the same time we claim to be trying to establish improved relations with China.

Just a few days ago, in an April 20 speech before an Associated Press luncheon, Secretary Laird reiterated his unyielding support for deployment of ABM and MIRV, reciting the standard hard-line dogma: "The fundamental driving force in an arms race is what one country perceives as possible objectives of another country's actions." He then went on to argue for ABM and MIRV as a necessary response to the "possible objectives" of the Soviet offensive build-up over the past five years—a build-up that still finds Russia today behind the U.S. in numbers of nuclear weapons. Of course, he did not consider it necessary to examine how Russia would perceive the "possible objectives" of our ABM and MIRV deployment, especially in light of our present superiority.

I have heard with interest earlier testimony before this Committee which disclosed the fact of a 1964 Air Force Manual advocating a U.S. first-strike. But let us not forget that the Secretary of Defense wrote a book as recently as 1962 advocating a first strike against Russia. The book was called "A House Divided." I quote: "What it means is serving credible notice, and meaning it, that we reserve to ourselves the initiative to strike first when the Soviet peril point rises beyond its interminable limit."

One must almost come to the conclusion that there are madmen in the Pentagon and madmen, who are very senior indeed, on the Armed Services Committee of both Houses. In fact, I am reminded of the madmen of the Confederate

States of America who led the South into the Civil War. It took the South 100 years to recover from that catastrophe. But if their successors have their way again, the world may well be destroyed by the disasters they lead us into.

Mr. Laird and Mr. Packard have told the Congress that ABM, in the words of Mr. Packard, "gives us another year in which to pursue SALT without ourselves exacerbating the arms control environment through actions on offensive systems."

But then the Secretary of the Air Force inadvertently let drop the news that the U.S. would deploy MIRV in June.

But that was not too big a surprise really. Only a few months ago, on the very same day the President *talked* favorably about a mutual moratorium on MIRV flight testing, the Air Force awarded General Electric $88 million to begin production of MIRV Missiles.

MIRV deployment can only provoke the Russians into further escalation, thus killing the best chance for freezing nuclear warheads on both sides at their present level which, God knows, is high enough.

But MIRV deployment would cause further complications in arms control negotiations. MIRV more than any other weapons system threatens to make both the United States and the Soviet Union incapable of determining one another's nuclear strength and capabilities. The major stumbling block to past arms control agreements—on-site inspection, which the USSR would never accept—is no longer in the way because of satellite and electronic surveillance. But MIRV deployment would make such unilateral, electronic surveillance much more difficult, and the inspection problem could again thwart agreements.

We must remember, as Ralph Lapp recently told us, that a limitation on strategic arms would represent a real threat to the Pentagon, and also to its industrial allies and to those members of Congress of the United States in both branches who have made a fetish over the years, through their activities on the Armed Services Committees and the Appropriations Committees, of advancing the interests of the military.

I am concerned that the Pentagon believes that if it can get the MIRV deployed before a SALT agreement is entered into, that it's probably home free. For the mere deployment of MIRV, and the inspection problems it raises, will make it more difficult to come to an agreement with the Russians on SALT. It follows that the Pentagon can blame the Russians for not being willing to permit on-site inspection, knowing in advance that they won't, and thus continue to deploy the MIRV and all the other lethal weapons which are referred to in Mr. Laird's posture statement.

While the President is believed to have given our SALT delegation authority to propose a comprehensive as opposed to a piecemeal plan for arms control, the press reports that our offer is coupled with a demand for on-site inspection, which in terms of calculated risk is in the last analysis unnecessary and which we know the Russians will not accept.

We can be thankful for small favors; but in view of the predominantly, hawkish nature of our delegation there is grave danger that the comprehensive approach will be dropped as soon as the Russians refuse on-site inspection as they promptly can be expected to do.

It is essential that a mutual freeze be placed on MIRV deployment. Otherwise the military will once again attempt to place the problem of on-site inspection as a stumbling block in the way of a truly meaningful, comprehensive arms control agreement. If MIRVs are deployed, it will be extremely difficult to reach any meaningful agreement on MIRV, due to the complex verification problems it raises. But if MIRV deployment can be frozen immediately, a limitation agreement on MIRV testing could then be reached, as testing can be verified by national inspection. Quoting Dr. Herbert Scoville, Jr., who testified before your Committee, "There is still time, but maybe only a little, to prevent deployment of MIRVs if a ban on testing and deployment can be achieved soon."

In conclusion, gentlemen, let me say that I am scared to death for my country by what is happening at the Pentagon with the ABM, the MIRV, and the arms race. I would like to leave you gentlemen, with a sense of fear, also; a sense that something must be done before these madmen in the Pentagon and their allies elsewhere lead this country to absolute and utter destruction.

Let me summarize, again, why I am scared for my country.

First, because I believe the Pentagon is determined to press forward with the further deployment of the anti-ballistic missile, the ABM. This is a serious error. First, because the weapon is no good and; secondly, because, despite the fact we know it is no good, the Russians are apt to react to its deployment by escalating the production and deployment of their own intercontinental ballistic missiles, the SS9–11 and –13, and thus escalate the arms race on their side. It is this kind of action-reaction cycle that has brought on the balance of terror we find ourselves in today.

Second, because the Pentagon has announced that it will deploy the MIRV in June. This, again, would assure a further escalation of the arms race, and would make it extremely difficult for the arms talks to succeed because of the problems of inspection which the deployment of the MIRV raises.

Third, because I believe that these activities, together with Mr. Laird's posture statement and the constant belligerent statements which are coming out of the Pentagon almost every day, make it abundantly clear that the Pentagon has no real interest in the success of the SALT talks, or in the United States meeting its commitments under Article VI of the Nuclear Nonproliferation Treaty.

Fourth, because of the clear danger that the belligerants in the Pentagon, with the aid of some of their colleagues in the White House, may yet sabotage the SALT talks. I don't mean that they will overtly oppose the President's basic decision to move forward in a positive manner. But in the intricate negotiations which will take place during the next few months, those of our delegates who really represent the Department of Defense could take so negative a position on specific issues that a reasonable and far-reaching agreement with the Russians could become almost impossible.

Fifth, because the defense budget and the posture statement supporting it by Mr. Laird indicate an irrevocable intention to run the military budget even higher than it was last year, discounting Vietnam, and to take from the starving domestic programs even more money than has been taken already. The inevitable result will be to bring about domestic disaster, without giving us any additional national security.

There remains to consider briefly what this Subcommittee can do. I suggest the following steps:

1. Write now a strong report spelling out the dangers I have been discussing.
2. Watch closely the behavior of the SALT delegation at Vienna to be sure that the instruction of the President and the desires of the Chairman of the delegation are fully carried out.

This Committee and the Senate must not abdicate responsibility for foreign policy and the chances for peace to the Generals and Admirals in the Pentagon. The Congress must assert itself and make it clear to the White House that the Pentagon's job is to implement policy, not to make it. We remember well how Congressional authority was pre-empted in Vietnam by the Executive Branch, and the disastrous consequences that followed.

There is complete lack of Congressional representation or involvement in planning U.S. policy and proposals for the SALT talks. None of the officials involved in preparing for the SALT talks can claim to represent the American people—not one of them has been elected.

Yet they are now determining whether the American people will live or die; whether we will spend countess billions of dollars on weapons development or on human development. A member of the Senate Foreign Relations Committee should be part of the delegation. At the very least a top staff officer of the Committee should be present at all the sessions.

3. Urge the delegation to take some realistic initiatives for peace at the SALT talks. The U.S. has been number one in the arms race and is now. We should be the first to move towards a relaxation of tensions, especially after our ABM and MIRV provocations. To couple a proposal for a "comprehensive arms control agreement" with a demand for on-site inspection which we know the Russians will not accept is disingenuous, to put it mildly.

Remembering that the Nuclear Test Ban Treaty of 1963 was signed only a few months after President Kennedy unilaterally suspended atmospheric testing, an interim freeze on ABM and MIRV deployment would seem to be a strong initiative that would show our good will and test that of the Russian's, without jeopardizing our security.

Definite far-reaching proposals, without crippling conditions, should come from the U.S. Serious consideration should be given to the following proposals:

(a) An immediate "in-place halt" on testing and deployment of new strategic weapons. This would give time for in-depth talks, and time is growing short.

(b) Negotiations to eliminate all land-based missiles. Submarine missile forces offer an invulnerable deterrent to both sides. The Soviet Union now has fewer submarines and submarine based missiles, but some compensation formula could be worked out.

(c) Revive discussions of General and Complete Disarmament at Geneva to eliminate all nuclear weapons by 1973. The two treaties submitted by the U.S. and U.S.S.R. in 1962 should be dusted off and brought up to date. This means conventional as well as nuclear disarmament.

And finally I urge you to speak on the floor of the Senate about these matters. Discuss the matter with your colleagues. Speak out across the country, and awaken our country to the deadly peril in which we are presently living, because of the unbridled power which the military-industrial complex has obtained over the government of the United States.

Mr. CLARK. Thank you, sir.

At that time I indicated that I was scared to death for my country, that I hoped the members of the subcommittee were scared to death, too, and if I could do anything to provoke their concern, I would have felt my testimony was well directed.

REASONS FOR CONCERN OVER PRESENT U.S. SITUATION

The reasons for my concern are so obvious that I do not think I will reiterate them. They are set forth at length in the earlier statement, and to summarize them briefly they are, first, because I believe the Pentagon is determined to press forward with the deployment of ABM and MIRV. This I consider a ghastly mistake in the interests of international agreements at SALT, in the interests of our national priorities, and because with respect to ABM almost all disinterested competent scientific opinion is in accord that it will not work.

Secondly, because MIRV is well on its way to being deployed. We saw in the newspapers 2 days ago that ground on the site has already been broken, and the delivery vehicle has been installed and all that is needed is to put the multiple warhead on it, and we are off to the races, and the chances of a meaningful agreement at SALT because of the Russians phobia about onsite inspection will have been very gravely damaged.

Third, because I am afraid that the Pentagon, despite its statements to the contrary, has no real interest in success at SALT. If it did I do not believe they would have coupled onsite inspection with the proposal for a comprehensive arms agreement at SALT, because they know, and you know, and I know, that the Russians are never going to agree to onsite inspection. Onsite inspection is necessary if we deploy MIRV but not if we don't.

And the fourth reason is because I am concerned that the SALT talks may in the end be sabotaged by the Pentagon. I am just not convinced that a delegation of which Lieutenant General Allison of the Air Force is a prominent member, and Paul Nitze, former Deputy Secretary of Defense, are perhaps the leading and certainly among the ablest of its members, can have a sincere interest in a comprehensive SALT agreement.

These, then, sir, are why I am concerned and scared about the situation in which our country finds itself.

TESTIMONY IN FAVOR OF ABM DEPLOYMENT

I have devoted in my testimony some pages to rebutting the testimony before this subcommittee of Defense Secretary Laird, but because of the unquestioned competence of the three witnesses who will follow me, I will not reiterate it here.

To me it is clear that the Secretary of Defense is taking an untenable position with respect to all of the subjects with which your subcommittee is concerned, and having made that rather rash statement I will leave to my friends who will follow me the detailed breakdown of what he had to say.

I would point out, however, that there is an article in the Reader's Digest of this month by our former colleague, Senator Henry Cabot Lodge, of Massachusetts, the Ambassador to Vietnam, and the gentleman who headed the delegation at Paris for a while, taking the position, and he is referred to in the Reader's Digest as a great patriot, which I am sure he is; but I yield to no man in my own patriotism, and I suppose the Senator from Tennessee would take the same position, so I think we are all patriots, and the article I commend to the members of the subcommittee is superficial exposition of a thoroughly untenable case.

Again I will leave to the gentlemen who will follow me such rebuttal as may be necessary to Senator Lodge's statement which I find full of factual inaccuracies, of conclusions which are not sound and of the "worst case" philosophy as a result of which, I believe, we have to do a great deal, as civilians, to prevent the military from overriding us.

That is the position which Dr. York exposed so clearly to your committee of taking the "worst case" and assuming the Russians are 12 feet high and are about to move for a first strike.

This, I believe, any calm and reasoned consideration by civilians would reject on the basis of the information which is available to us.

I also mention in my testimony the rather able statement made by Dr. Wohlstetter before the Armed Services Committee a few weeks ago. This former Rand Corp. executive, always closely identified with the Pentagon, has made perhaps the best case which can be made for the deployment of ABM. I suggest that Dr. Panofsky, who preceded him on the stand at the Armed Services Committee, made a much better case as to why we should not deploy ABM, and I know that Dr. Kistiakowsky, Dr. Wiesner, and Dr. Hornig will explain to you in some detail what I am sure you already know, that the deployment of the ABM at this point would be folly.

RAND CORP. STUDY ON PRESIDENTIAL ELECTIONS

Senator GORE. Speaking of the Rand Corp., did you see what appears to me to be wild imagination. It is a report that the Rand Corp. has conducted a study about the feasibility of calling off the presidential elections in 1972.

(The article referred to follows.)

[From the Distant Drummer, Philadelphia, Pa., May 21, 1970]

WILL '72 ELECTIONS BE CANCELLED?

(By Don Demaio)

The Nixon administration is studying the feasibility of calling off the 1972 presidential elections, according to reputable reports around the country.

The feasibility study is reportedly being done by the Rand Corporation "think-tank" people. Both the White House and the Rand Corporation have denied the report. But then one would not expect confirmation of a piece of information so potentially disruptive to internal security.

The first hint of the study was uncovered by a reporter for the conservative Newhouse newspaper chain. William Howard, of the Newhouse's Washington bureau, researched the story and it was published in a number of Newhouse newspapers on April 5. Newspapers in Portland, Oregon and Staten Island, New York, had also done research on the story and printed the item April 5.

Village Voice correspondent Ron Rosenbaum subsequently interviewed Howard, after the White House officially denied the report. Howard insisted that the sources for his story were "good," and he believes them despite the formal denials. Howard later revealed that some of his information came from the wife of an executive of the Rand Corporation.

According to Howard, the White House ordered a feasibility study of the cancellation of the 1972 elections because presidential advisors are "increasingly concerned about the country's internal security and the chances of radical elements disrupting governmental operations, including national elections."

The Rand study would "envision a situation where rebellious factions using force or bomb threats would make it unsafe to conduct an election, and would provide the President with a plan of action."

This sounds exactly like other Rand assignments: i.e., "Envision a situation where Chicago, New York, Los Angeles, and Washington are simultaneously under nuclear attack from the Russians, and provide the president with a plan of action."

On April 24, a week later the last item in a front page news column in the Wall Street Journal read: "Nixon men find a rumor hard to spike—that the Rand Corporation 'think-tank' is studying the idea of cancelling the 1972 elections if radicals threaten to disrupt it."

On April 27, the Nation magazine researched the item and decided to print it.

A few days later, the L.A. Free Press picked up the item. The Free Press interviewed persons close to the Rand Corporation of Santa Monica, California, who confirmed that the White House had ordered such a study. The sources said the White House issued instructions that anyone connected with the project is not to discuss it.

Free Press editor Art Kunkin speculated that Nixon was not beyond cancelling the election for the "sake of instituting a dictatorship and blaming it on the radicals, just as Hitler set the Reichstag fire and blamed the Communists."

Paranoia is always based on physical occurrences. The Nixon administration's complete failure to understand radicals in this country has led to the most trite name-calling game in history—the United States president actually calling radicals names. This communication failure has carried over into the straight press and, consequently, middle America.

As soon as paranoia enters middle America, it begins the final cycle. The White House looks at the paranoia, not recognizing it as the same disease it had fostered, and panics in the same way that everyone has panicked. The administration then does things like call off presidential elections or invade neutral countries.

Paranoia? We live with it.

Mr. CLARK. Yes, I did, Senator Gore: and I wondered whether this was serious. After reading the article I concluded that at least the author of it thought it was serious. My only surprise is that it was the Rand Corp. and not the Hudson Institute with Mr. Herman Kahn, who wrote the article.

Senator GORE. I can't believe this is a correct report, but I direct the staff to inquire of the Rand Corp. The Rand Corp. is subsidized and I want to know if the taxpayers' money has been used to finance this kind of study.

Mr. CLARK. I would be interested in that, too, and perhaps the reporter who wrote the article would have some information which would be of interest to your staff.

Senator GORE. Do you think the Attorney General will help us obtain that?

Mr. CLARK. What?

Senator GORE. Do you think the Attorney General could suggest some procedure by which we could obtain that?

Mr. CLARK. I think some of his able assistants might be interested in looking into the matter.

IMPACT OF CAMBODIA ON ARMS RACE

I think it is desirable to say a word about the impact of Cambodia on your work because as a former politician, it occurs to me that the uproar in this country resulting from the Cambodian invasion gives this subcommittee an even greater opportunity to take some pretty strong remedial action in terms of recommendations——

Senator GORE. If I may interrupt, we will let you refer to yourself as a former politician, but we will address you as a statesman.

Mr. CLARK. Thank you very much, sir. I appreciate the compliment.

With respect to Cambodia and the Church-Cooper amendment, the pending business on the floor of the Senate, which I believe has real impact on the arms race, indirectly to be sure; nonetheless, if we are going to continue the military adventures in Southeast Asia it is clearly going to be very difficult indeed to cut the military budget significantly or to be prepared to make the kind of mutual concessions with the Russians—and I stress the word "mutual"—at SALT which would curtail the arms race and result in some form of arms control.

I discovered 2 days ago to my chagrin that the Church-Cooper resolution does not prohibit the use of American troops as advisers to the South Vietnamese. It does not prohibit the use of American air support to the South Vietnamese in Cambodia nor logistical support.

I can well realize the difficulty at this point in attempting to amend an amendment which is going to have trouble enough getting through the Senate, but I call to your attention that if we are going to permit more Americans to be killed in Cambodia after June 30 perhaps this committee and the whole Foreign Relations Committee will want to give some consideration to proposing an amendment or legislation which would deny to our South Vietnamese allies the right to use American advisers and to call for American air support while they are in Cambodia.

CONSTITUTIONAL CRISIS DENIED

I would like to say a word about the so-called constitutional crisis. To me there is no constitutional crisis. To me it is very clear indeed from the provisions of the Constitution that the Congress has the sole power to lay and collect taxes, to pay the debts, and provide for the common defense. It has the sole power to declare war; it has the sole power to raise and support armies, with the interesting qualification that no appropriation of money for that use shall be for a longer term than 2 years—and I wonder how many of the appropriations which have been voted by the Congress in the past years for military budgets take a lot more than 2 years to spend—and that the Constitution provides that no money shall be drawn from the Treasury but in consequence of appropriations made by law.

Thus the power of the purse and of the creation and support of the military is clearly vested in Congress by the Constitution. The President can recommend but only the Congress can authorize and appropriate.

And I take it that practically every competent constitutional lawyer would agree that article II, section 2, subsection 1 of the Constitution, which makes the President the Commander in Chief of the Army and Navy of the United States, is a grant of power obviously subject to action by the Congress in raising and supporting the Army, Navy, and Air Force which he is to command.

It must appropriate the money necessary to pay for their pay and arms, and without action by the Congress the President's authority as Commander in Chief evaporates, because he has no forces to command.

I believe it is sophistry to suggest that the President's power as Commander in Chief takes precedence over congressional power to raise and support the Armed Forces and to provide funds for keeping in being.

It is an elementary principle of law, and known by all first-year law students, that you cannot mandamus a legislature to create the Armed Forces which the Congress does not desire either to raise or to support.

So I suggest to you, sir, that talk of a constitutional crisis is a phony suggestion. There is no such thing.

CUTTING MILITARY BUDGET FOR DOMESTIC NEEDS

I would like to reiterate what has been said many times before, that the investigations of the subcommittee, and the efforts of the full Foreign Relations Committee to withdraw from, to persuade the Administration to withdraw from Southeast Asia and to cut the military budget, which I hope the Congress will do significantly in the months ahead of us, is all lined up with the national priorities. Today I think it is practically a predominant opinion that the needs of our domestic society, whether it be feeding 15 million Americans who went to bed hungry last night or rehabilitating the badly cut Federal aid to education which is ruining many of our public school systems and indeed our universities having to close their doors and the need for air pollution control and water pollution control and the need to rehabilitate and rebuild our cities and their ghettos, should take a higher priority than unnecessary military expenditures, and I stress the word "unnecessary" because, in my opinion, there is about $30 billion in this military budget which could be eliminated without the slightest danger to our national security.

REPORT ON ALTERNATE DEFENSE BUDGET

In this connection, I was the chairman of a panel, the other members of which were former Secretary of Labor Wirtz and former Deputy Director of the Arms Control and Disarmament Agency, Adrian

Fisher, which heard six extremely competent and able witnesses, many of whom had worked earlier for the Pentagon on an alternate defense budget. We made a report, which has been sent to all Members of Congress, and I would like to have that report filed with my testimony today.

It indicates in some detail areas where it is obvious that cuts can be made in defense spending without the slightest injury to our national security, thus making available, I would have hoped, funds for these badly needed domestic programs; but now, as the economy continues to crash, funds to bring about that balanced budget, which is essential if we are to curb inflation, terminate unemployment, and put our country back on a healthy basis, I suggest to you, sir, there is no place except the defense budget where these funds can be obtained for those purposes unless the American people are prepared to urge on the Congress a massive increase in Federal taxation which, I think, the Congress would be loath to enact, unless they felt such pressure from the country.

(The information referred to follows.)

CITIZENS' HEARING ON AN ALTERNATE DEFENSE BUDGET FOR THE UNITED STATES

REPORT OF THE PANEL OF INQUIRY

Panel of inquiry

Hon. Joseph S. Clark, Chairman, Coalition on National Priorities and Military Policy; formerly U.S. Senator from Pennsylvania.

Dr. Ardian Fisher, Dean, Georgetown University Law School; formerly Deputy Director, U.S. Arms Control and Disarmament Agency.

Hon. W. Willard Wirtz, Wirtz & Gentry, Washington, D.C.; formerly Secretary of Labor of the United States.

Witnesses

Dr. Robert N. Anthony, Ross Graham Walker Professor of Management Control, Harvard University Graduate School of Business Administration; formerly Assistant Secretary of Defense (Comptroller).

Paul Warnke, Partner, Clifford, Warnke, Glass, McIlwain & Finney, Washington, D.C.; formerly Assistant Secretary of Defense for International Security Affairs.

Robert S. Benson, Western Regional Director, National Urban Coalition; formerly Assistant to the Assistant Secretary of Defense (Comptroller).

Dr. Seymour Melman, Professor of Industrial Engineering, Columbia University; author, "Pentagon Capitalism: The Political Economy of War", McGraw-Hill, June 1970.

Dr. Leonard Rodberg, Associate Professor of Physics, University of Maryland; formerly Chief of Policy Research in the Science and Technology Bureau of the U.S. Arms Control and Disarmament Agency.

Principles governing preparation of an alternate defense budget

The amount of the Federal budget submitted to the Congress depends on the final judgment of the President of the United States regarding the following considerations:

1. How much the Federal Government can wisely afford to spend in the coming fiscal year, in light of anticipated revenues and required expenditures. This judgment is reached after careful consideration of recommendations received from all spending and revenue agencies of the government, domestic as well as military.

2. Having reached this judgment, the President must determine the relative priorities of the various demands on the budget, after providing for irreducible claims such as interest on the national debt. He must consider the various requirements of the domestic economy and the basic needs of the military for national security.

In making his decision for fiscal 1971, the President has wisely ruled out (a) a tax increase—because it is politically not feasible, (b) a tax decrease—because the need for revenue is too great to permit it, and (3) a deficit in the budget—because the effort to prevent further inflation prohibits it.

In fact, at least a small surplus of receipts over expenditures on a cash basis was called for by the President's budget message. Accordingly, the President was faced with the requirement of dividing an inadequate amount of available revenue among competing domestic and military demands, none of which can be met in full.

Before these decisions were made by the President, assisted by the Director of the Budget, he had received from the domestic and military spending agencies of the government requests for many billions of dollars in excess of available funds.

These procedures and principles are sound. The difficulty is in the amount recommended in the budget for the Department of Defense.

How the defense budget was prepared

As Dr. Robert N. Anthony, formerly Comptroller of the Department of Defense, told the panel, the method of developing the budget request of the D.O.D. which goes to the President for incorporation in the overall budget is:
1. Start with actual D.O.D. spending in the recent past;
2. Consider the external threat in the light of current foreign policy, which may require both nuclear and conventional arms expenditures of a greater or lesser amount than previously. In assessing the threat, great emphasis is placed on the supposed capabilities of a potential enemy. Little consideration is given to enemy intentions in light of the current international political situation, except to assume the most belligerent attitude on the part of a possible adversary;
3. Give some thought to the needs of non-defense spending in light of overall budgetary considerations—thought, it should be noted, which is not apt to be very objective; and
4. Add as much as seems wise to take care of anticipated inflation.

A suggested new approach to defense budgeting

As pointed out by Paul Warnke, former Assistant Secretary of Defense for International Security Affairs, a wiser approach would be to start with a figure representing the maximum which could be spent for defense without sacrificing the requirements of domestic programs which have a high priority in terms of national well being. In his view, military spending should no longer have the top priority it has been given in recent years.

Warnke suggested that the President should determine the essential requirements of the domestic economy first. In his view, there would then be plenty left over for the military to provide for the national security. He stated his views succinctly: "The fact is that we are today faced with few external threats." And again: "Military force is an ineffective instrument for the conduct of American foreign policy."

Yet, as pointed out by Professor Anthony, the current defense budget, "eliminating Vietnam, is the highest in recent years," and "excluding the effect of other shooting wars, is the highest defense (as opposed to war) budget in history."

There is still time for the Congress to remedy this situation.

Responsibility of the Congress

The President, regardless of methodology and budget procedures, has made his recommendations to the Congress for fiscal 1971. It remains for the legislature, controller of the national purse strings, to determine to what extent, if at all, the President's budget should be cut. It is not likely to be increased, because of the unmet demands of the domestic economy of which the Congress is becoming increasingly conscious as demands of constituents make themselves known.

The needs of the domestic economy

Without resorting to dramatics, it seems established that:
1. There are many millions of Americans going to bed hungry each night whose hunger will not be alleviated from other sources, nor by appropriations requested by the current federal budget if it remains as recommended by the President.

2. The requirements of an acceptable educational system from grade to graduate school are not and cannot be met from state, local or private sources. The provisions for federal aid to education in the current budget are inadequate to close this gap.

3. Constantly increasing pollution of our lakes and streams to the point of endangering public health is not being remedied, nor is it likely it can be remedied without substantial additional federal support not presently available.

4. The air in and around most of our urban centers is polluted to an extent dangerous to public health and well being. There is little chance that this condition can be remedied without large additional federal appropriations not presently available.

5. Living conditions in our cities, and also in rural areas, for the less affluent members of our society are such that standards of health, safety and well being for millions of Americans are at a level below the minimum requirements of decency. There is little hope that these conditions can be remedied without the massive infusion of federal funds not available in the present budget.

6. There are a number of other areas, such as the problems of drug addiction and of public safety, where additional financial assistance from the federal government seems essential.

Conditions affecting the size of the defense budget

In the light of the foregoing discussion, let us consider the overall defense budget as recently justified by Secretary of Defense Laird. Relevant considerations would seem to be:

1. With regard to nuclear or strategic weapons, it is necessary for the immediate future to maintain a ready striking force sufficient to deter attack by Soviet Russia, and to discourage Mainland China from contemplating an attack on the United States. A "first strike" on our part should be ruled out. There is no need to produce or stockpile delivery systems or nuclear warheads in excess of the number needed for deterrence. While invulnerability of the deterrent is highly desirable, there is no need to build competing offensive systems if one is adequate. Nor is there a need for defensive nuclear weapons if the deterrent is adequate without them.

2. With regard to conventional forces our foreign policy for the immediate future dictates:

(*a*) A withdrawal of American forces from Vietnam at the earliest possible moment and the turning over of conduct of the war, if it continues thereafter, to the forces of the South Vietnamese government.

(*b*) No more Vietnams—intervention of American armed forces overseas in the future should be undertaken only as a part of international peacekeeping forces, not unilaterally.

(*c*) A reduction of conventional military forces and hardware to a level adequate to defend the territory of the United States against attack and to participate on an appropriate basis with other countries in peacemaking or peacekeeping efforts.

3. The ongoing effort to reach accommodation with the Soviet Union, after consultation with our allies, on a significant reduction in both nuclear and conventional armaments. This requirement is imposed on both Russia and the United States by the provisions of Article VI of the Nuclear Non-Proliferation Treaty recently promulgated simultaneously in Moscow, London and Washington.

4. An understanding of the present and probably continuing weakness of Mainland China—economically, politically and socially—which renders that country incapable of serious offensive action of a military nature outside its own borders.

5. In light of the current international situation and the heavy demands of domestic priorities, it would seem wise not to embark now on new and untried weapons systems which would put a heavy financial strain on the defense budget in future years.

Overall views of the witnesses

All of the witnesses who appeared before the panel were in substantial agreement on the foregoing principles and considerations. They differed rather substantially on the extent to which an alternative defense budget could make cuts in Secretary Laird's recommendation of a budget of $72.5 billion for Fiscal Year 1971.

Three witnesses, Professor Anthony and Messrs. Warnke and Benson, suggested a cut of $6.5 billion as reasonable but based their thinking, in part at least, on the view that in light of present public and Congressional opinion, as they viewed it, a larger cut was not politically feasible at this time. All three of these witnesses, it will be noted, served as executives in the Pentagon.

Dr. Rodberg felt "the elimination of dangerous and wasteful new weapons can result in savings of at least $10 billion this year. An additional $5 billion could be saved by eliminating obsolete weapons systems." He suggested large additional annual savings through adoption of a more moderate foreign policy. Dr. Rodberg was formerly Chief of Policy Research in the Science and Technology Bureau of the U.S. Arms Control and Disarmament Agency.

Dr. Melman, taking a more radical approach, recommended cuts in the President's budget of $54.794 billion in the current budget for fiscal 1970, and indicated his belief that a budget for 1971 of approximately $23 billion would be adequate to (a) operate a strategic deterrent force, (b) guard the shores of the United States, and (c) participate in international peacekeeping operations. Dr. Melman has, for some years, been a strong critic of the defense budget.

The accuracy of this last approach seems dubious to the panel. However, we believe the following review of cuts that might safely and wisely be made indicates the enormous sums which could safely be taken from the defense budget to provide adequate funding for domestic priorities.

Suggested areas for cuts in defense spending

1. Evidence indicates both the Russian and the American anti-ballistic missile systems, for a wide variety of reasons, are unlikely to be effective against a sustained attack. The projected cost seems out of line with any hoped for security benefit to our fixed land based missiles. ABM is useless for the defense of cities or submarines. The present budget contemplates no ABM defense of strategic air force bases.

2. MIRV, the independently targeted multiple nuclear warhead, is a lethal weapon which, if deployed, is certain to escalate the nuclear arms race, probably to the point of no return. Pending the results of the SALT—Strategic Arms Limitations Talks—with the Russians, it should not be deployed by the United States. It is unnecessary to our present adequate deterrent power. This is recognized in S. Res. 211, the Brooke-Cooper resolution, passed overwhelmingly by the Senate on April 9, 1970.

3. It would seem that, pending the results of the SALT talks, a significant reduction could be made in the huge sums requested by the Department of Defense for Research and Development.

4. A large cut-back in Vietnam expenditures would seem in order—from the $23 billion contemplated to be spent in fiscal 1970 to perhaps $16 billion for 1971, as suggested by Dr. Anthony. Nor should this saving be transferred to other military purposes as contemplated in the 1971 budget.

5. A significant cut in the size of our armed forces and supporting civilian personnel now totaling nearly 4,000,000 should be feasible, perhaps by as much as 1,000,000. This in itself, if accomplished, would make possible a cut of $10 billion in the budget.

6. The three present systems of strategic deterrence—land based missiles, submarine and manned aircraft—overlap. Regardless of the result of the SALT talks, it would not seem prudent, in the light of conflicting domestic demands, to keep all three at projected levels. Surely there is no present need for a new manned bomber (AMSA).

7. There are a number of obsolete, or at least obsolescent or ineffective, offensive and defensive systems which might well be phased out without prejudice to national security. Among these are:

(a) The SAFE early warning system of defense believed by many military experts to be ineffective under present conditions.

(b) The 14 attack carrier task forces now in being, and the 15th nuclear carrier for which funds are requested in the present budget. It is difficult to determine where such naval forces could be utilized under presently foreseeable conditions.

(c) The very expensive C-5A troop carrier airplane with respect to which it is contended we presently have enough for foreseeable emergencies.

(d) Futher expenditures for anti-submarine warfare, generally regarded as ineffective to identify enemy submarines and prevent them from attacking land targets.
(e) Chemical, biological and radiological methods of warfare.
(f) Anti-aircraft artillery, largely ineffective to protect against sophisticated attack, might well be reduced.
(g) The present numbers and quality of attack tactical aircraft are believed by many to be adequate to deal with presently foreseeable threats.

The members of the panel do not consider themselves experts in the field of weaponry, capable of passing final judgment on the necessity for either building or maintaining these weapons. We merely raise questions raised by others more competent than we as to their necessity in the light of our domestic requirements and national security.

Nor do we attempt to pass judgment as to an exact figure to be recommended to the Congress after considering the wide range of cuts in the President's budget proposed by the witnesses from $6.5 billion to over $50 billion.

We are satisfied, however, that very substantial cuts totaling many billions of dollars should be made by the Congress in the military budget. In fact, we believe such cuts must be made to assure a proper reordering of our national priorities. The Federal Government must play a larger role in meeting our domestic crises. And the military budget is the only feasible place to find the money.

Respectfully submitted.

JOSEPH S. CLARK.
W. WILLARD WIRTZ.
DR. ADRIAN S. FISHER.

The coalition on national priorities and military policy is a coordinating body for national religious, peace, liberal, labor and scientific organizations which seek to reverse the militarization of America's policies and resources. It serves affiliated organizations as a channel for communication and cooperative action to oppose deployment of new weapons systems, to support arms control and disarmament agreements and to redirect resources into programs to meet human needs at home and abroad.

The Coalition does not present policy positions for its affiliated organizations unless specifically agreed upon, since its function is not the making of policy but the coordination of action.

The Coalition is financed by contributions from organizations and from individuals. Formed in May, 1969, by twenty national groups, it continues to seek as affiliates additional organizations who share its concern and desire for action.

AFFILIATED ORGANIZATIONS AS OF APRIL 1, 1970

American Baptist Convention.
American Ethical Union.
American Friends Service Committee.
American Humanist Association.
Americans for Democratic Action.
Anti-Pollution League.
Business Executives Move for Vietnam Peace and New National Priorities.
Christian Church (Disciples of Christ), Department of Church in Society.
Committee for Community Affairs.
Church of the Brethren.
Executive Council of the Episcopal Church.
Federation of American Scientists.
Friends Committee on National Legislation.
Fund for New Priorities in America.
International Union, United Automobile, Aerospace and Agricultural Implement Workers of America, UAW.
Mennonite Central Committee.
National Council of Churches, Department of International Affairs.
National Education Association.
National Federation of Temple Sisterhoods.
SANE.

Society for Social Responsibility in Science.
Southern Christian Leadership Conference.
Teachers Committee for Peace in Vietnam.
Union of American Hebrew Congregations.
Unitarian Universalist Association, Department of Social Responsibility.
United Church of Christ, Council for Christian Social Action.
United Methodist Church, Board of Christian Social Concerns.
United Presbyterian Church. U.S.A., Office of Church and Society.
United States Catholic Conference, Division of World Justice and Peace.
William Penn House.
Women's International League for Peace and Freedom.
Women Strike for Peace.
World Federalists, U.S.A.
World Federalist Youth, U.S.A.

U.S. COMMITMENT TO COMPLETE DISARMAMENT

Then, finally, Mr. Chairman, I want to say what I suspect will be a mildly unpopular comment to my good friend, the Senator from Tennessee. I attended a meeting in New York the other day of extremely knowledgeable foreigners. The meeting was first addressed by Secretary General U Thant, and then by a number of others, Russians, English, French, and the like, and we had an observer there from the U.S. mission, but he did not speak. What impressed me was the consensus of opinion that through the brainwashing of the Pentagon the word "disarmament" had become unpopular in the Congress of the United States and indeed at the other end of Pennsylvania Avenue. The suggestion was that the United States is committed by many, many statements of the leaders starting with Christian Herter in 1960, going through with the three major speeches which President Kennedy made before his assassination, including the McCloy-Zorin agreement and the Treaty of General and Complete Disarmament which our country filed together with the Soviet Union in 1962. We are committed to general and complete disarmament under strict international control.

This is basic American policy and has been such since 1960.

The fact of the matter is that on March 5 of this year—I was present at the time, I think the Senator was, too—the treaty forbidding the proliferation of nuclear weapons was called into being in Washington by President Nixon, and he referred to the treaty as the law of the land. Article VI of that treaty commits all the signatories to make efforts in good faith to move as promptly as may be possible toward general and complete disarmament.

The reason I think that the statement may be unpopular with my friend from Tennessee is the word "disarmament" has been dropped from the title of the subcommittee where it was placed originally by our mutual friend, the then Senator Hubert Humphrey, and I would like to see you put it back because I think this is one of the critical matters which will confront us in the next few years.

GENERAL AND COMPLETE DISARMAMENT

Finally, Mr. Chairman, and I am practically through, may I call to your attention correspondence which is attached to my statement dealing with this problem of general and complete disarmament, and the fact that our Russian adversaries, if you wish to call them that, who I think sometimes are much better at public relations than we are, have announced that they will resume at Geneva this summer the discussion of a treaty of general and complete disarmament which they joined with us in submitting in 1962.

The Senator will recall at that time the principal obstacle to a goal, which was stated by both governments to be mutually sought, was the vexing problem of on-site inspection, and now because of the progress of the art of detection since 1962, the need for inspection has drastically decreased and there are many, and I suspect at least one of the witnesses who will follow me will concur with this view, many who believe that on-site inspection creates a less calculated risk of massive cheating of a disarmament or arms control agreement than continuation of the arms race.

So I would suggest that the time is now ripe to review these treaties to see to what extent on-site inspection is really necessary and perhaps to proceed pretty quickly with the first phase of those treaties which called in 1962 for a cutback to the tune of 30 percent in all arms and armaments of all of the parties to the treaty, including the Soviet Union, of course, as well as ourselves.

So I return to the correspondence which is attached to my statement which includes a letter from me to the President of the United States, another letter to the Secretary of State, a reply, and we are certainly downgraded, by a Deputy Assistant General Counsel of the Arms Control and Disarmament Agency, in which it has become clear, I think, that the United States has done no serious work on a treaty of general and complete disarmament since 1963, and does not intend to do so, despite the fact that the Russians state that they are going to bring this up for serious negotiation this summer.

I suggest that this correspondence will be of interest to the subcommittee.

I believe it is customary for politicians to say finally, and then add in conclusion, and I am now adding in conclusion.

Senator GORE. But not ad infinitum.

Mr. CLARK. But not ad infinitum; right.

RECOMMENDATIONS TO THE SUBCOMMITTEE

The recommendations to the subcommittee are contained on pages 12, 13, and 14 of my report and I think they are sufficiently important so that with your concurrence I will read them very briefly.

They are (1) support of Church-Cooper and, if possible, in due course amending it to prevent the American air support——

Senator GORE. I hope you won't mind omitting a discussion of the Church-Cooper because we have three very distinguished scientists to discuss ABM this morning.

Mr. CLARK. My friend, Senator Gore, may I yield to those three gentlemen at this point and urge you, sir, and the staff and the other members of the subcommittee and, indeed, the full committee, to read the eight recommendations which conclude my report?

Senator GORE. Fine.

Mr. CLARK. Thank you very much for your courtesy.

Senator GORE. Thank you, Senator Clark.

We appreciate your presence very much.

(Mr. Clark's statement follows.)

TESTIMONY OF JOSEPH S. CLARK, PRESIDENT OF WORLD FFDERALISTS, U.S.A., CHAIRMAN, COALITION ON NATIONAL PRIORITIES AND MILITARY POLICY

MAY 28, 1970.

I appreciate very much the opportunity to testify in person before this distinguished subcommittee. On April 23, 1970, I submitted a report to the subcommittee outlining my views at that time with respect to ABM, MIRV, SALT and the arms race in general.

A political approach to arms control

The subcommittee is about to conclude its hearings. This seems a good time to summarize the situation in the country and to make recommendations as to what the Committee on Foreign Relations might do to help the United States recover from the serious set-back in foreign relations it has suffered in the last several months.

My claim to some competence in discussing these matters comes from 18 years in elective public office, plus 4 years as an officer in the Army Air Force during World War II. My 12 years of service in the Senate including 4 years on the Foreign Relations Committee, and wide travels around the world to inform myself on our foreign policy perhaps qualify me to urge certain steps upon you.

Of all the witnesses who appeared before you in these hearings only one other, the Secretary of Defense, has ever held elective public office. This fact is one of the reasons why I asked your Chairman, Senator Gore, for permission to appear before you to comment on the political implications on the frightening situation in which our country finds itself.

Dismay at course of events

In my earlier report of April 23, I stressed the fact that I was scared to death for my country by what is happening at the Pentagon with respect to the ABM, the MIRV and the arms race. My concern is now rendered greater by what has happened in Cambodia and in our country since April 23. I would like to leave you gentlemen with a sense of fear also; a sense that the foreign policy of our country soon must be drastically revised before the madmen in the Pentagon and their allies lead our country to destruction through the polarization of our people.

The testimony of the Secretary of Defense

Nothing in the testimony of Secretary of Defense Laird before this subcommittee, which I had the privilege of reading and listening to, lessens my concern. The Secretary of Defense seems determined to proceed with the deployment of both ABM and MIRV. He bases his conclusion on an ever-mounting Soviet threat, largely from alleged continued Soviet buildup of SS-9 intercontinental ballistic missiles, which he says threatens a first strike against the United States which could destroy our country, leaving it with no effective second strike capability unless we, in turn, increase both our offensive and defensive nuclear capability ad infinitum.

The Secretary ignores the now well established intelligence reports that the Soviets built fewer SS-9's last year than in 1965, have constructed no new SS-9 sites since last August, and appear to be most anxious to reach a meaningful agreement with our negotiators at SALT.

Nor does he mention the fact that, even if the Soviets were able to destroy a major portion of our Minutemen Intercontinental Ballistic Missiles—a highly unlikely possibility—we would still have untouched our invulnerable Polaris submarine fleet with some 646 missiles directed on the Soviet Union, a 3 to 1 ratio over the USSR in this critical deterrence category, which cannot be touched by Soviet Intercontinental Ballistic Missiles.

Nor does he mention that the likelihood of the SS-9 destroying our strategic bombing force, equipped as it is with nuclear weapons, is extremely slight.

Nor does he mention that a preponderance of scientific opinion, outside those hired by the Pentagon, is convinced that the ABM just won't work under battle conditions.

Nor does he stress his own statement that our present deterrence with respect to the Soviet threat is quite satisfactory for the next five to seven years.

Nor does he give credence to the widely held belief that the deployment of ABM and MIRV will seriously damage the prospect of a worthwhile agreement at the SALT talks.

Nor does he mention that deployment of the MIRV by the United States is clearly provocative, escalates the arms race, and makes the inspection problem insoluble since no one can tell, once MIRV is fully tested and deployed, how many nuclear warheads are inside the missile.

Nor does Secretary Laird mention the heavy over costs of ABM development to date—$1.7 billion, even before the first ABM has been built and deployed, and the enormous cost, likely as high as $50 billion, which the comprehensive ABM system would entail.

The Secretary of Defense repeats the nonsense, demolished by every reputable scientist and political observer who has ever testified in Washington, that we need the ABM as a deterrent to a Chinese threat. That China is a paper tiger with a primitive nuclear capability which, for the foreseeable future, could be destroyed in a few hours by our strategic bombers is well understood by all except the ABM advocates in the Pentagon.

The determination to deploy both ABM and MIRV is a classic example of the mad momentum of the arms race under the direction of our Pentagon strategists. MIRV was initially intended as a response to the Soviet ABM around Moscow, a deployment which was suspended years ago. Now other reasons have to be given for continuing this mad folly in order to keep the military-industrial complex in business.

I suggest there is nothing in the testimony of the Secretary of Defense either before this subcommittee, before the Senate Armed Services Committee, or in many public addresses made during the last several months, which would justify a perceptive and cautious politician in advocating the enormous expenditures entailed by ABM and MIRV deployment. Deployment will inevitably result in taking food out of the mouths of hungry American children, eliminating desperately needed Federal aid to education, postponing essential aid in rebuilding our city ghettos, and short-changing all efforts to deal in time with ever more critical problems of air, water and soil pollution. To all these disastrous failures must be added mounting federal deficits, continuing inflation and increasing unemployment. The enormous military expenditures are perhaps the major cause for these conditions.

The most articulate and ingenious defender of the Pentagon's mad policy is Professor Wohlstetter of the Rand Corporation, a Pentagon financed research institution whose studies have supported for years the military-industrial complex in its efforts to obtain ever greater defense appropriations. But Professor Wohlstetter's testimony has, in my opinion, been effectively rebutted by the evidence of Dr. Panofsky before this subcommittee, and by the report of the American Assembly at Arden House, chaired by Dean Adrian Fisher of the Georgetown University Law Center, one of the most knowledgeable experts in the field of arms control this country has ever produced. And other witnesses before this subcommittee, notably Herbert York and Marshall Schulman, have in my judgment discredited the arguments made by Professor Wohlstetter.

An article by former Senator and Ambassador Henry Cabot Lodge, appearing in this month's Reader's Digest, is equally unpersuasive, based as it is on inaccurate facts and faulty logic. The Reader's Digest, a right wing journal, presents my school and college classmate as a "patriot" which, no doubt he is. But one may justly inquire does the right wing have a monopoly on patriotism? Is not peace as patriotic as war?

I would hope that the three extremely able former scientific advisors to our Presidents: Drs. Weisner, Kistiakowsky and Hornig, who will follow me today, would further bolster, with their scientific competence, the conclusions to which I, as a former politician, have come and which are stated above.

Tuesday morning's newspapers report that the first MIRV installation has already been set up and that full deployment is expected early in June. This, in my judgment, is a unmitigated tragedy. I would hope that an alert public opinion and the Congress, led by this subcommittee, would take adequate steps to prevent further work at this or other sites until efforts are made at SALT to reach an agreement banning the deployment of MIRV (and ABM), as urged in the American Assembly Report written by Dr. Fisher and which was placed in the Congressional Record by Senator Case on Monday, April 20. Congressional legislation halting deployment of MIRV warheads is even more important than stopping ABM.

Cambodia

Since my report to this committee, the President, without prior consultation with the Congress or, indeed, with many of his own Cabinet, has sent more than 10,000 American troops into Cambodia where hundreds have been killed and thousands wounded in the last month. This incredible action has created such a storm of public protest that the need to curb this Administration and the Pentagon has multiplied many times over. Just as one symptom, some 2 dozen brand new peace groups have arrived on the scene in Washington, many of them led by young people determined to see that an end be promptly put to the war in Indo-China. This stupendous outburst of public resentment against the President and our military leaders may well have changed completely the trend of American foreign policy, and I would hope that the Senate Committee on Foreign Relations would grasp time by the forelock and take advantage of the present condition of public opinion to revise quite drastically our entire foreign policy.

It is now clear that the American people want the war brought to a prompt end and our troops withdrawn from the land mass of Asia. As peace sentiment mounts, there is a great opportunity to turn our country away from international conflict and towards international cooperation.

Efforts made by this committee to cut the military budget, to readjust our national priorities, and to move towards meaningful cooperation with the Soviet Union in the area not only of arms control, but also of disarmament have multiplied.

There can be no denial of the fact that the actions of the President have polarized this country in the most undesirable way. Veterans groups are given access to the Senate Press Gallery to attack the patriotism of those of you who oppose the war. Construction workers supporting the President and waving American flags to evidence their patriotism, march in massive formation in New York, deriding and assaulting students who urge a contrary policy. And, on the other hand, the peace movement has grown enormously in strength during the month, catalyzed by the Cambodian invasion.

Just as the country is polarized, so is the membership in the House and in the Senate. I believe it is essential that a majority of the members of this body, which I believe represents a majority of the people of this country, should reestablish the constitutional responsibility of the Congress in the field of foreign policy and take adequate steps through the power of the purse to bring the war to an end and to encourage successful international negotiations to terminate the arms race.

There is no constitutional crisis

The President and a large segment of the press speak of a constitutional crisis in which the Congress, particularly the Senate, attacks the prerogatives of the President as Commander-in-Chief of the armed forces of the country.

This is indeed a phony issue. Nothing is clearer than the following:

Article I, Section 8, Subsection 1 of the Constitution gives the Congress the power to lay and collect taxes to pay the debts annd provide for the common defense of the United States.

Article 1, Section 8, Subsection 11 of the Constitution gives the Congress the power to declare war.

Subsection 12 authorizes Congress to raise and support armies "but no appropriation of money to that use shall be for a longer term than 2 years."

Article I Section 9, Subsection 7 of the Constitution provides that "no money shall be drawn from the Treasury but in consequence of appropriations made by law.

Thus the power of the purse and of the creation and support of the military is clearly vested in Congress by the Constitution. The President can recommend; but only the Congress can authorize and appropriate.

Article II, Section 2, Subsection 1 of the Constitution states that "the President shall be Commander-in-Chief of the Army and Navy of the United States * * *"

But the power of the President as Commander-in-Chief quite obviously is subject to action by the Congress in raising and supporting the Army, Navy and Air Force which he is to command. It must appropriate the money necessary for their pay and arms. Without action by the Congress, the President's authority as Commander-in-Chief of the Armed Forces evaporates because he has no forces to command.

It is sophistry to suggest that the President's powers as Commander-in-Chief take precedence over Congressional power to raise and support the armed forces and provide funds for keeping them in being. He surely cannot mandamus the legislature to create armed forces the Congress does not desire to either "raise" or "support." So the suggestion of a "constitutional crises" is a phony suggestion. If the Congress refuses to support the war in Southeast Asia with appropriations, the President has no alternative under the Constitution to withdrawing the troops.

The need for disarmament

We should move from arms control at SALT to disarmament at Geneva. This country has been committed to the goal of general and complete disarmament under strict international control ever since Christian Herter, as Secretary of State in 1960, laid down this policy. Mr. Herter's enunciation of the Doctrine was followed by three great speeches by President Kennedy reiterating that general and complete disarmament was our nation's goal and policy.

He acted on his rhetoric through the McCloy-Zorin 18 agreed principles for general and complete disarmament enunciated in the fall of 1961. He followed it up with the United States plan for a World Without War and with the draft treaty of general and complete disarmament filed in Geneva by our country in 1962.

Our commitment to General and Complete Disarmament was only recently reiterated when the treaty providing for the nonproliferation of nuclear weapons was called into being by President Nixon on March 5, 1970. Article VI of that treaty requires the parties to it to "undertake to pursue the negotiations in good faith on effective measures relating to cessation of the nuclear arms race at an early date and to nuclear disarmament, and on a treaty on general and complete disarmament under strict and effective international control."

There is a widespread feeling in many foreign countries that the constant erosion of Pentagon brainwashing has eliminated the word "disarmament" from the lexicon of the Congress of the United States. This subcommittee has been affected by this brainwashing, since it has eliminated the word "disarmament" from its title, where it was originally placed when former Vice President Hubert H. Humphrey was Chairman of this subcommittee. It is high time disarmament became respectable again.

The Soviet Union has never abandoned its expressed desire for general and complete disarmament and, whether or not their position is sincere, they have gained an unquestionable propaganda advantage with other nation-states by stubbornly insisting on advocating total elimination of all arms not necessary to maintain domestic order.

On April 21, the Soviet Union, through its Ambassador in Geneva, Aleksei A. Roshchin, announced that it was going to raise again, at the summer session on the Geneva Disarmament Conference, the question of negotiating a General and Complete Disarmament treaty based on the earlier drafts filed by it and the U.S. in 1962—no doubt motivated by the nonproliferation treaty. Shortly thereafter, I wrote the President and Secretary of State, urging them to meet the Russians half way. A reply dated May 19 was received from the General Counsel of the Arms Control and Disarmament Agency, to which I replied a few days later. Copies of this correspondence are being filed with this statement.

There should be an excellent chance to make a big start on General and Complete Disarmament this summer at Geneva. The vexed problem of inspection which resulted in the breakdown of negotiations at Geneva during President Kennedy's lifetime has been to a substantial extent, solved by the progress in the art of detection.

Many experts now believe that developments in the field of satellite, electronic, photographic, and seismographic intelligence make national inspection, as opposed to on-site inspection, quite adequate for the purpose of monitoring a GCD agreement. The calculated risk of massive cheating has been reduced to a point where it is significantly less than the callous risk of continuing the world as an armed camp, with nation-states constantly threatening to invoke force, either nuclear or conventional, as a solution to diplomatic problems.

One of the best analyses supporting this statement appears under the heading "Can the Communists Deceive Us?" by Jeremy J. Stone, which appeared in the volume "ABM," sponsored by Senator Edward Kennedy and edited by Abram

Chayes and Jerome B. Wiesner last year. While Dr. Stone was referring primarily to cheating on an arms control agreement, the same logic would obviously apply to the inspection problem under a treaty of general and complete disarmament.

National priorities

Behind discussion of ABM, MIRV, SALT and arms control lies the critical question of national priorities. There can be no doubt that millions of Americans go to bed hungry every night, that education is crippled for lack of Federal funds, that we are hardly out of the batter's box in our effort to make our cities decent places to live for all Americans, that we are slowly but surely being choked by breathing impure air, that our lakes, rivers and the oceans are being polluted to an extent which threatens the nation's water supply. It is equally clear that these problems can be solved only through a massive infusion of Federal funds and brains into these domestic areas.

There is no doubt that—eliminating the unlikely solution of a massive tax increase—these needed funds can come only from savings in the military budget.

It is apparent also that such savings can be made to the tune of tens of billions of dollars without the slightest danger to our national security and that, if a meaningful agreement can be made with the Russians at SALT, still more billions of dollars can be saved from military expenditures.

I am filing with this statement a Report of the Panel of Inquiry, consisting of former Secretary of Labor Willard Wirtz, Dean Adrian Fisher and myself, on an Alternate Defense Budget for the United States, which outlines the various areas where this saving could be made in the defense budget.

Recommendations to the subcommittee

In view of the foregoing, I would recommend that the Subcommittee take the following action:

1. Support the Church-Cooper amendment to the Military Sales Bill prohibiting the use of armed forces of the United States in Cambodia after June 30, 1970.
2. Support the McGovern-Hatfield amendment to the Military Procurement Authorization Bill, requiring the United States to withdraw from Vietnam by June of 1971.
3. Support the amendment to the Military Procurement Authorization Bill banning the use of funds for further development and deployment of the ABM.
4. Deny the Department of Defense authority to further deploy MIRV.
5. Support drastic cuts in the Military Appropriations Bills along the lines recommended in the Report of the Panel of Inquiry on an Alternate Defense Budget filed herewith.
6. Urge the President, the Secretary of State, Arms Control and Disarmament Agency, and our delegation at SALT to advocate the most far reaching arms control agreement with the Soviet Union including, as a first stage, the elimination of all land based missiles and ABMs and, ultimately, elimination and destruction of all nuclear weapons. On site inspection should not be a condition to such agreements.
7. Recommend to the President, the Secretary of State, and the Arms Control and Disarmament Agency a revival of negotiations for a treaty of general and complete disarmament under enforceable world law.
8. Encourage the diversion of funds thus saved to the solution of the domestic problems mentioned above which, for want of funding, are on their way to destroying the fabric of American civilization.

APRIL 28, 1970.

The PRESIDENT,
The White House,
Washington, D.C.

MY DEAR MR. PRESIDENT: You no doubt have been made aware of the recent remarks of Aleksei A. Roshchin, the Soviet representative to the Geneva Disarmament Conference, disclosing the Soviet Union's intention to submit a revised draft treaty on General and Complete Disarmament at the summer session of the Geneva Conference.

This new Soviet initiative is most encouraging and I assume your administration welcomes it and will offer revised U.S. proposals that could help lead to meaningful agreements which would serve the best interests of both the United States and the Soviet Union.

There is no reason not to move now on the negotiation of a comprehensive Treaty on General and Complete Disarmament. In fact, the Nuclear Nonproliferation Treaty, which you recently put into effect as "the law of the land," obligates both the U.S. and U.S.S.R. to "undertake to pursue the negotiations . . . on a treaty on general and complete disarmament under strict and effective international control."

The on-site inspection problem, which was the major obstacle to reaching an agreement in 1962, is no longer in the way because electronic detection and satellite surveillance have made verification of most any agreement possible through national means. I might add that Dr. Louis Sohn, your advisor on International Law, has suggested that the 1962 draft treaties of the U.S. and U.S.S.R. are substantially quite similar, and could be mediated by the 24 other nations represented at the Conference.

I urge you to direct Secretary of State Rogers and Arms Control and Disarmament Agency Director Smith to make this new hope for peace their very highest priority.

My thanks for your consideration and my best wishes,

Sincerely,

JOSEPH S. CLARK,
President.

APRIL 29, 1970.

Hon. WILLIAM P. ROGERS,
Secretary of State,
Washington, D.C.

DEAR MR. SECRETARY: Recent press dispatches from Geneva indicate that Mr. Roshchin, the principal Soviet negotiator at the 26 Nation Disarmament Conference, will press hard for negotiation of a treaty on general and complete disarmament in Geneva this summer. This is an understandable initiative from the Russians standpoint, since back in 1962–63 both our country and the Soviet Union filed, at the disarmament conference in Geneva, separate draft treaties of general and complete disarmament that, since the assassination of President Kennedy, have been gathering dust on the green baise at the tables at the conference.

In view of this initiative by the Russians, it occurs to me our response is a matter of some importance. I also would think our response must be for you, and not the Defense Department, to make after, of course, appropriate coordination with the National Security Council and Mr. Henry Kissinger, no doubt, and with the President himself.

May I point out that, going back to the Eisenhower Administration, Secretary of State Christian A. Herter, in 1960, publicly committed the United States to the principle of general and complete disarmament under enforceable world law. Shortly thereafter, John F. Kennedy was elected President, and in 1962–1963 he instituted the very strong peace offensive largely by three great speeches, two at the UN and one at American University, in which he urged the Russians and ourselves to engage not in a war race but in a peace race. He indicated his belief that the charter of the UN would have to be drastically revised and committed our country, the first President ever to do so, to the principle of general and complete disarmament under enforceable world law. The Russians are also committed to general and complete disarmament; their phrase is "under strict international control," but it would be difficult indeed for anyone except international lawyers to find any significant difference between the two phrases.

We start then with the premise, that ever since 1960 both the Soviet Union and the U.S. have been committed to general and complete disarmament under enforceable world law. Every year since then, the General Assembly of the UN has passed resolutions to the same effect. There can be little doubt that practically every nation-state of the world is strongly in favor of general and complete disarmament. There can be little further doubt that the obstacle to general and complete disarmament through the years has been first, the US and secondly, the Soviet Union. It would now appear that there is an opportunity to break the deadlock because of the Soviet initiative, and one would hope the US would not be far behind in picking up the challenge which Russia has laid down to us.

In this connection it is worth noting that Article 6 of the Nuclear Nonproliferation Treaty, proclaimed by President Nixon in Washington on March 5th, contains a specific requirement that parties of the treaty, including of course the

Soviet Union and the U.S., use their best efforts not only to turn the arms race downward, but also to move and promptly towards achieving general and complete disarmament. This section of the treaty was inserted, despite the fact neither the Soviet Union nor the U.S. wanted it. It was put in the Treaty because of the insistence of other countries, both at the Geneva Disarmament Conference and at the UN. It nonetheless has become a solemn obligation of the U.S. In fact, as President Nixon said when he called the treaty into effect, it is "the supreme law of the land."

I suggest, therefore, that the Department of State has a solemn obligation to move forward to meet the Russians at least halfway in terms of seeing where we can go to achieve an agreement on general and complete disarmament, under strict international control or under enforceable world law, as the case may be.

The principal problem on which the negotiations bog-down at the time the Soviet Union and the U.S. filed their draft treaties for general and complete disarmament back in 1962–63 was the vexed question of on-site inspection. The U.S. insisted on it. The Soviet Union refused to permit it.

However, progress in the art of detection since 1962–63 has been so very great that the problem of on-site inspection can no longer seriously concern anybody, except the military which depends for its existence on continuing the arms race.

As the testimony of many witnesses before the Gore Subcommittee of the Senate during the last few months has made abundantly clear, there is no reason why on-site inspection should be a requirement for the U.S. in proposing a treaty of general and complete disarmament. The progress of photographic and electronic satellite intelligence has been so great that we can now confidently assert that we can identify an object no bigger than a basketball on the streets of Moscow. While it is true that certain lethal weapons such as MIRV are not subject to national inspection, one would hope that their deployment, in fact their further testing, would promptly be barred by the negotiators at SALT in Vienna—particularly in view of S. Res. 211 which calls on the U.S. to take the initiative to assure that these weapons, MIRV and the ABM also, should not be further deployed pending the negotiations at SALT.

So I think you can well go along, although no doubt the Pentagon would refuse to, with the consensus of informed opinion that on-site inspection is no longer a requirement for a treaty of general and complete disarmament which would be acceptable to the U.S. In the end one has to consider what the calculated risks are; are the people in the U.S. in greater danger because of the continuation of the arms race which is urged by the Secretary of Defense and the Joint Chiefs of Staff, or would the calculated risk be substantially less if we were to agree on a treaty of general and complete disarmament with the Russians and the other major powers, including of course France and Communist China, assuming the principle that massive cheating is no longer a feasible alternative to meeting ones treaty commitments. I am sure you are aware of the persuasive arguments to this effect which have been made by a large number of knowledgeable experts, not only at hearings before the Gore Subcommittee, but also by Jeremy Stone in the book ABM published last year, by Ralph Lapp, and by a large number of other knowledgeable experts who are not on the payroll of the Pentagon.

Turning to the draft treaty which we filed in Geneva in 1962–63, one must admit that it is deliberately vague on a number of critical issues. So, too, was the Russian draft. Wide areas exist where negotiations will have to be conducted, and strenuous and hard-fought negotiations will no doubt be required before a treaty could be agreed upon.

I would suggest that the third edition of "World Peace Through World Law", published by Harvard University Press in 1966 and authored by Grenville Clark and Louis Sohn, gives an excellent specific draft from which our State Department could well work. I suggest this should be the basis of our policy position. In this regard it is most hopeful and interesting that Louis Sohn, co-author of the treaty draft above referred to, is presently a consultant on International Law for the State Department. I am confident that if you call him into consultation he will be able to guide you on appropriate lines leading to agreement on a mutually beneficial treaty which all the major military powers could accede to.

In the course of the determination as to what our policy should be, you of course have to determine the appropriate role of the United Nations in creating and monitoring the international institutions which will be necessary to make any treaty of general and complete disarmament effective. I would suggest that it is probably unlikely that the UN, in its present status, could agree upon the charter amendments necessary to make it an effective organization to monitor so widespread and so important a treaty. Of course, this is the year to attempt to revise the charter of the UN so as to make it capable of taking on this task.

Moreover the Commission for the Organization of Peace last summer issued, under the chairmanship of your Dr. Louis Sohn, 106 different changes in the practices, procedures and charter of the UN which in the opinion of the Commission were essential to make it an effective organization for monitoring the peace. Unfortunately, the State Department has been quite unwilling to move to accept the proposals which were made by this Commission. I would urge you personally to take a good hard look at them and see whether, in your calculated judgment, it is a feasible suggestion to revise the charter of the UN so as to make it the international institution that can become adequate to monitor a treaty of general and complete disarmament.

My own view is that it probably is not, and that it is not pragmatic to expect to revise the charter of the UN adequately so as to make it capable at this time of carrying-out the role of an international peacekeeper with power to prevent the outbreak of war. My own view is that the International Disarmament Organization, called for by both treaties filed by the US and the Soviet Union back 1962–63, could be developed into the institution capable of monitoring and enforcing world order. In the first instance, it would be comprised of representatives of the principal military powers in the world, and therefore would not need to pay much heed to the mini-states or the other perhaps 100 nation states which have no real direct interest in general and complete disarmament. In the second place, such an international disarmament organization would start free of the veto in the UN charter. Perhaps a new organization should be agreed upon which does not need to deal with the veto. Certainly it would not have one vote for each state regardless of its size or economic status. In the third place, such an organization should be able to devise methods of financing itself, which the UN so far has been incapable of doing.

You will recall that the first stage for general and complete disarmament set forth in both the Russian and US drafts of 1962–63 called for a 30 per cent across the board cut-back in both nuclear and conventional weapons. It occurs to us that this is a feasible objective to start the negotiations which hopefully will take place at Geneva this summer. Surely, in the present state of the world this is not too much to hope for.

In conclusion, may I stress again that in this matter so critical to the safety of the US and probably the most important question of foreign policy which will come before our country in the course of your tenure as Secretary of State, it is your Department and not the Department of Defense which should take the lead and which should control policy. While the National Security Council has of course a role to play to assure the US is not unnecessarily taking risks in terms of agreeing to such a treaty, it should be made elaborately clear that the phobia of the Defense Department against any constructive move towards arms control and disarmament and its ingrain philosophy of anticipating the worst from every conceivable opponent must not be permitted to guide the philosophy which will control the deliberations. I cannot stress too strongly that the lead in this area must be yours. This is a foreign policy issue, not a Defense issue. You will need, of course, to confer with the Secretary of Defense and the Joint Chiefs of Staff, but the fundamental decisions on the risks which the American people should be asked to take in this regard are *political* questions and not *military* questions. In this regard, I do hope that you and your colleagues in the State Department will take, with the President, an appropriate lead .

The foregoing is not intended to bypass or downgrade the role to be played by the Arms Control and Disarmament Agency. Mr. Smith and his colleagues of course have an important role to play in this regard, and it is even conceivable that he will be the head of our delegation at Geneva which would deal with these problems. Nonetheless, the ACDA is in a sense a ward of the State Department, although recently it has been considered far too much an appendage of the Defense Department. I am sure that you will find Mr. Smith most helpful in advancing the cause advocated in this letter. He has long been a staunch advocate of general and complete disarmament, but he has had very few friends, may I say candidly, either in the Defense Department or in the State Department. I would hope that you would extend a hand, a hand not only friendship but also of support so that the efforts of the ACDA can be backed up by State which in the end has the power with the President which the ACDA cannot be expected to wield.

I will be delighted to hear from you, Mr. Secretary, after you have had an opportunity to consider the contents of this letter.

Warm best wishes and regards.

Sincerely yours,

JOSEPH S. CLARK,
President.

U.S. ARMS CONTROL AND DISARMAMENT AGENCY,
Washington, D.C., May 19, 1970.

Mr. JOSEPH S. CLARK,
President, World Federalists, U.S.A.,
Washington, D.C.

DEAR MR. CLARK: The Secretary of State has asked me to respond to your letter of April 29, 1970 in which you refer to press dispatches from Geneva indicating that the Soviet representative, Ambassador Roshchin, will press for negotiation of a treaty on general and complete disarmament in Geneva this summer.

The question of general and complete disarmament will certainly be one of the issues discussed by the Conference of the Committee on Disarmament (CCD) this summer. During the spring session not only the Soviet representative but almost all delegations expressed the hope that the CCD would renew its consideration of general and complete disarmament. The U.S. representative made clear to the Committee that we believe this discussion "can play a useful role in the rededication of our efforts to broader goals and to the identification of specific measures which will be the milestones on the path to these goals." He also noted that "the best way to make progress towards the goal of general and complete disarmament is to concentrate on concrete and specific measures." Ambassador Roshchin similarly stressed the need to seek "agreements on partial measures which would put an end to the arms race and would create an atmosphere for carrying out measures which in the final analysis will lead to the achievement of general and complete disarmament." We expect that the CCD will approach the question of general and complete disarmament in these terms this summer and that it will not engage in negotiation of treaty texts on this subject.

The specific measures to which the CCD is devoting particular attention this year are the completion of a joint US-USSR draft treaty to ban the emplacement of nuclear weapons and other weapons of mass destruction on the seabed and the question of restraints on the use, development, production, and stockpiling of chemical and biological weapons.

We appreciate your continued interest in the field of arms control and disarmament.

Sincerely yours,

WILLIAM W. HANCOCK,
General Counsel.

MAY 25, 1970.

Mr. WILLIAM W. HANCOCK,
General Counsel. U.S. Arms Control and Disarmament Agency,
Washington, D.C.

DEAR MR. HANCOCK: Senator Clark has asked me to respond to your response to his letter to the Secretary of State regarding the negotiation of a treaty on general and complete disarmament which may or may not be considered in Geneva this summer.

Both Senator Clark and I feel that the treaties filed in Geneva need to have the dust shaken off them and we have been terribly disappointed that little or no work has been done on general and complete disarmament since 1962, and that since the McCloy-Zorin Agreement, the whole question has been a dead one from the standpoint of the United States. This bothers us so much that we fear for our country that we love and expect to see as a world leader in such activities.

Recently, at a high level meeting in New York attended by several important world figures, Senator Clark heard the United States take a severe beating from the participants who felt that we had done nothing in recent years to call attention to the grave problems relating to general and complete disarmament. If someone in your office could compile a checklist of United States activities in this area over the last five or so years it would be extremely helpful. We would be most anxious to see such a list.

We are, of course happy, that CCD will devote attention to the Seabed and CBW. In connection with the latter, we hope that ACDA will continue to press for action on senate ratification within the administration and continue to do everything it can to act as a countervailing force to the seemingly endless long grey line of hawks within the administration.

With best wishes

Sincerely,

WILLIAM F. CLAIRE,
Executive Director.

Senator GORE. With the very distinguished panel of gentlemen here, I don't know how to divide it other than to take you alphabetically. However, I invite all three of you to come to the table. I think the chairs are more comfortable.

Dr. Hornig, since you were last to arrive, we will let you be first. The first shall be last and the last shall be first.

STATEMENT OF DR. DONALD F. HORNIG, VICE PRESIDENT, EASTMAN KODAK CO., ROCHESTER, N.Y.

Dr. HORNIG. Thank you very much, Mr. Chairman. I should like to preface my remarks, sir, by commenting that one of the things we will discuss in connection with weapons systems such as Safeguard is the reliability of mechanical devices. Last week when I came down to testify before the Armed Services Committee my flight was canceled because the generator failed. This morning my flight was canceled because a pressure regulator failed, so I feel very keenly about the fact that even high reliability mechanical devices are only too prone to failure.

Senator GORE. Doctor, lest you be disturbed with that let me call to your attention that recently the wife of a Member of the Senate received her widow's annuity from the Social Security Board, a rather handsome check, which my colleague returned reluctantly. Computers as well as generators do make errors.

Dr. HORNIG. Yes. Well, of course, even such a well-tested device as Apollo 13 had difficulties which fortunately could be overcome.

IMPORTANCE OF SALT

It is a great privilege for me to be allowed to present my views on some of the problems we face in bringing the nuclear arms race under control. This is a particularly opportune time for careful consideration of these problems because the strategic arms limitation talks with the Soviet Union are presently going forward.

President Nixon has characterized these talks as the most important arms control negotiation that this country has ever entered. In this view I most heartily concur and it is precisely because SALT is so important that we must consider all the aspects of our strategic nuclear program, especially the question of whether and how fast we should deploy the Safeguard ABM and multiple independent reentry vehicles (MIRV's).

FUTILITY OF ARMS RACE

Anyone who surveys the course of the buildup of nuclear armaments in the last 25 years, whether or not it is characterized as a race, can only be struck by the insanity of the result. Each side has correctly perceived that potential weapons buildup or possible future technological developments on the other side could increase the threat to its survival. Each has responded with its own weapons buildup and accelerated technical development and research. Still, after spending fantastic sums neither has felt secure. In fact, as the potential scale of casualties constantly rises, as the weapons systems become more complex and subtle and less predictable, each side feels more threatened than before. This quarter century must surely go down in history as an exercise in futility.

To an observer from a distant planet this futile pursuit of actions which only increase the risks we face every day, which progressively threaten the existence of the civilization we have painfully constructed over 6,000 years, and which divert precious resources from things we badly need, must make the earth look like a vast insane asylum.

HISTORY OF THE ARMS RACE

The history of the last 25 years amply documents these extreme assertions. After 4 years of U.S. nuclear monopoly—1945-49—the Soviet Union produced its first fission weapon. The power of these weapons was measured in tens of thousands of tons of TNT equivalent. Further intensive efforts on both sides produced thermonuclear fusion weapons in the early fifties with a power equivalent to millions of tons of TNT. The United States developed a remarkably efficient delivery force under SAC with its B-52's and through the 1950's enjoyed decisive nuclear superiority.

But one can question how useful it was as an instrument of national policy. After all it did nothing to inhibit the Soviet attack against Hungary in 1956 or the North Korean attack on the south in 1950. The nuclear forces were only useful against each other.

Despite our enormous advantage the development of a small Soviet long-range bomber force worried us to the point of spending $10 billion over 10 years on an air defense net, SAGE (semiautomatic ground environment) which was never capable of preventing an attack. Of course, the Soviet Union wasted even larger sums on a still more elaborate air defense system which SAC was always confident it could penetrate.

We enjoyed decisive superiority in nuclear delivery power by aircraft in the 1950's so the Soviet Union turned in a new direction, rockets, and demonstrated their new abilities to us with Sputnik. That development led in turn to a U.S. crash program, actually started some years sooner, so that despite the illusory "missile gap" of the 1960 campaign, we soon enjoyed ICBM superiority through our Atlases, Titans, Polaris, and Minuteman.

What did this superiority mean to us? In peacetime military forces are an arm of political and diplomatic action and provide backup for such action. War is a confession of failure to achieve national purpose by other means. But the destructive power of this massive nuclear force on both sides was so out of proportion to any circumstance except a nuclear exchange that as far as I can see they exerted little influence on anything but the nuclear confrontation itself. This Alice in Wonderland drama affected nobody but the actors.

Senator GORE. And provided no additional security for either of the actors.

Dr. HORNIG. Absolutely.

By the middle 1960's we enjoyed a 3- or 4-to-1 advantage in our nuclear forces by any measure. We had Polaris submarines to provide a secure retaliatory force, Minuteman emplaced in concrete silos and an effective B-52 force in SAC. But what did this superiority do for us? It didn't inhibit Vietnam. It didn't make us sleep better at nights. Why? Because we knew the U.S.S.R. felt desperately threatened and would inevitably counter with new buildups of its own. I heard Marshal Malinowsky myself in Moscow on November 7, 1964, say that if the Americans thought they could destroy the U.S.S.R. they were wrong, and he proposed renewed efforts on their part.

At that time they may have thought we were approaching a first-strike capability.

At this same time we also felt threatened. We were being warned about Soviet first strikes and in any case were clear that in any exchange, no matter who initiated it, we would suffer tens of millions of casualties. Some of our defense specialists asked whether the U.S.S.R. was putting together a vast underground shelter system so that they could fight a nuclear war despite our superiority. You remember the brief flurry on our side when we almost started a home fallout shelter program—one in every backyard. Those were the days when some still thought a nuclear holocaust might be worth surviving.

So it went. Back and forth. Tens of billions of dollars each year whose only purpose was to counter the tens of billions on the other side. Each year we put more into nuclear destructive power than into our entire system of higher education.

Of course, I grant that survival dictated that we play this macabre game as long as the other fellow did. But he felt the same way and couldn't live with U.S. superiority.

So he started his catchup program with SS-9's, SS-11's, and SS-13's. He started an ABM system at Leningrad and abandoned it again. He deployed large radars which look like early warning radars for an ABM system. He deployed a massive new air defense system with new long-range rockets. He built an ABM system of very limited capacity to defend Moscow. He started his own ballistic missile submarine program, substantially like our Polaris submarines.

There is little question that he has blunted that decisive superiority which did us so little good. In some ways he has caught up. And once again we are asking about his intentions. Will he be content to catch up or does he intend to pass us by?

SECURE DETERRENT ON BOTH SIDES

More fundamentally, the question is whether this arithmetic is meaningful. Under most circumstances I think not because of the secure deterrent which has evolved on both sides. In brief, for some time now it has been clear to both sides that even if the other struck first they could still deliver a counterblow which would destroy a considerable fraction of the population and industry of the aggressor and effectively destroy his society.

That surely is what has given us some stability, whatever the details of warhead counts, megatonnage or what have you, whether we have parity or superiority.

It is implicit in this line of thinking that first strikes are directed against the enemy's weapons so as to blunt or eliminate retaliation, and retaliatory strikes are directed primarily against the population in cities.

Hence, so long as the cities remain hostage to nuclear retaliation, each side feels some security. Whatever new developments threaten the deterrent are dangerous because in a tense international situation they give the advantage to the one who strikes first.

CONCERN IS FOR THE FUTURE

Where are we now? The Secretary of Defense has recently stated before this committee, "We believe that today we do have sufficient forces for deterrence. However, we are very much disturbed by what we have observed about the character and rate of buildup of Soviet strategic forces.

"Thus, our concern is not about today, or even next year. Our concern is about what the future may bring."

He is certainly correct in that assessment. He would have been correct at any time in the last decade or more, and I venture to predict that unless SALT is successful, he will be correct a decade hence. He would also be correct if he were the Soviet Defense Minister.

Senator GORE. And at whatever level we madly push the armaments race.

Dr. HORNIG. Correct. That concern about what the future may bring highlights our dilemma.

If we now take the next step in this primitive ritual dance of perpetual action and reaction, will that assessment ever change? I think not. We live in a high-risk world and the risks are growing.

ONLY HOPE LIES IN SALT

The only hope of interrupting this dance lies in SALT and I hope we are prepared to take risks to end this competition which are at least a fraction of the risks we are taking if SALT fails. I hope the same is true of the U.S.S.R. But there must be people in the U.S.S.R. who also see the futility of the dangerous course we are both on. We have spent over $1,000 billion on this silly game since World War II. So have they. I hope we will add strength to those on their side who want SALT to succeed rather than fueling another round of military reaction on their part.

Right now we must make divisions on two scores: first, whether to deploy, or expand the deployment, of an ineffective ABM system, Safeguard, and whether we should deploy multiple independently targetable reentry vehicles (MIRV) which would enormously increase the number of nuclear warheads we could deliver.

DEVELOPMENT OF SAFEGUARD

First, let me discuss Safeguard. It is put together from hardware developed for the Nike X system, a city defense system which was rejected by the present and previous Administrations. Now that hardware is to be deployed away from the cities to defend Minuteman, to provide a thin umbrella against a light Chinese attack and to protect against an accidental launch.

No one can argue much about those purposes. But the question isn't whether we would like to defend Minuteman. It is whether Safeguard would in fact provide a defense commensurate with its cost. For years we have tended to talk about systems, paper systems, as if they did the things we said they were supposed to do. We talk as if the things we hope for are the properties of real weapons. One would have thought, after the experience we have had on a variety of complex weapons systems, that we would know better by now. Still we keep on indulging in this dream world.

What about Safeguard? My contention is that Safeguard will not do any of these things in the foreseeable future but is likely to add another impetus to the arms race. The technical criticisms of Safeguard have been presented by a variety of witnesses before several committees, notably Dr. Panofsky.

Many of the criticisms have been accepted by the Department of Defense and, if anything, the criticisms look more serious this year. I would like to look as the various roles separately since the requirements for each are somewhat contradictory.

POSSIBILITY OF THREAT TO MINUTEMAN

Although there is no present threat to the survivability of our Minuteman force, it is conceivable that one could develop in the future, as Secretary Laird has testified. Even then, it should be remarked that a threat to Minuteman cannot be equated with a Soviet first-strike capability. A first-strike threat would have to envisage a simultaneous attack against the Minuteman force, the SAC bomber fleet, and the Polaris-Poseidon fleet, on a time scale which is technically impossible because of U.S. early warning capabilities already in existence. Each of these forces independently can inflict retaliatory damage on an attacker which his society would be unlikely to survive.

Nonetheless, unless SALT succeeds, there is at least the possibility of an emerging threat against Minuteman. Even then we have several alternatives: (1) An ABM defense of Minuteman, (2) concentration of our deterrent in SAC and Polaris-Poseidon, (3) increasing the hardness of the Minuteman silos or providing mobility among several sites, and (4) increasing the number of Minuteman.

SAFEGUARD AS DEFENSE OF MINUTEMAN

The first is the choice which led to Safeguard deployment. However, granted that such a defense is desirable and nonproductive the following severe technical criticisms have been raised, and if you desire I will be glad to elaborate them. First, even if it performed as designed, it is small and the number of attacking missiles destroyed and the number of Minuteman saved would be negligible compared to the cost of the system.

Senator GORE. And also compared to the retaliatory capacity from other sources.

Dr. HORNIG. That is right. And also small compared to the possible attack. In fact it has the property that if the other side's attack is small we wouldn't need it because Minuteman would be safe. If the other side's attack is large it doesn't make an appreciable difference either. Only if the other side designs its attack to fit precisely the narrow range in which Minuteman would be effective would it do us any good. So we need the cooperation of the other side to make it any good.

Dr. WIESNER. If it worked.

Dr. HORNIG. And if it worked, yes.

Secondly, the defense of each Minuteman complex depends on a single, very expensive—about $200 million—radar. If this radar were to malfunction or be destroyed by enemy attack, then the whole system collapses. Attack on the radar is a very attractive tactic, therefore, for the enemy, especially since it is much "softer," that is, vulnerable, than the missile silos it defends. A consequence is that a substantial part of the already limited supply of defense missiles—Sprints—must be devoted to protecting the radar, that is, defending the defense.

Still worse, Soviet SS-11 missiles—which now are much more numerous than SS-9's, according to Secretary Laird more than 3 to 1—have sufficient power and accuracy to destroy the radar although they do not endanger the Minuteman silos. Thus, by using the SS-11's to take out the radars—MSR's—the Safeguard defense against the SS-9's, which might attack the Minuteman silos, would be negated. As far as I know, the Defense Department has never answered this objection.

Third, the computer system to automatically manage the engagement is so complex and the programing problem so staggering that those experienced with computers and computer programing have no faith that the system would actually work properly when called upon, particularly since it would never have undergone full-scale tests.

During this last year it has become clear beyond reasonable doubt that if the defense of Minuteman were the only, or even the principal, function of Safeguard, its deployment could not be justified. If the negligible protection now offered by Safeguard were increased by simply adding more missiles and radars of Safeguard type, the undertaking would be enormously expensive. Specifically, the cost per silo defended would be many times the cost of each Minuteman saved; the defense cost would also exceed the cost of the enemy missiles which could be intercepted with confidence. As a result, it would only provide an incentive for the attacker to increase slightly the number of his attacking missiles.

DEFENSE DEPARTMENT STATEMENTS ON SAFEGUARD

Apparently the Defense Department recognizes these criticisms; at least it has scaled down its claims since last year.

On April 16, 1969, Secretary Packard testified that he saw, "no feasible substitute for Safeguard." But on February 20, 1970, Secretary Laird stated:

If, in the future, the defense of Minuteman has to be expanded, new and smaller additional radars placed in Minuteman fields would be less costly than the Safeguard missile site radar—MSR—because they would not have to cover such large areas.

I should interpolate that this is absolutely right; it would be a much sounder approach.

> For this reason we will pursue a program to determine the optimum radar for such defense and begin the development of this radar and associated components in fiscal year 1971.

In a similar vein, Dr. Foster, Director of Defense Research and Engineering, testified last year before this committee:

> We think on the basis of these kinds of calculations that we can on an economic and practical basis defend the Minuteman field against anything the Soviets will throw at us.

While this year Dr. Foster states:

> If the Soviet threat to Minuteman should increase beyond levels that could be handled by the phase II Safeguard multipurpose defense, we might wish to augment the system by employing several terminal defense radars in each Minuteman field.

In short, Safeguard is vulnerable and not really designed to defend hardened Minuteman sites. The Defense Department belatedly recognizes that any hope of reasonably effective defense requires the development and deployment of a system specifically designed for the purpose rather than an adaptation of the Nike X and Sentinel systems which were designed primarily to defend cities.

If this is so, do we need Safeguard at all? If we need an airplane, should we build trucks because we happen to have the parts? Or should we design an airplane?

AREA DEFENSE AGAINST COMMUNIST CHINESE

Now I would like to turn to the problem of defending ourselves against the Chinese threat by erecting a "leaky" umbrella over the continental United States. What is the threat? Originally it was predicted that China would launch its first ICBM in 1967. Now Secretary Laird predicts the launch in 1970, so that by the late 1970's the Chinese might have a small ICBM force. Presumably it is this small force which may either threaten us or be used to blackmail others whom we might like to defend.

An immediate question, when we undoubtedly will have an overwhelming nuclear superiority over China for the foreseeable future, is whether the Chinese would choose to commit suicide? There is little recent evidence that the Chinese are any more foolhardy than others in military ventures.

Therefore, I do not see how anyone can take the threat of an outright, deliberate Chinese ICBM attack on the United States seriously.

Presumably our real concern is a different one. If we want to use our ICBM force to threaten the Chinese with nuclear reprisal, either to honor treaty commitments or to respond to a threat by China against one of its neighbors, we would like the Chinese to believe that threat, that is, to believe that we would carry it out, even at the risk of a few million deaths because a few Chinese missiles which survived the attack might be fired at the United States. Certainly a threat on our part would be much more credible if that risk could be eliminated. This is what I suppose the President means when he says we need the ABM umbrella if we are to have "a credible foreign policy in the Pacific area."

Senator GORE. I am not sure that is what it means, but I am glad to have an interpretation of it. It is the first one I have had.

Dr. HORNIG. I am sure there are many interpretations.

Unfortunately, present technology, and Safeguard technology in particular, cannot provide a reliable umbrella over the United States, against even the light Chinese attacks which might appear possible in the late 1970's. There are many reasons, among them:

1. Any system as complex as Safeguard which can never be tested is subject to many sources of failure—including human error.

And I have already cited the example of some much simpler systems this morning.

2. Since interceptor will never have perfect reliability there is a good chance that some enemy missiles will "leak" through.

3. An area defense is useless until all of the sites are installed. Otherwise the enemy simply targets on the unprotected areas.

4. Many devices, including ones as simple as fragments of the launch rocket tanks (and we did experiments blowing up Atlas tanks in the 1950s) are well known which can confuse the system and aid the penetration. There is no reason to believe that a nation which can build ICBMs and thermonuclear warheads will not have installed such devices even on their early missiles.

Although an area defense such as Safeguard will attenuate a Chinese attack, it can never be expected to achieve anything like total protection. Compared to the deterrence offered by our overwhelming ICBM force, I cannot see that Safeguard is worth even a fraction of the expense.

EFFECT OF SAFEGUARD ON THE ARMS RACE

As for the arms race, I cannot believe that Safeguard is provocative. Neither the ineffective defense of Minuteman or the "leaky" thin umbrella over cities need cause the Soviets any concern.

But still, why did we respond so strongly to the deployment of soft, vulnerable Soviet radars and the deployment of a defense around Moscow that we could easily penetrate and overcome?

We did respond by developing MIRV for our Minuteman and Poseidons.

The reason, of course, is that whatever the initial characteristics of the system, we were concerned about what it might become. In the same way, it seems likely that as we realize the vulnerability of our thin umbrella it will be beefed up. Pressure will arise to protect each area of the country against all of the Chinese force.

But such an expansion would worry the U.S.S.R., particularly since Sprints can be moved back to the cities, because it might cut down the effectiveness of their deterrent force. It seems quite predictable that they would redouble their efforts on penetration aids, MIRVs and other new weapons, not because Safeguard threatens them now but because it signals a move in a new direction which might threaten them a decade hence.

I presume they reason much like our Secretary of Defense on that score.

EFFECT OF MIRV ON THE ARMS RACE

I would like to spend only a few minutes on MIRV. It is a new weapons system which will enormously increase the number of independently targetable warheads we can shoot at the U.S.S.R. To be sure, it was developed to counter the possibility of a Soviet ABM which would degrade our deterrent. We regard it as a deterrent force, and so it is as long as it is not accurate enough to hit individual missile silos.

But how must it look from the Soviet side? They will see it as an important new step which will add many thousands of nuclear warheads to our arsenal. Despite our assurances to the contrary, any conservative Soviet defense planner must realize that if the accuracy were sufficiently improved, it might be we who are constructing a first-strike force. We cannot expect that the deployment of MIRV can have any effect except to force the U.S.S.R. to increase its own efforts. It must have the effect of accelerating the arms race. Since our deterrent is not presently threatened I can see no reason to rush to deploy MIRV before SALT has had a chance to succeed.

EFFECT OF MIRV ON SALT

It is sometimes argued that it will improve our bargaining position at SALT.

I am not an expert on Russian psychology but it really doesn't make sense to me to expedite arms control talks by deploying major new weapons systems. Nor does it make sense to spend billions of dollars to accumulate hardware so that we will have something to bargain away at the conference table. In fact, that seems downright wasteful and we don't have that much to waste right now—except, perhaps, in the Department of Defense.

Senator GORE. I suggested last year that this was a possible motivation of the proposed ABM deployment, and the Administration rushed a denial to the floor of the Senate. Yet it now appears to be the policy.

Dr. HORNIG. This argument keeps on being advanced in various quarters.

CONCLUSION

To sum it all up, for 25 years we and the Soviet Union have each expended vast treasure, all the while increasing the hazard to ourselves and future generations. Since prudent defense planning on each side must always overreact, and I say must, must always overreact to any move by the other, there seems to be no end in sight to this process unless the SALT talks succeed. For this reason, we must make progress if it is at all possible, even if we must take some risks in the process. After all, we are taking terrible risks if SALT does not succeed.

What I see now, in Safeguard, in MIRV, in the Soviet buildup of new weapons, is the beginning of a whole new round in the never-ending spiral. And frankly this scares me.

What should we do? Since I believe that Safeguard, on technical grounds, will not offer us substantial protection and is more costly than other means of doing so, I would abandon its deployment. Certainly I would not expand it before any construction on Phase I has been completed and no lessons at all have been learned. I would continue to support R. & D. which might give us a true nonprovocative defense of our deterrent missiles.

As to MIRV, I would delay deployment and put all my best efforts into making progress on SALT.

Finally—this is the time to halt the arms spiral, if possible. At best it is a prodigious waste of resources and it may be the road to the destruction of human civilization.

Thank you, sir.

Senator GORE. Doctor, I know that in the scientific world a disciplined mind is necessary for excellence in achievement. Your statement is particularly tightly well-reasoned.

Thank you very much.

If you will abide for a time, we will hear from your distinguished compatriots. We will hear Dr. Kistiakowsky next.

STATEMENT OF DR. GEORGE B. KISTIAKOWSKY, PROFESSOR OF CHEMISTRY, HARVARD UNIVERSITY

Dr. KISTIAKOWSKY. Thank you, Mr. Chairman.

It is a signal honor for me to be invited again to testify before your subcommittee, at this time on ABM and MIRV, and their relation to SALT and the continuing nuclear arms race.

DEPLOYMENT OF ABM AND MIRV IS AGAINST U.S. INTEREST

At the outset let me state my conclusion that the deployments of ABM and MIRV, and especially of both together, will disturb the comparative stability of the present nuclear peace maintained through mutual deterrence. Such deployments are provocative in the sense of stimulating the adversary to amplified reactions in kind. Thus they induce an acceleration of the arms race rather than encouraging meaningful arms control agreements.

The nuclear arms race (considered only in military terms quite apart from its effect of denying funds to vitally important domestic needs), is not strengthening but actually decreasing our national security in this world of ever-mounting nuclear armaments and capability of mutual destruction and overkill. I believe, therefore, that a determination to assume the initiative in massive deployments of ABM and MIRV, as seems to be happening now, before the possibilities for arms control agreements have been fully explored in SALT, is against the best interests of the American people—and I recommend against doing so.

These general conclusions are developed in considerable detail in an article written by G. W. Rathjens and myself and published last January by the Scientific American magazine. And if it pleases you I will be glad to submit it for the record.

Senator GORE. It will be printed in the record.

Thank you.

(The information referred to appears on p. 42.)

Dr. KISTIAKOWSKY. Now I propose to comment very briefly on Safeguard ABM, on MIRV and on SALT in that order.

SAFEGUARD AS DEFENSE OF MINUTEMAN DOUBTED

The last time I testified before your committee was 14 or 15 months ago when the first version of ABM deployment, utilizing Nike X technology and components, the Sentinel, was approaching its unlamented demise. Immediately thereafter the second version, the Safeguard Phase I, was proposed by the present Administration.

While the Sentinel was ostensibly planned to protect us from a Chinese attack utilizing ICBM's, which they are expected to develop shortly, the Safeguard Phase I deployment was purportedly to protect a small part of our Minuteman missile force from a preemptive attack by the Soviet Union, using its not-yet-in-being or tested, but expected, MIRV-equipped large SS-9 missiles. A number of highly competent witnesses appearing before your committee last spring and summer have brought out, however, that Safeguard was ill-adapted to the defense of hardpoint targets—Minuteman silos—scattered over large land areas. The technical arguments against the effectiveness of Safeguard as the Minuteman defender are extremely well presented, for instance, in the testimony of W. K. H. Panofsky before your and the Armed Services Committees, and I am referring to his testimony before your committee on April 13 of this year, and before the Armed Services Committee on May 19. And to spare your time, sir, I shall simply associate myself with his arguments. I shall only note by way of a summary that, if the Soviet Union were to acquire by the mid-70's the capability to destroy virtually completely our Minuteman force in a surprise attack using MIRV-equipped SS-9 missiles, then, even after the deployment of Safeguard at a cost to us of several billion dollars, it could still do the same less than a year later.

It would only have to continue during this additional insignificantly short time interval the same rate of deployment of its SS-9 missiles as it is asserted to be maintaining now and into the mid-70's.

Currently, the Administration proposes to continue with Phase I and to start Phase II deployment, although now conceding that Safeguard may not be a good defense for Minuteman unless the Soviet Union conveniently tailors its ICBM program to Safeguard capabilities. In the words of Secretary Laird—page 49, fiscal year 1971 defense program and budget statement, February 20, 1970, "the threat could actually turn out to be considerably larger than the Safeguard defense is designed to handle," but he then nonetheless proposes "to continue deployment of Safeguard because the additional costs needed to defend a portion of Minuteman is small if the full area defense is bought." I do not agree with his argument and may I submit that what may appear to be small to the Secretary of Defense looks very large to us civilians.

So I do not agree with his argument for the deployment and am disturbed by the fact that by now the justifications for ABM deployment have swung through almost a complete circle to those originally advanced for the Sentinel area defense against the Chinese attack. Meanwhile also, the decision seems to have been made to press for the deployment of the "full area defense" by the Safeguard.

SAFEGUARD AS AREA DEFENSE AGAINST COMMUNIST CHINA DOUBTED

My grave misgivings of a year ago about this kind of ABM deployment specifically are equally strong now because I am convinced that our reliance on an assured destruction through retaliation, as the real deterrent of a nuclear attack, must not be obscured by false hopes of damage prevention. Assuming that the leadership of the People's Republic of China would decide on a suicidal ICBM attack against the United States, it would have nearly a decade until the full area Safeguard defense has been deployed in which to develop sophisticated penetration aids and harden its ICBM warheads, guided by all the official disclosures and discussions in the United States. Forewarned that the Safeguard is to be deployed, the Chinese can make the penetration aids a concurrent part of their ICBM development program at a relatively small percentile increase in cost and time of readiness of the whole system. In our own case, and I speak from personal knowledge, the penetration aids were deployed only much later than our first ICBM's simply because such elaboration was not considered necessary in the earlier period.

As has been discussed in detail by your other witnesses, an area defense relying very largely on exo-atmospheric Spartan missile interception cannot assure protection against a well-planned attack, Chinese or otherwise, using reasonably sophisticated ICBMs with penetration aids. Some American cities of course would not be defended at all in the more immediate future and until the entire area deployment referred to before would be completed. Thus it is very difficult to see how the Safeguard could provide at any time anything like an infallible area defense against the hypothetical Chinese attack, and to assert this is to mislead grievously the American people. In the meantime, applying the well known "worst case" type of operational analysis, the Soviet military are likely to argue that since Safeguard may provide total area defense against the 50 or 100 Chinese missiles, they themselves need several hundred additional ICBM's to overcome Safeguard and preserve intact their assured destruction capability against the United States.

The consequences of this reasoning for the arms race are quite obvious.

I referred above to a possible "suicidal attack" by the Chinese. That, sir, it would certainly be, because but a small part of our offensive strategic forces would suffice to destroy the Chinese industrial establishment and, largely through fallout, for instance, inflict staggering population losses, since both the industry and the population are highly concentrated in the comparatively small area of maritime and other eastern provinces of China. The People's Republic of China is as vulnerable to nuclear attack as are other countries. Thus our deployment of the anti-Chinese form of Safeguard would have to be interpreted by the Chinese leaders as evidence that our Administration regards them as totally irresponsible, even though their past military record has been interpreted by experts as cautious and calculating. It is very difficult to visualize how in such a climate the relations between the United States and China could be gradually normalized, a stated objective of President Nixon.

In view of all these considerations, I can only reiterate my conclusion that the now proposed phase II deployment of Safeguard should not be authorized and that phase I should not be continued beyond fiscal year 1970.

SMALLER RADARS FOR DEFENSE OF MINUTEMAN SUPPORTED

While I oppose Safeguard deployment, I recognize that defense of land-based ICBM forces, so long as it is not convertible into a system to thwart the assured destruction capability of the adversary and does not appear to him to have this capability, could be an action that is not destabilizing to the nuclear arms balance. In fact it might be likened to measures to reduce the noise and otherwise to further improve the hiding ability of Polaris submarines. Therefore, the plans of the Department of Defense to develop smaller and less costly radars for the specific purpose of defending Minuteman (statement by Dr. J. S. Foster, Jr., DDRE, Feb. 24, 1970) should be supported. In general, I believe the development funds for maintaining the technology of ABM at the frontiers of scientific knowledge should not be spared.

DESTABILIZING EFFECT OF MIRV'S

I now turn to the problem of MIRV's, the multiple independently targetable reentry vehicles. As Dr. Herbert York explained in his recent testimony before your subcommittee, the original U.S. decision to go ahead with the development of MIRV's was based on the desire to have the most assured means of penetration of the Soviet ABM defenses that were beginning to take shape then. The Soviet Government eventually saw the futility of deploying its ABM and stopped that project, but our development of MIRV's has nevertheless continued and is reaching the stage of operational readiness.

The fiscal year 1971 budget proposal includes plans for accelerated conversion of Polaris into Poseidon submarines and the start of the deployment of MIRV-equipped Minuteman III ICBM's is to be advanced to this June according to the recent announcement by the Secretary of the Air Force. As is of course well known to your subcommittee, the destabilizing effect of MIRV's on the arms race arises because an adversary cannot know for sure how accurately the multiple warheads of the other can strike their targets and therefore he tends to assume the worst. If their accuracy and number of these warheads is high enough considering the explosive power of the warheads and the hardness of the targets, then one MIRV missile can theoretically destroy more than one of the adversary's missile silos. Thus to the war gamers a preemptive strike becomes far more tempting. This hypothetical threat invites the deployment of more nuclear arms to deter it and the arms race gets into even higher gear.

I am not aware of any claims that the first generation of our MIRV-equipped missiles will be effective against Soviet missile silos. However, recent statements by Pentagon spokesmen referred to their desire to improve guidance capabilities against hard targets. Thus, using again the so-called worst-case type of analysis, the Soviet military will probably argue that the United States is working on a preemptive first-strike force, just as Secretary Laird and various other Pentagon spokesmen have now argued for more than a year that this is what the Soviet Union is doing.

Considering the large numbers and great variety of our strategic weapons systems, a preemptive attack on these forces by any of our adversaries even if in possession of MIRV's will be, in the foreseeable future, a wholly irrational and suicidal action. Unfortunately, however, the worst-case arguments of the military planners about the threat of preemptive strike and the need for escalatory responses is likely to prevail as it has always prevailed in the past. One of the tragic but rather probable responses to massive deployments of MIRV's which Dr. Hornig has not described in his well-designed list, would be decisions by the nuclear-armed adversaries to "launch on warning" their land-based missiles. What is meant thereby is that missiles may be launched solely on receipt of signals, radar and otherwise, that an enemy has launched his missiles. This decision, of course, would enormously increase the chances of nuclear war by mistakes and thus would further endanger our own national security.

Therefore, it is my conviction that a deployment of MIRV's would be counterproductive, especially at a time when, as President Nixon has stated, he is desirous of changing the climate of confrontation into one of negotiation with the Soviet Union.

ENDORSEMENT OF SENATE RESOLUTION 211

Consequently I wish to express my endorsement of the spirit and purpose of Senate Resolution 211. The suspension of further deployment of all offensive and defensive nuclear strategic weapons systems while the Strategic Arms Limitation Talks are underway and the possibilities for more permanent arms control measures are being explored, can only be conducive to an early success of SALT. In fact, to make this proposal truly effective, I would urge that it be accompanied by a unilateral although strictly temporary suspension of such deployments by the United States, pending a favorable response by the USSR.

IMPORTANCE OF SALT

Mr. Chairman, having been personally involved with arms control problems now for quite a few years, I am very much aware of the staggeringly complex issues facing our (and Soviet) negotiators in Vienna (and whatever other cities the SALT meetings will move to, since, if they are productive, they will last for quite some time). Success of these meetings is overwhelmingly important for the future welfare and even survival of American and other peoples. Therefore, it is absolutely essential to create an environment at home which will reinforce rather than negate our sincere negotiators' efforts. The recommendations which I have made in this statement are intended to serve this purpose. I fervently hope that they will be put into effect.

Thank you very much.

Senator GORE. Thank you, Doctor, for a very eloquent and moving analytical statement.

Dr. Wiesner.

STATEMENT OF DR. JEROME B. WIESNER, PROVOST, MASSACHUSETTS INSTITUTE OF TECHNOLOGY

Dr. WIESNER. Mr. Chairman and members of the committee, I am pleased to be able to appear before you again and to participate in your inquiry into the possible effects of the ABM system, MIRV and SALT on the arms race and on efforts to stop it. I am pleased to be here for many reasons but particularly because in recent years discussions in your committee have been the focal point of a national effort to understand the arms race and bring it under control.

Senator GORE. Doctor, I would like to interrupt a moment to say that this effort of understanding has been directed first to ourselves, but also in the broader scale to the whole American public. The testimony of distinguished scholars, such as you gentlemen, has made this example of participatory democracy possible.

Thank you.

Dr. WIESNER. Right.

ARMS CONTROL AND DISARMAMENT

As an aside I would like to associate myself with Senator Clark's request, if that is what it was, that you consider the possibility of the reintroduction of the word "disarmament" back into the title of your committee. I think it is a sad thing when we allow ourselves to be frightened about the use of that word.

I think we have become just a little concerned about it.

Senator GORE. Doctor, in that regard, arms control is certainly the first step toward ultimate disarmament. Until we can achieve a considerably larger degree of arms control than is now feasible, total and complete disarmament is a dream.

Dr. WIESNER. Yes, I agree.

Senator GORE. It is a dream which we must continue to hold, but nevertheless a dream.

Dr. WIESNER. But partial disarmament steps which you might call arms control are not a dream. I think the two words are used interchangeably, and I think we have come to use arms control because we have been willing to allow the opponents to so taint the word of disarmament that we are afraid to use it and I think we shouldn't allow words to be captured, that is my point.

Senator GORE. Thank you for your suggestion.

Senator CASE. I think, if I may just say so here, that we all regard reduction of arms as a part of the job of this committee. We are not anxious, out of any false sense of purity, to attract any unnecessary argument against our cause which we think is a thoroughly sound cause.

Dr. WIESNER. Well, I was one of the first people who began to use the words "arms control" instead of disarmament because I thought maybe we could appease some of the people who worry——

Senator CASE. You are vulnerable to the people who, with or without sincerity, think you are talking about disarmament, laying ourselves bare to the enemy, and nobody is talking about that that I know of.

Dr. WIESNER. Nobody means that, of course.

Your hearings, as I have already said, not only filled a vital educational need but they have given us hope that peace has a chance. Those of us outside the Congress who are working to stop the arms race and create a more rational world take heart from the work of your committee. Our Nation is pleading for moral leadership and your committee is one of the few groups that is providing it.

Senator GORE. That is one of the finest compliments we have received. Thank you.

TWO COURSES OF ACTION IN SEARCH OF SECURITY

Dr. WIESNER. Most of our citizens have the same national security goals; we want peace and freedom for ourselves, for our allies, and I guess, in a general way this could be said to be our goal for all of the world. We have differing ideas about how to achieve these ends. For many years the United States has followed two courses of action in search of security, through international organizations, controls and agreements on the one hand and superior military force on the other. In recent years many of us have come to realize that these two routes are often incompatible; that an insistence on superior military force and the unilateral right to use it will in all likelihood foreclose establishing effective limitations on armaments and their use. We are forced to choose between these two courses as we plan our future and this takes deep understanding of the issues as well as considerable courage. For many years we have tried to have it both ways, in the case of nuclear weapons, to maintain a superior nuclear force and to get the Soviet Union to enter into an agreement which would preserve our superiority, to support the U.N. peacekeeping arrangements and yet be free to take unilateral military action when we deemed it necessary.

In the past as a consequence we have forfeited many opportunities to limit the strategic arms race, starting with Harold Stassen's efforts to limit bomber forces in 1955–56, because we have been afraid to accept balanced agreements. We have not realized sufficiently as Dr. Hornig and Dr. Kistiakowsky said, how much we had to gain from nuclear arms limitations nor that there are so many ways to insure our security that we could afford to be bold and imaginative in our approach. In fact, we almost always react from fear, fear of the Russians and in the case of many of our leaders, fear of our own people. For example, in 1961 at the start of the Kennedy administration, we had the opportunity to attempt to freeze the ballistic missile forces at the relatively low levels established by President Eisenhower. Soon after President Kennedy took office, we learned that the Soviet missile force was substantially smaller than earlier estimates which provided the basis for the so-called missile gap. We learned, in fact, that the United States probably had more missiles than the Soviet Union, a somewhat surprising and reassuring fact. At the time some persons, including me, proposed holding down the U.S. missile levels in the expectation that if the United States showed restraint, the Soviet Union could be persuaded to do the same and that in any event a force of 200–400 missiles, composed of missiles on the Polaris submarines, the existing hardened Titan II's and a few new Minuteman missiles, would be a mighty deterrent against any likely Soviet strategic force.

The Defense Department or at least Secretary of Defense McNamara's recommendation at the time was for 950 new Minuteman missiles. The Secretary of Defense thought that he was being modest because the Air Force wanted 3,000 new missiles. At the same time the Navy proposed increasing the Polaris submarine fleet to 41. The President's recommendation finally included 950 missiles and a force of 41 Polaris submarines. The explanation given by Secretary McNamara for his recommendation was that because the Air Force recommended 3,000 Minuteman missiles, 950 was the smallest number Congress would settle for. I believe that the failure to reach agreement on a nuclear test ban and the resumption of nuclear testing by the Soviet Union in the fall of 1961 were direct consequences of this buildup on our part.

For many years, the Soviet Union's leaders appeared to be willing to allow the United States to have a very substantial numerical superiority in strategic weapons. However, with the deployment of the large SS-9 missile and more SS-11's during the past two years, the Soviet Union may have surpassed the U.S. land-based missile force. Their decision to increase these forces must have been made sometime between 1962 and 1965 judging by the scale of their effort. At any rate that brings us to where we are today; we now have to face the question of an appropriate U.S. response to the latest Soviet response to an unnecessary U.S. response.

RECOMMENDATION FOR PRESENT U.S. COURSE OF ACTION

It is not only a time to think about a response, it is a moment to realize, maybe the last moment, that the United States has an opportunity to stop the upward spiral of the arms race by the proper response. We are not likely to stop the arms race with our present course of action which at the same time that it seeks an agreement to limit strategic weapons speeds up the deployment of ABM and MIRV. We are making the same old mistake again.

There is a simple, safe, sensitive course of action for the United States as has already been mentioned today. The United States and the rest of the world would be best served by a halt now in the deployment of the ABM system and a halt in the test and deployment of the MIRV system, coupled with a challenge for the Soviet leaders to show similar restraints. I believe that this would be the wisest course for our country to follow. It would also be the most sensible course for the Soviet Union—there is a symmetry here—and if the Soviet Union joined in such a moratorium it could be continued indefinitely. Otherwise future U.S. deployment decisions could be related to further Soviet reactions.

Incidentally, if MIRV testing was stopped now there would be little need for any inspection, a very important advantage.

VIEWS OF SECRETARY OF DEFENSE

The Secretary of Defense, Mr. Laird, has rejected this course of action in his 1971 Defense program and budget issued on March 2, 1970. He summarized his views in a talk to the Annual Luncheon of the Associated Press on April 20, 1970 when he said, "In my remarks today I will attempt to shed more light on the crucial subject of the strategic arms threat. In particular, I want to discuss with you editors, the nature and scope of the growing Soviet threat, recognizing full well that in Vienna, our negotiators have just begun round two of the Strategic Arms Limitation Talks commonly called SALT.

"I hope for success at SALT. I want to emphasize that point. I also want to emphasize that our top military leadership hopes for success at SALT. Where the security of the United States is involved, it is this objective—insuring national security—which is most important. A lower cost means to achieve that objective, lower compared to what otherwise may be required—if it can be achieved within tolerable risks—is obviously most desirable to all Americans, civilian and military."

We could all agree with this, but we would not agree that the course of action being followed is one that will either insure our military security or is a low cost option.

At that time then the Secretary went on to say, "as much as we might wish it otherwise, however, we must concentrate our attention on what the Soviet Union is actually doing. In the current situation of diminishing U.S. deterrent and Soviet momentum, we simply cannot base our plans and programs on what we hope the Soviet Union may do either unilaterally or in SALT. The Soviets have a momentum going both in strategic weapons deployment and in strategic weapons developments. If their strategic posture could be expected to stay at the operationally deployed posture which exists today, I believe we would have a tolerable situation. What must concern us, however, is the momentum the Soviets have established both in deployments and developments and where that momentum may carry them."

And on the basis of this reasoning, supported by considerable analysis and prediction of things to come, the Secretary has decided to proceed with phase two of the ABM and the MIRV deployments. Obviously, what constitutes tolerable risks is debatable. I believe that accelerating the arms race has major risks that should give us serious concern.

SOVIET MOMENTUM

Senator GORE. If I may interrupt just briefly, the Secretary advanced this same thesis to the committee. In other words, it was the momentum. He assumed that even after the Soviets may have achieved sufficiency that the momentum attained would in and of itself carry the Soviets into a degree of threat to the United States that we could not tolerate.

What would be your comment on the momentum? So much emphasis is placed on momentum.

Dr. WIESNER. I was going to talk a little bit about this later, Mr. Chairman.

Senator GORE. Okay.

Dr. WIESNER. But let me just comment briefly.

Why don't I go ahead with my discussion here and I think it will come out.

Senator GORE. Fine.

Dr. WIESNER. I will show that we do not need the MIRV and the ABM as insurance against the Soviet momentum and furthermore, that inspection is not needed to safeguard a freeze on MIRV's. There are three separate problems here, the military value of the ABM, the need for the MIRV as part of the deterrent force and the effect of the deployment of these weapons on the chances of success in the SALT talks and actually I could have a fourth which is implicit; what are the Soviets actually doing. I will talk about that too.

In my opinion, neither of these weapons systems can be justified now and their deployment will escalate the international military situation.

DIFFERENCES IN DOD TESTIMONY LAST YEAR AND THIS YEAR

Other witnesses before you today and in previous testimony have already pointed out the differences between the DOD testimony last year and this year, plus the contradictory intelligence estimates; nevertheless, I would like to emphasize a few points.

Last year, a DOD spokesman estimated that the Soviet Union had approximately 275 SS-9 missiles and that they would deploy approximately 50 more each year, so that by 1975 there might be 500 or slightly more of them. Recently, Secretary Laird stated that the Soviet Union did add approximately 50 SS-9 missiles to their inventory, so that last year's estimate was approximately correct. There is a persistent report circulating to the effect that no new SS-9 sites under construction, that is new starts of sites for bases, have been observed for several months. In addition to that Dr. Kistiakowsky has given me a chart, which you may have seen before, that shows the Soviet ICBM trends starting in 1966, I believe; and it is a curve which is leveling off. If one puts on to this curve the 1966, 1967, 1968, 1969 and 1970 curves it has almost flattened out. These are based on DOD figures.

If you add to that this intelligence story, which I think you should try to get to the bottom of, one would have to say that the last years' estimates of five hundred or more SS-9 missiles was very likely not to occur based on this evidence.

SOVIET ICBM TRENDS

Senator GORE. Dr. Kistiakowsky, if we may have your chart I would like to put it in the record at this point.

Dr. KISTIAKOWSKY. Yes, sir; you are very welcome to it. This is, if I may say, simply a plot of the numbers of ICBM sites as reported by the Defense Department in their posture statements. And although the Defense Department likes to draw a straight line indicating an indefinite rise, the actual points form a curve such as you would expect always from an incremental increase in a force. For instance, if we went to our own data on Minuteman sites in the past we would find this sort of stepwise growth curves.

Senator GORE. Thank you.

(The chart follows.)

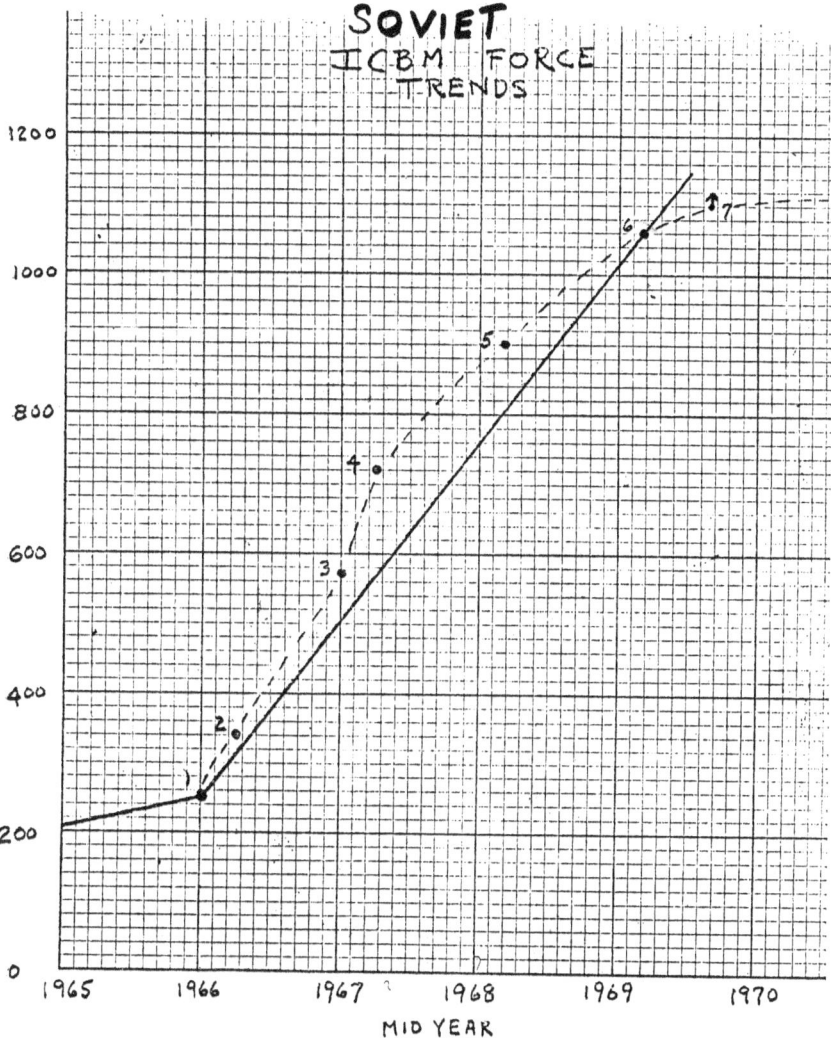

Solid curve is from p. 35, Posture statement for FY 71 budget.

1. (250), p. 103   Posture statement for FY 71 budget.
2. (340), p. 55   "   "   "   "   FY 69   "
3. (570), p. 102   "   "   "   "   FY 71   "
4. (720), p. 54   "   "   "   "   FY 69   "
5. (900), p. 102   "   "   "   "   FY 71   "
6. (1000), p. 102   "   "   "   "   FY 71   "
7. ("over 1100"), p. 35   "   "   "   "   FY 71   "

Senator CASE. Everything depends upon the accuracy of that last dot, doesn't it, otherwise the——

Dr. HORNIG. On that point, sir——

Dr. WIESNER. The point we are talking about goes through all the dots. If that dot was way up there it would disturb it. It would make a very different curve.

Senator CASE. It is very interesting.

Dr. WIESNER. It is very interesting.

Senator CASE. And these are all the points given by the Secretary.

Dr. WIESNER. It makes a very different conclusion possible than the Defense Department has been drawing—that is from their own information, which I think is terribly important.

Dr. HORNIG. As to that last dot, there have been reports in the newspapers that there have been no new Soviet starts in the last——

Senator CASE. Since August.

Dr. HORNIG. Yes. And I think this should be ascertained as a matter of fact by the committee.

PROJECTED SS-9 ATTACK ON MINUTEMAN

Dr. WIESNER. As you gentlemen may recall, last year I presented you with some calculations to show that, even if an SS-9 force of the projected 1975 size—that is the most extreme projection of the Defense Department—occurred, if there were 500 or somewhat more missiles, and these were used in a surprise attack against an unprotected Minuteman force, approximately 270 Minuteman missiles would survive such an attack. In my calculations I used DOD figures for missile reliability, kill probability, et cetera, and assumed that the SS-9's would be equipped with MIRV's. You may also recall that Dr. Foster criticized my assumptions and calculations. He estimated that only 50 Minuteman would survive such an attack, but to arrive at his figure he had to provide the SS-9 force with a technically very complicated retargeting capability and raise the single missile kill probability from the 0.8 figure to 0.9; so his figure of 50 Minuteman surviving an all-out Soviet attack in 1975 is clearly a very lower limit and I think that mine is much closer to being right.

Senator GORE. Even if he were right, I shouldn't think the Soviets would consider simultaneously 50 Minuteman with Poseidon.

Dr. HORNIG. It is worse than that because the Soviet planner can't afford to be optimistic about these figures. He has to ask how many Minuteman we might have left for retaliation and that number is likely to be bigger than Dr. Wiesner's.

Senator GORE. At least it would not be prudent for them to take the outside figure which Dr. Foster projects.

Dr. WIESNER. You may recall, in the same testimony I showed that even if the proposed Safeguard system worked as well as planned, and I presented detailed calculations on this, it would make very little difference in the number of Minuteman missiles that survived an attack. I didn't look the number up, but I think the number went from 270 to 300, something like that. I also showed, as has been stated by my colleagues before me here today, that it would be easy to increase the number of warheads on each SS-9 to overcome any reasonable increase in firepower in the Safeguard system. Dr. Kistiakowsky also pointed out that less than 1 year's production of the SS-9 would have done the same thing.

The testimony of last year also raised many questions about the Safeguard radars and its tracking computers. Many of us expressed strongly the opinion that the Safeguard system could not work as planned, and that in any event there was no way to test it realistically, so that the nation would be depending upon a complicated and untried system to work extremely well the first time it is used. In one way or another, most of these points have been admitted in this year's DOD testimony.

SAFEGUARD AS DEFENSE AGAINST COMMUNIST CHINESE

Some have argued, though, that it would do no harm and might even save a few Minuteman missiles that would otherwise be destroyed in an attack. But as some of our previous witnesses have indicated, this would be the least cost-effective system that anyone ever deployed except for those who don't work at costs. The only thing at risk then would be money, I suppose; but now we see that other justifications are being advanced again for the Safeguard, and these make it sound like a potential adjunct to a first-strike system against at least the Chinese, and when combined with the MIRV it could even frighten Soviet hawks. This certainly could hinder the SALT negotiations. In the March 2, 1970, defense report, Secretary Laird said, "President Nixon has assured our Asian allies that our nuclear shield extends to them. The credibility of that shield would be greatly enhanced if our Asian allies knew that because of a Safeguard defense the Chinese Communists had virtually no prospects of blackmailing the United States by threatening American cities." This is a very, very dangerous doctrine, as my colleagues have already pointed out.

No technical expert really believes that the Safeguard system could completely defend American cities against even a modest Chinese ICBM attack, and to construct a foreign policy on the belief that such a defense will be possible could lead to politically humiliating retreats or possibly even to the destruction of some cities. Furthermore, the belief that such a military-political strategy is possible will continue to distort our approach to Asian problems.

The reasons why the Safeguard system cannot be counted on to provide near-absolute protection against an even modest Chinese ICBM force were examined in detail last year and were reviewed here this morning by Dr. Hornig and Dr. Kistiakowsky and I will not repeat them unless you want me to go into them in some detail. The uncertainties regarding penetration aids, computer systems and so on I think are all well known.

Actually Safeguard looks worse today than it did a year ago to some people—it always looked hopeless to me—so the Chinese argument is a more important part of the rationalization of Safeguard than it was a year ago.

ABM NOT NEEDED IN VIEW OF U.S.-SOVIET OFFENSIVE FORCES

It is even more obvious than it was last year that the ABM will provide little protection for the U.S. deterrent. Even more important, it is clear that such protection is not needed. No matter what attack one imagines, using the forces projected for the Soviet Union in 1975, the extreme forces, a massive deterrent force would survive including more than 200 Minuteman missiles, a major fraction of the bomber force, the Polaris force and several thousand fighter bombers capable of carrying nuclear weapons. Furthermore, even if the Soviet Union did deploy an extensive ABM system, it is not possible for them to prevent an unacceptably large retaliatory strike.

This is the vital point. Given the offensive systems already in existence there is, I am convinced, no attainable combination of attack and defense which would prevent either the Soviet Union or the United States from having to face a devasting retaliatory blow if either one initiated a nuclear exchange. We have become so numbed by the number of games we play with nuclear weapons that we have lost track of their destruction power and of what fantastic damage each of them can do.

WHAT CONSTITUTES A DETERRENT?

It is hard to know just what constitutes a deterrent and so we go to extremes. The strategic analysts have a fairly sophisticated view of a deterrent wrapped in a concept called assured destruction which requires the clear-cut ability—on paper—to kill a large fraction of the Soviet population, say 40 or 50 percent, and destroy most of its industrial enterprise after the most sophisticated Soviet attacks have occurred on our forces we now maintain, or the Soviet Union has for that matter.

I tried to set a lower bound on the size of a deterrent force in a paper I presented to the American Association for the Advancement of Science last winter. Doing this obviously involves a guessing game but it is worth trying for the insights it provides. In the period immediately after World War II Stalin was obviously deterred by the existence of a very few 20 kiloton U.S. nuclear bombs. This level would undoubtedly leave us feeling worried in the face of the present massive Soviet forces. In my AAAS paper, I stated that I am firmly convinced that the probability that a nation was likely to have six out of ten of its largest cities destroyed and a substantial fraction of their residents killed will function as an effective deterrent against any but the most fear-driven action.

POSSIBILITY OF INTERCEPTING RETALIATORY ATTACK

The lower limit to a deterrent then, might be the force which clearly could deliver six modern nuclear weapons on city targets. Even this number seems high to me, but if it is too low for you, make it 20; and let's then examine the chances that we or the Soviets could prevent at least that number of warheads from reaching our respective cities by any of the actions that have been proposed or are even imaginable for 1975 or even 1980.

We have already seen that major U.S. forces would survive the best attack the Soviets could launch in 1975 using the forces that Defense Secretary Laird projects for them. This surviving force could include several hundred missiles—200 or more Minutemen and 300–600 Polaris missiles to be more specific—and at least several hundred aircraft.

I have tried to understand how defenses might change this situation and it is hard to be very specific about this, for we have to make so many assumptions about the crisis performances of untestable defense systems.

No expert expects the air defense to intercept as much as 50 percent of an attack, and the Vietnam experience would certainly support this. Remember that although aircraft may not be as good as missiles for carrying out a surprise attack, they remain an effective retaliatory weapon. Assume that Soviet air defenses are vastly improved and are 90 percent effective, and this is really giving credit for something nobody believes they can achieve. In fact, we doubt whether their defenses are 50 percent effective and certainly ours are less effective than that. Then if only a thousand of the U.S. attack aircraft available from our bomber force and fighter-bomber force were available, a hundred will reach their targets under this extreme action.

Now, as has already been said by my colleagues, there is as yet no sign of a new Soviet ABM system deployment beyond that at Moscow and it is presumed early warning radar, the so-called Hen House which we have known about for a great many years but has just been declassified this year, seems totally defenseless, so that the system appears to be easy to penetrate. But for the moment, let's assume that the Soviet Union was protected by a large-scale system and examine what the situation would be; and I will look at two different situations here. For argument's sake, I will assume that the Soviet ABM system is 50 percent effective, that is, intercepts half of the incoming objects, though I probably should not make such an assumption for it will be quoted against me someday. Actually, as I have already said, I don't believe that any ABM system so far developed would function at all against a substantial attack. But I have to assume something to make my argument. Of the 200 Minuteman and 325 Polaris missiles (half the fleet) available after the imaginary SS-9 attack, more than 250 would arrive at their targets in spite of the Soviet ABM. If the Soviet ABM system achieved a fantastic capability, say 90 percent, more than 50 U.S. missile warheads would still get through to their targets. In neither the Minuteman nor the Polaris case did I count the existing multiple warheads, so the attack would actually be larger.

The U.S. MIRV's are proposed as a means of assuring the U.S. missiles could penetrate a Soviet ABM system if it were deployed by increasing substantially the number of warheads that the ABM system would have to handle. My analysis has shown that a much more than adequate deterrent capability exists without this move.

SAFEGUARD AND MIRV ARE NOT NEEDED

Both of these escalatory steps, the Safeguard deployment and the MIRV, are clearly not needed. Here we have the arms race in its purest form. Not only is no response needed at this time to protect our deterrent forces, but the Safeguard ABM would be as poor a way as one could possibly find to insure their survival.

Neither ABM's nor MIRV's are necessary to insure the U.S. deterrent capability no matter what the Russians choose to do, and I think this point must be emphasized. If they want to waste their money on ABM's and hundreds more SS-9's and MIRV's, which incidentally I really doubt, well then we should let them do it.

It should be noted that adding present-day multiple warheads to the SS-9's would not further enhance their effectiveness against the Minuteman missiles and a great deal of additional testing of them would be needed before they would. This is one of the reasons that I don't believe, as I said earlier, that on-site inspection is needed as part of a SALT agreement.

Furthermore, the Polaris and the aircraft components of the deterrent are not vulnerable to MIRV-type weapons.

RECOMMENDATIONS

So to repeat my recommendations, which are the same as Dr. Kistiakowsky's in principle, we should halt all new missiles and the multiple warhead and MIRV testing and deployment and stop the Safeguard ABM deployment for all time. We should simultaneously ask the Russians to join us. If they do, the SALT negotiations should then be used to formalize such arrangements and, equally important, to seek agreements to reduce the size of the strategic forces. If the Russians don't join in formal arrangements to limit strategic armaments and if they don't even limit their own deployments unilaterally, we will have to reassess our posture. We can do this deliberately and slowly, for our deterrent force is secure and there appears to me to be no likelihood that any Soviet actions can change this situation. If the Soviets respond we could then cut down the strategic force a little bit and see if they would follow us down. If this worked we could go further, eliminating the vulnerable components of our forces, working toward a considerably smaller and more secure deterrent. Maybe we could even start a peace race. Thank you, sir.

Senator GORE. Doctor, thank you very, very much.

CONTRADICTORY OPINIONS ABOUT EFFECT OF ABM ON SALT

If the three of you will respond to what seems to me a crucial question, I will appreciate it.

The President, the Secretary of Defense, and all three of you gentlemen have expressed the hope that the SALT talks will succeed. How do you rationalize the completely contradictory conclusions of the Administration, on the one hand, and you, on the other? The Administration maintains that deployment of ABM would assist the SALT talks. You think it would harm the SALT talks?

Dr. Hornig, are you still first?

Dr. HORNIG. Well, as I state in my testimony, I am not an expert on Russian psychology and I really don't know how the Soviet Union will respond to the Administration's argument that it is good to negotiate from strength. I think we have the strength, so I am not sure that there is any merit to the argument that we need to acquire some extra pawns.

It seems to me the history of the arms race is such that either the circumstances are propitious now for negotiation or they aren't. It scarcely seems likely to me that military initiatives on our own side are likely to improve the climate for negotiations. It surely isn't true that our suspicions that the Russians were accelerating their deployment of SS-9's, which they may have thought of as negotiating from strength. It certainly hasn't improved the climate here for negotiating. So I simply find it very hard to believe that initiating new arms moves is the way to take steps toward arms reduction.

COMPROMISES IN GOVERNMENT IN INITIATING ARMS CONTROL PROPOSAL

Dr. KISTIAKOWSKY. Sir, my reply, of course, will have to be speculative because I wasn't there when all the arguments for and against this particular combination of deploying new weapons systems were going on, at the same time as the preparations for SALT, but I have been around the Government for many years, in the Pentagon and in the White House Office and in the Arms Control Agency. Therefore, I would submit, and I hope this doesn't sound too cynical, that as many times before a compromise had to be made, and in order to get an agreement on holding the SALT and progressing with these negotiations, the military and the defense officials had to be paid their price which was to go ahead with these deployments.

Senator GORE. Do you mean such things occurred when you were there?

[Laughter.]

Mr. KISTIAKOWSKY. Yes, sir.

Dr. HORNIG. I would assert from personal experience that I have seen it occur, too.

Senator GORE. Dr. Wiesner, have you witnessed such bargaining and balancing?

Dr. WIESNER. I have seen more arms limitations proposals destroyed by the compromises that had to be made to get them agreed to by everyone who had to agree to it in the Government, and very many times what one does in this process is to make a sort of treaty.

I used to say when I was working in the White House that we were fighting a four-front war when we tried to do something about arms limitations.

We had to deal with the Russians occasionally, but we had to deal with the Pentagon, we had to deal with the Congress and we had to deal with the public; and I was never certain which of these groups gave us more problems because we rarely got to deal with the Russians.

We were mostly dealing with ourselves. The kind of treaties one has to enter into to get into the position to negotiate with the Soviet Union were such, and I think they had the same problem incidentally that we frequently had, that when things looked very bad we would always agree if they looked really serious we could come back and change the most controversial aspects. We sometimes suspected they did the same thing, so we used to have a love-making game, I guess, in which one tried to find out the point of flexibility in each other's postures so that we could come home and say, "You know, if we had a little more flexibility to explore this," because we often were not even permitted to explore, and Dr. Kistiakowsky has been in this position, and I am sure Dr. Hornig has been, we would ask for things which were unreasonable and the Soviets would ask for the same thing. We would try to find the points of agreement so we could come back and fight for those parts which we thought were absolutely vital if we wanted to get agreement; and this is, I think, the normal situation that one finds in the Pentagon—which is a mighty powerful force in the U.S. Government, and at least in my day those of us who were trying to limit arms were a mighty weak force in the government.

We had a disadvantage, if there were people fighting for disarmament in government now, a new question, that they wouldn't have.

We did not have very many supporters in the Congress. There was not the strong support that there appears to be today, exploring these issues; and I think during both the Eisenhower administration and the Kennedy administration we were at least as concerned about the attacks we would get when we attempted to negotiate with some of the people in the Congress as we were from any of the other problems that we dealt with.

Wouldn't you agree?

Dr. KISTIAKOWSKY. Yes.

Senator GORE. This is not the first time that the principle of arming in order to parley has been advanced. It has been tried in history and found remarkably wanting.

ATTITUDE OF SCIENTIFIC COMMUNITY TOWARD WITNESSES' TESTIMONY

I have one more question and then I wish to yield to Senator Case. What is your impression as to the attitude of others of the scientific community, with the exception of course of those who are employed by the Pentagon or contractors for the Pentagon?

Any or all of you can respond.

Dr. HORNIG. My own impression is that with the exception of relatively few people there is remarkable unanimity in the scientific community along the lines of our testimony.

Dr. WIESNER. Even among many of the contractors, scientists and engineers I would say there is a general agreement with the positions that we take. Here again you do not always hear them, not quite as openly as some of us who are in a less exposed position, but we talk to them, and we find that there is generally very little disagreement with the kind of analysis that we have been making and presenting to you.

Senator GORE. Senator Case.

COMMENDATION OF WITNESSES

Senator CASE. Thank you, Mr. Chairman. I want to join with the Chairman in expressing the deep satisfaction that I feel, as he does, with the availability of men like you, and our appreciation for your coming not once but again and again and at great sacrifice to your own convenience and the giving of so much time in these matters. Without you we would be completely unable to do anything at all, and that is no overstatement.

NEED TO COMPROMISE IS UNFORTUNATE BASIS ON WHICH TO MAKE DECISIONS

On the last point that you were discussing with the Chairman, I noted that Dr. Wiesner, in his statement, explained why Secretary McNamara asked for 950 Minuteman missiles and 41 Polaris submarines and gives his explanation as to what that was, the smallest number that Congress would settle for. This bears upon the same thing you were talking about now with the Chairman.

I do want to say this is a terribly unfortunate basis for anybody to make a decision on and particularly a recommendation.

Is it necessary for us to ask everybody, is this what you really mean, or is this the least that you think we will accept?

Now I do understand the point that there was a greater weakness on the part of the limitation and arms reduction people then than now. I think that is true, and I can only testify for myself, because it was not then a primary interest of mine as it is now, and I would assume there are perhaps fewer people around to pick the thing up. But it is very unfortunate to have things affirmatively recommended, like, for instance, Secretary McNamara's—and I don't mean to be picking on him but he is the illustration that just came to us—recommendation of the ABM against China, the light ABM when he had just finished a most remarkable argument against any ABM at all. This kind of attitude, I can understand, and yet I think people would do better for the causes that they are interested in if they would really say what they mean and stick to it, and say it publicly.

Now, there is a limit on what a person can do when he is working for the White House. There is a limit on what anybody from the executive branch can do. He must follow Administration policy or else he leaves, I expect.

Senator GORE. There is a limit to what a Senator can do and get re-elected. [Laughter.]

Senator CASE. I don't mean to make it seem as if our job in our position is terribly extraordinary, but in a way it is. Maybe one Senator is vulnerable, and to that Senator that seems to be the most important consideration at the time; does it not, Senator, or almost the most important.

Senator GORE. At least he can't forget it.

Senator CASE. But collectively we are not. We do represent independence in the sense of representing quite a variety of different people and communities and we do have an obligation to try to do our job, and I just want publicly to express my unhappiness that at any time anybody would say something he really didn't believe in because he thought it was the least he could get away with when we are counting on him for an objective recommendation.

You wanted to say something about that, Dr. Hornig.

Dr. HORNIG. I was just going to say I think the kind of example Dr. Wiesner stated comes even closer to home. I was in Washington during the years 1966 and 1967 when some of the ABM decisions were made in the fall of 1966. There was the most extraordinary Congressional pressure, among others, to deploy Nike–X, the massive city defense system. I have never understood Secretary McNamara's 1967 speech, but I have always had the conviction that the Sentinel anti-Chinese system was sort of the minimum system that could be gotten away with and would withstand the pressure for a large Nike-X system.

Dr. WIESNER. Some of us used to believe it was an anti-Republican system.

Dr. HORNIG. I would like to finish by saying that the Sentinel system was in fact a downpayment on the Nike-X system.

Senator CASE. You said that: I didn't.

FACTORS AFFECTING MR. MCNAMARA'S DECISION ON MISSILES

Dr. WIESNER. I would like to say one thing about my statement as to the Minuteman in Mr. McNamara's defense. I wrote this rather reluctantly, actually, but it seems to me that we are dealing with matters on which the Nation's future depends; and unless some of us who have been involved in these things are willing to give examples from real life and explain what happened, we won't understand our past or be able to project our future properly. But I would like to maybe remind you of some of the other things that were going on at the same time that probably affected Mr. McNamara's decision about his relationship with Congress.

We had come into office under the most fantastic pressure to put the Nike-Zeus, the first ABM system, into operation, and a very substantial part of that pressure which Mr. McNamara, Mr. Kennedy and the rest of you resisted, came out of the Congress. We had just canceled the nuclear powered aircraft after it had wasted a billion dollars of the country's money. We were contemplating stopping the B-70 because we thought it was a poor investment, so there were many other issues involved in our on-going debate about our security posture; and I am sure these matters did influence the Secretary's decision.

But my point was not so much to pick on Mr. McNamara as to show there was no rational, no military basis for that very large number which has had very dreadful consequences for us and for the Russians and for the rest of the world in the decade since.

QUESTION OF PROPER DAMAGE LIMITATION

Senator CASE. I do appreciate that, and I am sorry. In a way it is I who picked it up, and I want to say this further thing, too, and please don't think I am doing it as a Republican. But I think I remember Dr. Kistiakowsky telling us General Eisenhower faced this problem and said, no, and it was in this connection that I just want to bring out this point about his attitude toward this whole question of what is proper damage limitation and all the rest of it. And when I think you or someone pointed out to him there are going to be at least 60 million people killed or something like that, we should save maybe 60 million or something of that sort, he said if that is the kind of a world we are going to be in there is no point in saving any lives, something like that.

Dr. KISTIAKOWSKY. That is very true, sir.

Senator CASE. I wish you would say it in your own words because I don't want to give the wrong impression and yet it has an awful lot to do with this whole question of the size of our relative forces and what we can do, and the justification sometimes given that if it only saves 10,000 lives or one life it is worth spending all this money and doing this whole business.

Dr. KISTIAKOWSKY. I think I was telling you, sir, privately about——

Senator CASE. I don't mean to impose on you.

Dr. KISTIAKOWSKY. A conversation I had with the then President Eisenhower quite alone in his office shortly after he came back from the disastrous Paris summit conference.

You will recall there was a sequence of the U-2 plane being shot down which was unfortunately handled so it led to a massive international incident. Then the summit conference in Paris which was a complete failure because Khrushchev came there clearly determined to make the maximum political capital out of the U-2 incident. President Eisenhower was terribly upset, and spontaneously began talking to me about how the central hope of his own in these last years of his Presidency was to advance the cause of peace, and how disastrous he therefore felt was this sequence of events. And then, perhaps because in those days the science adviser was to a very large extent also an adviser on national security affairs, he began talking about how unspeakably horrible the thought of all-out nuclear war was to him; and he did say what you mentioned, sir, namely, that seeing this as a national issue, he just couldn't see any great difference between, say, 60 or 80 million instant dead because the plain fact was that in either case our present society, the whole country, would disintegrate if that happened, and what was the point of living then.

Senator CASE. Well, I appreciate that, and in a very deep way I apologize for bringing up a private conversation or record of yours. But it seems to me this has a very important bearing on this whole question of national policy, and upon the moral and strategic judgments that we have to make here and that that insight is enormously helpful and enormously valuable in response to those who argue that if this only saves a few lives we ought to go in for it.

"RISKS" INVOLVED IN ARMS LIMITATIONS AGREEMENTS

The only other point I wanted to make, Mr. Chairman, if you will just permit one other intervention, is directed to your testimony, Dr. Hornig. Twice I think, perhaps more often, but twice I noticed you referred to taking risks, I am not sure just what that means. And it is not my impression that anything that any of you stands for or any of us stands for taking risks in the sense of laying ourselves again open to the enemy. If you have things that are specific in mind perhaps you would tell us, and if you don't maybe you would tell us what that meant when you said it.

Dr. HORNIG. I would be glad to answer, sir. I have sat through, as my colleagues here did, many discussions within the governments of the positions for potential arms talks. The argument that always comes up, for instance, with regard to verification or with regard to any agreement, is what if the other side cheats.

Now, of course, there is always some risk of the other side cheating. Even with the best verification system or any practical one there is a certain amount of risk in connection with cheating.

My own estimate is that these risks are very small, for the most part, compared to the risks of an escalating arms race. The reason I say that is that at least until one is down to the level of zero armaments, a weapon or two made in the back yard does not affect the deterrent balance appreciably. That is the risk I was referring to, the risk in any agreement that the other side might violate it in some conceivable way.

Senator CASE. Just to make the point before I yield to you, Dr. Wiesner; I know you have a comment you want to make. No risk that you even imagine would be a risk to our deterrent, to our retaliatory capacity.

Dr. HORNIG. Not given the totality of our technical capability.

Senator CASE. That is right; that is what I mean. Dr. Wiesner.

Dr. WIESNER. I think the word "risk" shouldn't be used by us in these very narrow senses because it conveys the wrong impression.

Senator CASE. It does.

Dr. WIESNER. We, for example, weren't prepared to take the risk of a small number of inspections to achieve a comprehensive test ban in 1963, and the Soviet Union wasn't prepared to take the risk of adding to the number they had agreed to. They were talking about three and maybe four and we were talking about six or seven, and none of us thought that the United States would ever carry out that many a year any way because it looked fairly complicated. But because the Nation was so focused on risk of cheating we didn't have the political maneuverability, and I understand Mr. Khrushchev didn't have it in his case to bring those things together.

Now the risks are essentially nonexistent in the sense that the deterrent could have been undermined by any cheating the Soviets could have done and yet we never were able to make that understood and clear. As a consequence of that, we had to go to a partial test ban agreement which was much less encompassing in terms of trying to stop the arms race, in terms of leading to other arms agreements, and so the risk of the war, which has been the consequence of not reaching that agreement, is probably very great in comparison.

Senator GORE. Doctor, when the security of the entire country, indeed of Western civilization, may be at stake, this popular concern in a popular government is unavoidable. Indeed it is commendable, and it must be weighed in the balance.

Dr. WIESNER. But it should be understood really and that is why I think these hearings contribute so much.

Senator GORE. Yes.

MEANING OF "RISK" IN ARMS LIMITATION

Senator CASE. That is right, because words are used, are turned against us, in ways that distort everybody's meaning. I am just very concerned not to use them unless we understand exactly what we mean by it. Dr. Kistiakowsky, do you have any comment on that point?

Dr. KISTIAKOWSKY. Well, I don't like the word "risk" in this connection and yet I don't know what other word to use.

Senator CASE. I know.

Dr. KISTIAKOWSKY. Because——

Senator CASE. Look, I am not trying to talk about or criticize anybody's English or literary style.

Dr. KISTIAKOWSKY. You are welcome to criticize mine, of course. [Laughter.]

But I see the meaning of the word "risk" in the sense that a situation is so complex that one cannot derive an exact mathematical formula to describe precisely what is going to happen in the future. It is somewhat like getting into an automobile to drive to some destination. There is a not wholly definable chance—or risk—of an accident on the way, but if one is aware of this and drives cautiously, the risk is minimal and wholly acceptable. On the other hand, if one were to get into a high-powered car with defective brakes and then races to the same destination, the risk would be much greater and to a reasonable person not acceptable.

To me, at any rate, the cautious driving is analogous to the arms control agreement policy and the unrestrained arms race is reckless driving with faulty brakes. Notwithstanding the old sayings to the contrary, the preparation for war by means of an unrestrained nuclear arms race means heading for war and not peace. That's why I say arms controls can mean a less risky future. I don't know as I make myself clear about risks, but I don't know what other word to use.

Senator CASE. Yes, you do; and I don't know either which word to use. But I do know that that word raises the hackles in many quarters.

Dr. KISTIAKOWSKY. Yes.

Senator CASE. And I would rather let the other fellow use it and make him say what he means.

Dr. KISTIAKOWSKY. I shall try to refrain in the future.

Senator CASE. That is all. I shouldn't put words into the mouths of emminent gentlemen like you. Thanks an awful lot. I appreciate very much what you have done and I will not detain you further, Mr. Chairman.

Thank you.

Senator GORE. Senator Pell.

Senator PELL. Thank you, Mr. Chairman. I apologize for not being here earlier. I look forward to reading the testimony of the witnesses. I am interested particularly in that of Dr. Hornig who is coming to our State as president of Brown University very soon, and we welcome you.

AMERICAN SECURITY COUNCIL QUESTIONNAIRE

I would like to take this occasion, Mr. Chairman, if I might, to mention to you a piece of mail I received yesterday from an organization called the American Security Council, and they very kindly said: "Dear Friend: Because you are an opinion leader in your community, you have been nominated to serve on the American Security Council's National Voter Advisory Board and to participate in our National Security Issues Poll."

I would like to put this letter of invitation into the record. Also I would like to put in the record, if I could, the questions they asked and then ask a couple of them of the witnesses. I thought, if you will permit me, I would read the questions.

Senator GORE. Yes.

(The letter and questionnaire follow.)

AMERICAN SECURITY COUNCIL
1101 17th Street, N.W. • Washington, D. C. 20036

JOHN M. FISHER, *President* (202) 296-4587

National Strategy Committee *
Gen. Paul D. Adams, USA (Ret.)
Former Commander-in-Chief
U.S. Strike Command

Dr. Harold M. Agnew
Los Alamos Scientific Lab

G. Duncan Bauman
Publisher
St. Louis Globe Democrat

Peter Bruce Clark
President and Publisher
The Detroit News

Adm. Robert L. Dennison, USN (Ret.)
Former Supreme Allied Commander—Atlantic

Adm. H. D. Felt, USN (Ret.)
Former Commander-in-Chief, Pacific

Patrick J. Frawley, Jr.
Chairman, Executive Committee
Eversharp, Inc.

Robert W. Galvin
Chairman of the Board
Motorola, Inc.

Clifford F. Hood
Former President
U.S. Steel Corporation

The Hon. William F. Knowland
President and Publisher
Oakland Tribune

Vice Adm. Fitzhugh Lee, USN (Ret.)
Former Commandant, National War College

General Curtis E. LeMay, USAF (Ret.)
Former Air Force Chief of Staff

The Hon. Clare Boothe Luce
Former Ambassador

Admiral Ben Moreell, CEC, USN (Ret.)
Former Chief of Civil Engineers

Dr. Robert Morris
President
University of Plano

Dr. Stefan Possony
Director of International Studies
Hoover Institute-Stanford University

Gen. Thomas S. Power, USAF (Ret.)
Former Commander, Strategic Air Command

Gen. Bernard A. Schriever, USAF (Ret.)
Former Commanding General
Air Force Systems Command

Adm. Lewis L. Strauss, USN (Ret.)
Former Chairman
U.S. Atomic Energy Commission

Dr. Edward Teller
Nuclear Scientist

Gen. Nathan F. Twining, USAF (Ret.)
Former Chairman
Joint Chiefs of Staff

Rear Adm. Chester C. Ward, USN (Ret.)
Former Judge Advocate General

Gen. Albert C. Wedemeyer, USA (Ret.)
Chief U.S. Strategist, World War II

Loyd Wright
Past President
American Bar Association

*Partial Listing

C. Pell
3425 Prospect Avenue N.W.
Washington, D.C. 20007

May 19, 1970

Dear Friend:

Because you are an opinion leader in your community, you have been nominated to serve on the American Security Council's National Voter Advisory Board and to participate in our National Security Issues Poll.

Of course, your nomination to the Voter Advisory Board is subject to your acceptance.

To insure accurate poll tabulation, I have assigned an identification code to each prospective Board Member. Your number is 326.

This poll is being strictly limited to members of our National Voter Advisory Board and Members of Congress.

We want to release the results of this poll to President Nixon, the Congress and the national press in a few weeks so please return your questionnaire today.

There are conservative and liberal voting indexes.

But no one puts out a National Security voting index. The ASC, with 15 years experience and a highly respected staff of internal security and foreign affairs experts, is uniquely qualified to prepare such an index.

For example, our staff is not only expert on strategic military affairs but is also very knowledgeable on the various forces at work internally to destroy our country, the Communist Party, the Black Panthers, SDS, etc.

Because of the ASC's outstanding reputation for sound research and accuracy, all previous ASC studies have received wide publicity in D.C. newspapers, magazines, radio and TV, as well as nationally. We can expect the same on this poll.

When completed, we'll give the results to each Member of Congress and ask that he complete his questionnaire.

Many voters are not aware of how some Senators, such as Kennedy, Gore, Muskie, Fulbright, Goodell, McGovern, Cranston and others, have taken positions on national security matters which weaken America in its fight against

Communism. For example, they all voted against the ABM.

So, we will also carefully analyze the actual national security voting record of each Member of Congress.

We will then compile a National Security Issues Index based on both the questionnaire and their actual voting record.

Key people in both the Republican and Democrat parties have told me that a well-publicized National Security Issues Index would be very influential in the 1970 elections.

If so, the report must be completed by July 1st. We can then have it printed by July 16th, and it can be mailed and in the hands of campaign workers of both parties by the week of July 20th.

But it will take a minimum of 655 hours of research to compile all of the information. The cost will be at least $68,000 and this includes researchers, printing, distribution and publicity for the Index.

An effective publicity effort to make national security one of the central campaign issues in key 1970 races will cost at least $143,500 more.

This crucial project is beyond our present budget so we'll need your help and the help of many concerned Americans to make this a success.

Some of the questions in this poll cover issues being hotly contested in Congress right now. For example, the ABM which passed by only one vote last year is again under attack.

We need your vote and your support. Let Members of Congress know where you stand and find out where they stand. The more Members represented on our Voter Advisory Board, the more influence it will have.

Please complete the enclosed questionnaire and return it to me as soon as possible. We ask each Member of the Voter Advisory Board to contribute a minimum of $10.00 to cover administration of their membership. Everything over $10.00 will be used toward making the poll a success. Your check should be made payable to: ASC Issues Index.

If you will do as much as you can, I promise you I will do all that is humanly possible to make the first National Security Issues Index a huge success.

Sincerely,

John M. Fisher

John M. Fisher

JMF/m

P. S. We believe that most Americans support a strong national defense against Communist aggression, but we can't prove it without your cooperation in this poll.

AMERICAN SECURITY COUNCIL
1101 17th St., N.W.
Washington, D. C. 20036

NATIONAL SECURITY ISSUES POLL—1970

Please check the one box which most nearly represents your position on each of the following 10 issues.

                                                                    Agree   Disagree   Undecided

1. The Safeguard Anti-Ballistic Missile Defense System (ABM) is necessary for the defense of the United States.   ☐   ☐   ☐

2. The United States should maintain military strength greater than that of the Soviet Union and Red China.   ☐   ☐   ☐

3. Communists and other revolutionaries should be permitted to teach in tax-supported educational institutions.   ☐   ☐   ☐

4. Communists and other revolutionaries should be permitted to hold sensitive positions in defense facilities.   ☐   ☐   ☐

5. The United States should have a national objective of victory in the Cold War.   ☐   ☐   ☐

6. The United States needs a "Freedom Academy" to train leaders for new forms of non-military conflict.   ☐   ☐   ☐

7. The United States should help the people of Czechoslovakia, Hungary, Cuba and other captive nations in their struggle for freedom.   ☐   ☐   ☐

(over please)

8. The United States should have a national objective of victory in Vietnam. ☐ ☐ ☐

9. The United States should give economic aid to foreign governments even if they are Communist or pro-Communist. ☐ ☐ ☐

10. The United States should extend diplomatic recognition to Red China. ☐ ☐ ☐

> This poll will be released to the national news media, but I will send members of the Voter Advisory Board an advance copy of the results before its release to the public. Please complete the rest of the form below and return it with the Questionnaire.

MEMBERSHIP ACCEPTANCE TO NATIONAL VOTER ADVISORY BOARD

Dear Mr. Fisher:

☐ To validate my poll, enclosed is my $10 for administration of membership to the National Voter Advisory Board.

☐ I want to do much more than serve on the National Voter Advisory Board. I am sending the amount checked below (which includes $10 for membership administration) to help you compile and publicize how the politicians voted on national security issues, as compared to the views of the Voter Advisory Board.

$1500.____ $1000.____ $500.____ $250.____

$100.____ $50.____ $25.____ $15.____ $10.____

Please make check payable to: **ASC Issues Index**

National Voter Advisory Board*_____(signature)

(Is your name and address correct on our records?)

---

* This poll is limited to members of the National Voter Advisory Board. Did you remember to enclose a minimum of $10.00 for administration of membership? This amount includes $5.00 to cover the cost of a one-year subscription to the prestigious Washington Report issued weekly by American Security Council.

Senator PELL. Thank you.

1. The Safeguard antiballistic missile defense system (ABM) is necessary for the defense of the United States.
2. The United States should maintain military strength greater than that of the Soviet Union and Red China.
3. Communists and other revolutionaries should be permitted to teach in tax-supported educational institutions.
4. Communists and other revolutionaries should be permitted to hold sensitive positions in defense facilities.
5. The United States should have a national objective of victory in the cold war.
6. The United States needs a freedom academy to train leaders for new forms of non-military conflict.
7. The United States should help the people of Czchoslovakia, Hungary, Cuba and other captive nations in their struggle for freedom.
8. The United States should have a national objective of victory in Vietnam.
9. The United States should give economic aid to foreign governments even if they are communist or pro-communist.
10. The United States should extend diplomatic recognition to Red China.

Some of these are what we call straw men. Obviously, we don't want to encourage revolutionaries to teach in our institutions, tax supported or not. Obviously, we would like to help the people of Czchoslovakia, Hungary and Cuba to achieve freedom, but the way these questions are set up seems to me a little biased, although I find myself in agreement with some of the objectives.

IS SAFEGUARD ABM NECESSARY TO U.S. DEFENSE?

I would like to ask these highly qualified physicists who are here today whether, with regard to the ABM—and I have not yet pursued your testimony—you believe the Safeguard ABM defense system is necessary for the defense of the United States Dr. Wiesner?

Dr. WIESNER. No.

Senator PELL. Dr. Kistiakowsky.

Dr. KISTIAKOWSKY. A flat no.

Senator PELL. Dr. Hornig.

Dr. HORNIG. A flat no.

Dr. WIESNER. I would like to add this statement that this American Security Council I think has sort of paraphrased its name on the official National Security Council, perhaps accidentally, and has a number of well known individuals on its board. One of them is Dr. Edward Teller, and you may recall that at the hearings here last year Dr. Edward Teller made the direct statement in answer to Senator Gore's question that he did not know whether or not an ABM system would work and that he regarded this whole thing as a giant experiment to find out.

Senator PELL. Thank you.

Dr. HORNIG. May I add one other point. Such questions are frequently meant to imply a different question such as are you opposed to any ABM system. Now I think the gist of all of our testimony has been that a non-provocative ABM system which defended our deterrent, if it worked, would be a very desirable thing.

It is the Safeguard ABM system that we have all said is not necessary.

Dr. WIESNER. Yes.

Senator PELL. It would be nice too if we could eliminate many of the nuclear weapons on both sides, but that would still be a little way off.

NATURE OF AMERICAN SECURITY COUNCIL QUESTIONS

The trouble with questions of this sort is that you can't argue too much with some of the objectives. Obviously victory is preferable to defeat.

One is impossible and the other one's hopes is avoidable.

Dr. WIESNER. But these are questions which don't necessarily have two answers that are right or wrong, and in accepting that implication, it seems to me, is to start on the wrong foot.

Senator PELL. I am so glad you said that because I felt this should be given more notice. I felt that these questions which cannot be answered simplistically should be made a matter of public record.

Let me ask that second question which you three gentlemen also——

Dr. KISTIAKOWSKY. If I may comment, sir, on what you just pointed out.

Senator PELL. Certainly.

Dr. KISTIAKOWSKY. My impression in listening to these questions and statements is that they have the same generic origin as that famous lawyer device of asking a witness "have you stopped beating your wife." A simple answer is impossible.

Senator PELL. That is correct.

(Laughter.)

Dr. KISTIAKOWSKY. Not if one is limited to yes or no.

SHOULD UNITED STATES MAINTAIN GREATER MILITARY STRENGTH THAN RUSSIA AND RED CHINA?

Senator PELL. The second question: The United States should maintain military strength greater than that of the Soviet Union and Red China.

Would you three be willing to hazard the dangerous step of a yes or no on that?

Dr. WIESNER. I don't know what it means. I don't think we want a standing army bigger than the Chinese standing army. If we have a bigger nuclear deterrent force than the Chinese, I think in spite of what this organization would say the mere numerical size, the size of the total deterrent force is bigger than the Russians. I personally have to be prepared and it seems to me our Government has been for a number of years to accept some rough form of equality if we want to freeze and if we want to cut back in the way that we have been talking about hoping that we can do in order to cut down the dangers of the arms race.

So that I don't believe in the nuclear case we should be striving for superiority. We have tried that for 20 years and that is how we got to where we are.

The Russians are prepared to match us. When you have got that situation it doesn't seem to converge.

QUESTION OF NEGOTIATION FROM SUPERIOR STRENGTH

Senator PELL. This point is so valid, too. Senator Gore may be too modest to mention it himself, but I remember when he took me with him to see Premier Kosygin. The point that came up in our conversation more strongly than anything else was, that negotiations from either side from the point of superiority were an impossibility.

Could you answer this question?

Dr. KISTIAKOWSKY. Well, I would certainly feel that a positive insistence on superiority inevitably leads to an unlimited arms race, because clearly the other side cannot accept a thesis that we will be superior to them. Thence within the limits of, and sometimes beyond the limits of, their economic capacity they would resist that position. So I would have to answer, no; that is not what our objective should be.

Our objective should be to have sufficient forces to preserve our national security.

Senator GORE. I would like to interject that when Senator Pell and I talked to Chairman Kosygin, President Nixon had just been elected. As a candidate for President he advocated as you will recall, superiority.

Fortunately, after becoming President he has changed this to sufficiently which I think is a great advance.

Secretary Laird says that we have a sufficiency as of now, but what he fears, as we alluded to earlier, is the Soviet momentum, to which we have already provided an answer.

Dr. WIESNER. That is why this curve is so important. It shows the momentum is dying.

Senator GORE. I didn't mean to interrupt.

Senator PELL. Dr. Hornig.

Dr. HORNIG. I devoted a good part of my testimony, which I hope you will have time to read, to this question of superiority.

Senator PELL. I will read it.

Dr. HORNIG. Or parity. I think for the most part one doesn't really know what those words mean. They certainly can't be arrived at simply by counting weapons. I would be inclined to answer by saying that we ought to have military forces sufficient to secure our national purposes. If our national purpose is to deter aggression that means military forces adequate to deter any conceivable aggression against us.

Senator PELL. I thank you.

When three men of your intelligence and academic qualifications have such a problem in understanding this question, it is obviously going to be even more complicated for simple opinion leaders in the Congress and elsewhere to be able to answer it and I think that you have answered these two questions of the poll better than anyone else could.

I will not burden you with the others because they are outside your own field of competence, but I would ask the chairman's permission that it be included in the record.

Senator GORE. I have seen one of these.

Senator PELL. Your name is mentioned.

Senator GORE. I know. So many people are marking me for extinction, particularly in 1970.

EFFECTIVENESS OF SAFEGUARD DEFENSE

I have one further question, which I think goes to the merit of this issue.

Secretary Laird says this:

"Safeguard is designed to provide us the options to fulfill any or all of several objectives," including: "to preserve the survivability of our land-based deterrent forces, to defend against the potential ICBM threat from China, and to defend against accidental launches from any source." It is a rather large order for Safeguard.

Now the question is does Safeguard provide the option of preserving the survivability of our land based deterrent forces. Does it provide the option of defending against the potential ICBM threat from China? Does it provide the option of defending against accidental launches from any source?

Which one of you will answer?

Dr. WIESNER. One no for each of us.

Senator GORE. All right.

Dr. HORNIG. I think the no would be an over-simplified answer. I think that we have already testified that we don't think it provides an effective defense, or I don't think it provides an effective defense of our deterrent forces.

It provides a negligible defense for our deterrent force.

Senator GORE. Did you say negligible?

Dr. HORNIG. Negligible. That is if it works. Surely if it works it can attenuate a Chinese attack. Some missiles may very well be caught. But it does not provide us with an infallible defense against the Chinese by any means at all.

As to accidental launches, again it may give us some defense, although to do that it must be maintained in a constant state of immediate readiness. The history of complicated systems working when called upon with no forewarning hasn't been very good in our own history, so that I have very little faith that even that purpose can be counted on.

Senator GORE. He took all three. Do you gentlemen concur?

Dr. WIESNER. On the last question, I think there is another more serious technical point and that is a command and control system that is capable of really preventing accidental launches of, and accidental firings of, the nuclear weapons that are involved in this defensive system, and at the same time would permit reliable quick response of the kind that is necessary to get a single accidental launch is probably very unlikely even if the quick response action that Dr. Hornig doubts could be achieved.

So that there is a fundamental problem, a fundamental technical question in addition to the general skepticism about whether one could maintain the kind of an alert day in and day out that would be necessary to have it available for that purpose.

Dr. KISTIAKOWSKY. I would subscribe to what Dr. Hornig and Dr. Wiesner said. The answer to the first is very definitely no. To the second one, the answer is yes, for a limited length of time there will be some attenuation, as Dr. Hornig puts it; in other words some Chinese missiles will not reach the targets. But the net effect of all of this is very questionable, and as regards the third question I think that to maintain this system in a state of such readiness that nuclear armed missiles are ready to be launched by an automatic system at any moment 24 hours a day after something like 15 minutes warning, seems to me a very unreasonable thing to plan for because the overall danger of nuclear explosions will be much increased thereby.

Senator GORE. Gentlemen, once again I wish to thank you. One of the rewarding experiences of my period of service has been to conduct the hearings on this technical, sophisticated and important issue.

I am particularly rewarded with the degree of public information and public opinion about it now. I think you gentlemen can feel rewarded in that though the battle was lost a year ago by a tie vote, the prospects are now that there will be no further ABM deployment.

Thank you very much.

(Whereupon, at 12:25 p.m., the committee was adjourned.)

ABM, MIRV, SALT, AND THE NUCLEAR ARMS RACE

THURSDAY, JUNE 4, 1970

UNITED STATES SENATE,
SUBCOMMITTEE ON ARMS CONTROL,
INTERNATIONAL LAW AND ORGANIZATION
OF THE COMMITTEE ON FOREIGN RELATIONS,
Washington, D.C.

The subcommittee met, pursuant to recess, at 10 a.m., in room 4221, New Senate Office Building, Senator Albert Gore (chairman of the subcommittee) presiding.

Present: Senators Gore, Fulbright (chairman of the full committee), Aiken, Case, and Cooper.

Senator GORE. The subcommittee will come to order.

On behalf of the subcommittee, I wish to welcome the large number of guests in the committee room. I am sorry those still in the hall can't find a seat. From the appearance of the audience, there must be a number of highly educated citizens who are our guests. If you have the same experience that members of the subcommittee have, it will test your capacity to grasp all that goes on here.

OPENING STATEMENT

This is the most sophisticated subject on which the Congress has ever attempted a public hearing. It is in my view an advance in anticipatory democracy.

The subcommittee has had a number of witnesses on this subject heretofore. They have testified on the Safeguard ABM system and the deployment of MIRV. All of these witnesses, except our distinguished Secretary of Defense, Secretary Laird, have said that in their judgment expanding Safeguard and deploying MIRV would be at best unwise and unnecessary, and at worst damaging if not dangerous in the effect that such actions would have on the arms race and on negotiations in that vital area.

These witnesses have included a former Director of Defense Research and Engineering, some of the most prominent scientists in the country, experts on the Soviet Union and China, and three of the four former Presidential science advisers.

On May 18 Secretary Laird appeared before this subcommittee and presented the case for expansion of the Safeguard system and also for the deployment of MIRV's.

Today we will hear further from Dr. John S. Foster, Jr., Director of Defense Research and Engineering.

Dr. Foster is a technician of recognized competence and experience and is equipped to testify on behalf of the Administration.

In Secretary Laird's statement on fiscal year 1971 Defense program and budget, before a joint session of the Armed Services and Appropriations Committees on February 20 of this year, he stated that if the Soviets deploy a MIRV on the SS-9, improve their ICBM accuracy, and do not stop building ICBM's at this time, the United States would be faced in the mid-1970's "with a threat which is much too large to be handled by the level of defense envisioned in the Safeguard system without substantial improvement and modification." Secretary Laird was thus conceding the point, I believe, made by witness after witness before this subcommittee, both last year and this year, that the very buildup postulated by the Department of Defense as a reason for the initial deployment of Safeguard will be in a few years greater than Safeguard can effectively counter.

In the very next paragraph of his February 20 statement, Secretary Laird stated, "We have further decided to continue deployment of Safeguard because the additional cost needed to defend a portion of Minuteman is small if the full area defense is bought." Was Secretary Laird saying in effect that we must agree to deploy a full 12-site area defense in order to justify the cost of Safeguard? Yet this full area defense has not yet been proposed to the Congress. If an ABM defense of our land-based missiles can only be justified if we go on to build and deploy other ABM's for other purposes, should not the executive branch propose or should not Congress now consider the full system? If the executive branch can no longer justify Safeguard with its principal purpose, the defense of Minuteman, then why should Congress not wait until the Administration makes a proposal that can be justified in its view for its own sake?

To put the question another way: Has the Administration changed its justification for an ABM to protect our Minuteman missiles? Is the real purpose of Safeguard now to lead us into a full-scale area defense or is it for our bargaining position at the SALT talks?

Dr. Foster, these are fundamental questions which have led to serious doubts about the wisdom of deploying Safeguard in the first place, doubts that apply to an even greater degree with regard to expanding that system and doing so at a time when we are attempting to negotiate with the Soviets some limitations on strategic arms.

These are some of the questions to which we hope you will supply answers today. You may proceed, please, sir.

STATEMENT OF DR. JOHN S. FOSTER, JR., DIRECTOR OF DEFENSE RESEARCH AND ENGINEERING

Dr. FOSTER. Mr. Chairman, and members of the committee, I welcome this opportunity to appear before you today. From our last appearance before you on May 18, I understand you have a desire to continue our discussion of the technical aspects of our strategic offensive and defensive forces. I realize that you are particularly concerned with the strategic arms limitation talks. The preliminary exchange at Helsinki and the Vienna talks, up to now, have been very encouraging, particularly from the point of view of the businesslike way in which the delegations have gone about their work. We are very hopeful that out of these negotiations will come some form of mutually acceptable limitation on strategic arms.

As you gentlemen fully realize, these talks are of a very delicate nature in that they deal with the vital interests of both nations and indeed can have great significance for all nations of the world. They concern proposed limitations and possible alterations of the strategic forces of both the Soviet Union and the United States. Because of the delicate and complicated nature of these negotiations, and because, as you know, both the Soviet Union and the United States are not discussing details publicly, I am sure you will agree that it would not be appropriate for me to go beyond the statements of Secretary Laird before this committee.

FUTURE ADEQUACY OF U.S. FORCES

In his statement before this committee on May 18, Secretary Laird laid out the very difficult problem we face in the transitional budget we are presenting before the Congress for fiscal year 1971. He noted our great sincerity in working to negotiate a mutually acceptable agreement with the Soviet Union. He noted also the very rapid buildup in Soviet strategic offensive weapons during the past 5 years and the fact that the United States, on the other hand, has maintained a virtually constant level of strategic offensive missile launchers during the same period. I will not repeat the facts that Secretary Laird presented, but wish to reiterate the concern he expressed, not about the present sufficiency of U.S. forces, but about their future adequacy, given the continued Soviet momentum they have displayed in recent years.

Our problem is simple to formulate but very difficult to solve when one considers the long leadtimes necessary from program initiation to deployment in the major weapon systems field. During this period of serious negotiations, I believe it is essential that we preserve sufficient flexibility to keep open strategic options that would be appropriate for the various possible outcomes of SALT.

Present Nixon and Secretary Laird have attempted, in the program presented for fiscal year 1971, to do what they judge is necessary to preserve the minimum flexibility needed on strategic programs for the future by a program that can be tailored to any possible outcome of the SALT negotiations:

1. For those programs that will still be required even if there is an agreement.

2. For those programs which we would need relatively soon if agreement is not reached, recognizing that we can stop or modify these programs if agreement is reached.

3. For the research necessary for programs that we might need in the future, regardless of the outcome of SALT.

However, we do not know what the details of a successful SALT agreement would be, nor do we know what the Soviets will do if there is no agreement. For these reasons, therefore, it is impossible now to describe a likely configuration of U.S. strategic forces in the future, with or without a SALT agreement.

U.S. CHANGES COUNTER SOVIET CHANGES

The changes that our forces are now undergoing have been programed for some years to counter changes in the Soviet forces. For the past 6 or 7 years the expansion of Soviet strategic military power has been very impressive. In this period they have enlarged and improved their already extensive air defense network. They have begun the deployment of an ABM system, and they have expanded their long-range missile forces to bring them from a position of significant inferiority to U.S. forces 6 years ago to a position now in which that inferiority has disappeared. They now have more operational ICBM launchers than the United States and we can expect that in about 2 years they also could have a larger total number of long-range missiles, ICBM's and SLBM's (submarine-launched ballistic missiles) than the United States. The military technology of the Soviet Union has also improved in a similar fashion.

Let me mention three U.S. programs that are designed to preserve our option to meet in a timely manner various aspects of the expanding Soviet threat to our deterrent. The SRAM (short-range attack missile) for strategic bomber penetration of air defense, which is still under development, should be effective against a number of forms of improved air defense. The deployment of the large number of reentry vehicles on our Minuteman III and Poseidon forces should counter any likely Soviet ABM's. The protection of the Minuteman and bomber forces that the Safeguard system would provide in the full Phase II deployment will help solve the problems of survivability which the land-based forces—bomber and ICBM's—could have due to the rapid Soviet buildup.

The Soviets have the ability to expand their strategic capability still further. This momentum, added to the expansion of the recent past, gives us little reason to relax. For instance, you have heard expressions of concern that the Safeguard defense of Minuteman can be easily countered by the Soviets. I am confident that, even if the Soviets apply the reasonably attainable technological improvements which we can expect to appear in the near future, such as MIRV deployment, improvements in accuracy, et cetera, the Minuteman defense will still be effective against a force of the size of the present Soviet "starts." However, if they should continue building and also make technological improvements, we cannot expect the defense we sized some 2 years ago to remain effective. As you know, we propose to start the design of a radar that could be fielded in quantity to supplement the MSR's (missile site radars) if the threat should continue to grow significantly, I believe a system that is a mix of larger radars such as the MSR and a new smaller radar will be superior to a system made up of only small radars or only MSR's.

U.S. STRATEGIC FORCE ACTIONS ARE NOT IRREVERSIBLE

However, it appears that some are concerned that the previously programed strategic force actions that we are continuing and the minimal addition to Safeguard proposed for fiscal year 1971 are irreversible, constraining the possible final outcome of an agreement. The changes that seem to give the most concern to some members of this subcommittee are apparently the deployment of the MIRVed missiles and the additional deployment of Safeguard. We have started the process of introducing Minuteman III missiles into operational use and phasing out the Minuteman I. The first of these missile conversions will be completed late this month. We are also continuing the overhaul of our ballistic missile submarines so as to convert them from the Polaris missile system to the MIRVed Poseidon missile system. We are just beginning construction of the facilities at Grand Forks, which will be the first site of the two-site Phase I of Safeguard.

None of these actions is irreversible. If the MIRV's were to be eliminated by an arms-control agreement, the Minuteman III and Poseidon systems could revert to a single-warhead configuration. Similarly, any Safeguard progress can be reversed. The construction at Grand Forks has only proceeded as far as ground excavation in preparation for a foundation, a quite modest advance. There is no reason that these excavations cannot be refilled with dirt—or, if the foundations have been completed, they could be either abandoned or ripped up.

At this point, Mr. Chairman, I would like to show you photographs of the excavations at Grand Forks as they looked about 2 weeks ago, if I may just present them to you.

Senator GORE. Yes.

Dr. FOSTER. Mr. Chairman, this is a photograph of the excavations for the PAR (perimeter acquisition radar) site, and you can remember that because I have written "PAR" on the back. And this is a photograph of the missile site radar, on which I have noted "MSR."

Senator GORE. Thank you. I will pass these along.

Senator AIKEN. Are these ours or theirs?

Dr. FOSTER. These are ours, sir—the excavations for U.S. Safeguard radar facilities at Grand Forks. One of them is for the perimeter acquisition radar; the other is for the missile site radar, the small one.

Senator GORE. I gather from the performance last night and yours today that the Administration is impressed with visual effects. [Laughter.]

Dr. FOSTER. Well, Mr. Chairman——

Senator GORE. That is nonpolitical, Doctor.

Dr. FOSTER. It has been noted a number of times that a picture is worth a great many words.

Senator GORE. Last year I used a homemade chart, and I have another one to present to you a little later today.

Dr. FOSTER. Very well, Mr. Chairman.

This site is not expected to be operational until 1974.

The PAR should look like the sketch that I am now showing. On the left, Mr. Chairman, is a sketch of what the first U.S. Safeguard PAR would look like in 1974.

By contrast, I show the Soviet Dog House radar, located near Moscow, that has been operational since 1969. These two sketches represent the two facilities approximately to the same scale.

(The information referred to follows.)

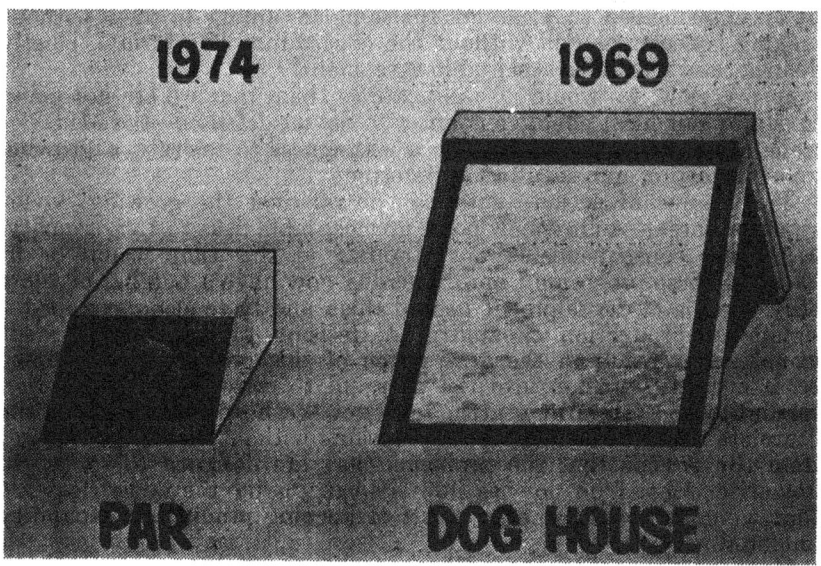

Senator GORE. What does the scale of the radar prove?

Dr. FOSTER. Mr. Chairman, I make just that point in the remainder of this paragraph.

Senator GORE. All right.

Dr. FOSTER. By way of comparison, the largest Soviet ABM radar near Moscow, the object we call the Dog House, is shown in the accompanying sketch; it was first operated last year. This should remind us that the time from a decision to proceed with some major change in strategic forces to the effective operating date of those forces is always a considerable amount of time—5 to 6 years.

I don't see how we can help the negotiations by assuming at this time we know the nature of the agreement and disrupting long-laid programs by unilateral moratorium-like decisions. It is my personal opinion that this type of action is more likely to damage the U.S. negotiating position than a determination to move forward as planned until a balanced and equitable arms-limitations agreement is consummated. To summarize, gentlemen, I do not believe any of the actions we are now taking are irreversible. We can at any time modify or terminate them if we have an agreement that dictates such changes. There would, of course, be some cost associated with reversion of the forces to a previous configuration, if that is required, but I am sure the people of the United States would be willing to pay that cost if a meaningful agreement to limit strategic arms is achieved.

CONSEQUENCES OF STOPPING PLANNED IMPROVEMENTS TO U.S. STRATEGIC FORCES

What, then, are the consequences of stopping planned improvements to our strategic forces? In my view, such a unilateral action on our part would indicate to the Soviets that they may be able to achieve a freeze of U.S. strategic arms without an agreement. It seems to me that lack of determination to proceed with programs deemed essential to preserve national security could hurt the possibility of reaching an agreement rather than help it. Why should the Soviets limit themselves by an agreement if they can get the same advantage to them without making concessions and without the constraints of a formal, clearly defined, and mutually acceptable agreement?

In my view, we would also indicate to them that we are not going to deploy our most effective counter to Soviet defenses—the MIRV—while at the same time signaling a willingness to tolerate a growing vulnerability of our land-based deterrent.

This course of action—with no control over the growing Soviet strategic threat—in my view poses unacceptable risks to U.S. security.

Another consequence of our stopping at this time would be financial. These programs I am discussing now have a number of years of research and development behind them and have also developed a significant production capability. A decision to delay deployment would either result in the destruction of this production capability or in a costly infusion into the program to convert the production capability to a standby status. I do not see how we can afford the complete abandonment of these programs without strong guarantees from the Soviets that the problems they are designed to solve will not arise. Also, I do not see how we can justify the added expense that would be incurred as a result of keeping production capability on standby.

UNITED STATES HAS THREE CHOICES

We have then three choices:
1. The abandonment of these programs with the accompanying grave risk to our security that would develop rapidly if the momentum of the growing Soviet threat continues.
2. An indefinite and expensive holding action with regard to these capabilities to guard against a possible failure of SALT, and a steady decrease in our security.
3. The determination to proceed with these programs until it is clear that we can arrive at some agreement, whose nature we understand, which will make these programs unnecessary.

Mr. Chairman, the President and the Secretary of Defense chose to follow the last course.

This concludes my statement. At this time, I would be pleased to answer any questions that you or your committee may have.

WISDOM AND URGENCY OF SALT

Senator GORE. Thank you, Dr. Foster. Many of your postulations I find agreeable. The question is one of judgment as to assumptions and to the future course of action. You have demonstrated, it seems to me, that both the United States and the Soviet Union have the capability of continuing the nuclear arms race ad infinitum. The question is where there is a place to stop.

You have said, as Secretary Laird did, that we think our strategic nuclear position is sufficient with present Soviet capability. That is correct, I believe.

Dr. FOSTER. Yes, that is correct, Mr. Chairman.

Senator GORE. The question you contemplate, as Secretary Laird did, is the danger that would occur to the United States in the event the Soviet momentum of buildup continues and accelerates. Therefore, you propose that we propose to match that continuing buildup.

This dramatizes the wisdom of the strategic arms limitation talks and the urgency of reaching an agreement.

EFFICACY OF SAFEGUARD PROTECTION OF MINUTEMAN QUESTIONED

One question to which you did not address your remarks was the the efficacy of the ABM system to meet such threat as you postulate in your assumption.

I have another chart on which I would like to ask your comments. This is putting the press in the dark. Can you see this, Dr. Foster?

Dr. FOSTER. Yes.

(The information referred to follows.)

**NUMBER OF ATTACKING WARHEADS
CERTAIN TO DESTROY M.M. SILO**

(Figure: Graph plotting number of attacking warheads (0–1200) versus year ('66–'80). Curves shown: "SS-9 — no MIRV", "Soviet MIRV's ?", "SS-11 upgrading ?", and a dashed line "Levelling off; SALT limitation ?". Shaded regions on the right labeled "Danger Zone with protection" and "Danger Zone without Safeguard Protection (Phase II-a)".)

Senator GORE. To begin with, as I understand the postulation of the Department of Defense, this would be the danger area. You assume or postulate the development of the Soviets. This line represents your current extrapolation of Soviet capability if continued. If slowed down it would be this. If SS-9 MIRVs it would be coming to this direction.

On the left is the capability of ABM's which shows that the danger area would be reached by your current postulations in 1980.

This raises the serious question of the efficacy of the ABM deployment even if the postulations you assume turned out to be correct.

I would like to read briefly a more detailed statement. I would like you to comment, if you will, upon this chart which has been prepared, not by my own staff, but by Dr. Panofsky. This chart, based upon DOD's unclassified figures, shows the Soviet threat against Minuteman now and what the threat could be over the next decade. It shows convincingly, I believe, how little protection, if any, of Minuteman a fully deployed Safeguard Phase II-a will provide. As I have pointed out, the chart shows on the left the number of attacking warheads of sufficient accuracy and explosive power which the Soviets have deployed or might deploy.

The heavy line indicates the SS-9 deployment at the present rate, which I have indicated here, if they continue their deployment as Secretary Laird suggested.

As you know, there is no evidence that the Soviets have a MIRV which can attack more than one Minuteman silo and, at the present, none of the other U.S.S.R. missiles has the power to endanger Minuteman, as I understand it.

The large rectangular area in the upper right hand area indicates, as I have said, the danger level. That is the time when the number of warheads capable of knocking out Minuteman silos reaches a danger level of 700, which you see upon the left.

Seven hundred is the danger level because the survival of Minuteman as an independent component of the U.S. deterrent forces might be in danger if only 300 Minutemen would remain to destroy the Soviet Union.

As you know, of course, 200 to 400 warheads is the number that has been given that would destroy the Soviet Union or its civilization. This doesn't take into consideration our submarines. We are talking now about Minuteman.

Extrapolating the rate of SS-9 deployment through 1980, we can see that the danger level would not be reached until about 1980. This is all we can say definitely from today's knowledge. Anything else is a speculative projection. Of course, speculative projection is something we must consider both on our own part and on their part, and that is all the more reason for the SALT talks.

The curve here shows a leveling off which might result because of SALT limitations, in which case ABM would not be needed.

If the Soviet MIRV the number of attacking warheads, it produces a sharply upturned curve as is indicated here.

The danger level would be reached before the middle of the decade and before Safeguard could be deployed. The same situation would result if the accuracy of the SS-11 is upgraded. It is clear that, if the Soviets MIRV and improve the quality of their SS-11's, Safeguard is not the answer to protection of Minuteman. This also underlines the necessity for preventing deployment of MIRV and ABM if we are to avoid a sharp upward turn in the arms race.

This, I hope, gets to the central question, Doctor. I will leave this here for you to comment upon.

Dr. FOSTER. Well, Mr. Chairman, I have considerable difficulty with this chart and I am in disagreement with it. It is misleading; let me just try to go through the various aspects of it for you.

The one part that I agree with is the number of warheads as a function of time with regard to the SS-9. That is a linear projection; it is a rough estimate; it does not take into account certain detailed and sensitive intelligence information—nor should it.

Senator GORE. I said it is based on nonclassified information which the Department of Defense has produced.

Dr. FOSTER. I understand, Mr. Chairman. I fully agree.

INTELLIGENCE COMMUNITY ESTIMATES OF SOVIET WEAPONS BUILDUP

But from there I believe it departs from the correct situation. Let me describe the situation as far as the intelligence community is concerned.

According to the intelligence community, the United States must assume that by 1972 or later, the Soviet SS-11 types, for example, could be accurate enough to attack Minuteman. That means that by 1973-75 we might have to reckon with the possibility of something like 1,100 incoming missiles. This is not some vague possibility, some curve that has no extension. This is a curve which by 1973, based on a prudent estimate on our part, will lie up here—just because of the SS-11 types—in this region of serious concern.

No. 2, the SS-9's——

Senator GORE. May I before you leave the SS-11——

Dr. FOSTER. Yes.

Senator GORE. If the assumption which you make with respect to the SS-11 is correct, then it seems to me you have effectively denied the adequacy of ABM deployment.

Dr. FOSTER. Not at all, Mr. Chairman. Let me just come to that in a moment.

With regard to the SS-9's, it is the intelligence community's position—and this is the advice that the President of the United States and the Secretary of Defense have been given—that we have to reckon not with the possibility that they now have MIRV—about which at the moment there is in fact doubt, and it cannot be proved one way or another conclusively—but with the fact that in the early 1970's they will have it. Therefore, in order to protect our deterrent, we can't go on some vague assumption about what is going on; we have to plan on a rather definite projection, made as carefully as this country can, of what the threat could be. The projection of that threat is agreed on by the community.

Senator GORE. Would that threat be met by the proposal on ABM now before this committee?

Dr. FOSTER. Yes, Mr. Chairman. If I may, sir, I would like to come to that in a moment, after I finish criticizing the chart.

Now, I agree with the numbers of SS-9 missiles. The difficulty I have, sir—if I may just finish——

Senator GORE. What you have said thus far is not a criticism of the chart. You have raised certain assumptions which you say intelligence estimates show. This chart is based upon the information supplied by the Department of Defense itself.

Dr. FOSTER. Yes, Mr. Chairman, but there is a strange inconsistency.

The Department of Defense supplies information with regard to what the Soviet SS-9's could do if they continued the current increase in numbers and what would happen if they leveled off. That information is provided. But nowhere is shown here any information—and that is also provided by the Department of Defense—that would project any of these trends into the danger zone. That is what is misleading about this chart, Mr. Chairman.

Senator GORE. No, I am sorry. Both the SS-11 curve and the curve showing MIRV's point directly to the danger area. The chart shows that the danger area would be reached with Soviet MIRVing their weapons in 1973 to 1974, and with an upgrading of SS-11's in 1975.

Dr. FOSTER. Yes, Mr. Chairman, I am simply saying it is misleading.

Now, again, with regard to the MIRV's on the SS-9, what we have to reckon with are the facts and their assessment, as given us by the intelligence community. We are told that by the 1973–75 period we will have to reckon with a Soviet MIRV capability.

PROTECTING U.S. SECURITY NOW OR LATER

That means we have to plan now to cope with it by around 1975; we have to plan now to provide for our security against something like 1,200 reentry vehicles. This we have to do.

Now, there are two ways we can do this: Either we can lay plans now to provide for America's security against such attacks or we can wait until our security is gone and say, "Now it is clear that we no longer have a deterrent, and we are all agreed that we must react."

I submit that is an unacceptable posture. I know of no way, Mr. Chairman, to cope with this danger without taking some steps now. The steps that are recommended by the President to the Congress are the deployment of MIRV and the deployment of Safeguard Modified Phase II.

Senator GORE. Would you yield there?

Dr. FOSTER. Certainly.

Senator GORE. I have no argument with the postulation that we need to be in readiness for future threats if future threats cannot be limited or contained.

ADEQUACY OF ADMINISTRATION'S RECOMMENDED PROTECTION QUESTIONED

The question I raise by this chart is the adequacy of the Administration's recommendation. ABM will not meet the threat if we have to face such a threat. If we don't face such a threat, then ABM is not needed.

Dr. FOSTER. You are quite right about the necessity for readiness, Mr. Chairman.

Senator GORE. Good.

Dr. FOSTER. I am in full agreement with you. So then the question is whether or not it is adequate.

Now let me discuss that, if I may.

The area labeled Phase II-a Safeguard, as it is shown here on the chart, would show the interception capability against roughly 100 missiles of the attacking force.

Senator GORE. This represents, according to this chart, the limitations of ABM.

Dr. FOSTER. Yes, Mr. Chairman, and I believe that is wrong. It is simply incorrect, and if you wish——

Senator GORE. Here you are arguing with Dr. Panofsky.

Dr. FOSTER. I certainly am, sir, if he is the one who made that estimate. I believe he is just wrong.

Senator GORE. It is based upon the information supplied by the Department of Defense.

Dr. FOSTER. No, sir, we have not supplied such information. We have supplied to this and other committees classified information dealing with the capabilities of the radars and the missiles, as well as the numbers of each, and that information does not lead to this kind of attrition.

Senator GORE. Then you find yourself at odds with Dr. Panofsky with respect to a conclusion based upon the same facts.

Dr. FOSTER. That is quite right, yes.

Senator GORE. Then the question is whether you and Secretary Laird are right or the overwhelming proportion of the scientific community of the country is right.

Dr. FOSTER. Mr. Chairman, I don't believe this is something that is settled by popular vote.

Let me tell you the nature of the problem, as I see it, sir. I think it is a very difficult one.

Senator GORE. I didn't say popular vote. I said the majority of scientific opinion, not votes.

Dr. FOSTER. I understand, Mr. Chairman.

DIFFICULTY OF INTERPRETING AVAILABLE INFORMATION

Let me try to describe the situation as I see it. We are faced, as you said in your opening remarks, with an extremely difficult technical problem, an extremely difficult military threat, and an extremely difficult political situation that demand judgments by other than scientific and military people.

Now, all of these known facts and all of our concerns make quite a large pile in fact; just the scientific information itself is voluminous. My point is this. If you compile these facts and then have a technical man, a very good technical man, come in and look at it with a feeling in advance about what he would like to find, it is possible for him to select a host of facts that will support his conclusion and make it look to the layman like an ironclad case.

Another good technical man can come in and select from that original pile another set of facts that suits his intuition, and he can thus make for our Congress, or others, an airtight case.

Let me tell you that the tough job is for the Administration, looking at all of these facts, to select those that make a case to provide for our security that can stand up against all of these outside attacks.

Senator GORE. The Congress itself also has a tough job.

Dr. FOSTER. You certainly do.

DANGER ZONE IN LIGHT OF ADMINISTRATION'S RECOMMENDED ABM DEPLOYMENT

Senator GORE. It equally shares these responsibilities.

Would you mind indicating to the committee on this chart where, in your opinion, the light area within the danger zone would be with your present recommendations of ABM deployment, and where it would be if the full-12-site deployment is made?

Dr. FOSTER. Mr. Chairman, I would like nothing more, but let me explain my problem, In order for me to give you an estimate of what the protection would look like, based on best judgment of the Department of Defense, I would have to tell you the following things: The capability of the radar, its reliability, its track-handling capability, the reliability of the missiles, the kill capability of the warheads, and the tactics for engaging various kinds of incoming objects.

All of this is sensitive information, eagerly sought by potential enemies. If I simply walked up and put my finger on a spot on that chart—I know the spot well, for we have calculated such spots many, many times—I would be giving away information sensitive to our security. I can't do that.

ADEQUACY OF SAFEGUARD PHASE II

Senator GORE. I don't ask you to do that. But this committee and the American people must make a judgment. The first two items you mentioned, of course, are the Achilles' heel of the whole system, and it seems to me what you are really saying is that Phase II is useless unless we proceed to deploy 12 sites. That is the conclusion I am forced to reach.

Dr. FOSTER. Mr. Chairman, we may not be using the same language, sir. There is nothing that I said that I understand to have any relationship to your statement. I believe that the Phase II deployment, particularly the modified Phase II deployment we are requesting for fiscal year 1971, will do the job described by the Department of Defense. I do not believe that it will be invulnerable to all attacks that could be made against it in the future. Any defense can be overwhelmed by a superior force, just as any offense can be defeated by a superior defensive force.

Senator GORE. In the light of your statements and this chart, will you address this committee on the statement I read from Secretary Laird: "With a threat which is much too large to be handled by the level of defense envisioned in the Safeguard system without substantial improvement and modification." What did the Secretary mean by that, if he did not mean that the proposal you now have made would not be adequate if the projection which you postulate for the Soviet Union is achieved?

Dr. FOSTER. Well, Mr. Chairman, both the Secretary's statement and my own dealt with that problem.

We have always said that the deployment we were proposing to the Congress would handle a certain range of threats, and that if the threat went beyond this—and we couldn't be sure that it would not—we would have to add to our defensive capabilities.

Now, with regard to the Minuteman system, the Phase II deployment will handle a certain level of threat, and I have described that in my statement; that is to say, if the Soviets complete their present starts and employ the technology that we believe seems reasonable in the next few years, then the Safeguard deployment can provide for an adequate number of surviving Minutemen.

Senator GORE. This is a matter of opinion.

Dr. FOSTER. Well, yes, I agree; people can differ on that judgment.

Senator GORE. Most scientists whom I have heard express their views completely disagree with you on that.

Dr. FOSTER. I believe one just has to select the scientists, and you can get a large number on either side.

Senator GORE. We haven't found a large number on but one side.

Dr. FOSTER. I can find a large number on the other side, sir.

Senator GORE. We would be happy to have them. We have not been able to find them.

IMPROVED DEFENSE AGAINST INCREASED SOVIET THREAT

Dr. FOSTER. We will be happy to assist, Mr. Chairman. If, however, the Soviet deployment of SS-11's continues to increase, if they employ MIRV, if they improve the accuracy of the SS-11's—these things would pose an additional threat to the Minuteman, and we would have to provide more defense.

Senator GORE. What kind?

Dr. FOSTER. In that regard over the last 10 years we have looked into the possibility of deploying additional large radars like the MSR's or deploying very small radars, much smaller, by perhaps a factor of two, perhaps even 10. In looking at this situation I have come to the conclusion—and so have a number of others—that the best solution is a combination of a large, very capable radar and a considerably smaller but less capable and certainly less costly radar.

Senator GORE. That is not what you now recommend.

Dr. FOSTER. We are recommending to the Congress in our fiscal year 1971 budget moneys to begin the design of a smaller radar.

Senator GORE. Yes, but we are discussing here deployment.

Dr. FOSTER. This radar would be needed only if the Soviet buildup continues in the later years.

PRESENT NEED FOR AND FUTURE ADEQUACY OF RECOMMENDED ABM

Senator GORE. You just confirmed my view if not my point, and I think both my view and the point. As presently designed and as presently recommended, ABM deployment would not counter a projected Soviet threat and is not needed with respect to present Soviet capability.

Dr. FOSTER. Mr. Chairman, I am afraid I must disagree. I think we are not talking about the same thing.

Senator GORE. Yes, I think we are, and I think we have reached a similar conclusion. You stated it in more sophisticated language.

Dr. FOSTER. Excuse me, Mr. Chairman. Currently the Soviet force in-being poses no threat to Minuteman, and Safeguard is not needed.

Senator GORE. That is what I said.

Dr. FOSTER. And that is not the issue. We don't have Safeguard. They don't have the ability to destroy all the Minutemen, and so we have a deterrent today.

Senator GORE. If I may take it step by step, as of now it is not needed.

Dr. FOSTER. That is correct, sir.

Senator GORE. It is only needed if the Soviets continue their buildup of strategic nuclear capability.

Dr. FOSTER. Let me be more precise here, Mr. Chairman, I think this is where we have to be quite careful. If the Soviets completed those starts that they have already made, and if they put triple MIRV's in the SS-9's and increase the accuracy of the SS-11's——

Senator GORE. Those are the assumptions. Excuse me.

Dr. FOSTER. Sir, they are not quite assumptions; they are the intelligence community's projections that we have to deal with.

Senator GORE. They are hypotheses. You say "if."

Dr. FOSTER. Someone in my position couldn't possibly come back to the Congress in 1974 and say, "Well, look, I am sorry, those were projections; we didn't know it was going to really happen. We didn't protect ourselves against it. We are now in a terrible shape." The Congress would simply turn around and say, "Gentlemen, you see the record of the predictions by the intelligence community. While they have underestimated time and time again in the past, they did estimate that by the early seventies there would be these characteristics. Now, why didn't you take them into account?"

Well, I am saying that we see these estimates, I concur in them personally and I have to take action that will provide for the survival of our deterrent should these actions come about.

Senator GORE. Have you just revealed to us that the intelligence estimate is that the Soviets will achieve MIRV capability within the early seventies?

Dr. FOSTER. Yes, sir, that is the intelligence estimate, and I stated it earlier. It is that the Soviets must be credited with a MIRV on their SS-9's in the early seventies, and improved accuracy on the SS-11 types in the early seventies.

Senator GORE. Then it would, it seems to me, logically follow that you have just told us that ABM as you now recommend it would be virtually useless to counter such a threat.

Dr. FOSTER. Now, Mr. Chairman, let's go at that question very slowly.

Senator GORE. I think you need to. I think you need to be careful with it.

Dr. FOSTER. Yes, sir, I certainly shall.

PRESENT AND FUTURE SOVIET STRATEGIC CAPABILITY

Senator COOPER. Mr. Chairman, I don't believe it will be in violation of any secret information, but if Dr. Foster would indicate the number of SS-9's in-being now, and tell us of any information he may have, of new individual silos and silo complexes being developed for SS-9's. If he would then work from that, to possible MRV or MIRV so we might find out what the threat might be at a certain time and when.

Dr. FOSTER. All right. Senator Cooper, while the chairman is occupied, if you wish, I will do that. If one takes a little over 400 SS-9's, which on this chart show up a little after 1974, and assumes three reentry vehicles, each about 5 megatons with an accuracy of about a quarter of a nautical mile—which is consistent with the intelligence community expectation for that time frame for the Soviets—then the number of surviving Minutemen is a few tens of missiles in the absence of defense.

Mr. Chairman, going back to your point, which I think is an extremely critical one——

Senator GORE. I agree. Let me just extrapolate it a little further in order that you may answer it fully. You used the word "revealed" just now. I did not know that this intelligence information had previously been made public. The committee was aware of it. It may have been made public and I raise no point of criticism. I wanted to add that it was because of this information I had reached the conclusion in my own mind that the projected deployment of ABM now before the Congress would be virtually useless as a counter to the threat which you project as a possibility of Soviet development.

You may answer the whole question. I wanted to add that to be clear.

Dr. FOSTER. Yes, Mr. Chairman, I do hope I can do justice to this question because it seems to me an extremely important aspect of this whole subject.

PRESENT U.S. DETERRENT

We start from the point that we described a moment ago, where the number of surviving Minutemen today, should there be an attack, is adequate; that is to say, the Soviets would have to reckon with a surviving number so large as to deter such an attack in the first place. That is our situation today.

Senator GORE. Would you just repeat that?

Dr. FOSTER. Today we have a number of Minutemen with a certain hardness. The Soviets have a number of missiles with certain yields and accuracies. If they were to target their forces in a reasonably sensible way, allocating them between attack of Minuteman and attack of other parts of the country, they would not have the ability to knock out our Minutemen so completely that the surviving force would not, in itself, be able to deliver an unacceptable blow to the Soviet Union. Therefore, today the Soviet Union should be deterred from such an attack.

Senator CASE. May I just make this point here, and that is entirely without regard to the submarines.

Dr. FOSTER. Yes, sir.

Senator CASE. And to our Strategic Air Force.

Dr. FOSTER. Yes, sir.

Senator CASE. They are, in addition, deterrent, counter weapons which would be in existence.

Dr. FOSTER. I understand, sir.

Senator CASE. This is solely the impossibility of the Soviets to knock out our missiles as a counter force.

Dr. FOSTER. Yes, sir, that is an extremely important point.

Senator GORE. I wish to yield to Senator Aiken who wants to ask a question.

U.S. ABILITY TO COMBAT GUERRILLA WARFARE

Senator AIKEN. I wonder if we could get out of space and down to earth for a moment.

We have been engaged in a rather costly war for the last 7 or 8 years, very costly indeed, and the end isn't quite in sight. In view of the fact that we probably have made progress toward a war in space or coming from outer space, has there been a corresponding improvement in our ability to combat guerrilla warfare, which seems to be a most serious and current difficulty?

Dr. FOSTER. Senator Aiken, you ask an extremely provocative question.

Senator AIKEN. I am trying to put first things first and that is with us now.

Dr. FOSTER. Yes, sir; I understand.

Well, Senator, I believe we have made considerable progress in antiguerrilla warfare. I believe that the equipment we have developed, for example, for use in Vietnam, has enormously increased the effectiveness of our fighting forces there. It has increased the effectiveness of the South Vietnamese forces. What is more, I believe that a number of these developments have a very general application. For example, as you know, we have developed a number of techniques for sensing on the battlefield, trying to uncover camouflaged materiel, trying to see at night, trying to detect people as they move at great distances, and then coordinating all of this intelligence—whether it was gathered by some local sensors, by radars, or by aerial systems—so that we have a real time picture of what is going on.

I have seen an enormous change in just the last 2 or 3 years in the actual capability of our forces in Vietnam.

Senator AIKEN. No doubt there has been great technical progress made, but we have been engaged there now 7 years. It will be some time—I hope not too long—before we are disengaged there. You know of the pressure which is being put upon the Government to involve itself in other parts of the world, which would be perhaps even more serious than Southeast Asia. Even Latin America is doing a lot of grumbling, and then there is Africa and other parts of the world. Suppose that these countries, these people, all decided to engage us in guerrilla warfare. Would we then be able to meet that challenge?

Dr. FOSTER. Well, I think I would be as disturbed as anyone if we had to cope with such a situation, but, as a matter of fact, Senator Aiken, I believe we are well prepared technologically to assist our friends and allies under the Nixon doctrine.

Senator AIKEN. It does seem more likely at this point than an atomic war. I don't question for a moment the desirability of looking ahead to any kind of a war, but we have this guerrilla-type warfare on our hands now which seems to have changed from time to time. I don't know. We might even return to where we may have to fight with slingshots and javelins, and bows and arrows and daggers.

Dr. FOSTER. It might be a good trend.

Senator AIKEN. It seems to me that it would be a very difficult task for the ABM or the SS-9's to compete in that kind of a war. Yet that is what we have. I was just trying to get back down to earth a little.

Dr. FOSTER. Thank you very, very much, Senator.

Senator AIKEN. Not that there isn't a future in outer space. I am sure there is, but we are here now.

Dr. FOSTER. Yes.

Senator AIKEN. That is all.

Senator GORE. Thank you.

Dr. Foster, I think in fairness you should be given time to complete your answer to the basic question I raised. Then, since I have used so much time, I will yield to Senator Fulbright.

PLANNING FOR FUTURE THREAT

Dr. FOSTER. Certainly, Mr. Chairman.

We have described the initial point, the position today. Then the problem is that, as one looks at the range of possibilities in the future, one makes a judgment of the type of threat with which we may have to cope—not an overstatement and certainly not an understatement—but a judgment concerning the likely range of threats with which we are going to have to deal.

Armed with that estimate, one lays out a plan; and the plan is intended to give us an opportunity to arrive at a position so that we will be able to cope with that threat.

Now, when you lay out the plan, it must have some starting point and must carry us some distance, which is, in a sense, perhaps a year or two or three.

What President Nixon did, with Secretary Laird's advice, was to recommend the plan for deploying a system to defend Minuteman, which will protect us during an admittedly narrow time frame. It is easy to say, "But, look, you project beyond that even more missiles and even more capabilities, and your deployment would be overwhelmed." That is true, but President Nixon also said that we will review this active ballistic missile defense program, Safeguard, each year from the point of view of the technical progress of the threat and the diplomatic context.

Senator GORE. That sounds very well, but it doesn't measure a test of feasibility and prudence when considered beside your previous statements that the present recommendation would not meet the projected threat.

Dr. FOSTER. Excuse me, there is some misunderstanding here, Mr. Chairman. The present deployment will take care of the situation that we predict for 1974. There is time now to make decisions regarding the deployments that would be made in 1975, 1976, and 1977 to take care of any possible growth between the years 1974 and 1977. There is time after that to make any deployments that are necessary between 1977 and 1978. We cannot decide now the right answer with regard to ballistic missile defense of Minuteman in 1978, for example, because, in fact, we don't know what the threat is going to look like by then.

We take only the minimum prudent action consistent with maintaining our security.

THREAT POSED BY SOVIET SS-11'S

Senator GORE. The statement you just made did not take into consideration, or at least you made no reference to, the SS-11 upon which you have previously indicated you possessed intelligence information.

Dr. FOSTER. Mr. Chairman, I have looked at that question in great detail. I have made calculations of the way I think the Soviets might target their forces. I have worked with the Joint Chiefs of Staff to see what their judgments are. I would be delighted to go into an executive session with you and write down what I think the allocations are.

Senator GORE. We will be glad to go into an executive session, but to take what——

Dr. FOSTER. My answer to your question is, yes, we have taken the SS-9 into our calculations.

Senator GORE. I said the SS-11.

Dr. FOSTER. Excuse me. I should have said we have taken the SS-11's into our calculations.

Senator GORE. You told us a few moments ago that the SS-11 would present a threat if development continues in 1973. The present recommendation you make with respect to ABM deployment would be inadequate, in my view, to counteract such a threat.

Dr. FOSTER. Mr. Chairman, I think there is a point here on which I could possibly have misled you. The time at which we judge the SS-11 type could have more accurate guidance is 1972 or later. That does not mean that the whole SS-11 force would be equipped with accurate guidance in 1973. I think that is an important correction.

Senator GORE. It could so mean.

Dr. FOSTER. No, I don't believe so, sir.

Senator GORE. That is an assumption of which you can't be sure.

Dr. FOSTER. No, and it is one I have worried about some. But now you are making the situation worse than our best intelligence estimate would sustain.

Senator GORE. Proceed and complete your answer and then I will yield to Senator Fulbright. I have taken too much time.

Dr. FOSTER. Well, Mr, Chairman, I think in the exchange we did finish that subject—at last. I hope we did to your satisfaction.

Senator GORE. Fine. Thank you.

That is an assumption I can't share. [Laughter.]

Senator Fulbright.

EFFECT OF SAFEGUARD PHASE II AND MIRV ON SALT

Senator FULBRIGHT. Mr. Foster, Secretary Laird, in his statement to the subcommittee on May 18, said, "We also want to insure that we do not complicate SALT by our own actions."

Could you say why the Defense Department is so sure that it is not complicating the SALT talks by going ahead with Phase II of Safeguard, and the deployment of MIRV's? What is the reasoning behind that?

Dr. FOSTER. Mr. Chairman, the reasons behind it are those given by Secretary Laird in his statement before this committee about 2 weeks ago. I have given my answers to your questions, sir, in my statement.

I also recall the exchange between you and Secretary Laird toward the end of the hearing when we last met. This was to the effect that it was your mutual judgment that these matters were really of a political nature and that scientists had no special competence or contribution to make in this area.

So in my statement, sir, I have tried to give my reasons, hoping that one would pay more attention to the reasons than to the fact that I hold some opinion—and, hopefully, leave it at that.

Senator FULBRIGHT. What concerns me is the fact that there are so many scientific authorities in the United States, those not in the employ of the Defense Department, and many people who are not scientists, but who are knowledgeable about Soviet relations and have studied them for many years, and also have studied disarmament matters, who do think this endangers the success of the SALT talks. In addition to that there is Premier Kosygin's statement regarding the effect of Cambodia on the SALT talks. It is very difficult for me to reconcile that with your statement because I don't know of any really responsible scientific authorities or others who have spoken out who have suggested that it doesn't endanger the SALT talks. It simply raises a very serious question.

You know, of course, Mr. Foster, that this country has spent over a thousand billion dollars on military affairs since World War II. You also know that every former Presidential science adviser is opposed to expanding Safeguard at this time.

We have had most of them testifying before this committee. Together with that there are such programs, which we daily read about, as the Cheyenne helicopter on which many millions of dollars have been spent, the Main Battle Tank, the C-5A and the F-111, and many other missile systems. The Sentinel system itself has been abandoned with enormous losses. The C-5A hasn't yet been abandoned, but the latest news is that there is something wrong with the wing and that it probably will be unless it is completely redesigned.

In view of this record, I don't see how you can be so confident of your judgment about these matters. It really shakes my confidence as to whether the Department is capable of an objective view of these matters.

Dr. FOSTER. Mr. Chairman, you have indicated the number of scientists who oppose this Safeguard deployment.

Senator FULBRIGHT. There are several grounds. They oppose it on the SALT talks alone. Then in addition they oppose it on the ground that it isn't technically feasible, at the present time at least.

AD HOC COMMITTEE OF SCIENTISTS ON SAFEGUARD

Dr. FOSTER. Well, Mr. Chairman, let me just simply point out that I asked a group of scientists to come together as an ad hoc committee and, before the Secretary of Defense made his recommendation to the President, review the program. I deliberately chose scientists who opposed the deployment of Safeguard as well as those who favored it.

In fact, as I recall, when they met there were more against it than for it. I had, however, one very simple instruction for them—to put politics aside and just ask the question: Will this deployment, with these components, do the job that the Department of Defense is trying to do? And I gave them a range of possible deployments, since the Secretary had not yet made up his mind.

There was considerable concern about this move, but the report sent to the Secretary of Defense said that this equipment will do the job that the Department of Defense wants to do. They had some recommendations; for example, they would like to add development of the smaller radars, a decision we had already made—at least, they concurred in that decision.

I think it is extremely important that, when you ask a scientist for his opinion, you make sure that you have found a way to rule out political factors, because, as you and Secretary Laird noted at our last hearing, the scientist doesn't have special competence in that area.

Senator FULBRIGHT. Who were the scientists that you had on this committee?

Dr. FOSTER. It was a group of scientists under the chairmanship of Prof. Larry O'Neill of Columbia University. I would be delighted to furnish the complete list.

Senator FULBRIGHT. How many were there?

Dr. FOSTER. About a half dozen, sir.

Senator FULBRIGHT. Can't you furnish them now? Don't you know who they were? Were they in the employ, directly or indirectly, of the Pentagon?

Dr. FOSTER. No, sir, generally they were not.

Senator FULBRIGHT. Who were they?

Dr. FOSTER. Prof. Sidney Drell, a close colleague of Professor Panofsky, who was mentioned earlier, at Stanford University was a member. It is so long ago I am embarrassed to say I have forgotten some of their names.

Senator GORE. You would have a record in the Department that you could supply.

Dr. FOSTER. Certainly, I have the list. There was Professor Goldberger of Princeton University; Prof. Allen Peterson, also of Stanford; Richard Latter of the Rand Corp. was a consultant. He is now over in Vienna on the talks. I don't have the others at the moment.
(The information referred to follows.)

AD HOC PANEL ON FISCAL 1971 SAFEGUARD PLAN

Professor Lawrence H. O'Neill, Chairman,
Professor of Electronic Engineering and
Director of Electronics Research Laboratory,
Riverside Research Institute,
632 West 125th Street,
New York, New York.

Dr. Lewis M. Branscomb,
Director,
National Bureau of Standards,
Washington, D.C.

Dr. Sidney D. Drell,
Stanford Linear Accelerator Center,
Stanford University,
P. O. Box 4349,
Stanford, California.

Dr. Marvin L. Goldberger,
Princeton University,
Princeton, New Jersey.

Dr. William G. McMillan,
The Rand Corporation,
1700 Main Street,
Santa Monica, California.

Mr. W. S. Melahn,
President,
Systems Development Corporation,
2500 Colorado Avenue,
Santa Monica, California.

Dr. Allen M. Peterson,
Stanford Research Institute,
333 Ravenswood Avenue,
Menlo Park, California.

Senator FULBRIGHT. These men are not in the employ of the Pentagon. They didn't have research contracts.

Dr. FOSTER. I don't know, Senator Fulbright, the degree to which Professor O'Neill has contracts from the Government, or Professor Drell or Professor Goldberger. But I understand that, as a result of section 203, Professor Goldberger lost his support from the Pentagon.

Senator FULBRIGHT. I want to talk about section 203 in a moment.
Senator CASE. Will the Senator yield just for a moment, please?
Senator FULBRIGHT. Yes.
Senator CASE. May I suggest we ask Dr. Foster to provide it later.
Senator FULBRIGHT. I would like it now. By the time it comes we will have long since passed on to something else.

MEETING OF AD HOC COMMITTEE ON SAFEGUARD

How long ago was this meeting.?
Dr. FOSTER. This was before the Secretary's decision.
Senator FULBRIGHT. Was it 6 months ago or a month or how long?
Dr. FOSTER. I believe it was in December.

Senator FULBRIGHT. How long did they meet?
Dr. FOSTER. For about a week.
Senator FULBRIGHT. Here in Washington?
Dr. FOSTER. Yes, sir.
Senator FULBRIGHT. In December.
You can supply them, but that will be long after the fact.
Senator CASE. No, I say would the Senator consent to an insertion of the report itself in the record.
Senator FULBRIGHT. That will be long after the impact of the hearing. It has happened before.
Senator CASE. Not before we vote on the ABM.
Senator FULBRIGHT. I think we will get it next fall.
Senator CASE. This is a matter we could follow up.
Senator FULBRIGHT. This matter came to the floor and I asked the chairman of the Armed Services Committee if in their deliberations they had ever invited any outside scientists to testify. He said no, he couldn't think of one. In other words this is just an in-house operation primarily and usually anyone outside the group is not consulted.
Dr. FOSTER. Senator Fulbright, I beg to differ with you on this. I went out of my way to select people who I believed were knowledgeable and, in fact, some of whom had formed opinions counter to that of the Department of Defense. And I asked them to serve. The only thing I asked them was to disregard their political feelings about the matter and to stick closely to the technical matters involved in which I personally believed they had great professional competence.

POLITICAL ASPECTS OF SALT

Senator FULBRIGHT. Are you suggesting that, in considering what kind of agreements they might come to at the SALT talks in Vienna, that political matters and relations between countries have no significance? Is this strictly and solely a technical conference?
Dr. FOSTER. Absolutely not, Senator Fulbright.
Senator FULBRIGHT. Of course not.
Dr. FOSTER. Political aspects, in fact, are dominant.
Senator FULBRIGHT. I think they are too.
How you can say that Safeguard and MIRV have no effect on SALT is beyond my comprehension. The political agency, the Senate, expressed very overwhelmingly its support of the Cooper-Brooke resolution which advised the Department and the Government not to proceed with the deployment of these. Of course, this has been ignored completely. Apparently no one has paid any attention to them at all. These are political judgments.
Dr. FOSTER. Excuse me, Senator Fulbright, with regard to this ad hoc group that I brought together, I was referring to the inclusion of technical people on both sides of the argument in an effort to review in advance the range of possible decisions that the Department of Defense might make with regard to Safeguard. It had nothing to do with SALT.

CHANGES IN WEAPONS SYSTEMS AND THEIR JUSTIFICATION

Senator FULBRIGHT. Mr. Foster, even on the technical side, the way that the Department of Defense has vacillated between the Sentinel and the Safeguard and the justification being the Chinese and then someone else, together with this well-known record on many other weapons systems, really doesn't lend a great deal of weight to the judgment of the Pentagon standing alone.

It seems to me in view of this record you should have some substantial outside confirmation of your judgment, on the technical and certainly on the political aspects of it.

Dr. FOSTER. Mr. Chairman, I beg to differ with you on this matter of vacillation. I have been with the program as long as it has existed, and it is my opinion that we have not vacillated. The changes have really been in the threat itself. Initially, when Secretary McNamara made his decision, he said that he was deploying the Sentinel system at that time to protect against the Chinese threat with an option to protect Minuteman should the SS-9 threat grow, and to protect against accidental launches from any source.

It subsequently happened that the Chinese threat was delayed, the Soviet SS-9's continued to increase despite intelligence predictions to the contrary, and the threat of the Soviet Y-class submarine continued to develop.

As a consequence of these developments, the Administration decided to deploy the Safeguard system, moving it away from the cities to make sure that the Soviets would understand that we were not trying to deny them a deterrent against the United States. And we placed our first sites at the Minuteman fields because the threat from the Soviet SS-9 had grown faster than that from the Chinese.

Senator FULBRIGHT. I don't want to renew the argument about the SS-9. We had testimony before that we considered and had, and deployed this type of missile and decided it as an inefficient way to use nuclear power, and abandoned it.

Dr. FOSTER. Sir, there was a difference in objectives.

Senator FULBRIGHT. I understand that.

Dr. FOSTER. The United States did not have as its objective the ability to knock out all of the Soviet military forces. If that kind of an objective had been made a matter of policy, we would have had a different force configuration.

SOVIET OFFER TO ABOLISH ABM'S

Senator FULBRIGHT. Mr. Foster, it was reported in one of the papers very recently that the Soviets have offered, or at least have discussed and tentatively offered, to abolish all ABM's and that the United States has declined and is insisting that we have at least one. To your knowledge, is that an accurate report?

Dr. FOSTER. Senator Fulbright, I can neither confirm nor deny any details associated with the SALT discussions at Vienna. I am very sorry. I think it is really in the interest of both countries, as I said earlier in the statement, that we decline any comment regarding those negotiations. I think we should give our negotiators every possible chance to come out with an early and equitable settlement.

Senator FULBRIGHT. I hope that report is not true.

EFFORT TO REPEAL SECTION 203 OF DEFENSE PROCUREMENT AUTHORIZATION ACT

If you don't wish to discuss it, I would like to ask you about section 203 which was put in last year's Defense Procurement Authorization Act and which requires that all defense research have a direct and apparent relationship to a specific military function or operation.

That was carried in the bill. On March 20 Secretary Laird began the effort to repeal section 203. Is that not correct? I will read you an article from Science Magazine of March 20. Secretary Laird was quoted as saying at the annual government-industry dinner of the Electronic Industries Association:

We are working with your industry in this area not only as far as industry-related research is concerned, but particularly as far as our colleges and universities are concerned, to repeal section 203.

Do you think it is a proper attitude for the Department of Defense to undertake to repeal section 203?

Dr. FOSTER. Senator Fulbright, I have done everything I could, the Secretary has done everything he could, and I believe the departments are doing everything they can, to implement section 203. It is the law; we are complying with it and will continue to do so.

Now, I have been very frank in discussing section 203 in each of the committee sessions at which I have had an opportunity to appear. First of all, I believe that section 203 has resulted in some benefits. It forced the Department of Defense, from the top down to the very bottom, to make an exhaustive review of every single contract that we had from the point of view of its relevance, as required by section 203.

Now, there were approximately 5,632 contracts with universities to look at, and almost 15,000 contracts altogether, so there was a lot of work.

Also there were some very difficult matters of judgment in trying to decide, "Is this really directly and apparently related?" And that ended with many difficult decisions and differences of opinion. But the important thing was that we did make a thorough review of several thousand programs, and I honestly think that was beneficial.

Senator FULBRIGHT. That isn't responsive to my question.

Dr. FOSTER. Well, sir——

Senator FULBRIGHT. I will put the whole article in the record. This is from the 20th of March Science magazine and describes the effort to repeal section 203. Is that a fact or not? Can you say yes or no that his policy is to repeal section 203?

Dr. FOSTER. Mr. Senator, you interrupted me just at that point.

Senator FULBRIGHT. You are rambling off on irrelevant answers.

Dr. FOSTER. No, sir.

Senator FULBRIGHT. We will get on if you will answer the question. Yes, or no?

Dr. FOSTER. I do not agree——

Senator FULBRIGHT. With what?

Dr. FOSTER. With the inclusion of section 203 in the fiscal year 1971 congressional action.

Senator FULBRIGHT. Then you are behind its repeal.

Dr. FOSTER. Yes, sir; I am.

Senator FULBRIGHT. You are undertaking to ignore it; you prefer to repeal it. That is all I wanted you to answer.

(The article referred to follows.)

[From Science Magazine, Mar. 20, 1970]

LAIRD SEEKS INDUSTRY AID TO DEFEAT MANSFIELD AMENDMENT

When Senate Majority Leader Mike Mansfield (D–Mont.) set out last year to restrict Pentagon-funded research, his amendment (Section 203) to the annual military authorization bill went almost unnoticed (*Science*, 14 November 1969).

Recently, however, concern about the effect of the amendment on academic institutions and other agencies of government has reached a high pitch, despite assurances from Pentagon officials that the monetary impact will be slight in the current fiscal year.

Last week Defense Secretary Melvin R. Laird announced that he actively opposes congressional attempts to impose restraints on research and development paid for by the Pentagon, and sought support from defense industries for an effort to repeal Section 203.

The Mansfield amendment requires the Pentagon to certify that research has "a direct and apparent relationship to a specific military function or operation."

Estimates of the impact of the amendment vary. Mansfield himself has indicated that all basic and applied research conducted for the Pentagon should be re-examined and, if necessary, terminated or transferred in an orderly fashion to the National Science Foundation or a more appropriate mission agency, such as the National Institutes of Health. Two weeks ago Representative Emilio Q. Daddario (D-Conn.), chairman of the House Subcommittee on Science, Research and Development, suggested that the Pentagon will cancel some $50 million in research because of the amendment. Daddario also expressed concern that other mission agencies might adopt similar policies (*Science*, 13 March).

But officials of the Office of Defense Research and Engineering last week said their rough, preliminary figures show that only about $8 million to $10 million worth of current basic research (out of a budget of $368.5 million) fails to meet the new criterion of military relevance. The officials privately guess that another $5 million to $10 million of applied research may also fail to pass the new test when the screening process is completed next month.

Although defense research officials have decided to administer the Mansfield amendment in ways that will minimize its disruptive effect on their programs, Laird chose to stress the maximum potential effect of the law in a speech on 11 March. He spoke at the annual government-industry dinner of the Electronic Industries Association (EIA), to an audience that included representatives of nearly half of the top 50 defense contractors. The Mansfield amendment, he said, "makes it impossible for us to continue the important program of basic research that the Defense Department must support in order for us to compete with the Soviet Union in the advances that they are making in the scientific and technological fields."

In a digression from the prepared text of the speech, Laird invited industry and the universities to help him defeat congressional efforts to restrict military research. "We are working with your industry in this area not only as far as industry-related research is concerned," he said (a reference to proposals to restrict "independent research and development"), "but particularly as far as our colleges and universities are concerned, to repeal Section 203." Laird said the relevance standard set by the Mansfield amendment "cannot be certified by me as Secretary of Defense as required by the United States Congress because in the basic research area we cannot tell as basic research starts out that it will have an overriding military significance."

In the prepared text, Laird merely expressed concern that the relevance requirement of Section 203 might "tend to discourage talented scientists from potentially productive research areas."

"We are complying with that requirement," he added.

Officials of the Electronic Industries Association were a little puzzled by Laird's appreciation of their efforts to defeat the Mansfield amendment, since they were not aware of having paid any attention to the matter. But, one official concluded, Laird "was telling us why we ought to become concerned" about Section 203, "and I quess we will."

A quick check last week also failed to disclose any signs of highly organized university opposition to the Mansfield amendment. But Pentagon officials and a number of congressional offices report frequent contacts with university officials who want to know what effect it will have on their budgets. Now it should soon become clear how far Mansfield and his supporters will be able to push their efforts to curb military influence by changing the pattern of federal science support.

In his address to the EIA, Laird opposed another legislative proposal which, like the Mansfield amendment, seeks to curb Pentagon support of research and development. The bill, sponsored by Senator William Proxmire (D-Wis.), would place tight restrictions on Pentagon payments to defense contractors for "independent research and development" (IR & D).

At present, about half of the annual $1.5 billion in research and development work initiated by defense contractors (IR & D) is allowed as an overhead cost on defense and space agency contracts. The principal beneficiaries of these payments, which totaled over $800 million in fiscal 1969, are the major defense industries, and they are up in arms against the bill. According to Proxmire, the Pentagon now permits wide latitude in the definition of allowable IR & D costs and makes no effort to control the growth of IR & D claims. Proxmire's staff claims to have evidence that companies have collected payments for work done to develop commercial applications of products produced under Pentagon contracts. The bill would apply the rule that now governs Atomic Energy Commission contracts to the Pentagon and to the National Aeronautics and Space Administration. The rule holds that the independent R & D costs may be covered by the government only if they are for work directly or indirectly of benefit to the purpose of the contract. "While I understand the concern of the Congress," Laird said, "I believe such restrictions would unnecessarily stifle new and imaginative efforts. The results would be to reduce the technological effectiveness of our defense-related industries."—ANDREW HAMILTON

DEFENSE DEPARTMENT RESEARCH PROJECTS

Senator FULBRIGHT. We will come to some of these specific research projects. You say there are 5,632 contracts. How much money is involved in those contracts?

Dr. FOSTER. I think I can find that for you, sir.

Senator FULBRIGHT. Don't you know? It is a very substantial amount. Is it not?

Dr. FOSTER. Yes, sir, it certainly is. Contracts with universities in the relatively basic research area amount to about $230 million.

Senator FULBRIGHT. Is that in the United States only or is it worldwide?

Dr. FOSTER. In the United States, sir.

Senator FULBRIGHT. What is the total of this worldwide?

Dr. FOSTER. The worldwide or foreign research figure is much smaller, just a few million dollars.

Senator FULBRIGHT. I understand, but this is taxpaying time.

Dr. FOSTER. Three million dollars is being requested in fiscal year 1971. It was $3.1 million in fiscal year 1970.

CLASSIFIED DOD LIST OF SOCIAL AND BEHAVIORAL RESEARCH PROJECTS

Senator FULBRIGHT. Last year the Department of Defense list of social and behavioral research projects given to the Congress to justify its request was unclassified except for a few projects involving policy matters.

In reply to my request for a listing of current and proposed social and behavioral science projects you sent me on April 25 a list on which every project is classified. I wonder if you would explain why that is so. I have the list here if you would like to look at it.

Dr. FOSTER. I would like to look at it, Mr. Chairman.

Senator FULBRIGHT. I didn't mean to delay it that much. I didn't think you would take that seriously. If you wish, you can see how bulky it is. I guess there are several pages, maybe 50 or 75 or a hundred, marked "Confidential." Aren't you familiar with that?

Dr. FOSTER. Yes, I certainly am, sir.

Senator FULBRIGHT. It was furnished to us by the Department.

Dr. FOSTER. I believe, sir, the reason for making that confidential—and I would support that classification—maybe because there are a few studies in the list that are considered classified, not so much their subject matter as their relationship to foreign countries. I would be pleased to go over the list, single out any I find in that category, and declassify the remainder, if you wish.

Senator FULBRIGHT. You don't think the purpose is simply to keep this knowledge from the Congress and the American public.
Dr. FOSTER. Absolutely not, sir.
Senator FULBRIGHT. You think it was intended to keep it from foreigners.
Dr. FOSTER. I think it was intended to avoid the embarrassment of the United States, sir.
Senator FULBRIGHT. I do too and particularly of the Defense Department on the floor of the Senate. [Laughter.]
Dr. FOSTER. No sir; I just disagree with you that there was such an intention. I think you are being misleading. I don't believe your accusation.

CLASSIFICATION OF GAO REPORT BY DEPARTMENT OF STATE

Senator FULBRIGHT. This isn't the first time the Pentagon or the State Department has done this. Anything that is the least bit embarrassing to them is classified. They are now beginning to refuse to allow the General Accounting Office to examine their accounts. I guess you are familiar with that?
Dr. FOSTER. No, sir; I am not.
Senator FULBRIGHT. I wouldn't like to take the time now, but that is a fact. The Department of State insisted that the GAO report to the Symington subcommittee be classified because it would embarrass the Department as to where the money went in the Philippines. They insisted it be classified. The report included statements that they refused the GAO the records. The extent of this is absolutely unbelievable as to the attitude of the executive branch toward the Congress and toward the GAO.
I have never heard of it before. I think it is strictly contrary to the basic law authorizing the GAO.

DEFENSE DEPARTMENT RESEARCH PROJECTS

Coming back to this list, I don't think it reveals anything that would embarrass you in the sense of security, only as to your judgment. You have such titles as this one: "What causes Navy men to like or dislike their work?" This is a very substantial research project. Do you think it has any relevance to the mission?
Dr. FOSTER. Yes.
Senator FULBRIGHT. What is it?
Dr. FOSTER. Yes, Senator Fulbright, I certainly do.
Let me tell you what the problem is.
Senator FULBRIGHT. What is it?
Dr. FOSTER. The problem is that Navy ships must be at sea for long periods. And this means the men are away from their families. The question concerns whether or not they care enough about national security and serving in the Navy that they are willing to stay away from their families for months and months on end. Let me just say——
Senator FULBRIGHT. Do you mean you had to have a research project to find that out? [Laughter.]
Dr. FOSTER. No, let me explain. On the average, an officer in his early years spends about 85 percent of his time at sea each year. Now that is a long time to ask a married man to stay away from his family, so questions of what motivates him in his work and what

doesn't motivate him are extremely important—and you are not going to find the answers just by asking peoples' opinion. Someone has to dig into it, get the facts, and see what we can do to increase the motivation of these Navy men. I think that is quite a reasonable, legitimate and, I think, apparent reason why such research should be conducted.

Senator FULBRIGHT. The trouble is, I think, that you in the Pentagon live so far removed from the ordinary life of the country that you don't realize that most of these are already common knowledge to most people. So many of these answers are perfectly obvious, it seems to me.

Some of the projects that you list look very childish but, above all, I don't understand why this type of thing has to be classified. If you think it has any merit, why do you want to classify it? What in fact you are saying is that it is illegal for us to discuss these things in this meeting or on the floor of the Senate. This is incredible to me.

Dr. FOSTER. Mr. Chairman, I would be pleased, if you wish, by this afternoon to come back with a list of those projects that are unclassified and available for your use anywhere, deleting only those that are of concern.

Senator FULBRIGHT. Of course we would like it. When I asked you for it in my letter, I certainly didn't ask you to classify it. I never anticipated you would. Last year it was not classified and this year you did classify it. I think it is obvious that you did it because of the inquiry that we mounted about it last year. It was the first time we seriously questioned this proliferation of 5,600 contracts. It seems absolutely outrageous that you feel you have to have research projects on that many different subjects. I may say these are all very substantial amounts of money, and that doesn't seem to impress the Pentagon. I cannot understand why you would classify it.

Dr. FOSTER. Well, Mr. Chairman, I will look into this immediately, as soon as I get back to my office.

Senator FULBRIGHT. Why didn't you look into it when you sent us the list? You waited until today. We wanted this list for purposes of examination.

Dr. FOSTER. May I ask, Senator Fulbright, when the list was received?

Senator FULBRIGHT. April, I told you.

Dr. FOSTER. Well, Mr. Chairman, if it caused you any trouble, I am awfully sorry you didn't let me know about it before now. I would have been glad to take care of it sooner.

Senator FULBRIGHT. I wrote you a letter asking about the list and you classified it. The list not having been classified before, I didn't think that it would even arise, that you would this year classify these types of programs.

(The information referred to follows.)

BEHAVIORAL SCIENCE WORK UNITS FISCAL YEAR 1970 AND 1971

The attached is a listing of behavioral science work units funded in FY 70 and projected for funding in FY 71. Those work units planned for FY 71 funding are indicated by an "X" in the FY 71 column. Planned FY 71 work unit funding has been deleted to declassify this document. Public release of *planning* figures identified to specific work units coupled with the listing of *all* work units in one area identifies subjects of potential emphasis and de-emphasis and is prejudicial to (1) contract negotiations contemplated or in progress and (2) long and short range plans to support work in given areas as required.

U. S. ARMY

6.1 Basic Research

Performer	Title	(Costs ($)) FY 70	FY 71
AIR/CRESS	Improving Communication Through the Associative Group Analysis Technique	65,000	--
AIR/CRESS	Communication Data on Korean Audiences	90,000	X
AIR/CRESS	A Social and Behavioral Science Information System Relevant to U. S. Army Overseas Activities (Formerly Applicability of Social and Behavioral Science Research to U. S. Army Activities in the Developing Countries)	105,000	X
AIR/CRESS	Intercultural Communications	165,000	X
AIR/CRESS	Strategic and Tactical Factors Underlying Internal Defense and Development	130,000	X
AIR/CRESS	Criteria - Military Assistance Program	--	X
HumRRO	Factors in Military Organizational Effectiveness (FORGE)	96,000	X
HumRRO	Development of Efficient Training for Soldiers of all Aptitude Levels (SPECTRUM)	159,000	X
HumRRO	Improving Ability to See Military Targets (BR-16)	63,000	X
HumRRO	Improving Race Relations in the Army (BR-20)	--	X
BESRL	Study of Response Systems in Enhancing Human Performance	25,000	--

U. S. ARMY

6.1 Basic Research

Performer	Title	(Costs ($)) FY 70	FY 71
BESRL	Optimization Models for Decision Making in the Manpower/Personnel Management Systems	50,000	--
BESRL	Characteristics of Image Interpretation Performance Measures	25,000	--
BESRL	Basic Research in Behavioral/Psychological Sciences	--	X
HEL	Human Sensory Processes in Military Operational Environments	32,000	X
HEL	Physiological Aspects of Emotions of Military Personnel	76,000	X
HEL	Endocrine Response to Stress	58,000	X
HEL	Keeping Track of Sequential Events	89,000	X
HEL	Relationship of Hearing Change to Acoustic Inputs	72,000	X
NATICK	Taste - Chemical Sense	70,000	X
NATICK	Regulatory Mechanism in Intake	70,000	X
	Total	1,499,000	

U. S. Army

6.2 Exploratory Development

Performer	Title	Costs ($) FY 70	FY 71
AIR/CRESS	ROKA Civic Action in Korea	45,000	X
AIR/CRESS	Criteria for Selection and Assessment of Military Civic Action Programs	85,000	X
AIR/CRESS	Improving Relations Between Military Units and Local Communities	40,000	--
AIR/CRESS	A Systematic Framework for Psychological Operations	115,000	X
AIR/CRESS	Development of Critical Target Analysis Information for US Strategic Psychological Operations	60,500	--
AIR/CRESS	Cultural Information Analysis Center (CINFAC)	300,000	X
AIR/CRESS	Characteristics of Selected Societies Relevant to U.S. Military Interests (U)	60,000	X
AIR/CRESS	Village Reconstruction Program on The Republic of Korea (DMZ (U)	90,000	X
AIR/CRESS	Roles and Mission of Military Police in Internal Defense and Internal Development	15,000	X
AIR/IRI	Research on Troop-Community Relations - Korea	182,000	X
AIR/IRI	Research on Troop-Community Relations - Thailand	114,000	X

U. S. ARMY

6.2 Exploratory Development

Performer	Title	(Costs ($)) FY 70	FY 71
HumRRO	Study of Soldiers in Lower Mental Categories: Job Performance and the Identification of Potentially Successful and Potentially Unsuccessful Men (UTILITY)	67,000	--
HumRRO	Training Strategies and Incentive Appropriate to Different Aptitude Levels for Selected Army Training (APSTRAT)	167,000	x
HumRRO	Determination of Reading, Listening and Arithmetic Skills Required for Major Military Occupational Specialties (REALISTIC)	119,000	--
HumRRO	Development of Improved Army Typing Training Program and Materials (TYPETRAIN)	80,000	x
HumRRO	Knowledges, Skills, and Thought Processes of the Battalion Commander and Primary Staff (CAMBCOM)	67,000	x
HumRRO	Small Group Instructional Methods for Military Training (INGROUP)	23,000	x
HumRRO	Combat Marksmanship (MARKSMAN)	88,000	x
HumRRO	Systems Engineering of Leadership Training for Officer Candidate Programs (OC LEADER)	23,000	
HumRRO	Training Methods for Forward Area Air Defense Weapons (SKYFIRE)	32,000	x
HumRRO	Aircraft Recognition Training (STAR)	58,000	--
HumRRO	Determination of Performance Capabilities and Training Requirements for Manual Command and Control Functions of Automated Air Defense Systems (MANICON)	88,000	x

U. S. Army

6.2 Exploratory Development

Performer	Title	(Costs ($)) FY 70	FY 71
Rowland & Co.	Experimental Training Methods in Republic of Korea Modernization Program	66,000	X
HRB-Singer Inc.	Evaluation of Psychological Operations in the Republic of Korea	102,500	X
In-House	In-House Social Science Research Laboratory	--	X
Undetermined	American Soldier in the 70's	--	X
HumRRO	Debriefing MAAG Advisors (DEBRIEF)	50,000	X
HumRRO	Foreign Language Training (AUTOSPAN)	50,000	X
HumRRO	Overseas Training Methods (COPE)	100,000	X
HumRRO	Local National Employees (EDGE)	110,000	X
HumRRO	Development of Training Management Procedures for Different Ability Groups (STOCK)	106,000	X
HumRRO	Analysis of Army Experience in Implementing a Mechanized Stock Accounting System (ACCOUNT)	62,000	X
HumRRO	Improved on-the-job Training for Logistics Personnel (JOBGOAL)	110,000	X
HumRRO	Training Techniques for New Night Vision Devices (NIGHTSIGHTS)	110,000	X
HumRRO	Tank Crew Performance During Periods of Extended Combat (ENDURE)	45,000	X
HumRRO	Training Guidelines for the US/FRG Main Battle Tank (MBT)	45,000	X

U.S. Army

6.2 Exploratory Development

Performer	Title	(Costs ($)) FY 70	FY 71
HumRRO	Improving Aviation Maintenance Training Through Task and Instructional Analysis (UPGRADE)	119,000	X
HumRRO	Human Information Processing Requirements in Manned Aerial Reconnaissance and Surveillance Tasks (MANPROBE)	36,000	X
HumRRO	Predicting Aviator Success in Training and Operational Assignments (PREDICT)	110,000	X
HumRRO	Modernization of Synthetic Training in Army Aviation (SYNTRAIN)	162,000	X
HumRRO	Supervisory and Managerial Skills Among Senior Enlisted Men from Different AFQT Levels (APTLEAD)	--	X
HumRRO	Curriculum and Instructional Improvements for the Air Defense Artillery Officer Advanced Course (SKYGUARD)	--	X
HumRRO	Training Requirements and Concepts for Air Cavalry Training (AIRSCOUT)	--	X
HumRRO	Characteristics of Men Tested in Work Unit UTILITY who remain in the Army (FOLLOWTHRU)	--	X
HumRRO	Development of Automated Programs to Improve Listening Skills Required in Army Jobs (LISTEN)	--	X
HumRRO	Methodology for Evaluating Reading Requirements of Army Jobs (READNEED)	--	X
HumRRO	Soldier Esprit (ER-74)	87,000	X
HumRRO	Methodology for Training Systems Engineering (ER-75)	44,000	X
HumRRO	Air Defense Officer Career Course (ER-77)	53,000	--

U. S. Army

6.2. Exploratory Development

Performer	Title	Costs ($) FY 70	FY 71
HumRRO	Reducing Errors in Logistics ADP (ER-79)	45,000	--
HumRRO	Methods and Media for Army Training (ER-80)	--	X
HumRRO	Training USASA Operators (ER-81)	--	X
HumRRO	Low-Cost Simulation in Military Training (ER-82)	--	X
HumRRO	GED Program for the Army (ER-83)	--	X
HumRRO	Retention of Army Flying Skills (ER-84)	--	X
HumRRO	Army Flight Skill Learning Curves (ER-85)	--	X
HumRRO	Technical Advisory Services	127,000	X
HEL	HFE Information Retrieval, Analysis and Design Guide Development	80,000	X
HEL	Human Error in Artillery Fire	110,000	X
HEL	Aircraft Handling Qualities and Control	80,000	X
HEL	Pistol Effectiveness Studies	60,000	X
HEL	Stress and Weapons Design	60,000	X
HEL	Human Factors Engineering in Support of Missiles, Communication and Engineer Equipment	130,000	X
HEL	Aircraft Station Equipment	70,000	X

U. S. ARMY
6.2. Exploratory Development

Performer	Title	Costs ($) FY 70	FY 71
HEL	General Human Factors Support for Weapon Systems	60,000	X
HEL	Aircrew Station Display and Information Processing	70,000	X
HEL	Human Factors Concept and Standards Development for Aviation Materiel	28,000	X
HEL	Auditory Threshold Changes as a Function of Weapon Noise Exposure	40,000	X
NATICK	Materials Research	50,000	X
NATICK	Cold and Tropic Environment	50,000	X
NATICK	Headgear and Head Protection	2,000	X
NATICK	Anthropometry	30,000	X
NATICK	Food Acceptance Testing	50,000	X
NATICK	Food Acceptance Methodology	60,000	X
NATICK	Control of Appetite in Man	50,000	X
BESRL	Interface Between Civilian and Army Enlisted Manpower Systems	108,000	X
BESRL	Classification of Army Enlisted Manpower	135,000	X
BESRL	Optimum Distribution of Abilities for Individual and Army Unit Effectiveness	108,000	X
BESRL	Prediction of Army Officer Performance and Retention	135,000	--
BESRL	Officer Performance Evaluation Systems	108,000	--

U. S. ARMY
6.2 Exploratory Development

Performer	Title	(Costs ($)) FY 70	FY 71
BESRL	Techniques for Use in Primary Army Officer Selection and Evaluation Programs	54,000	--
BESRL	Performance in Combat and Overseas Service	54,000	--
BESRL	Primary Officer Leadership Selection and Development	--	X
BESRL	Officer Assessment for Career Development	--	X
BESRL	Officer Performance Evaluation Systems	--	X
BESRL	Dependable Performance in Army Monitor Jobs	135,000	X
BESRL	Human Performance Experimentation in Army Tactical Night Operations	108,000	X
BESRL	Night Vision Data Acquisition System	12,000	X
BESRL	Dependable Performance in Army Tactical Controller Jobs	162,000	X
BESRL	Command Information Processing Systems	162,000	X
BESRL	Experimentation with TOS-MASSTER	--	X
BESRL	Tactical Scenarios and Simulated TOS	--	X
In-house	In-house Army Program of Research to Improve Military Training of Individuals and Chiefs	--	X
	Total	5,905,000	

U. S. ARMY
6.2 Exploratory Development

Performer	Title	(Costs ($)) FY 70	FY 71
Alfred Buck, M.D. Johns Hopkins University	Comprehensive Epidemiologic Studies in Developing Countries	88,332*	

*This amount not included in overall total for 6.2

U.S. ARMY

6.3 Advanced Development

Performer	Title	(Costs $) FY 70	FY 71
Human Resources Rsch Organization	Prototype of Computerized Training for Army Personnel (IMPACT)	630,000	X
To be determined	Prototype '70 Study (Vietnamese)	70,000	--
To be determined	Arabic Common Core Materials	70,000	
To be determined	Priority Two Test Series	210,000	
To be determined	Vietnamese Tactical/Modular Terminal Course	145,000	
To be determined	MAC Prototype		X
To be determined	Thai Tactical/Modular Terminal Course		X
To be determined	Russian Programmed Homework		X
To be determined	Laboratory Concept and Materials		X
To be determined	Vietnamese Maintenance Prototype		X
To be determined	Russian Maintenance Series		X
	Total	1,125,000	

U. S. ARMY

6.5 RDT&E, Management and Support

Performer	Title	Costs ($) FY 70	FY 71
RAC	Strategic Analysis of North Africa Middle East and South Asia (U)	139,000	X
RAC	Strategic Analysis of Europe (U)	83,700	--
RAC	Asia Defensive Postures (U)	96,800	--
RAC	Strategic Analysis of Northeast Asia (FOUO)	24,100	--
RAC	Japan's Defense Policy and the U.S. Military Role in Asia (U)	--	X
RAC	Communications Role in the Military Assistance Program and Contingency Planning for Stability Operations (U)	69,300	--
SRI	US, USSR, CPR Strategic Interactions and Response Patterns (U)	325,100	X
SRI	Strategic Forces Posture Applied Research (U)	258,200	X
RAC	Factors Influencing the Interaction of Communist Dominated Countries in East Asia (U)	--	X
RAC	Force Interface Study (U)	93,700	--
RAC	Political Implications of the Swing Strategy (POLISWING) (U)	--	X

U. S. NAVY

6.1 Basic Research

Performer	Title	FY 70 (Costs $)	FY 71
Columbia Univ.	Personnel Technology: Interpretation of Information Displayed on Sonar and Radar Equipments	31,000	X
Syracuse Univ.	Communications: Interpretation of Sound Signals by Navy Radio and Sonar Operators	19,000	X
U. of Denver	Personnel Technology: Factors Affecting Discrimination of Moving Compex Visual Stimuli in Radar-Like Tasks	0	X
Stanford Univ.	Communications: Fundamental Information to Guide the Design of Navy Auditory Displays	37,000	X
Brown Univ.	Personnel Technology: The Processing of Visual Information by Navy Weapons-Systems Operators	15,000	X
Cornell Univ.	Personnel Technology: Visual Problems of Personnel In Navy Vehicle Operations	20,000	X
Johns Hopkins Univ.	Personnel Technology: Investigate the Ways Human Process Information in Order to Improve Target Identification	27,000	X
Univ. of Texas	Personnel Technology: Limits of Binaural Interaction in Sonar-Like Tasks	0	X
Dunlap and Assoc.	Personnel Technology: Factors Which Contribute to Successful Carrier Landings	35,000	X
Control Image Corp.	Personnel Technology: Evaluation of an Experimental, Animated, Real-Time Sonar Display	27,000	X

U.S. Navy

Performer	6.1 Basic Research Title	(Costs ($)) FY 70	FY 71
Harvard Univ.	Personnel Technology: Advantages of Presenting "Texture" to Aid Visual Detection and Identification	23,000	X
Columbia Univ.	Personnel Technology: Target Characteristics Which Influence the Interpretation of Visually-Displayed Signals	26,000	X
Stanford Res. Inst.	Personnel Technology: New Principles for the Design of Man/Machine Control Systems	100,000	X
BioTechnology, Inc.	Personnel Technology: Analysis of Pilot Activity and Med-Evac Procedures in South East Asia	14,000	X
Ohio State Univ.	Communications: Intelligibility Factors in Naval Communications	20,000	X
Human Factors Res.	Personnel Technology: Overcoming Negative Attitudes Toward New Navy Equipment	13,000	X
Amer. Inst. for Research	Navy Vehicle Design: Human Engineering Guide to Equipment Design	0	X
General Electric Co.	Navy Vehicle Design and Construction: Machine Augmentation of Human Strength and Endurance	133,000	X
Dunlap and Assoc.	Personnel Technology: Measurement of Man-Machine Performance in Complex Navy Systems via Adaptive Techniques	32,000	X
Human Factors Res.	Surveillance: Methods for Enhancing the Detection and Classification of Sonar Signals	50,000	X
Life Sciences, Inc.	Navy Vehicle Design and Construction: Methodology for Human Factors Evaluation of Naval Aircraft and Systems	41,000	X

U.S. Navy

6.1 Basic Research

Performer	Title	(Costs ($)) FY 70	FY 71
Martin Marietta	Surveillance: Operator Performance in Air to Surface Target Acquisition as a Function of Viewing Conditions and Target Characteristics	40,000	X
Univ. of Illinois	Personnel Technology: Performance of Navy Pilots as a Function of Dynamic Movement Relationship in Attitude-Director Flight Displays	20,000	X
Human Factors Res.	Surveillance: Sonar and Radar Operator Performance in Target Detection and Tracking as a Function of Display Characteristics	30,000	X
	New work on men in weapons systems in response to unsolicited proposals		X
Princeton Univ.	Communications: Identify the Complex Characteristics of the Ear's Response to Sound to Aid in Design of Military Communications Systems	26,000	X
Univ. of Rochester	Personnel Technology: The Effects of Navy Hazardous Environments Upon Visual Tasks	25,000	X
Univ. of Texas Med. Branch	Personnel Technology: Performance Variability and Naval Personnel Effectiveness	30,000	X
Institute of Medical Sciences	Personnel Technology: Limits of Dynamic Visual Acuity in Critical Navy Tasks	16,000	X
Institute for Research	Personnel Technology: Drug Enhancement of Performance of Naval Personnel Under Stress	22,000	X
Harvard Univ.	Personnel Technology: Factors Which Enable Naval Personnel to Remain Alert	17,000	X

U.S. Navy

6.1 Basic Research

Performer	Title	FY 70 (Costs ($))	FY 71
Univ. of Illinois	Personnel Technology: Increasing the Precision with which Military Abilities are Measured	29,000	X
Univ. of Washington	Personnel Technology: Improvement of the Navy's Personnel-Management Decisions	43,000	X
Univ. of Rochester	Personnel Technology: Techniques for Encouraging Naval Personnel to Reenlist	61,000	X
Univ. of Calif (Irvine)	Personnel Technology: What Causes Navy Men to Like (or Dislike) their Work	65,000	X
Colorado State Univ.	Personnel Technology: Importance of Job Factors in Retention of Navy Personnel	20,000	X
Univ. of Minnesota	Personnel Technology: Improving the Career Motivation and Reenlistment Probability of Navy Men	178,000	X
Human Factors Res.	Personnel Technology: Techniques for Improving Proficiency of Sonarmen in Target Classification Aboard Submarines	101,000	X
Smithsonian Inst.	Personnel Technology: Scientific Consultation Services on Navy Personnel Research Problems	32,000	X
Univ. of Michigan	Personnel Technology: How to Introduce Needed Change in Navy Organizations	62,000	X
Univ. of Minnesota	Personnel Technology: How Navy Supervisors Deal with Problems	40,000	X
State University of New York/Albany	Personnel Technology: What Motivates the Effective Naval Leader	36,000	X

U.S. Navy

6.1 Basic Research

Performer	Title	(Costs ($)) FY 70	FY 71
Human Factors Res.	Personnel Technology: Determination of Body Chemistry Changes that Affect Target Detection Performance in Sonar Monitoring	45,000	X
Randomline, Inc.	Personnel Technology: The Effects of Ionized Air and Radio Energy Upon the Performance of Naval Personnel	21,000	X
Fort Custer State Home	Personnel Technology: Prediction of Inappropriate Aggressive Behavior of Members of Small Crews	30,000	X
Western Michigan Univ.	Personnel Technology: How to Prevent Unwanted Aggressive Behavior	35,000	X
American Institutes for Research	Personnel Technology: Analytical Method for Predicting Performance of Naval Personnel Under Varying Environmental Conditions	72,000	X
	New work on men under stress in response to unsolicited proposals		X
Univ. of Rochester	Personnel Technology: Improving the Effectiveness of Key Navy Personnel Through Management Training	50,000	X
Human Sciences Res.	Personnel Technology: Developing Combined Action Capabilities for Vietnam and Future Contingencies	91,000	X
Princeton Univ.	Personnel Technology: Techniques to Improve the Methods for Measuring Naval Personnel Performance	0	X
Educational Testing Service	Personnel Technology: Development of Techniques for Using Computers to Administer and Score Psychological Tests to Navy Applicants and Personnel	26,000	X

U.S. Navy

6.1 Basic Research

Performer	Title	FY 70	FY 71
Human Resources Res. Organization	Personnel Technology: Leadership Training for Future Naval Officers	0	X
Univ. of Florida	Personnel Technology: Intergroup Tensions in Military Units and Leadership Training	12,000	X
Univ. of Wisconsin	Personnel Technology: Identification of Factors which Improve Coordination among Complex Naval Organizations	13,000	X
	New work on men in personnel systems in response to unsolicited proposals		X
Univ. of Florida	Communications: Underwater Speech Communications	27,000	X
BioMarine Industries	Communications: Measures of Diver Performance Efficiency With and Without Speech Communication	47,000	X
Univ. of Texas	Navy Environment: Psychological Reactions During Saturation Dives	61,000	X
Whittenburg, Vaughan and Assoc., Inc.	Personnel Technology: Crew Performance in Swimmer Delivery Vehicle Operations	30,000	X
Man Factors, Inc.	Navy Environment: The Effects of the Underwater Environment Upon Work Efficiency on Navy Divers and Life Support Requirements	30,000	X
General Dynamics	Personnel Technology: Diver and Manipulator Operator Capabilities to Perform Undersea Tasks	21,000	X
Whittenburg, Vaughan and Assoc., Inc.	Navy Environment: The Influence of Environmental Factors on Diver Performance and the Design of Underwater Tools	30,000	X

U.S. Navy

6.1 Basic Research

Performer	Title	FY 70 (Costs ($))	FY 71
	New work on men in the sea in response to unsolicited proposals		X
New York Univ.	Personnel Technology: Limitations of Mental-Processing Speed of Tactical Information-Handling Personnel	35,000	X
Univ. of Pittsburgh	Personnel Technology: Instructional Strategies Tailored to the Needs of the Individual Navy Man	79,000	X
Florida State Univ.	Personnel Technology: Evaluating Recent Educational Technology for Navy Training	175,000	X
Bolt, Beranek and Newman, Inc.	Personnel Technology: Automated Monitoring of Instruction in Complex Operational Navy Skills	68,000	X
Univ. of So. Calif.	Personnel Technology: On-Line, Computer-Based Training of Naval Technicians	109,000	X
Stanford Univ.	Personnel Technology: A Computer-Based Approach to Navy Relevant, Foreign-Language Training	60,000	X
Northwestern Univ.	Personnel Technology: Defining the Conditions Which Control How Well Text Material is Learned and How Long it is Remembered	0	X
Univ. of Oregon	Personnel Technology: Increasing Cooperation Among Navy Crew Members	55,000	X
Stanford Univ.	Personnel Technology: Preventing Friction Among USMC Trainees	50,000	X
Univ. of Washington	Personnel Technology: An Investigation of Training Leading to Improved Adaptibility of Potential Navy Leaders	30,000	X
Purdue Univ.	Personnel Technology: Group Information Processing and Decision-Making in Complex Military Situations	0	X
	New work on men in training in response to unsolicited proposals		X

NAVY
6.2 Exploratory Development

Performer	Title	(Costs ($)) FY 70	FY 71
Navy Electronics Laboratory Center	Explosive Ordnance Disposal Influence Suppression Techniques Study	35,000	
Navy Electronics Laboratory Center	Ionizing radiation protection for Navy personnel at sea	235,000	X
Navy Personnel R&D Laboratory	Forecasting impact of new systems on personnel and training	128,000	X
Navy Personnel R&D Laboratory	Improving procedures for selection & procurement of Navy personnel	70,000	X
Navy Personnel R&D Laboratory	Navy personnel resources management	214,000	X
Navy Personnel R&D Laboratory	Man-machine system personnel and evaluation techniques	170,000	X
Navy Personnel and Training Res. Laboratory	Improved procedures for classifying and assigning Navy personnel	100,000	X
Navy Personnel and Training Res. Laboratory	Improving the career retention rate of Navy personnel	133,00	X
Navy Personnel and Training Res. Laboratory	Shipboard occupational analysis methodology	230,000	X
Navy Personnel and Training Res. Laboratory	Navy career structures	290,000	X
Navy Personnel and Training Res. Laboratory	Evaluating techniques for improving sonar operator training	85,000	X
Navy Personnel and Training Res. Laboratory	Methodology for developing/evaluating Navy training programs	410,000	X

NAVY
6.2 Exploratory Development

Performer	Title	(Costs ($)) FY 70	FY 71
Navy Personnel and Training Res. Laboratory	Exploring new technologies for designing Navy training courses	130,000	X
Navy Personnel and Training Res. Laboratory	Navy training management	100,000	X
Navy Electronics Laboratory Center	Swimmer/Diver Systems Analysis/Operations Research Studies		X
Navy Electronics Laboratory Center	Improvement on Man-machine interfaces in the Navy		X
Navy Electronics Laboratory Center	Optimizing Navy Man-machine Engineering design decisions		X

NAVY
6.3 Advanced Development

Performer	Title	(Costs ($)) FY 70	FY 71
Navy Personnel R&D Laboratory	Development of an Improved Navy-Wide System of Job Performance Standards	173,000	X
Naval Personnel & Training Res. Laboratory	Development of an Improved Navy-Wide System of Job Performance Standards	75,000	X
Naval Personnel R&D Laboratory	Manpower Requirements Prediction and Justification System	791,000	X
Mellonics Systems Division	Manpower Requirements Prediction and Justification System		
B-K Dynamics, Inc.	Manpower Requirements Prediction and Justification System		
Naval Personnel & Training Res. Laboratory	Manpower Requirements Prediction and Justification System	60,000	X
Naval Personnel R&D Laboratory	Computer Assisted Assignment and Distribution System - Matching of Manpower Requirements and Resources	86,000	X
Naval Personnel & Training Research Laboratory	Computer Assisted Assignment and Distribution System - Matching of Manpower Requirements and Resources	301,000	X
Naval Aerospace Medical Institute	Development of Improved Methods and Criteria for Predicting Success of Cadets in Training and in the Operating Forces	75,000	X
Naval Air Development Center	Aircrew Performance Criteria in Airborne Weapon Systems	115,000	X
Naval Air Development Center	Cockpit and Crew Station Performance	100,000	X
Serendipity, Inc.	Presentation of Information for Maintenance and Operation	100,000	

NAVY
6.3 Advanced Development

Performer	Title	(Costs ($)) FY 70	FY 71
Naval Ship Systems Command	Development of Human Reliability Prediction System	100,000	X
Naval Personnel & Training Research Laboratory	Application of Programmed Instruction, Television and Individualized Instruction to Navy Training	99,000	X
Westinghouse Learning Corp.	Application of Programmed Instruction, Television and Individualized Instruction to Navy Training		
Naval Personnel & Training Research Laboratory	Application of Computer Technology to Officer and Enlisted Education and Training	1,234,000	X
IBM, San Diego	Application of Computer Technology to Officer and Enlisted Education and Training		
U.S. Naval Academy	Application of Computer Technology to Officer and Enlisted Education and Training		
IBM, Data Processing Div.	Application of Computer Technology to Officer and Enlisted Education and Training		
Harvard University	Application of Computer Technology to Officer and Enlisted Education and Training		
Chief of Naval Air Technical Training	Application of Computer Technology to Officer and Enlisted education and Training		
Naval Personnel & Training Research Laboratory	Operationally Oriented Training	114,000	X
COMASWFORLANT	Operationally Oriented Training		
Naval Personnel & Training Research Laboratory	Development of Improved Navy-Wide Training System Integrating New Techniques	85,000	X

NAVY
6.3 Advanced Development

Performer	Title	(Costs ($)) FY 70	FY 71
Naval Personnel R&D Laboratory	Development of Improved Navy-Wide Training System Integrating New Techniques		
Navy Medical Res. Institute	Application of Systems Analysis to Improve Medical Training	709,000	X
Technomics, Inc.	Application of Systems Analysis to Improve Medical Training		
American Institutes for Research	Application of Systems Analysis to Improve Medical Training		
COMASWFORLANT	Development of Operational Performance Standards for Anti-submarine Warfare Operators	59,000	

NAVY
6.5 Studies and Analyses

Performer	Title	(Costs ($)) FY 70	FY 71
Center for Naval Analyses	Support/operating manpower relationships	102,000	
Center for Naval Analyses	Navy Manpower Analyses	102,000	X

U. S. AIR FORCE

6.1 Basic Research

Performer	Title	(Costs $) FY 70	FY 71
R. Hatch Decision System Assoc.	Research in Mathematical and Computer Based Methods of Simulating Air Force Personnel Systems	50,000	.X
Undetermined	Optimization of Personnel Assignment Procedures	50,000	.X
Undetermined	Development of Improved Techniques for Predicting Performance of Air Force Personnel From Aptitudes, Interests, Prior Education, and Experience	77,000	.X
Dr. S. Roscoe, U. of Illinois	Flying Training Research	145,000	.X
Dr. Calvin Taylor U. of Utah	Training in Problem Solving Techniques for Air Force Officers	20,000	
Undetermined	Validation of Curricula Content of Air Force Technical Training Courses	60,000	X
Dr. Harry Silberman Systems Development Corporation	Research on Natural Language Computer-Aided Instruction for Air Force Training Programs	90,000	X
Dr. Donald Forgays U. of Vermont	The Effects of Isolation on Human Performance		X
Dr. Charles R. Kelley Dunlap & Assoc., Inc. Santa Monica, Calif.	Studies of Predictive and Adaptive Processes in Air Force Control Systems	45,000	X
Dean Ralph Nevins Kansas State Univ.	The Effects of Environmental Extremes on Performance on Military Tasks		X
Dr. Raymond Nickerson Bolt, Beranek & Newman Cambridge, Mass.	Control of Speed and Variability in Air Force Operator Response	55,000	X

U. S. AIR FORCE
6.1 Basic Research

Performer	Title	FY 70 (Costs $)	FY 71
Undetermined	Flight Displays and Control Dynamics	49,000	X
Undetermined	Crew Workload Forecasting and Man-Machine Functions Allocation in Air Force Systems (Project 7183)	20,000	
Undetermined	Research on Head Mobility, Stability and Orientation Precision as Related to Head Aiming Devices		X
Undetermined	Effects of Optical Filters on Target Detection Performance Under Different Levels of Illumination and Contrast	25,000	X
Undetermined	Research on the Interaction of Illuminant Color, Illumination Level and Atmospheric Conditions on Visual Target Detection	40,000	X
R. W. Obermayer Bunker Ramo Corp. Canoga Park, Calif.	Comparative Study of Control and Feedback Techniques Applicable to Air Force Systems	30,000	X
Mr. T. Orne Penn. Univ. Hosp. Phil., Penn.	Research on Measurement and Control of Response to Stressful Situations		X
Dr. Jay Galbraith MIT Cambridge, Mass.	Information Processing and Uncertainty as Factors in Air Force Organization Effectiveness	48,000	X
Undetermined	Studies of Resistance to Stress Associated with Combat Operations, Captivity and Restoration to Service of Air Force Personnel	40,000	X

U. S. AIR FORCE

6.2 Exploratory Development

Performer	Title	FY 70 (Costs $)	FY 71
AFHRL	Administrative and Indirect Support Costs Associated with AFHRL Mission Accomplishment	656,900	X
Univ. Utah	Motivational Predictors of Pilot Trainee Performance and Attrition.	29,000	--
Undetermined	Procedures for Developing Job-Performance Aids as an Integrated Element of Weapon Systems.	--	X
AFHRL	Training for Critical Reconnaissance Tasks	16,000	X
AFHRL	Application of Systems Approach to Prototype Air Force Training Courses	16,000	X
AFHRL	Improved Techniques for Evaluating Job Performance	33,000	X
AFHRL	Facilitating Air Force Use of Technology of Job Performance Aids (F-111, B-1A, F-15, etc.)	17,000	X
Undetermined	Adjunct Programs for Air Force Courses	48,000	
Undetermined	Development and Evaluation of Improved Job Performance Tests for Technicians	--	X
AFHRL	Designing Training Capability within Operational Systems	8,000	X
AFHRL	Job-Performance Aids for Vietnamization (UH-1H, Etc.)	30,000	X
Conductron	Video Gunsight and Recording System for Training	500	

U. S. AIR FORCE

6.2 Exploratory Development

Performer	Title	Costs ($) FY 70	FY 71
System Research Laboratory	Support of In-House Studies of Desirable Characteristics of Training Media	45,000	X
Ritchie	Computer-Based Index of Training Literature	12,000	X
Systems Development Corporation	Application of Computer Techniques to System, Crew and Maintenance Task Information.	50,000	--
Applied Science Associates, Inc.	Job Performance Aids for AN/APN-147 and AN/ASN-35.	3,500	--
Applied Science Associates, Inc.	Data for Computer-Based, Fully-Proceduralized Job Performance Aids	37,000	--
Matrix	Symbolic Substitute Tests for Job Task Performance Tests (AN/APN-147 and AN/ASN-35)	46,000	--
Matrix	Field Tryout of Job-Task Performance Tests (AN/APN-147 and AN/ASN-35).	38,000	--
Undetermined	System for In-House development of Simulation and Media for Air Force Training.	50,000	X
Undetermined	Specifications and Guidelines for Preparing Fully-Proceduralized Job Performance Aids (Funded from Tactical Air Warfare Office, Aeronautical Systems Division.)	N/A	N/A
Undetermined	Computer-Based Diagrams and Schematics for Job-Performance Aids	--	X
Undetermined	Optimal Training Characteristics of Aircraft Simulators and Other Training Media	65,000	X

U. S. AIR FORCE

6.2 Exploratory Development

Performer	Title	FY 70 (Costs $)	FY 71
Undetermined	System for In-House Development of Simulation and Media for Air Force Training	255,000	X
AFHRL	Development and Test of Optical and Television Techniques for Visual Simulation in Pilot Training	42,000	X
AFHRL	Development and Test of Computer-Generated Imagery for Simulation in Undergraduate Pilot Training	21,000	X
AFHRL	Development and Test of Specialized Computer and Programming Techniques for Simulation in Pilot Training	21,000	X
AFHRL	Development of Radar Simulation Techniques for Observer-Navigator Training	14,000	X
AFHRL	Development of Self-Adjusting Simulation Techniques for Pilot Training	21,000	X
AFHRL	Engineering Support to AFSC in the Development of Training Simulation for Air Force Systems.	14,000	X
Melpar, Inc.	Dynamic Mathematical Models for Deriving Criteria for Use in Pilot Training	21,000	--
Farrand Optical Company	Optical Probe for Visual Simulation of Low Altitude Flying	61,000	--
Systems Research Laboratories	Ultra-High Resolution Camera for Aircraft Visual Simulation.	13,000	--
Undetermined	Radar Simulation Data Study for Aircrew Training	60,000	--

U. S. AIR FORCE
6.2 Exploratory Development

Performer	Title	Costs ($) FY 70	FY 71
AFHRL	Development of Simulation Techniques for Air Force Technical Training	14,000	X
AFHRL	Exploratory and Advanced Development in Support of the Flight and Technical Training Divisions of AFHRL	21,000	X
AFHRL	Mathematical Analysis of the Effects of Training on Reliability of Human Task Performance	13,000	X
AFHRL	Human Resources Data Handbook for Air Force Systems Engineering.	17,000	X
AFHRL	Relationships Between Subsystems Design, Training, Human Performance On-The-Job, and Air Force System Performance	19,000	X
AFHRL	Application of Advanced Computer Techniques to Human Resources Data Handling Methods in System Development	28,000	X
AFHRL	Development of New Techniques for Measuring Aircrew-Groundcrew Performance during Tests of New Air Force Systems (PSTE)	20,000	X
AFHRL	Development of Methods for Defining Components of Technology and Methods for Measuring Effects on Human Resources in Air Force Systems	5,000	X
AFHRL	Comparison of the Effectiveness of Technical Instructors with Field Experience Vs. Instructors without Field Experience	12,000	--
AFHRL	Application of Operations Research Methods to the Improvement of Human Resources Utilization.	--	X

U. S. AIR FORCE

6.2 Exploratory Development

Performer	Title	FY 70 (Costs $)	FY 71
AFHRL	Human Resources System Engineering Support to New Systems (F-15, B-1, Minuteman, F-4E, B-52, Space Systems Studies, and Others)	10,000	X
AFHRL	Vietnamization Project Support	9,000	X
Undetermined	Human Resources Data in System Design Trade-Off Studies	80,000	--
System Development Corporation	Application of Computer Techniques to System Crew and Maintenance Task Information	16,000	--
Undetermined	Development and Validation of Manuals for Application of Queuing Techniques to Selected Air Force and Army Operational Problems	34,000	X
Undetermined	Development and Validation of Models by Which Design Engineers and System Evaluators Can Predict Job Performance from Proposed Maintenance Design Characteristics	--	X
AFHRL	Application of Advances in Training to Simulation of New Base Civil Engineer Automated Management System	12,000	--
HumRRO	Inter-relationships of Military Experiences to Development of Occupational Skills and Occupational Goals of Men in Service	99,000	--
Undetermined	Occupational Analysis of Project 100,000 Personnel	50,000	--

U. S. AIR FORCE

6.2 Exploratory Development

Performer	Title	(Costs ($)) FY 70	FY 71
Undetermined	Selection and Utilization of Population Subgroups	--	X
AFHRL	Participation of Military Personnel in DOD Evaluation Program	3,000	X
AFHRL	Factors Associated with Outcomes of Remedial Training and Rehabilitation Program	5,000	X
AFHRL	The Relationships of Biographical Background Characteristics to Desertions from Military Service	5,000	X
Undetermined	Relationships of Military Skills, Occupational Goals, and Reserve Service	--	X
Undetermined	Development and Evaluation of an Individualized Multimedia Instructional Card for Air Force Precision Measuring Equipment Specialist	65,000	--
Undetermined	Evaluation of the Value of Competent Testing Procedures where Improving the Effectiveness of Air Force Technical Training	60,000	--
Undetermined	Development and Evaluation of Microform Materials for use in the Air Force Technical Training	60,000	--
Undetermined	Development and Evaluation of Innovation and Instructional Methods and Media for Air Force Technical Training	40,000	X
Undetermined	Instructional Carrel Design for Use in Evaluation Facility for Air Force Technical System Development	--	X
Undetermined	Development and Evaluation of Computer Based Training Simulators for Air Force Technical Training	--	X

U. S. AIR FORCE

6.2 Exploratory Development

Performer	Title	Cost ($) FY 70	FY 71
Undetermined	Procedural Guides for Air Force Instructional System Evaluation	--	X
AFHRL	Evaluation of Time-Compressed Speech Techniques for Use in Air Force Technical Training	500	X
AFHRL	Development of Audio/Visual Material for Air Force Medical-Helper Training Course	2,000	--
AFHRL	Application of Adjunct Programming Techniques in Air Force Technical Training	5,000	X
AFHRL	Comparison of Sound-Slide Equipment Configuration	3,000	--
AFHRL	Media Augmentation of CBPO Computer Assisted Instruction Course	10,000	--
AFHRL	Identification of Computer Assisted Instruction System for Use Within an Air Force Context	7,000	X
AFHRL	Air Force Career Development Course for Low Aptitude Personnel	5,000	--
AFHRL	Development of Measures of Student Attitude Toward Technical Training	2,000	--
AFHRL	Techniques for Facilitating Vietnamese Pilot Training	3,000	--
AFHRL	Determination of the Effect of Accelerated Training on Air Force Trainees	7,000	X
AFHRL	Use of Low Fidelity Simulators for Hands-on Technical Training	--	X
AFHRL	Survey of Vietnamese Air Force Technical Training, Phase II	--	X

U. S. AIR FORCE

6.2 Exploratory Development

Performer	Title	(Cost ($)) FY 70	FY 71
AFHRL	Investigation of Buddy Training Techniques for Use in Vietnamese Technical School	--	X
AFHRL	Collection of Information Concerning the Readability of Air Force Training Material	1,000	--
AFHRL	Survey of Vietnamese Air Technical Training, Phase I	3,000	--
AFHRL	USAF Student Pilot Performance Measurements	2,600	X
American Institute for Research	Techniques for Evaluating Pilot Performance Using Video Tape Records	2,600	--
Undetermined	Operational Combat-Ready Pilot Performance Measurement Techniques	1,300	X
Undetermined	Ground Trainer (GAT-1) as an Adjunct to VNAF's T-41 Training	1,300	X
AFHRL	Use of GAT-1 as Low-Cost Pre-Jet Pilot Selection	6,500	X
Undetermined	Factors Controlling Self-Elimination from Flying Training	--	X
Undetermined	Navigator/Observer Utilization Field Task Analysis for Undergraduate Navigator Training Program Design	42,600	X
U. of Illinois	Changing Structure of Basic Abilities as Flying Training Progresses	19,600	--
Undetermined	Improve VNAF Pilot Training Effectiveness by Exploiting Multi-media Techniques	1,300	X

U. S. AIR FORCE

6.2 Exploratory Development

Performer	Title	FY 70 (Costs $)	FY 71
AFHRL	Sound-Slide Presentation as an Effective Substitute for Live Briefings in UPT	2,600	X
Bunker Ramo	Application of Systems Approach to Cost-Effective A7D Training Program Design	18,300	X
Conductron	Video Camera Installation in A7D for Combat Crew Pilot Trainer Performance Monitoring	42,300	X
Undetermined	Optimizing Material for Flight Line Retrieval System: UPT and A7D	68,600	X
AFHRL	T-26 Ground Trainer Utilization - Effective Trainer in Increasing Student Skill in Transition from T-37 to T-38	6,500	X
AFHRL	Personnel Management Model Improvement	4,000	X
AFHRL	Mathematical Models To Test Impact of Personnel Policies	10,000	X
Undetermined	Mathematical Models to Test Impact of Personnel Policies	--	X
AFHRL	Personnel Management Information Display.	7,000	X
AFHRL	Computer Inquiry Techniques for Personnel Data	4,000	X
AFHRL	Personnel Management Information Display	4,000	X
AFHRL	Personnel Management Information Display	4,000	X

U.S. AIR FORCE

6.2 Exploratory Development

Performer	Title	FY 70 (Costs $)	FY 71
AFHRL	Computer Time-Sharing for Personnel Management	4,000	X
AFHRL	Mathematical Techniques for Personnel R&D	5,000	X
AFHRL	Advanced Computer Techniques for Personnel R&D	5,500	X
AFHRL	Personnel Data Reduction	10,000	X
AFHRL	Improvement in Air Force Personnel R&D Information	25,500	X
AFHRL	Improvement in Air Force Personnel R&D Information	25,500	X
AFHRL	Improvement in Air Force Personnel R&D Information	35,500	X
AFHRL	Expanding the Content of Human Resources Data Bank	10,000	X
AFHRL	Expanding the Content of Human Resources Data Bank	10,000	X
AFHRL	Costing Factors in Air Force Personnel Actions	10,000	X
Undetermined	Air Force Personnel System Simulation R&D	99,000	--
AFHRL	Air Force Personnel System Simulation R&D	20,000	X
AFHRL	Utilization of Economic Data in Force Projections	5,000	X
AFHRL	Enlargement of Force Simulation Model for Increased Power	3,500	X
AFHRL	Mathematical and Statistical Techniques for Personnel R&D	5,000	X
Undetermined	Improvement in Personnel Classification Methodology	--	X

U.S. AIR FORCE

6.2 Exploratory Development

Performer	Title	(Costs ($)) FY 70	FY 71
AFHRL	Improvement in Personnel Classification Methodology	--	X
AFHRL	Mathematical and Statistical Techniques for Personnel R&D	4,500	X
AFHRL	Mathematical Procedures for Combining Air Force Jobs into Jobtypes and Career Fields	--	X
AFHRL	Mathematical and Statistical Techniques for Personnel R&D	4,500	X
AFHRL	Identification of Personal Characteristics Indicative of Success in Air Force Training	25,000	X
AFHRL	Identification of Characteristics that Predict Human Reliability	25,000	X
AFHRL	Identification of Personal Characteristics Indicative of Successful Completion of Initial Tours	8,000	X
AFHRL	Development of Personnel Measurement Techniques Applicable to Low Ability Air Force Personnel	18,000	X
AFHRL	Improvement in Methods for Evaluating Air Force Job Performances:I	10,000	X
AFHRL	Improvement in Methods for Evaluating Air Force Job Performance:II	15,000	X
AFHRL	Improvement in Methods for Evaluating Air Force Job Performance:III	25,000	X
AFHRL	Improvement in Air Force Promotion Procedures	25,000	X
Undetermined	Improvement in Air Force Promotion Procedures	--	X

U. S. AIR FORCE

6.2 Exploratory Development

Performer	Title	(Costs ($)) FY 70	FY 71
AFHRL	Identification of Factors that Improve Retention of Personnel	25,000	--
AFHRL	Identification of Factors Leading to Volunteering for the Air Force	10,000	X
AFHRL	Improvement in Statistical Methods for Processing Selection and Assignment Information	35,000	X
Undetermined	Development of a Technique for Identifying Career-oriented Officers	30,000	--
AFHRL	Selection Measures for Career-oriented officers.	5,000	X
AFHRL	Joint Services Selection and Classification Programs	15,000	X
AFHRL	Improvement in Techniques for Identifying the Military-relevant Skills of Marginal Personnel	5,000	X
AFHRL	Optimizing the Utilization of Project 100,000 Personnel	20,000	X
AFHRL	Development of Specialized Personnel Selection Tests	20,000	X
Biotechnology Inc.	Investigation of the Usefulness of Psychomotor Tests in Air Force Personnel Selection	5,000	--
AFHRL	Psychomotor Tests in Air Force Personnel Selection	20,000	X
Research Associates Inc.	Development and Improvement of Airman Selection and Classification	6,000	--
AFHRL	Development and Improvement of Airman Selection and Classification	50,000	X

U.S. AIR FORCE

6.2 Exploratory Development

Performer	Title	FY 70 (Costs $)	FY 71
AFHRL	Development and Improvement of Air Force Officer Selection	40,000	X
AFHRL	Improvement in Procedures for Assignment and Utilization of Pilots	50,000	X
AFHRL	Conduct Analyses of Special Selection and Classification Problems	65,000	X
AFHRL	Development of Interest and Experience Indicators for Air Force Occupations	70,000	X
AFHRL	Procedures for Applying Selection Tests to New Air Force Jobs or Training Courses	10,000	--
AFHRL	Development of Measures of On-the-Job Performance (Work-samples)	30,000	X
AFHRL	Improvement in Air Force Recruiting through Selection for a Specific Job	45,000	X
AFHRL	Improvement in Air Force Recruiting through Nation-wide Quota Filling	15,000	X
AFHRL	Support of the Weighted Airman Promotion System	325,000	--
AFHRL	The Collection of Air Force Job Information	35,000	X
AFHRL	Procedures for Analyzing and Reporting Air Force Job Information	70,000	X
AFHRL	Determination of Feasibility of Evaluating the Performance of Airmen at the Task Level	35,000	X

U. S. AIR FORCE

6.2 Exploratory Development

Performer	Title	(Costs ($)) FY 70	FY 71
AFHRL	Improvement in Procedures for Processing Job Information	5,000	X
AFHRL	The Collection of Air Force Civilian Job Information	35,000	X
AFHRL	Application of Air Force Job Analysis Methods to Special Air Operations	2,000	--
AFHRL	Determination of the Difficulty Level of Air Force Jobs	45,000	X
AFHRL	Air Force Job Evaluation	50,000	X
AFHRL	Air Force Job Evaluation	40,000	X
Undetermined	Air Force Job Evaluation	--	X
AFHRL	Position Evaluation	10,000	X
Undetermined	Improvement in Procedures for Describing and Analyzing Officer Jobs	69,000	--
AFHRL	Improvement in Procedures for Describing and Analyzing Officer Jobs	10,000	X
AFHRL	Air Force Job Evaluation	5,000	X
AFHRL	Improvement in Computer Processing of Job Information	35,000	X
AFHRL	Improvement in Computer Processing of Job Information	10,000	X
AFHRL	Improvement in Computer Processing of Job Information.	5,000	X
AFHRL	Development of Methods for Increasing the Efficiency of Career Field Management	25,000	X

U. S. AIR FORCE

6.2 Exploratory Development

Performer	Title	(Costs ($)) FY 70	FY 71
AFHRL	Initiate Development of Experience Inventories and Reassignment Management Procedures	8,000	X
Undetermined	Initiate Development of Experience Inventories and Reassignment Management Procedures	--	X
AFHRL	Determine Capability of Supervisors to Rate Performance at the Task Level	25,000	X
AFHRL	Investigate the Specialization of Assignments over Time with Different Career Fields	10,000	X
AFHRL	Investigate the Impact of Work Assigned on Job Satisfaction and Career Decisions	6,000	X
AFHRL	Determine Actual Duties and Tasks Assigned to Low Ability Airmen	30,000	X
U. of Utah	Develop a Measure of Motivation for Pilot Training and Test its Potential for Reducing the Self-Initiated Elimination (SIE) Attrition Rate.	45,000	--
Undetermined	Development, Tests and Evaluation of Motivational Programs for Use in Air Force Education and Training.	56,000	X
Undetermined	Development of Quantitative Models and Alternative Systems for Determining and Validating Air Force Professional Education and Training Requirements.	10,000	X
AFHRL	Air Force Academy Faculty Studies on Air Force Human Resources Problems.	6,000	X
AFHRL	Development, Tests and Evaluation of Alternative Systems for Education and Training of Air Force Human Resources	--	X

U. S. AIR FORCE

6.3 Advanced Development

Performer	Title	(Costs ($)) FY 70	FY 71
Undetermined	Advanced Simulation in Undergraduate Pilot Training	(600)*	X
Undetermined	Advanced Instructional System	0	X
Undetermined	Non-Decision Job Performance Aids	(91)*	X

*Funds not yet released

U.S. AIR FORCE

6.5 RDT&E, Management and Support

Performer	Title	(Costs ($)) FY 70	FY 71
RAND Corp.	Soviet Military Policy	255,000	X
RAND Corp.	Military Representation in U.S. Missions	16,000	X
RAND Corp.	European Security Issues	76,000	X
RAND Corp.	Asian Security Issues	312,000	X
RAND Corp.	Air Force Personnel Research	239,000	X
RAND Corp.	Pilot Procurement and Training	80,000	--
RAND Corp.	Analysis of Systems for Air Force Education and Training	159,000	X
RAND Corp.	The Pilot as a Future Military Resource	50,000	X
RAND Corp.	Assistance to AFIT Students	4,000	--
RAND Corp.	Military Manpower Procurement	33,000	X

U.S. AIR FORCE
6.6 Studies and Analysis

Performer	Title	(Costs ($)) FY 70	FY 71
	The USAF Policy Planning Studies Program	348,000	X

Research Program for Office of
Assistant Secretary of Defense (M&RA)

Performer	Title	(Costs ($)) FY 70	FY 71
RAC	Development of Models for Projecting Military Manpower Supply	113,900	
IDA	Development of Models for Projecting Military Recruitment and Retention Rates	215,000	X
Survey Research Center, U. of Mich.	Research Survey on High School Youth Knowledge, Plans and Attitudes Concerning Military Service	77,868	
Performance Research, Inc.	The Use of the Armed Services Vocational Aptitude Battery in High School Counseling	20,000	
Unknown	Recruitment Market Research		X
Unknown	Design of Integrated Military Sample Survey Data Base for Longitudinal Storage, Retrieval and Analysis of Survey Data		X
Manpower Programs Office, AF Human Res. Laboratory	Military Manpower Research Studies and Analyses of Major Military Occupational Training Programs		X
Human Resources Research Organ.	Job Performance of High and Low Aptitude Army Personnel in Same Jobs	87,000	
Human Resources Research Organ.	Training Methods for Different Aptitude Level Army Personnel in Same Training Courses	105,000	X
Human Resources Research Organ.	Basic Literacy and Arithmetic Skills Required for Major Army Military Occupational Specialties	100,000	
BESRL	Optimum Balance of Army Personnel Abilities in Small Military Units	41,000	X
U.S. Naval Personnel & Training Research Laboratory	Research on Improved Selection and Classification of Lower Aptitude Naval Personnel	85,000	X

Research Program for Office of
Assistant Secretary of Defense (M&RA)

Performer	Title	FY 70 (Costs ($))	FY 71
U.S. Naval Personnel & Training Research Laboratory	Experimental Training Methods for Lower Aptitude Naval Personnel	100,000	X
U.S. Naval Personnel Research & Development Laboratory	Research on Attitude and Motivation of Lower Aptitude Naval Personnel	35,000	X
Manpower Programs Office, AF Human Res. Laboratory	Factors Relating to Service and Post-Service Performance of Project One Hundred Thousand Men and Other Military Separatees		X
U.S. Naval Personnel & Training Research Laboratory	Research on Job-Validated Selection Methods for Minority Group Officer and Enlisted Programs	85,000	X
Personnel Research Division, AFHRL	Research on Measurement of Job Performance at Level of Individual Job Tasks in Air Force Occupational Specialties		X
Information Concepts Incorporated	Development of Methods for Identifying and Recording Military Skill and Experience of Military Separatees	35,000	

1,099,858

ARPA - Overseas Defense Research

Performer	Title	FY 70 (Costs ($))	FY 71
RAND	Pacification and Termination	240,000	
RAND	CI Applied Research	200,000	X
not selected	Transfer Training (Vietnamization)	500,000*	X
Applied Scientific Research Corp. of Thailand	Tribal Data Center	10,000	
Applied Scientific Research Corp.	Strategic Trail Study - North Thailand	10,000	
in-house	Insurgent Studies - Thailand	25,000*	
AIR	Program Impact Assessment	454,000	X
AU of Beirut	Factors in Regional Change	150,000	
HumRRO	SIAF Training (Small Independent Action Force)	220,000	X
HumRRO	SIAF Selection of Personnel	220,000	X
in-house	N.E. Thailand Village Leadership Patterns	40,000	
in-house	Study of Strategic Minority in North Thailand (Ahka)	25,000	
in-house	Meo Handbook	5,000	
SRI	Defense Studies - Thailand	230,000	X

* FY 70 funds not yet obligated

ARPA - Behavioral Sciences

Performer	Title	FY 70 (Costs ($))	FY 71
M.I.T.	Computer Methods for Analysis and Modeling of Complex Systems	2,031,000	X
Raytheon	Feasibility of Use of ARPA Computer Network for Analysis of Defense Man-Machine Problems	25,000	
UCLA	Man-Computer Simulation of Crisis Management Decision Problems	1,837,000	X
Northwestern Univ.	Computer Simulation of Causes, Sequences and Effects of Conflict between Nations	84,000	
Univ. of Michigan	International Security Data Archive and Analysis Center	500,000	X
Univ. of Hawaii	Dimensions of International Conflict for Long-Term Prediction	200,000	X
Univ. of So. Calif.	World Event/Interaction Survey for Short-Term Conflict Prediction	112,000	X
Yale Univ.	Forecasting International Defense Alliances and Alignments	100,000	X
Rockefeller Univ.	Linguistic Bases of Command and Control Communications	55,000	
Univ. of Oregon	Improvement of Individual Operator Information Processing	419,000	X
NSF	Conference on Improved Self-Regulation of Physical and Psychological States for High-Stress Military Situations	10,000	
San Diego State Coll. Foundation and Naval Neuropsychiatric Research Unit	Improved Self-Regulation of Physical and Psychological States for High-Stress Military Situations	609,000	X

External Research Program

Performer	Title	FY 70 (Costs ($))	FY 71
RAND Corp.	Base Studies Opportunity Planning (US-Soviet Politico-Military Interaction) Cost Factors - Foreign Military Forces Command and Control Problems Contingency Studies General & Special Requests	400,000	X
IDA	Asian Regional Arrangements Opportunity Planning (US-Soviet Politico-Military Interaction) Canada and the Defense of North America	325,000	X
Univ. of Miami	U.S. Interests and Policies for Dissemination of Advanced Technology and Hardware with Security Implications	47,228	
Battelle Memorial Inst.	Technological Factors Affecting U.S. Policies for Dissemination of Advanced Technology and Hardware Related to Nuclear Weapons and Delivery Systems	29,000	
Univ. of Pennsylvania	The Implications of US-Soviet Strategic Parity on Western European Security and Arms Control	65,845	
Stanford Univ.	Sources of Threats to U.S. Security Interests from International Communist and Other Radical Organizations and Movements	70,000	
SRI	Quick Reaction and Computation (QRC) for Force Planning Strategic Nuclear Forces and Strategies in Enemy Initiated Limited Nuclear Exchange	135,500	
Drs. Franz Michael, Frank N. Trager and Gerald L. Steibel	Soviet and Chinese Operations in Support of Military and Strategic Doctrine	22,500	
	New studies	404,927	X

EFFORTS TO REPEAL SECTION 203

Senator FULBRIGHT. I certainly was somewhat surprised that you are undertaking to repeal section 203. This wasn't put in without any effort. It was a great effort, and it seems we were unable to make any progress or get any understanding with the Defense Department. We spent a lot of time putting section 203 in there. In the final analysis, most of the members of the Armed Services Committee went along with it.

DEFENSE DEPARTMENT RESEARCH PROJECTS

Here is another example of the types of projects. These involve very large amounts of money and they are spread all over the world. This is under research projects carried out abroad by U.S. contractors. You have: "The counter infiltration system," $342,000, in Iran, and "The waterborne traffic analysis," $16,000, "Iranian mobilization study."

I can't imagine why you are making contracts of this character for a foreign government. There are many others in here: Vietnam, of course, and Thailand. We are accustomed to those by the dozen.

Dr. FOSTER. Mr. Chairman, I am somewhat disturbed that it is readily apparent to you why those subjects are extremely important and ought to be studied. You see, I think the infiltration problem in the Middle East is a serious matter.

Senator FULBRIGHT. I suppose you could say every kind of search for knowledge is important in an abstract way, but it has no real relation to your mission. We have no treaty commitment with Iran that would justify this type of study. If you want to go to any country, they all have problems. Every State does. We have all kinds of problems now. You could, I suppose, have a project on the model cities program in North Little Rock. They are having trouble with it, but that isn't the point. It has nothing to do with the immediate needs or mission of the Defense Department.

Dr. FOSTER. Mr. Chairman, I believe that it does. The problem in the Middle East is associated with infiltration and raiding groups, and I believe that the progress we have made in dealing with infiltration in South Vietnam is extremely remarkable. I believe techniques have been developed that can be used in the Middle East situation to cool it down, and that is of immediate and direct interest to the Department of Defense and, in fact, the Nation.

Senator FULBRIGHT. It might be to the Nation, but, I don't think it is to the Department of Defense. Perhaps in the political field this may have some remote interest, but you are going so far all over the world and spending so much money. I suppose you would say the solvency of the United States isn't your responsibility and in a strict sense that is true, but it is the responsibility of the Senate. It is very difficult for us to make judgments when this type of program is undertaken. There are so many of them that it presents us with an almost insoluble problem simply because of their vast numbers.

The staff has looked at these as they did last year. We had quite a debate last year and this is the way you attract the contractors. I notice in his speech Mr. Laird solicited the support of the contractors in repealing section 203. I can imagine that the representatives of all the universities and manufacturers and everyone else involved are concentrating their efforts upon the Members of the Senate to try to repeal section 203.

INFLUENCE OF THE PENTAGON

This is part of the overwhelming influence that the Pentagon has exercised and is still exercising on the Congress. In fact, you really destroy the functioning of a democratic system when you follow this course, because there is nothing that can equal you. The very amount of your lobbyists who come here appealing to Senators and Congressmen in behalf of these programs, each one with his pet project makes it extremely difficult for the Congress to function at all. This is one of the troubles, I think, with our present situation and the reason why so many people have reservations about being able to make this system work.

I think this has a very great and direct relation to the frustration of the younger people or all those who feel that our democratic system is not working properly.

CLASSIFIED LIST OF DEFENSE DEPARTMENT RESEARCH PROJECTS

Since this list of projects is classified, I guess I can't put it in the record although I see no reason for the classification. There might be a half dozen in there that justify the classification on its real basis, but according to the list of foreign institutions being financed by the Department of Defense, there are projects being carried out in 39 countries. As you have already said, some $3 million is allocated or requested for these projects.

RESEARCH ON MOSQUITOES IN MALAYA

I have just one or two more items to illustrate what I have in mind. You have a project that is studying research at the University of Malaya on mosquitoes in Malaya.

What would be your justification for spending $27,000 for research on mosquitoes in Malaya? Are you preparing for an incursion into Malaya to protect our boys in Saigon?

Dr. FOSTER. No, Mr. Chairman.

Senator FULBRIGHT. What is the reason for it?

Dr. FOSTER. We are not doing any such thing, Senator Fulbright. Let me just point out the seriousness of the malarial problem.

Senator FULBRIGHT. I don't have to be told about the seriousness of the malarial problem. What does it have to do with the Defense Department and why is it your responsibility?

Dr. FOSTER. All right, I will tell you exactly what it has to do with the Defense Department.

Senator FULBRIGHT. That is all I want to know.

Dr. FOSTER. Should U.S. military men be sent to Malaya, it is important to know in advance whether or not the strains of malaria in Malaya—as you know, they vary in different regions of that whole area—are or are not amenable to available techniques for coping with them.

Our situation in Vietnam was very serious in the 1967–68 period. We were losing more people each week from malaria than from anything else. It was absolutely necessary, on a crash basis, to develop the necessary medical procedures and equipment to deal with the crisis which, otherwise, could have been extremely serious.

Now, that involved testing hundreds of various chemicals and drugs by trial and error. What we want to find out in Malaya is what strains of malaria are present. That is all. We are trying to find out about the local medical situation should we have to go there.

Senator FULBRIGHT. Do you have a contingency plan envisioning the invasion of Malaya?

Dr. FOSTER. Sir, that is not a proper question to address to me. I don't know.

Senator FULBRIGHT. You don't know.

Dr. FOSTER. I don't know.

Senator FULBRIGHT. Why then, if your justification has any merit, don't you undertake similar ones in all the countries in the tropics because something might occur sometime that would require the presence of American soldiers? This could happen in Chad, or in Upper Volta or in Paraguay or anywhere else? On your reasoning you could justify a research project in any country anywhere.

Dr. FOSTER. Senator Fulbright, it is not so easy to justify it, in a sense.

Senator FULBRIGHT. I don't think you do.

Dr. FOSTER. Let me tell you the problem in undertaking similar programs in all those other countries, we have very limited funding. Of every 10 requests that the Department gets for research of the type you are mentioning, we can only fund one.

DEFENSE DEPARTMENT SPENDING ON RESEARCH AND DEVELOPMENT

Senator FULBRIGHT. This isn't surprising. I mean you have such a reputation for handing out money in an indiscriminate way that I suppose everyone who needs money applies.

Dr. FOSTER. No, sir, I don't believe that the information I just gave you is at all consistent with you statement. We don't hand out money hand over fist and in an indiscriminate way when we can only fund one out of 10. We have nine dissatisfied people for every one who thinks he got what he duly deserved. It is just the other way around.

Senator FULBRIGHT. That is as sad as can be. It is very sad, but did it ever occur to you that this is taxpayers money, that the people in this country need money and that this country is in serious economic condition? This doesn't really come into your considerations at all, does it?

Dr. FOSTER. Senator Fulbright, it comes into my considerations every day.

Senator FULBRIGHT. It does.

Dr. FOSTER. The Defense budget available for research and development has been dropping for the last several years, and I am seriously concerned about it.

Senator FULBRIGHT. Yes; it is too bad you have only had a thousand billion dollars to spend in the Defense Department since World War II.

SOVIET RESEARCH AND DEVELOPMENT EFFORTS

Dr. FOSTER. Senator Fulbright, as you know, the current problem that we face is that the Soviet effort in research and development is already about 20 percent larger than that of the United States. It is increasing from 10 to 13 percent a year, has done so for the last decade, and is expected and predicted to continue increasing at least for the next few years. The U.S.R. & D. effort is declining.

I don't believe that the security of this country can be maintained if we allow this trend to continue indefinitely.

Senator FULBRIGHT. Really, Mr. Foster, you are more messianic than I ever believed possible for a scientist. We have 5,632 contracts. How many do the Soviets have?

Dr. FOSTER. I don't know, sir. Theirs is a closed society, and that is a major aspect of our problem.

Senator FULBRIGHT. Do you mean they classify their reports too? [Laughter].

Dr. FOSTER. We don't receive information that breaks down Soviet research efforts in anything like the detail in which the United States openly publishes its program.

Senator FULBRIGHT. You classify all your reports. What is the difference in a closed society or an open society?

Dr. FOSTER. We don't classify all reports.

Senator FULBRIGHT. It is not available to the Congress and the public.

Dr. FOSTER. Most of it is available to the Congress and the public. I would dearly love to have the defense report in the Soviet Union.

Senator FULBRIGHT. I think we are going to have to have a hearing on how difficult it is for this committee to obtain information from both the State Department and the Pentagon. I thought you might be aware of it.

DEFENSE DEPARTMENT RESEARCH PROJECTS

I have one last question, Mr. Chairman. Dr. Foster, What is your justification for spending $150,000 for a project entitled "Factors in Regional Change at the American University of Beirut in Lebanon."

Dr. FOSTER. I don't recall the details of that one, Mr. Chairman. I would be delighted to look into it and give you a reply.

(The information referred to follows.)

The purpose of this research effort is to increase our capability for understanding the political/social factors underlying the conflict in the Middle East. Tasks include (a) studies of technological development in Middle Eastern countries, (b) studies of patterns of "institutionalization" in the Middle East and (c) studies of the future political developments in the Arabian peninsula.

The research was fully coordinated with the Department of State and was strongly endorsed by the U.S. Ambassador to Lebanon in a message dated 26 February 1969 to the Secretary of Defense and the Secretary of State. This project is scheduled for termination in October 1970.

Senator FULBRIGHT. It occurred to me that this also might be a part of the contingency planning with regard to intervention in the Middle East.

Dr. FOSTER. No, sir; I don't believe it has anything to do with contingency planning for U.S. forces.

Senator FULBRIGHT. I haven't really looked at the list. Did you have any projects concerning the mosquitoes in Cambodia before you intervened there?

Dr. FOSTER. I don't recall any.

Senator FULBRIGHT. You don't recall it, but this would have been, it seems to me, much more appropriate than Malaya.

CONDUCT OF SUBCOMMITTEE HEARINGS

Senator COOPER. Mr. Chairman, I am going to raise a question.

Senator FULBRIGHT. I am through.

Senator COOPER. He has been trying to answer these questions as well as he can. I think we should have order in this room.

Senator FULBRIGHT. It is the chairman's responsibility to keep order in the room.

Senator GORE. Let there be order in the room.

Senator FULBRIGHT. I am through, Mr. Chairman.

Senator GORE. Senator Case.

Senator CASE. Mr. Chairman, I call attention to the fact it is now 12 o'clock. Dr. Foster took perhaps 15 minutes. Senator Aiken took, I think, five, and without questioning the propriety of it, I just note the fact that the balance of the time has been taken by the chairman and Senator Fulbright. This is something that is a continuing process, and I just note it for the record. I do that partly because the chairman of the full committee, Senator Fulbright, somewhat irascibly called me to account when he thought I had taken a little too long the other day in questioning a witness, and I would just like to make the suggestion that we do a little better job of evenhanded handling of these sessions.

REPORT OF AD HOC COMMITTEE OF SCIENTISTS ON SAFEGUARD

Now, Dr. Foster, you spoke about a report by an ad hoc committee of scientists that you had asked to make an examination of the antiballistic missile situation, and you mentioned Dr. Drell, Dr. Goldberger, and others as being members of that.

I would ask you if you will supply this committee with their report.

Dr. FOSTER. Senator Case, this was a report to the Secretary of Defense, and I believe before agreeing to that I should consult with the Secretary and see if we can make this report available to you.

Senator CASE. Will you do that?

Dr. FOSTER. Yes, sir, I certainly shall.

(The information is classified and in the committee files.)

Senator CASE. Mr. Chairman, I repeat what Senator Cooper said earlier. I think that this should be regarded as it should be, a serious inquiry.

What would your recommendation to the Secretary be on my request?

Dr. FOSTER. Senator Case, you are asking me to reveal to you the personal advice that I would give to the Secretary of Defense in my capacity as his science adviser on your question. I find that one a bit difficult to answer.

Senator CASE. Well, perhaps it is executive privilege in advance that you are suggesting. If that is the ground that you put it on, I don't question it. Let me get at it another way. What did they say?

Dr. FOSTER. The committee concluded that leaving aside political——
Senator CASE. Yes; you made that point before.
Dr. FOSTER (continuing). Political considerations, they believed that—and I have to paraphrase here.
Senator CASE. Sure.
Dr. FOSTER. They believed that the Safeguard approach was a reasonable way to try and accomplish the several objectives required by the Department of Defense—that is to say, defense of our strategic forces, the Minuteman and the bombers, protection against the light attacks such as might be launched from Communist China, and protection against accidental launches from any source.

SPECIFICATIONS AND RECOMMENDATIONS OF CONTRACTORS

Senator CASE. Now, you mentioned earlier, and I will come back to the requirements point, because I think we want to be somewhat more precise, and we haven't been at all in any of these discussions to what the requirements are. I want the specifications that were given to the contractors who have been asked to build these things. I would like to know now what you were referring to when you said they had certain recommendations to make.
Dr. FOSTER. They had recommendations, Senator Case, with respect to which additional site, or sites, should be chosen, and additional research and development that should take place to provide for additional capability should the threat require it. Those were the key points as I recall them.
Senator CASE. That is stated in very general points.
Dr. FOSTER. Yes.
Senator CASE. What recommendations did they make in regard to additional capability?
Dr. FOSTER. Senator Case, I am not yet sure that I can get Secretary Laird's agreement on supplying the document, and here we are in the process of your asking me for the details of the document. I find that a little awkward.
Senator CASE. Well, of course, I understand. I don't want any security information.
Dr. FOSTER. No, sir.
Senator CASE. But I do want the facts, and this we have been talking, I think, too much in generalities.
Dr. FOSTER. Yes.

SUBCOMMITTEE EFFORT TO ASCERTAIN IF SAFEGUARD WILL DO THE JOB

Senator CASE. This effort on the part of the chairman is a most worthwhile job to try to express in general terms what we regard as the problem. That is to say is the Safeguard designed to take care of a kind of threat, is it designed in the best way to accomplish that moneywise, and are there other choices that ought to be considered and dealt with? The chairman is trying, and this committee has been trying, it seems to us from unwilling witnesses, to drag it out, to get the basic facts, not just your conclusions, not just the recommendation that this be done, because we have very great doubt, not that you are not perfectly honest in what you say but that as to whether we really have something worth spending this enormous amount of money and time on, whether it will do a significant job, whether something else would be better. That is what we are trying to find out.

We have a strong suspicion, and you must know this; it is more than a suspicion in some cases, that what we are doing is just deploying something because it has been worked on for a long time, and that it is not calculated to do the job that we all want done. We are not, and we refuse to be put in this position. Speaking for myself, we want the best system we can get for the defense of our missile force, and for the defense of our strategic weapons systems overall.

We don't want to spend one nickel on something just for the sake of completing a program that is being kicked around for a long time under various names and because there are vested interests in getting this thing built. That is the question that we want this information to answer, and I don't see why we can't have this information since we have to authorize the money to pay for it.

Dr. FOSTER. Senator Case, if I may——

Senator CASE. You may.

Dr. FOSTER. I should like to respond to your statements. First of all, in closed sessions, I have spent perhaps 20 hours or more trying to gain the understanding of people such as you who care very much about your country. You want the answers you have been asking for and I believe we have given them to you.

Let me be very clear about it: Safeguard is not a solution that is looking for a problem.

The United States has a very serious defense problem, and Safeguard is the best solution that I know of that is within the available technology and is compatible with plans to meet the several objectives we had to face in the fiscal year 71 transitional budget.

Senator CASE. Now, Dr. Foster, I know you believe this, you have said it many times. But that is a conclusion.

Dr. FOSTER. I understand.

Senator CASE. What we want to find out in terms that we can understand and in terms that the public can understand is precisely just what we are talking about in factual terms as a basis for that conclusion, and we haven't got it. We haven't got it. And the reason that our doubts continue and continue to mount is that we have judgments from you, and we respect your judgment, but also recognize you are wearing several hats at the same time.

When we have people from the outside, who have had in the past the kind of experience that you have had, continually telling us that this is a poor solution, that it is a waste of enormous amounts of money, and that we ought not to authorize it, just on the ground of effectiveness and cost, to say nothing of other considerations, and other considerations do enter into this of a political nature, but I am not talking about political things. I am talking about effectiveness and costs of the Safeguard system for the various kinds of things that it is supposed to do.

REQUEST FOR SPECIFICATIONS FOR SAFEGUARD

First of all, I have tried to get a copy of the specifications that you have given to your contractors, so that we will know what it is that this is intended to do. It is all very well for the contractors to tell us, and they will, that they can do what they have agreed to do, but what have they agreed to do?

This I can't get. I asked the staff of this committee months ago to get from you a copy of the specifications for this thing. I don't know whether the request was ever made.

I ask you now, can you provide this to us, in confidence of course? I would like to know what the facts are, because we would do much better at getting sound answers if we can get the facts on this thing out on the table and know what we are talking about and not have to talk generalities from now until kingdom come.

Dr. FOSTER. Senator Case, I understand your point, and let me make my answer very clear. We can and will provide you with the specifications for the Safeguard system. By specifications, I understand you to mean not just the detailed characteristics of radar, but what the threat is that this system is supposed to cope with.

Senator CASE. You have to do it in terms that a layman can understand.

Dr. FOSTER. Yes, sir; I will do that.

Senator CASE. Because a layman has to make the judgment as to whether the money is to be spent for this.

Dr. FOSTER. Absolutely.

Senator CASE. And that is very definitely what I want, but not just judgments, but factual statements.

Dr. FOSTER. No, sir; I personally formulated the range of threats that I believed Safeguard would have to counter and sent that information to the Army on several different occasions, to make sure that they laid plans that could cope with that range of threats; so I am quite familiar with this question and am fully prepared to give you the answer.

Now, as you pointed out, a statement of exactly what the system will be able to cope with at various times is a sensitive matter, but it can be made available to you, sir.

Senator CASE. I ask now that you assemble it and then notify us when it is ready so that we can deal with it in depth because this I think is the heart of the question as far as most of the people of the country are concerned. Are we wasting our money? Are we getting something that is worth having? Is our effort in this direction impairing development of an effective ABM, or will we get something really worthwhile in the way of defense against strategic threats? That is the kind of question I am interested in and I think the public is too.

Dr. FOSTER. I quite understand, sir.

Senator CASE. So we will wait to hear from you when that is ready.

(The information referred to is classified and in the committee files.)

Now, Mr. Chairman, I shall not despite my remarks at the beginning of my questioning, take more than a couple of minutes because Senator Cooper has been waiting even longer than I.

Senator GORE. Would you yield just a moment?

Senator CASE. I want to make a point. Yes.

CONDUCT OF SUBCOMMITTEE HEARINGS

Senator GORE. We have never in this subcommittee had an agreed time limit. I tried to limit myself, although I didn't feel I had completed my line of questions. If the Senator raises a question of a time limit, this is something that the subcommittee will have to consider. I have followed the procedure of recognizing each member of the subcommittee and letting him proceed until he concludes and that is the case with the Senator from New Jersey.

Senator CASE. I can understand the value of an informal approach and I think it is a matter that is best if it can be worked. It requires a certain amount of consideration to make an informal situation like that work and I hope we can continue on that basis. I shall certainly do my best to cooperate, and to that end I will only ask you a couple of questions on a point that has been of great interest to me, a collateral one, if you will.

STRAY MISSILES IN EVENT OF SOVIET ATTACK ON U.S. MISSILE BASES

It seems to me the kind of thing that we often overlook, because we talk about these things in terms of gamesmanship, is what a Soviet first strike really means. We talk, for example, as if the Soviet strike against our missile bases would be sort of a neat surgical thing, that we can talk about hard point defense as being successful or not as separate from other considerations.

But the real point is, is it not, that if an attack is made against our missiles some of the attacking missiles are going to go off course. They are not going to hit our missiles; they are going to miss. And I am not now talking about anything except what happens to the strays. Whom do they hit? Wouldn't, for example, 50 percent be a pretty high success as far as hitting missile sites goes and where are the rest of the missiles going to go? They are going to land on the population maybe; are they not?

I wish you would talk to this point because it shows the kind of problem that we are dealing with. This is inconceivable and what do we do about it.

Dr. FOSTER. Senator Case, may I just at the outset call for a point of clarification? You are not concerned at the moment with the waywardness of the incoming missiles but the waywardness of the active defense missiles, is that correct?

Senator CASE. I am concerned with the waywardness of the incoming missiles.

Dr. FOSTER. The Soviet missiles.

Senator CASE. Yes; but not from the point of view now of the protection of our Minuteman. The thing I am talking about is the collateral question. What happens to the strays that come in and what are they going to do at the same time as we are sustaining an attack on our missiles?

Dr. FOSTER. You mean the stray Soviet missiles, should they be launched?

Senator CASE. Yes.

Dr. FOSTER. Yes.

Senator CASE. There will be no protection against this, I take it, by the Safeguard. That is to say the close-in radar would not protect against this and we have already determined there is no particular protection from the PAR.

DEFENSE AGAINST STRAYS IN ATTACK ON MINUTEMAN

Dr. FOSTER. Well, Senator Case, I believe the answer to your question is as follows:

First of all, our information on the Soviet ICBM's is such as to force us to conclude that they have a high reliability, so, unfortunately, should they attack the Minuteman force only, which I think is a very unlikely situation, the strays would be very few. Now should they attack only Minuteman at a time when, say, the full Safeguard Phase II system is deployed, then the area coverage provided by the full Phase II system would be able to intercept the strays.

Senator CASE. You mean the PAR would catch them.

Dr. FOSTER. Yes, sir.

Senator CASE. And the Spartans would kill them.

Dr. FOSTER. The PARS would acquire the wayward missiles, the MSR's would be used to track them and to guide the interceptors to points at which the detonation of their warheads would destroy the incoming objects.

Senator CASE. You are talking now about not a completed system with all, with the whole thing laid out that is going to take 10 years or more, but you are talking Phase II.

Dr. FOSTER. Yes, sir, it would take the 12-site deployment to complete area coverage of the United States to get the strays.

Senator CASE. Because the Spartans would not kill them.

Dr. FOSTER. Because the Spartans would kill them; yes, sir.

Senator CASE. You don't have to rely on the Sprint to kill them.

Dr. FOSTER. No, sir, we do not, not for strays.

Senator CASE. I see.

Dr. FOSTER. We do not have to rely on Sprint against a light attack such as might be launched from China or because of an accidental launch from any source. That can be handled adequately by the 12-site radar deployment and the Spartan missiles.

The reason we put Sprints at each of the 12 sites is to make sure that the enemy is not given an incentive to attack the radars. That is the only terminal defense we have in the 12-site system, outside of the defense of Minuteman itself.

Senator CASE. So that the Spartans would get these strays including any decoys that were involved, I take it, too.

Dr. FOSTER. We would not plan on attacking decoys that were analyzed as such by the radar.

Senator CASE. That would have to be as they entered the atmosphere, of course.

Dr. FOSTER. Yes, sir.

Senator CASE. So this again is a job for the MSR.

Dr. FOSTER. This is a job for the MSR.

Senator CASE. So your answer is that we need not be concerned about these strays once the full system is deployed.

Dr. FOSTER. That is correct, sir.

Senator CASE. Twelve sites and including the MSR's at the sites.

Dr. FOSTER. Yes, sir. Now there is another point: If the stray missile that might occur in a major attack on Minuteman alone—which, as I said, I believe is a very unlikely thing—was within a few hundred miles of the Minuteman field it could be intercepted by the Spartan. I suspect that a decision would be made to intercept it should it be heading for a populated area. Spartan would not, however, provide coverage to, say, 1,000 miles away from the Minuteman field.

SPECIFICATIONS AND REPORT OF AD HOC COMMITTEE OF SCIENTISTS

Senator CASE. Mr. Chairman, before I close, and I shall immediately, may I just repeat my understanding. Dr. Foster, you are going to ask, discuss with Secretary Laird, both the specifications and the report of these scientists as to whether they can be made available to this committee and, if so, whether in open or in secret session.

Dr. FOSTER. Senator Case—

Senator CASE. And you will advise us.

Dr. FOSTER. Yes, sir; with regard to the ad hoc group's report, I will discuss that with Secretary Laird.

With regard to the specifications, I will supply them, and if, when you receive them—and it will be in the near future—you find that there is something missing, just have your staff give me a call and I will be glad to provide the information in the form and in the completeness that you desire.

Senator CASE. May I just ask this on that point; is it appropriate for us to discuss these with scientists of the caliber of Dr. Panofsky, Dr. Kistiakowsky, and others so we may get some judgment and guidance from them in our understanding?

Dr. FOSTER. I would welcome that, Senator Case.

Senator CASE. You would. It would not be an impropriety in any case?

COMMUNICATION BETWEEN SCIENTISTS AND EXECUTIVE BRANCH

Dr. FOSTER. Not at all, sir. I, myself, have urged these gentlemen to come to the building and discuss these issues. I am not at all disturbed that these scientists come to the Congress and testify on either side. I think it is very beneficial.

I am a little concerned that most of those who object to the President's decision have not seen fit to come in and discuss their points of view with us.

Senator CASE. I do remember an occasion a year ago when we had four of the most eminent men here before us and I made the suggestion, blurted it out, I guess. It was a rather obvious thing, it seemed to me. This was an extraordinary assembly of talent, scientific advisers of three or four Presidents, and Dr. DuBridge, and so forth, and asked that the President see them that afternoon, and he did not, but he did assign Dr. Kissinger to see them and they had a discussion with him.

So they have been in. This is at least one occasion when I know they have done this, and made their concerns very explicit in person. And you know them as well as I, and perhaps better than; you know there would never be any hesitancy about talking to you and they have attempted to do this.

I have discovered myself, however, that sometimes—and I say this as a fact and without any bitterness at all—it is necessary to talk to the President and to his top advisers publicly rather than privately in order to have them, to have the confidence that you are being heard. Thank you very much.

Thank you, Mr. Chairman.

Dr. FOSTER. I quite understand, Senator Case.

Senator GORE. Senator Cooper.

DETECTION OF DEPLOYMENT OF MISSILES AND WARHEADS

Senator COOPER. Dr. FOSTER, as you know now all of us are concerned about the deployment of the ABM for two reasons. One, I believe—and I think most of us believe—that its deployment, and the deployment of a MIRV would put in doubt the coming to an agreement in the SALT talks with the Soviet Union. MIRV, as you say yourself, is being deployed.

Dr. FOSTER. Yes, sir; that is correct.

Senator COOPER. What?

Dr. FOSTER. That is correct, sir.

Senator COOPER. Can the Soviet Union determine whether MIRV is being deployed and to what extent without inspection on the ground, onsite inspection?

Dr. FOSTER. I am sorry, I missed the last words.

Senator COOPER. Without inspection.

Dr. FOSTER. Senator Cooper——

Senator COOPER. Put it conversely, if the Soviet Union should deploy MIRV's, MRV or MIRV, have we any capacity, any capability, of determining that fact other than onsite inspection of the missile itself?

Dr. FOSTER. Senator Cooper, this is a matter in which I have been intimately involved, and while I would like very much to try to gain your understanding of it I believe I must refrain from discussing details involving the negotiations. These matters of inspection and whether or not one could be sure that objects were MIRV'ed or maneuvering RV's, or multiple RV's, and the consequences and the possible arrangements to avoid such difficulties—I simply can't get into those in this session.

EFFECT OF MIRV OR MRV ON U.S.-SOVIET MUTUAL DETERRENCE

Senator COOPER. I think we would have to get into it. Would you agree with the proposition that the Soviet Union and the United States are now negotiating because there is some rough balance, as the chairman said, and that both know each has the capability to destroy the other. That mutual deterrent is the basis for the SALT talks.

Dr. FOSTER. Yes, sir, I agree with that position.

Senator COOPER. Do you consider that the mission of MRV or MIRV either by the United States or the Soviet Union causes any change in the stability of the deterrence? Doesn't that bother you at all?

Dr. FOSTER. As I have indicated, Senator Cooper, the deployment of MIRV by the United States does not threaten the Soviet deterrence.

Our deployment of MIRV does not add to the destruction that could be caused in the Soviet Union in an exchange if the Soviets had no defense. There are more warheads, indeed, but the number of missiles is not larger, there is not a larger number of megatons—in fact, it is considerably less. And there would be no increase in the effective military, industrial, urban damage that is done.

MIRV is used to penetrate defenses; that is its primary purpose. Thus it is to maintain our deterrent that we have decided to deploy MIRV.

Now the Soviet multiple reentry vehicles (MRV) pose a different problem, different because we do not understand the reason the Soviets are putting MRV's on their SS-9's. We question if it is to assist them in their deterrent capability, and there are several reasons why we question it. First, it seems to us there are far too many of these large SS-9 missiles, far too many to be required to attack U.S. cities. We haven't that many large cities requiring 10- to 20-megaton individual warheads or multiple 5-megaton warheads, so that bothers us.

Second, the SS-9 has rather good accuracy—better than that of their other strategic missiles anyway—and it doesn't make sense to us that they should put their best accuracy into the system carrying the largest yield or payload.

So that inconsistancy leads us to the conclusion that possibly the Soviets have in mind the development of a capability to attack multiple hardened points.

The only such targets that we know of in such numbers are our Minuteman sites; therefore, the possibility of a Soviet MIRV concerns us because it could nullify our deterrent. So we are deploying Safeguard in order to preserve a sufficient number of Minutemans to provide retaliatory capability.

Of our two actions, MIRV is to maintain the U.S. deterrent in the face of the Soviet ballistic missile defense, and Safeguard is to maintain our deterrent against a Soviet attack on it.

U.S. CAPABILITY TO INCREASE MISSILE ACCURACY

Senator COOPER. I understand the defense which has been made both for the deployment of MIRV and ABM. But you are assuming, of course, that the Soviets will believe that our intentions are perfect. I would just ask you this question. Isn't it possible for the United States with all its technology to develop an accuracy, better accuracy, both in our Minuteman, Polaris, and Poseidon missiles? We have that capability, do we not?

Dr. FOSTER. Senator Cooper, we do not have that capability, not in being; but it is technologically feasible, in my opinion, for the United States to develop sufficient accuracy that with multiple vehicles sometime in the future we would be able to attack silos in the Soviet Union.

However, we had a program of investigation along these lines and last year I canceled it. My purpose was to make it absolutely clear to the Congress and, hopefully, to the Soviet Union, that it is not the policy of the United States to deny the Soviet Union their deterrent capability.

Senator COOPER. But you say we could develop the accuracy and if that accuracy could be developed it could be a threat to their intercontinental ballistic missile, too.

Dr. FOSTER. Yes, sir, that is correct. It would be some time in the future, but I believe it is possible.

CAPABILITY OF ABM

Senator COOPER. I won't take very long, but I want to go into this question of the capability of the ABM.

As I understand your thesis, it is that you look at the worst possible case. At some point, I believe you said 1974, you estimate the number of SS-9's and what is the other missile the Soviets have in quantity?

Dr. FOSTER. SS-11's.

Senator COOPER. SS-11's, that the Soviets may have in being.

Then, second, you estimate the number of warheads those missiles would have in being if MRV or MIRV should be deployed. Is that correct?

Dr. FOSTER. Yes, sir, that is correct.

Senator COOPER. Then you say, taking that estimate, that you are developing an ABM to meet that threat.

Now, wouldn't it be clear that if you made such an estimate to have the best possible defense you could have, you would have to deploy a thick ABM then at all the 12 or 14 sites? You would have to plan deploying ABM at all of the proposed sites.

Dr. FOSTER. Senator Cooper, it might require it if the threat continued as we have projected it. This is not the worst case but simply an extension of present trends.

Senator COOPER. You have taken a case that threatens our deterrent, and my question is this——

Dr. FOSTER. Then it would call, sir——

Senator COOPER. If you estimate the worst case from the U.S. viewpoint or the best case from the Soviet viewpoint, then you have to make a similar kind of judgment as to the deployment of the ABM to meet that. My question is, wouldn't that require the deployment ABM of all of the phases that have been submitted to Congress— the full system?

Dr. FOSTER. Senator Cooper, this is, as I indicated to the chairman——

Senator COOPER. It is a fairly simple answer. The reason I ask it is this: Last year we were told that we should be very careful looking at this, these would be deployed at these sites, and now we are saying we have to make another mild restrained judgment. But don't you have to foresee that if this trend in the Soviet deployment continues, that you would have to deploy them at least at all of the other sites which have been named to the Congress?

Dr. FOSTER. Yes, sir, the short answer to that is, yes.

Senator COOPER. What?

Dr. FOSTER. The answer is, yes.

COST OF DEPLOYING SAFEGUARD PHASE II

Senator COOPER. I address myself to the question of cost. What would be the cost of deploying the full ABM system as described to the Congress?

Dr. FOSTER. The DOD acquisition cost associated with the completion of the defense around four Minuteman sites with Safeguard components only is, as I recall, about $6.4 billion.

Senator COOPER. Phase II.

Dr. FOSTER. Yes, sir. I think you are referring to the cost associated with the active defense of the Minuteman if we were to complete four sites.

Senator COOPER. First the Minuteman sites, with all of the facilities and weapons that are needed, including warheads. But you are not able now to give us testimony on that?

Dr. FOSTER. I can't give you an accurate number, but $6.4 billion is a good estimate. Those figures, Senator Cooper, have all been provided to the Congress previously.

EFFECTIVENESS OF SPRINTS AND SPARTANS IN DEFENDING MINUTEMAN

Senator COOPER. To be able to defend Minuteman against this level of Soviet offense that you estimate and taking into consideration that in addition to the warheads that may come in, and there would be other objects—penetration aids—in other words, you say that the number of Sprints that have been given to us would effectively meet an attack by them upon the greater part of our Minuteman silos, you think the number of Sprints and Spartans that you described to us last year would meet that threat including coping with the other objects that come in which would have to be met by the defensive warheads.

Dr. FOSTER. Senator Cooper, that is a very important point.

Senator COOPER. It surely is.

Dr. FOSTER. I will give you a quick answer. We have provided a number of Sprints to assure the survival of a critical number of Minutemans. We recognize that, in the attack that is postulated, hundreds of Minuteman will be destroyed, but it is important that a few hundred, of the total thousand, survive and form a deterrent.

Now that means that we use the Sprint missiles in the following way. The Sprints are fired at the warhead not before it comes into the atmosphere but after it has entered it and after the decoys and other objects are filtered out. If there are decoys that penetrate so deeply that the radar operator has to conclude from his information that those objects could be warheads and that they will land close enough to silos to destroy them, then Sprint missiles must be dispatched to attack them.

ESTIMATE OF 1974 SOVIET STRIKE CAPABILITY

Senator COOPER. Well, again I will make a rough estimate, but if your estimate of the incoming warheads, and considering the same rate that the SS-9's have been deployed, how many would be deployed by 1974?

Dr. FOSTER. The rough estimate is as given on the chairman's chart, Senator Cooper.

Senator COOPER. How many?

Dr. FOSTER. By 1974 there would be a little over 400 SS-9's.

Senator COOPER. If they were MRV's it would be 1,200.

Dr. FOSTER. Yes, sir, and if they were MIRVed and each had three RV's, there would be roughly 1,200.

Senator COOPER. It could be 2,000.

Dr. FOSTER. No, as I indicated, we do not take the worst case. It is true that the Soviet Union could next year decide to increase the rate at which they are deploying SS-9's, and under those conditions we would have to change our plans and accordingly come to the Congress with a different request.

Senator. COOPER. First, I want to take the case that you have given, 400 SS-9's. Now if they were MRV, what number of warheads could be delivered on our missile sites?

Dr. FOSTER. Well, sir, if they are MRV's that would mean they are not individually aimed. But if they are MIRV's——

Senator COOPER. How many warheads could be delivered on the United States then?

Dr. FOSTER. Then if they had 400 missiles around 1974 they would have 1,200 reentry vehicles. Perhaps something like eight-tenths of those might be successfully launched and arrive, so that means roughly 960 would arrive on targets in the United States. If the 960 were sent to the Minuteman fields, there would be a certain probability of their killing the Minuteman. Let's estimate for the sake of the example, that the probability that each would destroy a silo is nine-tenths. This leaves us with 800-odd Minuteman that would be destroyed and less than 200 surviving.

Senator COOPER. I remember the chart we examined and discussed last year in the closed session of the Senate. It was a chart which gave the information you are now supplying.

HAS DOD DECIDED TO INCREASE SPRINTS AROUND MSR'S?

I want to ask, since last year, has your department made a decision to deploy a greater number of Sprints around MSR's than the information you gave us last year?

Dr. FOSTER. Senator Cooper, last year when Secretary Laird came before you requesting moneys for Safeguard Phase I, he requested, as you recall, the sites at Grand Forks and Malmstrom, and there was also a request for some Sprints and Spartans at each site. This year we are coming before you, as you know, with a request for deployment of additional site, one at Whiteman.

In addition to that, we are asking for two other things: one, to increase the number of Sprints to be deployed at Malmstrom and Grand Forks; and, two, to request authority for the preliminary engineering work be done so that we can survey and gain an understanding of just what the best locations are around the country for an additional five sites.

Senator COOPER. You have not answered my question.

Dr. FOSTER. We have added Sprints.

Senator COOPER. Since last year the decision has been made to use more Sprints at the two sites than we were told last year would be necessary and that would be all that were needed.

Dr. FOSTER. Senator Cooper, in the Phase II plan, there always was a full complement of Sprints at Grand Forks and Malmstrom. We did not ask for the full complement of Sprints at Grand Forks and

Malmstrom last year. This year we are requesting funds to bring them to the full complement.

Senator COOPER. But last year though we were told by the supporters of ABM that the number asked for was entirely sufficient to take care of the job.

Dr. FOSTER. No; sir.

Senator COOPER. At a closed session, I suppose it is all right for me to tell what the representatives said, the debate hinged very largely on this issue, on this issue of whether the number of Sprints would be sufficient to protect the sites against an attack, and I believe we were assured that it was sufficient.

Now you say to us that since that time you are asking for more Sprints for these two sites.

Dr. FOSTER. Senator Cooper, in the request last year we asked for a certain number of Sprints and Spartans, and said those would be adequate to provide for the survival of a certain number of Minutemans in those sites.

Senator COOPER. Now I will ask you again.

Dr. FOSTER. Now the threat has continued to grow, and we have asked for an additional site and, at the same time, requested additional Sprints to bring those in the first two sites to their full complement.

Senator COOPER. I understand.

MODIFICATION OF RADARS AND INCREASE IN SPRINTS

Now last year questions were raised about the vulnerability of the radar and again we were assured that the plans of the Defense Department were correct. We were told that the arguments made by many scientists that we would need many small radars, if we were going to have an effective system. Is it correct that since that time you are planning to modify the system now, and you now will develop small radars? Is that correct?

Dr. FOSTER. Senator Cooper, we are requesting this year funds in the amount of about $58 million to begin the design of a small radar to complement the missile site radars in the defense of Minuteman—yes, that is correct.

Senator COOPER. You found it necessary to do that.

Dr. FOSTER. Yes, sir, we believe it is necessary not to make the deployment but to be prepared to deploy should the threat continue to mount.

Senator COOPER. Last year that argument which was made of the necessity for smaller radars was advanced by a number of scientists including Dr. Panofsky, was just brushed off. My conclusion is—I don't want to put words in your mouth—that the objections were made last year that there were not sufficient Sprints and that the single large radar, the MSR, would not be able to handle the traffic.

Now you have changed your mind in the Defense Department, and you now agree that many small radars and more Sprints should be added.

Dr. FOSTER. No, Senator Cooper, that description of our position is inaccurate.

Senator COOPER. But it is my understanding.

Dr. FOSTER. For 10 years we have looked at small radars. We have considered what kind we might design and when we might install them. There is no small radar system known that can accomplish the Safeguard mission.

Small radars sitting in a Minuteman field will not satisfy the area defense requirements of the Safeguard system.

Senator COOPER. I will come to area defense in just a few minutes.

Dr. FOSTER. When it comes to making an in-depth, extended defense of Minuteman against an increasing threat, I believe it will be necessary to add more radars and more missiles, and the request for development of the smaller radar is to give us the option to do that should the threat continue to grow.

WHAT IS INCREASED THREAT?

Senator CASE. Before the Senator goes to the other question, I wonder if on the points I think you just made, Dr. Foster, that the threat has increased from last year. Could you tell us just what you mean, because it has been my understanding that there have been no new sites observed for the SS-9, for example, since last August?

Senator COOPER. August.

Senator CASE. In what respect is the threat greater than it was anticipated when you came up last year before us?

Dr. FOSTER. Senator Case, the threat has continued to grow.

Senator CASE. But you anticipated it?

Dr. FOSTER. That is correct.

Senator CASE. Yes, so why——

Dr. FOSTER. In fact we took only the minimum step needed in fiscal year 1971. As long as the threat continues to grow, it will demand an additional step in 1972, and should the threat continue through 1973 and 1974 it will demand additional steps. I think it is quite clear from the President's statement that each year he will review Safeguard from the point of view of technical progress, changes in military threat and the diplomatic context.

ADEQUACY OF 1969 PROPOSAL QUESTIONED

Senator CASE. John, you take it from here. The point is, of course, that we understood you to tell us that not only what was proposed last year in the system designed for these two sites was adequate for them but was adequate for a projection of the Soviet deployment of its missiles as you saw it then, and I think there was no doubt about this. This we were told was adequate against many of the objections that many of us raised that it was not.

Dr. FOSTER. Senator Case, I am sorry. I believe then there was some misunderstanding.

Let me explain. The request in Safeguard Phase I involved only two radars and a very limited number of Spartans and Sprints. The number is so small that it would be very difficult to make much of an argument that a critical number of Minuteman would survive when the number of interceptors is very small and the threat very large and somewhat uncertain. So I would not have made any effort to persuade you of that case.

To the contrary, Secretary Laird and I have both said that the first step, Safeguard Phase I, requested in fiscal year 1970 was a start.

It was the minimum that we believed was necessary, judging the situation at that time.

Since the threat has continued to grow, we believe in fiscal year 1971 this is now the minimum that we need in order to cope with the future growth of the threat as we see it.

Senator CASE. Senator Cooper, I don't want to labor the obvious but as you saw it then, you saw then a continuation of the deployment, which has not increased over your then estimate.

Dr. FOSTER. That is correct.

Senator CASE. And so I think you say anything you want, but you cannot convince me that something that was expressed to us as adequate for its purpose ceased to be adequate just because something less than you then anticipated in the way of Soviet deployment has occurred since.

Dr. FOSTER. Senator Case, I think perhaps this approach would be helpful.

On requesting the fiscal year 1970 budget for Safeguard Phase I, we said it was the minimum needed at that time. We could, of course, have requested three or four sites, which was more than the minimum essential program. President Nixon has selected in each of the last 2 years the minimum necessary. That is the difference.

PURPOSE OF ADMINISTRATION'S REQUEST ON SAFEGUARD

Senator COOPER. I just say when I read Secretary Laird's first testimony before the House committee, I had no doubt at all that it was the purpose of the Administration to start and complete the whole 12–14 site ABM system.

But we were not told that new radars were necessary, and we were not told that an additional number of Sprints would be added. These things were not made public. Statements were made then to the effect of denying the very things I am talking about now which the Department of Defense says it now needs.

Dr. FOSTER. Senator Cooper, I can't speak for the impression that you gained, but it was very clear in my testimony—and I know it was in Secretary Laird's and Secretary Packard's—that we did not have a commitment to complete the 12 sites. We were only asking for the minimum that was necessary. In addition, in the several appearances last year, I took great pains to explain to the many committees that, if the threat should grow beyond those limits—in particular, the threat to Minuteman—it would be necessary to add more radars to the four outlined in Safeguard Phase II, and to add more missiles. I hoped it would be possible in deploying additional radars to reduce their size and capability in order to reduce the costs, in other words, to secure the defense of Minuteman at minimum cost.

DEFENSE DEPARTMENT EVALUATION OF SAFEGUARD ADEQUACY

Senator COOPER. I will ask this question. You have in your office an agency called an antiballistic evaluations office.

Dr. FOSTER. To my knowledge, sir, we don't have an agency by that name.

Senator COOPER. Do you have a group of men who are charged with the task of evaluating antiballistic-missile systems?

Dr. FOSTER. Yes, sir; we have two groups—one group in the Advanced Research Projects Agency that follows the offensive-defensive game and looks into the long-range research programs that are necessary to maintain a viable defense and to initiate new defenses.

We also have the Advanced Ballistic Missile Defense Agency in the Army that does a similar job.

Senator COOPER. Now, the advanced ballistic evaluations office in the Department of the Army——

Dr. FOSTER. The Advanced Ballistic Missile Defense Agency.

Senator COOPER. Now neither of these groups is the ad hoc committee that you talked about.

Dr. FOSTER. No, sir. The ad hoc committee was composed entirely of people from the outside.

Senator COOPER. I don't know whether you can answer this or not, but have any of these evaluations committees agreed with a study which advises that the Safeguard system was not adequate for its announced mission—is that correct?

Dr. FOSTER. The Advanced Ballistic Missile Defense Agency is conducting a study with regard to the best approaches to implementing the defense of Minuteman beyond the Safeguard Phase II portion.

They have not reached their final conclusions. Their report has not been presented to me. I expect to review it in the next 3 weeks very intensively.

Senator COOPER. Is one of the purposes of this study group to find out whether or not the Safeguard is adequate for its mission?

Dr. FOSTER. That group has already made that review over and over in previous years. Their charge at the moment is to come up with a range of options for me and for the Secretary of Defense to consider should the threat go beyond those levels with which the Safeguard Phase II defense of Minuteman could cope.

ADEQUATE SAFEGUARD AREA DEFENSES

Senator COOPER. I have just about three more questions, Mr. Chairman.

I will turn for a moment to the area defense aspect of this system. That is to protect against a Chinese threat, isn't it?

Dr. FOSTER. Yes, sir; against Chinese attack or accidental launch and to protect our bombers against an offshore attack by submarines with ballistic missiles.

Senator COOPER. If you were to have an area defense would it be necessary for the Department of Defense to name the areas, the community and facilities which will be necessary to protect?

Dr. FOSTER. I am not sure I fully understand your question, Senator Cooper.

Senator COOPER. If you have an area defense you would have to defend something—some localities, some areas.

Dr. FOSTER. Yes, sir; it would be the area of the United States.

Senator COOPER. If it is a missile site defense you would defend a missile site. You have to determine the cities, the communities and facilities that you felt it would be necessary to protect.

Dr. FOSTER. Yes, sir; and we would so designate them.

Senator COOPER. Has that been done?

Dr. FOSTER. No, sir; it has not been done. The reason is that we have not performed the engineering surveys that are necessary to determine which of the many possible sites are most acceptable from the point of view of the defense system.

Senator COOPER. I believe that we have had testimony that it has not been considered that the Chinese would develop for a number of years a ballistic missile system that would threaten the United States the same way that the Soviet missiles forces do. Now this would be chiefly to protect against so-called blackmail threats. Well, the blackmailer could deliver his force to any one facility or community, couldn't he? He could saturate a single area.

Dr. FOSTER. Yes, sir; it certainly could.

Senator COOPER. Well then, to make your defense adequate, credible, wouldn't you have to be in a position to protect every one of those facilities?

Dr. FOSTER. Yes, sir; we would.

Senator COOPER. Then you get the thick area defense, wouldn't you?

Dr. FOSTER. Senator Cooper, whether one considers the area defense, as specified in Safeguard Phase II, thick or thin depends on the nature of the attack. If one assumes that the Chinese, for example, were to get a capability comparable to that currently available to France or the United Kingdom, then there is no question that Safeguard Phase II could cope with those numbers of missiles.

If, however, one projects that the Chinese Communists will, in fact, deploy a force that becomes comparable to those of the Soviet Union and the United States, then Safeguard Phase II could not protect every community of the continental United States.

Senator COOPER. Would you then have to augment the system and provide for missiles or Sprints, Spartans?

Dr. FOSTER. I don't want to predict what the President might decide in 1980 or 1985, Senator Cooper. But President Nixon and Secretary Laird have said—and I believe it—that the Safeguard Phase II capability when fully implemented will provide protection of the U.S. population well into the 1980's against the projected Chinese growth capability as estimated by the intelligence community.

SOVIET VIEW OF SAFEGUARD AREA DEFENSE

Senator COOPER. You don't think the Soviet Union would consider that it might be an area of defense against an attack by the Soviet Union?

Dr. FOSTER. Senator Cooper, that is a serious point. As you know, last year President Nixon made the decision to deliberately pull the deployment of Safeguard sites away from cities, to make it crystal clear to the Soviet Union that we're not going to protect this country with Safeguard Phase I against a heavy deployment, and thus deny the Soviets a deterrent capability against the United States. In my view, the Soviets would have to view Safeguard as a relatively light defense, one that at best could absorb a very small fraction of their current strategic offensive capability.

QUESTIONS SUBMITTED FOR THE RECORD

Senator COOPER. I think this is my last question although there are a number of other questions, I wish we had time to ask them. I will submit the questions to you for classified answer if necessary and unclassified answer for the record.

Dr. FOSTER. I would be delighted, Senator Cooper, to give them my personal attention.

(The questions and answers referred to appear in appendix II.)

INCREASE IN SOVIET SS-9'S

Senator COOPER. How many SS-9's have been completed since last August and how many silos and silo complexes are being newly dug in addition to those that we have already seen?

Dr. FOSTER. Senator Cooper, the Defense statement on this is a matter of record and was given by Secretary Laird last fall and again this spring when he noted an increase. This extension of questioning, I am afraid, will lead us into the matter of the currency of our intelligence-collection capability, and I don't believe that is appropriate in an open session. If the chairman wishes, I would be delighted to discuss the details of the changes in the Soviet ICBM capability during the last 6 to 9 months.

SITES INVOLVED IN SAFEGUARD PHASE II AREA DEFENSE

Senator CASE. Will the Senator yield? Just this one question that was raised by Senator Cooper, I would appreciate your clarifying the matter for me, Dr. Foster. I think you said that the second stage, first and second stages, of Safeguard would take care of an area defense of the whole United States.

Dr. FOSTER. The continental United States?

Senator CASE. Continental United States.

Dr. FOSTER. Yes, sir.

Senator CASE. Against an anticipated Chinese capability. Now that second stage involves how many sites? It involves three sites, doesn't it?

Dr. FOSTER. Phase II would consist of 12 sites, sir.

Senator CASE. That is quite a different thing than we are asked to authorize this year, isn't it?

Dr. FOSTER. This year we are requesting authorization for a third site.

Senator CASE. Phase II, I am sorry by phase II you meant this year's appropriations.

Dr. FOSTER. No, sir.

Senator CASE. This year's appropriation will not do anything like that.

Dr. FOSTER. No, sir.

Senator CASE. We need all the 12 sites even for a thin defense against the Chinese.

Dr. FOSTER. That is correct.

Senator GORE. Which illustrates what I said last year to be correct that what you sought last year was a nose under the tent for the full scale ABM, wasn't it?

Dr. FOSTER. We made it clear, Mr. Chairman, that it was a start, to guard against deterioration of our strategic deterrent in the future and to provide protection against blackmail by the Communist Chinese when they achieve an ICBM capability.

Senator GORE. It is only this year that we hear about the fear of the momentum.

Dr. FOSTER. Sir, last year you will recall that Secretary Laird came before this Congress and expressed his concern about the growing capability in the Soviet Union. At that time there were many who felt that the Secretary was sabre rattling because the estimates that he gave were in excess of those provided just a year earlier by Secretary Clifford. This year he came again before the Congress and gave them estimates that were considerably above those last year, and so in retrospect he was conservative.

I hope that next year when he comes before the Congress he will be able to report a considerable dropoff, the kind of dropoff that has been projected year after year by the intelligence community but unfortunately has not, in fact, occurred.

Senator GORE. Perhaps several of us can take some satisfaction out of a view in retrospect.

I presented a chart last year which demonstrated, as I thought, the sufficiency of our nuclear strategic capability at that time. I am glad to find that you and the Secretary of Defense are this year agreeing with that.

You have been here 3 hours or a little better, and I thank you for coming.

You have been an able witness. I have many more questions I would like to ask. I will not do so, but I would like to make a very brief statement with respect to the SALT talks to which you can reply or not as you wish.

EFFECT OF INTERPLAY BETWEEN MIRV AND ABM ON SALT

I do this because the Administration has not invited Senate participation in preparation of the negotiating position, nor has it invited advice to the delegation or even an observer to the delegation. Nevertheless since I have been an active participant in this field for so long, I do feel some responsibility to suggest what appear to me to be some inconsistencies.

We have been told many times, and you have again related this morning, that the purpose of the United States in deploying MIRV was to proliferate our attack or our offensive capability so as to preserve our deterrence. That is MIRV is in response to Soviet deployment of defensive ABM's.

If in the SALT agreements we are able to eliminate ABM deployment, then what is the purpose of MIRV? This is a question.

On the other hand, we have been told many, many times that the 67 ABM sites deployed around Moscow would be ineffective as a defense because with our large number of strategic weapons, particularly when proliferated with MIRV warheads, our attack could simply exhaust or overpower the missiles around Moscow.

If the defense around the capital city of Moscow can be exhausted by a hundred or 68 or whatever number the United States should,

God forbid, launch upon Moscow, then would not a defense around the capital city of the United States be equally exhaustible by an attack by the Soviet Union?

The question I am raising and suggesting to the Administration is that this interplay between MIRV and ABM deployments is an intricate one, and unless we are very, very cautious then we box ourselves into the position where both sides must say that they must have both MIRV and ABM.

Dr. FOSTER. Mr. Chairman, I believe that a comprehensive statement in reply to your questions would involve details of the negotiations at SALT, and I believe I must refrain from discussing such matters.

Senator GORE. As I say, I was not asking you to make a reply, but I would not foreclose the opportunity. Would you pass these apprehensions along to whoever is making our policy with respect to negotiations?

Dr. FOSTER. I will be glad to pass your comments on to Secretary Laird, sir.

Senator GORE. It seems to me the suggestion that we only have one ABM system for the defense of the capital is about the most impractical ever made.

Senator Cooper, do you have something further?

Dr. FOSTER. I understand your concern.

Senator GORE. Thank you very much, Dr. Foster.

Dr. FOSTER. Thank you very much, Mr. Chairman and members of the committee.

(Whereupon, at 1:10 p.m., the committee was adjourned.)

ABM, MIRV, SALT, AND THE NUCLEAR ARMS RACE

MONDAY, JUNE 29, 1970

UNITED STATES SENATE,
SUBCOMMITTEE ON ARMS CONTROL,
INTERNATIONAL LAW AND ORGANIZATION
OF THE COMMITTEE ON FOREIGN RELATIONS,
Washington, D.C.

The subcommittee met, pursuant to recess, at 10 a.m., in room 4221, New Senate Office Building, Senator Albert Gore (chairman of the subcommittee) presiding.

Present: Senators Gore, Fulbright (chairman of the full committee), Symington, Case, and Cooper.

Senator GORE. The subcommittee will come to order.

OPENING STATEMENT

The Subcommittee on Arms Control, International Law and Organization is meeting today to hear testimony from Dr. Sidney D. Drell, deputy director, Stanford Linear Accelerator Center, and Dr. M. L. Goldberger, professor of physics, Princeton University. Both were, until recently, members of the President's Science Advisory Committee.

Dr. Drell and Dr. Goldberger were invited to appear before the subcommittee as a consequence of statements made by Dr. John Foster, Director of Defense Research and Engineering in the course of testimony before this subcommittee on June 4.

DR. FOSTER'S TESTIMONY ON AD HOC SCIENTIFIC PANEL

At that meeting, Dr. Foster told the subcommittee that an ad hoc panel of scientists, headed by Dr. Lawrence H. O'Neill of Columbia University, whom we are pleased to have in the audience this morning, had reviewed the Administration's plans for the Safeguard system and had reported to Secretary of Defense Laird that the equipment proposed for the Safeguard system would, in Dr. Foster's words, "do the jobs that the Department of Defense wants to do."

The clear implication of Dr. Foster's statement, as I read it, was that the panel supported the Pentagon's arguments justifying expanding the Safeguard ABM system.

When asked for the names of the members of the O'Neill Panel, Dr. Foster mentioned Dr. Drell and Dr. Goldberger, among others.

LETTERS FROM WITNESSES CONCERNING DR. FOSTER'S TESTIMONY

Subsequently, Dr. Drell and Dr. Goldberger wrote me and commented on Dr. Foster's testimony. Dr. Drell said in his letter that "Dr. Foster's remarks indicate that we made recommendations which in fact we did not make." He added that Dr. Foster's remark that the equipment proposed for the Safeguard "will do the job that the Department of Defense wants to do," was, "an incorrect statement since the report contains no such far-reaching conclusion."

Dr. Goldberger in his letter to me said that he presumed that the implication of Dr. Foster's remarks was that the "panel supported the arguments presented by Dr. Foster and the Department of Defense in justifying the next phase of Safeguard to your committee."

Dr. Goldberger added, "The report took no such position." I will include the letters from Dr. Drell and Dr. Goldberger in the record of this hearing.

(The information referred to follows.)

PRINCETON UNIVERSITY,
DEPARTMENT OF PHYSICS,
JOSEPH HENRY LABORATORIES,
Princeton, N.J., June 11, 1970.

Hon. ALBERT GORE,
*U.S. Senate, 1311 New Senate Office Building,
Washington, D.C.*

DEAR SENATOR GORE: I am writing to you in connection with the testimony before your committee presented by Dr. John Foster on 4 June.

Although I have not seen Dr. Foster's testimony, I have been informed that I was named as a member of a panel chaired by Dr. Lawrence O'Neill whose report was described by Dr. Foster as follows: ". . . the report was sent to the Secretary of Defense, and what it said was that this equipment will do the job the Department of Defense wants to do."

I can only presume that the implication here is that our panel supported the arguments presented by Dr. Foster and the Department of Defense in justifying the next phase of Safeguard to your committee.

The report took no such position. We were *not* presented with a definite deployment proposal with stated objectives against which systems performance could be measured. Our guidelines were only the original objectives for the Safeguard deployment made by President Nixon on 14 March 1969, and certain budgetary and schedule limitations. We analyzed certain alternative deployment options designed to maximize, insofar as possible, the effectiveness of defense against various threats. We did not address the question of the wisdom of continuing to obligate funds for ABM nor were we asked to recommend a level of funding for a next phase of deployment.

The extent to which any of the deployment options considered by the Panel meet The President's announced objectives is discussed in detail in the report which is classified Secret. I can therefore not describe them here but would strongly urge you to request a copy of the Panel report submitted to Secretary Laird on 27 January 1970.

I have spoken publicly in opposition to the proposed next phase of Safeguard deployment and would be happy to submit my views to you in writing or in person.

Sincerely yours,

(S) M. L. GOLDBERGER.

STANFORD UNIVERSITY,
STANFORD LINEAR ACCELERATOR CENTER,
Stanford, Calif., June 5, 1970.

Hon. ALBERT GORE,
*U.S. Senate,
Washington, D.C.*

DEAR SENATOR GORE: In his testimony of June 4, 1970 before your subcommittee Dr. John Foster, DDRE, introduced my name as a participant in a study [1] that

---
[1] Chaired by Dr. Lawrence H. O'Neill, president, Riverside Research Institute, and professor, electrical engineering, on leave of absence, Columbia University.

he initiated for the purpose of advising him on various possible Safeguard ABM programs for FY 1971.

I am writing this letter to make as clear as I can what were the scope and limits of the activity undertaken by this ad hoc panel because it seems to me that Dr. Foster's remarks indicate that we made recommendations which in fact we did not make. Of course these points would be totally clear if the panel report, submitted to Secretary Laird on January 27, 1970 and classified secret, were made available to you and your subcommittee.

(1) The panel was asked for its advice on the basis of scientific, technical, schedule, and budgetary considerations only, and on the assumption that the President and Congress, after review, decided to continue to approve the obligating of additional funds for ballistic missile defense. We were specifically *not* asked to judge the wisdom of such an assumed decision nor were we asked to advise on a sensible or desirable level of the additional funds.

(2) Dr. Foster remarked during his testimony that ". . . the report was sent to the Secretary of Defense, and what it said was that this equipment will do the job that the Department of Defense wants to do." *That is an incorrect statement* since the report contains no such far-reaching conclusion. What we did say in our report is classified secret and therefore I cannot elaborate further here; I do so under separate cover.

(3) Dr. Foster remarked that "they had some recommendations and, for example, they would like to add the smaller radars, a decision we had already made or at least they concurred in that decision." Along with most supporters as well as opponents of the Safeguard program we did indeed support the work on further development of the technologies based on smaller radars for an effective hard point defense of Minuteman—but the question of whether these are to be *added* to Safeguard hardware or are to *replace it* entirely for accomplishing this mission was not addressed.

(4) On May 6, 1970, I had the privilege of testifying concerning the Administration's proposed expansion of the Safeguard ABM system before the Subcommittee on Defense (Chairman—George Mahon of Texas) of the Committee on Appropriations (Chairman—George Mahon) of the U.S. House of Representatives. This testimony was given in closed session and both the formal testimony and the discussion following it were at the secret level. By separate mail I am sending you a copy of my full statement. I believe the transcript of this hearing will soon be printed. In the meantime I would like to quote several unclassified paragraphs from this testimony to make my own views clear in the light of Dr. Foster's testimony (italics added for present emphasis):

"Here I ask only whether Safeguard can accomplish an assigned mission of protecting Minuteman.

"My answer in substance is NO. *There have been extensive studies, and I believe it is fair to say that all now recognize that Safeguard, even working perfectly, and with a full nationwide Phase II deployment costing about $10 billion can be effective in preserving 300 Minuteman missiles, which is deemed adequate as a retaliatory force, against only a very narrow band of models of an assumed Soviet strike.*

"The trouble with Safeguard for *"hard point defense"* of the Minuteman system is that it is built exclusively of radar and missile components that were engineered for a *city defense* in the old Sentinel system."

*   *   *   *   *   *   *

"Today I am here to oppose strongly the proposed expansion not only because of the known technical inadequacies but because, in fact, we have yet to gain any of the experience motivating the Phase I decision that was promised as part of a phased deployment program. At this time no equipment is in place, no parts of the system are complete, and indeed its operating capability under a major attack is still under study. What then have we learned to support the expanded deployment?

"*All analyses of which I am aware make it clear that if defense of Minuteman is the principal or sole mission of Safeguard, its further deployment cannot be justified.* As I hope to have convinced you, it simply fails to respond to the Soviet threats postulated by the Pentagon. What I recommend is moving ahead vigorously with the development work on alternative technologies that we know at present can perform the hard point defense more effectively and economically in the mid to late 1970's, if needed."

*   *   *   *   *   *   *

"The Safeguard technology as we have argued is not well matched to the mission of hard point defense of Minuteman, nor to that of providing a thin area umbrella. What worries me is that the *technology* of Safeguard *is* best suited for providing a *thick* city defense if it is deployed extensively and with the shorter range Sprint interceptors near to the cities in order to back up the long range Spartans. An evolution in this direction, though technologically attractive, would be counter to the President's expressed goals and *must* be resisted in order to avoid escalation of the arms race to higher levels of cost as well as of potential destructiveness.

"In his speech of April 23, Dr. Foster spoke persuasively of our need to take "R&D hedges" in order to combat the great asymmetry between the USA and the Soviet Union as a result of their secrecy versus our openness in government programs. I support such R&D hedges as vital. What I oppose—and this is the thrust of my testimony—is the pressure to turn such R&D hedges into deployment decisions even if the results of the R&D have shown that the system is ineffective and wasteful of resources. I believe my testimony indicates that the Congress should resist that unwise further evolution of Safeguard.

"We must stop this heedless race soon and the best place to start is by stopping systems such as Safeguard that at best, as I have discussed, are wasteful, ineffective, and expensive. At worst they further propel the arms race by the action-reaction phenomenon described above."

* * * * * * *

I am available and would be happy to discuss in full my views on ABM and the Safeguard program with you and the Committee.

Very truly yours,

(S) SIDNEY D. DRELL,
Professor and Deputy Director.

SECRET CLASSIFICATION OF O'NEILL REPORT

Senator GORE. I should add that the subcommittee had requested Dr. Foster on June 4 to provide the O'Neill report. After repeated inquiries, the report was received over the weekend. I have this morning read the O'Neill report. Only a very small percentage of it appears to me to be justified as classified.

In my opinion, the conclusions reached by the report, if made public, would utterly destroy the rationale by which the present proposal is advanced.

Before we hear your prepared statements, would you two gentlemen comment on the secret classification of the report, in which you participated? Is it necessary? How much of this is genuinely secret information?

Dr. DRELL. Senator, I will comment that I believe there are several paragraphs in the report which makes specific technical remarks about our system and intelligence, remarks which are properly classified "Secret." But the main discussion, the main perception, we had of the Safeguard system and its limitations could very well be public.

Senator GORE. That is what I thought. The references to specific details, as you say, are properly classified, but the conclusions and recommendations do not contain such information. Do they?

Dr. DRELL. No.

Senator GORE. What do you think, Doctor?

Dr. GOLDBERGER. I agree completely. I see no reason why the bulk of the report could not be unclassified.

Senator GORE. Nor do I, except that if it were made public, the case for ABM expansion would go out the window. Since Dr. Goldberger's statement is more general in nature, will it be agreeable with you, Dr. Drell, if he goes first?

Dr. DRELL. Absolutely.

Senator GORE. Dr. Goldberger.

STATEMENT OF DR. M. L. GOLDBERGER, PROFESSOR OF PHYSICS, PRINCETON UNIVERSITY

Dr. GOLDBERGER. I am very pleased to have the opportunity to discuss with you today some of the issues associated with the proposed additional Safeguard deployment and more generally, problems of strategic weapons and arms control. I should state that I am testifying as an individual citizen who has been involved with defense matters in general for about 15 years, and ABM, in particular, for the past 10 years. The views I shall express are my own and do not necessarily reflect those of the various advisory groups I have been or currently am associated with.

There is very little which can be said about ABM and related issues which has not already been said in the 16 months which have elapsed since the President's announcement of phase I Safeguard on March 14, 1969.

TESTIMONY OF EXPERTS ON SAFEGUARD

I have studied much of the testimony presented to this and other committees of the House and Senate and am struck by two things. The experts who testified against Safeguard emphasized the technical shortcomings of the system in tremendous detail, got into hairsplitting arguments over whether it took 1,001 or 1,234 Soviet SS-9 missiles to knock out Minuteman, whether the system would or would not work when needed, et cetera, and in general conveyed an unfortunate impression of complexity and controversy that seemed to be beyond the grasp of all but the technical sophisticates.

In addition, they failed on occasion to distinguish sufficiently clearly between opposition to ABM in general as compared to opposition to Safeguard in particular. The civilian proponents of ABM presented by the Department of Defense to the various committees, in spite of explicit classified briefings which I know took place in certain cases, almost to a man avoided talking about the actual Safeguard system. The more charitable interpretation one can put on this remarkable fact is that they could not, as men of scientific integrity, defend the system that was being proposed.

They concentrated instead on the Soviet threat, the intransigence of the Chinese, national determination, the virtues of defensive weapons as extolled by Mr. Kosygin, et cetera, but never, never on the relation of Safeguard performance to the actual or projected threat.

The opponents of ABM, in my opinion, obviously won the debate, but they lost the battle.

WITNESS' OPPOSITION TO SAFEGUARD

I want to state at the outset that I am not unalterably opposed to ABM under all circumstances. I did, however, oppose the decision of last year to proceed with Safeguard phase I. I am not in favor of continuing the deployment at this time and am wholeheartedly opposed to the new Safeguard modified phase II deployment. I shall try today to put the technical and strategic-political issues involved in ABM deployment as simply and forcibly as I can. I want to associate myself completely with the technical presentation to this subcommittee that has been made recently by my professional colleague, Prof. W. K. H. Panofsky, and not emphasize these aspects too heavily.

DR. FOSTER'S TESTIMONY OF JUNE 4, 1970

Before I begin I wish to make a few comments on the testimony made to this subcommittee by Dr. John Foster on June 4, 1970. According to the uncorrected verbatim transcript which I have seen, Dr. Foster referred to my membership on an ad hoc panel convened by him to advise the Secretary of Defense on the next phase of Safeguard ABM deployment. This panel, chaired by Dr. Lawrence O'Neill, was reputed by Dr. Foster to have said that "* * * this equipment will do the jobs that the Department of Defense wants to do."

There is no such statement in the report, nor could there possibly have been because of the charge to the panel. Although we had been told when invited to join the panel that we would be presented with the Department of Defense recommendation for the new Safeguard deployment and that any objections we raised would be passed on to the administration along with the recommendation, this did not in fact happen.

Instead, when the panel actually met, we were asked to consider a number of deployment options that could be carried out within certain budgetary and schedule limitations. The only objective guidelines we had were the original goals for Safeguard that had been defined by President Nixon on March 14, 1969, which I will discuss further below.

The point is that since there was no specific deployment proposal presented to the panel and consequently no stated objectives, we could scarcely have concluded that "* * * this equipment will do the jobs that the Department of Defense wants to do." Since the report is classified and a privileged communication to the Secretary of Defense, I am not at liberty to discuss its actual content with you.

I might also note in passing that among the other members of the committee besides Dr. Drell and me referred to in Dr. Foster's testimony, Dr. Richard Latter was actually an ex-officio panel member, one whose presence during our deliberations I never fully understood. The actual panel members who signed the report were Lewis M. Branscomb, Sidney D. Drell, Marvin L. Goldberger, William G. McMillan, W. S. Melahn, Lawrence H. O'Neill, and Allen M. Peterson.

In summary, I would say that the implication in Dr. Foster's statement that the ad hoc panel had in fact concurred with arguments being presented by the Department of Defense in support of the new Safeguard proposal is very misleading and by no means expresses the considerable spread of opinion among the panel members on this issue.

U.S. POLICY OF DETERRENCE BY ASSURED DESTRUCTION CAPABILITY

Let me turn now to my substantive statement. Our national policy is one of deterrence of nuclear attack by maintaining the ability to inflict an unacceptable degree of damage against any aggressors at any time during the course of a nuclear exchange and, in particular, after absorbing a surprise first strike. This so-called assured destruction capability must be a real one and must be credible if it is to work: the enemy must understand that it will be used against him without question in response to a large attack. That it doesn't do us much short-run good to destroy the Soviet Union, for example, after we have suffered "unacceptable damage" is clear, but we must plan to respond and maintain the capability to do so. Certainty of suicide to an aggressor is the name of the deterrence game.

In the absence of meaningful arms control, the United States must maintain an adequate deterrent force against any plausible projection of the threat from the Soviet Union or the Chinese Peoples Republic. We have this deterrent now and I will discuss later the extent to which it is or is not being eroded.

PRESIDENT'S PROPOSAL OF SAFEGUARD ABM

On March 14, 1969, President Nixon in a policy statement proposed the so-called Safeguard ABM system. The initial deployment was to be at two Minuteman sites—Malmstrom and Grand Forks—and the system ultimately would consist of 12 installations. The purposes of the system were: (1) Protection of our land-based retaliatory forces against a direct attack by the Soviet Union, (2) Defense of the American people against the kind of nuclear attack which Communist China is likely to mount within the decade, and (3) Protection against the possibility of accidental attacks from any source.

He said also that any completed ABM should not be interpretable by the Soviet Union as threatening to their deterrent capability and that this deployment decision should not affect adversely the chance of success in the forthcoming talks with the Soviet Union on arms limitation, the so-called SALT talks.

He further acknowledges that U.S. strategic planners consider damage limitation in case of nuclear war an essentially hopeless strategy; prevention of nuclear war through a combination of deterrence and arms limitation remains our only real hope of survival in the nuclear age.

Finally, the President stated that future deployments of Safeguard would be influenced by the evolving threat and by the new operational experience gained from the initial two-site deployment.

I was very encouraged by these policy remarks in connection with SALT and the argument that the initial deployment of Safeguard, devoted as it was to Minuteman defense, should not exacerbate the arms race since it in no way threatened the Soviet deterrent. I was, however, deeply discouraged by the fact that what we were being offered was a technically makeshift system that bore little relationship to either the existing or projected threat or to the announced objectives it was to meet.

The bulk of the debate in the Senate centered around the threat to our land-based deterrent force—Minuteman—on whether the Soviet Union was building an offensive force of sufficient size to threaten our overall deterrent posture—referred to in the trade as acquiring a first-strike capability—and whether there were technical deficiencies in the Safeguard system made up of components designed for an area defense but whose initial deployment was to defend two hardened Minuteman complexes.

The reason for this emphasis on only one of the three announced Safeguard objectives was probably due to the emphasis in the original testimony of Defense Secretary Laird on the growing Soviet threat to Minuteman. Although there were and are cogent arguments about the irrelevance of the Chinese defense aspect of the Safeguard system, this was never really aired during the Senate hearings.

PROPOSAL FOR SAFEGUARD MODIFIED PHASE II

We are now presented with what is called the Safeguard modified phase II deployment still aimed at moving toward fulfilling all three of President Nixon's objectives, all being regarded as equally important. The new deployment is described by Mr. Laird as "the minimum we can and must do * * * to fulfill the President's national security objectives."

It is to add more missiles to the first two Safeguard sites and to proceed with defense of a third Minuteman complex at Whiteman Air Force Base in Missouri. In addition, preliminary work on five other sites is to begin.

It is perhaps worth noting that there has been no construction activity at the original two sites, no operational experience which was to guide the deployment expansion. Recent theoretical work has indicated that PAR, the perimeter acquisition radar, performance would be so degraded by the nuclear explosion environment produced by both offensive and defensive missiles that its contribution to Safeguard performance is highly questionable.

Senator GORE. May I ask you to identify the recent theoretical work to which you refer?

Dr. GOLDBERGER. There was a study that was presented to a panel, of which I am a member that was chaired by Dr. Robert LeLevier of the Rand Corp. I do not remember offhand under whose auspices this study was carried out, but it is on the basis of his analysis and discussions with other members of that panel that I am basing this statement.

In addition, problems have arisen in connection with the computer which would seriously limit the system's ability to handle large attacks. I will return shortly to the question of the changing threat and to the bearing of the proposed deployment on SALT.

ORIGINAL AND PROPOSED SAFEGUARD ARE SPHERICALLY SENSELESS

In trying to assess what is being proposed by the Department of Defense and the administration I would like to introduce a mathematical characterization of the familiar concept of a sphere. It is a closed surface which looks the same to an observer no matter what angle he views it from. In this same sense, I assert that the original Safeguard deployment and the proposed expanded deployment is spherically senseless. It makes no sense no matter how you look at it.

Let's try looking from at least a few directions. If we find that we get nonsense from enough angles perhaps we can conclude that the system is indeed spherically senseless.

WHAT IS THE SOVIET THREAT?

First, however, what is the Soviet threat? Mr. Laird has said that by mid-1970 the Soviets will have about 1,250 landbased ICBM's and about 300 submarine-launched ballistic missiles. The number of large SS-9's has increased roughly at the rate predicted last year although there are newspaper intelligence reports that there have been no new SS-9 complexes started during the past 9 months. Nevertheless, this continued expansion of offensive forces is surely worrying and rather puzzling.

I would like to speculate—which is really all anyone can do—about the SS-9 development. With its presumed 25 megaton warhead it may have been originally designed to destroy cities in the face of the old Nike-Zeus defense of ancient times. A more likely role was to attack launch-control facilities at Minuteman fields, a purpose essentially foiled by our development of measures to insure launch of individual missiles independent of the survival of the launch-control facility.

The next role for this essentially useless vehicle was heralded by the testing of SS-9's with three reentry vehicles, each presumably capable of carrying a sufficiently large warhead to destroy a Minuteman silo. This would be a much more reasonable role for the SS-9, but strangely enough it now seems less likely that the Soviets are actually moving in that direction.

Thus, although it is not unreasonable to assume that the Soviets would eventually develop a true MIRV capability, multiple individually targetable reentry vehicles, at the present time it still takes one SS-9 per silo attacked. It is perhaps worth remembering that we, too, went through the stage of going from one large warhead, the Polaris A-1, to the A-3, in order to improve our capability for penetrating crude terminal ABM systems. We obviously don't know why the Soviets are pursuing this continued SS-9 development. They, as do we, have an enormous excess of weapons over what is required for assured destruction. Perhaps it is not only us that are the victims of the "mad momentum of nuclear weaponry."

INEFFECTIVENESS OF SAFEGUARD DEFENSE AGAINST SOVIET ATTACK

So much for the threat. Now, what has Safeguard to do about it? It was widely and correctly argued last year that the Safeguard hard point defense composed as it was of the old Sentinel area defense components was unlikely to be very effective against a Soviet attack. The fundamental weakness of the system was the extreme vulnerability of the missile site radar, only one of which is at each defended Minuteman complex and the fact that there were only a very small, still classified, number of defensive missiles to protect both radar and Minuteman.

Clearly, this critical radar must be defended vigorously and it, in contrast to the hardened Minuteman silos, can be attacked by the very numerous SS-11 missiles which have a much smaller payload and less accuracy than the SS-9's. Now, it has been stated by Secretary Laird that there is less expensive and presumably more effective—than Safeguard—technology for carrying out the hard-point defense mission. Dr. Foster has also commented on studies of a new radar for a dedicated hard point system. Nevertheless we are being offered good old Safeguard.

Thus the Safeguard defense of Minuteman deemed highly vulnerable last year is being extended to a third site in the face of a larger Soviet force. The point last year was and continues this year to be the following: if there are enough highly accurate, large payload Soviet missiles to threaten Minuteman without any defense, the presence of the currently proposed hard-point component of Safeguard is irrelevant. In fact, the only thing which has actually changed since last year is the serious concern that the PAR radar may not contribute anything to the system performance.

We conclude then that from the angle of defense of our land-based deterrent, the current proposal makes no sense.

RESEARCH AND STUDY OF DEDICATED HARD-POINT DEFENSE SUPPORTED

It is perhaps worth remarking that with increasing missile accuracy and conceivable projections of missile numbers—it is important to emphasize that I am here referring to what could happen, not anything about which there is any hard intelligence—even a serious hard-point defense, as contrasted with Safeguard, might have only a limited lifetime. I, nevertheless, strongly support the idea of doing further research and, in particular, carrying out serious engineering studies of a dedicated hard-point defense. There are, in addition, a variety of alternate basing strategies currently under study which might be the only realistic long-range salvation for Minuteman survival.

EFFECT OF UNDEFENDED MINUTEMAN FORCE

There is something both reassuring and at the same time very scary about an undefended Minuteman force. The reassuring part is that the Soviets must always take into account the possibility that, no matter what public protestations to the contrary we might make, Minuteman can always be fired on warning of a massive attack. The scary thing is that fear of destruction could greatly increase the chances of all-out nuclear war by mistake or by panic.

CONCEIVABILITY OF 1975 SOVIET FIRST-STRIKE CAPABILITY

Let us ask now whether it is conceivable that the Soviet Union can get a first strike capability against the United States even without our deployment of hard-point defense in the 1975 time period—which is about as soon as we would mount a significant defense. A first-strike capability for the Soviet Union would require that they have the ability to destroy all the Polaris boats, decimate the strategic bomber force—to say nothing of tactical aircraft-carrying nuclear weapons—to such an extent that their air defense could handle the survivors, and knock out Minuteman completely.

Remember that they now have no significant ABM defense installation. Remember also that if the bombers are attacked first by sub-launched ballistic missiles the land-based missiles will be intact; if one attempts to attack the missiles by ICBM's and simultaneously hit the bombers, the latter can take off in the period between ICBM launch—with its 30 minute flight time—and SLBM arrival on target, a time interval of about 15 minutes.

This dual capability makes a first strike scenario sound implausible even without the existence of Polaris and may even raise questions of the need for Minuteman defense. Remember there is no intelligence information or any known technical invention that says that the security of Polaris is threatened. Such a threat would require an instant and reliable method to destroy all the boats simultaneously.

Finally, remember what a fearsome thing even a single B-52 or a single Polaris submarine is. There is no such thing as a small penetration of a defense when we are talking about nuclear weapons. I don't know what it takes to deter a country, but I sure wouldn't want to be in Moscow or Kiev if a few hundred B-52's were attacking.

I conclude from this argument that one cannot justify pushing ahead with the Safeguard defense of Minuteman with a sense of urgency on the basis of the Soviet Union acquiring a first-strike capability in the 1975 time period.

I should say that there is a scenario which involves destruction of most of the bomber force and all but about one-fourth of Minuteman and then utilizes the elaborate surface to air missile systems in the Soviet Union, the so-called SAMs—designed for bomber defense—to cope with Polaris and the degraded Minuteman and bomber forces. This is at least the scenario which is used to push ahead with U.S. MIRV—multiple individually guided re-entry vehicles—deployment, the beginning of which was recently announced. It is considerations of this variety that seem to drive the arms race inexorably. It is impossible to prove that such a threat to our deterrent violates the laws of physics. But does it follow that a conservative military planner must credit the Soviets with the capability?

Now, this SAM upgrade threat is too complex a problem to discuss in detail here today. I would just like to present three brief arguments which to me point out the implausibility of threat:

1. The creation of a make shift defensive system runs strongly counter to Soviet military practice.

2. The technical problems associated with inter-netting of radars and the computer and data handling processes involved in making this bomber defense into an ABM system are perhaps more complex than those we are having difficulty dealing with in Safeguard.

3. We are talking here about Soviet reliance on such a dubious system to give them a first-strike capability against the United States.

SAFEGUARD AS DEFENSE AGAINST COMMUNIST CHINESE

So much for the Soviet threat. How about the Chinese? The rationale for the Chinese defense has always been a difficult one for me to understand and I was very encouraged by the recent action by the Armed Services Committee of the Senate rejecting the anti-Chinese part of the current Safeguard proposal. However, experience has shown that arguments in favor of ABM have a curious resilence and I am not aware that the administration has changed its position on the issue. Consequently, I want to comment on the Chinese threat and Safeguard's relation to it.

We now have the capability to attack China without fear of nuclear retaliation. It is possible that the complete 12-site Safeguard deployment could extend this capability for some unknown but limited period of time after she gets ICBMs. However, the Chinese will be designing their offensive missile force in the face of our emplaced system whose operating characteristics will be precisely known. Since they are not noted for their stupidity, they will in all probability take steps to counter the defense by the use of penetration aids, or circumvent it entirely by, say, attacking Hawaii if they just want to kill people or using aircraft or ships to attack west coast cities with nuclear weapons.

There seems to be something wrong about the United States spending $12 billion or whatever the number is to purchase a defense against a nonexistent Chinese ICBM threat. Once this threat develops, there is no reason to believe that any ABM defense we build could be "virtually infallible." Suffice it to say that not every defensive missile can be perfectly reliable—there is always a good chance that some missiles will simply leak through.

Note also that the area defense against China is of no value until the full countrywide deployment is complete. It should also be said that the area protection to population centers provided by Safeguard is not as good as that of the old Sentinel deployment. Location of the PARS and Spartan-Sprint farms near cities in Sentinel made it more effective.

This is the inevitable price of trying to build a dual purpose system—it is maximized for neither the hard-point nor area defense role.

Finally, the idea of a blackmail threat by China in the face of our overwhelming forces seems extremely farfetched. I would hope that our concept of a low profile in Asia does not consist of trying to maintain a first-strike capability against China forever.

I conclude that the Chinese argument for ABM deployment makes very little sense. The senselessness is becoming more nearly spherical.

PROVOCATION OF SOVIET UNION

Now we argue that defenses of Minuteman should not be provocative to the Soviet Union because it does not threaten their deterrent. I agree. But how about a full scale area defense with a really substantial number of missiles? This must necessarily give the Russians pause. Consider our reaction to their miserable ABM around Moscow. If they think their deterrent will fall below whatever level they have decided upon, they will increase their offensive force. It is unlikely that we would not respond in kind. This is a virtual cost which should be added to the $12 billion. Thus from the standpoint of not provoking the Soviet Union, the present deployment, as a first step toward the full area defense, doesn't make much sense.

EFFECT OF PROPOSED SAFEGUARD EXPANSION ON SALT

The last angle from which I want to view the latest Safeguard proposal is in its relation to the SALT talks. It has been reported in the press that the Soviets have expressed considerable concern about our proposed ABM deployment. It has been also stated frequently that our decision to go ahead with Safeguard gives us an important "blue chip" to be used in the negotiations.

For example, in the discussion following Dr. Foster's June 4 statement to this subcommittee, he argued that it was important to go ahead with Safeguard at this time because the Soviets would not be inclined to limit ABM deployment by agreement if they can get the same advantages without one.

I am not an expert on Soviet psychology or on negotiations, so I won't speculate on the validity of this argument. A similar question, of course, arises in connection with our beginning MIRV deployment, another conceivable "blue chip." In connection with Safeguard, however, we should not insist on deploying an ineffective system just for bargaining purposes. Safeguard should stand or fall on its own merits. Should a SALT agreement be reached which precluded ABM, it is certainly just as easy to stop building or tear down an effective ABM system as a defective one.

Finally, in connection with SALT, I would be very concerned about our insisting in going ahead with a full area anti-Chinese defense. In an agreement, the corresponding Soviet defense would allow the disposition of many large radars over the Soviet Union which could then add considerable credence to upgrading air defense or clandestine missile defense deployment issues. This in turn would drive the United States to a position of having to make a full deployment of MIRV's in order to maintain our deterrent. And so on.

In plain language, this would be a continuation of the arms race, an escalation to a new level of danger, a new level of instability. Such a conclusion from SALT would be the ultimate in senselessness.

I conclude that the modified Safeguard phase II deployment proposal is indeed spherically senseless. What then should we do?

RECOMMENDATIONS

1. We must make an all-out effort to achieve at SALT an agreement which will limit offensive weapons at what now appears to be a condition of rough parity and ultimately and hopefully lead to a reduction from the present levels. No actions should be contemplated at this time which would endanger this opportunity to finally bring the arms race under some sort of control. I would personally have hoped that the deployment of MIRV would not have begun, but I am encouraged by the administration's expressed willingness to stop it under an agreement. I would also argue against any substantial ABM deployment proposal which might then tend to threaten the level of offensive weapon ceilings.

2. Under no circumstances should the modified Safeguard Phase II deployment go forward—it makes absolutely no sense. It would be consistent then in connection with the recent conclusion of the Armed Services Committee to abandon the anti-Chinese area component of the new deployment to, in fact, stop the deployment of Safeguard Phase I entirely. This was not a conclusion of the committee, but there is a widespread consensus that if the defense of Minuteman were the principal function of Safeguard its deployment cannot be justified.

3. In the absence of a meaningful SALT agreement, there are a number of alternate courses which should be followed: (*a*) Protect Minuteman by a realistic, dedicated, hard-point defense involving a large number of small hardened radars and a substantial number of defensive missiles per Minuteman complex; (*b*) Develop alternate basing strategies for Minuteman; (*c*) Study the possibility of the National Command Authority—Washington, D.C. Such a deployment should not be provocative in view of the Soviet ABM installation at Moscow and has a number of attractive features to it; and (*d*) Study the possibility of total reliance on Polaris—or an improved sea-based system—and our bomber force, the later augmented by a new bomber.

4. Under any circumstances continue active research programs on offensive and defensive weapon systems.

CONCLUSION CONCERNING THE ARMS RACE

Let me conclude with a few general remarks. It would be reasonable to believe that the profound qualitative change in strategic warfare brought about by nuclear weapons technology would have resulted in a complete rethinking and reevaluation of both strategic arms postures and arms control.

In spite of the fact that we have been living with nuclear weapons for a quarter of a century, there is little evidence that any reflection of this change has penetrated very far into the thinking of military strategists or world leaders, to say nothing of the man on the street.

The unbelievable wastefulness of the strategic and tactical arms race between the United States and the Soviet Union is mute testimony to the absence of thought and surely one of the great tragedies of all time. One sometimes gets the feeling that one is watching an unfortunately deadly serious soap opera with a completely ridiculous plot. One can only hope that it will be resolved in some future episode by real statesmen talking to each other. Perhaps the U.S. Senate will show the way.

To quote Robert McNamara in his speech of September 18, 1967, with a trivial modification of dates:

> In the end the root of man's security does not lie in his weaponry. In the end the root of man's security lies in his mind. What the world requires in the 25th year of the Atomic Age is not a new race toward armament. What the world requires in its 25th year of the Atomic Age is a new race toward reasonableness. We had better all run that race.

Senator GORE. Doctor, yours is an eloquent, closely reasoned statement, for which the subcommittee thanks you. We hope you will be willing for Dr. Drell now to give his statement and then participate with him in a panel in response to the subcommittee's questions.

Dr. Drell.

STATEMENT OF DR. SIDNEY D. DRELL, DEPUTY DIRECTOR, STANFORD LINEAR ACCELERATOR CENTER

Dr. DRELL. Thank you.

It is a privilege for me to have this opportunity to testify before you concerning the Administration's proposed expansion of the Safeguard ABM system. I speak here as an individual scientists who for the past 10 years has served actively in various capacities as an adviser and on working panels for the White House, the Department of Defense, and the Arms Control and Disarmament Agency.

Included in these activities have been numerous reviews of strategic problems and weapons systems such as ABM and MIRV. Dr. John Foster, DDRE, in his testimony before your subcommittee on June 4, 1970, introduced my name as a participant in one such study [1] that he initiated for the purpose of advising him on various possible Safeguard ABM programs for fiscal year 1971.

DR. FOSTER'S TESTIMONY CONCERNING O'NEILL PANEL REPORT

I want to comment specifically on this study at this point because Dr. Foster's remarks indicate that we made recommendations which in fact we did not make. Dr. Foster remarked during this testimony that "* * * the report was sent to the Secretary of Defense, and what it said was that this equipment will do the jobs that the Department of Defense wants to do." This is an incorrect statement. The report of the O'Neill committee contains no such far-reaching conclusion.

[1] Chaired by Dr. Lawrence H. O'Neill, president, Riverside Research Institute, and professor, electrical engineering, on leave of absence, Columbia University.

What we did say in our report is classified "secret" and therefore I cannot elaborate further here. I can say, however, that we were not presented with any one proposed program or specific deployment plan to analyze, endorse, or criticize. What the O'Neill panel was asked to do was simply to present its opinions about various proposed programs based on the assumption that the President and Congress, after review, decided to continue to approve the obligating of additional funds for ballistic missile defense.

We were specifically not asked to judge the wisdom of such an assumed decision, nor were we asked to advise on a sensible or desirable level of the additional funds. We made no recommendation about whether or not to expand or even to continue Safeguard deployments.

Also in his testimony, Dr. Foster remarked that "they had some recommendations and, for example, they would like to add the smaller radars, a decision we had already made or at least they concurred in that decision."

Along with most supporters as well as opponents of the Safeguard program, we did indeed support the work on further development of the technologies based on smaller radars for an effective hard-point defense of Minuteman—but the question of whether these are to be added to Safeguard hardware or are to replace it entirely for accomplishing this mission was not addressed.

I want it to be absolutely clear that I do not intend in any way to impugn Dr. Foster's integrity by these remarks.

Senator FULBRIGHT. Mr. Chairman, I do not understand that statement. What do you intend? You just said he is a liar. What do you intend to impugn?

Dr. DRELL. Senator, Dr. Foster, as I go on in my statement to say, has very many important responsibilities and it is not at all difficult for me to imagine that after a 6-month time lapse he does not have an accurate recollection——

Senator FULBRIGHT. Do you mean he is confused about it?

Dr. DRELL. I believe so.

Senator FULBRIGHT. That is a very charitable remark because we had him here specifically to answer these questions.

I do not know why you have to put in that statement when it denies what you have just said. It only leads to confusion in the public mind.

I can assure you that this is not the first time we have been lied to by Administration witnesses. There is no use in your feeling special about it. On the one hand you say that he came here and testified and said something that is not true, and then you say that you do not impugn his integrity.

Dr. DRELL. I can only speak for my own experience. I have been in positions like that at times with my own students, and my own business in my university. I always tend to be charitable unless I have evidence forcing me to a different conclusion.

TESTIMONY OF DR. FOSTER

Senator FULBRIGHT. I do not understand what you mean by that. This was not a casual meeting. In fact, we went to great lengths in getting him to come at all. We did it only by having Secretary Laird here in public and in public putting him on the spot, and making him agree to make Dr. Foster come. Otherwise he would not have agreed to come. He certainly had notice of what we were going to discuss. It certainly was not a casual slip of the tongue, if that is what you referred to in connection with your students.

You are not intimating that you deliberately mislead your students. Do you?

Dr. DRELL. No, not deliberately.

Senator FULBRIGHT. I believe it is a very critical remark. I do not know why you put it in here unless you are afraid of these people, which you well might be.

Dr. DRELL. I do not believe I am afraid. I merely say that I believe Dr. Foster has many reports and has a busy job.

Senator FULBRIGHT. He has entirely too many reports.

Dr. DRELL. Many reports in his office.

Senator FULBRIGHT. He may not know about a lot of them, but that is no reason to excuse his coming before this committee and misleading us and the public.

Dr. GOLDBERGER. May I make a statement, Senator Fulbright.

Senator FULBRIGHT. Yes.

Dr. GOLDBERGER. I think the issue that is involved with Dr. Foster's statement is not this quoted remark that the system will do what the Department of Defense wants it to do, but it is rather the implication of concurrence with a much larger series of arguments. That, in my mind, is the important point of our addressing this issue.

SECRET CLASSIFICATION OF O'NEILL PANEL'S REPORT

Senator FULBRIGHT. I think it is important too and it is all the more serious because this is not the first time. They have come before this committee and they insist on classifying this report. Every time they are caught in a misleading statement or whatever you want to call it, then it is classified to make it, as you say, "I cannot go further because it is classified."

There is no reason for this to be classified and you know there is not. The system of classification was based upon trying to protect our security from the enemy, not from the American public, and the Senate, but now they use it almost exclusively for this purpose. No one denies, I think, that the Russians know about our ABM. This whole business is getting to be ridiculous.

I noticed, Dr. Goldberger, that time and again, you said, "senseless." I do not know how many times you used the word "senseless." I agree with you. The whole operation seems to be senseless, and especially this game of having people like Dr. Foster trying to pull the wool over the eyes of the Senate and the people at this vast cost. I think it is time we speak frankly about it.

DR. FOSTER'S TESTIMONY

I do not see why you should throw in this statement that you do not intend to impugn his integrity. His intention is his business. Why don't you leave it open and let other people judge whether he intended to do it or not?

We have a long background with these people on the ABM. We had long hearings last year. The Senator from Tennessee held, I guess, 3-month hearings, and we had the ABM fight on the floor, as you know.

This is not something new and something casual about which Dr. Foster was not expected to be asked. You have to assume he intended to say what he said, that it was not just an accident, because there was a long background to it.

Very clearly on a number of occasions the question was raised as to whether they were being frank about it. This shifting from Sentinel to Safeguard and then shifting to the Chinese as being the reason, and then banning the Chinese has been on for a number of years. As Goldberger said, it is a senseless game.

NO JUSTIFICATION FOR SECRET CLASSIFICATION OF REPORT

Senator CASE. Mr. Chairman, may I just make one brief comment here. It seems to me that since the chairman of our committee has raised this, it is rather important for each of us to make a little comment at this point and on this matter.

I have just quickly read, as the chairman did, the report. I see nothing in it that justifies the characterization that Dr. Foster gave it. And, further, I see nothing in it that justifies its classification as "secret" or in any way confidential.

I would only like to make this further comment, and if it seems like an unusual characterization and one that required some preparation, that the report stated that the so-called Safeguard system would do what the Defense Department wanted it to do, it seems to me the only conclusion that one at this point can draw is that the Defense Department should be relieved of its responsibility for deciding what is necessary in this area.

Dr. DRELL. Senator Case, I concur both with your remark and that of Senator Fulbright about the lack of sense in this report being classified, and we remarked on that in response to a question by Senator Gore at the outset of the discussion this morning. I think that almost everything in the report could well be made public.

Senator CASE. I think it will have to be in order to eliminate this foolishness about what it contains and about what it means.

DR. FOSTER'S TESTIMONY ON CONCLUSIONS OF O'NEILL PANEL

Senator GORE. When he appeared before this subcommittee on June 4, Dr. Foster was asked several times in the course of the hearing what the O'Neill panel had recommended to the Secretary. I am sure each of you gentlemen have read the hearings. You have seen a portion of the transcript in which he answered that question the first time it was asked.

At a later point in the meeting on June 4 he was again asked what the committee had concluded, and Dr. Foster replied:

> That the Safeguard approach was a reasonable way to try and accomplish the objectives, the several objectives, required by the Department of Defense, that is to say, defense of our strategic forces, the Minuteman and the bombers, protection against the light attacks such as might be launched from Communist China, and protection against accident from any source.

Since we have had an interruption, I would like to ask you whether the O'Neill panel, on which you served, concluded that the Safeguard approach was a reasonable way to try to accomplish these objectives?

Dr. DRELL. No, sir. We drew no such conclusions.

Senator FULBRIGHT. "No, sir." Yet you say he did not intend to mislead this committee or you do not impugn his integrity. I do not know. I was asking Dr. Foster if there were any scientists of any reputation not in the employ of the Pentagon who agreed with his views. He was searching around, you see, to find a name. I think that is when he came up with the O'Neill panel. Once before we asked the Deputy Secretary of Defense, Mr. Packard if he knew of anyone other than his own employees who agreed with him. He finally said Dr. Panofsky.

Dr. Panofsky happened to be in town, and he immediately denied it.

Here I asked Dr. Foster did anyone other than his own employees, who did not dare cross him, agree with his view, and he was searching around, you see, and came up with this panel. Of course, this is directly misleading, Doctor. I submit this is not casual and it was not just an offhand remark. It was a direct misleading of the public and of this committee involving billions of dollars and the security of the country. I think it is a very serious offense.

Senator GORE. Will you proceed.

QUESTIONS INVOLVED IN PROPOSED SAFEGUARD EXPANSION

Dr. DRELL. In facing the question of whether or not to support the plan for expanding the phase I deployment of Safeguard to the modified phase II announced by Secretary Laird on February 23, 1970, we must ask the following: (1) Do we need it and, in particular, do we need it now? (2) Will it accomplish the mission it is assigned? (3) How will it affect the strategic arms limitations talks—SALT—in Vienna where the United States and the Soviets are now engaged in the vital attempt to stop the nuclear arms race that is a major tragedy of our times?

Each of these questions is very important. Just as we must maintain an effective, survivable and credible deterrent force vis-a-vis the Soviet Union so must we stop, as soon as possible, the extremely wasteful and dangerous nuclear arms race with the Soviet Union.

However, I will emphasize in my testimony the second of these questions—or what job will it do and at what cost? This is the question with the highest technical component and is therefore the easiest one to come to grips with. In contrast, our assessments of the Soviet threat and the risks we should be willing to take for peace in an arms control environment not only involve an inherent uncertainty on our part of the present Soviet capabilities, but must also reckon with Soviet intentions for 5 to 10 years into the future which is a weapon's system development cycle.

But the issue of whether the Safeguard ABM system will do the job can be met head on, on technical grounds, and it is on these grounds—which are the simplest ones according to Albert Einstein who remarked once that "Politics is much harder than physics"—that I want to analyze its engineering inadequacies.

SAFEGUARD MISSIONS

Much of the congressional debate last year centered on the growing Soviet threat to Minuteman and whether or not Safeguard could be supported for this mission on technical grounds. This year we are very much in the same position. The Soviet threat continues to grow in numbers of ICBM's and missile submarines. In his speech of April 20, 1970, to the Associated Press, Secretary Laird stated that we shouldn't rely only on the Polaris submarines for our retaliatory force, but should also defend part of our land-based retaliatory force.

In his words: "That is a major part of what the proposed minimal addition to the Safeguard defensive program is designed to do." I strongly endorse Secretary Laird's emphasis on maintaining the survivability of our retaliatory forces in the face of a growing Soviet threat.

Senator Stennis expressed the same emphasis in reporting the action of the Senate Armed Services Committee in killing the anti-Chinese thin area defense portion of the Safeguard program for fiscal year 1971. He remarked that "I'm really concerned in preserving our deterrent * * *" and commented further that the majority of his committee "* * * didn't think it was necessary now * * *" to add the area defense, that the Chinese threat was "* * * not immediate."

I particularly welcome this action of the Armed Services Committee striking out the anti-Chinese argument for ABM. Starting a thin area defense against China at this time may have the effect of constraining our SALT options, in particular by removing the possibility of zero ABM. I say this because I am troubled by the prospect of justifying to the American people an ABM expansion for its anti-Chinese capability and then negotiating with the Soviets in SALT to give it away. I am very pleased, and I strongly endorse President Nixon's statement that all our systems are negotiable in Vienna, and I hope they will so remain.

I would add in particular that there are technical limitations to a pure area defense of population centers such as provided by the full Safeguard Phase II plan. I believe these limitations preclude it from providing against China what President Nixon called a "virtually infallible" defense in his press conference of January 30, 1970. The President indicated that this capability was desirable in order to enable the United States to follow a "credible foreign policy in the Pacific areas."[1]

DEFENSE OF U.S. LAND-BASED RETALIATORY FORCE

So we ask again, does Safeguard have any significant potential for countering the growing threat to our land-based retaliatory forces, the SAC bombers and Minuteman missiles? Or are there other steps for protecting these forces that are less sensitive to the specific model of the threat, that can be implemented with more rapid response times, and that are less expensive for a given level of protection? To me, defense of our land-based retaliatory force is the crucial mission against which to measure Safeguard's capabilities and I am happy that the Senate Armed Services Committee agrees with me on this point.

Senator GORE. Incidentally, that was the position of this subcommittee a year ago.
Dr. DRELL. Yes, sir.
Senator GORE. So I too am encouraged.

---
[1] A more detailed presentation of my views on the value and technical limitations of a thin area defense against China or against an accidental launch can be found in my testimony before the Defense Subcommittee of the House Appropriations Committee on May 6, 1970.

Dr. DRELL. Consider first the SAC bombers which form one component of our land-based deterrent. The expanded Safeguard deployment through its long-range Spartan missiles plus some improved Spartans with longer ranges and smaller warheads that are now under design will afford some protection for SAC airfields against attack from the growing Soviet submarine based threat.

Technically, this argument may be sound although penetration aids associated with the incoming warheads can defeat the system. However, strategically a sea-launched attack against SAC airfields is not realistic on grounds of the required timing for such an attack. If Soviet submarines are to launch an attack against SAC airfields before the land-based Minuteman force is destroyed, then Minuteman, as well as the Polaris/Poseidon force could be launched in retaliation.

If an attack against Minuteman is launched before the bombers are attacked, then available warning times will be adequate to get the majority of SAC bombers off the ground before the SAC airfields can be attacked by submarine.

Moreover, an effective and more straightforward program to relocate some of the SAC aircraft in times of emergency to numerous subsidiary airfields removed further from the submarine threat is currently in active progress. Let us turn next to the defense of Minuteman.

Senator CASE. That means removed from the threat, just physically beyond the range of the submarine based threat?

Dr. DRELL. It is not physically beyond the range. It is further removed and would have more time for taking off, and also requires fewer launches of aircraft from the same runway because you have more airfields as a result of dispersal.

FUTURE THREAT TO MINUTEMAN

Let me turn then to defense of Minuteman. I have little doubt that the present land-based Minuteman force could be endangered by evolution both in numbers and quality of the Soviet missile threat sooner or later unless arrested by SALT. I conclude from what we now know that at this time we do not face a threat to the survival of our land-based deterrent.

I believe all concur on this point, although selective declassification by the Pentagon in recent months has appeared to attempt to raise false threats of a Soviet first strike plus a Soviet ABM capability to defeat all components of our strategic forces. However, it is technically feasible for such a threat to become real after 4 years or so unless halted by SALT.

Of course, whatever may be the fate of Minuteman, we have the other two components of our retaliatory forces to count on—the Polaris/ Poseidon submarines and the SAC bombers. Individually, each of these forces is in principle adequate to provide the deterrent capability.

SAFEGUARD AS DEFENSE OF MINUTEMAN

However, at least until SALT opens major new directions of policy I believe it is important to retain each of the three components of our deterrent force and so I ask whether Safeguard can accomplish an assigned mission of protecting Minuteman. Is Safeguard responsive to the projected or postulated threats?

My answer in substance is "No." There have been extensive studies, and I believe it is fair to say that all now recognize that Safeguard, even working perfectly, and with a full nationwide phase II deployment costing about $10 billion can be effective in preserving 300 Minuteman missiles, which is deemed adequate as a retaliatory force, against only a very narrow band of models of an assumed Soviet strike. Against lesser threats it is not needed and against greater threats it is ineffective.

The trouble with Safeguard for "hard-point defense" of the Minuteman system is that it is built exclusively of radar and missile components that were engineered for a city defense in the old Sentinel system. These radars and missiles have not been reengineered or technically altered in any way whatsoever to accomplish their new mission. They have simply been designated for deployment at different geographical sites and have been directed, by a policy fiat, to defend Minuteman in addition to providing the thin area umbrella against a Chinese attack or an accidental launch.

However, it is the mission of a hard-point defense to degrade or destroy partially the incoming missile attack by making low altitude intercepts at short range from hardened, blast-resistant targets. To accomplish this mission it makes use of the atmospheric drag to help sort out the incoming warheads from space junk accompanying them. A city defense, on the other hand, must totally remove, not simply degrade, the threat by high altitude intercepts at long range above most, if not all, of the atmosphere, where no sorting of warheads from space junk is possible. Only then can it protect the city, which is a soft, high-value target, from destruction.

For a city defense to have any effectiveness at all large, sophisticated, and expensive radars are required. However, these radars when used in the hard-point defense role become themselves the expensive, high priority, and vulnerable targets. In this case there is the gross mismatch of a few very expensive, very sophisticated, relatively vulnerable radars defending many missiles that are hardened and relatively cheap. In phase I of Safegard there are two long-range perimeter acquisition radars—PARs—and two missile site engagement radars—MSRs—one each for the defense of an entire wing of 150 Minutemen. The proposed step of extending Safeguard being considered this year calls for one more MSR for defense of an additional wing.

LIMITATIONS AND VULNERABILITY OF PAR'S

As the system has now evolved, there is grave doubt that the PAR will serve any purpose for Minuteman defense beyond that of supplementing other existing or planned systems that provide early warning of an enemy attack. There are two reasons for this. In addition to computer limitations in digesting information provided by the PAR and incorporating it into the engagement itself, recent studies have shown that the radio waves from the PAR are severely bent by the ionospheric disturbances accompanying high altitude nuclear bursts such as the detonation of an incoming ICBM—precursor burst—or of a defensive Spartan interceptor.

This effect is due to the fact that the PAR must have a relatively low frequency in order to see incoming objects at very large distances beyond 1,000 miles. The PAR performance is therefore seriously degraded in a nuclear environment, a point that is also of great importance in discussing the penetrability of the anti-Chinese umbrella.

Senator GORE. Could I ask a question? Is this vulnerability in ratio to the proximity of the ionospheric disturbance?

Dr. DRELL. This vulnerability is. I would characterize it this way. Above something like 60 kilometers in the air you deposit electrons which are freed by the energy released during the explosion, and now these electrons both absorb the radio waves of low frequency, and they introduce unpredictable fluctuations in the density, and this causes refraction or bending of the rays. It occurs at altitudes above 60 to 100 kilometers up.

It extends over very large regions of space.

Senator GORE. Would you like to comment on that?

Dr. GOLDBERGER. I think the point you are getting at is that one is concerned here with the high altitude Spartan defensive missile bursts and this issue of the refraction of the waves is not something that comes into play in connection with the lower altitude Sprint defensive missiles.

Similarly, high altitude detonation of offensive missiles would be the ones that would conceivably cause trouble for the PAR performance.

Senator GORE. Thank you.

VULNERABILITY OF MISSILE SITE RADAR

Dr. DRELL. This, then, leaves it up to the MSR only to accomplish the mission of Minuteman defense. One very expensive $200 million MSR that is relatively soft and vulnerable is the "eye" without which the entire defense of a Minuteman wing of 150 missiles is blind and would fail catastrophically. This vulnerability of the MSR is in complete contrast to the entire philosophy of the Minuteman system of having many hardened aim points—the silos and launch control facilities—no single one of which is crucial for the system's operation. As we argued above the reason for this lies in the historical roots of the Safeguard as the reoriented Sentinel city defense.

HARD-POINT ABM DEFENSE NEED NOT BE CRITICALLY VULNERABLE

Based on the correct technology a hard-point ABM defense need not have such a critical vulnerability. There is a qualitative difference in the distance scale of operation for a hard-point defense as contrasted to a city defense, that I would like to illustrate with my first chart. I believe you have it in the testimony.

(The chart follows.)

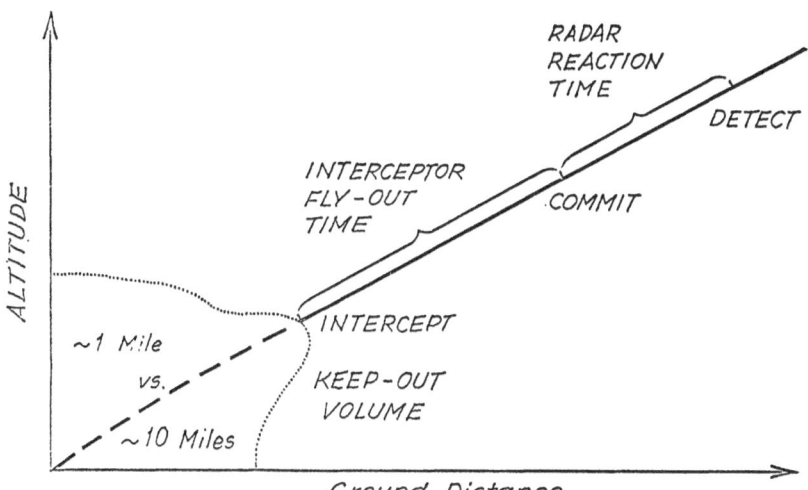

CHART I: This shows the factors determining how far out the surveillance radars of an ABM system must search so that the interceptor missiles can be launched and can reach an incoming ICBM before it enters the "keep-out volume", i.e., before the ICBM comes close enough to be able to destroy its target by blast from its warhead. For one of the 5MT warheads of an SS-9 triplet the dimension of this "keep-out volume" differs by a factor of about 10, depending on whether a city (~10-mile range) or a hardened Minuteman silo (~1 mile) is being defended. This change of scale of the "keep-out volume" leads to very different criteria for the required radar range.

This chart shows the factors that affect how far out a radar must see in order to initiate the engagement, and allow the interceptor missile to be launched in order to accomplish the intercept far enough away from the defended target so that a blast from the incoming ICBM cannot destroy the target.

If we are talking about the defense of the city, as the radars were designed for in the Sentinel system, the five megatons of one of the triplets of the SS–9 must be intercepted beyond the 10-mile range in order to prevent something like a blast overpressure of 3 p.s.i. from destroying wooden buildings or rigid steel frame buildings.

On the other hand, if we are talking about the defense of a hardened Minuteman silo from the same SS–9, keep-out distances are measured more like in the range of 1 mile rather than 10 miles. This distance determines the scale of the entire engagement and, therefore, determines the capability required of your radar which can be very much simpler for hard-point defense.

If you have a smaller scale then your radar need not react as fast nor see as far nor sort out as many objects.

INEFFECTIVENESS OF SAFEGUARD FOR PROTECTING MINUTEMAN

In addition to its vulnerability to catastrophic failure the Safeguard system is also ineffective for maintaining the Minuteman component of the deterrent even if it works perfectly as designed. I say this for two reasons:

1. Safeguard is effective against only a very narrow spectrum of threats. This is best illustrated by the following chart, presented to this committee earlier and prepared from open information, the background materials being Rathjens and Kistiakowsky (President Eisenhower's science advisers) in the Scientific American (January 1970). (The chart follows.)

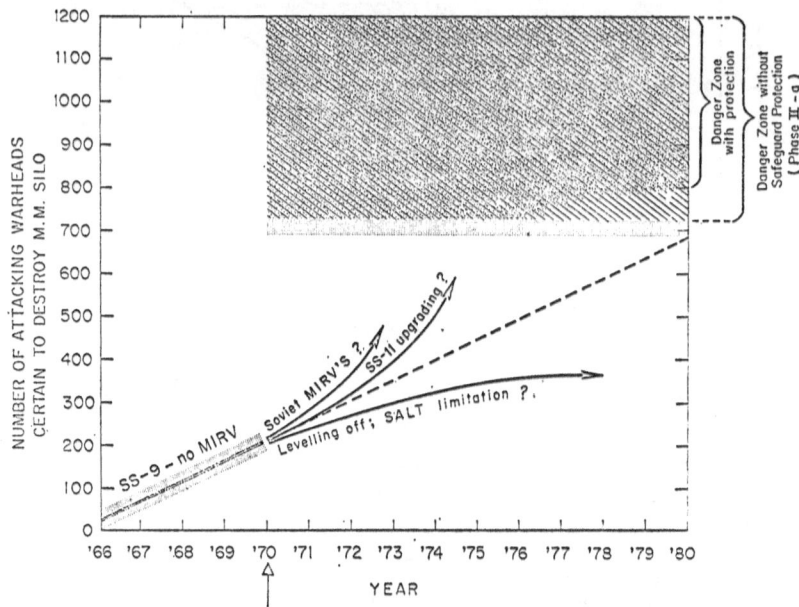

CHART II: This shows the growing Soviet threat to Minuteman and illustrates that Safeguard Phase II-A is effective in protecting 300 missiles as a retaliatory force against only a very narrow band of threats which follow along growth curves that enter into the small striped, but unshaded region. For a slower threat growth, Safeguard is not needed. For a more rapid threat growth it is both too little and too late. There is no intelligence information to distinguish along which of these possible curves to extrapolate the threat.

It shows the growing SS-9 threat in time. The number of warheads must reach up to a number like 700 or three times beyond its present level before one has to say that we have lost our Minuteman deterrent which we take to be a requirement that will be 300 Minuteman missiles surviving. So 1,000 minus 700 would be the 300.

Whether the threat will grow more rapidly than the straight line as a result of Soviet MIRVing or upgrading of the accuracy of their SS-11's or whether it will grow less rapidly due to SALT or will just continue along the present course, we have no reason to predict one path from the other on the basis of present intelligence.

The crucial point is that the capability of Safeguard to protect Minuteman as a component of the deterrent is limited to a very narrow band of threats that carries one into the striped, but unshaded region only. Any more rapid rise, Safeguard is too little and too late. Any slower rise, Safeguard is not needed.

Senator GORE. In a layman's words, does that prove that the proposed expansion of Safeguard is not needed against the present threat and would be inadequate if we assume a greater threat from either the SS-11's or the MIRVed SS-9's?

Dr. DRELL. That is right. It means that the threat, however the SS-9's or 11's evolve, would have to carry right into that small striped, unshaded region; in other words, for Safeguard to be effective, the threat model would have to be extrapolated into the striped, unshaded region. In any other region, Safeguard is ineffective.

DEVELOPMENT OF SOVIET THREAT

Senator CASE. It seems to me this is very important. It seems to me this is the heart of the thing, whether there is any worth or value in this system of defense, and I wonder whether you would develop it a little further, this area in time and for which a defense is possible.

Now, as I understand it, it is something like the middle of the seventies that this threat might come into being; is that correct?

Dr. DRELL. The threat—I would rather say, the only statement I can make is, I do not know when the threat will come into being because the present information does not give me any unambiguous signals whether the SS-11 is being upgraded in accuracy to be able to attack our Minuteman silos, something it cannot do now. I have no information that the SS-9's are being MIRVed, and I believe there is no information that they are being MIRVed so that the three warheads could attack three different Minuteman silos. I can quote Dr. Foster to that effect also; namely, they have not in their tests demonstrated the flexibility necessary to target three Minuteman silos with their SS-9's.

I think there is no disagreement on that.

So which curve to move along, I just have no hard information to go by, and it may be there will be no threat before 1980. The trouble is that no matter what, I cannot have Safeguard before 1975, and I get very little from the Safeguard Phase II as indicated by the striped, unshaded region.

Senator CASE. To lay the whole thing out clearly, it is a very narrow band, as you say, of threats that this will be effective against as well as necessary for.

Dr. DRELL. That is right.

ALTERNATIVE METHODS OF MEETING THREAT

Senator CASE. Now, as to alternative methods of meeting the threat, there are strategic ways of doing it by mobility and other things, apart from the question of an antiballistic missile defense. There is also the possibility of specifically designed missiles to serve this purpose more effectively.

Dr. DRELL. That is right.

Senator CASE. And I believe the general testimony in the scientific community is almost unanimous on this: that if such a defense is necessary that is the way it ought to be, because it will take care of a much greater range of threat.

Dr. DRELL. That is right; yes, sir.

GAP FILLER UNTIL ACHIEVEMENT OF HARD POINT DEFENSE

Senator CASE. There is one further question, it seems to me, and that is, is there a time when we can have this very limited defense when we cannot have the better defense, and how long is that timelag?

Dr. DRELL. I would say this is a point of contention among many of the technical people in and out of Government who have looked at the question of how to make the small radar, dedicated hard-point defense which is, I think, what you are driving at.

I believe, and I must say that the detailed analyses have not been carried through to the point that we have an equivalent understanding on these systems that we now do on Safeguard, so I recognize that the studies have not been made in that much detail; I believe that if we felt that we wanted to undertake as a gap filler in the middle 1970's, say, 3 years from now, if we wanted to have as a gap filler, on a shorttime basis for the defense of our Mintueman force, an active defense with small radars, I believe that upgrading of some of our present air defense equipment provides that gap filler.

It is distinctly a gap filler because it is the kind of system which the enemy, when he sees it, when he sees it coming into being, knows how to tailor his offense to negate. This is the nature of the game.

One side begins a deployment, and the other then responds by changing his parameters to beat his way through it, but for a short-range gap filler pending SALT, for example, I believe we have the ways to do that.

Senator CASE. And it would be much less expensive.

Dr. DRELL. Oh, much less expensive, much less expensive.

Now, a real dedicated hard-point defense system designed to have much more flexibility in growth as a defense would not be sooner. I believe that would be a year later, and I believe that is in agreement with the Defense Department.

Senator CASE. But you say this gap could be more cheaply filled and as effectively from the standpoint of defense than this other method?

Senator SYMINGTON. Mr. Chairman.

Senator GORE. Senator Symington.

Senator SYMINGTON. Dr. Drell, I was late, and wish I could have listened to your testimony and that of Dr. Goldberger. I have glanced at it, and want to be sure, based on the dialog you had with Senator Gore and Senator Case, that I understood.

EFFECTIVENESS OF PROPOSED CHANGES IN SAFEGUARD RADARS

When they shifted from Sentinel to Safeguard, Dr. Panofsky impressed me with the fact that the basic reason for his resistance was the vulnerability of the radar system and, therefore, its susceptibility to the SS-11, which we know they have a good many more of than they do of the SS-9's.

I noted with interest the conclusions this year of the Defense Department that the radar did have to be changed if it was going to be effective. Even if that radar is changed the way they plan, according to your knowledge, will that, in your opinion, justify the expense?

Dr. DRELL. Let me make sure I have gotten the correct thrust of the question.

I do not believe the Defense Department is designing major changes this year in the MSR. They have talked about adding to the Safeguard system if the growth in the threat requires it, a lot of small radars to supplement the Safeguard system.

Now, my statement there, if that is your question, is that I did not believe the case has been made that these small radars, dedicated small radars, should supplement Safeguard. It may very well be to replace it entirely; I am not aware of the case having been made to retain MSR in any form at all.

Senator SYMINGTON. Thank you.

Dr. Goldberger, would you comment on that, sir.

Dr. GOLDBERGER. I would like to concur with that. In Dr. Foster's testimony he argued, in fact, that there were virtues in having both the MSR and the smaller radars present in an improved dedicated hard-point system. I am unaware of any study which has come to that conclusion.

I am always a little suspicious of the game theorists' theoretical analysis that comes to that answer because if you ask a game theorist, you want X percentage of that and Y percentage of that, he never gets X or Y identically equal to zero, so he always concludes, "Well, it wouldn't hurt to have a little bit of MSR's around," and I do not believe that a technical case has been made for that.

Senator SYMINGTON. Mr. Chairman, I think this is very important testimony.

Last year the statement was made by at least two Members of the Senate that everything had been tested and was working in the entire system. This was difficult to understand because neither the software in the computer had been installed, let alone tested, nor had the PAR radar been built. All we want to do is just get the facts so that we can make a decision against those facts.

Thank you, Mr. Chairman.

Senator COOPER. May I ask a question, Mr. Chairman?

Senator GORE. Senator Cooper.

ADDITION OF SMALL RADARS TO SAFEGUARD

Senator COOPER. I believe it is correct, is it not, that Deputy Secretary Packard and Mr. Foster have both said that they intend to improve the Safeguard system by the addition of small radars of the type proposed by Dr. Panofsky, and with the addition of a number of Sprint missiles.

Is work now going forward on the small radars?

Dr. DRELL. The figure that has been quoted, $58 million of the request in this year's program, is to continue research and development work on the small radars for addressing the problem of how to back up Safeguard if the threat grows more rapidly than the straight line on that chart; that is right. There is also work going on in the Air Force.

Senator COOPER. In your judgment, could the small radars be developed as quickly, as speedily, as the MSR's?

Dr. DRELL. I believe that they could be developed much more quickly and speedily than they are now if there were really a true dedication in the Department of Defense to go this route. I have for a while been relatively unhappy at the fact that there is no real proponent of the dedicated hard-site radar system in the Defense Department, and I believe there are two reasons for this: one is that on the Army side they have come down the line so far on Safeguard that now there is a public political case involved with it, and any sign of faltering would be the kiss of death. Also I believe that in the other services, in the Air

Force, there are just jurisdictional problems of how the Air Force and the Army get in each other's way on something like that.

I have been unhappy with the way this case has been handled in the last 3 years because I do not believe it has been given the real impetus that it deserves.

USE OF SPRINTS IN HARD POINT DEFENSE

Senator COOPER. Would the Sprints proposed by the Defense Department be effective in a dedicated hard-point defense or does that need——

Dr. DRELL. It may be that the Sprints would be the missile.

Senator COOPER. What was that?

Dr. DRELL. It may be that you would end up with the Sprint as your interceptor or it may well be that a less advanced, less hot missile, one with less acceleration, would be the one to do the job because, remember, the Sprint was designed as a backup for city defense to keep the incoming warhead something like 10 miles away from the target, whereas it only has to be somewhere in the order of a mile or so to protect a hardened silo, to protect what has been its mission.

NO REQUIREMENT FOR PAR IN HARD POINT DEFENSE

Senator COOPER. Would an effective PAR be required for an effective hard-point defense?

Dr. DRELL. Absolutely not. PAR has little to do with a hard-point defense.

COMPUTER SYSTEM IN HARD POINT DEFENSE

Senator COOPER. What about the computer systems, is there any kind of effective research and development going on or was the computer system that has been proposed, designed for the Safeguard system, would it have to be redesigned for the small radars?

Dr. DRELL. I think the computer would be incredibly simpler if you had a hard-point defense system because when you have to look out several hundred miles, like the MSR radar does, you see traffic coming into an entire field or an entire wing of 150 Minutemen, for example, and you have to sort what is going where, what is junk and what is the real reentry vehicle. If you have a dedicated system which sees out an order of magnitude less, only 20 or 30 miles, to accomplish the intercept at 1 mile or 2 mile distance, then you see much less traffic, so the computer data processing requirements are very much reduced.

Senator COOPER. I ask, do you know whether or not the Defense Department is going forward with a design and development of the kind of computer that you say would be required?

Dr. DRELL. Yes; I think that is part of their program.

Senator COOPER. Could it be developed as quickly as, as speedily as, the computer system that the Defense Department talked so much about last year that they were working on for the Safeguard system?

Dr. DRELL. Let me make clear I am not saying that a real dedicated hard-point defense system starting now would be ready as soon as or sooner than Safeguard. So I want to be clear on that. I am not implying that, because I do not believe that is true. There are gap fillers that might do the job.

However, the computer problem for a dedicated hard-point system would be much easier and would not require the long lead time that presently paces the Safeguard deployment program.

SHOULD ADDITIONAL FUNDS BE AUTHORIZED FOR SAFEGUARD PHASE I?

Senator COOPER. One more question, Mr. Chairman. It concerns phase I, which was authorized and for which funds were appropriated. It was said that there would be great value in deploying phase I because the communications network would be in place and the knowledge and experience gained would be useful should additional funds be authorized and appropriated for phase I. In your judgment, both of you, do you believe additional funds should be authorized for phase I?

Dr. GOLDBERGER. Well, I addressed this question, Senator Cooper. In my opinion, if a decision were made that there would be no further deployment of ABM beyond phase I, then I would argue strongly against proceeding with phase I.

Senator COOPER. You would be against proceeding with phase I?

Dr. GOLDBERGER. That is correct. But if such a decision were taken I would say that phase I should be scrapped.

AVAILABILITY OF MEANS FOR OPERATIONAL EXPERIENCE

Senator COOPER. Is there any means now available for the kind of testing and communications and experience that it was argued last year were so badly needed? Would the facilities on Kwajalein be sufficient or would it be necessary to deploy a system on the mainland of the United States?

Dr. GOLDBERGER. This is a question which was widely discussed last year. I think there is a difference of opinion about it. It is undeniable that Kwajalein is a research installation, and the whole circumstances surrounding its operation do not effectively reproduce the conditions of an operational site, and I think one can make an argument for inability to acquire this sort of operation experience that is required.

From a technical standpoint, to find out really how the PAR passes over its information to the MSR, and so on, that can surely be accomplished, could surely be accomplished at Kwajalein.

Dr. DRELL. In terms of construction, you would have to build a PAR, whether you do it in Kwajalein or the United States because there exists no PAR, so that would still require a construction.

My own view on this—I was going to make a statement later on in my testimony, and I will make it now—and that is that I opposed the phase I decision last year because I felt that if you are not completely wedded to the Safeguard concept you would have more flexibility for modifying the system for doing real research and development if you did not cast your ideas in concrete on an operational site.

I recognize that Mr. Packard, who is a great expert in the area of how you produce things and has an expertise I do not care to challenge, said in terms of incentive, in terms of getting the program going, it was important to have it done at a real operational site. That was a judgment made last year, and I was not prepared to come in here this year and say let us undo that.

In fact, I consider that was something that was going ahead, and in the sense of Mr. Packard's calling it; namely, that it was a research and development installation. So be it. It is something now going on.

Senator GORE. Senator Symington.

SENATE'S DIFFICULTY IN OBTAINING INFORMATION

Senator SYMINGTON. Mr. Chairman, it seems the question that Senator Cooper asked presents one of the problems incident to this. I knew about the addition of Sprints, and I thought that this was classified, although I am sure it is not because he mentioned it, and he has had a chance to study this more than I have. But it illustrates the difficulties those of us in the Senate labor under when we try to push out this information so that the people can join in the ultimate decision which is going to cost so many billions of dollars.

OPPOSITION TO SAFEGUARD PHASE II

Dr. Goldberger, perhaps for parochial reasons, coming from Missouri, I would like to ask you about your emphatic negation incident to the proceeding with the first phase of Safeguard. Does that mean that you would favor going ahead with the second phase of Safeguard?

Dr. GOLDBERGER. It does not. I am opposed also to the second phase of Safeguard.

Senator SYMINGTON. How about you, Dr. Drell?

Dr. DRELL. I would comment in my testimony, in my statement, that I am opposed to the expansion this year because the basis for last year's decision, which I now accept; namely, getting on and learning things, finding out how equipments work, we have not gotten that experience yet, and the basis of using phase I for R. & D., as Mr. Packard told us, that can still proceed just using phase I alone.

Now we are told to go ahead with phase II in order to get program momentum. That is fine if it is the right momentum. Unfortunately, if it is the wrong momentum, and you are convinced it is the wrong momentum in the wrong direction, that is a bad argument.

Senator SYMINGTON. Thank you, Mr. Chairman.

FALLOUT ON CITIES FROM MISSILE EXPLOSIONS AT BASES

Before the hearing is over, I hope we can get into the question of the fallout. The farthest installation of the Whiteman Base is much closer than the center to Kansas City; and it is my understanding that whereas you get fallout that can be very serious—Hiroshima, Nagasaki experience—you would have fallouts considerably more serious if you had quite a few missiles hitting the ground and getting an infinitely more lethal effect as a result of the settling of dust incident to those explosions; is that correct?

Dr. DRELL. My statement on that, Senator Symington, is if Safeguard fails to deter the nuclear attack in the first place it has not saved anything and, in fact, whether the wind patterns would be such as to make the fallout quite severe in Kansas City or not is a matter of detailed atmospheric study. The winds generally go east. I think there would be a catastrophe if there is an attack with or without Safeguard, and the whole reason for Safeguard is not to either increase or decrease the fallout in Kansas City, but to prevent the attack.

Senator SYMINGTON. We have another city further east, St. Louis.
Dr. DRELL. St. Louis.
Senator SYMINGTON. Dr. Goldberger, would you comment.
Dr. GOLDBERGER. Yes, sir.
I think it is natural to be concerned about the whole spectrum of horrible nuclear wars. It would be much worse for Kansas City or even St. Louis to have a direct hit, of course. It is, of course, true that you can imagine a set of circumstances where there would be some desire to attack Whiteman, and it would actually draw fire, and then you would have the fallout being very serious because in order to maximize the effectiveness of the attack against hardened silos, there is a very high probability that they would be effectively ground bursts.

POSSIBILITY OF ERROR RESULTING IN DIRECT HIT ON CITY

Senator SYMINGTON. Just one more question. If that is true, if due to whatever the technical word is for ionization—technical results due to explosion farther out from incoming SS-11's or SS-9's or Sprints closer—then you might have an error that could result in a direct hit on the city itself; is that correct?
Dr. DRELL. Yes, sir.
Senator SYMINGTON. Dr. Goldberger, what do you think of that?
Dr. GOLDBERGER. It is possible.
Senator SYMINGTON. Thank you.
Thank you, Mr. Chairman.

MIXED VIEWS ON SAFEGUARD IN ARMED SERVICES ARE NOT VOICED

Senator GORE. Dr. Drell, before asking you to complete your statement, I would like to advert to some remarks you made a few moments ago about the division of the budget or missions or interservice rivalry or loyalty. I did not understand it. Would it be fair to interpret your statement to mean that this particular mission had been assigned to the Army, and since they want to preserve a major part in the defense role, they do not voice any doubts about this. Since they do not, and since within the service hierarchy this has been assigned to the Army, the Navy, and the Air Force, although not favoring this, remain quiet.
Dr. DRELL. That is an implication of my statement, sir.
Senator GORE. Do you think that is the case?
Dr. DRELL. I think that there is certainly an inhibition on various vigorous pursuits of alternate concepts created by the fact that this is an Army mission now in the way it stands.
Senator GORE. Is it not a fact that there are a number of officials in both the Navy and the Air Force who privately oppose ABM deployment? Would you know about that?
Dr. DRELL. There are in the services certainly mixed views about whether Safeguard is the right course; yes.
Senator GORE. This committee is unable to draw any of those mixed views from the Department of Defense. Everything that come here is pro-ABM.
We know privately that there are a good many people opposed to this system in both the Air Force and the Navy. We know also that there are a lot of doubts even in the Army Establishment, but you

cannot find anyone from the Defense Department who will come here and testify other than that this is grand and wonderful and that it must be approved.

Dr. DRELL. I wondered about this, and the only comment I can make is after these many years in which ABM has been trying to get the go-ahead, one has come so close to the point of making it, that altering the concept, going back to the drawing boards, bringing in competitive ideas might very well lead either to a considerable delay or the end of the program for the time being.

Senator GORE. It is on the basis of this that I said a long time ago that ABM was a missile in search of a mission.

Dr. DRELL. I believe that is a good statement.

Senator GORE. With that approval, will you complete your statement?

Dr. DRELL. Thank you.

COST OF SAFEGUARD DEFENSE EXCEEDS COST OF MINUTEMAN

I have another reason for saying that Safeguard is an ineffective way to maintain the Minuteman component of the deterrent. Safeguard is roughly an order of magnitude more expensive per Minuteman successfully defended than would be the cost of purchasing more Minuteman or Poseidon firepower should the threat grow at a greater than present rate as indicated on that chart (chart II). (The chart appears on p. 544.) This can readily be read from the same chart that sits over there. The estimated cost of the phase II-A program, the modified II-A program, is $7 billion.

The thickness of the striped, unshaded region on the chart is suitably fuzzed so that information is not too precise, but it shows something which is approximately like 100 warheads difference or 100 or so missiles saved. That means you save something like 100 Minuteman for $7 billion. In other words, if the system works, it costs $70 million per Minuteman defended successfully.

In contrast, the cost of a Minuteman III missile, using Secretary Laird's testimony of last year before the House Appropriations Committee, on a buy of 300 Minuteman III, the silos, complete with all required support costs, the cost is $8.3 million per missile compared with $70 million as computed above. Not only is the cost per silo defended many times the cost of each Minuteman saved, but it also exceeds the cost of the enemy missiles that could be intercepted with confidence. The ratio for Safeguard to Poseidon, to the Poseidon boat, is roughly 3 to 1 to 4 to 1 as opposed to the above $70 to $8 million.

VULNERABILITY OF MISSILE SITE RADARS

It makes matters even much worse for Safeguard's calculated capability to protect Minuteman if we now take into account fully the vulnerability of the missile site radars that conduct the engagement—that is, the MSR's—if they themselves are attacked. The MSR is much softer to blast than the Minuteman system it is defending. This means that the Soviets, in order to totally defeat Safeguard, need only target against the MSR's some of their 800 presently available smaller and less accurate SS-11 missiles which have no counterforce capability against our own ICBM's.

NEED FOR ALTERNATE PROGRAMS IF ARMS RACE CONTINUES

Clearly, if the arms race with the Soviet Union continues or accelerates we will want to turn to other programs if it is decided to maintain a land-based component of the deterrent force. What we need is a program or a mix of programs that can be implemented with shorter leadtimes, if needed, than the 4 to 5 years for initial Safeguard capability and that can also respond to a more extensive Soviet buildup of a counterforce capability should SALT fail.

Increasing the size of the offensive ICBM force would be just one possible step—and it is one that can be implemented at lower cost, as we have just illustrated, and with a shorter leadtime if needed. Other possibilities that have been studied include superhardening of the silos or creating more aim points by dispersal of a missile into one of several possible launch positions—that is, the mobile garage concept. There is, in addition, the alternate technology of many small radars, about which we have just been speaking, for providing an active, truly dedicated hard-point defense of Minuteman silos. Another option could be to go to sea with more Polaris/Poseidon boats or with a new longer range SLBM force.

There now appears to be a recognition of these blunt facts in the Pentagon that can be seen when we compare this year's and last year's statements on Safeguard effectiveness.

Thus in 1969 we were told by Secretary Packard in congressional testimony that there was "no feasible substitute for Safeguard," and that authorization of phase I will show the Soviets we "will protect our retaliatory forces now and in the future and do it effectively." In 1970 we are told that should the Soviet threat continue to grow, Safeguard will only be the "nucleus" of a Minuteman defense, to be supplemented by a true hard-point defense—HPD—with many cheaper, smaller, simpler, and less vulnerable radars—that is, to be supplemented by a newer system that is cheaper and more effective.

Why have things changed from 1969 to 1970? In fact, if it is admitted that, as a Minuteman defense, Safeguard will be only a nucleus to be supplemented by a dedicated hard-point defense, why do we need the Safeguard at all? I don't believe we do.

It has been shown conclusively in a number of studies that a truly dedicated, integrated hard-point defense system based on the engineering concept of many small radars can be built. The technology exists now for doing this. Such a system would, in fact, be more effective and cheaper than Safeguard for insuring survival of Minuteman against possible attack in the near future. Against various models of an extensively growing Soviet threat to Minuteman, in the event of a failure of SALT, one can deploy such dedicated systems at a much lower cost than required for a proliferated Safeguard deployment to provide the same protection.

Moreover, such a system would avoid the major problem of developing the computer programs for conducting the engagement with the MSR's, as I commented earlier with Senator Cooper. Work on these programs has proceeded satisfactorily during the past year, as reported by the Department of Defense, but it remains the pacing item for Safeguard deployment. It also severely limits the maximum size of the attack, including both real warheads and decor, that Safeguard can track and engage at any one time.

NO JUSTIFICATION FOR FURTHER DEPLOYMENT OF SAFEGUARD

Last year I was opposed to initiating deployment of Safeguard for the technical reasons enumerated. I recognize, of course, that that decision has been made and the program is now making good progress, with some onsite ground diggings recently begun. One major argument for last year's deployment decision as stated by Secretary Packard in testimony before the House Armed Services Committee on April 6, 1969, was that this is a very complex system and actual operational sites are needed to learn how to put together the complex computer and radar components into an actual operating system.

Today I am here to oppose strongly the proposed expansion not only because of the known technical inadequacies but because, in fact, we have yet to gain any of the experience motivating the phase I decision that was promised as part of a phased deployment program. At this time no equipment is in place, no parts of the system are complete, and indeed its operating capability under a major attack is still under study. What then have we learned to support the expanded deployment?

All analyses of which I am aware make it clear that if defense of Minuteman is the principal or sole mission of Safeguard, its further deployment cannot be justified. As I hope to have convinced you, it simply fails to respond to the Soviet threats postulated by the Pentagon, and furthermore it is not cost effective.

DEVELOPMENT WORK ON ALTERNATE TECHNOLOGIES RECOMMENDED

What I recommend is moving ahead vigorously with the development work on alternative technologies that we know at present can perform the hard-point defense more effectively and economically in the mid to late 1970's, if needed.

Thank you.

COMMENDATION OF WITNESSES

Senator GORE. Thank you, Doctor. Your statement is very impelling indeed. I wish that all Members of the Senate who must soon vote on this issue could have heard the testimony which you and Dr. Goldberger have given.

Gentlemen, today's hearing concludes the subcommittee's hearings.

The bill has been reported by the Armed Services Committee. We must now be prepared for the arena when this subject is presented to the Senate.

I think it is appropriate that the hearings conclude with your joint appearance. You gentlemen, until recently, were very important members of the President's Science Advisory Committee. You have served on a panel with access to all the secret information regarding this weapons system. Therefore, you bring to us a knowledge stemming not only from your own technical proficiency but from the standpoint of secret information in the White House and the Defense Department.

The statements you have given impress me. I think if they are read by our colleagues, they will be impressed. One purpose of this hearing is to inform the American people, insofar as we can, thus performing an educative function, an example of participatory democracy, to bring to bear the weight of public opinion.

With that statement, I have very few questions, and then I will yield to my colleagues.

LACK OF SCIENTIFIC SUPPORT FOR SAFEGUARD EXPANSION

Dr. Goldberger, you say in the first paragraph of your statement that the views you express do not necessarily reflect those of the various advisory groups which "I have been or currently am associated with."

Do you know of any advisory group with which you have served whose majority opinion supports the proposal to deploy phase II of Safeguard?

Dr. GOLDBERGER. I do not.

Senator GORE. This subcommittee has searched the scientific community. We have made public inquiries. We have asked the Defense Department to supply technical scientists who recommend phase II of Safeguard.

It was in response to such an inquiry of Dr. Foster that each of you were named. As a result of that, you were invited today.

Dr. Drell, would you respond to that question with respect to advisory groups with which you have served?

Dr. DRELL. I do not. If that is the right context, I do not know of any that is recommending the expansion of phase II.

Senator GORE. We have heard from the science adviser to President Eisenhower, the science adviser to President Kennedy, and the science adviser to President Johnson. We now have two distinguished scientists, recently members of the President's Science Advisory Committee, who were asked to participate in the panel to make recommendations to the Secretary of Defense. We have yet to find a scientific panel which has recommended, approved, or endorsed the deployment of phase II of ABM.

I will ask another question. Dr. Drell, you say in your statement, that you think it was "a healthy step for the Department of Defense to invite in outside critics to comment on their plans before recommending a program to the President."

Is it not true that most scientists would not concur with the recommendation made by the Department of Defense to the President with respect to Safeguard?

Dr. DRELL. I hesitate to answer because I have not systematically polled a broad community of scientists. I can only say that most of the scientists of my acquaintance oppose phase II.

Senator GORE. You know of no majority opinion of any advisory group or any assembled scientific body that has recommended it?

Dr. DRELL. I am not aware of any.

ADMINISTRATION'S DISREGARD OF OUTSIDE SCIENTIFIC ADVICE ON SAFEGUARD

Senator GORE. If, in your words, it is a healthy step to invite outside scientific opinion for advice, is it an unhealthy step for the Administration to disregard that advice?

Dr. DRELL. I made a remark also where I said Einstein said that politics is much harder than physics.

Senator GORE. Being a candidate, this is one thing on which I want to agree with Einstein. [Laughter.]

Dr. DRELL. I want to recognize that decisions on strategic systems involve many factors other than purely scientific ones, and I have always viewed the role of the scientist adviser as seeing to it that when a political, essentially political, strategic decision is made, the scientific technical component of that decision is correct. The President nor anyone else should be misled or should suffer from the deficiency of receiving less than the best possible caliber, the most far-seeing scientific advice.

So I am quite prepared to see that scientific advice may go one way and a decision may go another way because of other than technical considerations.

The problem with Safeguard is that the technical considerations here, I feel, are so overwhelming, and the different panels that I am familiar with do not disagree on the strategic or the political implications. I think most, if not all, of them, the scientists I know, endorse very strongly maintaining a credible deterrent, and many believe, as I do, that at this time the land-based component of that deterrent should not be abandoned, not, certainly, during the initial stages of SALT and, therefore, we share the same concern: How to preserve that deterrent.

So now we are on a technical issue, will Safeguard do it, and on this basis, really, I am puzzled to understand why, when there is such a strong scientific argument and a strong scientific representation as to the technical inadequacies of Safeguard, the Administration continues to push ahead with it.

Senator GORE. I find myself in agreement with that. Having studied this as earnestly and as fully as I have, I am impressed that if all members of the Senate studied it as diligently as I have, the proposed phase II would have very little, if any, support. Yet I know that there are some members who have studied the question carefully, and yet they approve it. So I am left troubled, but determined to fight. This would be wrong.

Dr. GOLDBERGER. I would like to comment on that. I agree completely with what Professor Drell said. It sometimes is frustrating, as a scientific adviser, to give what you consider to be perfect advice and have it ignored.

I think one of the problems that we face here is that there may be political, strategic, diplomatic arguments in favor of the abstract concept of ABM, and we do not—let me say I do not purport to be an expert on this. What I do, however, fail to understand totally is how one should insist on going forward with a system that has known technical deficiencies and, at the same time, having the opportunity to build a system without those technical deficiencies, and to confuse that with the strategic, political arguments that you are trying to use to come to a balanced decision.

It is for that reason I believe that many of the scientist advisers feel rather frustrated about the fact that their advice has not been taken on this particular issue, not the abstract one, but Safeguard phase II is what we are addressing.

UNITED STATES-SOVIET CONCERN IS OVER OFFENSIVE WEAPONS

Senator GORE. If I may, I will divert from the high-level exchange that we have had here. If we view it purely from the international political atmosphere or the internation strategic game, I doubt if the Soviets are very impressed with the deployment or proposed deployment phase II of ABM. They are advised of its deficiencies. They know that ABM has no power to reach them.

As an American citizen I am not particularly concerned about, nor do I fear, the ABM deployment around Moscow.

I do have some concern about their intercontinental ballistic missiles that can hit cities in the United States. I dare say the Soviets are concerned about the weapons we have that can hit them, but not those that perhaps can hit one of their missiles a few miles away from our cities.

Even from that viewpoint, to reduce it to the commonality of football strategy, the best defense is a strong offense.

With that learned dissertation, I yield to Senator Case. [Laughter.]

Senator CASE. Thank you, Mr. Chairman.

LIMITATIONS OF AND ALTERNATIVES TO SAFEGUARD

I just want to reemphasize, really, what came out during an exchange I had earlier with Dr. Drell, and to be sure I understand it. If he desires, Dr. Goldberger can comment on it as a conclusion.

The proposed use of Safeguard phase II for the defense of Minuteman would take care of a very limited range of threats to the survival of the Minuteman. Even that is based upon its working perfectly, and its vulnerability, particularly the vulnerability of the radar, would downgrade its value even for the defense against that narrow band of threats. Is that a correct statement?

Dr. DRELL. Yes, sir.

Dr. GOLDBERGER. Yes, sir.

Senator CASE. Nevertheless, it has at least theoretical value for defense against that narrow band of threats, and if you want an antiballistic missile defense as opposed to some other kind of defense it will be available a year or so sooner than it is anticipated that a better kind of antimissile defense, based upon a number of smaller radars, and so forth, might be developed. That is a fair summary of your statement; is that correct?

Dr. DRELL. That is right.

Senator CASE. Sometime.

Dr. DRELL. A gap filler could be available.

Senator CASE. That is right.

However, the defense of our Minuteman, if necessary, during that time could be taken care of by other means, in your judgment?

Dr. DRELL. Yes, sir.

Senator CASE. Including some kind of emergency development of existing antiaircraft defense, much cheaper and more surely than by this complicated system for this limited——

Dr. DRELL. As a gap filler that has very little, if any, growth capability, yes.

Senator CASE. This would be very much cheaper?

Dr. DRELL. Very much.

Senator CASE. And it would be just as effective, if not more effective, for that limited period that we are talking about Safeguard being useful?

Dr. DRELL. Well, I am talking about the middle 1970's, say, 1974 to 1976 or so, or 1977.

Senator CASE. That is right. The period before we could get into deployment of a really useful antimissile defense.

Dr. DRELL. Yes.

Senator CASE. So there are other ways of doing it even by antiballistic missile methods. In addition to that, there are strategic methods, whether by mobility or other things.

Dr. DRELL. Mobility or more missiles.

Senator CASE. More missiles.

Dr. DRELL. Yes.

Senator CASE. So at the very least what we are doing is an awful waste of money.

Dr. DRELL. That is right.

Senator CASE. Do you agree with those statements?

Dr. GOLDBERGER. Yes, I do.

Senator CASE. Dr. Goldberger, I am very much obliged to you.

Dr. DRELL. May I make one other remark, if I may?

Senator CASE. You may, indeed.

EFFECT ON ARMS RACE OF SAFEGUARD'S NATIONWIDE DEPLOYMENT OF LARGE RADARS

Dr. DRELL. It is not only a waste of money, but one of the things that worries me is that the Safeguard system introduces a nationwide deployment of very large radars.

Senator CASE. Oh, yes.

Dr. DRELL. We have the history of how the United States reacted to the very large radars the Soviet Union started deploying some 8 years ago, and Dr. Foster has recently spoken of these hen houses, the size of three football fields, and although many of us feel that, as an ABM system, their effectiveness is very poor, nevertheless, because there were large radars, because there was, therefore, concern that a nationwide ABM would compromise the penetrability of our deterrent force, we went into a MIRV development program which has now bloomed upon us as a MIRV deployment program.

So my statement is these large radars have shown us once how they maintained and accelerated the arms race, and some of us view it not only as ineffective but unfortunate. The large radars may trigger this reaction-action of the large radars threatening the deterrent, causing MIRV's, causing more offense to be built, and so forth.

BETTER AND LESS EXPENSIVE ALTERNATIVES TO SAFEGUARD

Senator CASE. I appreciate that comment, and I agree with it fully. But in order to keep this thing just as simple and as——

Dr. DRELL. Yes.

Senator CASE (continuing). And based upon hard scientific and economic facts that cannot be avoided by anybody, that cannot be matters on which you can have a difference of opinion even, I wanted you to make that point very clear, that there are other ways of accomplishing even better during this short period the defense of our Minuteman, and doing it much less expensively.

Dr. DRELL. As long as I make clear this is a gap filler with very little growth capability

Senator CASE. Absolutely. That is all this is.

Dr. DRELL. Yes.

Dr. GOLDBERGER. If I may comment on this, if you look at Dr. Drell's chart, the necessity of a gap filler even is based on making conjectures about the projections of the threat.

Dr. Foster, I think, correctly pointed out the difficult position of the military planner who, recognizing the technical capability to achieve a particular development, is one which the conservative military planner must cope with. But it is important, I think, to remember that someone is making a judgment that something will be done on the basis of technical capability, whether it is being carried out.

Senator CASE. I do understand that entirely. But I am trying to put this thing into a couple of propositions which cannot be controverted, even assuming the worst case, even assuming that at the highest level in this country, leadership comes and tells us, we need this. These are facts which cannot be dodged, that there are better ways of taking care of this threat, considering the worst case, at much less expense.

Dr. GOLDBERGER. It is also true if you look at those curves, it is conceivable that nothing we could do on the requisite time scale would protect this magic number of 300 Minutemen. I do not know how that number is arrived at. Why is it not 200, say, which just would make the whole danger area rise up a notch.

Senator CASE. I suppose the number is that number which will surely devastate or render or wreak unacceptable damage on the Soviet Union. That is that.

But in any event, there are other ways of taking care of that, mobility, and in addition, of course, we have our strategic bombers, and we have the Polaris, and such nuclear weapons of shorter range that are deployed around the Soviet Union, closer at hand.

Dr. Drell.

Dr. DRELL. I want to make sure if I err, I err on the side of the conservative field.

Senator CASE. I do, too, because we want to get this so clear and so hard that everybody has to accept it.

Dr. DRELL. Right.

Let me restate it: It is quite possible that we would perceive in the next year or two the Soviet development in their tests of their ICBM's of a MIRV'ed SS-9 capability, or of SS-11 upgrading that would lead to such sophisticated reentry vehicles, high speeds, and so forth, that the gap filler I am talking about really would not be adequate. I want to be clear that I am not saying that for anything that will happen in the next few years I know what to do.

It is quite possible that they would negate that course of action and force me, perhaps, to more mobility or, perhaps, more Minuteman.

Senator CASE. I understand that point. But my point is the alternative you suggest is this is much better than this one.

Dr. DRELL. This one (Safeguard) has no chance of doing anything essentially by 1974, when Malmstrom is the first installation.

TWELVE-SITE SAFEGUARD DEPLOYMENT NECESSARY FOR DEFENSE AGAINST COMMUNIST CHINESE

Senator CASE. One thing more, and this has no value as a Chinese defense until the whole 12 sites are deployed and operated.

Dr. DRELL. That is correct. To the extent I am concerned about 1975, 1976, Safeguard in no way alleviates these concerns.

Senator CASE. Right.

So what you just said now, in being completely candid, in no way is an argument for going ahead with Safeguard as presently planned.

Dr. DRELL. I believe so.

Senator CASE. Mr. Chairman, a couple of my colleagues have not had a crack at these wonderful witnesses yet, and I think I will wait and let them go ahead, reserving the right to come back to them.

Senator GORE. Senator Symington.

Senator SYMINGTON. Thank you, Mr. Chairman.

TRUE NATIONAL SECURITY

I would respectfully commend you gentlemen for your testimony this morning. For most of my adult life I have been involved in the problem of what might be true national security.

It seems to me that it is divided into three major component parts. The first is physical defense; the second is economic viability, a sound economy; and the third is the confidence of the people in the wisdom of their Government's decisions.

In this connection, I think these hearings, conducted by Senator Gore and this subcommittee, are tremendously important to the future true security of the United States. Surely by now we can tell that we cannot afford to do things that are not necessary.

EFFECT OF PUBLISHING O'NEILL PANEL REPORT

Now, one additional question. A staff member for whom I have great respect, said if the O'Neill report, which you two gentlemen signed, were published, as he put it, it would "Blow this whole thing out of the water." Thus if you can blow out of the water not spending $12 billion that is not necessary, or whatever the figure will be, why is it necessary to classify this report? Why shouldn't the American people be cut in on this decision, also? What are your comments on that, Dr. Drell?

Dr. DRELL. Well, I think that, as I remarked in the beginning, very much of the O'Neill report could and should be made public.

Senator SYMINGTON. I'm sorry, I was not here when you said that.

Dr. DRELL. In fact, as a general comment, the process of democracy would be well served by fewer closed, secret technical reports from which the people and many of their representatives are often shielded.

Whether it would blow the matter totally away or not, I am not sure, because what I have discerned is that the President announced three objectives for Safeguard. When you start putting it in trouble as the Minuteman defense, it blooms as the great anti-Chinese shield, and we are told it is not right to criticize it as a Minuteman defense.

Clearly if only Minuteman were the role, it would not be the thing to do, but it is in multimission aspects of it that it has its charm, we are told.

So, then, if you start technically criticizing the penetrability of the Chinese shield, it becomes the Minuteman defense or a SAC bomber defense, and so forth.

It also comes out wherever you are not punching at that moment.

I think multimission systems are great if you have not compromised their ability to do each one of the missions so bad in seeking the compromise you have made it ineffective.

Senator SYMINGTON. Dr. Goldberger, would you comment especially as to the importance of getting the O'Neill report out to the people?

Dr. GOLDBERGER. I think that you would probably find that it was not quite the equivalent of the invention of gunpowder. It would not, in my opinion, be quite as devastating a blow primarily because we concerned ourselves, as I said, with imagining possible responses to a variety of situations.

We did not analyze a specific proposal and attempt to come to grips with it.

Therefore, since we had prepared for a number of contingencies, I think you might find the structure of it a little looser than you might otherwise hope.

I do, however, believe that it was a serious panel, and addressed the problems quite honestly within very narrow framework, completely devoid of any political considerations on the part of the participants, and I think it would be a useful public document once a few relatively minor security matters were removed.

SAFEGUARD AS PROTECTION AGAINST ACCIDENTAL LAUNCH

I wanted to comment just a moment on one aspect of the three Presidential objectives, which none of us have addressed, and this is the one of protection against accidental launch. It is not a very frequently discussed subject, and I think the reason it is not discussed is because it is terribly difficult to define.

The full 12-site Safeguard system, if eventually deployed, could certainly protect against a very small class of extremely stupid accidents. However, a great, sophisticated accident would give that system very great trouble.

For example, a sophisticated accident that happened to be aimed at St. Louis, and it would hope to get protection from the Whiteman Air Force Base would be in pretty sad shape because the Sprint missiles won't reach out that far, and so if it is a good, sophisticated accident, you are not going to get much protection.

Senator SYMINGTON. Thank you, Doctor.

Thank you, Mr. Chairman.

Senator GORE. Senator Cooper.

Senator COOPER. Thank you, Mr. Chairman.

I might say, too, at the close of these hearings that I think our chairman should be congratulated for holding these hearings, for the quality of witnesses we have heard, and for your leadership in the investigation of this important issue.

We have had a number of distinguished witnesses, and I think today that both Dr. Goldberger and Dr. Drell have presented very well-reasoned and effective statements.

DR. LATTER'S PARTICIPATION IN AD HOC SCIENTIFIC PANEL

I would like to refer to the ad hoc panel on which both of you served. I noticed that Dr. Goldberger said he could not understand why it was Mr. Latter was on the panel. Was there any specific reason for that?

Dr. GOLDBERGER. Well, there may be a specific reason why. I do not understand it.

Senator COOPER. Is he a scientist?

Dr. GOLDBERGER. He is a scientist, a man who is deeply knowledgeable at defense matters, who contributed a good deal to the liveliness of the discussion and to various technical parts of it. He was, however, not a panel member, and there was no reason why Dr. Foster should have quoted him as being such. He did not sign the report; he did not associate himself with the deliberations of the panel. However, he did participate in the discussions.

Dr. DRELL. May I clarify, just add one note there?

Dr. Latter participated in the discussions and contributed to the report, and the discussions that went into it, as Dr. Goldberger said. It was felt by him it would be inappropriate for him to sign a report when he is currently engaged actively in our SALT negotiating team in Vienna.

Senator COOPER. I note yours——

Dr. DRELL. So his views are not to be taken—to what extent those views are his, there was no unanimity in the committee, and it was a matter of protecting his own views and flexibility.

AD HOC SCIENTIFIC PANEL'S CONTACTS WITH EXECUTIVE BRANCH

Senator COOPER. As I understand it, you were required to report to the Secretary of Defense. Did you, or did your group, meet with Deputy Secretary Packard and discuss your work and your findings?

Dr. GOLDBERGER. We were scheduled to meet with Secretary Laird, but he was called to the White House at that time and, consequently, we met with Deputy Secretary Packard.

Senator COOPER. You did meet with Deputy Secretary Packard?

Dr. GOLDBERGER. That is correct.

Dr. DRELL. In detail with Dr. Foster, also.

Senator COOPER. Was Safeguard discussed when you met with Deputy Secretary Packard?

Dr. GOLDBERGER. We presented the conclusions of our panel and we discussed only those issues. We did not stray off from that.

Senator COOPER. Your charge, as Dr. Goldberger said, was to consider a number of deployment options.

Did you discuss, was the effect of your talk with Deputy Secretary Packard, to recommend that these options, deployment options, be considered, which are superior to Safeguard?

Dr. GOLDBERGER. Senator Cooper, I hesitate to pursue this because I am not sure of the propriety of my response to the question. I do not feel it is appropriate for me to divulge the contents of that report——

Senator COOPER. At any time has this panel met with Secretary Laird?

Dr. GOLDBERGER. Not to my knowledge.

Senator COOPER. With Dr. Kissinger?

Dr. GOLDBERGER. This particular panel did not meet with Dr. Kissinger.

Senator COOPER. I assume you did not meet with the President?

Dr. GOLDBERGER. No.

Dr. DRELL. No; that is right.

DEPLOYMENT OF ABM SYSTEM AROUND WASHINGTON, D.C.

Senator COOPER. One witness, I believe it was Dr. Goldberger, said that the deployment of an ABM defense system around Washington had some attractive qualities.

Dr. GOLDBERGER. Yes. I think, I believe, that is the case. One has to invent scenarios, of course. For example, if there were an accident to be aimed at Washington, you might like that there would be someone at the other end of the hot line to make a comment about it. And, in general, if you consider any number of situations, the importance of maintaining the command and control system, the Commander in Chief, and the whole command structure would be very valuable, for example, to bring to an end conceivably an encounter if one should, unfortunately, occur.

I think you have to stretch, perhaps, at scenarios, but I think you can make them up. You can make two arguments.

One, is a madman attacking the United States, would want to attack Washington and wipe out the command and control structure and kill the President, and so on.

You could also argue that, of course, he would not want to do that because he might want to have someone to talk to at the end of the blackmail operation. I do not know how you come out on that.

SOVIET RESPONSE TO U.S. ALTERNATIVE DEVELOPMENT OF OFFENSIVE WEAPONS

Senator COOPER. Both of you said a more effective and cheaper alternative would be the deployment of more ICBM's, more Polaris-Poseidon-type submarines, and a new bomber, and mobile basing for ICBM's.

Now, particularly with regard to building more ICBM's and more Polaris-type submarines and, I assume, bombers, the argument has been made to us that the development of offensive weapons could cause the Soviet Union to respond, and could cause them to believe that we were threatening a first strike. This point of view was compared to the nonprovocative building of a defensive system.

What about that argument?

Dr. GOLDBERGER. Well, it seems to me that basically you cannot be seriously accused of effecting, trying to achieve, a first strike capability when you have zero city defense.

Now, I mean, in order to really seriously threaten a first strike, when you, yourself, have no defense capability, you have to be awfully sure that you can knock out a fantastically high percentage of the enemy's offensive strength.

I mean, I think these numbers, like 300, to provide an assured destruction capability are too high by a significant amount. I do not know what the number is, but I think to imagine anyone interpreting our attempting a first strike advantage in the absence of significant ABM's, just does not make any sense, and I think Dr. Drell alluded to this earlier. That is the terrible instability of an ABM system, a large ABM system, which is that it poses a threat of removing the enemy's deterrent capability, and that is why, in my opinion, a widespread Soviet deployment of ABM's around cities would be so terribly worrying, much more worrying, in my opinion, than their continued deployment of SS-9's.

POSSIBLE CONVERSION OF SOVIET SAM INTO DEFENSIVE ABM

Senator COOPER. Some in the Senate and some Department of Defense witnesses have stated that the widespread Soviet SAM system has the capability of being quickly converted into an ABM defensive system, and that would pose great concern. Is that a concern to you?

Dr. DRELL. May I comment on that? I think, my belief would be, the following:

At this time it does not pose a concern to me. On the other hand, if, for example, we were to go ahead with Safeguard with its large radars, and the Soviets were to respond with a comparable large radar system, which their present one is not comparable to, then that union of large sophisticated radars and their many and widely deployed SAM systems, I think, would be a problem that I would worry about.

I think that again it is another one of these difficult technical analyses, but I believe that at the present time the Soviet air defense system does not pose a threat to the U.S. deterrent.

On that line may I comment on just one other remark about building more ICBM's. Remember, the ICBM's threaten each other, but the sea-based component of the deterrent is not threatened by ICBM production. That is why building more, say, U.S. Minutemen, if a growing Soviet threat curved up and made it look quite ominous, the threat does not exist today, does not in my mind cause as much perturbation on the arms race as a major nationwide radar deployment does.

UNITED STATES WOULD HAVE TIME TO RESPOND TO CONTINUING SOVIET BUILDUP

Senator COOPER. I am of the impression that both of the witnesses believe that there could be a time, if development of the Soviet nuclear systems continue, when a threat would be posed to the U.S. deterrent to which we would have to respond.

Dr. DRELL. Yes.

Senator COOPER. I think that was probably the reason in the Senate why our efforts to halt ABM deployment were defeated last year, because there was a feeling we had to do something, we ought not to leave this country unprotected. At least the Safeguard system is something, they said, was ready to deploy, and it would be in place if the Soviet threat develops and if this production of Soviet missiles continues.

Now, I know this Safeguard ABM is not any good and, therefore, it is no protection. But let me ask you, if we assume that the Soviet continues its deployment of defensive weapons, and of offensive weapons, would the United States have the time to provide additional offensive weapons, such as ICBM's, Polaris and Poseidon submarines, and bombers, which additions would protect our deterrent? Would there be time?

Dr. DRELL. Sir, if I may remark, the Polaris-Poseidon and the SAC bombers independently each have the capability of serving as a deterrent even if we were to lose our Minuteman force. That is statement 1.

Statement 2. I believe if the Soviets did continue their buildup or accelerate their buildup there would be time to take steps to provide the land-based missile components of our deterrent in a more effective way than Safeguard.

Dr. GOLDBERGER. I would concur in that. Throughout this discussion of what an appropriate response to an increasing Soviet buildup would be, we are making the assumption that we do have to have all three deterrent systems because as far as we know the increased number of Soviet ICBM's does not threaten Polaris, and it becomes a matter of judgment as to how long you insist on having three separate forces.

I agree that at the present time, since we have that capability, and we can maintain it without unbelievable difficulty, it is prudent to do so. It simply increases the stability in an otherwise rather unstable world.

LEVEL OF MISSILES NECESSARY FOR DESTRUCTION

Senator COOPER. This is my last question: I think Dr. Goldberger said he could not understand why the number of 300 warheads is used as the level for destruction of the U.S.S.R. or the United States.

Is there any other number of missiles you can think of that if targeted by the United States on the Soviet Union, or conversely by the Soviet Union on the United States, would destroy the countries, that is, civilization as we know it.

Dr. GOLDBERGER. In my opinion, Senator Cooper, nobody really knows how to answer that question. We really have no concept of a post-nuclear-war situation. All of the analyses that have been carried out, to my knowledge, are completely unrealistic. They are more dictated by the size of the computer you have at your disposal than the actual size of the threat. There are very complicated nonlinear, almost uncomputable effects, that are so hard to estimate that I do not think any serious person can pick a number that is meaningful. It seems to me 300 would be devastating.

Senator COOPER. Do you have some idea of how many SS-9's, would you say, if targeted upon the city of New York would be required to destroy it?

Dr. GOLDBERGER. It depends. If you are talking about the putative 25 megaton SS-9 or the 3 MRV with a conjectured 5 megaton yield. Now, Professor Drell happens to have this slide rule, which I can never read under moments of stress, and he can probably tell us what a 25 megaton would be at 2 p.s.i. or something.

Dr. DRELL. I think, my unit, being from Stanford, is San Francisco. One Minuteman would leave very little of San Francisco.

Dr. GOLDBERGER. That is one.

Dr. DRELL. I daresay a 25 megaton bomb on New York or three 5 megaton bombs dispersed on New York would leave very little.

Dr. GOLDBERGER. It might even hit Princeton.

Senator COOPER. I assume the Minuteman would have a comparable impact on Moscow; is that correct?

Dr. GOLDBERGER. Yes.

Dr. DRELL. The Minuteman, of course, is a much lower yield, and probably we would think in terms of Moscow, the Moscow complex is larger than San Francisco, which is a compact city, in terms of several Minutemen.

DEPLOYMENT OF SAFEGUARD AS BARGAINING ISSUE AT SALT

Senator COOPER. One last question. I know you want to proceed further. What about the strength of the argument that the United States would have a bargaining issue in the SALT talks if we continue to go ahead with the deployment of the, so-called deployment of, ABM?

Dr. DRELL. I would prefer to turn that question over to a diplomat, but Dr. Goldberger made a remark earlier that bargaining chips should be something that are worthwhile, and the argument that we make about Safeguard is that it is not very worthwhile because it is so unresponsive to the threat, is effective in such a limited band and, therefore, I do not see why it should be that important as a bargaining chip.

Senator COOPER. I thank you all very much.

EFFECT OF MIRV DEPLOYMENT ON SALT

Senator CASE. Senator Cooper has been suggesting, while he has to go, that he would like to have an answer to his question as to whether, in your judgment, the deployment of MIRV has an important bearing on the SALT talks. Do you have any comment you would like to make on that general area?

Dr. GOLDBERGER. Well, let us both respond. I might say that I feel that the beginning of our deployment of MIRV greatly complicates any sort of agreement that we might hope to achieve in connection with the SALT talks. These points have been aired so many times I do not think it is worth going into them in detail.

I think it is bad stuff. I believe that we should have withheld the deployment of MIRV. In my opinion that would have made the job of the negotiators much more simple.

Dr. DRELL. My comment would be that I do not think MIRV has as strong an impact on SALT as do ABM's, and that is because ABM, if it works, or particularly if it has a nationwide large radar deployment, poses a potential threat to the entire deterrent force to the other side.

MIRV, on the other hand, is an additional threat only to the land-based component of that force, because MIRV's accurate missiles can be used to attack only the hardened silos, not the submarines.

So, as long as we have a large sea-based component and a launchable air-based component, and the Soviets are developing their sea-based component, larger than they have had in the past, which was considerably smaller than ours, but rapidly developing, as long as they have other than hardened missiles as their deterrent force, then I think the MIRV issue is less serious than the ABM one because again it attacks only the land-based component of the deterrent.

My only point would be that I think we are losing a real opportunity as far as MIRV is concerned, because I believe that there is a real asymmetry at this point in time between the United States and the Soviet position with regard to MIRV. We have developed MIRV's. We can deploy MIRV's. We are deploying MIRV's.

The Soviet Union has not tested MIRV's; they have not developed MIRV's, to the best of our knowledge, and they cannot deploy them.

It seems to me that at this time there was an opportunity while SALT is in progress, either publicly or privately, through low key to try in some way to maintain this asymmetry, and that is why I would have preferred to see us not go ahead with MIRV's, but, perhaps, use that as a bargaining card at SALT.

WITNESSES' SUPPORT FOR S. RES. 211

Senator CASE. I take it that both of you would have voted for the resolution which we passed in the Senate several months ago?
Dr. DRELL. Enthusiastically.
Senator CASE. Since a nod does not appear in print——
Dr. GOLDBERGER. I would concur.
Senator CASE. You both agree?
Dr. GOLDBERGER. Yes.

READER'S DIGEST ARTICLE BY HENRY CABOT LODGE

Senator CASE. I wonder if, for the record, you would be willing to comment on an article which former Senator Lodge, Henry Cabot Lodge, wrote in the June issue of Readers' Digest on this matter and, particularly, on several questions which the staff has prepared related to that article. I do not ask you to do it now, because we only have just a very few minutes before our vote, but if you would be willing to do that, I would be most grateful, and I know the chairman would, also.

(The article and the information referred to follow.)

[From the Reader's Digest, June 1970]

A CITIZEN LOOKS AT THE ABM

THE CHOICE IS CLEAR, SAYS THIS RESPECTED PATRIOT: UNLESS WE PROTECT OUR VULNERABLE RETALIATORY FORCES, THE CHANCES FOR WORLD PEACE WILL BE PLACED IN SERIOUS JEOPARDY

(By Henry Cabot Lodge)

HENRY CABOT LODGE—politician, soldier, ambassador, statesman—has served his country long and well. He was first elected Senator from Massachusetts in 1936, and as a much-decorated Army officer in World War II was the first Senator to see battle action since the Civil War. He served as U.S. Representative to the United Nations (1953–60), ran unsuccessfully for Vice President in 1960 on Richard Nixon's ticket, was ambassador to South Vietnam (1963–64, and again in 1965–67) and last year was chief U.S. representative at the Paris peace talks.

Once again the vexing question of how far and how fast to proceed with a defense of our country by anti-ballistic missile (ABM) is before Congress and the nation.

Last summer the decision to make a limited start with our anti-ballistic missiles—Safeguard—cleared the Senate by a single vote. That decision, fiercely disputed, authorized the Defense Department to go only as far as deployment of the first two anti-missile installations.

This summer Congress is debating whether to carry the deployment somewhat further. The Administration wants funds to add a third site and to do the advance work on five more sites so as to be ready should an urgent expansion of the country's defenses against a nuclear attack be needed.

Our security needs were stated by President Nixon on March 14, 1969, when he disclosed the three functions that a "measured" deployment of the Safeguard system was intended to serve. The system, if fully extended, would provide:

1. A shield, or cover, for the land-based Minuteman intercontinental ballistic missile (ICBM) force and the Strategic Air Command's B-52 bombers against a direct attack.

2. A defense of American cities from a terroristic nuclear fusillade of the kind that could be mounted with relatively primitive nuclear ICBMs during the 1970s by a nation not in the first rank of nuclear powers.

3. A guard to ward off a nuclear shot or volley fired by accident or as a demonstration of force, or a warning shot "across the bow."

For a number of reasons, including the hope that the current disarmament talks with the Soviet Union may eventually slow the accumulation of long-range nuclear weapons, the Nixon Administration has refrained from attempting to go to a full Safeguard system immediately.

Safeguard and Stabilization.—Our current strategic land-based offensive systems consist of two main elements: SAC B-52 manned-bomber wings are deployed across the United States; the Minuteman force, some 1,000 ICBMs in deep concrete silos, are arrayed in six wide fields in five states. The first two Safeguard complexes are separately to cover the Minuteman squadrons in place around Malmstrom Air Force Base in Montana and around Grand Forks Air Force Base in North Dakota. The third complex called for in this year's budget is to cover the Minuteman field near Whiteman Air Force Base in Missouri. These three complexes protect about half of the entire Minuteman force.

While the major function of the Safeguard system that Congress is now being asked to strengthen is to defend Minuteman, there is also a need to provide cover for our manned bombers. They are increasingly exposed on their fields to missiles launched by submarines in positions just off our coasts. All that is requested in the new budget for this important function is funds for advance work on forward defenses.

Heretofore, one of the principal arguments against our investing seriously in a missile defense was that such an action, by "destabilizing" (as the jargon goes) the condition of mutual deterrence, would "goad" the Soviet Union into still heavier deployments of ICBMs. It was argued that the Soviet Union was maneuvering only for ICBM equality with the United States, in the interest of making a condition of mutual deterrence absolutely certain.

The fact which challenges this assumption is that the Soviets show no signs of stopping the arms race.

In mid-1966, before the debate in the United States over the ABM became serious, our intelligence credited the Soviet Union with 250 land-based ICBMs, then deployed, with a growth rate of about 150 missiles a year. These reports said further that an unusually powerful new ICBM, the SS-9, was also undergoing test firing.

Only a year later the count rose to 570. Last September the Soviet ICBM force in being passed 1,000. If Soviet deployments continue at the present pace (a new ICBM every other day), the ICBM force in operational readiness will number more than 1,300 nuclear long-range attack vehicles by the end of this year. This compares with a total of about 1,000 weapons in the U.S. Minuteman force, which was leveled off four years ago on the assumption that it was already big enough.

The Deepening Shadow.—Numbers alone, however, are not the only reason for the deepening shadow which this expansion casts across the prospects for American security. Last year Defense Secretary Melvin Laird predicted that the Soviet force of huge and ready SS-9 missiles, which then numbered 150, could grow to about 230 missiles by this summer if the pace continued. The Soviets are reaching that goal. (Far bigger than the Minuteman, the SS-9 is believed to be able to hurl either a 25-megaton warhead or a cluster of three 5-megaton warheads more than 5000 miles and strike a target at a so-called miss-radius of less than half a mile.)

The experts believe that 400 SS-9s (with MIRV, independently targeted multiple warheads), launched more or less simultaneously, could with the benefit of surprise destroy 95 percent of the entire Minuteman force if it were left unprotected.

The continuing expansion of the Soviet land-based ICBM force has been paralleled by the growth of a Polaris-type submarine force, the so-called Y class. Last year the Soviet navy sent no fewer than six and perhaps as many as nine of these craft to sea. Since then, several more have been launched and as many more are under construction. Like our Polaris, the Soviet subs are each armed with 16 missiles. Military experts conclude that the Y-force is capable of destroying the SAC bombers, based for the most part only a few miles back from our coasts. The warning interval available to bomber crews on alert would be shrunk to minutes if the attack were to come from submarines launching a rain of flat trajectory warheads from concealments in the ocean close to the American shore.

The Soviets, according to reports, have also been experimenting diligently with a strategic-attack space machine, an orbiting version of the ICBM designed to respond on command and attack a ground target.

Nuclear Pearl Harbor. This fast-emerging threat last spring caused Secretary Laird to warn that the Russians seem to be headed for a first-strike capability; that is, the capability of destroying our total retaliatory force in one sudden strike—in a nuclear Pearl Harbor from which there could be no recovery. I know of no one who even suggests that the Soviets intend to do such a thing—to use a first-strike capability. What is important in maintaining world peace, however, is that no power have a capability such as this which it *could* use, without our having an adequate defense.

In the span of three or four years, while Americans have been absorbed in domestic strife and the Vietnam war, it appears to those in a position to know that our margin of strength in strategic-nuclear-weapons systems—the basis of our deterrent against attack—has been seriously reduced. It is thus no longer only the American cities that lie under nuclear threat, but our retaliatory defense as well. We thus can no longer afford the luxury of debating the ABM in abstract terms.

Obviously, the decision before us can be crucial to our survival. According to the respected Rand Corp, strategist, Dr. Alfred Wohlsteter, if the American Minuteman force should be left undefended; and if before 1975—the year the proposed initial elements of Safeguard should be in place—the Russians should match the accuracy and reliability already attained in our own systems; and if, too, the Russians should continue to add SS–9s while bringing on modest numbers of MIRV-type warheads for it—*then it is mathematically certain that by the middle of this decade virtually all the Minuteman force could be wiped out in a matter of minutes.*

Balance of Terror. A fresh look must therefore be taken at the two principal assumptions which, through the early and mid-1960s, regulated the U.S. approach to the strategy of mutual deterrence and which rejected the ABM as an essential reinforcing elements in such a strategy.

One was the expectation that the Soviet Union would stop accumulating strategic offensive nuclear weapons as soon as equality was reached with the United States. Instead, as noted earlier, the Soviet Union is pushing ahead to numerical superiority.

The other assumption was that each nuclear super-power could achieve a balance of terror by leaving its cities in hostage to the other. So long as both the Soviet Union and the United States retained a capacity to retaliate by inflicting "assured destruction" equal to wiping out (by former Defense Secretary Robert McNamara's estimates) from one fifth to one third of the attacker's population, they would stand mutually self-deterred. Correspondingly, for one side or the other to start investing seriously in city-defending anti-ballistic missile systems would, by this theory, have the practical consequence of taking the hostages off the board. That would, presumably, unsettle the strategic balance, loosen the rein of self-deterrence, and spur the adversary into either following suit or putting more capital into the strategic strike forces. But now the argument that any ABM is "destabilizing" is, in the face of the rapid Soviet buildup of offensive systems, no longer valid.

The further argument that a decision by us to move ahead with an ABM would either frighten the Soviets out of discussing limitation of strategic offensive systems or would provoke them also has no validity. The Senate vote last year to proceed with the initial phase of Safeguard was followed by an immediate Soviet decision to join the disarmament talks at Helsinki in November. Indeed, one might argue that the U.S. decision helped bring about these talks.

Glassboro and "Galosh."—The most authoritative reports available of the meeting at Glassboro, New Jersey, in mid-1967 between President Johnson and Premier Kosygin are that the meeting was largely concerned with the ABM question. The year before, the Soviets seemed to be constructing around Moscow what was eventually identified as a full-blown and unmistakable ABM system, named "The Moscow System"; it materialized as a grouping of four huge installations, each intended to serve 16 "Galosh" anti-missile missiles, depending for guidance upon elaborate radar-computer combination.

That the Soviets became engrossed in the science of missile defense almost as soon as they grasped the science of offensive missiles was well known to American intelligence. Evidence gathered in the winter of 1961–62, after the Soviets broke the nuclear-test moratorium of 1958, established that their rocket forces had, with some success, attempted to intercept and destroy another rocket with a nuclear explosion at high altitude. There is also the so-called Talinn system, which became and remains, for American technicians, a subject of controversy: whether it is designed to shoot down U.S. bombers, or ICBMs, or possibly both, is in dispute. But it appears that there never was any serious doubt about the purpose of "Galosh," the first true anti-missile missile to become operational.

At Glassboro, according to the most authoritative reports, Secretary McNamara tried to persuade the Russians not to press on with the "Galosh" system. He is said to have made the argument against "destabilizing" the strategic balance. At that point, we Americans were holding back a prototype ABM system of our own. (This was the Nike X concept, from which have come most of the fundamental subsystems of Safeguard: the elaborate "phased-array" radars for tracking and identifying dozens of oncoming missiles individually; the long-range Spartan missile for intercepting and destroying nuclear warheads hundreds of miles out, above the earth's atmosphere; and the short-range, low-altitude Sprint for attacking nuclear warheads inside the atmosphere.)

Evidently the Soviets did not consider the ABM "destabilizing." Premier Kosygin was quoted in London in the same year as saying that a defense system had the merit of saving lives and that under no circumstances could such a mechanism be blamed for the arms race.

In the aftermath of Glassboro, the decision was made to deploy our first ABM system, named Sentinel. The deployment was aimed primarily at providing an area defense for American cities against the expected ICBM threat—albeit primitive—from other countries not in the front rank of nuclear powers. Secretary McNamara did, however, wisely foresee a possible need to provide a specific defense of the Minuteman force if the Soviet ICBM force kept expanding. That provision proved timely.

The Soviets, for their part, remain engrossed in the Moscow ABM System—probably to be refitted with a superior defense missile. They thus already have a fully operational system.

Tipping the Balance.—Why have the Soviets invested so heavily in an ABM system of their own? Looking at it from their point of view, and setting aside a possible intent to achieve a first strike, we see they may well believe it necessary to have protection against an irresponsible, terroristic attack from some "minor" nuclear power. This is quite understandable; our experts feel a similar need. For that reason, the Soviets do not view their ABM system as speeding up the nuclear-arms race, but rather believe their ABM to be essential to their defense.

But in a world where so much is delicately balanced, even an understandable action must be scrutinized. Even if we assume that the Soviet ABM is built as a protection against a near neighbor, its existence, coupled with the Russians' increasing offensive capacity, can upset the strategic balance between the Soviets and ourselves.

What can we do to stabilize the situation without provoking another step down a dangerous road? We could, if we had to, increase our offensive capability to compensate for the new Soviet offensive and defensive systems—an invitation to further escalation. Or we could, as the President wishes to do, "stabilize" defensively—by building an ABM system that protects the United States.

Amid all the confusing terminology and sophisticated chess-playing, a certain common-sense fundamental stands out: *The only time an arms race can be controlled is when both sides feel "safe," and the only time both sides feel safe is when neither side has an offensive or defensive advantage.*

Another basic question arises: can we afford it?

The best information available to me indicates that the Administration's ABM program, in its second phase, would not unreasonably burden the American economy. Capital outlays for the total system thus far requested add up to $5.9 billion. This compares with the cost of $20 billion for putting a man on the moon.

Meanwhile, the reviewing arrangements set up by President Nixon will allow him to halt the project completely, or stretch it out, or turn it in a new direction as the technological situation might require. Furthermore, this flexibility will enable him to try a diplomatic initiative in the current disarmament talks, or as world political conditions might dictate.

Summing up.—Judged by these standards, Safeguard seems a modest program. Defense Secretary Laird said in February that what is contemplated really represents "the minimum we can and must do, both in cost and system development, to fulfill the President's security objectives."

The case, then, for moving on with Safeguard seems clear-cut. Safeguard holds out these propositions:

It provides a shield for the Minuteman and B-52 forces at a juncture when their retaliatory credibility is coming into jeopardy.

It offers the President a hedge against a hostile threat at a time when he has deliberately withheld production money from new strategic offensive forces.

It protects us from "nuclear blackmail" and the possible catastrophe of an attack from an irresponsible third power.

It widens the choices open to the United States if the disarmament talks should fail or be extended for a protracted period.

Finally, maintaining the development of ABM should strengthen the American trading position in the disarmament talks. As it is, their ABM strength is now greater than ours.

For me, therefore, the evidence is persuasive that the President's requests are wise.

In sum, what is at stake here is nothing less than protecting the deterrent forces of the United States and thus the survival of the country. In the face of this awesome proposition, four arguments are heard.

The first is that the ABM is technically faulty. This is an argument on which no layman can pass. The judgment of the expert officials whose solemn duty it is to pass on such matters is clearly favorable to ABM. Furthermore, the Soviets have perfected such a system. Can it be that our scientists are any less capable?

The second argument is that both sides have so much capacity to "overkill" each other's populations that ABM is not necessary. This is the so-called "balance of terror." But if party A can actually overwhelm party B's weapons, party B will have lost his capacity to kill anything. There will be "terror," but no "balance."

The third argument is that it would be better to spend the money which is asked for ABM on domestic peacetime pursuits. We can all agree that it would be more satisfying to spend the money on housing or anti-pollution but, almost at the same moment that we say this, the question presents itself: If our country is not secure, what do domestic programs avail? Professor Hans Morgenthau, assuredly no hawk, was quoted recently as saying: "A nation which refuses to accept the primacy of foreign policy over domestic politics has doomed itself."

Much as we may hope that other nuclear powers will live quietly within their own borders, common sense tells us that we cannot accept a state of affairs in which these powers are superior to us in nuclear missiles. Surely in a matter involving the survival of the nation, the burden of proof must rest on those who contend that the international order is so lamb-like that such superiority is acceptable.

It is bleak to have to admit that the international order is dangerous, disorderly and complicated, and that we therefore must expect that life will consist of a series of alerts—as it has for a large part of the 20th century. It is only human to exclaim, as many have done: "I don't want to live out my life in this kind of a world!" This human cry is understandable, but our chance of survival is greatest if we see the international order as it is—not as we would wish it to be. In all of this we, of course, are keeping the door open in the event that the disarmament talks should produce some sort of an agreement or new opportunity.

Far from criticizing ABM, should we not recognize that it is perhaps one glimmer of light in an otherwise bleak prospect? The ABM is defensive: it can attack no country. It can be actually "de-escalatory"; it could work toward a shrinkage—a slowing—of the arms race, an easing of the tension.

The fourth argument—that for us to undertake this ABM program would be provocative—seems unconvincing. Whatever force it may once have had has been wiped out by the Soviet gains, by their obvious determination to build a system for their own protection, by the defensive character of the ABM, and by the fact that the President can modify or suspend the program entirely if it seemed that by so doing he could reach a satisfactory international agreement.

It can thus be a force for peace making. It might even augur the beginning of a more stable international order.

This being said, can we prudently turn away?

JULY 6, 1970.

Hon. ALBERT GORE,
*U.S. Senate, New Senate Office Building,
Washington, D.C.*

DEAR SENATOR GORE: In his article "A Citizen Looks at the ABM" appearing in the June 1970 issue of *The Reader's Digest*, Henry Cabot Lodge argues in support of the Administration's proposed program for expanding SAFEGUARD in FY 1971. In this letter we present a rebuttal of Mr. Lodge's position. The technical basis of our arguments can be found in our testimony to your subcommittee on 20 June 1970.

We share Mr. Lodge's concern about the growing Soviet nuclear missile capability and the potential threat it may pose to our land-based retaliatory forces unless arrested. Although the growing numbers of Soviet ICBM's and missile-carrying nuclear submarines do not at this time pose a threat to the survival of the MINUTEMAN component of our deterrent forces, they could indeed endanger MINUTEMAN should the Soviets continue to increase their numbers and improve their quality by MIRV'ing the SS-9's or improving accuracy of the SS-11's. We disagree strongly, however, with the idea that SAFEGUARD has any significant value in providing a defense of MINUTEMAN. Mr. Lodge's article mixes elements of the Soviet threat, Soviet psychology, abstract ideas about ABM and offensive vs defensive systems. What it does *not* do is address the relevance of SAFEGUARD to any of these questions.

In the absence of meaningful arms control agreements, we feel that it is important to maintain the invulnerability of MINUTEMAN. It is precisely this issue, the ability of the system to defend MINUTEMAN, against which SAFEGUARD must be measured. It is our opinion, unchallenged by any studies of which we are aware, that not only is SAFEGUARD a cost ineffective response to the present or potential Soviet threat but it is also technically incapable of preserving any substantial component of our ICBM force. The point is simply that a Soviet force large enough to seriously threaten more than seven hundred MINUTEMAN missiles would scarcely be affected by the presence of SAFEGUARD. Another way of saying this same thing is that SAFEGUARD, working perfectly and with the full nationwide 12-site deployment costing in excess of $10 billion, can be effective in preserving 300 MINUTEMAN missiles, which is deemed adequate as a retaliatory force, against only a very limited and narrow band of models of an assumed Soviet strike.

We turn now to a point by point analysis of Mr. Lodge's article.

1. Mr. Lodge asserts that a MIRV'ed force of 400 SS-9's could destroy MINUTEMAN. Assuming the requisite combination of payload capability and accuracy, so that each MIRV'ed SS-9 can destroy three MINUTEMAN silos, one cannot quarrel with this statement. We note that this postulated force is pure conjecture, unsubstantiated by any hard intelligence and is a very large extrapolation beyond the present threat. The Soviets are currently credited with about 275 SS-9's (both operational and under construction) and they have yet to demonstrate a true MIRV capability—their current multiple warhead program has not demonstrated the flexibility to target individual silos. But the point again is that SAFEGUARD would have little to do with negating Lodge's conjectured attack: A system with the capability to destroy no more than 100 or so of the presumed 1,200 incoming warheads, less than 10% of the threat, can scarcely be called effective.

If the arms race with the Soviet Union continues, what will be needed are (a) programs to preserve MINUTEMAN which can be implemented, if needed, in less than the 4–5 years required for the *initial* SAFEGUARD deployment; and (b) programs that can realistically respond to a massive Soviet buildup of counterforce capability. Programs of both sorts exist. They include the following possibilities if needed:

(1) Increasing the size of the offensive ICBM force. If needed this could be implemented with a shorter lead time, and also at a much lower cost. Thus Secretary Laird testified before the House Appropriations Committee on November 17, 1969 that a buy of 300 new MINUTEMAN III missiles in silos, complete with all required support equipment is $2.5 billion, or $8.3 million per missile. In contrast, the cost of the proposed modified Phase II–A of SAFEGUARD designed primarily for MINUTEMAN defense is given by DOD as $7 billion. If it is effective in saving roughly 100 or so MINUTEMAN silos, this works out to an expense of $70 million per successfully defended missile. Thus the cost to defend and save a silo is almost nine times

the cost of each MINUTEMAN saved. Moreover, this cost exceeds the cost of the enemy missiles that could be intercepted with confidence.

(2) Superhardening of the silos to withstand larger blast overpressures.

(3) Creating more aimpoints by dispersal of a missile into one of several possible launch positions.

(4) Developing more mobility of the missiles either on land or by going to sea with more POLARIS/POSEIDON boats or with new longer range underwater launched missiles.

(5) Developing and deploying the alternative technology of a dedicated hard point active ABM defense system with many simpler, cheaper, less vulnerable and smaller radars for the MINUTEMAN silos. As we testified, this can be done.

2. Mr. Lodge comments on the growing Soviet nuclear submarine threat and remarks that the force of Y-class submarines ". . . is capable of destroying the SAC bombers based for the most part only a few miles back from our coasts." There are two points we would like to make on this point:

(1) *Technically* it is true that the expanded SAFEGUARD deployment will offer *some* protection to SAC air fields against attack from the growing Soviet submarine-based threat, although penetration aids associated with the incoming warheads can defeat a system that relies only on an intercept capability above the atmosphere as is the case with SAFEGUARD for this mission. However *strategically* a sea-launched attack against SAC bases is not realistic on grounds of the timing requirements for such an attack. If the submarine launch occurs at the same time as the Soviet ICBM launch against our MINUTEMAN force, then there will be at least 15-20 minutes or so after the SAC bases have been destroyed to assess this fact and to launch the MINUTEMAN force—in addition to the POLARIS/POSEIDON force—in retaliation. If, on the other hand, the Soviets launch their ICM's and their submarine-based missiles in an attack coordinated to arrive on target at the same time, early warning of their ICBM launch will allow us enough time to get most of the SAC bombers off the ground.

(2) Currently, the U.S. has in progress an effective and more straightforward program to relocate some of the SAC aircraft in times of emergency to numerous subsidiary air fields further removed from the submarine threat.

3. Mr. Lodge remarks that the "fast emerging threat caused Secretary Laird to warn that the Russians seemed to be headed for a first strike capability . . . a nuclear Pearl Harbor from which there could be no recovery." We disagree with the implications of this statement. A threat against the MINUTEMAN silos or the SAC air bases is not synonymous with a first strike capability against the U.S., let alone the intent of a first strike. A first strike against the U.S. would have to accomplish a simultaneous attack against MINUTEMAN, the SAC bombers, and the POLARIS/POSEIDON fleet. Technically it is impossible to envisage this possibility because of U.S. early warning capabilities. Under existing U.S. policy, moreover, each of these three U.S. retaliatory forces is designed with the capability to inflict unacceptable damage on the Soviet Union and on Mainland China—i.e. each, even after absorbing a first strike, is designed to meet the requirements of a deterrent force.

In spite of this, Mr. Lodge says that "while Americans have been absorbed in domestic strife and the Vietnam war . . . our margin of strength in strategic-nuclear weapons systems—the basis of our deterrent against attack has been seriously reduced." He concludes that "we can thus no longer afford the luxury of debating the ABM in abstract terms." In our opinion, the U.S. deterrent is not *seriously* threatened by any combination of Soviet offensive or defensive weapon systems about which we have any intelligence. Furthermore, it is Mr. Lodge who is talking about ABM in abstract terms: Even if the Lodge allegations were correct, SAFEGUARD would do virtually nothing to change the situation as we have argued. What could be more abstract than advocating the deployment of an ABM system that makes no sense?

4. Mr. Lodge quotes the concerns of Dr. Alfred Wohlsteter to the effect that the SAFEGUARD decision is crucial to our survival: "According to the respected Rand Corp. strategist, Dr. Alfred Wohlsteter, if the American Minuteman force should be left undefended; and if before 1975—the year the proposed initial elements of Safeguard should be in place—the Russians should match the accuracy and reliability already attained in our own systems; and if, too, the Russians should continue to add SS–9s while bringing on modest numbers of MIRV-type warheads for it—then it is mathematically certain that by the middle of this

decade virtually all the Minuteman force could be wiped out in a matter of minutes."

While we agree that the Soviet threat could evolve during the next three or four years in such a way as to endanger survival of our MINUTEMAN force, we have argued above that SAFEGUARD is not effective for meeting this threat. We oppose the proposed extension of the SAFEGUARD deployment neither because we disregard Dr. Wohlsteter's concerns nor because we oppose the concept of ABM. We oppose the administration's proposal because we believe that SAFEGUARD, which is made of equipment engineered for city defense and not for hard point defense, will not be effective in accomplishing the defense of MINUTEMAN. DOD spokesmen who defend SAFEGUARD on grounds of its multi-mission capabilities (defense of the land-based retaliatory forces; thin area defense against China; defense against accident) ignore the fact that the compromises in the system that are designed to enable it to meet all these missions have made it relatively ineffective in accomplishing *each* one individually.

5. Mr. Lodge comments on the Soviet ABM system around Moscow, noting that "The year before, the Soviets seemed to be constructing around Moscow what was eventually identified as a fullblown and unmistakable ABM system, named "The Moscow System"; it materialized as a grouping of four huge installations, each intended to serve 16 "Galosh" anti-missile missiles, depending for guidance upon elaborate radar-computer combination"; and later on, "The Soviets, for their part, remain engrossed in the Moscow ABM System—probably to be refitted with a superior defense missile. They thus already have a fully operational system."

Our comment on this is that a U.S. ABM is not necessarily the proper response to a Soviet ABM program. Our response to the 64 launchers around Moscow was to develop MIRV's for U.S. missiles to ensure their penetration of possible Soviet capabilities. In fact the present Soviet ABM ring at Moscow has very limited defensive capability and poses no significant threat to the U.S. deterrent capability. It follows in no way from the Soviet experience that deploying ABM is a useful course for the U.S. Indeed the Moscow ABM ring shows a major danger with going ahead with ABM. In this case, the Soviets gained no increased security—they merely triggered a U.S. response in the form of the MIRV program and thus simply perpetuated and escalated the arms race to a greater level of cost and destructiveness.

6. Mr. Lodge comments that "Judged by these standards, Safeguard seems a modest program. Defense Secretary Laird said in February that what is contemplated really represents 'the minimum we can and must do, both in cost and system development, to fulfill the President's security objectives.'"

As we have argued in this letter, the extension of the SAFEGUARD ABM system is not a wise course to follow simply because it is not responsive to projected or postulated Soviet threats, except for a very narrow band of threat models as we described in our testimony before your subcommittee on June 29, 1970.

7. Mr. Lodge dismisses the argument that the ABM is technically faulty by noting that: "This is an argument on which no layman can pass. The judgment of the expert officials whose solemn duty it is to pass on such matters is clearly favorable to ABM. Furthermore, the Soviets have perfected such a system. Can it be that our scientists are any less capable?"

Our response to this is as follows:

(1) Concerning the statement that expert officials judge ABM favorably, we again remark that we are aware of no independent analysis of the SAFEGUARD system by scientists outside of the Pentagon that endorses the proposed program for its stated missions. Our own criticisms have been reviewed above in response to earlier comments by Mr. Lodge.

(2) By judging the SAFEGUARD to be technically faulty for defending MINUTEMAN silos, we in no way imply or agree that U.S. scientists are less capable than Soviet scientists. We are simply saying that the engineering solution of SAFEGUARD, designed as it was for defense of cities which are soft and high value targets, is the wrong solution for hard point defense of MINUTEMAN silos, which are very hard and individually low value targets. We indeed believe that we can build an effective and much cheaper hard point defense based on the alternative technology of many small radars, each much simpler, cheaper, and less vulnerable than the very expensive $200 million dollar MSR engagement radar which in SAFEGUARD is the single "eye" responsible for defense of *an entire wing of 150 MINUTEMAN missiles.* We believe that the U.S. should be "getting on" with the job of designing this dedicated hard point defense system so that we can have it if needed in the

face of a growing Soviet threat. SAFEGUARD in our view is an engineering mistake grafted from the city defense role in the old SENTINEL system, and is ineffective for hard point defense.

8. Mr. Lodge asserts that ". . . it (ABM) is perhaps the one glimmer of light in an otherwise bleak prospect. The ABM is defensive; it can attack no country. It can actually be de-escalatory." He goes on to say the argument that ABM is provocative is "unconvincing."

This argument is contrary to U.S. experience of the past 10 years. We have already commented that our decision to go ahead with our MIRV program was provoked exactly by Soviet ABM activity at Moscow. Should the Soviets respond to the deployment of SAFEGUARD by a similar substantial ABM deployment with large radars throughout the Soviet Union, this would certainly be interpreted as a threat to our deterrent. To be specific, a deployment of large radars comparable in capability with the full 12-site SAFEGUARD installations would cause grave concern to U.S. planners. It would also lend credence to the possible utilization of their extensive air defense systems in an ABM role. The capability of such a defense to deal with a U.S. force degraded by a Soviet first strike would surely cause us grave concern and would provoke a response involving expansion of our offensive forces. Why should the Soviets react any differently to our deployment of a nationwide ABM system?

In summary, we find that there is absolutely nothing in Mr. Lodge's article which makes a convincing case for the SAFEGUARD Modified Phase II deployment.

Very truly yours,

SIDNEY D. DRELL,
Deputy Director,
Stanford Linear Accelerator Center,
Stanford University.

MARVIN L. GOLDBERGER,
Professor of Physics,
Princeton University.

HOLDING SAFEGUARD PHASE II FUNDS IN ESCROW

Senator CASE. There have been press reports over the weekend that have said that some Senator may suggest sort of an escrow method of dealing with the authorization of the modified phase II Safeguard under which the funds would be authorized and appropriated but held in escrow for a certain period of time to see whether the negotiators at SALT are able to reach an agreement that would make phase II-A unnecessary or even prohibited under an agreement.

What is you reaction to this hypothetical possibility?

Dr. GOLDBERGER. My reaction would be Safeguard modified phase II or phase II-A, as you referred to it, is not going to look any better 6 months from now than it looks now. It is not going to age like wine and, consequently, I would be strongly opposed.

Senator CASE. You would not even put the money in escrow?

Dr. GOLDBERGER. That is correct.

Seantor CASE. How about you, Doctor?

Dr. DRELL. I agree, for the same reason.

FULL AREA DEPLOYMENT OF SAFEGUARD TO JUSTIFY COST

Senator CASE. In his statement on the fiscal 1971 defense budget and program, known as the Posture Statement, Secretary Laird stated that, and I quote now:

> We have further decided to continue deployment of Safeguard because the additional cost needed to defend a portion of Minuteman is small if the full area defense is bought.

In your opinion, does that statement mean that we must agree to buy the full 12-site area defense in order to justify the cost of using this Safeguard to defend the Minuteman, as you implied?

Dr. GOLDBERGER. I would say that is a strong implication in that statement.

Dr. DRELL. In my testimony I gave the figures that phase II–A, the defense of Minuteman, was something like $7 billion in the Defense Department statement, and that is a large fraction of the cost of the full phase II, which is a little more than $10 billion or $11 billion, once you include Atomic Energy Commission costs.

Senator CASE. So, in general, you believe that is the implication of this statement?

Dr. DRELL. Yes.

Senator CASE. For the record, Dr. Goldberger?

Dr. GOLDBERGER. Yes.

Senator CASE. For the record, the inaudible response was yes.

Dr. DRELL. The cost per Minuteman defended, as I testified, if you do nothing but defend Minuteman with Safeguard is something like $70 million, is the rough arithmetic, compared with the cost of a new Minuteman of about $8 million.

Senator CASE. $8 million in the case of the Minuteman.

COST OF DELAYING SAFEGUARD PHASE II

I would be interested in having your comment on the following statement that Dr. Foster made when he appeared here on June 4, and these are his words:

> Another consequence of our stopping at this time would be financial. These programs I am discussing now have a number of years of research and development behind them and have also developed a significant production capability. A decision to delay deployment would either result in the destruction of this production capability or in a costly infusion into the program to convert the production capability to a standby status.

I would like to have your comment on that statement, if you have a comment.

Dr. DRELL. I have not studied the management flow in detail to in any way challenge the statement. It seems reasonable that the program has been developed up to now to anticipate an orderly growth, because that is what the proponents want, and I believe it is true what he says. But that does not negate the argument, if you are doing the wrong thing it is still more expensive to continue to invest in a bad program.

Senator CASE. Have you anything to add to that?

Dr. GOLDBERGER. No; I would agree. We discussed this issue at various times over the year about the cost in both time and money of delaying a proposal under the assumption we might want later to take it up, and also it seems to be extremely expensive, an extremely expensive thing, to stop anything.

I do not know whether it is more expensive to continue a program or to bring it to a close. It does not seem reasonable.

DR. LATTER'S PARTICIPATION IN O'NEILL PANEL

Senator CASE. Dr. Goldberger, I gather from your statement about Dr. Richard Latter in your prepared statement that Dr. Foster erred in telling this subcommitee that Dr. Latter was a member of the O'Neill panel.

By virtue of what office was he an ex officio panel member?

Dr. GOLDBERGER. I am not sure of precisely whose—I do not know exactly who invited him. He did not regard himself as a panel member, however, although he was present during the entire session and engaged in the discussions with us. He insisted that he was not a member of the panel.

Senator CASE. Why do you suppose he was there?

Dr. GOLDBERGER. Dr. Latter is an extremely knowledgeable man on defense issues. He is deeply involved with a variety of programs within the Department of Defense, and I would imagine, at least in part, the idea was that he could be of assistance to this panel on technical issues.

Senator CASE. Have you anything to add to that Dr. Drell?

Dr. DRELL. No. I think—he was a very active member, and I suspect—the reason he is in this limbo of a nonsigner was because he is engaged actively on the SALT team, and it would be inappropriate for him to be in any way officially associated with a report that made a recommendation in any form.

I want to be clear there is no implication here that he supported any statement or was against any statement in the report. He talked with us 2 days, and he sat and probed our thoughts.

Senator CASE. I am very glad to have your additional comment on that.

SOVIET DEPLOYMENT OF ESSENTIALLY USELESS SS-9

Dr. Goldberger, you said in your statement that the SS-9 was an essentially useless vehicle. If that is so, why do they continue to deploy it over there?

Dr. GOLDBERGER. Well, I feel that it is essentially useless, in the first place, because it carries too big a warhead to be of any use under any circumstances as we can now conceive it.

Now, it is possible, as I suggested, that the decision was made to work on it at a time when we were talking about the Nike-Zeus defense, which was a defense with very limited capabilities, one that could have been, in fact, defeated by the high-altitude explosion of a very large weapon, and I do not know how long it takes the Soviet Union to turn off a program. But my reason for referring to it as a senseless weapon is that its yield is too great for any job which it is now capable of addressing itself to.

Its accuracy is not sufficient, at the present time, at any rate, for an effective attack on more than one Minuteman silo, and it certainly is not needed, in the absence of any ABM defense in the United States, for attack on the cities.

Furthermore, the Soviet Union themselves seem to have come to a similar conclusion in that their largest deployment of weapons has been for the smaller SS-11's.

Senator CASE. We came to that conclusion a long time ago, didn't we?

Dr. GOLDBERGER. Yes, indeed.

Senator CASE. Not to go ahead.

Dr. GOLDBERGER. Not to go ahead with the Titan.

Senator CASE. Go ahead with the larger one.

Dr. DRELL. I must say the SS-9 puzzles me; not only puzzles me but it disturbs me because it is the kind of weapon that could provide Russians with a very extensive MIRV capability if they were to develop it, and I think that is why there is a certain concern, and proper concern, among many people within and without the Department of Defense. We have not seen, as Dr. Foster has said, and as I certainly believe, them develop the MIRV capability, so that one SS-9 could attack many Minuteman silos.

But given a very good weapon like this, with a very large throw weight, this capability might in the future evolve, and we have to watch out for it.

Senator CASE. And, of course, nothing—your whole opposition to Safeguard is not in any way based upon any contempt or downgrading of SS-9.

Dr. DRELL. No, sir.

Senator CASE. Or of the Soviet capability in the field.

Dr. DRELL. No, sir. It is merely a contempt of the capability of the Safeguard.

Senator CASE. Exactly. I think that is terribly important to me.

RECENT SELECTIVE DECLASSIFICATION BY PENTAGON

Dr. Drell, you refer in your statement to selective declassification by the Pentagon in recent months which has raised the false threats of a Soviet first strike. I wonder if you could comment on that, or expand on it, without violating any confidence?

Dr. DRELL. Well, I refer here to the statement of the following type. For example, we have heard a lot in the statements of the Pentagon about these three streaks in the sky that represent the SS-9 triplets and its possible evolution as a MIRV counterforce threat.

We have heard a lot about their large radars, the Hen House has been identified publicly; something called the Dog House has been identified publicly, these large nationwide radars, which together with extensive air defense systems might be the components of an ABM capability that they have. These are not new disclosures. I mean these are—this is not new knowledge. It is just at this time of the debate we are learning that there are various things that may have ABM capabilities, if we think only casually about them, or may have MIRV implications that if you only think casually about them but, in fact, if you think about them in detail there is no MIRV capability. I referred to those types of disclosure.

Senator CASE. And the kind of information which the Pentagon has not yet declassified, you might include in that report that your panel made. Is that a fair statement?

Dr. DRELL. Yes, that would be a declassification of our own system, yes.

Senator CASE. But I mean that is where they refused to declassify. You are talking about a selective declassification which involves refusal to declassify.

Dr. DRELL. Including additions to Safeguard.

Senator CASE. And that is the kind of thing you have in mind, and it exists, in fact?

Dr. DRELL. Yes.

COMPUTER LIMITATIONS IN DIGESTING PAR INFORMATION

Senator CASE. What are the computer limitations, Dr. Drell, you are talking about in your statement, digesting information provided by the PAR?

Dr. DRELL. How many information bits can be processed by the data processor per second. You can get many bits of information, and we are talking about bits measured in units of millions, when you talk about the latest computers, of bits of information per second.

The more millions of bits you can put through your data processor per second, then the more objects coming in you can analyze and see whether they are booster fragments or real RV's or decoys or what have you.

So when we are referring to the limitation of the numbers of the bits of information you can process, that gives you how large a threat you can engage in your Safeguard.

Senator CASE. And there are limits?

Dr. DRELL. There are certain limits. No matter how good a job is done, and I must say the American computer industry has outstripped the rest of the world, and the Defense Department's competency is excellent, I think there are just physical limits, given the equipment available.

IMPACT OF SAFEGUARD EQUIPMENT ON SALT

Senator CASE. If Safeguard doesn't work, why do we worry about its impact on SALT?

Dr. DRELL. Well, this is the question of large radars and how they are perceived by another nation. I refer here only to the history of the Russian analog. That is, they developed large radars, the Hen Houses, and its impact on the U.S. military posture was for us to develop and now deploy MIRV's.

The point is that the type of equipment that we are dealing with with Safeguard, I have argued, is not well suited to the defense of Minuteman, and although I did not argue here in detail, we claim it is not well suited to the defense of the cities in its present deployment because the Sprints have been moved away from the cities.

Yet once you put the long-lead-time construction items like the PAR's around the country, and you start developing MSR's it is going to, unfortunately, be too small a step, I fear to bring the MSR's and the Sprints back in toward the city, and then you would have a one-two punch, the area components backed up by the terminal components, which could grow into a city capable defense and would be threatening to the Soviet deterrent, and that is the type of evolution we would hope to stop at SALT.

The counter to that is, to conclude, would be if the Russians were to imitate our Safeguard phase II with 12 sites with large radars being deployed around the Soviet Union, they would certainly give our planners, and me included, concern as to the problem of all their widely deployed air defenses being tied in together with big sophisticated radars like that.

I would be much more concerned then about the upgraded potential of their air defense and a threat to our deterrent. It would be another layer of armaments, and another very serious problem I feel for the arms control folks.

RUSSIAN CONCERN OVER RESPONSE TO FULL SAFEGUARD DEPLOYMENT

Dr. GOLDBERGER. If I could go back to your original question and respond directly to that, I cannot believe that the Russians are dismayed and upset about our defense of Minuteman with Safeguard. But I think the thing that has them upset is they do not believe that that is where the defensive system is going to stop, and that is the basis of their concern because the full system would, in my opinion, require a response from them in the structure of their offensive forces, not that they would be unable to penetrate even the full Safeguard deployment, but they would have to take certain steps in restructuring their forces in order that they would be confident of their deterrent capability.

Senator CASE. I want to express again the thanks of the subcommittee and the Senate to both of you for coming and for your extensive preparation for this appearance.

It has been enormously helpful.

Thank you.

(Thereupon, at 12:55 p.m. the hearing adjourned, subject to call of the Chair.)

APPENDIX I

BIOGRAPHIC SKETCH OF MARSHALL D. SHULMAN

Born.—April 8, 1916, Jersey City, New Jersey.
Education.—University of Michigan, A.B., 1937; Harvard University, student, 1939–40; Columbia University, M.A., 1948; Russian Institute, Certificate 1948; Columbia University, Ph. D., 1959.
Experience.—1937–38: Newspaper reporter, Detroit News. 1938–39: Writer, National Safety Council. 1940–42: Vice-President, Council for Democracy. 1942–46: U.S. Army Air Force (Private to Captain): Glider pilot, psychological warfare officer. Decorated: Bronze Star; 1949–50: Information officer, U.S. Mission to the UN; 1950–53: Special Assistant to Secretary of State; 1954–62: Associate Director, Russian Research Center, Harvard; 1956–60: Lecturer, Department of Government, Harvard; 1962–67: Research associate, Harvard; 1961–67: Professor, International politics, Fletcher School of Law and Diplomacy; 1963–64: Visiting research scholar, Carnegie Institute; 1967—: Professor, Government; Director, Russian Institute, Columbia University.
Awards and Memberships.—Recipient, Rockefeller Public Service Award, 1953–54. Fellow, American Academy of Arts and Sciences; Member, International Political Science Association.
Research and Publications.—Author: Stalin's Foreign Policy Reappraised, 1963; Beyond the Cold War, 1966.
Address.—622 West 113th Street, New York City, 10025.

BIOGRAPHY OF MCGEORGE BUNDY, PRESIDENT OF THE FORD FOUNDATION, 320 EAST 43RD STREET, NEW YORK, NEW YORK 10017

McGeorge Bundy was born in Boston, Massachusetts, March 30, 1919, son of Harvey Hollister and Katharine Lawrence (Putnam) Bundy. He received his preparatory education at the Dexter School, Brookline, Massachusetts, and the Groton (Massachusetts) School and was graduated A. B. in 1940 from Yale University. In the following year he became a Junior Fellow at Harvard University.

Mr. Bundy entered the U.S. Army as a Private in 1942 and was advanced through grades to the rank of Captain prior to his discharge in 1946, participating in Operation Husky, the invasion of Sicily, and Operation Overlord, the invasion of France.

Following the war he served during 1946–48 as Assistant to Henry L. Stimson, who was readying the manuscript of the book, "On Active Service In Peace and War" (1948), of which Mr. Bundy was co-author.

Early in 1948 Mr. Bundy served as a consultant to the programs division of the Economic Cooperation Administration, which administered the Marshall Plan. In September, 1948, he served as research analyst for foreign policy on a committee recruited by the Republican presidential candidate, Thomas E. Dewey. He then served as a political analyst for the Council on Foreign Relations, New York City, in a study of the Marshall Plan.

In 1949 Mr. Bundy returned to Harvard University as visiting lecturer in government. He was advanced to Associate Professor in 1951 and to Professor of Government in 1954, maintaining the latter position until 1961. He also was Dean of the Faculty of Arts and Sciences at Harvard University from 1953 to 1961.

In December, 1960, Mr. Bundy was appointed by President-elect John F. Kennedy to the post of Special Assistant to the President for National Security Affairs. In this capacity Mr. Bundy served as a staff officer on foreign and defense policy for Presidents Kennedy and Johnson until March 1, 1966 when he became President of the Ford Foundation.

Mr. Bundy is editor of "Pattern of Responsibility" (1952), and the author of "The Strength of Government" (1968). Honorary LL.D. degrees have been conferred upon him by Brown University, Harvard University, Oberlin College, Hofstra College, the University of Notre Dame, Brandeis University, and Boston University, and an honorary L.H.D. degree by Yale University. Mr. Bundy is a member of Phi Beta Kappa, the American Political Science Association, and the Council on Foreign Relations.

Traveling and playing tennis are his principal avocations.

Mr. Bundy was married at Beverly Farms, Massachusetts, June 10, 1950, to Mary B. Lothrop of Boston, Massachusetts. They have four sons, Stephen, Andrew, William and James.

BIOGRAPHY OF DR. HERBERT YORK, DEAN OF THE GRADUATE SCHOOL, THE UNIVERSITY OF CALIFORNIA AT SAN DIEGO, SAN DIEGO, CALIFORNIA

Born.—November 24, 1921, Rochester, New York.

Education.—University of Rochester, B.A., 1942; M.S. 1943; University of California, Berkeley, Ph.D., 1960; Case Institute of Technology, D.Sc. (hon.), 1960; University of San Diego, LLD (hon.), 1964.

Experience.—1943–58: Member research and teaching staffs of Lawrence Radiation Laboratory, University of California, Livermore.

1952–58: Director of Above. 1957–58: Member of the President's Scientific Advisory Committee. 1958: Research administrator of Institute for Defense Analyses, Washington, now trustee. 1958–61: Director of Defense Research and Engineering, Department of Defense, Washington, D.C. 1961–64: Chancellor of University of California at San Diego, La Jolla, California, now professor. 1964–67: Member of the President's Scientific Advisory Committee (Vice Chairman 1965–66); Consultant government and industry; Trustee Aerospace Corporation, El Segundo, California. 1968– : Dean of the Graduate School, the University of California at San Diego.

Awards and Memberships.—Recipient Ernest Orlando Lawrence Memorial Award of AEC, 1962. Member of American Physics Society, International Academy of Astronautics, Phi Beta Kappa, Sigma Xi.

Research and Publications.—Research and publications in application of atomic energy to national defense, elementary particles, high energy physics, nuclear weapons and power defense research.

BIOGRAPHICAL SKETCH OF ALICE LANGLEY HSIEH

Born.—March 30, 1922, College Point, New York. Widow.

Home address.—7109 Matthew Mills Road, McLean, Virginia 22101, Phone: 703/356–6631.

Education.—B.A., Queens College, Flushing, New York, 1943 (History and Political Science) (Queens College Scholar).

M.A., Clark University, Worcester, Massachusetts, 1944 (History and International Relations).

Graduate Work: Stanford University, 1944–45 (Royal Victor Fellowship, History, U.S. Foreign Policy); George Washington University Law School, 1946–1951; University of California at Berkeley, 1956–57 (Chinese).

Experience (Abbreviated).—International Relations Officer and Foreign Service Officer, Bureau of Far Eastern Relations, Department of State, 1945–1955, dealing primarily with political-military problems in Japan, Korea, and other areas in Far East.

Member of the U.S. Delegation to the Far Eastern Commission, 1946–1952.

Special Assistant to the U.S. Political Adviser to the Supreme Commander for the Allied Powers, Tokyo, Japan, 1951.

Consultant to The RAND Corporation, 1955–1958.

Member of the Senior Staff (Political Scientist) of the Social Science Department of The RAND Corporation, 1958 to August 1969 (Communist China's foreign and military policies, military developments, and internal Army-Party relations; Sino-Japanese relations; international political and security relations in the Far East).

Research Staff Member, International and Social Studies Division, Institute for Defense Analyses, September 1969 to present.

Visiting Professor in Political Science at Mount Holyoke College and Visiting Professor in Government at the University of Massachusetts under the Four-College Asian-African Studies Program, spring semester, 1966. (Graduate seminar and undergraduate course on government and politics of contemporary China.)

Visiting Scholar at the National Defense College, Tokyo, Japan, September-October 1968, lecturing on Communist China's military policy, doctrine, and strategy.

Governmental Committees.—Member of the Social Science Advisory Board to the U.S. Arms Control and Disarmament Agency, 1964–

Member of the Department of State's Panel of Advisors for East Asia and Pacific Affairs, 1966–

Member of the Department of State's Panel of Advisors on China, 1968–

Publications.—

Books

Communist China's Strategy in the Nuclear Era, Prentice-Hall, Inc., Englewood Cliffs, New Jersey, 1962. Translated into Japanese and published by *Mainichi Shimbun*, Tokyo, 1965. Spanish edition published by Editorial Letsas, S.A., Mexico, D.F., 1966.

Contributions to Books

Essay on "Communist China and Nuclear Force," in R. N. Rosecrance, ed., *The Dispersion of Nuclear Weapons*, Columbia University Press, New York and London, 1964.

Essay on "Communist China and Nuclear Force," in Associates in Political Science, U.S. Air Force Academy, eds., *American Defense Policy*, The John Hopkins Press, Maryland, 1965.

Essay on "The Sino-Soviet Nuclear Dialogue: 1963," in R. Gartoff, *Sino-Soviet Military Relations*, F. Praeger, New York, 1966. Also published in *The Journal of Conflict Revolution*, and *Survival*, 1964. Condensed version in *Bulletin of the Atomic Scientists*, January 1965.

Articles and Essays

"Japan in Transition," *Foreign Service Journal*, March 1952.

"Communist China and Nuclear Warfare," *The China Quarterly*, April–June 1960. (Reprinted in *Survival* and *Military Review*.)

"China, Russia, and the Bomb," *New Leader*, October 17, 1960.

"China's Secretary Military Papers: Military Doctrine and Strategy," *The China Quarterly*, April–June 1964. (Reprinted in *Military Review*.)

"The Position of Communist China and the Problem of Disarmament," *Disarmament*, No. 2, 1964.

Remarks on Sino-Soviet frontier in collection of papers on "Russia and China: Non-Ideological aspects of Their Relationship," presented at Far Western Slavic Conference, Claremont Graduate School and University Center, Claremont, April 11, 1965, and published by School of International Relations, University of Southern California, Los Angeles, March 1966.

Foreword to the Japanese Edition of *Communist China's Strategy in the Nuclear Era: Implications of the Chinese Nuclear Detonations*, June 1965. (Also published in *Military Review*, March 1966.)

"Communist China's Military Policies and Nuclear Strategy," in *Hearings* before the Subcommittee on Military Applications of the Joint Committee on Atomic Energy, Congress of the United States, November 6 and 7, 1967.

Talk on "The Military Confrontation in Asia: The Chinese Viewpoint" to the joint conference—JASON, ISSD, ISDA—on the United States and the Chinese People's Republic, at La Jolla, California, August 14–15, 1968. (Being prepared for publication.)

"Communist China's Military Policies, Doctrine, and Strategy," *Boei Ronshu* (*The Journal of National Defense*), National Defense College, Tokyo, Japan, No. 3, 1969 (also National Defense College, Tokyo, Japan, available as P–3960, October 1968, The RAND Corporation).

Unclassified RAND studies, not otherwise published or published in full.

"The Significance of the Chinese Communist Treatment of Khrushchev's January 14 Speech on Strategy," RM–2534, February 1960.

"The Chinese Genie: Peking's Role in the Nuclear Test Ban Negotiations," RM–2595, June 1960.

Co-author with C. Zoppo, "The Accession of Other Nations to the Nuclear Test Ban," RM–2730, March 1961.

"The Role of the Military in Communist China's External Policies: A Study Kit for the American Association of University Women," P–3412, July 1966.

Biography of Mr. A. Doak Barnett, Senior Fellow, The Brookings Institution

Born.—October 8, 1921, Shanghai, China.

Mr. Barnett served in the Marine Corps from 1942 to 1946 and as a correspondent on China and Southeast Asia for the Chicago Daily News foreign service at three different times: 1947–50, 1952–53, and 1954–55. He was the head of Department of Foreign Area Studies, Foreign Service Institute, Department of State, from 1956 to 1957. He was a research fellow at the Council on Foreign Relations in 1958–59. From 1959 to 1961 Mr. Barnett was employed in the Ford Foundation's international training and research program. From 1961 through July 1969 he was a professor of government at Columbia University. He was Acting Director of Columbia's East Asian Institute and a member of the University's Research Institute on Communist Affairs. Mr. Barnett has been a Senior Fellow at the Brookings Institution since July 1969.

Publications.—
Communist China: The Early Years, 1949–55.
Communist Strategies in Asia: A Comparative Analysis of Governments and Parties (edited by A. Doak Barnett).
China on the Eve of Communist Takeover.
Communist China in Perspective.
Communist China—Continuing Revolution.
Communist China and Asia: Challenge to American Policy.
Communist Economic Strategy: The Rise of Mainland China.
Turn East Toward Asia: A Report on the Sixth National Conference, United States National Commission on UNESCO.

W. K. H. Panofsky, Director, Stanford Linear Accelerator Center Professor, SLAC

Degrees:
1938   A.B., Princeton University.
1942   Ph. D., California Institute of Technology.
1963   D. Sc. (Hon), Case Institute of Technology.
1964   D. Sc. (Hon), University of Saskatchewan.

Experience:
1942–3   Director, Office of Scientific Research and Development Project, California Institute of Technology, Pasadena.
1943–5   Consultant, Manhattan District, Los Alamos, New Mexico.
1945–6   Physicist, Radiation Laboratory, University of California at Berkeley.
1946–8   Assistant Professor of Physics, University of California at Berkeley.
1948–51   Associate Professor of Physics, University of California at Berkeley.
1951–63   Professor of Physics, Stanford University.
1953–61   Director, High-Energy Physics Laboratory, Stanford University.
1961–   Director, Professor, Stanford Linear Accelerator Center, Stanford University.

Special fields: X-rays and natural constants; accelerator design; nuclear research; high-energy particle physics.

Activities:
1945–60   Division of Military Application, U.S. Atomic Energy Commission.
1954–58   Member, Physics Panel, National Science Foundation.
1955–57   U.S. Air Force Scientific Advisory Board.
1951–   Radiation Laboratory, University of California.
1958   Stanford Research Institute.
1960–64   President's Science Advisory Committee.
1959   Office of Director of Defense Research and Engineering (member, Ad Hoc Group on Detection of Nuclear Explosions).
1959   WAE Foreign Service Officer, Department of State: Chairman, U.S. Delegation (Geneva), Technical Working Group on High-Altitude Detection; Vice-Chairman, U.S. Delegation (Geneva), Technical Working Group 2.
1958–60   Member, High-Energy Commission of International Union of Pure and Applied Physics.
1958–60   Review Committee for the Particle Accelerator Division and
1963–   Energy Physics Division, Argonne National Laboratory.

1959-61 Advisory Council, Department of Physics, Princeton University.
1958-62 Advanced Research Projects Agency.
1964 Advisory Committee, 200-BeV Accelerator Study, Lawrence Radiation Laboratory, Berkeley.
1965– Consultant, Office of Science and Technology, Executive Office of the President.
1965– Steering Committee, JASON Division, Institute for Defense Analyses.
1967– Member, High-Energy Physics Advisory Panel to the Atomic Energy Commission.
1968– Advisory Committee, Brookhaven National Laboratory.
1968– Advisory Committee, Cambridge Electron Accelerator Laboratory.
1969– Advisory Committee, CalTech for Physics, Mathematics and Astronomy.
1969– Stanford-Mid-Peninsula Urban Coalition; Co-Chairman.

Societies: Phi Beta Kappa; American Physical Society (Fellow and Member of Council, 1956-60); Sigmi Xi; National Academy of Sciences; Amer. Acad. Arts and Sciences.
Awards: Guggenheim Fellowship (1959); Ernest Orlando Lawrence Memorial Award (1961); Richtmyer Lecture (1963); California Institute of Technology—Alumni Distinguished Service Award (1966); California Scientist of the Year Award, 1967; National Medal of Science, 1969.
Publications: Classical Electricity and Magnetism (with M. Phillips), Cambridge, Addison-Wesley (1955); 2nd edition, 1962; numerous scientific papers in professional journals.
Personal data:
  Name: Wolfgang Kurt Hermann Panofsky.
  Born 24 April 1919, Berlin, Germany.
  Entered U.S. September 1934; naturalized April 1942.
  Married (Adele Irene DuMond).
  Children:
    Richard Jacob, October 13, 1943.
    Margaret Anne, October 13, 1943.
    Edward Frank, April 19, 1947.
    Carol Eleanor, January 12, 1951.
    Steven Thomas, December 13, 1952.
  Home address: 25671 Chapin Ave., Los Altos Hills, Calif. 94022.

BIOGRAPHIC SKETCH OF DR. HERBERT SCOVILLE, JR.

Born: March 16, 1915; New York, New York.
B.S., Yale, 1937. Graduate work in Physical Chemistry at Cambridge University, England, and University of Rochester culminating in Ph.D. in 1942.
1941–45: Worked on variety of National Defense Research Committee contracts at the University of Rochester, Northwestern University, and University of Illinois, and the National Research Council.
1946–48: Senior scientist AEC Los Alamos contract.
1948–55: Technical Director of the Armed Forces Special Weapons Project.
1955–June 1963: CIA, Assistant Director for Scientific Intelligence and later as Deputy Director for Research.
1963–69: Assistant Director, Science and Technology, U.S. Arms Control and Disarmament Agency.
1969–Present: Director, Arms Control Program, Carnegie Endowment for International Peace.
1957–63: Consultant to the President's Science Advisory Committee.
1955–62: Member of the Air Force Science Advisory Board.
In 1958, member of U.S. Delegation to the Geneva Conference of Experts to Study the Possibility of Detecting Violations of a Possible Agreement on the Suspension of Nuclear Tests.
1966–68: Chairman, U.S. Delegation, NATO Disarmament Experts' Meetings.
1967–68: Chairman, U.S. Delegation, U.S.-Japan, U.S.-Australia and U.S.-S. Africa Experts' Conference on the Non-Proliferation Treaty.
1970: Author with Robert Osborn, *Missile Madness*, Houghton Mifflin.

BIOGRAPHY OF DR. ADRIAN S. FISHER, DEAN OF GEORGETOWN UNIVERSITY LAW SCHOOL

Born.—January 21, 1914, Memphis, Tennessee.
Education.—A.B., Princeton, 1934, LL.D., 1965; LL.B., Harvard, 1937.
Experience.—Admitted to Tennessee State bar, 1938; law clerk to Supreme Court Justice Brandeis, 1938, law clerk to Justice Frankfurter, 1939; attorney various government agencies, 1939-41; Assistant Chief Foreign Funds Control Division, U.S. Department of State, 1941-42; Assistant to Assistant Secretary of War, 1944; Solicitor, U.S. Department of Commerce, 1947-48; general counsel, Atomic Energy Commission, 1948-49; legal adviser, Department of State, 1949-53; Deputy Director, U.S. Arms Control and Disarmament Agency, 1961-69.
Activities.—The legal adviser to U.S. Delegation to the United Nations, Paris, 1952; member President's Commission on Immigration and Naturalization; member U.S. Panel Permanent Court Arbitration. Technical adviser to U.S. judges, International Military Tribunal, Nuremberg, Germany, 1946. Served as navigator, U.S.A.A.F., 1942-43, 45, discharged as Captain. Awarded Legion of Merit. Phi Beta Kappa.

BIOGRAPHIC SKETCH OF THE HONORABLE JOSEPH S. CLARK

Former Pennsylvania Senator Joseph S. Clark was elected President of United World Federalists by the 72-member National Council meeting in Washington, D.C., March 14, 1969. The nationally-known Democrat succeeds James G. Patton, who has been President of UWF since December 1967 and will continue that office until April 1st when he will return full time to private business.

Clark was elected to the United States Senate in 1956 and re-elected in 1962. Prior to that office, he was elected City Controller of Philadelphia and, in 1951 was the first Democrat to be elected Mayor of Philadelphia in 67 years. He was defeated for reelection to the Senate in 1968 by Senator Richard Schweiker, former Republican Congressman from Pennsylvania and a member of UWF.

While in the Senate, Clark's committee assignments led him to specialize in manpower, unemployment, poverty, housing, education, foreign relations, and Congressional reform. His record in seeking ways to set up the machinery for peaceful settlement of conflicts is amply documented, particularly his role as a member of the Senate Foreign Relations Committee.

He introduced the United Nations Peacekeeping Resolution to create a U.N. Peacekeeping force. Twenty-one Senators co-sponsored that Bill. Since 1959 his record shows consistent performance in submitting resolutions in the Senate calling for far-reaching revision of the Charter of the U.N. so as to make that body a more effective force for peace. He submitted the Planning for Peace Resolution; and co-sponsored the International Cooperation Year Resolution, which passed without record dissent by both the Senate and the House.

The former Senator's role is equally as vigorous in the area of international law, arms control and disarmament, nuclear non-proliferation, the comprehensive test ban treaty, control of fissionable material, nuclear free zones, reduction and limitation of the deployment of strategic arms, curbing the arms race, security for less developed countries, European security arrangements, and many other facets of the question of war versus peace.

Since retiring from the Senate, he has been an adjunct professor at Temple University and a visiting lecturer at Haverford College and the University of Pennsylvania. He holds honorary degrees from nine institutions of higher learning, including Harvard, Haverford, and the University of Pennsylvania.

Clark was educated at Middlesex School in Concord, Mass.; Harvard College (graduated magna cum laude, Phi Beta Kappa, 1923); and the University of Pennsylvania Law School, 1926. He practiced law in Philadelphia until August 1941 when he was commissioned a captain in the United States Army Air Forces where he served until shortly after V-J Day in September 1945; being retired with the rank of colonel.

Senator Clark was born in Philadelphia on October 21, 1901.

A BIOGRAPHIC SKETCH OF DR. DONALD F. HORNIG

Dr. Donald F. Hornig was born in Milwaukee on March 17, 1920, the son of C. Arthur Hornig and the former Emma Knuth. In 1943, he married Lilli Schwenk and they have four children: Joanna, Ellen, Christopher and Leslie.

A graduate of Harvard University, where he received his B.S. degree in 1940 and his Ph.D. in chemistry three years later, he was awarded a Guggenheim grant and a Fulbright scholarship for research at St. John's College, Oxford University, England, in 1954-55, and in 1955 he was appointed the first Bourke Overseas Lecturer by the Faraday Society of London.

After receiving his doctorate at Harvard, Dr. Hornig spent a year as a Research Associate at the Woods Hole Oceanographic Institution in Massachusetts. From 1944 to 1946 he was a Group Leader at the Los Alamos Laboratory in New Mexico and in the latter year he joined the faculty at Brown University as Assistant Professor. Three years later he became an Associate Professor and Director of the Metcalf Research Laboratory. He was promoted to the rank of Professor in 1951 and the following year became Associate Dean of the Graduate School. Subsequently he was Acting Dean. In 1957 he joined the faculty of Princeton University and was appointed Chairman of the Department of Chemistry in 1958. Dr. Hornig was the first incumbent of the Donner Chair of Science at Princeton, established in 1958 by the Donner Foundation, Inc.

Dr. Hornig has been an Associate Editor of the *Journal of Chemical Physics* and a member of the Editorial Advisory Boards of *Spectrochimica Acta* and *Molecular Physics*. He was President, from 1945 to 1947, of Radiation Instruments Company, and served as Chairman of Project Metcalf of the Office of Naval Research in 1951-52. Before coming to Washington in 1964, he was a member of the Advisory Committee, Office of Scientific Research, U.S. Air Force. In 1959 he was appointed to the Space Science Board of the National Academy of Sciences, on which he served until February 1964. In 1960 President Eisenhower appointed Dr. Hornig to his Science Advisory Committee, and he was reappointed by President Kennedy in 1961. In late 1960 he served on the Kennedy Task Force on Space to help formulate policy in this field for the new administration.

In 1962-63 Dr. Hornig served as a member of the U.S. Delegation headed by Dr. Hugh Dryden which negotiated the agreement with the U.S.S.R. for cooperation in certain space activities.

Dr. Hornig became Special Assistant to President Johnson for Science and Technology on January 24, 1964, and was simultaneously named by the President to be Chairman of the Federal Council for Science and Technology. On January 27, 1964, the Senate confirmed the President's nomination of Dr. Hornig as Director of the Office of Science and Technology in the Executive Office of the President. He also served as the Chairman of President Johnson's Science Advisory Committee.

In January 1969, Dr. Hornig was appointed by President Nixon as Consultant-at-Large to the President's Science Advisory Committee. Also in January 1969, Dr. Hornig became Vice President of Eastman Kodak Company and since February 1969 has served as a Director of the company. He is also a member of the faculty of the University of Rochester as Professor of Chemistry.

Dr. Hornig was elected in 1954 to a three-year term on the Executive Committee, Division of Physical and Inorganic Chemistry, American Chemical Society. He is also a Fellow of the American Physical Society (Member, Executive Committee, Division of Chemical Physics, and Chairman 1957-58); a Fellow of the American Academy of Arts and Sciences; a Fellow of the Faraday Society, London, and was elected a member of the Washington Academy of Sciences in 1967. He was elected to the U.S. National Academy of Sciences in 1957, and in 1964 he was named a member of the Board of Overseers of Harvard University. He was elected an Honorary Member of the Rumanian Academy of Sciences in February 1965. Dr. Hornig is a member of the American Philosophical Society (1967); in February 1967 was awarded the Engineering Centennial Award by PMC Colleges, Chester, Pennsylvania; was the recipient of the 1967 Charles Lathrop Parsons Award of the American Chemical Society on November 30, 1967; and was the recipient of the first Mellon Institute Award on May 10,.1968, at Pittsburgh, Pennsylvania. Dr. Hornig was awarded the Order of Civil Merit (the Moranjang Medal) by the Korean Government in September 1968. Dr. Hornig became a member of the Board of Directors of the Overseas Development Council in February 1969.

Dr. Hornig has published about eighty papers in the *Journal of Chemical Physics*, *Journal of the Optical Society of America*, *Journal of Physical Chemistry*, *Review of Scientific Instruments*, *Physics of Fluids*, *Molecular Physics*, *Spectrochimica Acta*, *Discussions of the Faraday Society*, etc., on molecular and crystal structure, infrared and Raman spectra, shock and detonation waves, relaxation phenomena and fast chemical reactions at high temperatures.

Dr. Hornig has been awarded honorary degrees by: Temple University (LLD 1964); Yeshiva University of New York (Doctor of Humane Letters 1965); University of Notre Dame (LLD 1965); Rensselaer Polytechnic Institute (Doctor of Science 1965); University of Maryland (Doctor of Science 1965); Ripon College (Doctor of Science 1966); Boston College (Doctor of Laws 1966); PMC Colleges (Doctor of Science 1967): University of Wisconsin (Doctor of Science 1967); Worcester Polytechnic Institute (Doctor of Engineering 1967); University of Puget Sound (Doctor of Science 1968); Syracuse University (Doctor of Science 1968).

BIOGRAPHIC SKETCH OF GEORGE BOGDEN KISTIAKOWSKY

Born: November 18, 1900, Kiev, Russia.

Education: Kiev public schools until 1918; University of Berlin, Ph. D., 1925; Harvard University, D. Sc., 1955; Williams College, 1958; Oxford, 1959; University of Penna., 1960; University of Rochester, Carnegie Tech., 1961; Princeton University, Case Institute of Technology, 1962.

Experience:
  1926–28: International Research Fellow, Princeton.
  1928–30: Research associate, Princeton.
  1930–33: Assistant Professor of Chemistry, Harvard University.
  1933–37: Associate Professor of Chemistry, Harvard University.
  1937–59, 1961—: Professor of Chemistry, Harvard University.
  1959–61: Special Assistant to the President for Science and Technology.
  1961—: Chairman Science Board, Director of Itek Corporation.
  1957–63: Director of the Cabot Corporation and Member of the President's Science Advisory Committee.

Awards include:
  1946: Medal for Merit.
  1948: British Medal for Service in the Cause of Freedom.
  1958: Priestly award.

Memberships: Honorary Fellow of the Chemical Society (London); member of the Royal Society, National Academy of Sciences (Vice President, 1965–69), American Academy of Sciences; American Chemical Society, American Philosophical Society.

Research and Writing Activities: Contributor of numerous articles to scientific journals. Research in chemical kinetics; thermodynamics of organic molecules, shock and detonation waves; molecule spectroscopy.

Address: 12 Oxford Street, Cambridge, Massachusetts.

A BIOGRAPHIC SKETCH OF DR. JEROME B. WIESNER

Dr. Jerome B. Wiesner, who became Provost of the Massachusetts Institute of Technology on July 1, 1966, is the senior academic officer reporting to the President and also has responsibility for the interdisciplinary activities of the Institute's five schools.

Returning to M.I.T. in 1964, after having been Special Assistant for Science and Technology to the President of the United States for three years, Dr. Wiesner served as Dean of the School of Science and was responsible for seven academic departments—Biology, Chemistry, Geology and Geophysics, Mathematics, Meteorology, Nutrition and Food Science and Physics.

Before his appointment by President Kennedy as Special Assistant for Science and Technology on January 20, 1961, Dr. Wiesner was Director of the Research Laboratory of Electronics, one of the largest interdisciplinary laboratories at M.I.T., in which a broad spectrum of reasearch is conducted by professors and students from various departments. He also had been actively concerned with national problems involving science and engineering and became a member of the President's Science Advisory Committee in 1957, the same year that Dr. James R. Killian, Jr., then President of M.I.T., went to Washington as the first to hold the title of Special Assistant for Science and Technology. Dr. Wiesner remains a member of the committee. He was made Director of the Office of Science and Technology when that agency was established in 1962 and resigned at the beginning of 1964. In 1958, he served as Staff Director of the American Delegation to the Geneva Conference for the Prevention of Surprise Attack.

Dr. Wiesner was born in Detroit, Michigan, May 30, 1915, and received the degree of Bachelor of Science, Master of Science and Doctor of Philosophy from the University of Michigan in 1937, 1938 and 1950 respectively. While a student at the University of Michigan he was Associate Director of the University's broadcasting station and assisted in developing modern electronic techniques for use in the Speech Correction Department. He also served as a teacher of radio techniques at the summer National Music Camp at Interlocken, Michigan.

In 1940, Dr. Wiesner was appointed chief engineer of the Acoustical and Record Laboratory in the Library of Congress, Washington, D.C. There, under a Carnegie Corporation grant, he assisted in developing sound recording facilities and associated equipment.

Shortly after the beginning of World War II, Dr. Wiesner joined the staff of M.I.T.'s Radiation Laboratory as associate leader of the radio frequency development group. Later he became project engineer of a key radar development program and a member of the laboratory's steering committee. He was group leader of Project Cadillac, assigned to devise an airborne radar system. In 1945, Dr. Wiesner joined the staff of the Los Alamos Laboratory, where he served for a year, returning to M.I.T. as Assistant Professor of Electrical Engineering. Dr. Wiesner was advanced to the rank of Associate Professor of Electrical Engineering in 1947, and full Professor in 1950. He became Director of the Research Laboratory of Electronics in 1952. He has held the title of Institute Professor since February 1, 1962.

Dr. Wiesner's scientific contributions, particularly in the fields of microwave theory and communication sciences, have been notable. He was one of the principals in the conception of scatter transmission and in the application of statistical methods to communication engineering. He has participated in several summer studies of great importance to national defense, as well as in a number of international conferences devoted to the subject of disarmament. He was chairman of the Institute's steering committee for a Center for Communication Sciences established in 1958.

Dr. Wiesner has published technical articles in *Science, Proceedings of the IRE, Electronics, Physical Review, Journal of Applied Physics, Astronaut:..., IBM Journal of Research and Development*, as well as *Daedalus, Scientific American* and *L'Onde Electrique* and is the author of the book, *Where Science and Politics Meet*.

Eta Kappa Nu Association, the electrical engineering honor society, voted Dr. Wiesner an honorable mention as a outstanding young electrical engineer for the year 1947. In recognition of "outstanding services to his country," he was awarded the President's Certificate of Merit, the second highest civilian award, in 1948. In 1952, Dr. Wiesner was elected a Fellow of the Institute of Radio Engineers for his "outstanding contributions to radio or allied fields." He is a Fellow of the American Academy of Arts and Sciences, a member of the Acoustical Society of America, the National Academy of Sciences and the National Academy of Engineering.

Dr. Wiesner is married to the former Laya Wainger and they have four children, Stephen J., Zachary K., Elizabeth A. and Joshua A. Wiesner. They live at 61 Shattuck Road, Watertown.

BIOGRAPHY OF SIDNEY D. DRELL

Date and Place of Birth: September 13, 1926, Atlantic City, New Jersey.
Marital Status: Married, 3 Children.
Education:
    1946: A.B., Princeton.
    1947: M.A., University of Illinois.
    1949: Ph. D., University of Illinois.
Employment Record:
    1949–50: Research Associate, University of Illinois.
    Summer 1950: Visiting Physicist, Oak Ridge National Laboratory.
    1950–52: Physics Instructor, Stanford University.
    1952–53: Research Associate, Massachusetts Institute of Technology.
    Summer 1953: Visiting Physicist, Brookhaven National Laboratory.
    1953–56: Assistant Professor, Massachusetts Institute of Technology.
    Summer 1955: Visiting Physicist, Brookhaven National Laboratory.
    1956–60: Associate Professor, Stanford University.

Summer 1958: Visiting Scientist, CERN, Switzerland.
1960–63: Professor of Physics, Stanford University.
1961–62: Visiting Scientist and Guggenheim Fellow, CERN, Switzerland.
Fall 1962: Visiting Professor and Loeb Lecturer, Harvard University.
1963– : Professor, Stanford Linear Accelerator Center (Theoretical Physics).
1969– : Deputy Director and Executive Head of Theoretical Physics, Stanford Linear Accelerator Center.

Consultantships:
1956–64: Los Alamos Scientific Laboratory.
1968– : Los Alamos Scientific Laboratory.
1960– : Jason Division, Institute for Defense Analyses, Arlington, Virginia.
1960– : Office of Science and Technology, Executive Office of the President.
1966–70: President's Science Advisory Committee.
1969– : Arms Control and Disarmament Agency.

Societies:
1. Professional and Scientific:
   Fellow of the American Physical Society.
   National Academy of Sciences.
2. Academic Honorary:
   Phi Beta Kappa.
   Sigma Xi.
   Phi Kappa Phi.

Professional Activities:
1960–62: Member of the Board of Editors of "The Physical Review."
Summer 1962: Lecturer at the International School of Physics, Enrico Fermi Summer School (XXVIth) Course, Lake Como, Italy.
1963–65: Member of the Visiting Committee to the Laboratory of Nuclear Science, Massachusetts Institute of Technology.
Summer 1963: Lecturer at Ettore Majorana International School of Physics, Erice (Sicily), Italy.
1964: Member of the Panel on Elementary Particle Physics of the Physics Survey Committee, National Academy of Science-National Research Council (Pake Committee).
Summer 1966: Lecturer at the 7th Scottish Universities Summer School in Physics, Edinburgh, Scotland.
1966–69: Member of the Advisory Council of the Department of Physics, Princeton University.
1967–69: Chairman of the Advisory Council of the Department of Physics, Princeton University.
1967: Member of the Board of Editors of "Reviews of Modern Physics".
1967–68: Member of the National Accelerator Laboratory Physics Advisory Committee.
1967–69: Correspondent, "Comments on Nuclear and Particle Physics".
1969– : Member of the Board of Advisors of "Comments on Nuclear and Particle Physics".
1969– : Member of the Editorial Council of "Annals of Physics".
Summer 1969: Lecturer at Ettore Majorana International School of Physics, Erice (Sicily), Italy.

BIOGRAPHY OF DR. M. L. GOLDBERGER

Marvin Leonard Goldberger, Born 10 October 1922 in Chicago, Illinois. Attended elementary and high school in Youngstown, Ohio. Entered Carnegie Institute of Technology, Pittsburgh, Pennsylvania in 1940, graduated with B.S. in Physics 1943. U.S. Army, 1944–1946 assigned to Manhattan Project. Entered graduate school, University of Chicago 1946, received Ph. D. in Physics 1948. Rose from assistant professor to professor, University of Chicago 1952–1957. Since 1957, Eugene Higgins Professor of Physics, Princeton University. Member American Academy of Arts and Sciences, National Academy of Sciences. Married, 1945, Mildred Ginsburg, two children.

Consultant to Atomic Energy Commission, Department of Defense, other government agencies since 1955. Chairman, Jason Division of IDA 1959–1966. Member, President's Science Advisory Committee 1965–1969.

INSTITUTE FOR DEFENSE ANALYSES,
Arlington, Va., April 15, 1970.

Hon. ALBERT GORE,
U.S. Senate,
Washington, D.C.

DEAR SENATOR GORE: I am taking this opportunity to offer my views on Soviet attitudes, incentives, and perceptions relevant to the ongoing US-Soviet strategic arms limitation talks in Vienna. These views and comments are based on research in Soviet military and political problems conducted over the years at the RAND Corporation, and more recently, at the Institute for Defense Analyses. It is my purpose within the limitation of time and space, to suggest how Soviet arms control attitudes and policies are influenced by: perception of the United States; US-Soviet strategic balance; internal Soviet bureaucratic politics; and some related Soviet policy interests.

I am also attaching a recently completed paper on some general and specific Soviet interests in SALT, on some alternative outcomes of SALT, and some postulated implications of such alternative outcomes. This paper is part of a larger study on Soviet arms control interests which will be published as a book by the Johns Hopkins Press this summer.

I would like to suggest that the views expressed in these materials are my own and do not necessarily reflect the views or interests of IDA.

Sincerely yours,

ROMAN KOLKOWICZ.

(The papers follow.)

1. We enter the 1970's at a crucial time in U.S.-Soviet relations:
—for the first time both the U.S. and the Soviet Union are strategic equals
—both contemplate or pursue massive new arms programs
—both are aware of the potentially destabilizing effects of these weapons
—both are aware of the diminishing utility (political and military) of these new weapons and technologies
—both are pursuing strategic arms limitation talks

Thus we perceive a peculiar dilemma of superpower, where, in the words of President Nixon "the traditional course of seeking security primarily through military strength raises several problems in a world of multiplying strategic weapons," while at the same time, in the words of Mr. McGeorge Bundy "the same political leaders who know these terrible weapons must never be used, and who do not run the foolish risks of nuclear gamemanship abroad still do not hesitate to authorize system after system." There is, indeed, a "curious and distressing paradox in all this."

We must, nevertheless, seek more understanding of how Soviet leaders look at these problems, because an arms control agreement is presumable a "non-zero-sum game" situation: both participants must be assured that they both stand to gain and that their essential security and policy interests would not be jeopardized in the process. We would, therefore, want to know how the Soviets see the rules of the game: the opportunities, risks, costs, and limitations inherent in their arms programs and in potential arms control arrangements.

2. Certain political, cultural and psychological characteristics of the Soviet system contribute to high levels of "threat expectation." A combination of militant ideology and a perception of a hostile international environment has instilled in most Soviet leaders a form of political paranoia in general, and a profound mistrust in the West in particular. It has also engendered in them a strong expectation of threat and a corresponding reliance in their own defense capabilities. It has further led to a militarization of national priorities in which the defense sector is almost invariably given primacy; a sense of internal vigilance and mobilization of resources and manpower in anticipation of threat; and a basic mistrust in agreements which might impinge on their freedom to pursue optimal defense policies. Soviet leaders were raised on the Leninist philosophy of a basic "Bolshevik belief that enemies strive not merely to contain the Party . . . but rather to annihilate it." Thus, Stalin spoke of basic contradictions between the two camps, capitalist and socialist, and concluded that "Who will defeat whom? that is the essential question." Khrushchev maintained that the "imperialists walk around the fence of the socialist countries like hungry wolves around a sheep pen." He also warned that "some people watch us with greedy eyes and think how they can disarm us. But what would happen if we disarmed? We would certainly be torn to pieces." Brezhnev alluded to the "dangerous intrigues by the enemies of peace" while Shelepin warned that "the Soviet Union has no right to ignore the constantly threatening danger of a new military attack by the predatory imperialists."

Among the reasons for the near-paranoid attitude of Soviet leaders are their perceptions of a hostile international environment and "punitive" Western policies. Soviet leaders grew up in a society marked by such anti-Soviet policies as:
—"Cordon Sanitaire"
—"Capitalist Encirclement"
—Roll-back
—Massive Retaliation
—Containment
—Asserted Western Strategic Superiority

The Soviet Union existed for many years being surrounded by a ring of US military bases, making Russia vulnerable to US retaliatory attacks, while during much of that time the US remained virtually invulnerable. Moreover, the Soviets were "educated" by the West to the fact that credible strategic superiority can be translated into various kinds of political, strategic, and diplomatic advantages. This particular "lesson" did not fail and the primary Soviet objective since the Cuban missile crisis was to climb out of the pariah position of strategic inferiority and to obtain at least parity with the United States.

3. In examining current approximate US-Soviet strategic parity, we ought to consider briefly a related important factor: that for the first time since the war, US and Soviet military capabilities, postures, and doctrines have become roughly symmetrical, they have come into-phase. They have been asymmetrical during the past two decades, out-of-phase. This, I submit, is a vital factor in current Soviet interests in arms control: Soviet leaders would not be likely to seek serious arms control agreements from a clear position of strategic disadvantage, since a stabilization of such arms ratios would permanently "freeze" Soviet military capabilities at a position of disadvantage. Such a proposition would also be politically unpalatable to the several powerful bureaucratic institutions in Russia, chiefly among them the Soviet military.

Let us briefly compare the evolution of American and Soviet strategic capabilities postures and doctrines:

United States	Soviet Union

US and Soviet strategic *capabilities* did not come into phase until the past year or two:

United States	Soviet Union
Nuclear Monopoly	Marginal Strategic Capabilities
Strategic Superiority	Strategic Inferiority
Parity	Parity

US and Soviet strategic *doctrines* were also out-of-phase until recently:

United States	Soviet Union
Massive Retaliation	Obsolete Stalinist Doctrines
Flexible Response	"Massive Retaliation"
Flexible Response	Flexible Response

Soviet military *posture* remained out-of-phase relative to ours until recently:

United States	Soviet Union
Global, Offensive	Continental, Defensive
Global, Deterring	Mixed: Strategic forces were in global deterring posture; conventional forces in continental, defensive posture
Global, Deterring, Flexible	Global, Deterring, Flexible

This coming into-phase of Soviet military capabilities, postures, and doctrines is important to our understanding of current Soviet attitudes toward SALT and arms control. The current parity relationship of Soviet and US forces satisfies a basic precondition for Soviet arms control interests, i.e., to negotiate from military and political equality and not from a position of acknowledged inferiority. Thus, SALT would seem to logically satisfy this and several other basic Soviet objectives and interests.

Among other Soviet interests that would be logically served by SALT are: the prevention of the possibility of a Soviet "two-front" confrontation, China in the East and NATO/US in the West; it might possibly prevent a potential US "overreaction" to recent Soviet strategic buildup reminiscent of the missile-gap era; and, finally, the current and foreseeable Soviet strategic capabilities are deemed by many Soviet political and some military people as being adequate. A continued escalating strategic arms program would by these considerations create great pressures on Soviet resources in the face of severe economic problems within the Soviet Union, while adding little to their security or political interests.

4. If the above considerations suggest why the Soviets view SALT as desirable and as serving several of their major interests, we ought to also mention several countervailing trends which make meaningful outcomes of the talks questionable. First, the obvious skepticism and resistance of the Soviet military toward SALT. Their military establishment strongly distrusts diplomatic settlements of major defense issues and generally subscribes to the "worst plausible case" approach to military problems. Secondly, the fact that the presumed propitious timing for meaningful arms control arrangements is rapidly disappearing. Let me elaborate on this point.

Before the appearance of MIRV, SS-9 and the possibility of a "thick" ABM system, US and Soviet capabilities satisfied several basic security requirements. They each possessed credible, nearly invulnerable retaliatory, second-strike capabilities, thus creating stable deterrence. Moreover, for purposes of arms control, such systems had further clear advantage. Modern reconnaissance technology could assess adversary capabilities with a comfortable margin of assurance against any surprises and could provide a credible assessment of adversary testing techniques, deployment programs, etc. This was important since the Soviets (and to a large extent the United States) resist and oppose on-site inspection as part of any arms control agreements. In sum, the deterrence system was relatively stable; the element of uncertainty was tolerable; there were low incentives for first-strike considerations; and arms control was theoretically feasible.

The prospect of a deployed MIRV, SS-9 and "thick" ABM systems injects a highly destabilizing new factor into the situation. First, they can be used in principle as a counterforce, first-strike weapon; second, they can theoretically saturate the defenses of the opponent, and thus render him even more vulnerable; third, they cannot be accounted for by the usual means of detection and thus introduce a new strong element of uncertainty, which reenforces the "worst plausible case" approach to security and politics. The role of the ABM in the context of MIRV and SS-9 is ambiguous. In the prevailing strategic parlance, the argument against a "thick" ABM is that it is both very expensive and militarily futile since the enemy would presumably saturate the defenses with massive salvoes of warheads, and at the same time it is unnecessarily provocative, motivating the adversary to strengthen his efforts to make sure that he can annihilate such defenses, thus adding further to the arms race.

5. If we assume that the Soviets are seriously interested in SALT, and that several basic conditions for such Soviet interest have become satisfied we may want to inquire how SALT fits within broader Soviet policy interests and objectives. We would want first, however, to examine certain entrenched Western beliefs and misapprehensions about the Soviet Union and US-Soviet relations. Among these beliefs are:
—that we can "bleed" them to death economically, by forcing them to keep up with us in an intensive arms race
—that we can still attain meaningful strategic superiority
—that we can expect an internal political and social upheaval in the Soviet Union or in the communist bloc

I would suggest that such beliefs are unrealistic and are to some extent wishful thinking. It may be more realistic to assume that
—the Soviet Union is going to continue its arms program, if necessary, to ensure strategic equality
—that the Soviet Union is not seriously interested in first strike or surprise attacks on the United States
—that the Soviet Union is interested in stabilizing the expensive arms race and would seek to avoid confrontations with the United States in areas of vital interests
—however, the Soviet Union is also going to selectively probe in the soft areas of the world for opportunities and expansion, regardless of the SALT outcomes

Thus, while SALT is a desirable Soviet objective, it is not the one-and-all objective of Soviet policy. As a matter of fact, one would argue that Soviet interests in SALT, while presumably realistic and serious, are part of a larger policy schema, which I call a Hold-and-Explore policy for the seventies. The postulated objectives of this policy are:
—*Hold* and stabilize their Western flank (NATO, US) through SALT, European Security Conference, etc.
—Obtain greater freedom to deal with China (thus also prevent a two-front confrontation)

—*Explore* opportunities south of Russia, via a capillary expansion in the regions of Middle East, Mediterranean, and North Africa.

Such a policy is seen by many Soviets as one of low risks, low costs, and potential high payoffs; while a continued confrontation and arms race with the West is seen as one of high costs, high risks, and low payoffs.

6. Whether reasonable and useful arms control arrangements will be obtained will depend on many factors. Key among them will be a reciprocal understanding regarding common concerns and common needs. A useful arms control agreement should obviate the need to trust one another, because the basic utility of such an agreement is obtaining mutually acceptable objectives that transcend mutual trust. Moreover, a workable arms control agreement is, in essence, a formalization of certain rules of behavior among states. It also serves as a way of communicating to the adversary present and likely future intentions regarding the uses of economic and technological resources for military and political purposes.

In conclusion, it is important to consider the history of Soviet technological and military development. The Soviets have over the past two decades sought to systematically and with considerable success to overcome deficiencies in their military technologies. They ended US atomic monopoly several years earlier than most Western experts expected; thermonuclear weapons were developed almost simultaneously in both countries; and the Soviet Union was the first to test an ICBM successfully in flight. While the Soviet Union lagged behind the United States in the procurement of ICBM systems, this was the result more of political calculations than of an inability to do. This "gap" has been closed in recent years and the Soviets have come close in equaling US strategic capabilities.

It would be imprudent at present, therefore, to assume that the Soviet Union is not capable of making great and rapid strides in the development and deployment of military technologies, if circumstances should demand it. We must not forget the rather sanguine assessments in 1965 by very knowledgeable American leaders (McNamara et al) that the Soviet leaders "have decided that they have lost the quantitative race and they are not seeking to engage us in that contest * * *. There is no indication that the Soviets are seeking to develop a strategic nuclear force as large as ours." Current US assessments of Soviet strategic capabilities offer a rather melancholy negation of those projections.

Thus since the Soviet Union seems serious about realistic arms limitation talks, and since such talks and possible arrangements would also serve US interests, it seems reasonable to suggest that such talks should be actively pursued and that actions which jeopardize them should be avoided. At the same time we should remain alert to the fact that strategic arms limitation is not an end in itself to Soviet leaders, but rather a key objective in their current policy orientation: to stabilize an expensive and essentially unproductive arms race at mutually agreeable levels, while gaining greater freedom to pursue policy opportunities in other areas. The United States may want to consider how challenging such two-pronged Soviet policy might be and if the Soviets may be persuaded to subordinate some of their other interests to that of SALT. This, I believe, is not impossible.

Finally, it would be imprudent of the United States to base its security interests and policies on expectations of Soviet technological and economic backwardness. The Soviet Union has in the past shown an impressive ability to make great strides in catching up with, matching, and at time surpassing Western progress in the development and deployment of strategic forces. It would be equally imprudent to assume that the current Soviet leadership is planning to commit its economic and social systems to vast arming programs with the intent to go to nuclear war. The constraints of the deterrence relationship and some current domestic constraints on Soviet leaders seem to argue against such an assumption. Therefore, a strategic arms control agreement which would serve both countries would seem a useful way of also serving their individual needs.

SOVIET INTERESTS IN SALT

Soviet arms control motives are complex and ambiguous. Moreover, arms control issues involve a variety of technological, military, political, economic, and psychological factors which are frequently at odds with one another. Indeed, the impetus for arms control is rather fragile and ephemeral: if the circumstances for initiation of such negotiations are propitious at one time, they may be rapidly overtaken by events, by the inexorable march of technology and shifts in the psychological milieu.

Certain recent developments, however, contribute to a climate conducive to arms control. Key among them is the realization in the words of President Nixon, that "the traditional course of seeking security primarily through military strength raises several problems in a world of multiplying strategic weapons." President Nixon went on to enumerate the problems: "Modern technology makes any balance precarious and prompts new efforts at ever higher levels of complexity. Such an arms race absorbs resources, talents, and energies." Higher levels of complexity lead to ever greater levels "of uncertainty about the other side's intentions," and "the higher level of armaments, the greater the violence and devastation, should deterrence fail."[1] Similarly sober views on the futility and dangers of building ever greater and newer strategic inventories are constantly echoed by the Soviet leaders and by the Soviet press. Yet, as McGeorge Bundy asserted "there is a curious and distressing paradox in all this. The same political leaders who know these terrible weapons must never be used and who do not run the foolish risks of nuclear gamesmanship abroad still do not hesitate to authorize system after system."[2]

While Bundy's observation about the gap between political rhetoric and policy behavior is well founded, it seems too harsh. The fact is that proposals for US-Soviet arms control measures are cast in a world conditioned by intense East-West hostility, by past and current major conflicts of vital interests, by psychological resistance to trusting the adversary, and most of all, by deep uncertainties about the implementation and outcome of such unprecedented potential arrangements. Moreover, such proposals evoke profound uneasiness among the major institutions whose past *raison d'être* has been to create fear in the adversary, lest he consider aggressive measures.

The wall of distrust must be scaled, however, if for no other reason than because the world of the seventies will be different in many ways from that of past decades. The basic fact contributing to the change is that the United States and the Soviet Union are strategic equals and whatever the technological and numerical advances achieved in either country, their relationship will not change significantly in the foreseeable future.

FACTORS MOTIVATING SOVIET ARMS CONTROL INTERESTS

The likely motivations for serious Soviet interest in arms control can be broken down into three groups: objective motives (derived from perceptions of likely gains in military, political, and economic areas); subjective motives (generated by uncertainties and concerns about a new unchecked arms-race cycle); and manipulative motives (aimed at creating "favorable" political and psychological conditions in the West relevant to arms control).

Many Soviet leaders see a new arms race with the United States as both militarily and politically unproductive—and possibly counterproductive—while at the same time creating new and undesirable demands on their internal resources. They seem to believe that since both superpowers now possess assured destruction capabilities (though asymmetrical ones), it makes little sense to continue to increase significantly their strategic offensive and defensive forces in an open-ended manner. Therefore, since both superpowers are vitally concerned about retaining a stable and credible deterrence relation, it is useless and possibly dangerous to consider the actual deployment of potentially destabilizing weapons systems. Such an eventuality could possibly provoke the reemergence of the surprise-attack fears that pervaded the security perceptions of both superpowers during the 1950s when the "balance of terror" was considered indeed "delicate."

A stabilization of the arms race at mutually acceptable levels would tend to enhance other Soviet policy interests and actually increase the options for dealing with them. Soviet policy interests and external commitments have increased in recent years. The Soviet Union has extended its political and military influence in the Mediterranean and the Middle East, and its interest in the Persian Gulf and North African areas is mounting. Moreover, the deteriorating situation on the Sino-Soviet border and related complications have introduced new demands and stresses on Soviet military capabilities. Thus, Soviet defense capabilities are being spread out, both for offensive and defensive reasons, in the face of new demands on resources in connection with the US-Soviet armed balance. A stabilization of the strategic arms competition would logically ease the pressures on Soviet resources and commitments, since current and foreseeable Soviet policy interests necessitate largely the support of conventional, rather than strategic nuclear, forces.

Turning to the assumed subjective Soviet motives, it appears that Soviet leaders are becoming concerned with certain developments in the United States

---

[1] A report to the Congress by Richard Nixon, President of the United States, *US Foreign Policy for the 1970's: A New Strategy for Peace*, p. 142.
[2] McGeorge Bundy, "To Cap the Volcano," *Foreign Affairs*, No. 1, October 1969.

which harbor potential challenges to them. Policy decisions concerning the expansion of the Safeguard ABM system and the potential deployment of the Poseidon and Minuteman III MIRV systems suggest to the Soviets a renewed hardening of the U.S. position. Various public statements by leading U.S. governmental figures are interpreted by the Soviets in this light and suggest to them a return to an alleged policy "from a position of force," a search for strategic superiority and renewed threat of first-strike planning. The fact that their own expanding SS-9 missile system, in addition to increases in the number of Polaris-type missile weapons and the continuing deployment of such ICBM weapons as the SS-11 and the SS-13, is causing grave concern in the West seems to escape Soviet awareness.

Finally, the Soviets have been mounting a vigorous public campaign on behalf of SALT in order to create a political-psychological climate in the United States which would militate against expensive new military programs whose very utility is controversial. It also serves Soviet interests to establish the impression of their peace-loving, sane and conciliatory position before and during the negotiatory process. Thus, if such talks should become bogged down or fail, the Soviet Union could accuse the United States of bad faith and perfidy.

SOVIET NEGOTIATORY POSTURE AND TACTICS

The Soviet Union's declaratory policy, prenegotiation tactics, and initial negotiatory evidence suggest a negotiatory "profile" which reflects several underlying objectives: the retention of a credible and stable deterrence relationship with the United States: the avoidance of a "two-front" confrontation involving China in the East and the United States and NATO in the West; and the avoidance of dangerous situations deriving from potentially incendiary tensions in the Middle East, Europe, and Asia. It is clear that as the Soviets pursue their various interests around the world, they must calculate the intensity and method of their policy pursuit so as not to compromise the above objectives. Moreover, the Soviets would seek to retain a wide range of options to deal with these policy interests, even in the event of useful strategic arms control talks with the United States.

The Soviet negotiatory posture includes insistence upon the following points:
(1) Separation of strategic arms control issues from other policy issues.
(2) Exclusion of matters pertaining to conventional forces from strategic arms control talks.
(3) Preferability of exclusive bilateral talks between the superpowers.
(4) Unfettered continuation of research and development programs if production, testing, and deployment of strategic weapons are curtailed.
(5) Retention of the principle of "territorial integrity," which rejects proposals for supranational inspection.

This posture gives the Soviet Union a good bargaining position in the negotiations, since some of these points are presumably open to trade-offs with the United States.

ALTERNATIVE SOVIET ARMS CONTROL OBJECTIVES

The general approach to strategic arms limitation maintains that the Soviet Union has "no desire to receive additional unilateral advantages for itself relevant to safeguarding just its security alone." [3] Beyond this broad concept lies a multitude of possible negotiatory variations on the basic theme of stabilizing the arms competition. The Soviets, however, for their own reasons, refrain from going deeply into the specifics of their negotiatory position.

On the U.S. side, there appears to be a similar though not identical vagueness concerning concrete and feasible negotiatory positions, although President Nixon did describe three negotiatory alternatives. First, limit the number of missiles stockpiled, which would place a ceiling on the quantity of missiles without restricting "qualitative improvements." Second, limit the number and capabilities of missiles, which would also limit their "capabilities, including qualitative controls over such weapons as MIRVs." Or third, reduce offensive forces without qualitative restrictions, "on the theory that at fixed and lower levels of armaments the risks of technological surprise would be reduced." Thus, the United States and, according to President Nixon, the Soviet Union, are approaching the arms limitation talks on the basis of "building blocs" for several different positions depending on "what might prove negotiable." [4]

[3] "Observer," *Pravda*, Mar. 7, 1970.
[4] President Nixon, *U.S. Foreign Policy for the 1970s*.

Before the emergence of the MIRV weapons (which are being tested and are rapidly approaching the deployment stage) and the SS-9 missile (which is being deployed in sizable numbers and has undergone MIRV testing), it seemed reasonable to accept the proposition that a freeze on the number of launchers on both sides at mutually agreeable levels (which would allow for trade-offs in a symmetrical systems) would satisfy both sides and would be easily verified. The prospect of deployed MIRVs and expanded ABM systems on both sides changes this strategic equation. Thus, we have to postulate several contingent contextual situations for arms control in which to examine Soviet objectives.

CRITICAL AND TOLERABLE CONDITIONS AFFECTING ARMS CONTROL PROSPECTS

There are a number of likely or hypothetical developments which could profoundly affect the perceptions, conduct, and outcome of arms limitation talks. These likely developments have been broken down into two broad categories—those considered "critical" and those considered "tolerable." It is assumed that critical developments could (a) imbalance severely the strategic relationship between the protagonists, thus tending to create a new "superior-inferior" relationship between them; (b) undermine the political and psychological climate necessary for negotiations; or (c) threaten a high-value objective of one or both superpowers forcing them to seek recourse in "extra" levels of deterrence capability. On the other hand, tolerable developments would be likely to have a less-direct and less-significant impact on decisions for going ahead with strategic arms control talks, although they would still in various ways create or maintain periods of high tension. Moreover, some of these tolerable developments could rapidly become critical, depending on a variety of technological, military, political, and psychological factors.

The critical and tolerable developments listed below are not to be taken as exhaustive or equally relevant. They are merely suggestive of the kinds of problems that could affect the arms control talks.

CRITICAL DEVELOPMENTS RELEVANT TO ARMS CONTROL

- US or Soviet deployment of a credible MIRV system
- US or Soviet decision to proceed with a "thick" ABM system
- Continued Soviet deployment of ICBMs and SLBMs substantially beyond present levels
- Rapid development of a significant Chinese strategic nuclear capability

Any one of the above developments would, in effect, raise doubts about the stability of deterrence and the assumed vulnerability of second-strike capabilities. It might therefore also raise the specter of surprise attacks and of a renewed search for "superiority." Deployment of a significant FOBS, MIRV, or SLBM capability by either power would negate a vital precondition for possible arms control, namely, the high credibility of verification of Soviet and US offensive and strategic quantitative and qualitative levels of armament. In the event of such a deployment, it would be almost impossible to rely on extraterritorial verification methods. Moreover, even if deployment is not undertaken, but testing programs are satisfactorily concluded, this would create severe concerns lest one or the other side clandestinely modify its "conventional" missiles into MIRVs. It would thus give impetus to those groups in the opposing country which are unwilling to accept strategic and technological "inferiority."

- Serious crises in areas of the Middle East, East Europe, Central Europe, or Asia
- Radical shifts in the Soviet or U.S. leadership which would bring forth more militant and less reconcilable personalities into positions of power.

These developments would exacerbate the present international situation and erode the necessary preconditions for bilateral arms control negotiations. Specifically, they would result in shifts of policy priorities with a renewed stress on "Vigilance," readiness, and mobilization of the nation for likely hostilities or intense political conflict.

TOLERABLE DEVELOPMENTS RELEVANT TO ARMS CONTROL

- U.S. deployment of a "thin" ABM system
- Anticipated low-rate progression of Chinese strategic nuclear capabilities
- Certain type of nuclear proliferation

Such developments, though they might create tension and uncertainty, would not materially affect the credibility of U.S. or Soviet deterrents or their second-

strike capabilities. While such developments contain "nuisance" value, and while they may complicate the balancing of relations between the superpowers, they would not, in the final analysis, create serious obstacles or challenges to the security needs of the two countries.
- Protracted but low-level conflicts and tensions in the Middle East and Asia
- "Police actions" in superpower zones of influence

While it is probable that such developments would not adversely affect the basic security interests of the superpowers, and therefore should not, in principle, undermine the proposed strategic arms control negotiations, much would depend on the superpowers' perceptions of the intensity and direction of such developments. In an atmosphere of high tension, poor communication, and high expectations of deterioration of the political milieu, for example, it is conceivable that events could snowball and lead to imprudent actions and commitments by the parties involved.

It may be argued that even certain "critical" conditions do not necessarily jeopardize the probability of arms control negotiations. Some argue that for negotiatory purposes it is useful to go into such talks with a "full pocket" of bargaining points which can be traded off reciprocally. Others maintain that, even in the absence of formal agreements on the limitation of strategic forces, the Soviet Union and the United States would forego plans to push on with continuous production, testing, and deployment of larger or newer strategic systems. However, such arguments are not very persuasive in the light of historical evidence. Once a weapons system has been proven to be viable and "useful," it is highly improbable that either side would agree to abandon it. The reasons for such hesitancy are many, including institutional pressures, distrust of the adversary, difficulty in verification, and much of the "mad momentum" of modern war technology.

However, if ideal and total solutions to the arms debacle are not possible, it is still useful to contemplate certain negotiatory arrangements which would at the very least affirm the rules of the game at potentially higher thresholds of strategic capabilities. Thus, the Soviets would likely seek such negotiatory objectives as a freeze on the number of missile launchers and thereby obtain one broad limiting parameter in the arms competition. Next, they would likely press for a moratorium on MIRV testing, after their own tests, which are behind those of the United States, have been successfully accomplished. They would also be likely to seek a moratorium on MIRV deployment with some form of verification, which by the nature of the art will be less than satisfactory. They may also seek some trade-offs in the US strategic bomber/Soviet MRBM-IRBM ratios.

At the heart of the Soviet position seems to be the belief that once political equality as well as strategic equality is obtained with the United States, a basic premise becomes established for political solutions to strategic problems. The Soviet Union, like the United States, possesses three independent types of deterrence systems, each of which could potentially inflict vast destruction on the opponent, although possibly less than what strategic parlance calls "unacceptable damage" running into tens of millions of casualties.

The three systems are an offensive, land-based strategic force (SS-9, SS-11, SS-13); a growing sea-based deterrent force of SLBMs (presently inferior to that of the United States); and a significant IRBM-MRBM land-based force, which keeps West Europe, and possibly China, as "hostage." (Soviet strategic bomber forces are inferior to those of the United States.) Thus, counting on their "assured destruction" capability as sufficient to deter the United States, the Soviets are likely to consider various stabilizing arms control measures which would be less than optimal, but nevertheless tolerable.

ALTERNATIVE OUTCOMES OF STRATEGIC ARMS LIMITATION TALKS

Realistic analysis suggests that even at their most productive point, U.S.-Soviet arms control negotiations will not profoundly alter their adversary relationship, nor will they measurably affect the range of their traditional political interests and objectives. The negotiations would, however, stabilize and formalize U.S.-Soviet relations and thus affirm some new rules of the game for the superpowers in the 1970s. This in itself would be a major step in the right direction which could possibly create a proper political and psychological climate for further political negotiations.

At the same time, we ought to consider some of the less desirable general implications of a potential limited arms control agreement. In any such agreement, both parties will want to retain broad options as a hedge against the eventuality that the agreement, once reached, would fail. These options would no doubt include undertaking sizable research and development programs which would aggregate new technologies and techniques and which could, in turn, generate pressure for political decisions for going ahead. As long as the relations between the parties to an arms control agreement remained fairly stable, such pressures could presumably be contained. In the event, however, of a serious deterioration of relations, there would be considerable hesitation to deny self-access to available military technologies, some of which might be considered in the nature of "breakthroughs."

Let us now examine several possible outcomes of strategic arms control talks and their likely implications for superpower interests.

POSITIVE, COMPREHENSIVE AGREEMENTS

Optimal negotiatory arrangements in the current US-Soviet strategic arms control talks would include a freeze on land-based missile launchers at mutually acceptable current levels, a moratorium on MIRV deployment (a potential moratorium on MIRV testing seems rather unpromising), and a limitation on future expansion of ABM systems beyond reasonable levels, which would still leave them in a "thin" configuration. Moreover, such an optimal arrangement would presumably fix ceilings on further deployment of SLBMs and arrive at some understanding of equitable strategic bomber-IRBM/MRBM trade-offs. Such a postulated set of negotiatory agreements would stabilize the strategic balance at approximate parity levels, while slowing down and eventually arresting the production and deployment momentum of weapons systems on both sides.

Given the assumed Soviet negotiatory profile, it is fair to speculate that such an arms control arrangement would leave the Soviets free to pursue, rather vigorously, their hold-and-explore policy in the 1970s. It would permit them, under the umbrella of stabilized mutual deterrence, to reorder their priorities and allocations to the advantage of their nonstrategic capabilities and afford them a stronger political and military posture for the pursuit of their defensive (Chinese) and offensive (Middle East, Mediterranean, North African) policy objectives. It is doubtful, however, that the Soviets would become reckless in the use of their conventional forces for political and military exploration and expansion. Although they would have gained a stabilized strategic parity relationship with the United States, the Soviets would still expect a high U.S. resolve to deter and contain any aggressive Soviet expansionistic moves by conventional U.S. forces and, if necessary, by threats to use strategic nuclear forces.

EFFECTS ON ALLIANCE COMMITMENTS

One of the reasons for the Soviet pressure for bilateral arms control talks at the superpower level is an implicit desire to preserve the existing superpower ascendancy in the international system. Although the Soviets are fully aware that the idea of a superpower condominium raises concerns among their own and American allies, they can afford to be more sanguine about it than the United States because Soviet influence over its allies is more direct and reinforceable by threats of coercion or use of force. While both the United States and the Soviet Union would meet with suspicion and resistance from their respective allies in the event of a bilateral superpower agreement on arms control, it would seem that the Soviets would stand to lose less in this respect than the United States.

After all, it is the Soviets who sought to deny the West Germans (and Japanese) access to nuclear weapons in any form or shape. Moreover, much of the cohesion of the NATO alliance stems from expectations of "threats from the East" and the corollary reliance on the United States to protect and support West European interests which involve the Soviet Union. Hence, the possibility of a bilateral agreement for arms control could create concerns among some West European countries about the future credibility of US commitments to protect their national interests.

Moreover, the Soviet Union has another advantage: Soviet allies in the Warsaw Pact have expressed no interest publicly in nuclear weapons, they do not seek or expect any nuclear-sharing agreements with the Soviet Union, and they have no plans for any kind of regional nuclear-shared force. On the other hand, some West Europeans are considering the latter eventuality as an alternative to continued and uncertain dependence on US deterrence. In short, a superpower arms control agreement would affect Soviet alliance commitments and obligations to a much lesser extent than those of the United States.

PROLONGED NEGOTIATIONS WITH PARTIAL RESULTS

Another potential outcome of the arms control talks is one of extensive and largely fruitless negotiations, paralleled by the constant march of military technology, resulting in some partial and essentially "tokenistic" agreements. Given the currently contemplated and planned arms programs, it is fair to assume that if the talks continue over a period of about one year or more, there will be enough internal pressure in both countries for going ahead with the implementation of such programs. Thus, one could assume the successful completion of MIRV tests in the United States and the Soviet Union, partial or extensive deployment of MIRV systems in both countries, expansion of current ABM programs and SLBM systems, and a general active pursuit of their respective arms programs. Such an eventuality seems logical, since both sides would seek to strengthen their negotiatory posture as the talks continue; moreover, the action-reaction momentum would dictate resolve on either side not to fall behind the other side's arms programs.

What might be the effects of this parallelism on the outcome of the talks? At the very least, it would continue to reduce the margin of negotiatory options, as either or both sides continue to test and deploy weapons systems. Thus, there might likely be created a progressive hardening of respective negotiatory postures, while the urgency for negotiating would increase and thereby add a sense of urgency and tension to the negotiatory situation. A likely outcome might be some agreements on *what is*, that is, legitimizing external developments by giving them the imprimatur of concessionary agreements. Such agreements might include a freeze on the number of launchers, without agreement on the "qualitative" improvements of the weapons, i.e., MIRVs. Another feasible agreement may be a new ceiling on ABM systems, with the understanding that an anti-Chinese, incremental expansion be tolerated.

While such outcomes are not to be dismissed out of hand as useless, since they would at least establish some understanding about the limitations, parameters, and sets of tolerances about adversary initiatives, they would on the whole be of limited utility. Essentially, they would represent forms of unilateral constraint on either side in their arms programs under the guise of mutually agreed upon negotiatory concessions. Moreover, they would leave the strategic relations of the superpowers in a state of high tension and uncertainty and thus contribute little to a fuller stabilization of their relations.

NEGOTIATIONS BREAKDOWN

Another possible outcome of the arms control talks is an early stalemate and eventual breakdown of the negotiations. This eventuality is most disturbing since it would free the action-reaction momentum to move on unrestrained, it would tend to heighten the sense of insecurity and mistrust on both sides, and it would also reinforce the arguments of those groups which demand security by superior force of arms. Having tried diplomatic means to stablize their arms race, and having failed, both sides would most likely seek to ensure their basic interests through unilateral, available means, i.e., intensive arms programs.

The breakdown of the talks, however, would not necessarily imply a return to a war-like international milieu, nor would it necessarily mean that either or both sides would pursue irrational, unimpeded arms programs. It is very likely that some form of unilateral constraint would be imposed by economic, political, and social inhibitions, as well as by perceptions of the finiteness of arms utility beyond certain points. It may be argued that a breakdown of arms control talks, and the corollary pressures on the Soviets to "keep up" with the United States, would impose greater hardships on Moscow than on Washington. This assumption is based on the premise, articulated earlier, that a basic objective of the Soviets is to keep the United States engaged in talks and to seek reasonable agreements in order to stabilize their Western flank and free themselves to pursue other policy opportunities elsewhere. A breakdown in such talks would jeopardize these assumed objectives and would force the Soviets to spread their resources and attention quite widely, thus stretching their capabilities rather severely.

A final note is in order on the concept of unilateral constraint and its likely utility. Unilateral constraint in a highly unpredictable situation with a high probability of strategic-technological surprise, is not a very sound basis for defense policy decisions. It could be fairly assumed, therefore, that sooner or later such constraint would give way to doubts and pressures and would result in a search for higher levels of security. Such a search would encompass parts or all of the presently available and possible panoply of weapons systems.

A "thick" ABM or an extensive MIRV deployment, or an improved FOBS, would tend to destabilize the deterrence relationship and would create added tensions in international relations. The possible effects of such deployments on nuclear "threshold" powers could range from a sense of resignation leading to the abandonment of nuclear options to a heightened desirability of exercising such options through independent or regional nuclear forces for safeguarding their national security interests. If such a deployment of new strategic systems created high levels of tension and uncertainties about credible deterrence, it might also lead to unilateral revocation of earlier arms control agreements such as the test ban and non-proliferation treaties.

CONCLUDING REMARKS

The Soviet Union's arms control interests are shaped on the one hand by concerns about its basic and current security needs and, on the other hand, by its short-range and long-range policy objectives. The former motivates Soviet leaders to seek formal stabilization of U.S.-Soviet strategic relations from a position of equality; the latter motivates them to seek a wide range of options which will ensure the flexibility necessary for the pursuit of their broad policy interests, including options for dealing with contingencies in the event the arms control talks fail, and even if they yield agreements.

On balance, it seems reasonable to suggest that relative equality in US and Soviet strategic capabilities is a useful basis for arms control negotiations, and in a broader sense, a reasonable basis for the pursuit of US security interests. As indicated earlier, policies in pursuit of strategic superiority have in the past resulted in expensive and politically detrimental destabilizations of international relations; they have created action-reaction trends which resulted in accelerated arms programs that canceled out the initial advantage; and they have also resulted in overreactions by one or the other protagonist which only propelled the arms race further. Moreover, large and growing strategic weapons systems have limited applicability to problems and issues that involve nonnuclear countries, since the latter are undeterred by such capabilities in pursuing their national objectives, relying instead on the superpowers to maintain a stable deterrence relationship. Consequently, a freeze of strategic offensive and defensive weapons at current or future force level seems useful to US interests. For such an agreement to be realistic and viable, however, it should be coupled with a formal or informal US-Soviet understanding on several issues:

Regulation of R and D Levels and the Testing of New Weapons Systems.—Verification and control of R and D programs is a highly difficult and complex problem that has strong political overtones. It is unlikely that either partner in the talks would desire to curtail such programs sharply, since they provide necessary options and fall-back positions in the event of an abrogation of agreements. Procedures for examining budgetary allocations may offer a minimal control device for the verification of R and D levels. The testing of new weapons systems is, in principle, more verifiable. Some kind of agreement would be necessary to ensure that weapons tests did not involve weapons prohibited by any arms control agreements.

Termination of Currently Ongoing Programs for the Deployment of Offensive and Defensive Weapons Systems.—The Soviet Union is presently involved in active production and deployment programs of weapons systems including SLBMs and ICBMs. Both the Soviet Union and the United States have been testing MIRVs and/or FOBS'. It is important that these programs are taken into account in the early stages of the talks, lest they make such arms control talks academic.

Countermeasures Regarding Third Parties Who May Seriously Threaten an Agreed Upon Strategic Stabilization.—The problem of how to go about assuring a superpower strategic stabilization which may be threatened by an aggressive or irresponsible third nuclear power is complicated by a host of domestic, political, and military problems that would be involved. While such an arrangement is not absolutely necessary for successful arms control talks, it may be useful to consider the matter in connection with the range of other issues relevant to arms control.

Augmentation of Conventional Forces, Either Independently or in Regional-Defense Alliances.—It is assumed here that in the event of a strategic arms freeze the Soviet Union would be motivated to strengthen and upgrade its conventional forces, and would likely employ them more actively for defense and policy purposes. The West must retain wide options for dealing with such likely contingencies as they emerge.

Finally, it would be imprudent of the United States to base its security interests and policies on expectations of Soviet technological and economic backwardness. The Soviet Union has in the past shown an impressive ability to make great strides in catching up with, matching, and at times surpassing Western progress in the development and deployment of strategic forces. It would be equally imprudent to assume that the current Soviet leadership is planning to commit its economic and social systems to vast arming programs with the intent to go to nuclear war. The constraints of the deterrence relationship and some of the current domestic constraints on Soviet leaders seem to argue against such an assumption. Therefore, a strategic arms control agreement which would serve both countries would seem a useful way of also serving their individual needs.

APPENDIX II

DEPARTMENT OF DEFENSE RESPONSES TO QUESTIONS SUBMITTED BY SENATORS CASE AND COOPER

Note: Sections of the following have been deleted at the request of the Department of Defense. Deleted material is indicated by the notation "[Deleted]."
  1. President Nixon said that the SAFEGUARD System has three objectives:
      1. To protect land-based retaliatory forces.
      2. As a thin area defense against a possible ICBM attack from China.
      3. Protection against accidental launch.
  (a). The second and third purposes of President Nixon require a full twelve or fourteen site system to be effective; is that not correct?
  Answer. The full SAFEGUARD deployment calls for twelve sites. This is the number required to provide effective area protection of the entire continental United States against a Chinese ICBM attack or an accidental ICBM attack from any source.
  1. President Nixon said that the SAFEGUARD system has three objectives:
      1. To protect land-based retaliatory forces.
      2. As a thin area defense against a possible ICBM attack from China.
      3. Protection against accidental launch.
  (b). The first purpose could be better done by a dedicated hard point defense. The Department of the Army, I understand, has recent studies that conclude that a dedicated hard point defense using many small radars could provide more effective defense of MINUTEMAN than SAFEGUARD and could be installed within this same time frame.
  Answer. First, our land-based retaliatory forces include strategic bombers as well as ICBMs. Without an effective area defense, these bombers would be vulnerable to a Soviet SLBM attack. A "dedicated hard point defense" is not optimized for bomber defense.
  Development of new hard site defense radar and its associated computer will commence in FY 71 as a hedge against further increase in the Soviet threat to MINUTEMAN which might exceed the threat which the presently proposed SAFEGUARD defense is designed to counter. However, this system would not be operationally available until several years after the Modified Phase 2 of SAFEGUARD can be deployed.
  In other words:
      1. Area defense is needed to defend part of our land-based deterrent, the strategic bombers, against SLBM attack.
      2. Dedicated hard point defense is *not* available in the same time frame as SAFEGUARD defense of MINUTEMAN.
      3. Dedicated hard point defense is intended as an augmentation of SAFEGUARD for high threat levels.
  (c). Could you supply for the Committee a copy of the Panel Report chaired by Dr. Lawrence H. O'Neill, dated January 27, 1970.
  (The information is classified and in the Committee files.)
  2. Is it not true that SS-9's without MIRV in being or in progress do not pose a serious threat to our present MINUTEMAN force and if not MIRVed will not pose a threat until 1980 at present rates of development.
  Answer. As I stated before your subcommittee, on June 4, 1970, "Currently the Soviet force in being poses no threat to MINUTEMAN." With respect to the projected increase in SS-9's, I testified that I was in agreement with the numbers shown by the dashed trend line on the chart displayed by Senator Gore, but only as a "rough estimate." This trend line showed about 700 "attacking warheads certain to destroy a MINUTEMAN silo" in 1980. I then pointed out that the chart did not take into account a MIRV capability (which would at least triple the number of SS-9 enemy warheads), nor the probability of an improved SS-11 capable of effectively attacking MINUTEMAN silos. Both of these are well within Soviet capability and are likely developments by the middle 1970s.

(Committee Note: The chart appears on page 430. It does take into account the possibility of MIRVS on SS-9s and a possible increase in SS-11 accuracy. In commenting on the chart, Senator Gore pointed out that if MIRVs were to be installed on SS-9s, or if SS-11 accuracy were to be upgraded, Safeguard would not be "the answer to protection of Minuteman." Page 431)

3 (a). How many starts of SS-9s have there been since August?

Answer. There have been SS-9 starts since August, 1969. Details cannot be supplied because of classification.

(Committee Note: In response to other questions the Defense Department provided classified information which then had to be deleted from the published hearing record. No classified information was provided, however, in response to this question or to question 3(b).)

(b). How many starts on new complexes of SS-9s have there been since August?

Answer. This question can not be answered because of classification.

(c). How many SS-9 complexes have been completed since August?

Answer. [Deleted.]

4(a). Is it not true that the relatively low frequency of the PAR required to see 2,000 plus miles ahead can be degraded in a nuclear environment?

Answer. The PAR operates at a relatively low frequency [deleted] compared to the MSR [deleted] and it is therefore more susceptible to performance degradation in a nuclear environment than the MSR. The extent of this performance degradation, which depends upon many factors such as number, altitude, location, type, size and timing of the nuclear detonations which generate the increased ionization levels in the upper atmosphere, has been extensively studied in the context of SAFEGUARD system performance. The results of these studies indicate that SAFEGUARD will be able to accomplish its defensive missions.

(b). High altitude nuclear bursts by SPARTAN interceptor, for example, can cause ionospheric disturbances which could degrade the PAR so that it is not reliable; is this correct?

Answer. Uncontrolled high altitude intercepts (nuclear bursts) of the SPARTAN interceptor could, if allowed, degrade PAR performance unnecessarily. [Deleted.] In this way the temporary ionospheric disturbances do not interfere with PAR detection. This example is given as an illustration of the detailed analyses that have been made of how SPARTAN intercepts can be made without seriously degrading PAR performance. These analyses have been used in SAFEGUARD system design. It should also be pointed out that the system utilizes more than one PAR along the Northern Boundary, and attacking ICBMs can generally be seen simultaneously by more than one of these PARs. Any one PAR can adequately track the incoming ICBM to SPARTAN intercept. Thus, more than one PAR must be degraded, or "blacked out", simultaneously to degrade significantly system performance.

(c). Is it not true that the computer problems of the PAR are of such an order that the data provided by the PAR cannot be used by the PAR for interceptor engagement?

Answer. No. The PAR is designed to search a large spatial sector and acquire and track incoming ICBMs together with accompanying objects—tankage, "junk", etc. The PAR data processor has enough capacity to handle adequately the PAR search and tracking data, including tracking for SPARTAN launch.

(d). Is it not, therefore, true that the MSR must handle the assignment of MINUTEMAN defense by itself and if the MSRs are knocked out, the interceptors placed for defense of MINUTEMAN are without guidance and therefore useless?

Answer. Normally the MSR does not handle MINUTEMAN defense by itself although it can operate autonomously. The PAR in the SAFEGUARD defense of MINUTEMAN will serve two purposes. First, it will provide the target information for SPARTAN engagement planning and SPARTAN launch. Second, [Deleted.] The PARs and SPARTANs will make a significant contribution to the defense of MINUTEMAN.

The MSR is capable of operating autonomously if the PARs are lost. If the MSR is lost the remaining interceptors cannot be used. However, this is unlikely because of the SPARTANs and SPRINTs in the MINUTEMAN fields can defend the MSR. In any event, the attacker cannot be confident of destroying the MSR without first exhausting the interceptor stockpiles, and he must target his force accordingly.

(e). The number of interceptors planned for Phase 1 and your projected Phase 2 is so small that the SAFEGUARD defense would hardly be significant in the event of the possible Soviet threat you yourself project. Would you provide the Committee with details of the number of interceptors you plan to deploy?

Answer. The number of interceptors planned for Modified Phase 2 or full Phase 2 is significant in countering the projected Soviet threat to MINUTEMAN.

For SAFEGUARD Phase 1 deployment, [deleted] SPARTANs and [deleted] SPRINTs would be deployed at each of the two sites, Grand Forks, North Dakota and Malmstrom AFB, Montana.

For SAFEGUARD Modified Phase 2 deployment, [deleted] SPARTANs would be deployed at each of the three MINUTEMAN defense sites, Grand Forks, Malmstrom and Whiteman. In addition, the complement of SPRINTs at Grand Forks would be increased to [deleted] and at Malmstrom to [deleted]. At Whiteman the complement of SPRINTs would be [deleted]. The total for Modified Phase 2 would then be [deleted] SPARTANs and [deleted] SPRINTs.

The full Phase 2 defense of MINUTEMAN would add [deleted] more SPARTANs and [deleted] more SPRINTs at Warren. The total interceptor complement for the projected full Phase 2 deployment in defense of MINUTEMAN is [deleted] SPARTANs and [deleted] SPRINTs.

(Committee Note: The chart on page 430 indicates the narrow band of protection that Safeguard would provide and also indicates that if SS-9s are MIRVed Safeguard will not provide adequate protection for the deterrent.)

(*f*). *Are the number of SPRINTs and SPARTANs to be deployed at Malmstrom and Grand Forks the same as last year's planned deployment? Please evaluate the increase over last year's planned deployment and why the number has been increased?*

Answer. There has been no change since last year in our plans for deployment of SPRINTs and SPARTANs at Malmstrom and Grand Forks. The additional [deleted] SPRINT missiles for Grand Forks and [deleted] SPRINTs for the Malmstrom were requested under the Modified Phase 2 deployment to raise the Phase 1 complement to that which was contemplated last year for the Phase 2a deployment.

(Committee Note: This Committee was not informed last year of any plan for additional Sprints and Spartans at Malmstrom and Grand Forks.)

(*g*). *In order to completely defeat SAFEGUARD, is it not true that only a relatively small number of the now existing SS-11's could be used by the Soviets to destroy the few very soft MSR's through exhaustion of defensive interceptors and taking out the radar and thereby render the whole system inoperative?*

Answer. No it is not true that only a relatively small number of now existing SS-11's could be used by the Soviets to destroy the MSR's through exhaustion of defensive interceptors. Under the Phase 2 deployment a total of [deleted] SPRINT and SPARTAN interceptors would be deployed at 4 MINUTEMAN sites. Against an SS-11 attack all these could be used for intercepts in defense of either the MSRs or the MINUTEMAN silos. In addition the SPARTANs at Grand Forks and Malmstrom can be used to preferentially defend either their collocated MSRs or the Whiteman and Warren MSRs. Thus, the Soviet Union would have to allocate SS-11's as though those SPARTANs were used at two sites, raising the apparent and effective interceptor complement to [deleted]. We estimate the reliability of the SS-11 to be [deleted]. Therefore, even if the attacker believes he will achieve a kill probability of 1 against the MSRs with a penetrating SS-11, he will have to allocate [deleted] SS-11s to achieve high confidence kill of the 4 MSRs.

5. It is not true that computer programs for the MSR remain the pacing item for SAFEGUARD?

Answer. The schedule for deploying SAFEGUARD is not controlled by software (computer programs) availability. Earlier during SENTINEL, based on a more accelerated construction and deployment schedule, software development was the controlling factor in achieving the scheduled operating capability for the *first SENTINEL* site. Reorientation of the ABM program from SENTINEL to SAFEGUARD resulted in an extension of time for other than software availability reasons in the deployment schedule. Based on the SAFEGUARD schedule, more time is available for the construction, installation and testing of equipment and software. This stretchout has also reduced the pressure on software development schedule, and consequently, we do not believe the initial site deployment schedule is paced more significantly by software development than by hardware production and construction. As the software is essentially the same for the early SAFEGUARD sites, software development has considerably less influence on the deployment pace after the first site is completed.

(*a*). *The maximum site of attack that SAFEGUARD computer systems can track and engage at one time is limited.*

(*1*) *Would you please indicate what that capacity is?*

(*2*) *How many ICBM missiles with penetration aids can a single MSR handle?*

Answer. [Deleted.]

6(a). *Please detail the on-site experience gained from Malmstrom and Grand Forks that was to be a criteria for going ahead with Phase II.*
(b). *What has been learned at those sites to support an expanded deployment of Phase II?*
(c). *When would actual construction at the sites begin?*

Answer. On March 17, 1969, President Nixon outlined the criteria which would be used in going ahead with phased deployment of SAFEGUARD. On-site experience from Malmstrom and Grand Forks was not among the criteria listed by the President when he stated: "I believe that because of a number of reasons we should have a phase system. That is why, on an annual basis, the new SAFEGUARD System will be reviewed, and the review may bring about changes in the system based on our evaluation of three major points. First, what our intelligence shows us with regard to the magnitude of the threat, whether from the Soviet Union or from the Chinese; and, second, in terms of what our evaluation is of any talks that we are having by that time, or may be having, with regard to arms control; and finally, because we believe that since this is a new system, we should constantly examine what progress has been made in the development of the technique to see if changes in the system should be made."

We have gained from the Phase 1 program during the past year substantial experience in deployment planning and production. The primary system experience to be obtained from Phase 1, however, that cannot be obtained from our R&D test program, is the test of site activation procedures and the test and operation of an internetted multiple radar, multiple site system. This valuable Phase I experience will be available for application to the installation, test and integration of the Modified Phase 2 Whiteman site or other subsequent sites. The equipment readiness dates for the two Phase I sites and the Modified Phase 2 Whiteman site have been deliberately selected to be a minimum of four months apart so that advantage can be taken of the experience gained at the early sites.

Site construction has started at both Phase I sites. At Grand Forks, the construction contractor was given notice to proceed in April 1970 and at Malmstrom the contract was awarded for initial construction activities in May 1970. The construction award for the Whiteman site is tentatively scheduled for March 1971, subject, of course, to Congressional approval of the deployment. Initiation of construction at other sites would be scheduled as determined necessary during the annual review of the phase deployment program established by the President.

7(a). *Please discuss how the various components of the U.S. deterrent force—ICBMs, bombers, submarines—could simultaneously be attacked?*

Answer. The primary threat to our MINUTEMAN is from the Soviet ICBM while the primary threat to our strategic bomber bases is from the Soviet SLBM employing depressed trajectories to minimize time of flight. The attacking ICBMs and SLBMs could be launched simultaneously. The attack then would arrive in two waves: the first, an SLBM wave, could attack both the bomber bases and MINUTEMAN, destroying the bombers before takeoff [deleted.] The second wave, an ICBM attack, would be directed at the MINUTEMAN force. The SLBM requirements for such an attack are well within the projected capabilities of the Soviet Y-Class submarine.

In the case of our POLARIS/POSEIDON submarine force, we have every confidence in its survivability for some time to come, and do not feel that it can be successfully attacked now. We cannot preclude the possibility, however, that the Soviets in the next several years may devise some weapon, technique, or tactic which might increase its vulnerability. If this condition existed, we would then be susceptible to simultaneous attack of all three deterrent forces.

(b). *If our POLARIS force, which by itself can destroy the Soviet Union, is susceptiable to simultaneous attack of all three deterrent forces.*

(b). *If our POLARIS force, which by itself can destroy the Soviet Union, is thought of as a retaliatory force only, why do you believe the much smaller Soviet nuclear submarine fleet is a first-strike threat?*

Answer. The question refers to ". . . our POLARIS force, which by itself can destroy the Soviet Union, . . ." It should be noted that the Soviet ABM deployment, which could be expanded over the next few years, together with the on-going Soviet ABM deployment program introduces uncertainty into the idea that our submarine launched missile force by itself will be able *in the future* to destroy the Soviet Union.

Furthermore, the Soviet nuclear submarine fleet is growing and now consists of 25 boats launched or under construction, whereas we have 41 boats and no program to build more. Of course, if the Soviets continue to build nuclear submarines at the rate they have been building them they could exceed our force level in the 1970s.

The concern over the Soviet threat to our land-based deterrent is not based on their submarine fleet alone, nor is it based solely on their forces already deployed. It is the combination of their growing ICBM force, their growing SLBM force, and their continued testing of new and/or improved ABM components that gives cause for concern. As Secretary of Defense Melvin Laird testified before the Senate Armed Services Committee on May 12, 1970:

"We are concerned about the future because of the momentum in this Soviet buildup. The rapid Soviet buildup in the past five years has reached the point where there is reason to wonder what the Soviet goal is. It also raises a serious question in our minds about the future adequacy of our forces. Advances in Soviet deployments and technology could threaten the survivability of our ICBM's and bombers."

(c). *Do you believe the SAFEGUARD system can provide a "virtually infallible" defense against China?*

Answer. In the period of time up to the 1980's, the SAFEGUARD system in its 12-site configuration (full Phase II) will be able to limit damage from a Chinese attack to a very low level, probably zero. This means that for each Chinese ICBM launched against the U.S., there is a very high probability each will be destroyed by SAFEGUARD, and, since the number of Chinese ICBM's will be small and their reliability questionable, that there is a very high probability that all of the Chinese ICBM's will be destroyed.

8(a). *Can the Chinese at their discretion respond to a fully deployed 12–14 site SAFEGUARD system costing $20–$50 billion by use of penetration aids or (b) bypass SAFEGUARD completely by suitcase bombs or freighter-borne nuclear devices?*

8(a). Answer. First, SAFEGUARD has never been proposed as more than a 12-site system. The department of Defense acquisition cost for this system is not $20–$50 billion but $10.7 billion (in December 1969 purchasing power). If we add the Atomic Energy Commission costs for SAFEGUARD, exclusive of the Modified SPARTAN warhead, which has not yet been selected, the $10.7 billion is increased by $1.2 billion to a total of $11.9 billion. Even taking into account the AEC costs for Modified SPARTAN estimated to be within the range of $0.2 to $0.5 billion, and also taking into account a reasonable estimate of inflation, the projected cost of the 12-site SAFEGUARD system is still well below the $20–$50 billion level.

Second, with regard to the possible Chinese development of penetration aids, Deputy Secretary of Defense Packard stated on April 8, 1970, before the Subcommittees of the Committee on Appropriations, House of Representatives:

"Another possibility is that the Chinese might develop and deploy penetration aids. Relatively simple devices like tank fragments have a limited ability to deceive a sophisticated defense system like SAFEGUARD. Even to achieve that crude capability, the Chinese would have to construct an extensive radar and instrumentation capability simply to be assured that in-flight fragmentation of the tank could be properly carried out. Moreover, without very detailed knowledge of the operating characteristics of SAFEGUARD, it is not possible to design a penetration system in which they can have confidence. More complex penetration aids require much more complex range instrumentation together with the efforts of hundreds of highly skilled technical people. We spent about a decade developing effective penetration aids for our own missiles. It is believed that the Chinese have no such range instrumentation and they may not be able to build it for many years. Thus penetration aids, even the simplest kinds, require technical effort, including testing, which will complicate and delay what might, in the absence of a U.S. ABM defense, be the relatively rapid acquisition of attack capabilities.

"If we look beyond these obstacles to Communist Chinese weapons development toward a later time when they could develop more sophisticated reentry systems for their ICMSs, we would still have ways of maintaining our capability to defend against them. We have a vigorous ABM research and development effort (outside the SAFEGUARD program) which is today working on ways of extending the useful life of SAFEGUARD against a more sophisticated Communist Chinese threat. Those measures would not involve a general thickening of the system in ways which might appear provocative to the Soviet Union."

(b). Answer. The question suggests that ballistic missile defense is ineffective because it cannot meet all possible nuclear threats regardless of the method of delivery. SAFEGUARD can, however, meet the most probable threats, ones that we know other countries are working on. Both the U.S. and Russia, the two most experienced countries in nuclear weapon technology, have chosen to rely on ICBMs and SLBMs as their principal offensive weapons—on the grounds of reliability and because they are amenable to effective command and control.

9. *In order to prevent "leakage", the back-up of the exo-atmospheric interceptor by SPARTAN interceptor missiles would require the implacement of SPRINT batteries*

near cities as a protection against Chinese attack. This deployment would increase the likely Soviet interpretation that a so-called anti-Chinese system was also anti-Soviet. The 2000 plus interceptor system plan of the 12-site SAFEGUARD system is a massive response to the 64 interceptors contained in the Moscow system; is it not?

Answer. There are misconceptions and errors in the above question.

1. It is *not* necessary for the foreseeable future in defending against the Chinese to put SPRINT batteries near cities and there is no plan to do so. One of the major changes in going from the SENTINEL to the SAFEGUARD system was to move the batteries *away* from the cities. This was based on careful calculations that we could defend effectively against the Chinese threat until at least the 1980's—and do so from these battery locations. Locations near cities are only required if we are trying to defend the cities against a massive attack such as the Soviets might launch.

2. The Soviets are very familiar with ABM deployment considerations and can easily see that our deployment, insofar as the defense of cities is concerned, is not aimed at them, but rather against the Chinese.

3. The 12-site SAFEGUARD system does not have 2000 interceptors, [deleted] to be exact.

4. SAFEGUARD is not a response to the Soviet ABM and the number of SAFEGUARD interceptors bears no relation to the number of Soviet interceptors. It is set by considerations of the Soviet *offensive* threat against our strategic offensive forces and the Chinese threat against our population.

10(a). The Chinese satellite launch last month used an IRBM launcher; is that not correct?

Answer. The launch vehicle used for launching Communist China's first space satellite cannot be stated with confidence. It probably was an IRBM class; however, it is possible it was an ICBM class.

(b). How long have you been predicting that the Chinese would launch an ICBM?

Answer. The intelligence community's initial estimate of the Chinese capability to launch an ICBM was made in 1967. This judgment was based on knowledge of the construction of a large ballistic missile launch facility.

11. Please comment upon the testimony given before this Committee by Mrs. Alice Hsieh and Doak Barnett?

(a). Would you comment on the assertion made by them that the anti-Chinese orientation of the SAFEGUARD system would adversely affect U.S. interests in the Pacific?

Answer. I find that the testimony of Mrs. Alice Hsieh and Doak Barnett deals with political rather than technical issues. Since I have no special knowledge concerning foreign political issues I feel that I am not qualified to comment.

12. If the SAFEGUARD System is necessary for our defense against China, how can we bargain it away in the SALT talks?

Answer. The relative value of an ABM defense against Communist China and arms limitation agreement with the Soviets has to be weighed and the most advantageous course of action chosen. No more can be said without discussion of the details of SALT, which would be detrimental to the success of those important negotiations.

13(a). Is it not true, as many scientists have asserted, that the "fireball" effects on the PAR are so great that the use of the PAR for SPARTAN interceptors could be considered unreliable?

Answer. The system has more than one PAR along the Northern Boundary, and attacking ICBMs can generally be seen simultaneously by more than one of these PARs. Since any one PAR can adequately track the incoming ICBM and the PARs are interconnected, one PAR can look around a fireball that temporarily obstructs an adjacent PAR. Thus, more than one PAR must be degraded, or "blacked out", simultaneously to degrade significantly system performance. It should be remembered that the fireball is a "bubble" of very hot gas and, consequently, it rises rapidly in the atmosphere. This rapid rise quickly carries the fireball up to altitudes where it does not interfere with PAR detection and tracking of distant targets at low elevation angles.

(b). Can you be certain that the PAR will have any reliable function beyond a supplement to our existing early warning system because of the serious technical problems caused by the "fireball" effect?

Answer. We are confident that the PAR will perform reliably its intended functions. Our detailed studies, analyses and computer runs on anticipated engagements with expected nuclear effects modeled as accurately as available knowledge allows show that the SAFEGUARD defense capability is limited by interceptor stockpile exhaustion rather than by "fireball" effects on the PAR. Even against an attack where the enemy sets off deliberate precursor bursts designed to blind the PARs while other attackers penetrate, the PAR/SPARTAN system charges a high price to the attacker before it can be overcome. This price follows because the attacker must simultaneously (within tens of seconds) and reliably blackout more than one PAR in order to keep any one PAR from looking behind the fireball set off to blind another PAR.

14. *It has been asserted that Soviet "henhouse" radars might be part of a future Soviet ABM system.*

(a). *Is it not true that the Soviet "henhouse" is even more vulnerable to attack than the PAR, being of lower frequency, more susceptible to exo-atmospheric distortion, and even softer than the PAR?*

Answer. The Soviet "henhouse" is, because of its lower frequency, more susceptible to degradation caused by nuclear bursts than the PAR. [Deleted.]

(b). *Are the "hen house" radars presently defended by an ABM?*

Answer. [Deleted.] The Soviets have deployed their ABM–1 (Moscow) System only at Moscow. The four complexes of this system have reached their initial operational capability and have a total of 64 launchers.

[Deleted.]

(c). *Is it not true that these "henhouse" radars have been targeted out of existence by U.S. offensive forces?*

Answer. This question can not be answered because of classification.

15(a). *What are the costs now of the SAFEGUARD ABM System as compared to last year's estimates?*

Answer. The DOD program acquisition cost growth of the 2-site deployment was provided to the Congress in May 1970. At that time, Congress was informed that the total acquisition cost of the Phase 1 deployment had increased $409 million or about 9¾ percent, from $4.185 billion (the Phase 1 cost estimate furnished Congress last year) to $4.594 billion. Of this total, $136 million was due to price level inflation which occurred between December 1968 and December 1969; $137 million was due to stretchout of the time until deployment can be completed (requiring longer retention of the production base); and $136 million was due to design changes and refinement of cost estimates.

Should the full 12-site deployment be authorized, the total DOD acquisition cost would be about $10.7 billion (at December 1969 price levels) as compared with the $9.1 billion (at December 1968 price levels) estimate reported to Congress last year. The increase of $1.6 billion is due to several causes: the inflation in price levels that occurred between December 1968 and December 1969, a stretchout in the time until deployment can be completed, certain design changes found necessary during the year, and more detailed estimates for the work earlier contemplated. Of the total increase, $395 million or 4 percent is due to inflation, $575 million or 6 percent is due to the longer period of deployment, and $650 million or 7 percent is due to design changes and to more detailed estimates.

(b). *What are the total costs of ABM since 1958?*

Answer. In the period beginning with fiscal year 1958 and extending through fiscal year 1970, there has been about $5.7 billion approved for Army development and deployment of ballistic missile defense systems.

(c). *What would be the full system cost of the SAFEGUARD System if all 12 sites were deployed? Please include:*
  1) *full R&D and ten-year operation costs,*
  2) *warhead R&D and*
  3) *production cost and*
  4) *full O&M cost.*

Answer. For the full Phase 2 deployment of 12 sites, the DOD acquisition cost would be $10.7 billion (December 1969 price levels). This includes $2.9 billion RDT&E, $5.9 billion PEMA, and $1.9 billion MCA funds.

Based on information furnished by the Atomic Energy Commission, the estimated AEC costs of SAFEGUARD missile warheads for the full Phase 2 (12-site) deployment is slightly less than $1.2 billion. These costs are for SPRINT and standard SPARTAN warheads. The cost for substituting modified SPARTAN's for an equal number of standard SPARTAN's has not been included since the warhead design has not been selected, however the AEC has furnished an estimate of a total cost ranging from $200 million to $500 million for Modified SPARTAN nuclear warheads.

The above stated estimates are exclusive of operating costs which, currently, are running about $34 million per year and which, for the period after the completion of deployment, are estimated to be about $350 million annually if the full Phase 2 were authorized and deployed.

16(a). *Is it not true that to deploy ineffective weapons systems such as SAFE-GUARD will detract from technological development because changes in systems becomes more difficult once military crews are trained and hardware goes into a production line basis?*

Answer. SAFEGUARD is not an "ineffective" weapon system. In fact, the very extensive research and development and test program on SAFEGUARD components has already given high assurance that the system will work.

Problems relating to component design have largely been solved. The state-of-the-art is such that all technical areas have been developed to the point where the remaining effort is largely a matter of production engineering. The matter of technological obsolescence has been carefully explored, and the radar-guided missile intercept concept, which the SAFEGUARD System employs, is the latest and best technology presently available in the field of ballistic missile defense. No other technology promises any better system in the near future.

Development of trained military crews and establishment of production lines does not preclude required system modifications and SAFEGUARD improvements can be made as needed.

(b). *Since nothing has been learned at the Grand Forks and Malmstrom sites, why not continue R &D at Kwajalein and other test sites and laboratories until an effective system is developed?*

Answer. The assertion that ". . . . nothing has been learned at the Grand Forks and Malmstrom sites . . . ." is incorrect. On 10 April 1970 Deputy Secretary of Defense David Packard furnished the following testimony before the House Appropriations Committee. "We have gained from the Phase I program during the past year substantial experience in deployment planning and production. The primary system experience to be obtained from Phase I, that cannot be obtained from our R&D test program, is the test of site activation procedures and the test and operation of an internetted multiple radar, multiple site system. This valuable experience from Phase I will be available for application to the installation, test, and integration of the Modified Phase 2 Whiteman site. The equipment readiness dates for the two Phase I sites and the Modified Phase 2 Whiteman site have been deliberately selected to be a minimum of 4 months apart so that advantage can be taken of the experience gained at the early sites."

During the same hearing, I furnished the following information in response to a question regarding possible reduction of uncertainties and saving of money by delaying the Phase 2 deployment for a year or more: "In a strictly technical sense delay of Phase 2 deployment at this point in the program would not serve to reduce so-called program uncertainties and would certainly result in a considerable cost increase and, more importantly, would not be responsive to the growing threat."

I also testified that, "Postponement for a year of a decision to authorize more than Phase I would increase both the cost and risk to the United States. For example, if no additional deployment were authorized in fiscal year 1971, but the full 12-site Phase 2 deployment were authorized in fiscal year 1972, the total DOD acquisition cost of $10.7 billion would increase by about $0.3 billion and completion of the full deployment would be delayed by at least 6 months and probably for a much longer period. Although continuation during the next year of only the SAFEGUARD research and development program and the two Phase 1 sites would continue the development, production and construction programs now underway, if the decision to commence Modified Phase 2 is delayed by a year, "gaps" would appear in these programs as Phase 1 work is completed. As these gaps occur, we would be forced to reduce production and engineering capability, especially highly skilled manpower, to avoid waste. With a later, possibly fiscal year 1972, authorization to complete additional site deployment we would have to rehire and retrain personnel in order to rebuild production and engineering capacity. It is not possible to estimate, therefore, how much more than 6 months' delay would occur. Such a delay would add to the risk to the United States, since we would be unable to protect ourselves against the threats expected to exist before the deployment would be completed."

17. *Assuming that the Soviets design an attack to reduce our Minuteman force to 300 surviving launchers, and assuming the Soviets use penetration aids which successfully negate Spartan, how many Minutemen beyond 300 would survive if Safeguard Phase 2A, as now proposed by the Administration, operated as designed?*

(The information referred to had not been received as of the date of publication.)

1. *Questions about SAFEGUARD in its area defense mode (that is, with SPARTAN missiles and Perimeter Acquisition Radar—PAR).*

(a). *How many incoming objects per unit of time can be detected and discriminated and tracked by PAR? Against how many objects can PAR fulfill these functions and also fire and guide SPARTAN missiles to the selected targets?*
Answer. [Deleted.]

(b). *With what probability of success can the PAR track and discriminate among these objects to identify actual warheads?*
Answer. [Deleted.] The probability of successful discrimination is very high for crude penetration aids such as the Chinese might be expected to use initially.

(c). *To what extent is the ability to track objects and to make this discrimination determined by the construction/design of the radar itself or by the hardware or the software of the computer.*
Answer. The ability of the PAR to track a large number of objects is a function of the design and construction of both the radar itself and the computer. The number of objects on which the radar can make measurements is limited by its average power because only a fraction of the average power can be directed at each object and there is a certain minimum power per object needed to track at adequate distances from the radar. The capacity of the computer speed and memory also can limit the number of tracks which the computer can file and update.

The PAR radar-processor combination has been designed and will be constructed so that the radar and computer are balanced. In other words, the computer is designed to keep up with the maximum tracking capacity of the radar itself.

(d). *How many PAR's and SPARTAN missiles are associated with each of the contemplated SAFEGUARD sites in the area defense mode?*
Answer. It should be noted (see next question) that some of the PAR's and SPARTAN missiles contribute to the defense of MINUTEMAN in addition to forming a light area defense. Numbers of PARs and SPARTANs by site are:

Site	Par	Spartan/modified Spartan
Grand Forks AFB, N. Dak.	1	
Malmstrom AFB, Mont.	1	
Whiteman AFB, Mo.	0	
Northeast	1	
National Capital area	0	
Northwest	1	
Michigan/Ohio	1	[Deleted]
Warren AFB, Wyo.	0	
Texas	0	
Southern California	1	
Central California	0	
Florida/Georgia	1	

The PAR, being a long range radar acquires targets and predicts the targets' impact. These data are then transmitted to the appropriate MSR site. Consequently, any one site may receive data from more than one PAR or one PAR can supply data to several different MSR's.

(e) *What roles are the PAR and the SPARTAN missiles designed to play in the defense of our MINUTEMAN sites? Will the PAR and SPARTAN contribute significantly to MINUTEMAN defense?*
Answer. The PAR in the SAFEGUARD defense of MINUTEMAN will serve two purposes. First, it will provide the target information for SPARTAN engagement planning and SPARTAN launch. Second, [Deleted.] The PARs and SPARTANs will make a significant contribution to the defense of MINUTEMAN.

(f). *How many interceptors (either SPARTAN or SPRINT or both) are presently planned to be deployed (a) at each of the 12 SAFEGUARD sites, (b) at the two Phase 1 sites?*
Answer. Type and Number of Missiles at SAFEGUARD Sites:

Site	Spartan	Sprint
Grand Forks AFB, N. Dak.[1]	⎫	
Malmstrom AFB, Mont.[1]	⎪	
Whiteman AFB, Mo.	⎪	
Northeast	⎪	
National Capital area	⎪	
Northwest	⎬ [Deleted.]	[Deleted.]
Michigan/Ohio	⎪	
Warren AFB, Wyo.	⎪	
Texas	⎪	
Southern California	⎪	
Central California	⎪	
Florida/Georgia	⎭	

[1] Phase 1 sites (parenthetical numbers are phase 1 totals).

(g). Given your answers to the above questions, how many PAR's and SPARTAN missiles would be needed to give 80% protection to an American city if the Chinese fired 20 missiles at that city with (a) single warheads, and (b) with simple penetration aids?

Answer. If the Chinese Communists attempt to launch 20 ICBMs at a major U.S. city the number requiring engagement by the SAFEGUARD defense might be an expected maximum of 10 to 12 RVs. This difference in number of ICBMs on-launcher and the number of RVs arriving is due to the ICBM reliability. Given this size of attack, a high probability of preventing a penetration of the defense can be achieved. For example, if two SPARTANs are allocated to each of the 12 RVs for a total of 24 SPARTANs, this will provide an expected probability of no penetration of about 0.97. Essentially the same capabilities can be maintained against this level of attack if the attacker fragments the tanks of his ICBMs.

The full twelve site SAFEGUARD Phase 2 defense includes a net of five PARs across the northern part of the Continental U.S. These PARs provide overlapping coverage of ICBM approaches and have sufficient capability to accommodate the Chinese Communist threat of non-penaided or tank fragmentation threats.

Against the more distant future possibility of more sophisticated Chinese Communist penetration aids the DOD has an aggressive research and development program to design counters to preserve defense capability without significantly increasing the number of interceptors.

(h). Do you consider that the SPARTANs and the PAR can provide a "virtually infallible defense" against China "perhaps 10 years from now" (quotes from President Nixon's press conference of January 31, 1970).

Answer. In the period of time up to the 1980's, the SAFEGUARD system in its 12-site configuration (full Phase II) will be able to limit damage from a Chinese attack to a very low level, probably zero. This means that for each Chinese ICBM launched against the U.S., there is a very high probability each will be destroyed by SAFEGUARD, and, since the number of Chinese ICBM's will be small and their reliability questionable, that there is a very high probability that all of the Chinese ICBMs will be destroyed.

(i). Considering the fact that the Chinese have launched a satellite successfully, do you consider it technically unlikely that the Chinese could develop decoys and penetration aids adequate to penetrate the area defense of SAFEGUARD in one decade?

Answer. We see no direct relationship between likelihood of development of decoys and the Chinese satellite launch. With regard to Chinese capability to confuse SAFEGUARD by using penetration aids, Deputy Secretary of Defense Packard stated on April 8, 1970, before the Subcommittees of the Committee on Appropriations, House of Representatives;

"Another possibility is that the Chinese might develop and deploy penetration aids. Relatively simple devices like tank fragments have a limited ability to deceive a sophisticated defense system like SAFEGUARD. Even to achieve that crude capability, the Chinese would have to construct an extensive radar and instrumentation capability simply to be assured that in-flight fragmentation of the tank could be properly carried out. Moreover, without very detailed knowledge of the operating characteristics of SAFEGUARD, it is not possible to design a penetration system in which they can have confidence. More complex penetration aids require much more complex range instrumentation together with the efforts of hundreds of highly skilled technical people. We spent about a decade developing effective penetration aids for our own missiles. It is believed that the Chinese have not such range instrumentation and they may not be able to build it for many years. Thus penetration aids, even the simplest kinds, require technical effort, including testing, which will complicate and delay what might, in the absence of a U.S. ABM defense, be the relatively rapid acquisition of attack capabilities.

"If we look beyond these obstacles to Communist Chinese weapons development toward a later time when they could develop more sophisticated reentry systems for their ICBM's, we would still have ways of maintaining our capability to defend against them. We have a vigorous ABM research and development effort (outside the SAFEGUARD program) which is today working on ways of extending the useful life of SAFEGUARD against a more sophisticated Communist Chinese threat. Those measures would not involve a general thickening of the system in ways which might appear provocative to the Soviet Union."

(j). *Could the PAR track and discriminate the total number of incoming threatening objects from, say, ten incoming Chinese ICBM's if the Chinese choose to detonate the propulsion tank? (As we have done in our ATLAS program).*

Answer. Yes. This particular penetration-aid tactic has been considered in some detail and [deleted].

2(a). *Are PAR's and SPARTANs as well as Missile Site Radars (MSR's) and SPRINT missiles to be deployed in the SAFEGUARD defense of MINUTEMAN? What roles will each of these four components play in defense of MINUTEMAN?*

Answer. PARs and SPARTANs as well as Missile Site Radars and SPRINT missiles are included at each of the four SAFEGUARD sites located in the MINUTEMAN Wings.

The PAR in the SAFEGUARD defense of MINUTEMAN will serve two purposes. First, it will provide the target information for SPARTAN engagement planning and SPARTAN launch. Second, [deleted.] The PARs and SPARTANs will make a significant contribution to the defense of MINUTEMAN.

The Missile Site Radar has the primary functions of terminal tracking of attacking missiles and launching and guiding both SPARTANs and SPRINTs to intercept. The SPRINTs provide a heavy terminal defense of the MINUTEMAN silos in the vicinity of the Missile Site Radar and the same SPRINTs are also capable of defending the PARs and Missile Site Radars.

(b). *To what extent has the PAR been found subject to degrading of its performance by nuclear bursts?*

Answer. The effects of nuclear bursts on the PAR have been extensively analyzed over the past several years. As a result of these analyses, it has been determined that nuclear bursts can cause reduction of the PAR detection and tracking sensitivity and degradation of the accuracy of the positional data measured by the PAR. In a worst case situation a single nuclear burst could degrade the performance of a PAR to the extent that for a period [deleted] and over a limited volume in the direction of the burst it would be unable to detect or track. However, the system has more than one PAR along the northern boundary and attacking ICBMs can generally be seen simultaneously by more than one PAR. The PARs are interconnected, and one PAR can look behind a nuclear burst that temporarily obstructs an adjacent PAR. Thus more than one PAR must be degraded or "blacked out" simultaneously to degrade the system.

The extent to which a particular deployed PAR will be subject to these types of performance degradation is dependent upon the number, type and size of the nuclear weapons that are detonated, the altitude and time of the bursts, and the location of the bursts with respect to the PAR and the incoming warheads. Numerous studies have been conducted which have evaluated the SAFEGUARD system performance in nuclear burst environments resulting from a multitude of offensive and defensive options which have included various levels of precursor attacks. The overall results of these studies are: (1) the impact of nuclear detonations due to our own warheads can be made small by correct system design and (2) the cost to the offense in terms of number of missiles required to defeat the defense by offense precursor bursts turns out to be so large as to make the tactic extremely unattractive.

(c). *How many incoming objects (warheads or decoys) per unit of time can each MSR detect and discriminate and track?*

Answer. [Deleted.]

(d). *Against how many incoming objects per unit of time can the MSR fulfill the functions listed in the previous question and also fire and guide SPRINT missiles, that is if the attack were of a kind that might endanger our MINUTEMAN force?*

Answer. [Deleted.]

(e). *To what extent is the ability to fulfill the functions listed in the two previous questions determined by the construction/design of the MSR itself or by the hardware of software of the computer? Explain. By what year will computer programs be ready to perform against an attack of the kind that might endanger our MINUTEMAN force?*

Answer. The MSR and its computers form a balanced design to perform the tasks described in the previous answer. In other words, the computer size is generally determined by how much data will be supplied to it by the radar itself. Similarly, the software structure is determined to a significant extent by the type and quality of information that can be supplied by the radar and, vice versa, the software is structured to manage the radar resources and the most efficient way for the task at hand. The MSR antenna aperture and the peak transmitter power radiated determine how small an RV can be detected at how long a range. The average power of the radar determines the number of pulses transmitted per second and this value together with the required listening time determines the number of object tracks which can be computed per second and the size of the computer memory unit determines the number of tracked objects that can be stored and correlated with up-dated track information as the engagement progresses.

The programs are scheduled to be checked out, thoroughly tested, and ready for operational use by October, 1974, the Equipment Readiness Date (ERD) of the first MSR site at Grand Forks. The computer programs for subsequent sites in the MINUTEMAN fields would be almost identical with the Grand Forks program, so readiness dates for these sites are determined by building construction and hardware installation schedules, not software.

(f). *If there were two MSR's per MINUTEMAN defense complex, would this increase the number of objects that could be detected, tracked, and attack by SPRINT?*

Answer. Yes, two MSR's per MINUTEMAN defense complex would increase the number of objects that could be detected, tracked and intercepted by SPRINTs, but at increased cost.

(g). *In the design specifications for SAFEGUARD radars, what radar cross-section of incoming targets was assumed? Would improvement in reentry vehicle design, and possible reduction of radar cross-section, necessitate changes in radar design and/or computer programming in order to detect, discriminate, and track such reentry vehicles? How difficult and costly would these changes be? Are such design improvements likely to be made by the Soviets or the Chinese?*

Answer. [Deleted.]

(h). *How many Soviet warheads, each having 100% kill probability against MINUTEMAN, are required to attack MINUTEMAN such that only 300 MINUTEMAN would survive for retaliation? Please provide the answer if (a) MINUTEMAN were undefended; (b) MINUTEMAN were defended by SAFEGUARD Phase 1; (c) MINUTEMAN were defended by SAFEGUARD Phase 2a now before Congress.*

Answer. If the Soviet objective, as assumed in the question, is to destroy only 700 MINUTEMAN leaving 300 survivors and the Soviet threat level is constrained accordingly, [deleted]. The objective of the SAFEGUARD defense of MINUTEMAN is to provide [deleted] MINUTEMAN survivors against a Soviet threat which could, if undefended, reduce the MINUTEMAN survivors below the objective level. An example of such an attack is given in the table below and the following defense cases are included: no defense, the two site limited interceptor inventory SAFEGUARD Phase 1 deployment, the three site Modified Phase 2 deployment and the four site SAFEGUARD defense of MINUTEMAN.

The results in the table are based on Soviet ICBM forces with 5.0 MT warheads, an assumed reprogrammable force reliability of 0.81 with a post-boost and warhead reliability of 0.95, and a kill probability of [deleted] on a MINUTEMAN silo provided by a [deleted] accuracy. The attacker is assumed to exhaust interceptor stockpiles by firing at the radars.

MINUTEMAN survivors for [deleted] RVs on launcher

Undefended MINUTEMAN	[Deleted]
Phase 1 SAFEGUARD	[Deleted]
Modified Phase 2 SAFEGUARD	[Deleted]
Four Site SAFEGUARD	[Deleted]

(i). *If some of the present air defense systems now deployed in the U.S. or abroad were adapted for MINUTEMAN defense, would they have any capability against the present SS-9 threat?*

Answer. As has been pointed out before, the *present* SS-9 threat does not require defense of MINUTEMAN because there is no deployed MIRV or MRV and there are not at present enough SS-9s with single warheads to cause unacceptable damage to MINUTEMAN. However, as a result of concern over future threats to MINUTEMAN [Deleted.]

(*j*). *What is the kill probability of an incoming SS-11 missile in its present configuration against MINUTEMAN silos? What is the kill probability of an incoming SS-11 missile against the MSR? How many SS-11's do the Soviets have? If the Soviets were willing to dedicate the SS-11 towards destroying the MSR and thereby "blind SAFEGUARD", could they do so?*

Answer. In my 26 February 1970 statement before the Joint Committee on Armed Services and Defense Subcommittee on the Appropriation Committee, U.S. Senate, I discussed the size of the Soviet SS-11 force as follows: "As of February 1970, the Soviets are believed to have over 275 SS-9's under construction or operational, and over 800 SS-11's."

Assuming that the Soviets were willing to retarget the SS-11 force, the Soviets could, after exhausting the SAFEGUARD interceptors, destroy the SAFEGUARD MSRs now planned for defense of MINUTEMAN. Similarly if the Soviets improved the SS-11 guidance system they could retarget it to destroy MINUTEMAN silos. In either case, the Soviet SS-11 targets other than MINUTEMAN (or MINUTEMAN defenses) would either receive a lighter attack or no attack at all.

(*k*). *If it were decided to expand the SAFEGUARD defense of each MINUTEMAN squadron by doubling the number of MSR's and SPRINTs would the increased cost be larger or smaller than the additional number of MINUTEMEN which could be saved under Soviet attack?*

Answer. It is difficult to give a general answer independent of the threat and the exact deployment of the defense. However, an additional SPRINT interceptor and its prorated share of an MSR costs less than a MINUTEMAN and if a new dedicated hardsite radar were used instead of the MSR the cost of the defense would be even less.

It should be noted that the DOD has no plans to provide a defense of each MINUTEMAN squadron with MSR and SPRINT and therefore has not investigated the cost to implement such an action. The total number of planned MSRs for the defense of MINUTEMAN is the four multiple-objective SAFEGUARD defense sites of the Full Phase 2 deployment. DOD plans to initiate development in FY 71 of a new hard site defense radar and data processor to augment the SAFEGUARD MINUTEMAN defense in the event the Soviet threat to MINUTEMAN should in the future require additional defense of MINUTEMAN.

(*l*). *In defending MINUTEMAN does the computer use the information from the PAR radar to assist it in giving the guidance command to the SPRINT about the flight path of the enemy warhead?*

Answer. [Deleted.]

(*m*). *A newspaper article has alleged that the emissions from SAFEGUARD radars are so powerful that they could interfere with the effective firing of our own MINUTEMAN deterrent force. Would you please comment on this?*

Answer. The possible effects of SAFEGUARD radars on the entire MINUTEMAN system, including the missiles, has been a subject of investigation by the Army, Air Force, and the Electromagnetic Compatibility Analysis Center (ECAC) over the past two years, and close working relationships at the technical level have been established for that purpose. These investigations have identified no potential interference problems that cannot be solved by operational procedures or, at most, inexpensive fixes.

(*n*). *Assuming other than an accidental launch or very small attack, in which the President might be expected to withhold immediate firing of SAFEGUARD, what amount of time for decision would be available to the President between initial detection of RV's and the latest point (a) at which SPARTANs could be launched and (b) at which SPRINTs could be fired with a reasonable expectation of success?*

Answer. Approximately [deleted] minutes time should be available at the National level to decide upon and authorize employment of the SAFEGUARD system against a ballistic missile attack originating from the Soviet Union or the CPR. The SAFEGUARD System is specifically engineered to assure near instantaneous exchange of data with National Command Authorities. The reaction time available to the President prior to firing a SPRINT is a few minutes longer because of the shorter time of flight for the SPRINT.

3. *The Department of Defense has said that the SAFEGUARD System was to be implemented in phases according to the threat facing the U.S. Yet DOD has also said*

that it was a necessity to have a full 12-site system to meet the Chinese threat. This seems to throw into doubt the original claim that SAFEGUARD could be built in phases and that construction would proceed only according to need. Would you comment on this apparent contradiction?

Answer. We adhere to our statement that SAFEGUARD is a phased program by requesting Congressional approval, not for the full 12-site system, but for two SAFEGUARD sites last year and one site this year (plus advanced preparation at five additional sites). All of these sites are part of the full 12-site system and allow us to build toward it as the threat develops. As Deputy Secretary of Defense Packard, on April 8, 1970, in testimony before the Subcommittees of the Committee on Appropriations, House of Representatives, in referring to the present request to Congress for SAFEGUARD, stated: "The proposed program maintains the President's options to move further toward a 12-site Full Phase 2 SAFEGUARD system, if necessary, or to curtail the deployment if threat developments permit. This deployment continues orderly, controlled, progress toward the objectives set forth by President Nixon and yet does not commit us to Full Phase 2 deployment without further review and further decisions. The deployment can be modified as required by changes in the threat, arms limitation negotiations, or unilateral actions of the Soviets or Chinese Communists."

There is no "contradiction" in the statement that SAFEGUARD is a phased program.

4. Secretary Laird testified on May 8, 1970, that the U.S. MIRV is needed solely as a penetration device: "It is a question of penetration that is involved, rather than anything else." As the USSR has only a crude ABM system deployed, and only around Moscow, what is the necessity of deploying the U.S. MIRV now?

Answer. We do not consider the Soviet ABM to be a "crude" system. Its effectiveness is limited not by technical deficiencies but by the fact that they have chosen to deploy, up to now, very few interceptors. This deficiency, however, could be overcome by the Soviets in a comparatively short time—much less than that required to install all the necessary radars.

Also, although the Soviet ABM is now deployed "only around Moscow", the geographical location is such that, when coupled with the long range capability of the Galosh missile, a very substantial portion of western Russia is covered—comparable to the U.S. eastern "heartland."

Finally, a very real potential exists for using the numerous Soviet SAM systems, the SA-2 and the SA-5, as ABMs in the same ABM network of radar which the Galosh utilizes.

It is for these reasons that it is necessary to deploy our MIRVs to insure continued U.S. capability of penetration.

5. Please tell me, also, on what grounds Secretary Laird based his recent remarks that he can "predict" reaching an arms agreement at SALT if we deploy MIRV—and possible SAFEGUARD? (a) Have the Soviets told us to go ahead and deploy MIRV? (b) Do they want us to do this? (c) Do you claim success at SALT as the only reason we have to deploy MIRV?

Answer. Secretary Laird, on May 12 before the Senate Committee on Armed Services, stated the following in a series of questions and answers with Senator Henry Jackson:

"Senator JACKSON. Thank you, Mr. Secretary, for a very fine statement.

"Mr. Secretary, in his press conference Friday night, President Nixon commented on the SALT talks. He said, and I quote: 'I will predict that there will be an agreement * * * of great significance.'

"Could you comment further on this remark of the President? I have received a number of inquiries about it.

"Secretary LAIRD. I certainly agree with the President's prediction. I think that his prediction can be met, provided we carry out the program that has been set forth by the President of the United States not only as far as the ABM is concerned, but also as far as MIRV deployment is concerned.

"I believe it is most important that we continue these programs as we negotiate with the Soviet Union. And I predict that we will have success if we are able to maintain our posture and if we receive the necessary support from the Congress of the United States.

"Senator JACKSON. You feel very strongly, then, that the maintenance of our strategic posture is essential to attaining the goal expressed by the President?

"Secretary LAIRD. I feel very strongly, Mr. Chairman, that we must maintain our position, and that for us to take unilateral action at this time by stopping our previously planned deployment, would, I think, jeopardize any kind of an agreement."

The President, the Secretary of State, the Secretary of Defense and Members of the Congress have stated that this nation's negotiating positions should not be matters of public debate. In that context, I don't feel I can comment further and I believe Secretary Laird's statement speaks for itself.

6. *Secretary Laird has said that the United States must deploy SAFEGUARD and MIRVs or go to new offensive systems.*

(a). *What new systems are being considered and by what year might they be deployed? and MIRVs or go to new offensive systems. What new systems are being considered and by what year might they be deployed?*

Answer. ULMS (Underwater Long Range Missile System), now starting in development, is the new sea based strategic missile system being considered. At present it is estimated that the earliest deployment would be [deleted].

The new land based strategic missile systems being considered are primarily the hardened shelter systems (random location of the missile in a group of shelters), increased hardness silos with and without hard point defense, and hard point defense of present MINUTEMAN silos. These systems could be deployed [deleted].

(b). *What is the increase in the threat since May 1969 that causes you to say this?*
Answer. [Deleted.]

7. *Given the following statements concerning the wisdom of building Phase I of SAFEGUARD before proceeding to further construction—*

A. *President Nixon has said, "We will take maximum advantage of the information gathered from the initial deployment in designing later phases of the program;"*

B. *Secretary Packard has said, according to the Washington Post, that the SAFEGUARD sites at Malmstrom and Grand Forks will be built first to test ABM technology;*

C. *Dr. Gordon MacDonald, who as you know was vice president of the Institute of Defense Analyses and a member of the Defense Science Board, said last year before this subcommittee that we should "insist" "that the experience gained in the first two (sites) be fed back into the program" and that we should review the R&D before going to further deployment;*

D. *Secretary Laird's testimony last year, that it is only wise, no matter how often the sub-assemblies and components have been individually tested, that they be assembled in as close to operational conditions as possible for systems tests:—*

On what grounds does DOD intend to move to Phase II and the construction of a third site at Whiteman without any of the knowledge that would result from the completion of Phase I?

Answer. As Secretary Packard testified before the House Appropriations Committee on 8 April 1970: "We have gained from the Phase I program during the past year substantial experience in deployment planning and production. The primary system experience to be obtained from Phase I, that cannot be obtained from our R&D test program, is the test of site activation procedures and the test and operation of an internetted multiple radar, multiple site system. This valuable experience from Phase I will be available for application to the installation, test, and integration of the Modified Phase 2 Whiteman site. The equipment readiness dates for the two Phase I sites and the Modified Phase 2 Whiteman site have been deliberately selected to be a minimum of 4 months apart so that advantage can be taken of the experience gained at the early sites."

During the same hearing, I furnished the following information in response to a question regarding possible reduction of uncertainties and saving of money by delaying the Phase 2 deployment for a year or more: "In a strictly technical sense, delay of Phase 2 deployment at this point in the program would not serve to reduce so-called program uncertainties and would certainly result in a considerable cost increase and, more importantly, would not be responsive to the growing threat.

"In the development of a large weapons system such as SAFEGUARD, the answer to the question of whether or not the system development has progressed to the point where deployment can be justified must necessarily be based upon the research and development testing progress of the major system components. The major SAFEGUARD system components, Perimeter Acquisition Radar (PAR), Missile Site Radar (MSR), SPRINT missile and SPARTAN missile have all undergone extensive research and development (R&D) testing which has already progressed to the point where the design of all critical items, that is, ones with large cost impact or long leadtime, has been validated. The development testing of each major subsystem—that is, the MSR at Meck Island, the SPRINT at White Sands Missile Range, and the SPARTAN at Kwajalein—has progressed very satisfactorily to the point where it is essentially complete. There is a high level of confidence that there are no major problems, and the next step, system integration testing of these components at Meck Island, is underway. High confidence in the development progress of the other major system component, the PAR, has been achieved from the very successful performance history of a radar of similar technology (AN FPS/85) at Eglin Air Force Base, Fla., and by the design validation of the PAR subsystems prior to production release in a Limited Engineering Development Model (LEDM), which has been constructed and operated at the Syracuse General Electric plant. A decision to delay the Phase 2 deployment for a year or two simply would not increase further the high confidence levels which already justifiably exist in regard to the design adequacy of the major SAFEGUARD system components.

"Also, the experience gained as we move further ahead in our Phase I activities will reinforce our confidence in system performance. By the time Phase I is completed, multiradar, multisite internetting will be accomplished. This will provide a means of system testing wherein two sites, each with both PAR and MSR can be checked out to verify site integration. Further, if we maintain our currently planned activation schedules for Whiteman, by the time site activation procedures there progress to the point of component and integration testing, highly valuable experience will have been gained from tests already completed at Grand Forks and Malmstrom. The equipment readiness dates for the first three sites in our currently planned schedules have been deliberately picked to be a minimum of four months apart so that the contractor may apply the knowledge and experience gained at the first sites to the later sites.

"Postponement for a year of a decision to authorize more than Phase 1 would increase both the cost and risk to the United States. For example, if no additional deployment were authorized in fiscal year 1971, but the full 12-site Phase 2 deployment were authorized in fiscal year 1972, the total DOD acquisition cost of $10.7 billion would increase by about $0.3 billion and completion of the full deployment would be delayed by at least 6 months and probably for a much longer period. Although continuation during the next year of only the SAFEGUARD research and development program and the two Phase 1 sites would continue the development, production and construction programs now underway, if the decision to commence Modified Phase 2 is delayed by a year, 'gaps' would appear in these programs as Phase 1 work is completed. As these gaps occur, we would be forced to reduce production and engineering capability, especially highly skilled manpower, to avoid waste. With a later, possibly fiscal year 1972, authorization to complete additional site deployment we would have to rehire and retrain personnel in order to rebuild production and engineering capacity. It is not possible to estimate, therefore, how much more than 6 months' delay would occur. Such a delay would add to the risk to the United States, since we would be unable to protect ourselves against the threats expected to exist before the deployment would be completed."

8. *On what grounds do you base your assessment that the Chinese would risk, indeed court, the elimination of their industrial base and millions of persons in a nuclear exchange with the United States?—given that destruction of China's ten major cities would reult in 30–35% loss of its industrial capacity (compared to 33.1% for the U.S.) and most of the human talent that goes with this base.*

Answer. We are not sure that the Chinese would "court" a nuclear exchange with the U.S. or any other nation. However, there are several fundamental differences in the problem of deterring Communist China with our strategic offensive forces as compared with deterring the Soviet Union.

While it is true that a large part of the Chinese industrial capacity is concentrated in a relatively few cities, Communist China, in contrast to the Soviet Union, and for that matter the United States, is predominantly a rural society and only a relatively small proportion of the population is urban.

Some have contended that a relatively small number of warheads detonated over China's 50 largest cities could destroy half of their urban population and more than half of their industry, as well as most of their key government officials and a large majority of their scientific, technical and skilled workers. This amount of destruction, they maintain, should be a sufficient deterrent to an attack by Communist China on the U.S.

However, there are ways the Chinese Communists might use their nuclear capability—as a threat to the U.S. or our friends in Asia—and while the fact that we can destroy a sizeable proportion of Chinese urban population and industrial capacity is important, it may not necessarily be decisive in this latter case.

China is predominantly a rural society where the great majority of the people live off the land and are dependent only to a limited extent on urban industry for their survival. The key government officials and even the skilled workers could be evacuated from the cities in time of crisis. The Chinese are taking steps to decentralize their industry.

In contrast to China, our population is heavily concentrated in a relatively few large cities—25 percent in the 10 largest cities. Consequently, they could inflict on us a proportionately greater number of fatalities in a small attack than we could inflict on them in a very large attack. Finally, in any nuclear confrontation with Communist China, we would still have to maintain a sufficient deterrent against the Soviet Union.

We recognize apparent Chinese ambitions for political hegemony in Asia, and their indicated hostility towards the U.S. However, we do not expect them to resort to overt aggression to achieve their political purpose in Asia. Nevertheless, in view of the nature of the developing Chinese nuclear threat, it is imprudent on our part to rely on our deterrent forces only—if a reasonable alternative is available.

A flexible SAFEGUARD defense to negate possible Chinese attempts at nuclear blackmail would serve a future President far better than only a rigid offensive capability. SAFEGUARD provides the option for a more complete counter than deterrence alone to this potential Chinese threat.

9. *The President, in asking for SAFEGUARD II, asked that "long lead time advanced preparation work" be done on five sites.*
(a). *What does "long lead time advanced preparation work" mean?*
(b). *How does this square with Secretary Packard's testimony last year that site survey and preparation, including engineering, takes 6 to 9 months?*
(c). *With what confidence can you go ahead with the procurement of long lead time components without having completed Phase I and the attendant R&D?*

Answer. (a). Long lead time advanced preparation work includes such activities as site survey and engineering, land acquisition and advanced procurement of items to avoid delay in undertaking production and construction for the site should it be authorized later for deployment.

(b). This definition is consistent with Secretary Packard's testimony of last year. As indicated, "site survey and preparation, including engineering", constitute part, but not all, of the work associated with advanced preparation. Land acquisition and advanced procurement are also part of advanced preparation and would require additional time.

(c). We can proceed now with the procurement of long lead time components with a high degree of confidence. As I testified before the House Appropriations Committee on 8 April 1970, "In the development of a large weapons system such as SAFEGUARD, the answer to the question of whether or not the system development has progressed to the point where deployment can be justified must necessarily be based upon the research and development testing progress of the major system components. The major SAFEGUARD system components, Perimeter Acquisition Radar (PAR), Missile Site Radar (MSR), SPRINT missile and SPARTAN missile have all undergone extensive research and development (R&D) testing which has already progressed to the point where the design of all critical items, that is, ones with large cost impact or long leadtime, has been validated. The development testing of each major subsystem—that is, the MSR at Meck Island, the SPRINT at White Sands Missile Range, and the SPARTAN at Kwajalein—has progressed very satisfactorily to the point where it is essentially complete. There is a high level of confidence that there are no major problems, and the next step, system integration testing of these components at Meck Island, is underway. High confidence in the development progress of the other major system component, the PAR, has been achieved from the very successful performance history of a radar of similar technology (AN FPS/85) at Eglin Air Force Base, Florida, and by the design validation of the PAR subsystems prior to production release in a Limited Engineering Development Model (LEDM), which has been constructed and operated at the Syracuse General Electric plant. A decision to delay the Phase 2 deployment for a year or two simply would not increase further the high confidence levels which already justifiably exist in regard to the design adequacy of the major SAFEGUARD system components.

"Also, the experience gained as we move further ahead in our Phase I activities will reinforce our confidence in system performance. By the time Phase I is completed, multiradar, multisite internetting will be accomplished. This will provide a means of system testing wherein two sites, each with both PAR and MSR can be checked out to verify site integration. Further, if we maintain our currently planned activation schedules for Whiteman, by the time site activation procedures there progress to the point of component and integration testing, highly valuable experience will have been gained from tests already completed at Grand Forks and Malmstrom. The equipment readiness dates for the first three sites in our currently planned schedules have been deliberately picked to be a minimum of four months apart so that the contractor may apply the knowledge and experience gained at the first sites to the later sites."

10(a). *What is the estimated, longest period of time that can be consumed between the detection of an incoming possible warhead and discrimination that it is or is not an actual warhead?*

Answer. For SPARTAN intercepts a period of [deleted] is allowable for exoatmospheric discrimination and designation after detection. For SPRINT defending against large radar cross-section RVs even more time is available for exoatmospheric discrimination. For endoatmospheric discrimination, assuming small radar cross-section RVs with precision decoys, a period of [deleted] is available.

(b). *What is the estimated, longest period of time between the moment discrimination is achieved and*
(1) A SPARTAN missile would have to be fired to have an 80% possibility of intercepting the incoming warhead?
(2) A SPRINT missile would have to be fired to have an 80% possibility of intercepting the incoming warhead?

Answer. For intercepts within the interceptor's specified range and altitude capabilities, either SPRINT or SPARTAN has a probability of intercepting the incoming warhead [deleted].

For the SPARTAN missile, latest possible launch would be [deleted] after PAR exoatmospheric discrimination of simple penetration aids (such as the Chinese might have initially).

For the SPRINT missile, if discrimination were done exoatmospherically by the PAR, latest launch would be [deleted] after discrimination. However, the more likely event that SPRINT launch is preceded by endoatmospheric discrimination by the MSR, latest possible time of launch would be [deleted] after discrimination.

In the practical application of this information it should be noted that interceptor launch would not normally be delayed until the latest possible moment.

11. *CEP, or circular error probable, means, as I understand it, that 50% of the time a single missile will hit within the radius of a designed circle. This means, of course, that 50% of the time, that warhead will strike somewhere else. I have several detailed questions about this.*

Discussion. The errors associated with target misses have what is called a "normal" statistical distribution, and most of them are clustered around a central value, and the number of scores declines sharply as you move away from the central value. The 50% circle, or CEP, is merely a convenient way of specifying the accuracy of a missile system. The CEP is, by definition, the radius of a circle within which 50% of the missiles which work reliably can be expected to fall. It is believed, however, that the questions below have little to do with this statistical clustering of misses about an aim point, but rather with unpredictable "strays" which fall completely outside of normal behavior. A "stray" missile's error is not included in the CEP calculations. If, for example, 19 missiles fell within one mile of the aim point, and the 20th one fell 1000 miles away, the 1000 mile error would not be considered in the CEP determination. Rather, such a large error would have to be the result of a malfunction or failure which would affect the estimated reliability of the missile and not its estimated accuracy.

The "normal" distribution indicates that almost all warheads attacking MINUTEMAN will fall in or very close to MINUTEMAN silos. As an example, the "normal" distribution indicates that 90% of the missile warheads would fall within a circle which has a radius of about 2.4 times the 50% circle radius and 99% with about 4 times the 50% circle radius. In order to be effective against a MINUTEMAN silo the present Soviet warheads have to be delivered with CEP's of less than one half a nautical mile. Therefore 99% of the missile warheads would fall within a few miles of the target. Thus it is to be expected that warheads falling significantly outside of the MINUTEMAN fields would be the result of guidance system malfunction. Their number would be extremely small and they must be considered very similar to one of a few accidental launches.

(a). *What are the distances from CEP of predictable, stray warheads?*

Answer. A "stray" represents a reliability failure of the attacking system and its impact point is unpredictable.

(b). *What is, and has been, the maximum error from CEP of a single firing event?*

Answer. Excluding malfunctions, maximum error is [deleted.]

(c). *On how many firings, how big a sample, is the probable distance of stray based?*
Answer. To determine the CEP (not "strays") several tens of missiles are fired. The probable distance of a "stray" cannot be determined.

(d). *How many of these calculations were based on operational, as separate from test firings.*
Answer. The development test program demonstrates the approximate CEP capability of a system. The operational test firings and follow-on operational test firings, using the deployed system (with dummy warheads) and conducted by the operational crews, after the system is deployed provides a continuing check on the deployed force CEP capability and adds to the confidence in the estimated CEP value. These operational test launches are conducted on a continuing basis. For a force that has been deployed for a number of years, such as MINUTEMAN I or TITAN II, which have a large number of operational test results available, the CEP estimates are based on the operational test results.

(e). *How many Strategic Air Command operational firings have been performed since ATLAS, TITAN, and MINUTEMAN missiles have been deployed? Of these firings, what has been the actual error in range? I mean where did the missiles hit in relation to the bulls-eye?*
Answer. ATLAS is no longer operational. A total of 60 TITAN II, MINUTEMAN I and MINUTEMAN II missiles have been fired to gather CEP data. CEP's are [deleted].

(f). *Were the actual results of the firings compared with the theoretical CEP? What was the result?*
Answer. Yes. In the context of these questions, the actual firing results are in close agreement with the estimated CEP's.

(g). *Is our estimate of the CEP of Soviet missiles based on the same methodology, or is it based on observation?*
Answer. Our estimates of Soviet CEP are based on [deleted].

(h). *What is the probability of perfect functioning within CEP design of incoming Soviet or Chinese warheads?*
Answer. As noted previously almost all Soviet warheads would fall into the MINUTEMAN fields and by definition one half will fall within the CEP of the intended aim point. As most reliability failures occur during the propulsion (boost) phases, most of the malfunctioning missile impact zones would be outside of the U.S. Soviet ICBMs are believed to be [deleted].

The technical characteristics of the Chinese missile force may be estimated by analogy to the early U.S. ICBM systems. Thus it is possible to estimate the Chinese CEP to be [deleted] and the reliability to be about [deleted.] However area defense, by its very nature, is designed to defend an entire country, in this case the continental United States, and is thus capable of handling variations in the attacker's CEP and "strays" which would impact on the continental United States.

(i). *Therefore, I ask, also, if it is not more than likely that a Soviet strike intended to hit only our missiles would also incinerate millions of Americans simply by the accidents of stray missiles.*
Answer. No, it is not likely—first, because as discussed above, Soviet strays are quite unlikely, and, second, because even if a "stray" did occur, impact on a large population center is also very unlikely—particularly if the "stray" were originally aimed at the sparsely populated MINUTEMAN fields. Again, it should be noted that the SAFEGUARD area coverage (12 site deployment) could engage and destroy "strays" headed for any part of the continental U.S.

(j). *What degree of protection would SAFEGUARD offer against this, and I mean shooting down strays during an actual full attack on our missile bases?*
Answer. The SAFEGUARD area coverage capability would be used to protect against strays which would impact outside of the silo fields and inside the SAFEGUARD coverage. However, we think the occurrence of strays to be quite unlikely. I stated on June 4, 1970, before your subcommittee, ". . . should the stray missile that might occur in a major attack on MINUTEMAN—which, as I said, is a very unlikely thing, I believe—should the stray missile be within a few hundred miles of the MINUTEMAN field it could be intercepted by the SPARTAN, and I suspect decisions would be made to intercept it should it be aiming for a populated area. SPARTAN would not, however, provide coverage, say, a thousand miles away." My statement refers to the SAFEGUARD defense of MINUTEMAN only and for the full 12-site SAFEGUARD deployment the entire continental United States would be so protected.

12. *Would you please now give us the Defense Intelligence Agency's best estimate of the numbers of (1) SS-9s, (2) SS-11s, and (3) SS-13s that the Soviet Union is most likely to have at the end of 1970, 1971, 1972, 1973?*
Answer. [Deleted.]

13. *Would you comment on the substance of the following two paragraphs?*

In Secretary Laird's most recent testimony before the Senate Armed Services Committee, he said that "We cannot rule out the possibility that the Soviets have given or will give this system, called the SA-5 or Tallinn system, an ABM role. We believe such a role is technically feasible for this system."

Yet we have expert testimony from inside and outside the government that Tallinn continues to be an anti-aircraft defense, that it would need extensive modification to become an ABM system, if this could be done at all, and that even if this could be done, the result would resemble our SPRINT missiles, which are not an escalatory, area defense, or a threat against us. Additionally, we are told that any effort to modify Tallinn into an ABM system we could detect by national means of verification.

Answer. [Deleted].

14(a). *When the two sites of Phase 1, SAFEGUARD, are completed, how many persons, military and civilian will be employed to keep them in operational readiness? And what would be the annual costs?*

Answer. When the two sites of Phase 1, SAFEGUARD, are completed and become fully operational, it is estimated at this time that approximately 2900 military and 2260 civilians for a total of about 5160 government employed personnel will be required to keep them in operational readiness. These totals include the operating personnel required physically on-site as well as other personnel required to perform the support functions of RDT&E, training, logistics, and command and control. The total annual direct personnel costs (i.e., pay and allowances) for these strengths would be about $23 million for military personnel and $30 million for civilians.

(b). *If all twelve sites were in operational readiness, how many persons would be required (1) to man them, (2) to keep the entire system in operational readiness—this includes persons not at sites who are involved in RDT&E, command, control, operational maintenance of all ancillary equipment. And what would be annual costs?*

Answer. If all 12 sites were in operational readiness, it is now expected that some 7250 military and 4500 civilians for a total of about 11,750 government employed on-site personnel would be required to man and operate the tactical sites only. It is currently estimated that a total of about 9550 military and 9250 civilians or about 18,800 government employed personnel would be required to keep the entire system in operational readiness. These total figures include government employed personnel required to man and operate the tactical sites and to perform the support functions of RDT&E, training, logistics and command and control. The total annual direct personnel costs (i.e., pay and allowances) related to the total strengths above would be about $64 million for military and $123 million for civilians.

15. *Has a complete PAR yet been tested in that configuration in which it is intended to be used? Has a complete PAR yet been built?*

Answer. No. However the design of the PAR is well within the current state of the art. A similar radar, the FPS-85, has been built and successfully operated at Eglin Air Force Base in Florida. A limited engineering development model of the PAR was constructed and is being operated and tested at the Syracuse New York General Electric plant during 1969. This model was developed for the purpose of verifying the design of each of the PAR components. We have encountered no serious technical difficulties in this development, and we have confidence of meeting the presently scheduled Equipment Readiness date for the first PAR site. The first PAR built will be a tactical design at Grand Forks, N.D.

16. *How many pounds of PSI overpressure can a PAR presently withstand; how many can an MSR withstand?*

The numbers given in each case in your answer are equal to the PSI generated by a one megaton burst at what altitude and at what distance from the radars?

What is the hardness ratio between a MINUTEMAN silo and a PAR and an MSR?

Answer: [Deleted].

INDEX

EXAMINATION OF WITNESSES

Aiken, Senator Goeorge D.:   Page
  Foster, Dr. John S., Jr _____ 427, 438–439
  Hsieh, Mrs. Alice Langley _____ 127–129
Case, Senator Clifford P.:
  Barnett, A. Doak _____ 146, 158–161, 163–166, 168, 172–174
  Brooke, Senator Edward W _____ 16–18
  Bundy, McGeorge _____ 99–100, 103–108, 115–117
  Drell, Dr. Sidney D _____ 537, 540, 545–546, 557–559, 560, 567, 575–569
  Fisher, Adrian S _____ 235, 239, 248, 255–256, 258–259, 262, 265, 267–269
  Foster, Dr. John S., Jr _____ 438, 501–508, 514–515, 518
  Goldberger, Dr. M. L _____ 558–559, 566–567, 575–577
  Hornig, Dr. Donald F _____ 407
  Hsieh, Mrs. Alice Langley _____ 143, 173–174
  Kistiakowsky, Dr. George B _____ 411
  Laird, Secretary Melvin R _____ 303–306,
                    308–314, 318–319, 322–325, 328–330
  Panofsky, Dr. Wolfgang K. H _____ 181,
              184–185, 190, 193–194, 201–204, 213–215
  Scoville, Dr. Herbert, Jr _____ 265–270
  Shulman, Marshall D _____ 16, 27
  Wiesner, Dr. Jerome B _____ 400
  York, Dr. Herbert _____ 102, 104–106, 108
Cooper, Senator John Sherman:
  Barnett, A. Doak _____ 160–163
  Brooke, Senator Edward W _____ 34
  Bundy, McGeorge _____ 114, 116
  Drell, Dr. Sidney D _____ 547–548, 564–566
  Fisher, Adrian S _____ 244–245, 256–257, 259
  Foster, Dr. John S., Jr _____ 508–518
  Goldberger, Dr. M. L _____ 549, 561–563, 565–566
  Hsieh, Mrs. Alice Langley _____ 149–151
  Panofsky, Dr. Wolfgang, K. H _____ 186, 195–197, 208–211, 216–217
  Scoville, Dr. Herbert, Jr _____ 262–265, 270
  Shulman, Marshall D _____ 35
  York, Dr. Herbert _____ 110–113
Church, Senator Frank:
  Brooke, Senator Edward W _____ 31–33
  Shulman, Marshall D _____ 28–33
Gore, Senator Albert:
  Barnett, A. Doak _____ 157, 165–169, 172
  Brooke, Senator Edward W _____ 9–12, 16, 34
  Bundy, McGregor _____ 97–101, 106, 115
  Clark, Joseph S _____ 362, 370
  Drell, Dr. Sidney D _____ 524, 537, 539, 542, 544, 551–552, 554–556
  Fisher, Adrian S _____ 234–238, 241, 243, 255
  Foster, Dr. John S., Jr _____ 427–441, 518–520
  Goldberger, Dr. M. L _____ 524, 528, 534, 542, 555–556
  Hornig, Dr. Donald F _____ 406, 420
  Hsieh, Mrs. Alice Langley _____ 125–127
  Kistiakowsky, Dr. George B _____ 405
  Laird, Secretary Melvin R _____ 274–285, 301–303, 306, 311–312
  Panofsky, Dr. Wolfgang K. H _____ 176–177,
          179, 181–184, 187–189, 192–193, 211–213, 215–216

Gore, Senator Albert—Continued

    Page

Scoville, Dr. Herbert, Jr	221–225, 231–234
Shulman, Marshall D	23, 27
Wilsner, Dr. Jerome B	397, 405, 419–420
York, Dr. Herbert	97, 100–103, 108–109

Fulbright, Senator J. W.:

Barnett, A. Doak	145–147, 152–153
Brooke, Senator Edward W	12–15, 16
Bundy, McGeorge	92–96
Drell, Dr. Sidney D	535–536, 538
Fisher, Adrian S	239–248, 253–255
Foster, Dr. John S., Jr	343–344, 441–446, 448–450, 497–501
Goldberger, Dr. M. L	536
Hsieh, Mrs. Alice Langley	141–145, 147
Laird, Secretary Melvin R	290–301, 330–334, 336–352
Moorer, Adm. Thomas H	332, 338, 340–341
Panofsky, Dr. Wolfgang K. H	184–185, 189, 197–201
Shulman, Marshall D	30
York, Dr. Herbert	96–97

Javits, Senator Jacob K.:

Shulman, Marshall D	40

Pell, Senator Claiborne:

Hornig, Dr. Donald F	417
Kistiakowsky, Dr. George B	417–419
Wiesner, Dr. Jerome B	417–419

Symington, Senator Stuart:

Brooke, Senator Edward W	36, 39
Drell, Dr. Sidney D	546, 550–551, 560–561
Goldberger, Dr. M. L	547, 550–551, 561
Laird, Secretary Melvin R	316–318, 320–321, 325–328
Panofsky, Dr. Wolfgang K. H	186–177, 194, 204–208
Shulman, Marshall D	24, 33, 36–39

○

www.ingramcontent.com/pod-product-compliance
Lightning Source LLC
Chambersburg PA
CBHW020629230426
43665CB00008B/95